Psychological Development Through the Life Span

Under the Editorship of GARDNER MURPHY

Psychological Development
Through the Life Span

By SIDNEY L. PRESSEY

PROFESSOR OF PSYCHOLOGY
THE OHIO STATE UNIVERSITY

and RAYMOND G. KUHLEN

PROFESSOR OF PSYCHOLOGY
SYRACUSE UNIVERSITY

HARPER & ROW, PUBLISHERS

New York, Evanston, and London

Library of Congress catalog card number: 57-6267

L-O

CONTENTS •

Preface   xxi

1. Development in the Changing Modern World   1
   Values of a Life-Span Perspective
   The Rapidly Changing World Context of Human
     Development
   The Double Task of a Developmental Psychology of the Life
     Span
   Summary
   Bibliography

Part One: ABILITIES, TASKS, AND ACHIEVEMENTS

2. Growth, Change, and Decline in Physique   27
   Growth in Height and Weight
   Change in Proportion and Tissues
   Changes with Age in Strength, Quickness, and Skill
   Health and Organic Functioning at Different Ages
   Major Conclusions Regarding the Physical Organism at
     Different Ages
   Summary
   Bibliography

3. Growth and Change in Abilities as Shown by Tests   70
   "General Ability" Through the Life Span
   Analyses of Changes of Abilities with Age
   Factors Related to Ability
   Major Trends, Problems, and Applications
   Summary
   Bibliography

4. Development of Abilities as Indicated by Achievement and by
     Mental Disease: Perspective by Contrast   123
   Ages When Notable Achievements Are Most Commonly
     Made

v

Factors Involved in Notable Achievement
Mental Disease and Ill-Health as Indicative of Change and
    Decline with Age
A Larger View of Abilities and Their Development
Summary
Bibliography

5. Education Through the Life Span   165
    The Growth of "Life-Span" Education
    Three Major Psychoeducational Problems
    Educational Problems of the Handicapped and the Mentally
        Inadequate
    A Much Fumbled and Critical Problem: Education of the
        Most Able
    Major Developmental Needs and Problems in Education
    Summary
    Bibliography

6. The Work Life   216
    Gross Date Regarding Workers and Jobs
    The Course of the Work Life
    The "Way of Life" and Work
    Major Needs Indicated from a "Developmental" Study of
        Work
    Summary
    Bibliography

Part Two: DYNAMIC AND SOCIAL DEVELOPMENT

7. Changing Motivation During the Life Span   271
    Constitutional Factors in Motivation
    Changing Social Motives
    Pressures of Time and Money: Major Factors in Human
        Motivation
    Broad Significance of Adjustment to Basic Needs
    Summary
    Bibliography

8. Emotional Development: Unresolved Tensions, Aggressions,
        Fears and Anxieties   322
    Nature and Nurture in Emotional Development

Anger and Aggressive Tendencies
Age Changes in Fears and Anxieties
Developmental Trends in Anxiety and Emotional Stress
Constructive Adjustments Reduce Stress
Summary
Bibliography

9. Satisfactions in Life Activities: General Interests and
    Recreation   372
    Happiness and Basic Satisfactions in Life: Overall
      Perspective
    Play, Recreation, and General Interests
    Recreation and Entertainment via the Media of Mass
      Communication
    Development and Contrasts in Interest Patterns
    Interests and Adjustment: Problems and Potentials
    Summary
    Bibliography

10. Moral, Sociopolitical, and Religious Values and Behavior   436
    Moral Values and Behavior
    Sociopolitical Attitudes and Behavior and Law Observance
    Religion and Philosophy of Life
    Age Trends in Conservatism: Cause and Possible Remedy
    Summary
    Bibliography

11. Social Interaction: Developmental Trends in Interpersonal and
    Group Relations   506
    Interpersonal Relations in Childhood and Adolescence
    Interpersonal Relations and Status in the Adult Years
    Social Interaction in Groups
    Racial, National, and Religious Biases in Interpersonal
      Relations
    Personality and Other Factors in Attitude Development and
      Modification
    Summary
    Bibliography

12. Heterosexual Development, Marriage, and Family
    Relationships   569

Dating and Courtship: From First Date to Marriage
Adjustment During Marriage
Changes in Sex Interest and Sex Life
Parent-Child Relationships During the Course of Life
Summary
Bibliography

Part Three: PREFACE TO A "LIFE-SPAN" PSYCHOLOGY OF THE FUTURE

13. Retrospect and Prospect: Major Concepts and Problems as Seen
        Integratively in the Life-Span View   633
    The Changing Person in the Rapidly Changing Scene
    Psychological Reinterpretations
    Certain Reintegrated Applications
    Some Possible Personal Applications to the Reader

Index of Names   649

Index of Subjects   651

LIST OF FIGURES •

1. Average Length of Life from Ancient to Modern Times. 4
2. Survivors from Birth to Successive Ages and Expectation of Life According to Life Table for the United States. 5
3. Age Composition of the Population. Percent Distribution of Total Population by Age, United States 1850 to 2000. 6
4. Estimated Growth in the Population of the World and of Each Continent. 7
5. National Output and Labor Input. 9
6. Radio and Television Sets, Automobiles, etc., in Use. 11
7. Changes in Average Family Income. 12
8. Estimated Number of Persons 65 Years of Age and Over Receiving Income from Specified Source, December, 1930—December, 1952.
9. Marriage, Birth, and Divorce Rates, 1870–1954 and Percent of Married Women Employed 1910–1951. 15
10. Increase in Newspaper Space Given to Sports. 17
11. Changes in Mean Height and Mean Weight with Age. 28
12. Average Gains Each Year in Height and Weight for Boys and Girls. 29
13. Maximum Growth Age in Relation to Total Growth Curves. 31
14. Standing Heights of 167 Girls at Ages 8, 12, and 16. 32
15. Changes in Body Proportions with Age and Sex Differences 37
16. Edison at 12, 32, 58, and 81 Years of Age. 38
17. Changes in Weight of Various Organs with Age. 39
18. Individual Differences in Physical Development. 41
19. Increases from Age 6 to 18 in Rate of Tapping and Strength of Grip. 45
20. Right-Hand Grip of Early and Late Maturing Boys and Girls. 45
21. Contrasts Between the Ten Strongest and Least Strong Boys on Certain Traits. 47
22. Changes with Age in Strength and Quickness. 48

23. Changes in Rate of Block Sorting.   51
24. Age and Accidents in Auto Driving.   51
25. Limitations of Activity and Liability to Falls of Old People.   52
26. Age of Outstanding Professional Athletic Accomplishments.   53
27. Relation of Age to Visual Accommodation and Visual Acuity.   55
28. Changes in Hearing with Age.   56
29. Number, of 1000 Cases in Each Age Group, Who Were Ill and
    Who Died.   57
30. Physiological Change with Age.   59
31. Change in Sexual Vigor with Age.   60
32. Relationship of Maternal Age to the Incidence of Physically
    Defective Children and to Stillbirths.   60
33. Curves of Growth in General Ability.   73
34. Distribution of Mental Ages of 167 Girls at Ages 8, 12, and 16.   74
35. Standard Scores of Four Children on Successive Testings.   75
36. Average Scores on Wechsler Individual and Otis and Alpha
    Group Scales.   76
37. Initial and Later Mean Scores on the Concept Mastery Test.   80
38. Alpha and Wechsler Subtests Showing Most and Least Decline
    with Age.   83
39. Mean Number Attempted on 120 Item Vocabulary Test.   84
40. Learning Curves of an Infant.   86
41. Number of Lines of Poetry Learned in 15 Minutes by Children
    of Different Ages.   88
42. "General Ability" in Relation to Civilian Occupation—World
    War II.   97
43. Relation of Social Status to Intelligence.   99
44. Effects of Relatively Slight Differences in Socioeconomic Con-
    ditions.   101
45. Three Cases Showing Changes in General Ability from 2–18
    years.   108
46. Age of Most Outstanding Creative Work.   124
47. Age Differences in Types of Superior Literary Productivity.   125
48. Relation of Quality and Quantity in Artistic Production to Age.   126
49. Relation of Age to Number of Important Chemical Contribu-
    tions.   127
50. Age of Leadership in Government.   128
51. Age of Leadership in Organizations and Institutions.   128

52. National Differences in Contributions to Medicine and Philosophy.   136
53. First Admission Rates for Selected Diagnoses by Age.   149
54. Resident Patient Rates for Selected Diagnoses by Age.   149
55. Percentage of Young People in School and College.   167
56. Growth of a Boy at a High Level of Ability and a Boy at a Low Level of Ability.   171
57. Percentage of Students in Each Grade Marking Different Poetic Variants Best.   173
58. Scores on a Spanish Vocabulary Test.   180
59. Scores on a Test Battery Supposedly Covering the Essentials of a College Education.   181
60. School Survival Rates in the United States.   183
61. Social Structure of a Small Sixth-Grade Class.   186
62. Labor Force, Employment, and Unemployment—Annual Averages.   217
63. Labor Force as a Percentage of the Total Population of Each Age Group, 1890 and 1953.   218
64. Career Patterns of Different Occupation Levels.   226
65. Injury Frequency Rate in Relation to Age.   236
66. Absenteeism and Illness at Different Ages.   236
67. Informal Associations of Managerial and Office Staff.   251
68. Age and Interest Inventory Scores for Semiskilled Workers.   259
69. Curves Showing the Relation of Activity to Age in Laboratory Rats.   277
70. Responses of Introverts and Extroverts to Praise and Blame.   287
71. Percentage of Teachers and Factory Workers with Vocational Interests at Various Ages.   289
72. Changes in Goals with Increasing Adult Age.   291
73. Expansion and Restriction of Life Activities.   293
74. The Differential Threat of Aging for Various Economic Groups.   295
75. Age Trends in Major Activities and Roles.   300
76. Age Changes in Amount of Leisure Time.   302
77. Differentiation of Emotions During the First Two Years of Life.   323
78. Age Changes in Frequency of Anger Outbursts During the Preschool Years.   330

79. Relative Frequency of Various Fear Situations During the First Six Years. 339

80. Age Trends in Worries and Anxieties During the Adolescent Period. 343

81. Waxing and Waning of Conflict in Adolescent Adjustment. 345

82. Age Trends During Childhood and Adolescence in Frequency of Worries and Emotional Episodes. 350

83. Relationship Between Age and General Adjustment. 354

84. Changing Behaviour Patterns Through Adolescence. 382

85. Age Trends in Hobby Participation. 390

86. Changes with Age of Men Liking Active or Sedentary Diversions. 393

87. Progress of the Sexes Toward Maturity of Interests. 413

88. Adult Age Trends in Masculinity and Femininity of Interests and Attitudes. 417

89. Interest Profiles for Men in Selected Occupations. 418

90. Trends with Age in Adjustment of Youngsters. 423

91. Distribution of Scores on Tests of Honesty, Cheating, and Helpfulness. 437

92. Honesty Profiles of One Girl and One Boy. 439

93. Age Trends in Basic Values in the American Culture. 441

94. Percentage of Children Answering Variously the Question, "Are there cases in which lies are necessary?" 443

95. Changes from Grade Six to Senior Year in College in Moral Values. 446

96. Contrasts Between Three Generations in Their Reliance on Types of Moral Standards. 451

97. Juvenile Delinquency Rates at Each Year of Age. 469

98. Percentage Distribution of Religious Conversion According to Age.

99. Age Trends in Importance of Ideology and Philosophy of Life. 493

100. Growth Trends in Certain Aspects of Social Behavior. 507

101. Increasing Stability of Social Relationships with Age. 509

102. Percentage of Children Choosing the Opposite Sex under Various Conditions. 512

103. Perception of Own and Others' Sociometric Status for Various Ages. 514

104. Change of Interest in Social Activities and Interests with Increased Age. 522

105. Social Grouping Among 15-Year-Old Girls.   532
106. Social Grouping Among 15-Year-Old Boys.   533
107. Organizational Activity as Related to Age.   541
108. Extent to Which Negroes and White Children Prefer Their
      Own Race.   548
109. Average Number of Love Affairs per Person During Various
      Age Periods.   575
110. Mean Happiness Scores According to Length of Marriage.   589
111. Divorce Rates for Married Couples.   590
112. Accumulative Incidence of Orgasm.   601
113. Age Trends in Reported and Preferred Frequency of Sexual
      Intercourse.   605
114. How Emancipation from Parents Might Best Develop and
      How It Probably Does Develop.   613

LIST OF TABLES •

1. Percentage at Each Weight in Each Age Group from 12 to 80.   33
2. Age of First Menstruation of 1313 Girls as Found in Five Investigations.   40
3. Age of Menopause.   43
4. Percentage in Each Age Group from 12 to 80 Showing Different Degrees of Strength in Pull.   49
5. Leading Causes of Death, 1949.   58
6. Army Alpha Intelligence Test Scores.   79
7. Age Differences in Ability to Learn.   89
8. Average Proficiency of Three Age Groups in Various Learning Tasks.   90
9. Percentage Loss of Persons Aged 60–69 on Various Memory Tests.   91
10. Correlations Found Between Related Pairs of Persons.   94
11. Relations of Scores on Tests of General Ability.   98
12. (a) Good and Poor Foster Homes and (b) Age of Placement. Effect on IQ.   102
13. Effects of Nursery School Upon General Ability.   104
14. Numbers of Elementary, Secondary and College Students, 1890–1950.   166
15. Number of Right Choices of "Best" Verse.   173
16. Age of Receiving the Ph.D. in Science in the United States and in Germany.   174
17. Median Point–Hour Ratio, etc., of Students Who Graduated at Different Ages.   176
18. Age of Graduation and Success in Adult Life.   178
19. Relationships of Age of High School Graduation to Adjustment and Later Educational and Vocational Success.   195
20. A Comparison of Women Who Graduated in Three Years or Less with Those Who Graduated in the Regular Time.   196

21. Percentages of Pupils Who Mentioned Various Subjects or Activities as Liked Best in School.   206

22. Percentage of Various Age Groups Who Enrolled in Home Study Courses for Specific Reasons.   209

23. Percentage of Population Economically Active According to Age Group (Selected Countries).   219

24. Percentage of Total Workers Engaged in Different Types of Occupations.   220

25. Average Annual Earnings in Different Industries, 1932 and 1953.   221

26. Types of Male Initial Work Period Jobs.   224

27. Causes of Leaving Employment.   232

28. Percentages of Employees Having Certain Traits.   233

29. Distributions of Net Appraisals of Workers of Different Ages.   235

30. Numbers of Part-Time Saleswomen Hired at Different Ages, and Days Available.   236

31. Frequency of Different Types of Farm Accidents by Ages.   237

32. Injury Frequency and Severity Rates in Various Occupations, 1949.   244

33. Meanings of Work in 5 Occupational Groups for Older Workers.   247

34. Percentage in Various Occupational Levels Reporting (1) Work Associates of the Same Background, (2) Various Mean Social Participation Scores.   249

35. Categories into Which Goals of High School Students Were Classified.   281

36. Percentage of Cases in Which Needs or Motives Played a Role in Vocational History.   283

37. Distribution of the Hours in a Week Among Teen-Age Boys.   298

38. Expenditures for Personal Consumption, United States, 1950.   306

39. Age Changes in Earnings by Level of Income and by Sex, United States, 1950.   307

40. Age Differences in Financial Pressures Among Teachers.   308

41. Percentage of Children of Various Ages Showing Behavior During Anger.   332

42. Sex and Grade Differences in Frequency of Various Fears.   344

43. Ages at Which Worries Characterized Businessmen and Psychologists.   347

44. IQ Ratings of Matched Groups Compared for "Adaptive" and "Consecutive" Methods of Testing.   358

45. Percentage of Individuals Over 65 Who, in Retrospect, Designated Various Periods of Life as the Happiest.   373
46. Frequency of Responses When Children Described "One of the Happiest Days of My Life."   375
47. Percentage Distribution of Reasons Given for Major Happy Episodes.   376
48. Adult Age Changes in Leisure-Time Activities.   387
49. Variations According to Income in Activities in Which Families Participate and Percentage Believing Program Satisfactory.   389
50. Type of Activities Participated in by People Over 70.   392
51. Age Changes in Reading, Radio, and Movie Interests.   396
52. Changes in Time Spent on Each Medium After Purchase of TV Set.   397
53. Percentage of Various Items in Newspapers Read by Members of Various Age Groups.   399
54. Percentage of People of Various Ages Who Reported That They Regularly Read Comic Books.   401
55. Percentage of Pupils in Various Grades Who Indicated Preferences for Various Types of Radio Programs.   405
56. Percentage of Various Groups Who Indicated Preferences for Types of Radio Programs.   406
57. Interrelationships Among Interests and Attitudes and Their Patterning with Respect to Certain Drives.   421
58. Comparative Mean Scores of Boys and Girls on Moral Knowledge Tests.   442
59. Percentage Frequency with Which Boys and Girls Mentioned Various Types of People as Their "Ideals."   447
60. Adult Age Differences in Moral Attitudes and Behavior.   449
61. Percentage Prevalence of Handicaps, Characteristics and Conditions Among Youngsters of Varying Degrees of Honesty.   453
62. Adult Differences on Social and Political Issues.   458
63. Percentage of Married Male and Female College Graduates Who Participated in Specified Political Activities.   460
64. Percentage of Married Male and Female College Graduates Who Participated in Specified Civic Activities.   461
65. Effect of Participation in a School Program on Community Behavior of Children.   463
66. Relationship Between Urban Occupational Strata and Politico-Economic Attitudes.   466

67. Percentage of a Sample of Adults of Various Groups Who Voted in the 1948 Presidential Election. 467
68. Contrasts Between Delinquents and Nondelinquents: Family Characteristics and Relationships. 472
69. Contrasts Between Delinquents and Nondelinquents: Personal Characteristics, Attitudes, and Habits. 473
70. Percentage Distribution of Certain Offenses Within Age Groups. 476
71. Changes in Specific Religious Beliefs During Adolescence. 482
72. Types of Religious "Awakening" Experienced by People of Different Social and Religious Backgrounds. 485
73. Religious Practices of Catholics in a Southern City. 487
74. Changes in Religious Attitudes and Activities in Later Maturity. 489
75. Coefficients of Correlation from Two Studies Showing the Similarity Between Mutual Friends. 510
76. Behaviour Traits of Residents in a "Training School for Girls." 516
77. Social Class of Self and Class of Listed Best Friends by Number and Percent. 517
78. Degree of Companionship in Old Age, by Age Periods. 525
79. Social Acceptability and Average Scores on Recreational Activities, Usefulness, and Happiness of the Residents of a Community for Old People. 526
80. Contrasts Between Upwardly Mobile and Nonmobile Unmarried Career Women. 528
81. Percentage of Men and Women Over 65 Who Were Upwardly or Downwardly Mobile by Age 50 Compared to Parents' Status, and Who Were Upwardly or Downwardly Mobile from Age 50 on. 529
82. Extent of Participation in Various High School Activities of Children from Different Social Levels. 539
84. Adult Age Trends in Bias Toward Various Groups in a Sample of College Graduates. 551
85. Adult Age Differences in Attitude Toward Minority Groups as Revealed by Public Opinion Poll Questions. 552
86. Mean Ethnocentrism Score of Members of Various Organizations. 554
87. Percentage Frequency with Which High School Freshmen and Seniors Had Dates. 570

88. Attitudes of Parents Toward First Dating as Reported by College Students.   571
89. Progress Toward Mate Selection with Progressive "Affairs" as Suggested by Emotional Components Reported by College Students.   576
90. Percentage of 409 Couples Reporting Various Degrees of Present Adjustment in Marriage.   593
91. Median Age of Husband and Wife at Each Stage of the Family Cycle, United States, 1940 and 1890.   594
92. Percentages of a Group of College Students Who Stated They Had Obtained Sex Information from Various Sources.   603
93. Median Number of Times per Week Orgasm Is Experienced, from All Causes, Among Single and Married Males and Females Who Are Sexually Active.   606
94. Percentage Distribution of the Criticisms of Mothers and Fathers Offered by Adolescent Offspring.   611
95. Percentage Distribution of Causes of Quarrels with Parents Reported by Boys and Girls.   612
96. Percentage of Husbands and Wives Reporting Attitudes, Judgments, or Behavior with Respect to "In-Laws."   617
97. The "In-Law" Named by Respondents as Representing the Most Difficult In-Law Relationship Experienced.   618
98. Percentage Distribution of the Roles of Grandparents and Great-Grandparents.   621
99. Percentage Distribution of a Sample of People Over 65 According to Living Arrangements.   622

PREFACE •

IN 1939, the writers collaborated in a volume (*Life: A Psychological Survey*) which was believed unique in two respects: it was a developmental psychology covering the life span with emphasis on the adult and older years; and it emphasized socioeconomic and cultural more than biological environments and backgrounds. Since then, a number of texts have appeared also covering the life span. However, these treatments have tended to minimize development and change past 20. And they have minimized socioeconomic and cultural backgrounds and influences which the writers feel are cumulatively, in the adult and older years, of great importance.

Since 1939, and especially in the last 10 years, gerontology has become not only a major field of professional interest for many psychologists, biologists, and sociologists, but also a subject of general public discussion. Important studies having to do developmentally with the young adult and middle ages, such as the Kinsey reports, and Lehman's studies regarding age of achievement, have appeared. There has been much recent relevant sociological, economic, and anthropological research. Needs for a long developmental perspective seem increasing in a variety of areas—in educational and vocational guidance, in industrial psychology, in most of the many types of work psychologists are doing in governmental agencies. A more adequate time dimension seems desirable in treatment of sundry topics in general psychology. In this era of longer life and increasing numbers of older people, a full-length picture of human life might be declared a need of every well-informed person. The writers have, therefore, again attempted a developmental psychology of the life span, taking account of the vast total of new work in and related to the field.

This total is so extensive that some limitation from the scope of the earlier volume seemed necessary. Socioeconomic and cultural backgrounds have, therefore, been much less stressed, and the several chapters in the first volume emphasizing certain broad applications have been omitted. The treatment in the present volume thus becomes, much more than before, a developmental psychology rather than a broad survey. But it again attempts to give what is believed a desirable emphasis on socio-economic and cultural as well as biological backgrounds. And it goes much more extensively than before into psychological topics, with a life-span approach.

To this task the writers bring not only the experience in the earlier collaboration but also continuing professional activities in gerontology, in adult education, and in wide-ranging research projects having to do with growth and change of abilities, interests, and attitudes through child-hood and adolescence and into the older years. Perhaps it might be said that their professional careers have been consciously directed in terms of a life-span developmental perspective. As mentioned above, and stressed in the first chapter, they feel that such a treatment can be of very direct personal value to a reader, of relevance in most fields of applied psy-chology, and also of decided perspective-giving value in consideration of a variety of topics in general psychology. It has been said that the psy-chology of the first part of this century had as a distinctive characteristic the emergence, and the assimilation into the larger body of professional knowledge, of research on growth through childhood and adolescence. Certainly that work has made its contributions to larger thinking in the total field. The writers venture the prediction that the middle period of the century may well see a similar contribution from study extending developmentally through the years of maturity.

A word remains to be said regarding the structuring of the treatment. An introductory chapter seeks to indicate purposes and to outline very broadly certain basic socioeconomic and cultural settings considered es-sential for understanding human development and change in today's world and especially today's America. Five chapters then attempt to indicate the most significant features of physical development and change through the life span, to bring together diverse material into something of a reformulation of current concepts regarding abilities, to stress cer-tain educational issues often involving long-term developmental factors or problems, and to view the work life in analogous fashion. The five chapters have been grouped in a first part, as dealing with organic po-tentials and major tasks. For the first six chapters, and the last, the first author has been primarily responsible. Chapters 7–12 (the work of the second author) are concerned with motivation and emotion, values, and social relationships, and have been grouped as a second part of the entire volume. The final chapter is an effort to make certain integrations and applications and to stress certain issues seen as most vital in the total volume. The division of labor (but with joint planning throughout, and frequent conferences and correspondence) is believed to have given more adequacy than one person could well achieve—and has resulted also in certain differences in style and mode of presentation and occasionally in point of view, from one part to the other, which should make for more variegated, interesting reading. The chapters are long but carefully organized, in the belief that a life-span view calls for a treatment substantial and closely structured. Seen in the long perspective, every major phase of life needs to be seen both in its complexity, and whole.

SIDNEY L. PRESSEY
RAYMOND G. KUHLEN

January, 1957

• Psychological Development
Through the Life Span

CHAPTER 1 •

• Development in the Changing Modern World

THIS volume has, it is believed, two major special characteristics: it deals with psychological development and change throughout the life span, with emphasis on the adult years, and it attempts to see that development in its social and economic and cultural environment, an environment which is rapidly changing. These two special features need to be examined more fully.

Values of a Life-Span Perspective

A developmental psychology covering the human life span and with emphasis on the adult years may, the writers believe, serve the reader in two ways: it may help a person in seeking more adequate self-understanding and in meeting present and future problems; and it may help a student who desires to see various phases and specialties of psychology in long developmental perspective.

SELF-UNDERSTANDING AND PLANNING FOR ONE'S TOTAL LIFE

Suppose the reader is in his early twenties. He very likely has a vocational choice to be made, or at least to be matured and carried through. In this connection, he needs any help he can find for self-appraisal and for judgment regarding his possible choices, in terms not only of total possible career but also total related adult life experience. He very likely still has before him the problems of choice, of adjustments, and of family living involved in marriage. As he becomes adult, he will have responsibilities of community living. Very likely he will have problems both of child-rearing and of adjusting to and perhaps helping older members of the family. As he gets older, a successful career may bring enlarging, often new, psychological relationships, or disappointment in life work may force very trying problems of acceptance and psychological "down-grading." As children leave home, relationships with spouse and with friends may be substantially reconstituted. Retirement may be a major crisis, and old age may be an empty, purposeless loneliness. The young adult should have some awareness of these issues of the future; the older reader may find value in discussion of them which brings immediate problems into the proportion of a life view. An adult of any age should try to see his life as a whole and understand others as whole personalities at different stages in the total developmental process.

CONTRIBUTIONS OF A LIFE-SPAN PERSPECTIVE TO GENERAL PSYCHOLOGY

A life-span perspective *should,* the writers contend, be a basic mode of viewing almost every phase and topic in psychology. For instance, abilities are almost always considered in terms of their growth through childhood and adolescence. But it is now increasingly being appreciated that in adult life some abilities may decline, while others perhaps increase, and the total constitution of the intellectual capacities substantially changes. Not only are these various changes after 18 or 20 of importance in themselves, but they may well force reformulations of basic theory regarding abilities. Somewhat similarly, long-term consideration of the growth of some interests and the decrease of others, and changes in motivational strength and patterns throughout the span of life, should give a better understanding of the extent to which the lively dynamic of youth is primarily a biological phenomenon of growth and the decrease thereafter biological and inevitable. Or may the changes and perhaps much of the decreases in the strength of interests in the adult and older years be quite as much an outcome of changes and limitations involved in social role and expectation, of decreasing range and availability of opportunity, and of boredom and timidity? Yet, more broadly, personality is a totality which can hardly be adequately appraised in childhood and youth, because the outcome of trends in those years is not yet known. And somewhat different phases or perhaps types of personality may be appropriate at different ages. In fact, it would seem essential in any consideration of personality to know how it develops and changes throughout life. Problems of childhood personality need to be seen not alone in the context of child life but with relation to possible inadequacies in young adulthood; their seriousness may not be manifest until a crisis of menopause or senescence brings out starkly an inadequacy that was largely concealed through middle life. Or, there may be a splendid triumph of character in age, showing strength not before appreciated.

THE LIFE-SPAN VIEW IN APPLIED PSYCHOLOGY

In applied psychology, even more than in general psychology, the life-span point of view would seem valuable in sundry applications of the subject. Surely, educational guidance in youth should be with reference to plans in adult life, and appraisal of such guidance should be in terms of the ways those plans work out. Industrial personnel workers obviously should be concerned with any age changes in the competence of workers, with adjustments of work to age, with problems of advancement or down-grading, or with retirement—all basically issues of development and change in the adult years. Marriage counseling needs, more than it often has, the long perspective, as well as insights regarding any immediate problem situations. The psychologist specializing in clinical work or in counseling should recognize, more than some do, the many counseling and clinical problems in maturity and old age as well as in young adulthood. The opinion will even be ventured that a psychology of the life span has more to contribute to such related special fields as social case-work and psychiatry than any briefer segment in psychology considered by itself. In short, the writers believe that a developmental psychology with life-span range, but with emphasis on the years after 20, has distinctive interest and distinctive values to a wide range of possible readers.

The Rapidly Changing World Context of Human Development

It is a commonplace that now is a time of almost universal rapid change. This fact has bearings in many ways on an adequate developmental psychology of the life span, which must take account of major influences affecting that development.

LENGTHENED LIFE AND MOUNTING POPULATIONS

Indeed, the first topic to be considered involves the extension of that span—with possible consequences that are both encouraging and frighteningly difficult! Figure 1 exhibits a major and unique feature of the world today—average length of life has, especially in the Western world over the last 50 years, been extraordinarily lengthened. Data for early times are, of course, only rough estimates, based on tombstone inscriptions and other scattered evidence. But gradually, vital statistics have become more adequate. There is no doubt that since 1900 the average length of life in this country has increased almost 20 years.

This lengthening is due primarily to reduction of mortality in infancy

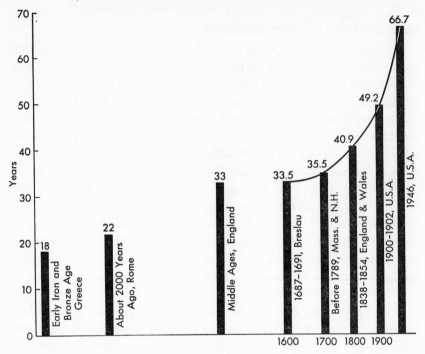

Figure 1. Average Length of Life from Ancient to Modern Times. (Adapted from L. I. Dublin, A. J. Lotka, and M. Spiegelman, *Length of Life* (rev. ed.), New York, Ronald Press, 1949.)

and childhood by conquest of such diseases as diphtheria. Many more persons now than formerly thus survive into adult life. But since relatively little progress has been made in dealing with diseases of the middle and older years, such as cancer and hardening of the arteries, there is little more expectation of life for a person at 60 now than there was a century ago. Now, the average person who lives to be 60 will average about 17 more years of life—about two more years than in 1900. Figure 2(upper and lower parts) shows, for two dates, numbers out of 100 born who survived to successive ages and the expectation of life remaining at each age. From the lower part of Figure 2 the reader can (for what satisfaction it may give him) read off the number of years of additional life he may hope for before he dies. But there can be this added cheer: with reasonable self-care, he should be able to better the average, and advances in medical science from now on should help him to do it.

Lengthened life might be expected to increase the proportion of adult

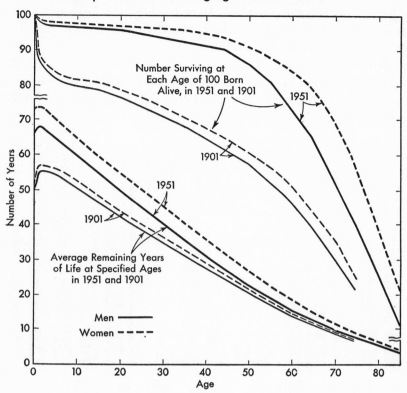

Figure 2.   Survivors from Birth to Successive Ages and Expectation of Life According to Life Table for the United States. (From Abridged Life Tables, U.S. Office of Vital Statistics, Washington, D.C., U.S. Government Printing Office, April 30, 1954.)

and older people in the population. Figure 3 shows the age composition of the population of this country over a 100-year period, with estimates for the near future. Evidently in 1850 this country had indeed a young population—over half the people were under 20. In 1950 less than a third were this young. But the proportion of people 65 and over had increased about three times. In the last 50 years the population of this country has doubled, but the number 40 through 65 has tripled, and the number 65 and over has quadrupled. These changes have been caused not only by lengthened life but also by other factors. Fifty years ago great numbers of young adults were immigrating into this country from Europe, but more recently immigration has been drastically restricted. Until recently, the American birth rate had been dropping, the younger age group in consequence not being replenished. More recently, the birth rate has increased, thus increasing the numbers of children and young people. Thus, some influences are countering the trend to an older population. But the number of people who are living into the older years also continues to mount. Lengthened lives and increasing numbers of the adult and old as well as of the young would thus seem to call for a developmental psychology covering all these ages.

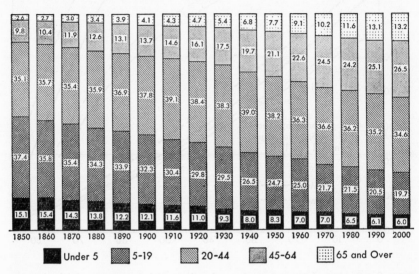

Figure 3.   Percent Distribution of Total Population by Age, United States 1850 to 2000. (1850 to 1940 from U.S. Census enumerations; 1950 to 2000 from estimates by the Bureau of the Census, 1947.)

Contrasting conditions, especially in the Near and Far East, should be noted. For example, a recent report showed a death rate of 34 per thousand in Egypt as compared to 11 in this country—and only 8 in still healthier New Zealand. In the United States, in 1939–1941, about 95 out of every 100 persons born survived to the age of 5; in India only 60 survived to the age of 5 and only 15 lived to be 60, as compared to 67 in this country.

Lengthened life spans and increasing proportions of older people have come about especially in Western Europe and North America. But, in other countries there have been sufficient reductions in deaths from disease, famine, and war to increase their population growth substantially. In total, the population of the world has doubled in the last 100 years; in the last 300 years it has increased almost four times. This tremendous and accelerating upsurge of world population, with most rapid growth in the last 50 years, is indeed a phenomenon of frightening importance. It is well shown in Figure 4. Though for a while Europe and North America grew rapidly in number of people, Asia has grown, too, and it continues to have the majority of the world's population.

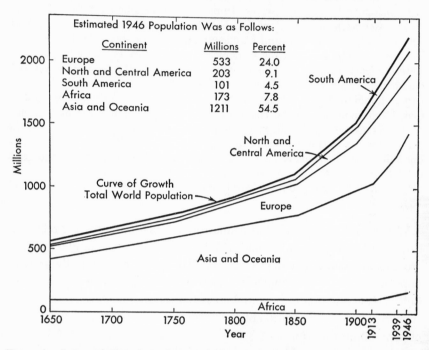

Estimated 1946 Population Was as Follows:

Continent	Millions	Percent
Europe	533	24.0
North and Central America	203	9.1
South America	101	4.5
Africa	173	7.8
Asia and Oceania	1211	54.5

Figure 4. Estimated Growth in the Population of the World and of Each Continent. (Adapted from A. M. Carr-Saunders, *World Population*, Oxford, Clarendon Press, 1937, and W. S. Thompson, *Plenty of People*, New York, Ronald Press, 1948.)

The shifting comparative rates of population growth must be stressed. For more than a century, up until about 1900, the Western Europeans and "their migratory descendants overseas" increased most rapidly. But then their population growth began to slow up. The population of France remained stationary from 1900 to 1950; The population of Ireland decreased 7 percent. But the population of the Soviet Union has increased 59 percent. China and India have grown 30 and 49 percent respectively. Indonesia, the Philippines, and Thailand have doubled their populations in the last 50 years (*15*).

In general, the most advanced countries economically and culturally have grown slowly or actually decreased. And within a given country there has been a similar perverse tendency for those segments of the population which might be thought of as most desirable in sundry respects to show the lowest increase. Thus, in 1935 the fertility rates for 1000 wives in families having incomes of $5000 or more was only 78—100 being the number of children required to maintain a population. But 1000 wives on total relief had 147 children. One thousand wives of professional men had 94 children, and wives of businessmen had 86; but wives of unskilled workers had 115 offspring. The "White Replacement Index" of San Francisco was 53 and that of New York City was 63; but of rural farm families it was 154. In short, the families who had the most children had the least means to take care of and educate them, were the least competent occupationally, and were in the least culturally rich environments. There is evidence also that the least able mentally have the largest families. And some investigators have presented evidence suggesting that, in consequence, in the countries in which these trends are most prominent, average general intelligence may be slowly decreasing (2). Recently, the population of this country has been growing faster than had been estimated— but still slower than many backward countries. And "fertility of college graduates throughout the United States continues upward. . . . But they are not yet contributing their pro-rata share to the quota of next generation's children" (8).

Western European and North American populations, growing relatively slowly or actually declining, and with increasing numbers of older people, are thus in mounting conflict with much larger and more rapidly growing populations which have much larger proportions of younger people. Here, indeed, is a situation of potential crisis that needs intensive study, which should include consideration of psychological differences in the dynamics of populations thus different. Surely, the outnumbered and aging Western peoples need to consider the characteristics and potentialities of their populations to the end that, in their greater stability and maturity, distinctive strengths might possibly be found and adjustments might be made to any weaknesses.

TECHNOLOGY

Clearly, one resource in the above situation might be found in the extraordinary developments in American technology, especially in the last 50 years—changes often so taken for granted that the total impact of them may not be adequately recognized. Figure 5 includes diverse information, indicative of little less than a revolution as regards the nature of living and resources therefor (the reader will note that progressive reduction in scaling for the higher percents makes the changes appear less than they really are). From 1890 to 1950, there occurred a drop of about 25 percent in average hours of work but an increase of over 450 percent in output per man-hour. And this increased efficiency, plus an increase of about 280 percent in number of employed workers, has resulted in almost an 800 percent increase in the gross national productivity!

Increased productivity was a result, in large part, of the increase in use of power. Even in 1900, half the work of America was done by the

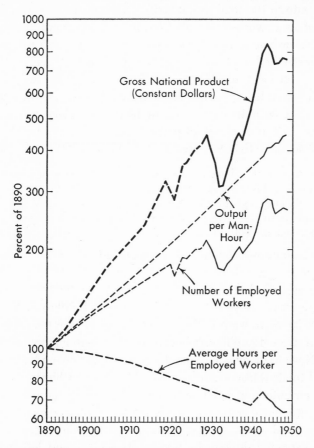

Figure 5. National Output and Labor Input. Our long-run production achievements have been more the result of increased productivity than of increased employment. Output per man-hour has more than quadrupled in the last 60 years. (From Department of Commerce, Department of Labor, and Council of Economic Advisors, *The Economic Report of the President*, Washington, D.C., January, 1950, p. 76.)

muscles of animals and men. By 1944 animals supplied only 2 percent of our work energy and human beings only 4 percent; the rest came from such sources as coal, oil, gas, and water power. But increases in productivity have come not only from more power but also from use of that power through marvelous machines and carefully planned utilization of workers and devices for maximal total effectiveness. These devices serve mightily in almost all types of work—farming, mining, lumbering, as well as manufacturing. Such various gains as hybrid corn, cows that produce more milk, hens that produce more eggs, and trees that bear more fruit all contribute to the total productivity. "During the nineteen forties the number of farm workers shrank from 9½ million to only a little over 8 million. Nevertheless, farm production increased by 25 percent" (*1*, p. 192). Work in the homes was also made easier. In 1900 only a few homes were wired for electricity, but by 1935, 21 million were wired; by 1950, 48 million homes had electricity. In 1920, electric refrigerators were rare; now there are 50 million of them. In 1900, rural electrification had not begun; "by 1935 only about 10 percent of American farms were electrified; by 1950, more than 85 percent were" (*1*, p. 191).

In contrast with the above situation, the level of production of most of the people in the world is lower than that of this country in 1890. The great present American efficiency (as illustrated by Figure 5) has enabled this country to produce and consume one-third of the world's goods and services, although it has less than one-fifteenth of the world's population.

Advances in transportation and communication have been indeed spectacular. Once again, the extraordinary progress of the last 50 years can be well summarized in a graph. In the whole United States only 13,824 automobiles were registered in 1900 as compared with over 40 million in 1950. In 1900, there were slightly more than a million telephones, but in 1951, there were 45 million. Twenty-five years ago air travel was an adventure. Now, to many, a lurching train seems as slow and uncomfortable compared to air transportation as the old-fashioned buggy seemed compared to an automobile. Radio and television are tending to make the whole country one community, in which vast numbers may listen together to one voice and watch one scene. To an extraordinary extent, experience has been extended directly by increased mobility and less tangibly by the long reach of communication. There result psychological problems and psychological benefits in profusion: children become so absorbed with TV that a teacher resigns in disgust, declaring herself unable to compete, but home-bound old people find in the same medium a return again into the world which revitalizes their spirits. As shown in Figure 6, recent increases are greatest.

The treatment has stressed the great rapidity of change since 1900. A grandfather is almost literally correct when he says that he grew up in a different world from now. A developmental psychology covering the life span should, at the outset, clearly recognize this fact. Moreover, in the last 15 years, advances seem to have been particularly rapid. Automation is bringing new marvels of production. "Ford's automatic engine plant turns out twice as many engines as an old-style plant, with one-tenth the manpower."[1] The atom in peace may bring wonders as great as in war.

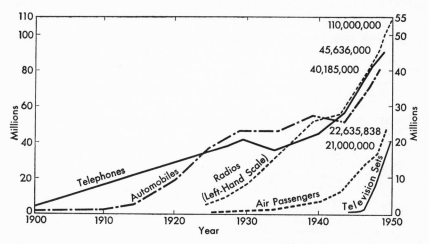

Figure 6.   Radio Sets in Use (Left-Hand Scale) and Television Sets in Use, Automobiles, Registrations, Telephones, and Passengers on Domestic Air Lines (Right-Hand Scale), 1900–1952. (Automobiles, telephones, and air passengers: U.S. Bureau of the Census, *Statistical Abstract of the United States, 1954* (75th ed.), Washington, D.C., U.S. Government Printing Office, 1954, pp. 496, 460, 530. Air Passengers also U.S. Bureau of the Census, Continuation to 1952 of Historical Statistics of the U.S. (1789–1945), Washington, D.C., U.S. Government Printing Office, 1954. Radios and television: *Broadcasting Telecasting,* 1952, 53rd and 54th issues.)

The reader should note that most of the preceding graphs have shown changes proceeding *increasingly* rapidly. Almost everything seems to be moving (the hope must be) to new crescendos of marvelous living—or, conceivably, of explosive disintegration, if affairs go awry. It would seem that any adequate psychology must take account of these facts of the environment of modern living.

ECONOMIC CHANGE

The increase in productivity in the last 60 years has already been exhibited as a gain in technology. It may well be put in purchasing power and in resources for living. In terms of 1947 prices, it has been estimated

[1] Quoted from *Newsweek* in *Automation* (*14*).

that, in 1900, American workmen earned 27 cents an hour; in 1920, 56 cents; in 1940, $1.21; and in 1944, $1.40. In 1960, an estimate of $1.74 has been made. The income of the average family has been calculated as $4460 in 1950 as compared to $3320 (in 1950 dollars) in 1929, or a gain of 1½ percent a year (*19*). These are indeed great gains that may well be contrasted with earnings in other countries. Thus, it has been estimated that in the second half of 1950, an American would have to work about 33 hours to earn a man's wool suit, but a Frenchman would need to labor 86 hours for the same purchase, and an Italian would have to

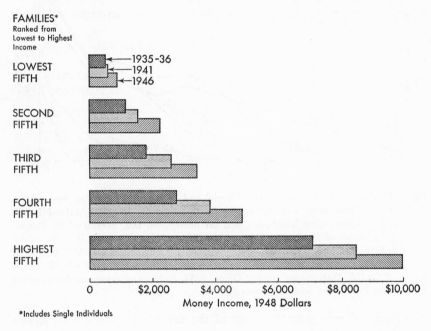

*Includes Single Individuals

Figure 7. Changes in Average Family Income. The average family income of all groups has increased greatly from the prewar period. The fifth of families having highest incomes received the largest increase in dollars but smallest relative increase. (Statistics from National Resources Planning Board, Department of Labor, and Department of Commerce, and Council of Economic Advisers.)

work 208 hours. Earnings in more primitive countries would, of course, be even lower.

The above figures are averages. Figure 7 shows something as to the range of incomes in this country (in terms of dollars of 1948 purchasing power) in 1935–1936 and 1948. In 1935, the lowest fifth of families had an annual income of only about $600; in 1948, the lowest fifth was still not well off, but its income was almost doubled. And it must be remembered that in the lowest group are the handicapped, the old, and those under temporary financial difficulties. In addition, their problems are cushioned in large part by measures of social security shortly to be mentioned. The second fifth of families was, in 1948, receiving much more income than 12 years before. Over this period, all segments of the population seem to have gained substanstantially in resources for living. And since 1948 (as will be mentioned in consideration of the work life), these trends have gone further.

As mentioned above, various protections against economic need are now available. Figure 8 shows the growth of some of these programs. The

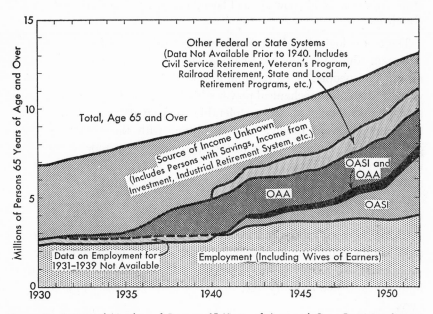

Figure 8.   Estimated Number of Persons 65 Years of Age and Over Receiving Income from Specified Source, December, 1930, to December, 1952. (U.S. Bureau of the Census, *Statistical Abstract of the United States, 1954* (75th ed.), Washington, D.C., U.S. Government Printing Office, 1954.)

growth in coverage and in total benefits has been great in the following areas: industrial accident compensation, unemployment compensation, private pension plans, old age and survivors insurance, and aid for the aged (OASI and OAA or Old Age Assistance).

Not only have incomes risen and protections against need in cases of failure of income increased, but also conditions of work have greatly improved, tasks have been made easier, and the workday and the work week have been shortened. Child labor has almost been done away with, and early in old age, retirement with pension is possible. In total, these gains make life very different now as compared to a generation or two ago. And today's worker returns to a home with comforts which would have indeed seemed luxurious 50 years ago. However, in many countries of the world, workers still toil long hours, from childhood through old age, in burdensome drudgery, living in city slums or rural hovels.

This résumé of the merits of the American economy may seem trite. But a developmental psychology reaching from young to old must consider the varying circumstances of people's upbringings and appreciate how unique many of the conditions of life now are and how different the conditions are from life elsewhere.

The technological and economic changes mentioned in the last pages also seem admirably adopted to a population that is living longer and has more older people. A more comfortable life, greater security in older years, and greater mechanical power which results in less need for manual strength and shorter and more tolerable work conditions are all changes that, indeed, seem timely. In competition with the surging younger populations of many other countries, such changed economic conditions might even put the United States into an advantage because of the matured stability, experience, and resourcefulness of its people.

CHANGED SOCIETY AND CULTURE

Changing more subtly, but in many respects as markedly as the economy, are the American society and culture. Certain of these changes are so intimate, so pervasive and powerful in their effects on the nature of human experience at every age, that they must be briefly touched upon here.

Changes in the family are indeed changes in the basic unit of society. Figure 9 summarizes three gross changes over the past 80 years: the falling then rising birth rate, rising marriage and divorce rate, and mounting increase in proportion of married women who are employed. Probably a better indication of the divorce rate than is given in the graph is the number of divorces in proportion to the number of marriages in a given year. In 1870, there were 3 per 100 marriages; by 1900, 7; in 1945, a peak of 32 was reached; and in 1950, the rate was 24—about 1 divorce for every 4 marriages. The increase in divorce plus the great increase in number of wives employed makes clear a great change in the family and in family life.

The shift in attitude has been tremendous. The family, formerly a unit strongly knit together, protecting, comforting, encouraging each member, forming a bulwark against the vicissitudes of life, and existing as long as its members lived, now tends to be thought of as a joining of two individuals, each of whom has, to be sure, a large stake in the undertaking but either of whom has tacit permission to withdraw if the marriage does not meet individual expectations. . . . Remarriages occur without prejudice. Nor do those who remain married seriously disapprove of those who terminate their marriages. Under other circumstances, might they not also have acted likewise? (3, p. 11.)

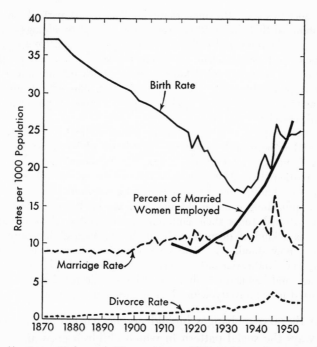

Figure 9. Marriage, Birth, and Divorce Rates, 1870–1954, and Percent of Married Women Employed 1910–1951. Note: The curve for employment has been smoothed. (Adapted from R. S. Cavan, *The American Family*, New York, Crowell, 1953, pp. 19 and 534, with extensions from recent U.S. Statistical Reports.)

Also of great importance is the shift from what has been called a kinship to a conjugal family. The older kinship family included in the intimate family circle, often living together, not only the young married couple and their children but also one or more grandparents and perhaps a maiden aunt. In a large country home the relatives could often be useful in the work of the house or farm. And since very likely all had grown up and been long resident in the community, they were easily part of it.

Now, young married people and their children are likely to live in small apartments or houses in a community strange to *their* parents or other relatives. They frequently move, and they no longer think of other relatives as really part of their own small conjugal group. Problems are thereby presented as regards the mode of living of the elderly or others economically dependent. The essential nature of the family has, especially for older people, basically changed.

In most societies . . . the immediate family . . . is part of an extended kinship system, so that the child is structurally related to siblings and parents but also to grandparents and collateral relatives descended from common ancestors (uncles and aunts, cousins of various degrees). . . . The child remains a member of the same extended kinship group, with definite and continuing rights and responsibilities, even through marriage, parenthood, and old age. . . . The aged in such a system tend to acquire increasing power and responsibility, with correlative security.

The extreme conjugal family stands in marked contrast . . . the family into which a child is born and family into which his children are born are two quite different units. . . . Old people have no definite claim . . . for support and social participation. The primary obligation of each brother and sister is to his or her own family, and the same is true for married children. . . . Persons now in or approaching inactive old age . . . are likely to be kinship-oriented to a degree that disturbs their children and bewilders their grandchildren. . . . There is a kind of deep tragedy in the vagaries of the normative patterns as they now stand. . . . The same complex process loosely called "urbanization" and "industrialization" has made it possible for more people to reach old age and has made it difficult or impossible for the aged to be used and supported in conformity with older patterns and values. (6, pp. 34–39.)

Though the above changes hit old people hardest, they also involve in many ways the social pattern in which children grow up; they make adult life not a pattern into which the person can settle back, but rather a series of roles, all demanding, and with the act, the stage, and the players frequently changing. Study of personal-social development throughout the life span seems indeed called for in hope of better understanding of this complex and rapidly changing situation.

Present-day shorter hours, beginning work at a later age, retiring at an earlier age, and manifold conveniences have yielded time for leisure and energy for its use to an unprecedented degree for the great masses of people. Figure 10 is a simple and straightforward display of growing interest in sports as evidenced by the space given in a great metropolitan newspaper and in a daily in a midwestern city. Especially to be noted are the gains in attention to collegiate and then secondary school sports, as these become interests not only for the young people immediately involved but for the community. The development of interests of various types will be returned to later. Here it is important only to emphasize the rapid growth of leisure in recent years and the doubtful worth of

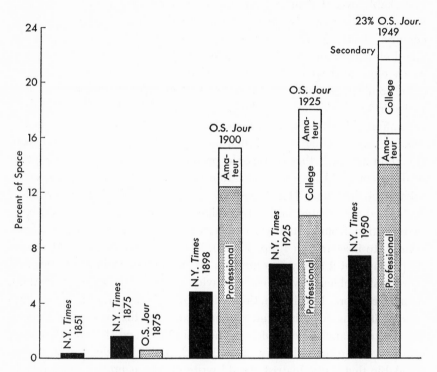

Figure 10. A Century's Increase in Space Given to Sports News. (Adapted from S. L. Pressey and W. E. Crates, Sports and the public mind, *School and Society*, 1950, 72:373-374.)

many leisure activities. Also, recreation seems to be largely (at least so far as the participants are concerned) for the youth; the new leisure of adult life and the vast leisure of the older people still do not seem to be constructively provided for. Surely a task of the immediate future is to find ways of using leisure with some larger profit and adapting leisure to fit the needs of those at each stage of the new, long life span.

Reviewing his own long life, shortly after the turn of the century, Henry Adams wrote that "In essentials like religion, ethics, philosophy; in history, literature, art and the concepts of all science . . . the American boy of 1854 stood nearer the year one than to the year 1900" (Adams quoted in Lynd, *10*, p. 53). But since this last date, changes in the total American scene have moved at a continuingly accelerated rate. They have been "all but convulsive." Surely, Americans who have lived through recent years might agree that the "American mind" has also changed remarkably over that time. Certainly, there have been pervasive changes in mood. "The most significant fact about the changes in the past half century," Bruce Bliven has declared, has been "the alteration in the moral climate from one of overwhelming optimism to one which comes pretty close to despair" (*1*, p. 261). This came not only from the wars, atom bombs, and continuing conflicts that are global in scope and pervasive in ideologies. By 1950 Americans "had all but banished God from their affairs," but they did not know "who or what they would put in His place. . . ." They had relaxed their moral standards and habits "but were uncertain as to whether they could preserve themselves from corruption or decadence." "American civilization was urban, but it was not yet an urbane civilization." Her "economy of abundance" had nevertheless "witnessed the greatest and most prolonged depression." There had been "a transition from certainty to uncertainty, from faith to doubt, from security to insecurity" (*4*, pp. 406 ff.). The American mind might not be despairing, but it surely was facing a greater range of more complex and more vast problems, with fewer convictions and assurances to hold to, than ever before. In this situation, with nostalgic desperation "many lawyers, politicians, scientists, and economists occupy themselves by suggesting the minimal changes which are necessary to stand still; yet the status quo proves the most illusory of goals (*12*, p. 370). Indeed, it is understandable that a psychiatrist should write of "the neurotic personality of our time."

If the changes of the last half century have been confusing and disrupting of older ideas and ideals in this country, then how much greater must be the frustration and distress of those involved in the cataclysmic events in Germany, the upheavals in Russia and China, and the disorders and changes in India. Governmental, economic, social, and cultural changes which in the past have taken centuries have all swept through in a few years. The German mind, the Russian mind, the Chinese mind—to what extraordinary bruising and disintegrative forces they have been subject. Through what bewildering changes of attitudes, ideals, beliefs, loyalties, and views of life and the world have the older members of these countries gone! And how largely without guidance from accepted past custom or mode of thought are the minds of their younger generation developing!

SOCIETY AND CULTURE AND THE LONGER VIEW IN DEVELOPMENTAL PSYCHOLOGY

It is a commonplace of psychology that usual situations can be met with little thinking by established habits, but that an informed intelligence is necessary to deal with changed or new situations where the organism does not know what to do. The preceding paragraphs have suggested that American society, and the complex of ideas and attitudes and purposes broadly called the American mind, have been pervasively and rapidly changing and that in most of the rest of the world, change and confusion have been even greater. To have some understanding of the differences between older and younger people in their ideas about the family and relations between the sexes, use and abuse of leisure, and philosophy of life may ease tensions by substituting an intellectual for an emotional reaction to these differences. An understanding of the ways these differences have developed in the lives of different generations, and of constitutional differences between older and younger personalities, should suggest tolerant adjustments.

Increasingly, historians, anthropologists, and sociologists have stressed these facts and problems and considered them in terms of their subject matter. Developmental psychologists should do the same thing, and this volume attempts to do so—often from an interdisciplinary point of view, in the belief that a developmental psychology stressing the adult and older years has much to gain from these other social sciences and that they can find much of service to them in such a broad-based psychology of the whole life span.

The Double Task of a Developmental Psychology of the Life Span

The diversity of material in the preceding pages has, the writers believe, a double unity in its implications regarding subject material and regarding needs.

There is indicated, it is believed, a developmental psychology which is substantially new in its total Gestalt. It is a new phenomenon for most people in favored countries to live out most of a biological life span. New, therefore, is a psychology not only of the last part of that span but of the first part as seen with relation to the later outcome. A modern developmental psychology is also substantially a new subject because the physical circumstances of life, and also current and coming culture and ideology, are largely new. The child growing up in the age of radio and television, air travel, and atomic destruction is surely a somewhat different child in his present existence, and his probable future growth and change, from the youngster of the leisurely, isolated, horse-drawn age of a half-century ago. A present-day developmental psychology of the life span must describe a creature who in his life course and in his environment is a type of person that never existed before.

In view of all that has been said and the extraordinary mounting potentials of change, this new person has new needs. The young person has the need for learning to live with old people whose number will grow to be legion. He has the need for planning for middle and old age and living wisely through these periods. He will probably live his older years not in the family circle, like the comparatively few grandparents of a century ago, but in a largely independent age class, whose social, economic, and ideational characteristics have still largely to be determined. The *average* 20-year-old now will (unless civilization destroys itself) live past the year 2000! Even a vivid imagination hesitates to try to conceive what life will be like then. There is need to replan education and replan industry with reference to this new human who will usually live his life span through, and in a world of such rapid change. There is need for a reconstituted ideology for people of all ages, living together, yet having desirable independence and significant purposes congruent to these new times. A broad developmental psychology alert to these facts and these needs would seem of basic importance in this situation.

And the double task is urgent. The present appears to be one of the major crisis times of history, the global East-West conflict being of enormous portent and putting the West under terrible handicap of man power. Only by superior use of its more limited populations might the West survive. It cannot keep up in any population race with the Orient. Only by making its peoples more competent over a longer life, and using them more wisely, would any effective continuance—certainly any important advances—of Western civilizations seem possible.

Summary

This volume has two special characteristics: first, it deals with psychological development and change throughout the life span (not simply in childhood and youth), with emphasis on the fact that change and de-

velopment go on after the growth years; second, it sees that development in its rapidly changing socioeconomic and cultural environment—
not simply as a biological phenomenon.

1. Such a treatment is believed to have special value in (1) aiding
self-understanding for seeing one's life as a whole, and so planning it,
(2) giving a life-span perspective to topics in general psychology which
results in significant long-term interpretations, and (3) making much in
applied psychology more useful.

2. During the first half of this century, length of life in this country
increased by almost 20 years (to about 68 for men and 70 for women),
and the composition of the population has shifted so that in 1950 there
were over 12 million in this country over 65. While the population has
doubled since 1900, the number of people who are 65 and over has
quadrupled. These phenomena of lengthened average life span and of
aging of the total population are common in all the Western European
countries. For the first time anywhere in the history of the world, people
may hope to live out substantially a full life span, and the middle-aged
and old people are major elements in the population. In contrast, high
death rates in the Orient keep down the average length of life. But
death rates have been reduced enough, while the birth rate continues
high, so that the population growth has resulted in overwhelmingly large
populations in Asia. And world population has doubled in the last hundred years; an explosive population pressure may result.

3. In this country, production per man-hour has increased 450 percent
in the last 60 years; at the same time, hours of work per week have been
cut about a quarter, and work has been made easier. Drudgery in the
home and on the farm, as well as in the factory, has also been greatly
reduced. Marvelous advances in transportation and communication bring
almost every section of the country within easy reach of every other,
and television, as it were, brings millions together at one scene. But in
most parts of the world, lifelong burdensome toil for long hours has remained the lot of the people, and transportation has continued by ox-
cart. Thus, because technology in this country seems to be advancing at
an accelerating rate, the contrast with backward countries is becoming
more marked and perhaps more critical.

4. Average real income in this country has increased almost seven
times in the last hundred years. Moreover, distribution of income is now
far more equitable than in 1850 or 1900 or even in 1930. Such measures
as industrial accident insurance, unemployment insurance, pension plans,

and aid for the aged give support in times of economic need. These changes bring a degree of comfort and security that were never before enjoyed, anywhere. They make an economy better suited than before to the longer span of life and the increasing numbers of old people.

5. American society has been rapidly changing. Marriage is becoming a relationship that is permanent only with mutual continuing assent; the family is a unit of parents with children while they are growing, rather than a lifelong aggregation of grandparents, parents, and children. Each generation largely goes it alone, and the oldest often is lost. Leisure time has grown—and it has become filled haphazardly with diversions often of dubious worth and little suited to the newly numerous middle-aged and old people who are left with empty time. And the "American mind" seems dizzied and dismayed by the swirling changes through which it has moved. A broad developmental psychology of the life span, which sees the individual at each age in his society and his developing intellectual world, should make major contributions to his orientations at each life stage.

6. In his longer life and his modern world, the modern man is in total a largely new phenomenon. And he has largely new needs. He lives in a world in crisis. Adequate study of his growth and change and decline, in relation to his world, should make major contributions to his better adjustment to the world and himself. To attempt some contribution to this end is the aim of this volume.

BIBLIOGRAPHY

1. Allen, F. L., *The Big Change*, New York, Harper, 1952.
2. Burt, C. I., Intelligence and fertility, *Occasional Papers on Eugenics*, London, Hamish, 1946.
3. Cavan, R. S., *The American Family*, New York, Crowell, 1953.
4. Commager, H. S., *The American Mind*, New Haven, Yale University Press, 1950.
5. Council of Economic Advisors, *The Economic Report of the President*, Washington, D.C., 1950.
6. Derber, M. (ed.), *The Aged and Society*, Champaign Illinois, Industrial Relations Research Association, 1950.
7. Dublin, L. I., Lotka, A. J., and Spiegelman, M., *Length of Life* (rev. ed.), New York, Ronald Press, 1949.
8. Gamble, C. J., and Kibbee, B. N., College study report, *Population Bull.*, Washington, D.C., Population Reference Bureau, June, 1955, Vol. 11, No. 4.

9. International Labor Office (Geneva, Switzerland), *Year Book of Labor Statistics, 1954,* London, Staples Press, 1954.
10. Lynd, R. S., and H. M., *Middletown,* New York, Harcourt, Brace, 1929.
11. Pressey, S. L., and Crates, W. E., Sports and the public mind, *School and Society,* 1950, 72:373–374.
12. Riesman, David, *The Lonely Crowd,* New Haven, Yale University Press, 1950.
13. Thompson, W. S., *Plenty of People,* New York, Ronald Press, 1948.
14. UAW–CIO Education Department, *Automation,* Detroit, 1955.
15. *United Nation's Reporter,* July, 1952, Vol. 24, No. 9.
16. United Nations, *Statistical Yearbook, 1955,* New York, United Nations Publications (Columbia University Press), 1954.
17. U.S. Bureau of the Census, *Continuation to 1952 of Historical Statistics of the U.S. (1789–1945),* Washington, D.C., U.S. Government Printing Office, 1954.
18. U.S. Bureau of the Census, *Statistical Abstract of the United States, 1954* (75th ed.), Washington, D.C., U.S. Government Printing Office, 1954.
19. U.S. Department of Commerce, Office of Business Economics, *Income Distribution in the United States by Size, 1944–1950,* Washington, D.C., U.S. Government Printing Office, 1953.
20. U.S. Department of Commerce, Office of Business Economics, *National Income, 1954 Edition,* Washington, D.C., U.S. Government Printing Office, 1954.
21. U.S. Department of Labor, Bureau of Labor Statistics, *Handbook of Labor Statistics (1951) Supplement,* Washington, D.C., U.S. Government Printing Office, 1952.
22. U.S. Department of Labor, Bureau of Labor Statistics, *The Workers' Story, 1913–1953,* Washington, D.C., U.S. Government Printing Office, 1953.
23. Woytinsky and associates (20th Century Fund), *Employment and Wages in the U.S.,* Baltimore, Lord Baltimore Press, 1953.

PART ONE •

• Abilities, Tasks, and Achievements

CHAPTER 2 •

• Growth, Change, and Decline in Physique

ADEQUATE study of mental growth and decline through life requires knowledge of physical growth, change, and decline. The life history of abilities, interests, emotions, and attitudes can be understood only if the upsurge and then gradual decrease of physical vigor, the delicate balances of the ductless glands, and the changes in physical strengths and skills are kept in mind. Such factors are the physiological foundation of the mental life. They also are an ever-present, often dominant element in the individual's thinking and feeling. The child shy in the presence of adults twice his size, the adolescent embarrassed by his evident changes in physique, the young man confident in the full attainment of his strength, and the old person timid with the infirmities of age all show the effects of stages of growth on attitudes and on behavior. It is thus essential that data on physical growth, change, and decline be first considered.

Not only growth but change and decline must be studied—these last phases are most neglected and need emphasizing. The course of the physical life is not simply a growing to adult level and then riding on that level until old age. In certain respects, growth proceeds until the middle years, and in certain other respects, decline has already set in by that time. From before birth to death there is continual change not only in the gross proportions and appearance but also in metabolic activity and in delicate physiological balances which pervade and may often dominate the whole mental life.[1] First, however, what are the gross changes in physique through life?

[1] To emphasize both the continuity and the variety of these changes, much use will be made of graphs, especially in this chapter.

Growth in Height and Weight

It might be hoped that satisfactory data would be available regarding such elementary features as height and weight. But material regarding adults is very inadequate, and only within the last few years have individual growth patterns in the first two decades of life been followed through.

CHANGE IN HEIGHT AND WEIGHT WITH AGE

Figure 11 shows height and weight from childhood to old age. The curves for the first 20 years are a compounding by one of the writers of extensive surveys in various parts of this country and may be thought

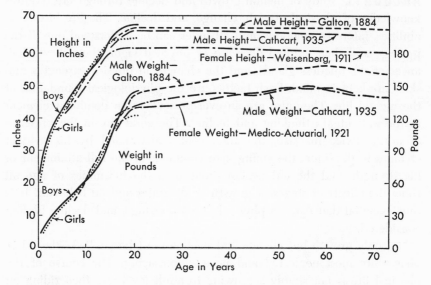

Figure 11. Changes in Mean Height and Weight with Age. Galton: 7000 British males who voluntarily attended a Health Institute held in London; Schwartz: 2162 American males, New York City, ages 3 to 50; Cathcart: 10,593 English males in manual occupations; Medico-Actuarial: 136,504 American insurance policy-holders; Weisenberg: 1000 cases, German; boys and girls: 1943 composite of American studies. (From H. A. Ruger and B. Stoessiger, Growth curves of certain characteristics in man, *Annals of Eugenics*, 1927, 2:76–110 plus data in references 3, 8, 55 of bibliography.)

of as representing average American growth trends. Data regarding adults are much more meager and are from special groups. Thus, Galton's volunteers were (it might be guessed) chiefly well-fed, middle-and upper-class Englishmen.

The curves show similar growth in height and weight for both sexes during the first 12 years or so; then some acceleration, especially in weight, with substantially greater gain for the male; and a leveling off around 18 to 20. But there are changes after 20. Average weight increases until about 50 and decreases in the older ages. In old age there is slight decrease in height, probably due partly to less erect posture and partly to a settling together of the vertebrae. But since the adult groups were special, these last trends must be regarded as only approximate. Better diet and dieting and other changes in mode of living might somewhat modify the trends. More representative groups might show slightly different averages.

In order to cover the entire life span, these curves are so condensed that variations in rate of growth during the first 20 years are not readily noted. Figure 12 makes clear, however, that there are such differences.

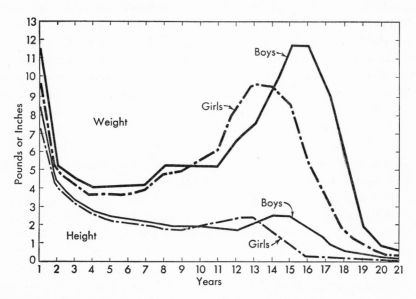

Figure 12. Average Gains Each Year in Height and Weight for Boys and Girls. One division on the chart equals 1 pound, 1 inch, or 1 year. (Pressey and Robinson, *Psychology and the New Education*, p. 14.)

It shows the yearly increments in height and weight for both sexes from birth to maturity. The figure shows rapid growth in infancy. But the most striking feature is the great increase in growth rate in the early teens—an upsurge which comes about two years earlier for girls than for boys. It might well be presumed that an organism thus rapidly growing might have physiological problems of growth and psychological repercussions to these problems.

But the situation is even more complicated than Figure 12 indicates. As will be seen shortly, puberty may come for one girl at 11 but for another girl at 16, and the big upswing in growth rate is just before and at the time of puberty. Presumably, a girl of 11 thus growing rapidly is in a very different total situation as regards her physical self, and her psychological reactions to that self and its changing, from another girl of the same chronological age who is still growing at the childish rate and for whom this upsurge in growth and sex maturing does not come for another five years. The situation is yet more complicated, however. Figure 12 shows cross-sectional data—that is, at a given time, youngsters at the different ages were studied. Repeated measures of the same children show that the boy or girl who reaches this pubertal upsurge in growth early is likely to be at that time somewhat heavier and taller than average, and his upswing in growth is likely to be especially rapid. The child whose puberty comes late is likely to be smaller than average and to show a slower pubertal change. Figure 13 shows something as to how all this works out, the material being from a longitudinal study—that is, from an investigation in which the same youngsters were measured year after year. The year of maximal growth (MG age) was used to indicate the beginning of pubertal change.

At 8 or 9 years of age, the early-maturing boys are evidently taller and heavier than those maturing later; but by the ages of 14 and 15 the differences between them are very much greater. By 18 the differences are less—the slow maturers have somewhat caught up—but those maturing early are still a bit taller and substantially heavier. The girls show somewhat less difference at all ages between the early and late maturers; and after 16, these last cases get taller than those who mature early. The slow-growing boys, however, do not appear to catch up. All this may seem unimportant detail. But evidence, shortly to be presented, will emphasize that these phenomena often largely determine social status and personality development in youth and even after. The early-maturing boy usually has an advantage. Being bigger than average in childhood, he does well in the rough-and-tumble play of that period. His earlier marked increase in height and weight and masculinity may bring athletic or other prominence in high school, and he may move into adulthood confident and assertive, as compared with a slow-maturing lad who throughout childhood and adolescence has been at a handicap in physical size. But in curious contrast, slow maturing tends to be advantageous for a girl. As a petite child she may be made more of than an overbig girl. Her late puberty gets her into adolescence at about the same time as the boys who are her age mates—and who then tend to like a slim,

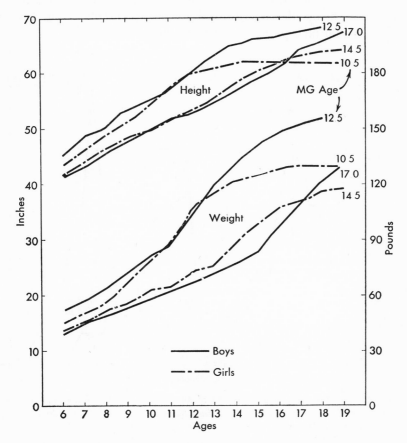

Figure 13. Maximum Growth Age in Relation to Total Growth Curves. (Adapted from F. K. Shuttleworth, The physical and mental growth of girls and boys age 6 to 19 in relation to age of maximal growth, Monogr. of the Society for Research in Child Development, 1939, Vol. 4, No. 3.)

small girl rather than one maturing early who is possibly bigger and embarrassingly more mature.

The fact that some youngsters, and most commonly those bigger in childhood, have their maximal growth period several years earlier than others brings about a phenomenon that is very important for those who deal with adolescents: individual differences are greater in the early teens than either before or after. And this fact appears clearly in longitudinal studies, as illustrated by Figure 14. The 167 girls in this study scattered out much more in height when they were 12 than when they were 8 or 16. And what is thus definitely shown for height appears to hold also for many other physical and psychological traits. Greatest range for boys would be expected about two years later.

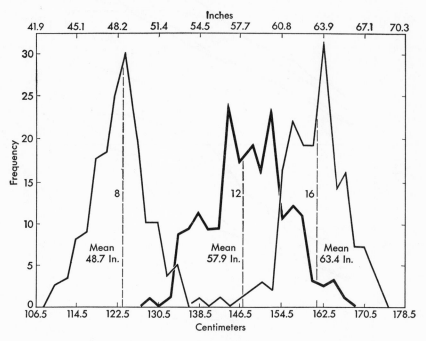

Figure 14.   Standing Heights of 167 Girls at Ages 8, 12, and 16. (Adapted from J. W. Rothney and W. F. Dearborn, *Predicting the Child's Development*, Cambridge, Science-Art Publications, 1941.)

The above material indicates something as to the complicated character of growth patterns around puberty and the interrelations with development of personality. Different individuals reach a given stage of development at different ages; they do this because of differences in growth rate which are probably in large part constitutional and perhaps related to constitutional body type and partly influenced by nutrition and health. In school systems which insist on grouping pupils according to chronological rather than developmental age, youngsters at different stages are thrown together. Largely as a consequence of this practice, in the American culture which emphasizes athleticism in the adolescent male and slim attractiveness in the girl, sundry personality outcomes follow. The assumption seems reasonable that analogous, careful longitudinal studies of women around the time of the menopause would show

TABLE 1.   Percentage at Each Weight in Each Age Group from 12 to 80, About 6000 English Males

Pounds	12	14	16	18	Age 20–29	30–39	40–49	50–59	60–69	70–79
236 up									3	
229								1	1	
222							1		1	
215						1	2	2	1	
208						1	1	5	2	3
201						1	3	4[b]	5[b]	10[b]
194						2	4[b]	4	3	6
187				1		3	5	7	6	3
180					2	4[b]	6	8	10	6
173			1	1	2	6	10	10	10	10
166				1	5[b]	6	12	9	13[a]	21[a]
159				3	7	10	10[a]	11[a]	8	13
152				9[b]	13	13	12	8	6	3
145		1	3	12	16	13[a]	10	8	9	3
138		1	11[b]	15	18[a]	12	10	9	9	10
131		3	14	18[a]	16	11	6[b]	6[b]	6[b]	6[b]
124		3	20	19	10	9[b]	4	4	3	3
117		7[b]	17[a]	12	7[b]	5	3	2	3	
110		6	17	6[b]	2	2	1	1	1	
103		14	6	3	1	1				
96	8	14	6[b]	1				1		
89	13[b]	16[a]	4							3
82	21	17	1							
75	37[a]	11[b]								
68	5	5								
61	8[b]	2								
54	8									
	100	100	100	100	100	100	100	100	100	100

NOTE: The letter "a" shows approximate location of mean, and the letter "b" shows approximate 10 and 90 percentiles. Note that 12, 14, 16, and 18 are for single years and thereafter data are grouped in 10-year intervals. The small ranges at 12 and 70 to 79 are probably due in part to the small number of cases (38 and 32) at these ages.

SOURCE: After Galton. Adapted from H. A. Ruger and Brenda Stoessiger, Growth curves of certain characteristics in man (males), *Annals of Eugenics*, 1927, 2: 84.

similar differences in age of reaching this stage, analogous causes, and even more complicated sociological and cultural interrelations.

The old and otherwise unsatisfactory cross-sectional data on weight summarized in Table 1 are too gross to reveal such phenomena as mentioned above, but they do show the increasing range with age in the adult years which appears characteristic of many physical and mental traits and also the great overlapping at all ages—thus there are 14-year-old boys as heavy as the average 25-year-old man. The fewer very heavy men in the seventies might be a result of their earlier death, loss of weight in old age, or inadequate number of cases.

INFLUENCES AFFECTING HEIGHT AND WEIGHT

What are the causes of differences in size and in rate of growth? As mentioned above, the basic factor is presumably constitutional; some children naturally are bigger and grow faster than others. But numerous studies indicate that various favorable or inadequate conditions may play a part. Children in crowded one-room tenements have been found to be, on the average, shorter and lighter than those in apartments of three rooms or more. Undoubtedly, many factors are involved in this finding. Not only might children in tenements suffer in various ways from the congestion, but their families were presumably more poverty-stricken and had less adequate diet and medical care. The families in the most crowded slums might have been recent immigrants who were of smaller stock (64, Sect. I, Pt. I, p. 288). A fall has been reported in rate of increase in weight of young children in families which suffered severely in the Great Depression of the nineteen thirties, though children in families which at that time remained well-to-do or poor showed no shift. Disturbances of family morale, as well as changes in diet or living conditions, presumably might be involved here (45).

The devastations and disruptions of war may affect child growth. The First World War is reported to have slowed the development of French children from one to five years, with delay in pubescence (64, Sect. I, Pt. I, p. 286). In Paris, in 1941-1942, 12.8 percent of 23,000 children lost weight (more than 300 grams) and 21.2 percent did not gain weight during the year, as compared with a normal incidence of no weight gain in only .5 to 2 percent of school children in 1939 (27, p. 996). In general, weight was affected more than height and older children and adolescents more than younger children. In Stuttgart, measurements of school children since 1910, and records of annual consumption per head of main foods in 1913, 1932, and 1938, showed height and weight down during both world wars but tending up afterward. Ultimate effects on adult level were not covered (23). Fortunately, the human organism is resilient and may catch up somewhat, if conditions improve. One group of investigators concluded "that the food crises of the 1940's in many parts of the world, if they are not of too long duration, will probably have no permanent effect on the generation of growing children" (27, Chap. 45). Judicious restrictions in diet may even contribute to health and longevity (35).

In general, American children from socioeconomically superior homes are, on the average, larger than children from poor homes. A recent résumé (38) suggests differences of 2 inches in height and 5 pounds in weight. Adolescent boys and girls in school average taller and heavier than youngsters of the same age who are working, and they reach maturity in size earlier than the working children. But all these differences may be largely constitutional rather than environmental in origin; for example, employed adolescents may be from recently immigrated, smaller stock.

Nationalities may differ in height and weight; differences have been reported even in the newborn. Presumably, racial, climatological, nutritional, and other related socioeconomic factors may all play a part. Japanese children born and raised in America are larger than children of the same racial type in Japan. And American-born children of immigrants seem to be superior in growth to children of the same age and racial type in Europe.

If diet and living conditions are thus important for growth, it might be expected that with improvement in such respects people generally would become larger in succeeding generations, and much evidence is to that effect. Studies in places as far apart as Brisbane, Australia (46), and London, England (50), have found children taller and heavier in 1950 than in 1911 and in 1949 than in 1938; the English children in 1949 were about ¾ inch taller and 1¾ pounds heavier than 11 years previously. It might be presumed that improvements in income of the poorer classes, equalizations of diet with rationing, and "socialized medicine" all contributed to these gains. At Harvard, sons have been found about 1¾ inches taller and 10 pounds heavier than their fathers; in four eastern women's colleges, the superiority of daughters over mothers was 1.1 inches in height and 3.9 pounds in weight (7); however (most fortunately), the daughters, although taller and heavier, were more slender. Stanford

University women students increased 1 inch in height in 70 years (9). But the situation may be complicated. A very extensive compilation of heights of about two million Englishmen from 18 to 50 years of age, from 1845 to 1948, indicated that youth are now taller than formerly but fully grown younger, with average adult height there not changing. The present earlier maturing might be attributed to better diet, less child labor, and so on. Adult decline in height may come earlier (41).

What various factors influence height and weight after 20? Malnutrition is to be found in slums among adults as well as among children, but the last-mentioned investigation shows that final height might not be much affected. That emotional strain may reduce weight is a common observation; that overeating, injudicious diet, and underexercise are major factors in overweight is generally accepted. Presumably, relationships might be found between presence in a neighborhood of an adult class in diet and hygiene, or provision for adult physical recreation, and optimum weight. There may be relationships between intelligence and wise weight. Presumably, as provision is made for recreation and education for old people, control of weight and posture in old age will be more common. Perhaps, in the older ages, as is now the case with vigorous young people, there may be pride in erect leanness. As one energetic, elderly woman has said in criticizing other old people, "They should not slouch, and they should not be so indolent or so fatalistic."

It is common knowledge that tallness and shortness, fatness and thinness, more special characteristics such as tendency to take on weight or remain thin with advancing years, and innumerable other characteristics tend to run in families. Thus, the heights of fathers and sons have been found to correlate .51; of brothers, .51; of fraternal twins, .64; of identical twins, .93 (42). But not all this resemblance is due to constitution. Living conditions, diet, and other circumstances are usually similar for members of a family. And a correlation of .50 between heights of fathers and sons indicates only a rough general relationship, not a close one. Considerable differences in height between father and son are common.

Change in Proportion and Tissues

PROPORTION

It might be said that increases in height and weight are, relatively, only minor in the total process of growth; most important are the changes in the organism going on throughout life. Figure 15, picturing sample ages from infancy to old age, illustrates well that even in gross proportion the body does not simply grow but also changes. The figures are all drawn the same height so that comparisons as to proportion may readily be made.

In the baby, head and body are large and legs are short. The boy of 15 is slim and gangling, the mature man is broad-shouldered and strong-limbed, and the old man is stooped and paunchy, with the limbs shrunken. The extent to which changes continue, even after maturity

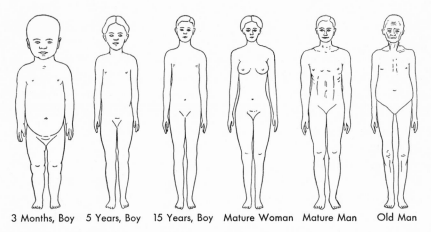

3 Months, Boy　5 Years, Boy　15 Years, Boy　Mature Woman　Mature Man　Old Man

Figure 15.　Change in Body Proportions with Age and Sex Differences. (From C. R. Bardeen, The height-weight index of build in relation to linear and volumetric proportions and surface area of the body during postnatal development, *Contributions to Embryology*, Carnegie Institute of Technology, 1920, 9:483–554.)

has been reached, must be emphasized. Thus, the head continues to grow until the fifth decade; the cranial wall maintains a continuing slow process of thickening and is slightly thicker at 70 than at 30. The face grows and changes so strikingly throughout life (but especially at adolescence and the beginning of old age) that a person's age is commonly estimated with some accuracy from facial appearance. With age, the face becomes longer and the nose and mouth become larger, and the total effect changes in ways that are hard to describe though generally recognized. The hair becomes grayer and more sparse, and the skin becomes roughened and wrinkled. Figure 16 (see p. 38), showing pictures of Edison from the ages 12 to 81, will illustrate these various changes.

TISSUE

Figure 17 shows how different organs of the body develop at different rates. Early in life the brain grows rapidly in weight, shows no gross change at puberty, and is heaviest around the age of 20. The thymus weighs most before 10 and begins a decline soon thereafter. The thyroid grows slowly through childhood and very rapidly at puberty, reaches a peak around 35, and falls off in weight only very slowly thereafter. In the growing girl, the weight of the uterus, nevertheless, does not appreciably increase through childhood but mounts very rapidly at puberty and more slowly after 20, until it is heaviest at 40; after that age, it rather rapidly declines. Not only the sizes of the different body organs but also their proportions relative to each other change greatly from childhood to adolescence to maturity and then into old age. Related changes in personality might be expected. And the figure leaves out much. The skeleton has been found to weigh most at 35, to get lighter and more porous slowly until 65, and thereafter to decline more rapidly. At birth the voluntary musculature in one set of cases was 23 percent of total body weight, while at 25 it was 44 percent, the big increase following pubescence. In adult life, amount of fat may increase.

Further, the nature of many tissues changes substantially with age. After puberty, skeletal muscles contain more solids and until about 50 have been found to increase in bulk and density; a little later, degenerative changes begin to appear. However, smooth muscle has been re-

Figure 16.   The first picture is of Thomas A. Edison at 12, when he became a railroad newsboy. The stories of his enterprise in selling papers giving Civil War news, and of his chemical experiments in the baggage car, are well known. The next photograph shows him with the first form of the phonograph which he had invented some two years before and in the year (1879) when he succeeded in making the first incandescent electric lamp; already to his credit were numerous other important inventions, beginning with the patenting of an electric vote recorder for legislative assemblies when he was 21. At 58 he was internationally famous and perhaps the best-known and most-admired American, with an extraordinary record of inventiveness, including methods for the generation of electric light and power, an electric railway, magnetic methods of concentrating iron ores, moving pictures, and forerunners of the radio tube and wireless telegraph; at the time this picture was taken, he was especially interested in devising a new kind of storage battery. The last picture shows the aged Edison demonstrating that he still had some skill with a telegraph key. When a lad of 15 he had become a telegrapher, and soon became known as one of the best. In this same year—when 81—he took out his last patent, making a total of 1033! He died three years later.

The pictures were chosen not only because they are interesting portraits of a famous American and because each picture can be related to a stage in his career, but also because they exhibit age changes exceptionally well. Each shows the face fairly full on—plump in boyhood, slimmer in intense young manhood, full near 60, somewhat sunken and wrinkled at 81. The hair is thick at 32 but thinned and fine in old age, the mouth and nose are larger at 58 than 26 years earlier. Carriage is erect at 58 but stooped with the head forward in old age. And by 81 the hands are gaunt, though full-fleshed 23 years before. (Reproduced by permission of Underwood and Underwood.)

ported to change little from childhood to old age. Changes in the skin with age involve not only wrinkling but histological changes, slower healing after injury. In the later years, the thyroid gland not only decreases in size but shows decrease in size and number of secretory cells.

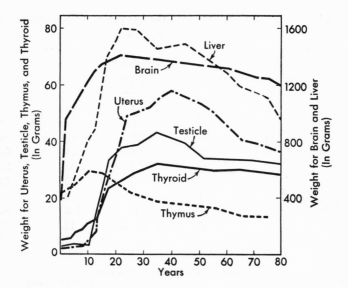

Figure 17. Changes in Weight of Various Organs with Age. (Adapted from E. J. Stieglitz, *Geriatric Medicine: Diagnosis and Management of Disease in the Aging and in the Aged*, Philadelphia, W. B. Saunders, 1949, p. 89.)

The amount of renal tissue appears to decline after about 60. With age, the brain becomes shrunken, more convoluted, and there appears to be cellular change and a decrease in the number of cells (*66*). All these appear to be "normal" changes with aging, not the result of injury or disease —this last topic will be returned to later (*31, 66*).

TRANSITION PERIODS—PUBERTY, MATURITY, MENOPAUSE

Though development and decline are continuous processes, there are times of especially rapid change. At puberty, not only do the sex organs mature quickly, but, as shown by earlier figures, there is a total upsurge of growth in height, weight, strength, and a general readjustment of the organism. The various secondary sex characteristics appear in both sexes. Table 2 shows the great individual differences among girls in age of first menstruation. A 10-year-old child may be frightened by menstruation at that age; another girl may be unduly alarmed by delay until 16.

The average year is around 13, but a couple of years earlier or later is not uncommon.

For boys, puberty comes about two years later, with similar individual differences.[2] Almost any group through the secondary school period

TABLE 2.   Age of First Menstruation of 1313 Girls as Found in Five Investigations; Percentages Who Reached the Menarche at Various Ages

Age	Investigator				
	Shuttleworth	Abernethy	Engle	Boas	Nicolson
16 up	1	2	1	2	
15	3	6	7	7	4
14	11	25	27	13	9
13	36	35	35	31	28
12	34	23	22	32	37
11	12	8	8	13	18
10	3	1		3	4
Number	248	487	250	236	92
Average age	13.0	13.5	13.5	13.1	12.8
Standard deviation	1.1	1.1	1.1	1.2	1.1

NOTE: Age 10 means from the tenth to the eleventh birthday, etc.

Kinsey (29, p. 81) lists average age of first menstruation for nine studies including the first three above as ranging from 13.0 to 13.9, these all being direct reports or examinations at the time. The recall data of his investigations average 13.1 with a range from 9 to 17 (p. 131). Nicolson and Hanley list eight studies, with means from 12.6 to 13.5 and S.D.'s from 1.1 to 1.4.

SOURCE: From F. K. Shuttleworth, The adolescent period: a graphic atlas and a pictorial atlas, Monogr. *Society for Research in Child Development*, 1951, Vol. 14, Nos. 1 and 2, pp. 265, 269; and Arline and H. C. Nicolson, Indices of physiological maturity, *Child Development*, 1953, 24: 3–38.

is likely to include some individuals who are still prepubescent children and some who are physically and emotionally adult. Figure 18 shows how great the differences between boys of the same age may be. As stated earlier, boys above average in height and weight tend to reach pubescence earlier, and with pubescence comes marked increase in growth. These two factors thus combine to cause striking physical differences in size and maturity during the adolescent years.

Average age of puberty is a little earlier for youngsters with good

[2] For boys, there is no definite dating by an event so determinable as first menstruation; but age of maximal growth comes about two years later in boys, and the total picture of pubertal change (in dentition, skeletal change, appearance of secondary sex characteristics) is about that much later than for the typical girl. And development can be noted in terms of appearance of pubic hair and other changes, as reported by various investigators and shown in the photographs of Shuttleworth and Stoltz (29, 57, 60).

rather than with poor socioeconomic status and for city than for country children. Although it has been supposed that girls in the tropics reach pubescence earlier than those in cold climates, research indicates earlier pubescence occurs in temperate climates, with later occurrence in both hot and cold areas. As already mentioned, unfavorable conditions such as malnutrition tend to delay puberty. Puberty in this country may be averaging a little earlier (perhaps five months) than 20 years ago

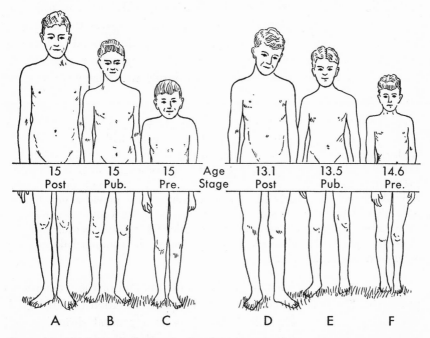

| 15 Post | 15 Pub. | 15 Pre. | Age Stage | 13.1 Post | 13.5 Pub. | 14.6 Pre. |
| A | B | C | | D | E | F |

Figure 18. A Concrete Illustration of Individual Differences in Physical Development. The three boys to the left (A, B, C) are all 15 years of age. A is post-pubescent; B is pubescent, and C is prepubescent. The three to the right (D, E, F) have chronological ages in reverse order to their physical size. D is 13 years, 1 month old and post-pubescent; E is 13 years, 5 months of age and pubescent; F is 14 years, 6 months of age and prepubescent. (Adapted from H. S. Dimock, *Rediscovering the Adolescent*, New York, Association Press, 1937.)

(*12, 17, 19*) possibly because of better nutrition and other conditions favoring physical development. It is also conceivable that, in part, greater frankness about sex and even stimulation thereof may tend to further rather than retard sex maturing.

The second time of marked change shows the most sweeping and consistent shift of the entire life span in the direction of development —and yet it is ordinarily hardly noted in discussions of growth! This is the time, around 18 to 20, when growth is finished and adult life begins —when all the increases in total height and weight cease, and in the size of most of the body organs also, and there is a leveling off or the beginning of a decline. As will be seen shortly, growth in strength and quickness also levels off at about this age. Chapter 3 will show intellectual capacities quite similarly increasing, then tending to reach a level. Almost all types of growth go forward relatively steadily and rapidly during the first 18 or 20 years; then, rather quickly, all stop together. The reader need only glance back and also forward over the figures in this and succeeding chapters to appreciate this little-stressed fact. Being little mentioned, the possibility of marked changes in personality at this time has also been little considered. Surely such changes might be expected.

Figure 13 has indicated that whereas girls who reach puberty early tended to stop growing so promptly that they remained somewhat short, early-maturing boys seemed to maintain a childhood superiority in height into adult life. This finding illustrates the probability that intensive investigation of "maturity" (as this time of change from growth to adult level will from now on be called) very likely will show intricate interrelationships with previous growth and with adult status. For instance, may the early-maturing youth have not only early-acquired confidence and status with adults but also a certain maturity of personality, making him especially impatient of the continued dependency of long-extended schooling?

The menopause or "change of life" marks the end of the woman's reproductive life. It is characterized chiefly by the cessation (usually gradual) of the menses. Physiologically, there is a general shrinkage and cessation of function in the sex organs; the ductless glands, especially the thyroid, become less active. Many general changes (slowing down, decline of sex urge) begun well before menopause may be considered caused by this change in sex functions; often this is mostly because they are brought sharply and especially to attention at this time by general physiological readjustment. Hot and cold flashes, sweating, sensitivity to hot and cold, instability of pulse, feelings of suffocation may be experienced. There may also be a tendency to magnify any ailments. There may be periods of depression, irritability, and restlessness. Healthy, well-balanced women may pass through the period with relatively little difficulty and emerge into a calm afternoon of life which is rich in satisfactions. Instead of decreasing, with the passing of the danger of conception, sex life may be less constrained. Kinsey states (28,

p. 735) that "in our sample, it would be difficult to identify any reduction of sexual response or activities which could be considered the consequence of any change at menopause."

Mean age for the menopause appears to be about 47; various studies have shown average ages from 44 to 49. Table 3 emphasizes the great range of ages over which the menopause may occur. Two or three women out of 100 may reach menopause in their early thirties and a few not until the late fifties.

TABLE 3.   Age of Menopause; Percentages of 903 German Women and 407 American and Canadian Women Reaching the Menopause at Various Ages

Age	German (Percent)	American (Percent)
55–59	2	4
50–54	30	31
45–49	44	40
40–44	20	18
35–39	4[a]	5
30–34		2[a]
	—	—
Total	903	407
Mean	47.1	46.9

[a] Includes all cases before 40 (Germans) and before 30 (Americans).

NOTE: Kinsey (28, p. 719) reports a range in age of onset of the menopause from 40 to 60 with median at 49. His data on this matter seem, however, not clear.

SOURCE: From K. I. Sane, The age of menopause, A.M.A. *Transaction* (section on obstetrics, gynecology, and abdominal surgery, 1918, pp. 259–282.

The consensus of experts seems to be that there is no male climacteric, but rather a gradual, slow diminution of sexual vigor. Certain data to this effect will be presented shortly. If there is any "climacteric," it apparently is more a product of emotional stresses or problems of health that occur in the forties or fifties and are given an undue sex reference.

Some individuals seem to go through a fourth change point, usually in the seventies, when they move out of the seasoned vigor of what may be called later adulthood into the time when handicaps or diseases of old age begin to press down upon them. The curve for weight presented earlier showed some falling off after 65 or 70. Some curves for strength and quickness will later be found to show a little sharper drop in the seventies or thereabout. Perhaps there is skeletal sagging and the beginning of deafness and of some chronic illness; the physique tends to become somewhat dilapidated. This may be thought of as a time when the stresses of past accidents and illnesses and present hardships begin to break through the organism's resistance, rather than a time when there seems to be an inherent constitutional change. If there is indeed a natural life span, however, it might be expected that there would be a change time when the organism moved into the end phase of that span. And, surely, many people seem to have a distinct period of old age with a more or less differentiated time of beginning. But others seem to remain essentially intact—though in sundry respects enfeebled—until death is close upon them.

Changes with Age in Strength, Quickness, and Skill

Data regarding strength and skill are of great importance and have numerous relationships to everyday problems. Might mastery of basic skills like walking come earlier with intensive training? Are fine movements so ill controlled at six or seven that instruction in handwriting is premature? Is the development of high school youngsters so incomplete as regards muscular strength and coördination, as well as stamina, that competitive athletics are, on the whole, undesirable? Within what ages may maximum skill and strength be expected, and is it useless to attempt to excel at ages other than these? Is there, after 45, such a decrease in quickness or strength as would warrant refusal to employ men after that age on an assembly line? Are people past 60 for the most part industrial liabilities? Research on changes in skill and strength over a period of years has thrown important light on numerous such questions.

BASIC DEVELOPMENT IN THE EARLY YEARS

The newborn infant is a strangely incoördinated, helpless mite of humanity. Its very first years are devoted to the fascinating but difficult problem of getting control of its own body. At the age of four months, babies can usually lift their heads while lying in their cribs; at six months they can usually hold their heads erect while sitting. About one-half sit alone at the end of six months, and the majority can stand alone at one year. At the age of four months most infants can move themselves about on the floor; by nine months about two-thirds of them can creep, and a few with help can walk; by a year and a half almost all can do so. Climbing and walking are well-developed skills usually by the age of three, and at four years most children can go up and down stairs in the adult manner. By four or five they can jump, skip, hop, and dance.

Can these skills be reached earlier by special training? Apparently, not much, if any, continuing advantage is thus gained, though a temporary superiority is brought about. For instance, one group of 10 children (ages 24 to 36 months) was given extensive practice in climbing stairs, buttoning, and cutting with scissors over a 12-week period, and by the end of this training the group had improved markedly. A control group, equivalent as to age, sex, measured intelligence, and initial ability in these skills, was given no training over this period, *but in one week* of intensive practice it attained the level of performance reached by the practiced group. Practice or training thus contributed to the performance, but evidently the important factor was the maturing of the total neuromuscular system which went forward at an established biological rate that could not be hurried (22). However, malnutrition or disease, and marked restrictions on activity, or lack of stimuli to activity probably may retard behavioral development to some extent. Clothing permitting easy movement, fond parents who encourage and admire—all such factors play a part in helping a child to realize the potentialities which each stage of maturity makes possible.

The figures presented earlier in this chapter showed growth to proceed very rapidly during these first years. It seems reasonable to assume that the advances in strength and skill going forward during these years are also to be thought of as notable. It is a most difficult task to get control of oneself. And from that sprawling helplessness of the first month to the five-year-old's exuberance of movement and speech is indeed an advance.

DEVELOPMENT OF STRENGTH AND QUICKNESS IN CHILDHOOD AND YOUTH

Figure 19 shows increases in simple tests of quickness and strength during the childhood and adolescent years. Gains are marked. Thus boys' rate of tapping about doubled and strength of grip increased about five times, from the age of 6 to 18. Sex differences are evident.

Figure 19 is made up from cross-sectional data. Figure 20 (p. 47) shows the value of longitudinal studies; it summarizes certain measurements of the same 60 boys and 56 girls in California, tested at regular intervals from the ages of 11 through 17. The heavy middle line for boys shows their very marked increase in average strength of grip; over the six-year period the averages more than double—from 24 to 53. The upper heavy line exhibits increases for the 16 boys of the total 60 who were earliest in skeletal maturing, being at age 15 at least one year advanced; the dot-dash heavy line shows increases for the 16 at least a year retarded. The first group shows the beginning of a pubertal upswing in

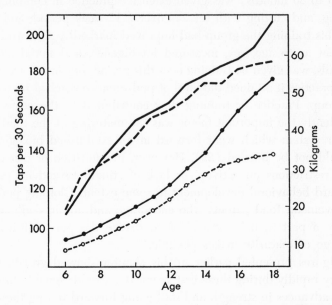

Figure 19. Increases from Age 6 to 18 in Rate of Tapping and Strength of Grip. (Adapted from F. D. Brooks and L. F. Shaffer, *Child Psychology*, Boston, Houghton Mifflin, 1937, p. 157; and H. E. Jones, The development of physical abilities, in National Society for the Study of Education, *Yearbook*, 1944, vol. 43, part 1.)

growth at the age of 12 but the second not until 14, when the early group is half again as strong and obviously at a great advantage in the physical competitions of boyhood society. And though by 17 the slow ones are increasing in strength faster, they have not caught up to the average. Whether they do later remains to be seen from later measurements.

The average line for the total 56 girls in this study shows only about half the gain made by the boys. At 12 boys are only slightly stronger than the girls, but by 17 they are far ahead and still increasing in strength, while the girls seem to have reached adult level. Sex differences both in age of maturing and in strength at maturity seem clearly indicated. And there appears to be a further sex difference. The light dotted lines show that by the age of 17 both the 16 slowest- *and* the 16 fastest-developing girls are below the light "average" line. The late-developing girls have remained there from their initial slow start, and those reaching pubescence early appear to have suffered the same early cessation of growth in strength which appeared in connection with height.

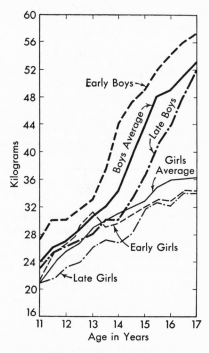

Figure 20. Right-Hand Grip of Early and Late Maturing Boys and Girls. (Adapted from H. E. Jones, *Motor Performance and Growth*, Berkeley, University of California Press, 1949, pp. 58, 63.)

The above are anthropometric phenomena. That these may have important psychosocial relationships is well indicated by Figure 21, from the same study, showing ratings by child-study experts of the personality and social adjustment of the 10 strongest and 10 weakest boys (as of age 17) in the total group. In grade school the two groups were quite similar in such traits as "generalized tensions" and popularity, though the strong group was superior in family adjustment and "emotional buoyancy." But by the end of senior high the strong group had gained relatively over the earlier appraisals in almost every trait, and the weaker boys had dropped behind. Clearly, rate of development of strength is, for boys, a very important phenomenon affecting personality.

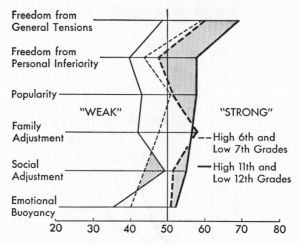

Figure 21.   Contrasts Between the 10 Highest and the 10 Lowest of 78 Boys on Total Score on Strength Tests at 17.5 Years. Popularity and emotional buoyancy as rated by staff observers during "free-play" activity; general tensions, personal inferiority, and adjustment as shown on a personal-social inventory filled out by the boys. The chart shows the 10 strongest boys to have been high on freedom from general tensions in grades 6–7, and yet higher in grades 11–12, but the 10 weakest are more inferior in this respect in grades 11–12 than earlier. (Adapted from H. E. Jones, *Motor Performance and Growth*, Berkeley, University of California Press, 1949.)

CHANGES IN STRENGTH AND QUICKNESS THROUGH ADULT LIFE

Material in Figure 22 comes from various sources, from tests given at the London exposition by Frances Galton 80 odd years ago (as already mentioned) to recent findings in this country. The similarity in trends in all the instances may be thought of as largely confirmatory of them. There is a rapid, steady growth through the growth years, a peak around the ages of 20 to 30, and, thereafter, a slow decline which may somewhat accelerate in the later years. The decrease in speed with age may well be most fundamental, as indicating slowing and perhaps decreased effectiveness of central nervous processes (5).

The drop in averages with increasing age does not mean that every older person is less strong or quick than the average person in his prime. Table 4 shows two men in their sixties who are as strong as the stronger 20-year-olds. The two strong old men may have declined from very great strength in their youth, or they may have maintained themselves physically while most older people let themselves get soft.

Figure 22 and Table 4 report simple tests of grip, pull, or quickness. Industrial tasks presumably are somewhat more complicated but often relatively simple and repetitive. A recent English study with a block sorting test is relevant here. In their first sorting, men over 65 took much

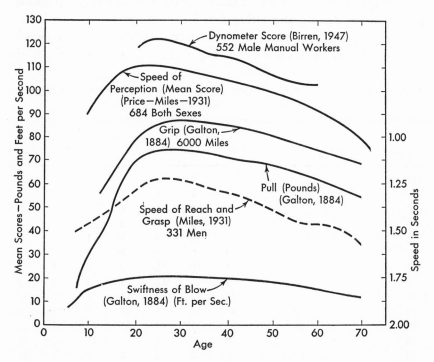

Figure 22. Changes with Age in Strength and Quickness. (Adapted from M. B. Fisher and J. E. Birren, Age and strength, *J. Appl. Psychol.*, 1947, 31:490–497; W. R. Miles, Measures of certain human abilities throughout the life span, *Proc. Nat. Acad. Sci.*, 1931, 17:627–633; and H. A. Ruger and B. Stoessiger, Growth curves of certain characteristics in man (males), *Annals of Eugenics*, 1927, 2:76–110.)

longer than those under 25. But as the task was continued, the oldest group seemed to get over its initial slowness; in later trials they were only slightly slower than the youngest group, and the men 45 to 64 were fastest. This investigator has also stated that "as we go up the age scale, we find that differences between people of the same age at the same task get greater . . . a man well over seventy was the third quickest in a group with ages ranging from 20 to 69." Figure 23 summarizes the findings.

Problems of physical competence with relation to age are indeed complicated, as is indicated by Figure 24 which deals with frequency of automobile accidents at different ages. The heavy black line emphasizes the great frequency of accidents among young drivers. However, younger drivers also drive more miles. And if, as shown by the bottom curve, the data are handled in terms of accidents per 100,000 miles, the younger drivers appear somewhat less at fault, and the very oldest group also appear to be accident-prone. Other data have indicated that older drivers drive more slowly. Appraisal of competence in driving is thus a complex problem. But it seems clear that greatest safety is, on the whole, in the

TABLE 4.   Percentage in Each Age Group from 12 to 80 Showing Different Degrees of Strength in Pull—About 6000 English Males

Pounds	Age									
	12	14	16	18	20–29	30–39	40–49	50–59	60–69	70–79
110					1					
105				1	1	1	1			
100				1	2	1	1		1	
95				1	2	2	2		1	
90			1	2	4	4	3	1		
85			1	3	9b	8b	7b	4		
80			2	5b	13	13	10	4	1	
75			3	9	15	15	13	8b	3	3
70			5b	14	16a	14a	17a	9	7b	
65		2	11	16a	14	17	17	17	11	3
65		3	18	21	12	13	15	25a	23	10b
55		8b	20a	14	7b	7b	9b	17	22a	21
50		13	17	5b	2	4	3	9b	13	21a
45		14	11	5	1	1	1	2	11b	13
40	16b	16a	6b	2	1		1	2	3	13
35	26	23	4	1				1	2	3
30	29a	8	1						1	13b
25	21b	12b						1	1	
20	8	1								
	100	100	100	100	100	100	100	100	100	100

NOTE: The letter "a" shows mean of each distribution; the letter "b" shows 10 and 90 percentiles. Note 10-year grouping from age 20 on; also, first four columns are for even ages only. Smaller ranges at 12 and 70 to 79 are probably due in part to the small number of cases (38 and 30) at these ages.

SOURCE: After Galton. Adapted from H. A. Ruger and Brenda Stoessiger, Growth curves of certain characteristics in man (males), *Annals of Eugenics*, 1927, 2:84.

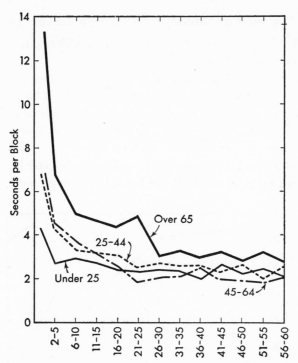

Figure 23. Change in Rate of Block Sorting from Beginning to End of Task, with Age. (Adapted from A. T. Welford, *Skill and Age*, London, Oxford University Press, 1951.)

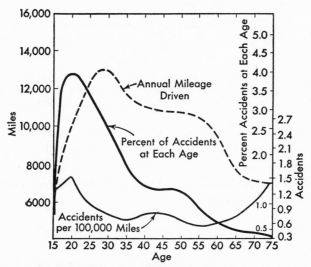

Figure 24. Miles Driven per Year by Iowa Males, Accidents per 100,000 Miles and Percent of All Accidents Occurring at Each Age. (Adapted from A. R. Lauer, Age and sex in relation to accidents, *Highway Research Board Bulletin*, National Research Council Offprint, January, 1952; and *Iowa State College Driving Laboratory News*, April 22, 1953.)

middle and older years. Material on industrial accidents, to be presented later, is also to this effect.

Figure 25 brings out a matter of practical importance with regard to the welfare of old people: they are increasingly subject to falls—perhaps as a result of middle-ear disease, incoördination in motor movement, or other related factors. In any event, liability to falls seems to begin shortly after 65, and the proportion getting about freely drops off very rapidly from around 80 on. The reader should note that this chart begins at 60. Note also that up to 80 over half are still active enough not to be limited

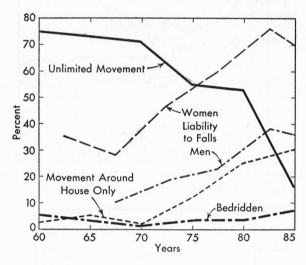

Figure 25. Limitations of Activity and Liability to Falls of Old People. (Adapted from J. H. Sheldon, Medical social aspects of the aging process, *The Aged and Society,* Industrial Relations Research Association, December, 1950, pp. 222, 230.)

in their moving about and only 5 percent of those 85 and over are bedridden. Also, the number of falls could probably have been substantially reduced if many stairways had not been steep, without handrails, and poorly lighted and if other remediable handicaps had not reduced safety in the community studied.

AGES OF WINNING ATHLETIC CHAMPIONSHIPS, AS EVIDENCE OF TIME OF GREATEST PHYSICAL COMPETENCE

The material immediately preceding has attempted to outline the rise and then the slow settling back of neuromuscular functioning over the life span. A further type of evidence brings together practically all factors involved in total physical efficiency, with reference to the question as to when they are at their peak. Ages when athletic championships are won would seem to give a rough measure of such climax of physical adequacy in those physically most able. Figure 26 exhibits such information for two active professional sports—boxing and baseball—and two sports involving less gross effort but greater skill and nicety of coördination—billiards and golf. Data regarding these sports were chosen as representative of a great amount of such material compiled by Dr. Harvey Lehman, all of which came to substantially the same conclusion. The graph makes clear that championships in very demanding sports are won most frequently in the twenties, although they are sometimes won a little later. Sports like billiards involving accuracy rather than strength or endurance may have champions who maintain their superiority well into their forties, but most championship contests, even in billiards, are won by contestants in their twenties.

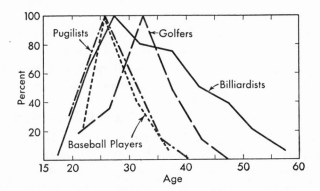

Figure 26. Age of Outstanding Professional Athletic Accomplishments: 156 World Champion Pugilists; 63 Golf Champions in Britain and America; 136 World Billard Champions; and Best Batting Averages of 303 Baseball Players. Note: For each field, the number of contributions at the age group where most occurred (for the athletes then alive) was considered 100 percent, and number of contributions at other ages expressed as a percent of this. (Adapted from H. C. Lehman, Chronological age vs. proficiency in physical skills, *Amer. J. Psychol.*, 1951, 64:161–187.)

The method of constructing Figure 26 was essentially simple. For each sport, records were gone over to find the age of the winner in each championship contest. The age when most championships were won was considered the base of reference and the number of championships won at that age was assigned a value of 100; the value for each other age was the ratio between the championships won at that age and the championships won at the base age expressed as a percent. In the calculations, account was taken of the number of people of the champion group who were alive at each age. This same method, in essence, will appear in a later chapter in connection with somewhat analogous data on age of notable intellectual accomplishment.

It was said that in less physically demanding sports, championships might be won in the forties or even after. But outstanding athletic accomplishment may come as early as the later or even middle teens. Thus, Marlene Bauer was playing fine tournament golf at 14, as was also Bobby Jones. Helen Wills was a tennis star at 15, and Barbara Ann Scott was internationally known for her figure skating while still a teen-age girl. As will be mentioned later, such early extraordinary physical accomplishment has possible significance regarding early accomplishment in other fields. However, as a counter to these "wonder kids" it should also be mentioned that Walter J. Travis did not take up golf until he was 37 and won four national golf titles after he was 40. Grover Cleveland Alexander saved a world series for the St. Louis Cardinals by his pitching in his fortieth year, and Devereux Milburn was considered one of the two best polo players in the country at 46. The "age of champions" thus seems to extend from 20 or a little before to around 40 or 45, with most championships being won in the middle and later twenties and early thirties.

Health and Organic Functioning at Different Ages

Sickness and death are such important elements in human experience that some data regarding them would seem a necessary part of any attempt to describe life through its whole span. And such material should be of great value in evidencing changes in vitality and energy through the years—changes which might have important relationships to intellectual vigor and to personality. More specifically, it is desirable to consider any available evidence regarding the functioning of various organs of the body as of both practical and general significance.

CHANGES WITH AGE IN SENSORY ADEQUACY

It is common knowledge that as people get older, they are increasingly likely to need glasses and may become deaf. Actually, changes in vision and hearing go on throughout life. Figure 27 shows, first, that from childhood there is a steady decrease in range of accommodation of the lens, with relative rigidity beginning around 60 and, second, that beginning around 40 (there is little change before), visual acuity declines. The size of the pupil decreases about a third from the twenties to the sixties, thus decreasing the amount of light admitted to the retina (6). With increasing age, glasses for close work and increasing illumination are likely to be needed. After the age of 50, sensitivity of the eye in the dark decreases. After 30, some narrowing of the visual field may begin. Obviously all these decreases in visual efficiency may handicap in various ways; in such tasks as driving an automobile or flying a plane at night, they might sometimes be of critical importance (36).

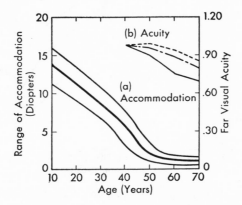

Figure 27. Relation of (a) age 10–70 Years to Visual Accommodation, the Heavy Line Showing the Mean and Lighter Lines Maximal and Minimal Values, and (b) Decline in Mean Visual Acuity from 40 on (When Appreciable Decline Begins) as Shown in Three Investigations. (Adapted from R. A. McFarland, *Human Factors in Air Transportation*, New York, McGraw-Hill, 1953, p. 378, data of Duane and Friedenwald.)

The average person suffers a progressive loss of ability to hear tones of high pitch from childhood on. Figure 28 shows practically no decrease in ability to hear low tones at 60, but a loss on high tones is clearly evident at 40. (Women lose the ability to hear less than men do, perhaps because they do less noisy work.) In older people, there is, therefore, decreasing sensitivity to the full richness of complex musical tones—less value in high fidelity recordings. Since most consonants in speech involve high tones, difficulty in understanding conversation results from a considerable loss of this faculty. One investigator has reported that about 1 percent of people 20 years old are deaf enough to have some difficulty with telephone conversations, 2 percent at 35 years, and 9 percent at 65 (31).

The number of taste buds appears to decrease somewhat in the older years, and perhaps sensitivity to sweet decreases somewhat. Scattered research indicates that sensitivity to touch, pressure, pain, and movement declines after 50 (66). In short, it seems literally true that things look, sound, taste, and feel somewhat different at different ages. As a person gets older, the senses dull somewhat and become less adequate. And these losses are not simply decrepitudes appearing near the end of life.

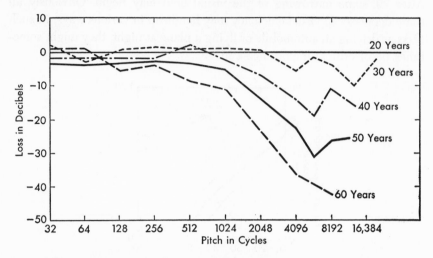

Figure 28.   Changes in Sensitivity of Hearing with Age. Note the lack of hearing loss for pitches up to 512 cycles for all age groups. (After Bunch. From A. T. Poffenberger, *Principles of Applied Psychology*, New York, Appleton, 1942.)

Rather, they seem part of the total complex processes of development and change, progressing gradually from the early prime, or even from childhood, through the middle and older years.

MORBIDITY AND MORTALITY

Figure 29 shows two types of evidence regarding total physiological vigor and soundness at different ages. The bottom two lines show frequency of deaths per thousand in each age group. The death rate is relatively high in infancy but quickly drops, fewest deaths occurring around 10 and in the early teens. There is only a slow rise until about 40, but the increase is more rapid from 60 on. Fewest males are ill at about 18, with little rise till 40; women show an increase around 22 because of childbirth and related malaise. In general, healthiest years are from the teens to about 40 to 50, with number ill on a given day increasing substantially at 50 and more rapidly at 70. But these last figures may give an exaggerated impression as to the number of old people who are ill, since illnesses tend to be longer in old age, and that fact pushes up the above frequencies. The "Prairie City" survey reported 8 out of 10 of those over

65 were "fairly well and vigorous"; and "no more than 1 in 10 was so ill or feeble as to need help from relatives or nurses."[3]

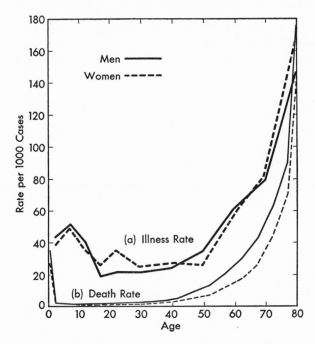

Figure 29. Number, of 1000 Cases in Each Age Group, (a) Who Were Ill on the Survey Date, and (b) Who Died During 1950 in the United States. (Health survey in Baltimore, 1938–1943. From office of Vital Statistics, November 2, 1953, and Public Health Reports, December 14, 1951.)

It is generally appreciated that some illnesses are especially characteristic of certain ages. Table 5 makes clear that important causes of death differ from one period of life to another. The causes differ very much in the older years as compared with childhood or, indeed, even with middle age. Such degenerative conditions as heart disease, hardening of the arteries, and cancer are the great killers after 45, the first having a rate for 65 years and over of 2771 per 100,000 population. In general, the causes of death under 5 years (except for accidents) are not important after that age. Accidents are the most important cause of death all the way from 1 year to 24. But accidents are largely of a different nature at different ages. Thus, fatal burns are relatively more common among

[3] R. H. Havighurst and Ruth Albrecht, *Older People*, New York, Longmans, Green, 1953, p. 65.

young children than at any other age until past 65. And of the 222 fatal accidents per 100,000 population in this oldest age group, 166 were falls, as compared with only 2 fatal falls in ages 5 to 14. No disease is frequently

TABLE 5.   Leading Causes of Death, 1949

		Rate per 100,000 Population
Under 1 year	Immaturity	725
	Congenital malformations	422
	Postnatal asphyxia	385
	Birth injuries	358
	Pneumonia	329
	Gastritis, enteritis, colitis	165
	Accidents	108
1 to 4 years	Accidents	39
	Pneumonia	18
	Congenital malformations	12
5 to 14 years	Accidents	23
	Cancer	6
	Poliomyelitis	4
15 to 24 years	Accidents	52
	Tuberculosis	15
	Cancer	9
25 to 44 years	Heart disease	51
	Accidents	44
	Cancer	40
45 to 64 years	Heart disease	527
	Cancer	271
	Vascular lesions affecting brain	125
	Accidents	61
65 years	Heart disease	2771
	Vascular lesions affecting brain	883
	Cancer	842
	General arteriosclerosis	235
	Accidents	222

SOURCE: Adapted from material of the National Safety Council, from data of the National Office of Vital Statistics.

fatal from 1 to 24 or indeed to 45. In short, it seems very clear not only that the organism is at its best healthwise from the teens through about 40 or 45, but also that organic resistances and weaknesses are very different from one age group to another.

AGE AND FUNCTIONING OF THE VITAL ORGANS

Are there important changes with age in the functioning of various vital organs of the body? Figures 30 and 31 bring together examples of substantial change in lung capacity, blood pressure, digestive fluids in the stomach, and male sex activity. These curves all show consistent changes with age, and the changes are of the nature already much evidenced—optimal functioning in the twenties, then the beginning of a

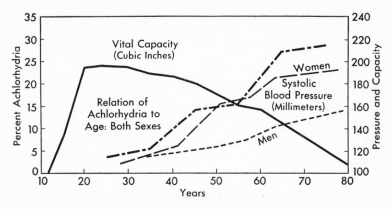

Figure 30. Physiological Change with Age. (Adapted from E. V. Cowdry, *Problems of Aging,* Baltimore, Williams and Wilkins, 1939, pp. 207, 634; and D. Wechsler, Intellectual changes with age, mental health in later maturity, Federal Security Agency, U.S. Public Health Service, Supplement No. 168, Washington, D.C., U.S. Government Printing Office, p. 44.)

slow decrease, with perhaps greater falling off in the older years. Thus, male sex functioning according to Kinsey is at its peak in the late teens and early twenties, falls off slowly thereafter without any accelerated drop at a "menopausal" time, may somewhat remain into the seventies; impotence becomes increasingly more common from 55 on. Lung capacity is greatest around 20, then slowly decreases; there may also be a slow decrease in hydrochloric acid in the digestive juices and an increase in systolic blood pressure, especially in women from the forties on.

Material regarding age of the mother as related to abnormality in the offspring is of interest in its own right, insofar as it indicates desirable age of marriage and childbearing. The findings, presumably, also have greater significance as evidence of age in relation to total organic vigor

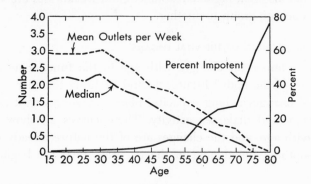

Figure 31. Change in Sexual Vigor with Age. (Adapted from A. C. Kinsey *et al., Sexual Behavior in the Human Male,* Philadelphia, W. B. Saunders, 1948, pp. 221, 236.)

and mother's developmental stage. Figure 32 shows that a healthy child is most likely to be born to a mother in her twenties. Beginning around 35 the risk of a stillbirth or a congenital deformity (or a mongoloid child) increases—though fortunately the expectation is always of a normal child. Risks to the mother also increase. In part, these risks result from previous childbearing, but analyses indicate that they are in part products of aging,

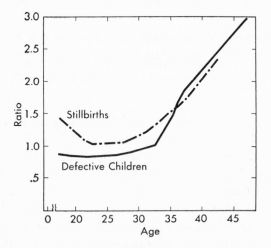

Figure 32. Relationship of Maternal Age to the Incidence of Physically Defective Children and to Stillbirths. (Adapted from L. M. Hellman, Effect of aging on the course and outcome of pregnancy, *J. Gerontol.,* 1946, 1:418–425.)

independent of such factors. Just before World War II, 14 percent of all births were occurring to mothers 35 years or older.

Electroencephalographic measurements have shown a gradual maturing, in rate and pattern, of potentials in the nervous system or "brain waves" until around 20 and a slowing in old age (66).

The preceding material has reported a variety of changes with age. But some tissues seem to function about as well in the later years as earlier. The smooth muscles show little change and normally operate about as well in older people as in the young; so the digestive systems of most old people may continue to operate reasonably satisfactorily. And if there is no special strain or crisis, all these various body functions may serve reasonably well even into old age.

HOMEOSTASIS

Of vital importance throughout life are certain processes of adjustment within the body which maintain essential stabilities as of body temperature, blood sugar level, and acid-base balance of the blood. Throughout adolescence and early maturity all these conditions are held relatively stable unless there are excessive strains. However, after about the age of 40, regulation of body temperatures becomes more difficult in a cold environment as a result of lowered metabolic activity and muscular vigor and more difficult in a hot environment because of limited ability to dissipate heat through skin in which capillaries may be degenerated, sweat glands may be deficient, and arterioles may be contracted. So in cold weather, old people dress more warmly, shiver more readily, and go south in large numbers. In hot weather, more old people die of heat stroke.

There is progressive lessening of tolerance of glucose following injection, and impairment of kidney function. Under stiff exercise there is less increase in heart rate with increasing age and thus reduced adjustment to the exercise. Reaction to various drugs may change. In short, with increasing age the organism shows decreasing ability to maintain normal conditions in the body and greater difficulty in recovery if these internal conditions have been disturbed (31).

Major Conclusions Regarding the Physical Organism at Different Ages

In total, the writers believe that the preceding diverse material makes the following contributions toward discriminating appraisals of the human organism over the life span with reference to psychological issues of major import.

MAJOR PERIODS OF LIFE

The material emphasizes, it is believed, the great and psychologically important differences between major periods of total life development. The first 20 years are one continuing surge of growth—punctuated at puberty by some change in rate and nature of the growth process. Then comes the most marked and most consistent change in the entire life span, the cessation of growing and leveling off into the adult period at maturity around 18 or 20. A period then comes which may well be called "the prime," when growth has just ceased but the great growth energies perhaps briefly continue, and the sex and other energies of the young adult are at their peak. About 45 or 50—around the age of the menopause in women—vitality and energy begin to decrease (usually very gradually with men), and a period follows which might be called later adulthood, often a time of continuing and seasoned vigor but nevertheless one of slow physical regression. And there may be a last change time, around 70 or later, when the regression turns into the weakness of old age. The growth period (childhood and youth), adulthood (the prime and later adulthood), old age—these three major periods seem differentiated from each other in developmental direction, dynamics, physical appearance, and physiological functioning. And the subperiods are quite clearly differentiated from each other. It is believed that it is useful to differentiate between the periods and subperiods in later consideration of psychological phenomena—abilities, interests, personality traits. The concept of developmental periods is well recognized in child and adolescent psychology; it is believed of greater value than heretofore appreciated in psychological study of the full life span. But whether or not this concept of periods is accepted, the fact of important changing throughout life seems clear. And psychological changes would be expected.

The above viewpoint sees different periods in the total span of life having different characteristics and having an organically determined duration. So, growth lasts around 20 years, and the prime has a duration, well recognized in women, of about 25 years more. The total possible length of life might similarly be considered biologically determined and limited. "By some inexorable law, still to be discovered and clarified, nature has allotted to man a life span of about 100 years" (Dublin in *31*, p. 220). According to this concept, all that medical science might hope to do would be to lengthen more lives to somewhat nearer this limit (and to make that living healthier), but not to extend lives longer.

The preceding pages have suggested that as the human organism moved from one period or subperiod to the next (as from childhood to adolescence within the growth period) there was a change time, sometimes involving special physiological stresses. Studies of puberty have shown the organic changes occurring then to be complicated and substantial; these biological changes have relationships (often poorly coördinated) with educational programs, social customs, and culture patterns; and the organic changes, the relationship, and the incoördinations all involve psychological changes and problems. As studies are made of other change times—as of maturity, around 20; the end of the prime, around 45 or 50; and any beginning of old age—the hypothesis is ventured that these times may be found to involve organic readjustments now inadequately understood and that vocational and social coördinations with these changes are also often very unsatisfactory. Thus, psychological inquiry regarding these matters would be found richly rewarding.

It may be doubted that men have a change time around 50. But it does seem true that a man of 60 is different from a man of 40 in capacity for great physical exertion (as in sports and possibly winning championships, in likelihood of degenerative disease, and in general physical vigor); and the opinion is tentatively ventured that more of these changes are going on more rapidly around 45 or 50 than just before or after. The many who are feeble in their last years may, in these years, be considered in the period of old age, and the time when health broke thus becomes the change time from later adulthood to old age.

The question has been raised as to whether healthy, vigorous people have a period of old age distinct from later adulthood; some seem to continue essentially intact physically and mentally even into the nineties—then go quickly. The writers' opinion is that these persons do usually somewhat settle back into a period involving a certain disengagement from close grips with life and a mellowing and that this is not entirely a cultural phenomenon but includes pervasive physiological correlates—increasing slowness, unsteadiness and fatigability, and, presumably, less tonus and homeostatic responsiveness, often proceeding almost imperceptibly.[4]

[4] Designation of the last period of life as senility or senescence has been avoided as implying a decay this last group does not show. Bernard Baruch and Herbert Hoover at 80 certainly were not senile and hardly senescent. Simply to say that such people are old seems best. The above designation of periods and change times must

The life-span view brings up its own problems; and it gives new significance to issues hitherto viewed less adequately. Thus, McCay has presented evidence that a spartan diet makes for a long life. Does it lengthen the prime? Research, taking account of long-time cumulative effects, seems to be discovering serious, long-delayed consequences of supposedly innocuous indulgences, such as lung cancer resulting from habitual smoking. Psychosomatic medicine often finds illnesses of the middle and later years stemming from emotional stresses reaching back into childhood. But some childhood stresses and psychosomatic difficulties seem to fade away in adult life. What factors are involved here? What about life-span programs of sports and recreation? It is not only important to consider the effect of athletics in youth on health after 40, but also to consider what the best sports and recreations are for the later years. The writers believe that, for the most part, they have still to be invented. Are the stresses of work really a substantial factor in later debilities? In the life-span view, all such factors become cumulatively important, and constructive dealing with them becomes cumulatively valuable.

The previous chapter indicated that the great and growing number of older people in this and other Western countries was a new phenomenon and that they should become a distinctive asset rather than a burden, if the huge masses of the younger populations of Asia are to be countered. Vigorously constructive programs for the furtherance of optimal development throughout the life span seem vital in this situation.

Two points seem worth mentioning here. In the first place, certain declines with age are usually of little practical importance, or can be compensated for. Thus, it is usually of little practical importance to a man of 60 that he cannot run as fast as at 20; at all ages, the usual pace in self-locomotion is a walk. And in this country especially, means of conveyance are so plentiful that he usually need not even walk far. Modern industry provides improved conditions of work, simplified tasks involving little physical strain, and shorter hours which in total should make it possible for older persons to continue economically productive longer than even

---

not be understood as a segmentation of life. Life is a continuum, and the gradualness of many changes is one of their most important characteristics. But there are changes, and their rate is not always the same, and these facts are to be noted. Perhaps it is better to overstress them slightly than to neglect them—for instance, simply to say that from 20 to 65 is one long, presumably unchanging period of maturity.

30 years ago. In home and in place of work, winter heating and summer air conditioning are a help, particularly to older people, in maintaining homeostasis. Better spectacles, hearing aids, and noise control aid the older people. And as differences between the different ages become better and more generally understood, personnel managers and others involved can better allow for these differences. In the second place, increasing numbers of old people who do really take care of themselves illustrate that a seasoned vigor is possible into old age. Advances in medicine are bringing new health into the older years. It is the hope of the writers that a broad and practical psychology of the entire life span can make contributions to the self-understanding of the intelligent individual and to educational, industrial, and welfare programs, which will foster still more the potentialities of each age and conserve physical and psychological capacities throughout life.[5]

Summary

The chapter attempts (with much use of graphs to show both change and continuity) to summarize material about physical development throughout the life span which might be helpful in structuring and interpreting psychological development through life. The following evidence regarding physical growth, strength, and health appears of significance for these purposes.

1. Measurements of height and weight show a continuous upsurging growth during the first 18 or 20 years of life, with acceleration of growth rate at puberty; at around 20, growth ceases, though weight may slowly increase until old age and then drop. At every age there are great individual differences, not only in size but also in age when a given stage of growth is reached and in relation to previous and later stages. Around adolescence, these features have been shown to have important influences on the development of personality. They probably do at other ages also.

[5] Very old people (especially centenarians) seem to give fascinating glimpses as to what might be hoped for and also as to what the problems might be. Some of these very old people seem to continue largely intact in personality and abilities, and as far as physical capacities are concerned, seem able to get about somewhat. If one can escape or weather the diseases and hazards of life (and has a good constitution), perhaps one might before long hope to reach the century mark and in a reasonably coherent condition. Perhaps by the year 2000 many will live to that age—many present-day 20-year-olds might hope to live to the year 2036. But what is to be done with life from 70 to 100? Thirty years is a long time! And *is* the human constitution such that, as Dublin says, it cannot hope to last beyond the century mark? The separate bodily organs seem mostly to have a longer potential (31). But if some persons should last still longer, what will they be like at the age of 120? And what will they do or what will be done with them?

2. Throughout life, the body is in constant change. In gross proportion and in comparative size and functioning of the different internal organs, the adolescent is very different from the child, the woman of 50 from the girl of 20, the 70-year-old from the man of 45. Changes are especially rapid at certain times, such as at puberty, maturity, menopause, and perhaps at the beginning of old age. There are substantial individual differences in the age at which these changes occur and in their rapidity. These changes may involve or cause important psychological problems. And subtle changes in personality might be presumed from the great changes in the total physiology from one period of life to another.

3. Strength and quickness increase through the growth period and increase especially rapidly in adolescence, level off in early adult life, and then slowly decline. Maximal total physical effectiveness as shown by championships in sports appears in the twenties and earlier thirties. Individual differences in all the above phenomena are substantial.

4. Susceptibility to illness and death varies with the years, and the nature of illness and causes of death vary also. Thus, here again is evidence of the rise and the slow fall of the organism's vitality and of changes in constitution. Fortunately, there is much evidence to indicate that morbidity may be lessened and vitality conserved. From childhood, there are changes in sensory adequacy. Functionings of the vital organs also show age changes. With increasing age, the delicate balances of homeostasis are more difficult to maintain.

5. All the above evidence is consistent in indicating that the normal life appears to move through three major periods: growth (childhood and youth), adulthood (the prime and later adulthood), and old age, each needing careful and differentiating study and each with times of change (such as at puberty, maturity, the menopause) involving special physiological and psychological stresses. Such a life-span approach gives perspectives to problems of health and optimal physical welfare and should be of great value in efforts to increase understanding of abilities, interests, and personality at each age.

BIBLIOGRAPHY

1. Alvarez, W. C., *Nervousness, Indigestion and Pain*, New York, Harper, 1943.
2. Association of Life Insurance Medical Directors and the Actuarial Society of America, *Medico Actuarial Mortality Investigation*, New York, 1912. Vol. 1.
3. Bardeen, C. R., The height-weight index of build in relation to linear and

volumetric proportions and surface area of the body during post-natal development, *Contributions to Embryology*, Carnegie Institute of Technology, 1920, 9:483–554.

4. Bick, M. M., and Birren, J. E., Age changes in the light threshold of the dark-adapted eye, *J. Gerontol.*, 1948, 3:267–271.

5. Birren, J. E., and Botwinick, J., The relation of writing speed to age and to senile psychoses, *J. Consult. Psychol.*, 1951, 15:243–249.

6. Birren, J. E., Casperson, R. C., and Botwinick, J., Age changes in pupil size, *J. Gerontol.*, 1950, 5:216–221.

7. Bowles, G. T., *New Types of Old Americans at Harvard and at Eastern Women's Universities*, Cambridge, Harvard University Press, 1932.

8. Cathcart, E. P., Hughes, D. E. R., and Chalmers, J. G., The physique of man in industry, *Report No. 71*, London, Medical Research Council, Industrial Health Research Board, 1935.

9. Chenoweth, L. B., Increase in height and weight and decrease in age of college freshmen, *J.A.M.A.*, 1937, 108:354–356.

10. Collins, S. D., A general view of the causes of illness and death at specific ages, *U.S. Public Health Report*, U.S. Public Health Service, Treasury Department, 1935, 50:237–255.

11. De Silva, H. R., Age and highway accidents, *Sci. Mont.*, 1938, 47:536–546.

12. Dimock, H. S., *Rediscovering the Adolescent*, New York, Association Press, 1937.

13. Droller, H., Falls among elderly people living at home, *Geriat.*, 1955, 10:239–244.

14. Dunbar, Flanders, *Mind and Body: Psychosomatic Medicine*, New York, Random House, 1947.

15. Fisher, M. B., and Birren, J. E., Age and strength, *J. Appl. Psychol.*, 1947, 31:490–497.

16. Ford, C. S., and Beach, F. A., *Patterns of Sexual Behavior*, New York, Harper, 1951.

17. Garn, S. M., Physical growth and development, *Amer. J. Physical Anthropol.*, 1952, 10:169–192.

18. Gilbert, Jeanne G., *Understanding Old Age*, New York, Ronald Press, 1952.

19. Gould, H. N., and M. R., Age of first menstruation in mothers and daughters, *J.A.M.A.*, 1932, 98:1349–1352.

20. Gray, H., Increase in stature of American boys in the last fifty years, *J.A.M.A.*, 1927, 88:908.

21. Hellman, L. M., Effect of aging on the course and outcome of pregnancy, *J. Gerontol.*, 1946, 1:418–425.

22. Hilgard, J. R., Learning and maturation in pre-school children, *Ped. Sem. and J. Genet. Psychol.*, 1932, 4:35–36.

23. Howe, P. E., and Schiller, M., Growth responses of the school child to changes in diet and environmental factors, *J. Appl. Psychol.*, 1952, 5:51–61.

24. Jones, H. E., Development of physical abilities, *43rd Yearbook*, National Society for the Study of Education, Pt. I, 1944, pp. 100–122.
25. Jones, H. E., *Motor Performance and Growth*, Berkeley, University of California Press, 1949.
26. Kaplan, O. J. (ed.), *Mental Disorders in Later Life* (2nd ed.), Stanford, Stanford University Press, 1956.
27. Keys, A. B., *et al.*, *The Biology of Human Starvation*, Minneapolis, University of Minnesota Press, 1950, 2.
28. Kinsey, A. C., *et al.*, *Sexual Behavior in the Human Female*, Philadelphia, W. B. Saunders, 1953.
29. Kinsey, A. C., *et al.*, *Sexual Behavior in the Human Male*, Philadelphia, W. B. Saunders, 1948.
30. Klineberg, Otto, *Race Differences*, New York, Harper, 1935.
31. Lansing, A. I. (ed.), *Problems of Aging*, Baltimore, Williams and Wilkins, 1952.
32. Lehman, H. C., The most proficient years at sports and games, *Res. Quart.*, American Association of Health and Physical Education, 1938, 9:3–19.
33. Maranon, G., *The Climacteric*, St. Louis, C. V. Mosby, 1929.
34. McCance, R. A., *et al.*, Studies of undernutrition, Wuppertal 1946–1949, *Special Report No. 275*, Medical Research Council, London, Her Majesty's Stationery Office, 1951.
35. McCay, C. M., *et al.*, Nutritional aspects of aging, *J. Gerontol.*, 1952, 7:448–463.
36. McFarland, R. A., *Human Factors in Air Transportation*, New York, McGraw-Hill, 1953.
37. McGraw, M. B., *Growth: A Study of Johnny and Jimmy*, New York, D. Appleton-Century, 1935.
38. Meredith, H. V., Relation between socio-economic status and body size in boys 7 to 10, *Amer. J. Diseases of Children*, 1951, 82:702–709.
39. Miles, H. H. W., *Case Histories in Psychosomatic Medicine*, New York, W. W. Norton, 1952.
40. Miles, W. R., Measures of certain human abilities throughout the life span, *Proc. Nat. Acad. Sci.*, 1931, 17:627–633.
41. Moraut, G. M., A discussion on the measurement of growth and form, *Proc. Royal Society of London*, Series B, Biological Sciences, 1950, 137:443–452.
42. Newman, H. H., Freeman, F. H., and Holzinger, K. J., *Twins—A Study of Heredity and Environment*, Chicago, University of Chicago Press, 1937.
43. Nicolson, Arline, and H. C., Indices of physiological maturity, *Child Development*, 1953, 24:3–38.
44. Ohlson, M. A., and Roberts, P. H., Dietary practices of 100 women from 40 to 75, *J. Amer. Dietet. Assoc.*, 1948, 24:286–291.
45. Palmer, C. E., Height and weight of children of depression poor, *U.S. Public Health Report*, U.S. Public Health Service, Treasury Department, August, 1935, Pt. 2, 50:1106–1113.

46. Patrick, P. R., Heights and weights of Queensland school children, *Medical J. Australia,* 1951, 2:324–331.

47. Paul, G. A., Summary of physical findings of employees over sixty years of age, *Industrial Medicine and Surgery,* 1949, *18*:360–364.

48. Peraza, G., Mental and physical benefits of a well-balanced diet on a group of undernourished children, *J. Amer. Med. Woman's Assoc.,* 1946, *1*:256.

49. Pinner, M., and Miller, B. F., *When Doctors Are Patients,* New York, W. W. Norton, 1952.

50. Pirrie, G. D., Heights and weights of London school children, *Monthly Bull. Univ. of Health,* 1950, 9:247–252.

51. Poffenberger, A. T., *Principles of Applied Psychology,* New York, Appleton, 1942.

52. Rothney, J. W., and Dearborn, W. F., *Predicting the Child's Development,* Cambridge, Science-Art Publishers, 1941.

53. Ruger, H. A., and Stoessiger, Brenda, Growth curves of certain characteristics in man (males), *Annals of Eugenics,* 1927, 2:76–110.

54. Sane, K. I., The age of menopause, *A.M.A., Transactions* (section on obstetrics, gynecology, and abdominal surgery), 1918, pp. 259–282.

55. Schwartz, L., Britten, R. H., and Thompson, L. R., Studies in physical development and posture, *U.S. Public Health Bull.,* U.S. Public Health Service, Treasury Department, 1928, *179*:124.

56. Sheldon, J. H., *The Social Medicine of Old Age,* London, Oxford University Press, 1948.

57. Shuttleworth, F. K., The adolescent period: a graphic atlas and a pictorial atlas, *Monogr. Society for Research in Child Development,* 1951, Vol. 14, Nos. 1 and 2, pp. 265, 269.

58. Shuttleworth, F. K., The physical and mental growth of girls and boys age six to nineteen in relation to age at maximal growth, *Monogr. Society for Research in Child Development,* 1939, Vol. 4, No. 3.

59. Simonton, K. M., Presbycusis: the hearing loss of old age, *Geriat.,* 1955, *10*:337–338.

60. Stolz, H. R., and Lois M., *Somatic Development of Adolescent Boys,* New York, Macmillan 1951.

61. Stuart, H. C., *Healthy Childhood,* New York, D. Appleton-Century, 1933.

62. Wechsler, D., *The Range of Human Capacities* (rev. ed.), Baltimore, Williams and Wilkins, 1952.

63. Welford, A. T., *Skill and Age,* London, Oxford University Press, 1951.

64. White House Conference on Child Health and Protection, Growth and Development of the Child, Sect. I, Medical Service, Pts. I–IV. New York, D. Appleton-Century, 1932, 1933, 1932, 1932.

65. Williams, Judith R., and Scott, R. B., Motor development and its relationship to child rearing processes in two groups of Negro infants, *Child Development,* 1953, *24*:103–122.

66. Zubek, J. P., and Solberg, Patricia, *Human Development,* New York, McGraw-Hill, 1954.

CHAPTER 3 ●

● Growth and Change in Abilities as Shown by Tests

THE previous chapter reviewed evidence of various types regarding physical growth and change through the life span. Results of measurements of various types—of height, weight, strength, quickness—were considered. Certain information regarding physical accomplishments of various sorts was also glanced at; particular attention was given to ages when championships in sports were most often won, as indicating the time when the organism might be considered to reach its peak potentialities. Data on morbidity and mortality were also summarized, as indicating the organism's disabilities and weaknesses at different ages. A somewhat similar plan will be followed in considering the growth of mental abilities and their possible change and decline in the adult and older years. But these psychological topics must be given more extensive treatment. The present chapter summarizes results of attempts to measure the development and change of mental abilities throughout the life span and to determine factors involved. Chapter 4 will report evidence regarding age of superior accomplishment and will present data regarding the age incidence of mental diseases as indications of mental vitality and health at different periods of life. Chapter 6 on the work life will also have bearings on this topic. From the total discussion, it is hoped that larger perspectives than have heretofore been gained may be obtained regarding diverse problems of education, of guidance in school and after, and of most effective utilization of human resources by industry and government.

"General Ability" Through the Life Span

The natural first question is as to the findings obtained with tests of "general ability" from individuals of different ages from childhood to old age. The great mass of test data, as might be expected, is from children and young people in school. But adults have also been tested in a variety of places from Army camps to institutions for the aged. Recently, adults who were first thus appraised in childhood or youth have been retested, and the abilities of the same individuals have been measured at regular intervals from infancy into adult life. As an outcome, earlier ideas regarding growth of abilities, and change and possible decline in the adult and older years seem in process of substantial revision.

NATURE OF THE TESTS

Examinations which can be given to entire classes or other groups have been most widely used because large numbers of cases can be quickly tested. In fact, they have been so widely used that their nature is a matter of common knowledge. These test blanks contain large numbers of questions of which the following are samples (answers are indicated by checking or other simple means so that a large number of questions can be covered in a short time):

Are apples good to eat? Yes No
The day before Thursday is (a) Wednesday (b) Tuesday (c) Friday (d) Sunday.
Cheese comes from (a) plants (b) eggs (c) milk.
What is iron never without? (a) coldness (b) polish (c) weight (d) rust.
Head is to hat as hand is to: foot, glove, shoe, coat, wrist.
New York is larger than Berlin because it (a) has more railroads (b) has more millionaires (c) is better located.

In general, the questions call for "common sense," practical information, or the solution of simple problems and try to avoid material that would be familiar only to people from a particular part of the country or in a particular occupation. The tests try to deal with ideas which are common property in the average American community. They also assume ability to read. If an individual has lived in an isolated district and his schooling has been very meager, or as an adult, his work has been unskilled and his reading minimal, then he may conceivably be so handicapped as to reading skill and general fund of information that the tests are unfair to him. But a person who has grown up in the usual American community is presumed to have had such advantages and maintained such literacy as will permit him to take the tests without difficulty; he will (it is inferred) deal effectively with these common ideas in proportion to his native ability. It is also assumed that largely verbal materials, as distinct from tasks calling for actual dealing with things or people, are reasonably adequate for differentiating general ability. These assumptions will be returned to later but will be tentatively accepted for the present.

The above statement has to do with group tests. Tests to be given informally by an examiner to one individual at a time may also be used. Most widely known are various forms of the Binet scale. Little tots are asked simple little questions, such as to identify common objects shown to them; older children may be requested to define abstract terms or solve common-sense problems in arithmetic. The Wechsler-Bellevue scale, a test instrument designed especially for use with adults, has five verbal and five performance tests (a revised form has recently been issued). The first verbal test asks general information questions, such as "What is a thermometer?" "How tall is the average American woman?" and "What is the Apocrypha?" The general comprehension test asks "Why are shoes made of leather?" and "Why are people who are born deaf usually unable to talk?" The arithmetic test includes such questions as "How many oranges can you buy for 36¢ if one orange costs 4¢?" A similarities test asks in what way orange and banana, wagon and bicycle, praise and punishment are alike. Performance tests call for arranging in the right order a series of pictures which tell a story, telling what part is missing in pictures having one part gone, putting together pieces of a puzzle, and writing under a series of symbols the number which, according to a key at the top of the page, goes with each.

GROWTH OF "GENERAL ABILITY" DURING THE FIRST TWENTY YEARS

The first topic to be discussed is the development of abilities during the growth years. Figure 33 brings together several studies which made use of tests of the Binet type. The major curves, from an investigation by an English psychologist (16) who used his own adaptation of the Binet scales, show that superior youngsters who were recipients of scholarships increased rapidly in ability, but the dull and the defective grew much more slowly in mental ability. The two bottom curves, from an American investigation, show the minimal abilities of imbeciles and idiots and apparent early beginnings of a decline. For contrast, and a sample of successive testings of a single individual, the dotted highest curve shows mental growth for a boy who averaged an IQ of 181 in several tests.

Figure 33 shows, for example, that when chronologically 20 years old, Burt's "mentally defective" group made only as good a score as the average child of 8, or had a "mental age" of 8. In striking contrast, when only 9 years and 6 months in age, the very bright boy scored a "mental age" of 17 years and 5 months. The IQ or intelligence quotient was found by dividing the mental age (in months) by the chronological age—209 divided by 114— giving an IQ of 183. As a contrast, the average mental defective in the figure when 5 years old had a mental age of only about 3 or an IQ of 60.

Figure 33 makes clear that the first two decades of life are a period of great mental as well as physical growth. Also, mental as well as physical growth seems to level off around 18 to 20. It would appear (the topic will be returned to later) that a basic organic growth process was exhibited here, similar in course (except for absence of prepubescent growth

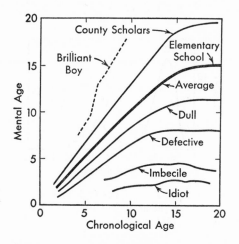

Figure 33.   Curves of Growth in General Ability, as Shown by Binet-type Tests, of Children of a Wide Range of Brightness from Very Brilliant Boy in a New York Private School and Scholarship Winners in England to Idiots in an Institution for the Feeble-minded. (From G. Hildreth, Three gifted children: a developmental study, J. Genet. Psychol., 1954, 85:239–262; C. Burt, The Backward Child, New York, Appleton-Century, 1937, p. 650; and Kuhlman, Results of repeated examinations of 639 feebleminded over a period of ten years, J. Appl. Psychol., 1921, 5:195–224.)

spurt) to growth in height. Figure 33 also shows a great and increasing total range in ability. Thus, by the age of 20, the county scholars average some five years in "mental age" above the general run of "elementary school" pupils, and the "mentally defective" are some six years in "mental age" below these, i. e., they have a mental age of only about 8 though they are chronologically 20. But these curves are for groups of children; individuals might be expected to vary even more as is evidenced by Figure 34 which shows the distributions of mental ages for the same group of 167 American girls in the Boston area when given certain mental tests at the ages of 8, 12, and 16.

These school girls, whose families were sufficiently established so that they remained in the same locality throughout the years covered by the investigation, averaged in mental age above their chronological age at each testing. As a group, they thus appear to be somewhat superior in ability. Nevertheless, when they were 12 years old, they ranged in mental age from 9 to 18! It would seem evident that in almost any group of youngsters one might expect differences in mental ability so great as to call for differences in school programs and methods and in educational and vocational plans. The distribution for age 12 is also obviously wider than for age 8; if the tests used at age 16 had had a high enough "ceiling"

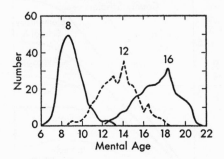

Figure 34.   Distributions of Mental Ages of 167 Girls at Ages 8, 12, and 16. (Adapted from W. F. Dearborn and J. W. Rothney, *Predicting the Child's Development*, Cambridge, Science-Art Publications, 1941, p. 325.)

for the ablest girls fully to show their superiority, the distribution for the 16-year testing would probably have been even wider. In short, as youngsters get older, the need for differentiated school programs, taking account of their differences in abilities, becomes greater.

To what extent do children maintain their relative abilities? What likelihood is there that a little girl who tested as very bright when in nursery school will rate as only average when in the sixth grade or that a boy whose IQ at 6 was 80 will have an IQ of 110 when 16? Longitudinal studies, in which the same youngsters have been tested every year or so over a considerable period of time, yield clear evidence on this point. One such study has followed the same 40 children from infancy to 18 years of age. Figure 35 summarizes findings for four of these cases, the results being expressed as variations (sigma differences) from the average for the group at each testing.

Obviously, test results in infancy are very erratic, but from about 6 on they are much more stable. Some slow trends up or down, or occasional more marked variations, may still occur, however. A later figure will show more variant cases. Variations averaged about one-third of a standard deviation, or five or six IQ points. In considering the graph, it must be kept in mind that this also was a somewhat superior and select group; if the

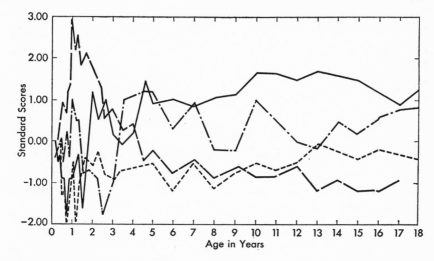

Figure 35. Standard Scores of Four Children on Successive Testings from Infancy Through 18 Years (Sigma Scores for Distribution of Scores for Berkeley Groups). (Adapted from N. Bayley, Consistency and variability in the growth of intelligence from birth to 18 years, J. Genet. Psychol., 1949, 75:188–189.)

total range of abilities in an entire school population had been included, the fluctuations over that entire range would probably have been relatively less.

For 27 cases for whom most complete data were available, correlations of tests given at various ages with test score at 18 (obtained with the Wechsler scale) were as follows:

Age	1	2	4	7	9	11	15
Correlation	.14	.39	.52	.68	.80	.87	.84

Evidently the testing at 1 year, using the California first-year scale, gave no indication as to ability at 18, and the California preschool scale at 2 and 4 predicted only roughly, but the Stanford-Binet at 7, 9, and 11 and Terman-McNemar at 15 gave scores quite closely related to the 18-year score. And the average scores for years 17 and 18 correlated only .41 with the average scores of 10, 11, and 12 months, .62 with the average scores for 42, 48, and 54 months, and .86 with the average scores for 5, 6, and 7 years (8).

CHANGES IN "GENERAL ABILITY" DURING THE ADULT AND OLDER YEARS

The above material has made quite clear that general ability grows during the growth years and that individual differences increase, but that after early childhood relative standings remain fairly constant. What happens to abilities through the adult years? Do they continue somewhat to rise, or do they level off and then slowly fall, like strength and quickness? The dash line in Figure 36 summarizes a pioneer investigation (50) bearing on such questions—an attempt to test all the individuals between the ages of 10 and 60 in certain New England communities. Procedure involved a shrewd appeal to Yankee thrift and fair play. A free moving picture show was offered in a community hall. Then, during an intermission, the audience was asked to take the Army "Alpha" test used with soldiers during the First World War. Individuals who did not attend the free movie were visited in their homes and, if possible, wheedled (and bribed!) into taking the test there. In all, 1191 persons were tested.

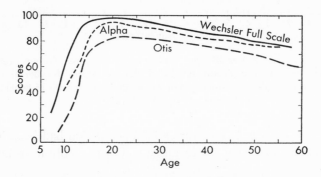

Figure 36. Average Scores on Wechsler Individual and Otis and Alpha Group Scales and Variability on Wechsler. Cases from New York (Wechsler). California (Otis), and Vermont (Alpha). (Adapted from H. E. Jones and H. S. Conrad, The growth and decline of intelligence: a study of a monogeneous group between ages of 10 and 60, Genet. Psychol. Monogr., 1933, 13:223–298; C. C. and W. R. Miles, The correlation of intelligence scores and chronological age from early to late maturity, Amer. J. Psychol., 1932, 44:44–78; and D. Wechsler, The Measurement of Adult Intelligence (3rd ed.), Baltimore, Williams and Wilkins, 1955.)

The dash line in Figure 36 shows the average of the mean and median for each age group in this survey; it indicates that ability develops rapidly and at a fairly constant rate up to about 16 and then more slowly until a highest point is reached between 18 and 21. After this, a very gradual decline sets in, which by the fifty-fifth year reaches about the level attained by school children of 14. However, the range of ability at each age was, as will be seen shortly, very great. There was evidence that some of these adults did not put forth their full effort and also that the time limits on the tests handicapped progressively the older adults because of their tendency to work slowly. Moreover, certain of the items would hardly interest, or be understood by, older people in small New England villages.

This last point might lead one to the inference that older persons in cities would not show so much decline, being more widely informed and more alert. However, another early study, using an urban population and in a different part of the country—California—reported very similar results. Some 820 persons ranging from adolescence to old age in two small cities, one of 12,000 and one of 15,000 population, were tested individually with the Otis self-administering test (a brief test intended for both adults and high school students). The long-dash line in Figure 36 shows the means. Again the peak is around 20, and the subsequent slow decline parallels very closely that found in the first-mentioned study. Trial of this test without time limits showed, however, that the drop through the middle years was due in considerable part to slowness rather than less capacity to solve problems (66).

The solid line in Figure 36 summarizes data obtained with the 1939 edition of the Wechsler individual scale (95), which, as already mentioned, was designed to be used especially for adults. The adult cases tested were mostly in the New York area but were so chosen as to be roughly representative of the country as a whole in respect to occupation and education. Again the average scores rise to about the age of 20, and thereafter there is a gradual falling off. (Scores on the revised Wechsler scale show the curve topping a little later—around 30 for the verbal half —and dropping somewhat more slowly than did scores on the first form, but the results are largely similar in nature.) Are basic biological trends exhibited here, and must one accept as constitutionally inevitable a crest in intellectual capacity at 18 or 20 (or a little later) with a decline beginning shortly thereafter? To anyone over 35, such conclusions must be distasteful! The problem is clearly of enormous practical importance. Much of this chapter and the next will be devoted to it.

Certain very general factors might be expected to affect adversely the showing made by adults in the usual test of general ability. One has already been referred to; a slowing down seems characteristic of increasing age. Muscular responses in reading or marking a test sheet might be slower or more awkward. There might be a slowing of the central nervous processes.

Students, and young people who have recently been in school, are accustomed to taking tests, but middle-aged and older adults are not. To them, the many diverse, unconnected, and apparently purposeless questions and the objective methods of the group examinations may be odd and confusing. Moreover, the tasks involved in the usual intelligence tests are largely clerical and somewhat academic (perhaps, also, as will be seen shortly, weighted in favor of the middle-upper socioeconomic classes) and thus call for abilities which are developed and kept in practice in school but are less exercised in most adult occupations. In this general connection it is also important to keep in mind the very substantial difference in educational background of average persons of 20 and 60, for example. The average 20-year-old of today is a high school graduate; but in the 60-year-old's young days, the average person had only a grade school education. Further, the typical young person of today has been about, geographically and otherwise, more than his grandparent; reading matter has been more diverse, and movies, radio, and television have enlarged his understandings. Quiz programs might even be said to coach him for testing!

In part because they sense their handicaps as test-takers, adults may often not coöperate as well as young people. In fact, one investigator reported that only about one-half the adults he wished to test were willing to be tested. Adults may be suspicious that test results might be used in some way prejudicial to them; for instance, a low score might handicap them in being considered for a job. Older people may be increasingly timorous lest findings reveal possible weaknesses. They may doubt the value of these curious tasks or disdain them as childish or academic. In short, the low scores in the later adult years might be indicative of poor coöperation rather than poor ability.

Though inadequate schooling and slowness in clerical tasks may handicap the average older adult in taking tests, some of the older people presumably were well educated and are clerically facile; do the detailed results of test surveys show some adults scoring high as a result of their educational advantages or otherwise favored circumstances or constitution? Table 6 presents the scatter of scores at each age, the results being from the New England towns in which the Army Alpha test battery was used.

The range of scores at every age is great. Thus, three 10-year-old children scored up with the average 16-year-olds. The range increases with age during the growth years; thus, the distribution of scores is wider at 18 than at 12. And throughout the adult years the distribution is wide. Even in the oldest group tested, an occasional individual score is up with the very highest in the earlier ages. And this is true in spite of the fact

TABLE 6. Army Alpha Intelligence Test Scores of 1191 Individuals in Age from 10 to 60 in Certain New England Communities

Score	10	12	14	16	18	19–21	22–24	25–29	30–34	35–39	40–44	45–49	50–54	55–59
200						2								
190							1	1	1					
180				1	2					1				
170				2	6			2	3	3	4		1	1
160			1	2	2	1	2	2			3	2	2	
150				5	2	4	3	4	2	1	4	1	2	2
140				4	1	5		4	5	4	6	5	1	1
130			2	6	3	1	3	1	9	7	7	3	2	1
120			1	6	1	6	4	1	7	8	5	1	7	
110		2	4	8	6	6	4	8	7	6	6	5	3	1
100		1	4	3	1	3[a]	3	6	5	5	5	3	3	2
90	3	2	5	5[a]	5[a]	9	3[a]	12[a]	2	7	9[a]	4	3	2
80		8	13	10	3	5	2	10	11[a]	11[a]	10	7[a]	2[a]	5
70	1	7	1[a]	5	3	10	6	12	12	5	5	5	4	2[a]
60	5	5	9	5	8	7	3	6	8	5	7	8	5	5
50	2	10[a]	7	5	1	11	2	9	8	9	8	11	6	2
40	8[a]	9	4	4	5	1	4	3	7	6	5	3	6	2
30	4	16	3	4	1	6	3	3	6	8	3	4	7	6
20	7	4	2	3	1	1	1	1	5	7	3	2	3	
10	2	1					1	2	5	3	6	4	2	
0–9	2		1	1				1	1			1		
Total	34	65	56	75	46	87	44	88	106	96	97	68	59	33
Mean	44	57	76	93	97	101	92	90	87	85	92	81	81	79

NOTE: The mean for each age group is indicated by the letter "a."

SOURCE: Adapted from H. E. Jones and H. S. Conrad, the growth and decline of intelligence: a study of a homogeneous group between ages of 10 and 60, Genet. Psychol. Monogr., 1933, 13:240.

that tests in this scale had time limits which probably hampered most older persons and that much of the test material was of doubtful suitability for older adults.

Clearly, longitudinal studies, comparing the same individuals in youth and in adulthood, should be of great value here, and a few have appeared. One persistent investigator has followed cases from infancy to the age of 25, at which age the average was still continuing to rise a little (8). Another investigator (70) was able to retest in their fifties 127 men who had taken the Army Alpha test when they were college freshmen some 30 years earlier. The recent tests averaged clearly higher. There was uncertainty as to whether the gain came in the college years or after.

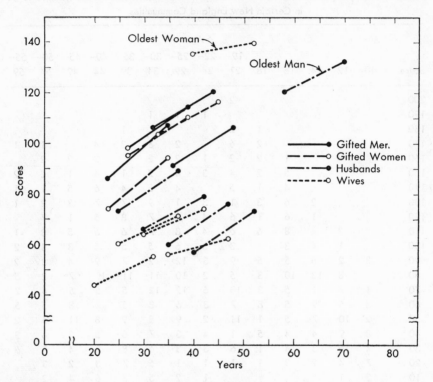

Figure 37. Gains in Scores with Age of Gifted Adults. Initial and later mean scores on the "Concept Mastery" test, of Terman's gifted group and their spouses, grouped according to age at first testing and with first and second scores for each group connected. Also scores of oldest of each sex. (From N. Bayley and M. H. Oden, The maintenance of intellectual ability in gifted adults, J. Gerontol., 1955, 10:91–107.)

But a follow-up on Terman's gifted cases and their spouses showed gains in middle life on a "concept mastery" test involving analogies and like verbal material, as shown in Figure 37. Even the oldest case showed gain. It would appear that well-educated, intellectually active adults do not lose in such verbal abilities but may improve with age.

Several investigators who have tested adult feeble-minded individuals, some of these being repeated testings of the same cases, report the general finding that in adult life mental defectives show a decline in general ability which begins earlier than for average individuals, though repeat testing may show some gain even with some of the mentally inferior (19, 52, 88). The two bottom curves of Figure 33 suggest such a trend. Congruent with these findings, are the facts that mental defectives tend to die earlier than normal people, and the greater the defect, the earlier death is likely to come. Thus, there is evidence that the mentally inferior tend to be also physically inferior. In contrast, several investigators have found the intellectually superior to be also physically superior and longer-lived than the average individual.

General intellectual ability thus seems to grow rapidly through the growth years to about 18 or 20. Early investigators found that a decline began soon after 20, which was indeed distressing to anyone over 35 and seemed contrary to almost all everyday observations. The 1955 revision of the Wechsler scale shows growth continuing a little longer (to around 30) and declining more slowly. Recently, some longitudinal study has shown continuing rises, with mentally superior individuals gaining on certain types of tests even in middle life, though practically all investigators report a tendency for "mental growth" at best to slow down around 20. In such a somewhat confused and indeed complex situation, analyses to determine whether different types of tests show differences in growth and possible decline seem certainly called for.

Analyses of Changes of Abilities with Age

Unfortunately, the concept of "general" ability has so dominated research that all too few analytical studies have been made. What has been done, however, distinctly broadens and illuminates thinking as to the probable nature of intellectual changes through the years.

CHANGES IN THE COMPOSITE OF ABILITIES THROUGH THE GROWTH YEARS

A gross fact must first be stressed: for special abilities as well as "general intelligence," the first two decades are growth years. Various tests of mechanical, artistic, and manipulative ability all show similar rises through those years and a tendency to level off in the later teens.

Mental growth may, nevertheless, have somewhat different characteristics at different times over these years. Bayley's continuing intimate study of a group from birth through 18 years of age found a marked decrease in variability of test scores at 1 year of age, as have other investigators. This finding she explained on the ground that "The mental processes which are developing during the first year are largely sensory-motor in character. . . . By the end of the first year most of the slow developers have caught up with those who were precocious in these simple coördinations. The SD's thus become restricted to individual differences in mature functions," whereas before that time they had included also variations in rate of development (7, pp. 178–179). Some studies show another contraction of variability at the age of 6 years; presumably, this could roughly mark the close of another stage of mental development—perhaps described as devoted especially to achieving familiarity with the home environment and readiness in colloquial speech. Variability of mental test scores of Bayley's group was greatest around 11 years but had substantially decreased by 16—a phenomenon noted in the previous chapter for growth in height and weight. Presumably, these years involved other somewhat different stages of mental growth, which different children went through at different rates, but which most had largely completed by the time they had reached 16 to 18. That this concept of stages of growth seems congruent with the facts of physical growth is suggested by common observation and is exemplified in the content of such scales as the Binet. If the concept of stages of mental growth becomes established, then attempts to find stages in the mental life through the adult and older years would seem warranted. This point will be returned to.

Through the growth years, mental traits in a given child also tend to become more diverse and independent. Thus, one investigation (37) found that average "intercorrelations on tests of memory, verbal, and number abilities for ages 9, 12, and 15 were, for boys, .30, .21, and .18, and for girls, .27, .30, and .10." Other studies have shown similar results (78).

ANALYSES REGARDING CHANGES AFTER TWENTY

Early users of Binet-type scales with adults noted that their pattern of responses differed from that of children. Adults did especially better than children on tests of vocabulary and comparatively poorly on learning and immediate recall of rote material.[1] However, not until the exten-

---

[1] It is believed that one of the present writers was the first to present data on this issue and to suggest that a measure of deterioration might be obtained in this connection. (S. L. Pressey, Distinctive features in psychological test measurements made upon dementia praecox and chronic alcoholic patients, *J. Abnorm. Psychol.*, 1917, 12:130–139; also Are the present psychological scales reliable for adults?, *J. Abnorm. Psychol.*, 1919, 14:314–324.

sive data of Jones and Conrad and of Wechsler were available was it possible to analyze changes systematically from childhood to the older years. The Alpha examination used by Jones and Conrad is made up of 8 subtests and the Wechsler scale of 10; both studies include data for each subtest. Figure 38 shows the most distinctive findings for the present discussion: the average score for each age group, for that test of each scale on which the older individuals did best as compared to the younger adults, and for that test of each battery on which the older individual did worst. Recent Wechsler data from the California State Prison at San Quentin are shown, as well as the earlier Alpha and Wechsler curves.

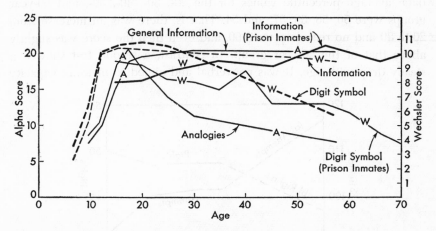

Figure 38.   Alpha (A) and Wechsler (W) Subtests Showing Most and Least Decline with Age in Different Groups. Note: Median alpha, means Wechsler scores, curves smoothed except for prison data. (Adapted from H. E. Jones and H. S. Conrad, The growth and decline of intelligence: a study of a homogeneous group between ages of 10 and 60, *Genet. Psychol. Monogr.*, 1933, 13:251–252; D. Wechsler, *The Measurement of Adult Intelligence* (1st ed.), Baltimore, Williams and Wilkins, 1939, p. 222; and R. J. Corsini and K. K. Fassett, Intelligence and aging, *J. Genet. Psychol.*, 1953, 83:257.)

All four tests show a rapid rise through the childhood and adolescent years and cresting in the late teens, as did the other subtests not included in Figure 38. These trends appear to be usual through the first 20 years. But after that, results for different tests are increasingly dissimilar. The older persons showed practically no decline on the general information test of the Wechsler and a similar test of the Alpha battery; both may be thought of as measuring the accumulations of past learning. In fact, the penitentiary survey shows some rise with age. The older groups do poorest on the Wechsler digit-symbol test (learning that certain numbers go with certain geometrical designs) and on an analogies test; the first calls for rote learning and the second for unusual and rather artificial association of words. Some evidence indicates that those who survive into the seventies and eighties maintain many abilities in these years fairly well (10).

Most of the above tests had time limits. Those used in an excellent English investigation (32) did not. About 2000 Scottish industrial employees, mostly skilled workmen, ranging in age from 15 to 65, were first given a test for vocabulary to measure general fund of information. Percentiles for the 20-year-old group were used as base in handling the data; average percentile values for the 20-, 30-, 40-, 50-, and 60-year groups were 50, 58, 58, 57, and 54. That is, there was an increase from 20 to 30 and no real drop until 60, and even then the score was slightly above that of the 20-year group. In contrast, a second test showed a steady drop with age. It was nonverbal and aimed to measure capacity

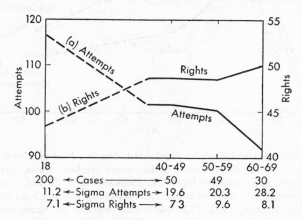

Figure 39.   Mean Number (a) Attempted on 120-Item Vocabulary Test, and (b) Correct of First 60. (Adapted from A. M. Christian and D. G. Paterson, Growth of vocabulary in later maturity, *J. Psychol.*, 1936, 1:167–169.)

to make comparisons and analyze logically, and it might perhaps be considered somewhat artificial and special for these workmen. Results were handled in the same way, and average percentile values for ages from 20 to 60 ran as follows: 50, 48, 43, 40, and 38. Another English investigation, using a test of "capacity to understand and to apply a fresh method of thinking" with some 8000 cases from childhood into the sixties, found that the ablest decline only slightly after the twenties, but the duller people decline more (74).

Progressive loss in speed with age but gains in general information and accuracy are well exhibited in Figure 39. An objective test of vocabulary was given to 329 college and evening school students, ranging in age from 18 to the sixties. The number of answers marked, whether rightly or wrongly, within the time limit decreased from about 117 to 92 tries or attempts, and there was a decrease also in total number of right answers. However, the number of answers right was next counted on the first 60 questions only, this number having been finished by practically everybody, even in the oldest group. This score, which does not include a speed factor, shows the highest average for the oldest group. Also to be noted is the consistent increase in range (sigmas) with age for both attempts and rights—though the smaller range of the younger cases might be the result of a test that was too easy for the ablest to go as high as they could (21).

A clever study dealt with an older group presumably distinctly superior, with a control group of younger individuals of the same general type (85). Forty-five older faculty members in two universities, their ages ranging from 60 to 80, with a mean of 66, were compared with 45 members 25 to 35, with a mean age of 31, the cases being paired as to professional background so that an older chemist was compared with a younger man in the physical sciences, and so on. The test battery included eight tests, some having time limits and some not, but all the tests were sufficiently difficult to challenge the abilities of these men; the younger group averaged three hours for the entire examination while the older took 50 minutes more. Mean total score on the whole battery was 428 ± 29 points for the younger and 373 ± 46 points for the older group. There is a drop in average, but one of the highest scores was made by an 80-year-old. However, the older men did better than the younger on a synonym-antonym test and about as well on a word meanings test; they did poorest on two time-limit code-learning tests. Tests which were timed but without time limit showed the usual slowing with age; thus the younger men averaged 56 minutes on an ingenuity problems test and the older 77 minutes.

The evidence of slowing appears in a great variety of tasks. Thus, when asked to write as many words as they could, beginning with a given letter, 31 persons aged 20 to 29 wrote a mean of 25 words beginning with "S" in a minute, this being 52 percent of their rate of copying words, whereas 30 oldsters aged 70 to 79 wrote a mean of only 6 words, and this was 36 percent of their copying speed (13). English investigators have stressed slowing as a major change appearing in almost every ability; the slowing may be slight, however, in familiar, practiced tasks. Further, older persons may use other methods than younger, often somewhat compensating for this slowness. And they may be more careful and accurate (97). The old also have more difficulty with new tasks and learn with more difficulty. This matter is so important that it must now be given special attention.

CHANGE OVER THE LIFE SPAN IN ABILITY TO LEARN

There is abundant evidence of a growth in ability to learn through the growth years. The great variety of such learning and the possibilities of interrelations of learnings in various ways may well be stressed. Figure

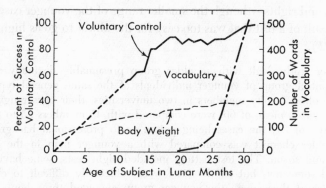

Figure 40. Learning Curves of an Infant in Vocabulary and in Voluntary Control of the Bladder. (From C. L. and B. I. Hull, Parallel learning curves of an infant in vocabulary and in voluntary control of the bladder, Ped. Sem., 1919, 26:272–283.)

40 shows, to the right, growth in vocabulary in childhood. The baby, although it had very likely heard people talking during most of its waking hours, and although the doting parents presumably tried to teach it to talk from early infancy, began to learn words about the eighteenth month, and then only very slowly. However, vocabulary increased very rapidly from about the twenty-fifth month. That is, the baby did not begin to use and understand language until its nervous system had matured to the point where it had "readiness" for such learning. Learning to control the bladder had begun earlier, however, then went on a plateau of no progress when the exciting new experience of language began. Clearly, learning can be of various types—of inhibition as well as action, of internal organic adjustment as well as of social and symbolic acts—

which may begin at different ages and proceed at different rates. The steady rise in weight was an indication that body growth was proceeding well throughout this period.

Similarly, "reading readiness" appears to develop at about 6 years of age in the average child, or even a little later, and efforts to teach reading earlier may be wasteful of time and effort. Youngsters may not be ready for the abstract learnings of algebra until around 14, and some may never be. Attempts to teach Shakespeare in high school may be premature. As will be shown in Chapter 5 on education, the norms for the Abbott-Trabue test for appreciation of poetry do not get substantially above chance scores until the later teens. Exceedingly important social learnings cannot come until adolescence, and they may then interfere with other learnings. The concept that a particular piece of learning cannot profitably go forward until the learner is in readiness for it is of great importance. The concept mentioned earlier, of stages of mental growth, is again suggested. Not only with the appearance of language, but again with mastery of the printed symbol, there may be a somewhat new type of learning. "There are probably a number of different kinds of learning. . . . It is quite probable that the different kinds of learning follow different laws" (45, p. 330).

Figure 41 shows another fact of great importance. It is probably misleading in its implication that learning is a single, essentially simple process and without such stages and phases as mentioned above. But it shows a basic phenomenon. At 16 twice as many lines of poetry were learned in 15 minutes as at 8 years. The leveling off in the late teens is also to be noted.

Increase in ability to learn through the growth years seems a basic fact. It does not seem true, for instance, that foreign languages are more readily learned in junior high school than in senior high. Experiments show that, hour for hour, the study of foreign languages is quite clearly more efficient in senior high school. Such findings do not mean that all education should be postponed until later adolescence. They do show a need for adjusting tasks to ability and planning school work with reference to the child's total development.

The writers venture the opinion that the slower memorizing at the younger ages and the less effective foreign-language study indicate less docility for doing a task considered of little value, quite as much as less "neural plasticity." And surely the competence of 12-year-old boys with such scientific hobbies as radio shows that children *can* master difficult material, if it appeals to their interests and is congruent with their abilities. In fact, the writers would say that the capacity for such learning was a great undeveloped natural resource. And instead of delaying educational programs until the pupil is older, the writers will shortly urge that education may well encroach less on the prime adult years and accomplish more in childhood and adolescence by instituting certain changes in educational programs and methods.

The digit-symbol (or simple rote learning) test of the Wechsler scale showed rapid rise to about 18 and a decline beginning shortly thereafter. A much greater variety of information about adult ability to learn is

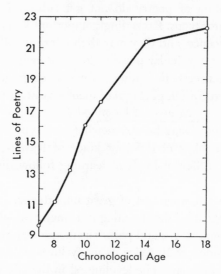

Figure 41.   Number of Lines of Poetry Learned in 15 Minutes by Children of Different Ages. (From J. B. Stroud and R. Maul, The influence of age on learning and retention of poetry and nonsense syllables, *Ped. Sem.* and *J. Genet. Psychol.*, 1933, 42:242–250.)

needed, however. Some learning tasks should be similar to those met in real life, since results will then have a more practical bearing, and the tasks will then seem to adults to be more worth while. And various types of individuals should be experimented upon, since these problems affect everyone. Table 7 summarizes certain research which attempted to meet these difficult requirements.

The study included learners of various sorts, from university students to Sing Sing prisoners. Some tasks were very simple. In one experiment the subjects drew lines of a prescribed length while blindfolded. First the average number correct was found in 600 trials without knowledge as to success; this average was used as a base from which to measure the

TABLE 7.   Age Differences in Ability to Learn: Percentages Which the Gains of Groups 35 Years or More in Age Were of the Gains of Groups Under 25 Years of Age in Various Types of Learning

Group	Material to Be Learned	Percent Which Gain of Oldest Group Was of Gain of Youngest	
University students	Drawing lines of prescribed length		64
	Hand-writing with wrong hand		72
	Substitution (transcribing words)		81
	Learning code		61
	Esperanto		79
	Digit-nonsense syllables association		64
	University studies	over	100
Prisoners in Sing	Substitution (1, 2, etc., for a, b, etc.)		104
Sing	Elementary school subjects		88
	Addition practice		96
Evening high students	Algebra, civics, English, etc.		87[a]
Secretarial students	Typewriting	about	95[a]
	Learning stenographic symbols	about	100[a]

[a] Age here was 30 and over for older group; elsewhere it was 35 and over.

SOURCE: Adapted from E. L. Thorndike, et al., Adult Learning, New York, Macmillan, 1928, p. 103.

effects of a seven-day training period. The training consisted of 600 trials per day in which the information "right" or "wrong" was given after each attempt. The end test, again of 600 trials with no knowledge of success, indicated that the older group had learned only about 64 percent as effectively as the younger group. In code learning, the learner simply transcribed words into a code, without mention being made of learning the code. On an end test, the amount of incidental code learning was found to be 10 elements for the younger group and 6 for the older. Table 7 shows in each instance what percentage the average gain of the older students was of the average for the younger.

In general, the older (really only middle-aged) group did not do as well as the younger. However, in some instances (as in learning typewriting and stenography or school subjects) the older did about as well or even better, possibly because of greater interest and motivation. A comparison of children and adults in learning Esperanto showed that the oldest group (average age 42) was about 20 percent less effective than the young group (average age 22), but the oldest still did almost twice as well as private school pupils aged 9 to 18 after over twice as much class study.

Another investigator (75) compared 40 youngsters aged 12 to 17 with 40 adults aged 34 to 59 and with another 40 adults aged 60 to 85. Table 8 shows that the youngest group did best on all the tasks. And as in the previous investigation, the oldest did poorest when changed methods (as mirror drawing) or nonsensical learning was asked. On straightforward learning of sensible and familiar material (as paired associates like man-boy, stem-bud) they were only 18 percent below the youngest group.

TABLE 8. Average Proficiency of Three Age Groups in Various Learning Tasks of More or Less Congruence with Established Habits. Results Expressed as Percentages of the Averages for the Youngest Group

Test	Young (12–17)	Middle Aged (34–59)	Old (60–85)
Motor learning			
Direct vision	100	98	84
Mirror vision	100	96	54
Verbal learning			
Paired associates (man-boy, etc.)	100	90	82
Nonsense equations ($E \times Z = G$)	100	80	48
False multiplications ($3 \times 5 = 25$)	100	72	47

SOURCE: Adapted from F. L. Ruch, The differentiative effects of age upon human learning, Ped. Sem. and J. Genet. Psychol., 1934, 11:261–286.

More recent findings have been largely to the same effect. An English investigator (97) found only slight decrease in competence from the twenties to the forties in learning to operate a relatively simple apparatus, but men in their sixties needed more than twice the number of trials and made over three times as many errors in about four times as much time, as compared to the youngest group.

Research regarding memory has yielded largely similar findings. A clever investigator compared 174 persons in their twenties with 174 paired with them on vocabulary test scores but in their sixties, the hypothesis being that since vocabulary seems to remain quite constant after 20, the older group would thus be made largely comparable in original ability and literacy to the younger. As shown in Table 9, the older group did poorer (21 percent loss) on reversed digits than on simple recall of an auditory series of numbers (12 percent loss), poorer on memory of a paragraph than of a sentence, and most poor on the strange Turkish vocabulary. Various other investigations have shown decline in recall of movies, especially after 40, and less forgetting of old than of recent matter (79).

TABLE 9.   Percentage Loss of 174 Persons Aged 60 to 69 on Various Memory Tests as Compared to Scores Made by 174 persons 20 to 29 and Paired with Them on the Basis of Vocabulary Test Scores.

Material to Be Remembered	Loss
Visual memory span for digits	8
Auditory memory span for digits	12
Reversed digit span	21
Sentence repetitions	21
Retention of paragraph	40
Memory for designs	46
Retention of paired associates	55
Retention of Turkish-English vocabulary	60

SOURCE: Adapted from J. G. Gilbert, Memory loss in senescence, *J. Abnorm. and Soc. Psychol.*, 1941, 36:73–86.

Perhaps some softening of these conclusions may be warranted, however. Suppose one is oldish and weary and rather disillusioned with life, and an impersonal young man asks one to learn that $E \times Z = G$ or that $3 \times 5 = 25$; does less application to this bizarre task than is given by a youth of 20 mean less capacity to learn, or is it more a different feeling as to what is really worth while trying hard to do? Are the tasks in these experiments on which the older people do best—as learning paired associate words—of a kind to elicit the best evidence as to the most effective learning these older people are capable of? Best learning presumably would be of matter that was of a familiar type for which the learner already had some perceptual background and method of attack in learning. The task should be congruent with the learner's status and role and should be undertaken comfortably, with confidence that accomplishments of significance to the learner and his fellows are possible. For these older sales people and mechanics and housewives, paired associates and even Esperanto hardly seem very indigenous to their lives.

In his *Theories of Learning*, Hilgard protests the narrow artificialities of matter and method in most research regarding learning of children and laboratory subjects. He urges that investigators "break through the rigidity which makes us think of nonsense syllable lists, mazes, conditioning experiments and target-practice as exhausting the phenomena of learning." Instead there should be an effort to "pick problems out of real life situations. . . . It would probably be desirable for someone to . . . take a notebook and follow a child around for hours at a time. What are the circumstances under which he learns? What performances provide for recall? for recognition? for problem-solving? What tasks are left half finished? What kinds of forgetting are there? What motives can be inferred? Such observations would be like a breath of fresh air in most learning laboratories" (45, pp. 351–352). But if such vigorous empiricism is needed in studies of children, it would seem even more called for, to assure close contact with the real facts, in work with older adults. Notebook jottings of the moment-by-moment doings of salesmen and mechanics and housewives might be expected to suggest tests and experiments very different from those now usual. Perhaps it may not be possible to determine whether adults really are less able than youngsters to assimilate something new that is appropriate to their particular worlds until new materials and methods are developed for use especially with adults.

Thus, ability to learn clearly appears to increase through the growth years and begin a slow decline rather soon thereafter. But most research regarding learning in the adult and older years has lacked congruence with the real tissue and color of adult experience and attitude. Research firmly rooted in empirical study of adult experience might well yield information of great practical significance regarding adult learning, and it might also distinctively contribute to a more adequate understanding of the learning process.

Factors Related to Ability

A comprehensive consideration of factors affecting abilities throughout the entire life span may be expected to emphasize both the variety of such factors and their cumulative effects. It is to be hoped that suggestions might be obtained for furthering desirable development and retarding unfortunate decline which could be of broad significance for education and for industry, as well as of some help in planning one's own career and in understanding one's associates.

PHYSIQUE AND ABILITY

The simplest question concerns the relationship of ability to height and weight. Careful studies have shown that, on the average, intellectually superior children are superior physically. Most substantial are the re- sults of Terman's continuing appraisals of his large group of gifted young- sters. They averaged 1 to 3 inches taller at all ages than the general run of children, with an average adult height that was 2 inches above the normal adult; the Terman group were also 5 to 12 pounds heavier, the young adult weight being 10 pounds more than average. The rather common assumption that intellectually superior children are physically small and inadequate is clearly not correct. The misconception may have arisen from comparisons of accelerated bright children with older classmates, from failure to differentiate unhappy average children who are trying to compensate for maladjustment by intensive school work from really bright youngsters, and perhaps from jealousy of the bright. Further, dull children have been found to average 2 or 3 inches shorter and 5 to 8 pounds lighter than the norm; but their physical inferiority may not be recognized because they have dropped back to classes with younger children. Feeble-minded individuals in institutions tend to be below normal in height and weight, and the more defective they are mentally, the more inferior they are likely to be physically.

Moreover, bright children tend to develop physically a bit more rapidly than average and reach puberty a little sooner (87), while the physical development of the mentally inferior is likely to lag. Nevertheless, all these correlations between physique and intellect are so low (usually around .10 to .20), and there are so many exceptions, that no inference is permissible regarding an individual's ability from his physical measurements.

Evidence regarding relations of physique and ability in the adult years leads to the same general conclusion. Years ago, Galton reported that notable men tended to be superior in physique and energy. An American questionnaire study compared executives with lesser men in the same field; it was found that 81 bishops averaged 2 inches taller and 17 pounds heavier than preachers in small towns, 58 university presidents averaged 1 inch taller and 17 pounds heavier than presidents of small colleges, 25 city school superintendents were 1 inch taller and 21 pounds heavier than 28 small-town school principals, and so on.[2] Even allowing that a bit of the extra weight might be due to greater age (or heartier dining), it seems that the more important man tends to be physically bigger. Greater size and physical impressiveness might, of course, help toward an executive position independent of ability. Terman's follow-ups of his gifted group into adult life show continuing physical superiority (87).

FAMILY, SEX, RACE, AND ABILITY

Table 10 summarizes a dozen different investigations having to do with familial resemblances in abilities and significantly relates them to anal-

[2] E. B. Gowin, *The Executive and His Control of Men*, New York, Macmillan, 1916.

ogous data bearing on physical resemblances. In gross physique, parents tended not to be very much alike, but correlations between physical measurements of parents and children were substantial, were of about the same amount for brothers and sisters (siblings), were slightly higher for nonidentical twins, and were very high indeed for same-egg twins.

TABLE 10.   Correlations Found Between Related Pairs of Persons, Northern European Stock, in Twelve Different Investigations

	Physical Measures	Mental Measures
Unrelated children		−.19 to .09
Cousins		.27
Parents	.00 to .15	.46 to .49
Parent-child	.42 to .53	.45 to .55
Siblings, same home[a]	.42 to .53	.45 to .55
Nonidentical twins	.58	.53 to .70
Identical twins	.91	.88 to .97

[a] A correlation of only .25 in intelligence has been reported for siblings who had spent at least four years in different homes, with the similarity dropping to .19 when the homes were of different socioeconomic level. And the longer the siblings had been apart, the greater the differences tended to be (36). For identical twins in the same home, Binet mental ages correlated .92 but for identicals reared apart, .64; for the Stanford achievement test battery the correlations were .96 and .51. For weight they were .97 and .89 and for height, .98 and .97.

SOURCE: Adapted from E. B. Green, *Measurements of Human Behavior,* New York, Odyssey Press, 1941, p. 716.

Correlations of abilities of parents are higher than correlations of physical measures, as might be expected on the assumption that people who tended to marry had somewhat similar interests and activities and often became acquainted in situations (as at school or work) where people of similar abilities were likely to be together. Parent-child and sibling correlations in abilities are about the same as the correlation between the parents, with closer similarities for nonidentical twins and very high correlations for identical twins.

Slightly higher correlations for mental traits than physical traits might be presumed to be due to similarities of home environment; similarities would usually be great for nonidentical twins, since they are the same age and usually are in school and play together, and especially great for identical twins, since they are necessarily of the same sex and often so similar in appearance as to be confused with each other. But how similar will identical twins be if they are reared apart? Naturally, such cases are rare. But persistent investigators have managed, by extensive publicity and prizes awarded twins willing to be investigated, to obtain evidence in this matter. Even when twins have been reared apart under very different circumstances, startling resemblances often remain, even into old age (51). But differences may appear. Differences in schooling and social experience may bring differences in manner and readiness in social contacts and sometimes substantial differences in scores on mental tests. In short, even for identical twins, a favorable or handicapping environment can make an appreciable difference. And if this is true for twins, it could obviously be more true for siblings reared apart who are not twins, as indicated by the footnote to Table 10. It should also be remembered that the same home may nevertheless be a very different place for different children in it. Thus, the oldest and youngest child may have very different relationships to parents and to other children in the family and have differences in opportunity and responsibility.

It is also important to remember that correlations between siblings and between parent and child are not so high that marked differences cannot ofter appear. Serious problems may then arise. A dull child of bright parents may be under great pressure to do better in school or career than he can, especially if there is a bright sibling. A bright child in a family of mediocre abilities may be neither appreciated nor given desirable opportunities.

A hundred years ago—and during almost all previous history—it was generally assumed that women were less able than men. Certainly women's record of achievement suggested that conclusion; almost all the great doers and thinkers in history had been men. Thirty years ago psychological opinion tended to the conclusion that the male showed more "variability": males were more common not only in lists of notables but also in institutions for the feeble-minded! However, in the last century women began to make their way in the world of affairs, where their previous failure in notable accomplishments came to be seen as possibly a result of the burden of childbearing and the organization of society rather than any inherent mental inferiority. Then intelligence tests showed girls usually averaging a bit higher than boys (as might be expected in view of girls' more rapid physical development), and having the same variability; tests given to adults, though unsatisfactory for such comparisons, have yielded no evidence of sex differences in general ability. However, there appear to be some sex differences in special abilities. The average girl begins to talk earlier and from then on to maintain a verbal superiority— in oral and written expression and in reading—over the average male. Girls and women appear to have more manual dexterity, but males have more speed and coördination of gross movements, and perhaps more mechanical aptitude.

Are there racial differences in ability? Eight studies of Negro children indicated an average IQ about 10 points below whites. But other comparisons must be included before any conclusions are drawn. American-born children whose foreign-born parents were Polish Jews or Swedes have been reported to average about 103 in IQ, whereas children of French-Canadian and Italian parentage averaged 87 (2). In Hawaii, children of Japanese and Chinese parents tested up near white norms, but Portuguese, Filipino, and Hawaiian children tested lower. Racial groups compare somewhat differently according to the type of test used. Various investigations have agreed in finding Japanese, Chinese, Indian, Mexican, and Italian children doing better on performance than on verbal tests. Even though they are born and raised in this country, children of immigrants apparently have some language handicap.

Selective migration may be a factor in certain of the above differences. On a nonverbal test battery planned especially for international and interracial use, Danish-Americans scored substantially above Italian-Americans. But on these same tests, Italian children in Rome tested slightly above Danish children in Copenhagen (2). Intelligence tests in the Army during the First World War, and numerous studies since, have shown Negroes in the North averaging above those in the South. This fact might be due to selective migration north of the more capable Negroes. However, a study of the IQ's of Harlem Negro children showed that those who had lived in New York for one or two years averaged 72, while those who had been in the metropolis nine years or more averaged 94; moreover, the school records of all those children in the South before migration averaged about the same (55). Better schooling and other advantages in the North appeared to be the important factors.

Subtle cultural differences may influence test results. Thus, on every one of certain form-board puzzles a group of Indian children took more time but made fewer errors than a group of white children. To the Indians, time meant little, but a mistake was considered very distressing and to be avoided. Another Indian group considered it improper to try to score high. In short, attempts to compare nationalities and races by means of tests have emphasized issues already met in comparisons of older and younger adults. Pervasive differences in fund of information and mental organization, in methods of attacking problems, in feelings of confidence or timidity, and in standards of work and goals may subtly affect test results. Hilgard's remark has been quoted that field studies need to be made of (American) children's learning. To appraise the abilities of Navaho or Hindustani or Chinese children, field studies of their lives would seem called for, and it would be necessary to construct appraising devices as indigenous to their environments and cultures as American tests are to ours. If that is ever done, it will indeed be interesting to see how Iowa or Brooklyn youngsters score on Navaho or Hindustani tests! If broadened approaches are needed for comparisons of the abilities of children of different nationalities or races, obviously there is much greater need for a broader approach in making comparisons of the adults in these groups. It is conceivable that there may be some differences in average ability between certain racial groups. However, the dominant feature of every study is of individual differences and overlappings between race groups. There are able and stupid individuals in all groups, and discriminations against individuals on the basis of race are clearly without scientific justification.

SOCIOECONOMIC STATUS AND ABILITIES

Tests of general ability given to men in the armed forces in both world wars have shown marked differences in average scores made by men in different types of occupations; professional men averaged highest and unskilled workers lowest. This finding would be expected; requirements as to training and abilities would select the more able for the professions,

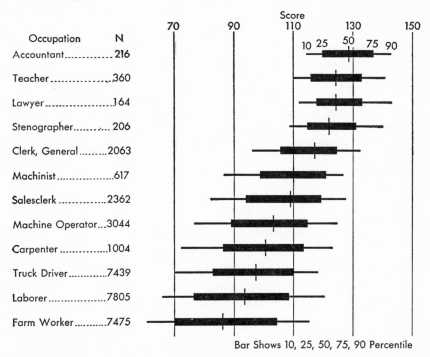

Figure 42. "General Ability" in Relation to Civilian Occupation—World War II. (Data from N. Stewart, A.G.C.T. scores of Army personnel grouped by occupation, Occupations, 1947, 26:5–41.)

and both his own ambition and selective personnel practices in industry would tend to move the able laborer up the occupational ladder a bit. But the difficulties in testing adults mentioned earlier in this chapter must be kept in mind in interpreting these results. Men of substantial education and in professional or clerical work might be considered to have unfair advantage on tests calling largely for clerical skills and verbal information over a manual worker who left school early. One must not promptly conclude that most people in this country rise to the occupational level of which they are capable. Thus, Figure 42 shows the upper 10 percent of the machine operators above the median for the lawyers.

Comparisons of the test scores of children classified according to the occupations of their fathers might be expected to help elucidate the situation. The children might be thought of as having had largely similar experiences and education. And since it has been shown that the intelligence of children is substantially correlated with that of their parents, clearer indication of the comparative general abilities of different groups might thus be obtained. Table 11 shows the mean IQ's on the revised

TABLE 11.   Relations of Scores on Tests of General Ability as Shown by (1) Stanford-Binet IQ's of Very Young and Older Children and (2) Scores on a Group Test of Kansas College Undergraduates

| Father's Occupation | Mean IQ | | Mean Percentile |
Age in Years	2–5½	15–18	College Students
Professional	116	116	59
Clerical, skilled worker	108	110	54
Farmers	99	94	47
Unskilled	94	98	37

SOURCE: Adapted from L. M. Terman and M. H. Merrill, *Measuring Intelligence: A Guide to the Administration of the New Revised Stanford-Binet Tests of Intelligence*, Boston, Houghton Mifflin, 1937, p. 48, and M. Smith, University student intelligence and occupation of fathers, *Amer. Soc. Rev.*, December, 1942, pp. 764–771.

Stanford-Binet scale of the youngest and oldest age groups of almost two thousand children who were classified according to their father's occupation. Children in all age groups covered whose fathers were professional men averaged from 115 to 118 IQ, while children of day laborers averaged 94 to 98. The differences are about as great for the younger children as the older; if favorable home environment rather than constitutional mental capacity were a major factor, greater differences might be expected in the older years. The last column shows analogous differences in a college population (*86, 81*).

Though the occupation of the father may usually be the most important single indication of the socioeconomic status of a family, more adequate appraisals are desirable. In a research (26) involving detailed analyses, in a midwestern city, the families of over two thousand 9- and 10-year-old children and about the same number of 13- and 14-year-olds were rated as to social class on four "status characteristics." The first was occupation: if the head of the family was in a profession or had a managerial position in a large business, a rating of "1" was assigned; semiprofessional or high-status white collar workers were given a rating of "2"; and other types of work were ranked down to "7" for unskilled workers. The education of the parents, the house in which

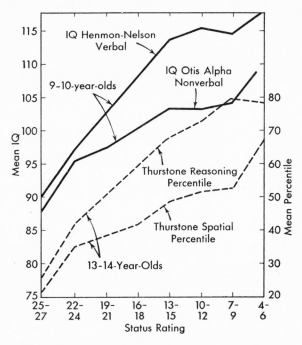

Figure 43. Status Rating. (Adapted from K. W. Eells, *Intelligence and Cultural Differences,* Chicago, University of Chicago Press, 1951, pp. 146, 148.)

the family lived, and the neighborhood were similarly rated from "1" for excellent to "7" for very poor. For each family, the sum of the four figures gave its total status rating. Figure 43 shows certain relationships between these ratings and scores on certain tests of general ability which were given to the four thousand children.

On the Henmon-Nelson verbal-type test, the 9- and 10-year-olds with low-status ratings of 25 to 27 averaged 90 IQ, but those of high-status ratings of 4 to 6 averaged 118. The same low-status cases scored about the same (88 IQ) on the Otis nonverbal test, but results with this test showed less rise with socioeconomic status. Quite similar trends were shown by the two thousand

13- and 14-year-olds on the two somewhat similarly contrasting tests, as also shown in Figure 43. It should be added that there were four times as many children in the two lower- as in the two upper-status groups, and so there were a greater number of children in the lower two groups with IQ's on the Henmon-Nelson scale above 115.

For further analysis, records of children either of whose parents was foreign born were eliminated, leaving only those knowing English as their native tongue. Of these, about 12 percent were considered of high status and 18 percent of low status. Detailed comparisons were made of the responses of these two groups on each question of the verbal tests given them. Many of these questions showed clearly significant differences in favor of the high-status group. There might be vocabulary or literary expressions more commonly found in upper-class magazines or in college preparatory courses or information more likely to be gained by youngsters who went to summer camps or were taken to concerts. To a substantial extent, the higher scores of the upper-class youngsters appeared due to an unconscious loading of the tests with middle- and upper-class material by the middle- and upper-class test builders!

Very broad and diverse factors indeed may play a part in socioeconomic differences on tests. A fascinating study (60) made a broad comparison of southern mountain with New York City children as to the total nature of their lives. The enormous differences between the Tennessee village and Manhattan in variety of experience, challenge, and tempo need hardly be mentioned. But the handicaps of the mountain children were pervasive. Their diet was inadequate. They did not get enough restful sleep because families were large and houses were small. In summer the weather was hot, and in winter the houses were cold and the clothing inadequate so that the family kept around the stoves. In both seasons, the mountain children romped and engaged in diverse outside activities less than did the New York boys and girls. As they got older, the mountain youth felt so much a part of the big family group and the little community that they were shy about going to other places for work or visits or pleasure trips. There was inbreeding culturally as well as biologically. Presumably as a cumulating result of all their multiple limitations of experience and physical vigor, and their chronic lassitude and easy complacency, the IQ's of mountain children have been found to fall lower with increasing age. In average communities, children in "lower-class" families may be somewhat analogously isolated from many experiences and ideas, at odds with the schools, rejected socially—a people largely apart, even in democratic America (46). Figure 44 summarizes evidence that children from such homes may show some progressive loss in IQ with increasing age—and isolated mountain children show more of a loss—and also that lessened isolation and improved conditions may reduce the drop with age, as indicated by the 1940 curve.

Numerous investigations have shown that the average scores of rural children are somewhat below city children, and the difference in scores increases with age. So the 1937 Stanford-Binet standardization sample showed median IQ's of 106 for urban and 101 for rural children 2 to 5½ years old but 108 and 96, respectively, for cases 15 to 18. Analyses have shown that rural children do especially poorly on certain items more

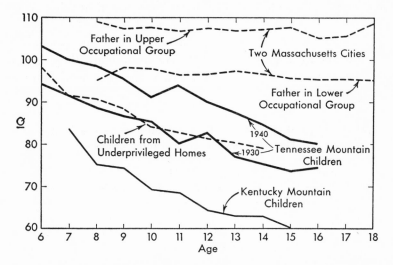

Figure 44. Effects of Relatively Slight Differences in Socioeconomic Conditions (Top Two Curves), Very Meager Rural Environment and the Same After 10 Years of Improvement (Heavy Lines), Yet More Limited Mountain Condition (Bottom Curve), and City Slum Area of Underprivileged Homes. (Adapted from E. J. Asher, The inadequacy of current intelligence tests for testing Kentucky mountain children, J. Genet. Psychol., 1935, 46:480–486; H. M. Skeels and E. A. Fillmore, The mental development of children from underprivileged homes, Ped. Sem. and J. Genet. Psychol., 1937, 50:427–439; and L. R. Wheeler, A comparative study of the intelligence of East Tennessee mountain children, J. Educ. Psychol., 1942, 33:321–334.)

common in towns or requiring speed but excel on other items. And on a special scale made up of these last types of materials, country children scored higher than urban (2, p. 827).

If a very poor environment may retard the growth of ability as measured, may an improved environment bring gain? The balance of the evidence seems to be that at least a little improvement may be hoped for. Table 12 summarizes certain findings of an early but excellent study of this problem. A group of 74 children from underprivileged homes were tested shortly before being placed in foster homes and again after an average of about four years in the new home. Average age at first testing was eight years. The first part of the table shows that children placed in good foster homes improved somewhat (5.3 IQ points) in the four years, but those placed in poor homes did not. These last were, it may be noted, the duller children to begin with—apparently the better foster homes tended to get the brighter youngsters. The lower part of Table 12 indicates that the younger children benefited more from foster home placement than the older. All may have improved in health or conduct or other respects not appraised here. Other evidence indicates that even earlier adoption would probably have brought greater gain. Though foster homes are usually considered better than institutions, there is similar evidence that good orphanages may bring similar gain, if entrance is relatively early.

TABLE 12.   Effect of (1) Good and Poor Foster Homes and (2) Age of Placement on Gains in IQ of Foster Children

Foster Home Rating	Number of Cases	IQ Before Placement	IQ After 4 Years	Gain
Good	33	95.2	100.5	5.3
Poor	41	88.0	88.1	.1
Age on 2nd Test				
Over 12 years, 4 months	37	89.7	89.3	−.4
Under 12 years, 4 months	37	92.8	98.0	5.2

SOURCE: Adapted from F. N. Freeman, K. U. Holzinger, and B. C. Mitchell, The influence of environment on the intelligence, school achievement and conduct of foster children, National Society for Study of Education, 27th Yearbook, 1928, Pt. I, pp. 103–217.

Various investigators of effects on measured ability of foster-home and institutional care of children have been assiduous in considering factors of selection and experimental design but have given comparatively much less attention to influences making for gain. Available evidence emphasizes the importance of friendly contacts. The adequacy of the methods of inquiry has, however, been questioned. In an institution for feeble-minded women, dull babies placed there as "guests" were made much of and gained in IQ, while a control group, also of orphanage children, lost (80). It might be hoped that extensive studies of such influences might yield constructive suggestions of great value for child-rearing and institutional management.

A clever investigation yielded evidence that early childhood stimuli, apparently not noticed and certainly not understood, might have long-continuing effects. A father repeatedly read certain passages in Greek to a 15-month-old baby. And when the boy was 8½ years old he learned the passages heard in infancy with fewer repetitions than other passages not heard before. Even when he was 14, some effects remained. (17). Presumably more relevant matter, heard early and continuing over a period of time, could be even more influential. A cultured home would thus have, beginning at an early age, cumulative effects on ability.

For various reasons, relationships of socioeconomic status to ability in adult life would surely be expected. Childhood status often would continue, and effects would be cumulative. Adults would be directly subject to continuing occupational and other socioeconomic appraisals and selection. They would cumulatively be subject to any stimulating or limiting effects their socioeconomic environment might have and would also get into more specialized environments. Adults' abilities might therefore tend increasingly to be more closely related to socioeconomic status the longer they lived with that status. Very limiting rural or poverty-striken environments might be expected to continue the curves in Figure 44 showing cumulative effects of such conditions in children. If most tests of general ability are class weighted, then they become increasingly less satisfactory for those not in the middle and upper classes. The data mentioned earlier, showing superiority of adults in professional and managerial work over unskilled labor on current tests of so-called general ability, clearly exaggerate differences between occupational and socioeconomic classes in basic intellectual capacity, therefore. It seems particularly desirable to develop tests which will locate superior minds in less privileged social groups.[3]

EDUCATION AND ABILITY

The preceding section reported evidence that marked improvement in the total environment of young children (transfer from a poor home to a good foster home or institution) tended to be followed by increases in measured general ability. May increases be brought about by educational programs when children remain in the same family and neighbor-

[3] Since (as mentioned earlier) more children are in lower middle and lower social classes, the total number of mentally superior children may be greater there, even though the percentage is smaller. For example, the Elmtown study (46, p. 175) reported 8 children with IQ's of 120 and up in social classes I and II (of a total of 35) as compared with 11 in class IV (of a total of 229) and 19 in class III (out of 152 youngsters there).

hood environment? Table 13 summarizes two of the considerable number of investigations which have been made of the effects of nursery school programs. The first set of figures indicates that such a program did somewhat increase the IQ's of a group of underprivileged orphanage children who were initially somewhat below average in ability. Seventeen orphans just entering nursery school were paired with 17 other orphanage children as to sex, chronological age, standing in the Merrill-Palmer scale of mental tests, and institutional experience. After the first group had been in the school about eight months, all the children were tested again. The control group showed a little gain, perhaps as a result of experience with the tests. But the nursery school group gained substantially more.

TABLE 13.   Effects of Nursery School upon the General Ability of (1) Below-Average Children from a Poor Environment and (2) Above-Average Children from a Superior Environment

	Orphanage IQ			University Area IQ		
	Number of Cases	Begin-ning	End	Number of Cases	Begin-ning	End	3½ Years Later
Nursery school	19	92	113	29	112	126	129
Control	17	93	98	52	112	123	125
Difference		−1	15		0	3	4

SOURCE: Adapted from F. N. Freeman, K. U. Holzinger, and B. C. Mitchell, the influence of environment on the intelligence, school achievement and conduct of foster children, National Society for Study of Education, *27th Yearbook*, 1928, Pt. I, pp. 103–217.

Why did the nursery school benefit these orphanage children? It may have had more toys and other facilities and more freedom to do many things which were hardly feasible in the disciplined orphanage. Particularly the friendly teacher and the encouragement to do and talk and express oneself could be important. There is evidence that orphanage children are decidedly hampered as to speech by lack of the opportunity to talk and to be talked to which is usual in a home (15).

The right-hand side of Table 13 summarizes another investigation which was similar in method but was of bright children from good homes. The 29 who went to nursery school entered at about 30 months of age and were tested when they began school. They attended an average of about five semesters and were thereafter tested at various intervals up to about

8 years of age. With them were paired two control groups, totaling 52 cases, on the basis of IQ at the beginning and of parents' education. The control group showed a gain of 11 points, but the nursery school pupils gained only 3 more at the end of the nursery school attendance and 1 more additional point 3½ months later. Both groups thus gained substantially, presumably because of "increasing assimilation of the relatively high cultural levels" of their superior homes and the "intrinsic growth characteristic of an innately superior group" as well as experience with the tests. The nursery school program added only negligibly to these gains. The inference is that a good nursery school program may compensate somewhat for a lack of a good home environment (and may be needed more by duller children), but it adds little to the intellectual stimulations which bright children from good homes obtain anyway. These last children may be benefited in many other ways by attending nursery school, as by better adjustment to other children, but their favorable home and neighborhood environment appears to develop their abilities about as fast as their rate of biological maturation will permit.

Analogous investigations to determine whether elementary, secondary, or collegiate education might affect measured ability have been largely lacking. Through the ages of required school attendance, a control group making possible the comparison of no schooling with some could obviously hardly be found. Comparisons of school programs that are superior or distinctive in some way (as of a progressive type) with average or conventional programs have failed to demonstrate that the special programs brought any increase in general ability; however, gains may have occurred in effectiveness or range of learning, in broadened attitudes, in social adjustment, or in enjoyment of school (68, pp. 351–361). Further, the schools with these special programs served bright youngsters from good homes. Conceivably, underprivileged children of less ability might have shown some gain, as appeared to be true for such children in nursery schools.

There is abundant evidence that increases in the length of schooling tend to be associated with higher scores on tests of general ability, but it is uncertain as to how this association is to be interpreted. In 1917–1918, a correlation of .74 was found between scores on the Army Alpha test of general ability and the extent of schooling of recruits. And analyses of test data showed a correlation of .72 between the average Alpha test score of the white draftee in each state and an index of the adequacy of the educational program of that state (based on average length of school year, school expenditure per pupil, etc.) (4). Soldiers of World War II averaged decidedly higher on tests of general ability than did those of World War I; a sample comparison showed 768 enlisted men of the last war making a median score of 104 on the Army Alpha examination for which the median in the first war had been 62. Eighty-five percent of the scores of the recent group were above the median of the first group (93). And over the 25-year period there had been an increase of about three years in average length of schooling. This gain over a quarter of a century probably is the result of other factors also, however. In the nine-teen forties, young men were much more used to tests. More reading matter, the multiple stimuli of movies and radio, and more travel made possible especially by automobile and plane all might make people more widely informed. Though a much larger proportion of all youngsters are now going to high school, tests given recently show no significant dif-ferences from 15 and more years ago in averages or variabilities. Much the same finding holds for college students (99, p. 173).[4]

A retesting in 1941 of 131 young men with an average age at that time of 34, who had taken other tests indicative of general ability in 1921–1922 when boys of 14, showed on the second test increases proportional to the amount of schooling they had had since the first date. Thus, in 1921, 45 boys scored within 10 points of each other; 5 of these later completed the eighth grade, and they averaged 26 on the 1941 test; another 5 had a total of 17 or more years of schooling (one or more years after college graduation or the equivalent), and they averaged 46 on the 1941 test. Roughly, it ap-peared that 7 or 8 years of schooling had added about 2 years of mental age (62). It is hardly surprising that so much schooling beyond a minimum, plus continuing experience in work of a professional or clerical type such as 17 years of education would usually lead to, would bring higher scores in 1941 on group tests requiring reading and somewhat academic types of vo-cabulary and information and arithmetic problem-solving. However, better tests might have more clearly shown gains of a more basic nature, such as knowledge and understanding of things that have proven to be of importance in the adult world, skill in differentiating adequate evidence from hearsay or propaganda, and habituation in systematic methods of attack upon a problem. Just as good diet, health care, living conditions, and emotional adjustment may bring superior physical development, surpassing previous less favored generations, so superior educational programs might bring realization of con-stitutional intellectual potentials beyond what has yet been proven possible.

Whether interpreted more or less broadly, the preceding materials

[4] Bayley has reported high correlations between mid-parent education and child in-telligence as tested—a finding interpretable in various ways, but indicative of test-schooling relationships.

indicating higher scores following more schooling again raise questions as to the adult level of ability and the age when this is reached. In the early days of Binet testing, 14 was commonly considered the adult mental age. Later, the adult level was raised to 16, on the basis of more recent findings that the tested ability of the average individual did increase up to that age. Was this later finding a product simply of the increase of about two years in the schooling which the average person of the more recent norms has had? Other investigators have found increases in scores on tests of general ability up to 18. Data from college students suggested an adult level for them somewhere between 21 and 25 years (90). But these apparent interrelationships between schooling and adult level emphasize even more the need for tests and methods of research which would explicate the situation. More recently the picture has been further confused by the results of Wechsler's revised test which indicate increases in score until around 30, by Bayley's longitudinal data which show rises still continuing at 25, and the increases in middle life of Terman's gifted cases.

Might programs of adult education favorably affect ability? There is a little evidence to that effect. In one university, a vocabulary and a paragraph-reading test were given to 641 part-time students ranging in age from 16 to 70. Vocabulary was found to increase with age, and reading ability showed no decrease in this group who were thus trying to "keep up" mentally. And elementary school teachers who had come back to the university for additional professional training after long absence from such training were compared by similar tests with other teachers who had more frequently attended summer sessions. The first group showed some decline, but the second showed none, at least up to 50 years. But the less able may have tended less to continue schooling (82).

Such findings seem too perfect a vindication of the work of university teachers, of whom the investigator was one! But at least for teachers, vocabulary and other paper and pencil tests cannot be considered too academic or vocationally irrelevant—teachers might thus be called the ideal group to whom such tests should be given to investigate shifts in ability through the adult years. And perhaps it may be true that going to school occasionally *is* good for an adult. Settling back into the routine of the job, with leisure spent on the sports page and television, is easy and may lead to mental stagnation. But to keep on learning may keep ability limber and maintain "habits of wide application, the tools which can serve in an enormous number of situations, and those subtle habits which we usually call ideals, attitudes, methods of procedure and the like" (*89*).

The preceding pages have attempted to differentiate the relationships of some one factor—as family or education—to the development of abilities. Intensive longitudinal studies are beginning to show how the inter-

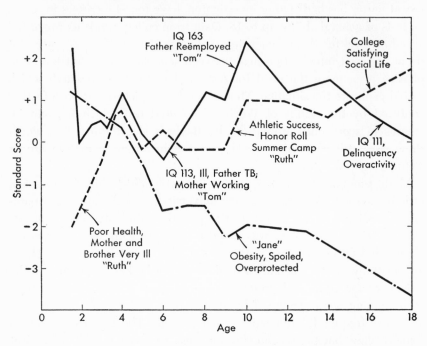

Figure 45. Three Cases Showing Changes in General Ability from 2–18 Years. (Adapted from M. P. Honizik, J. W. MacFarlane, and L. Allen, The stability of mental test performance between 2 and 18 years, *J. Exp. Educ.*, 1948, *17*:319–320.)

play of all these influences affects the abilities of each individual. As indicated in Figure 35 successive measurements of a youngster's general ability usually show rather consistent test ratings after the first five or six years. But there may be downward or upward trends or marked variations, and often the case history gives some hints as to possible factors. In Figure 45 the girl showing a steady fall in ability from an IQ of 133 to 77 was an only child born when the mother was 40 and the father 37, the mother having an estimated IQ of 64 to 70 and the parents having gone to school only until the age of 14. The child began in late preschool years to show marked obesity which increased until medical advice was finally obtained at 14; weight was finally got back to normal by 17. However, these last changes were not reflected in variations in ability as measured. The girl was always overindulged by the mother, who was always complaining that the daughter did not appreciate her. Mediocre constitutional capacity, possible glandular or nutritional disturbance, maternal indulgence, and an unstimulating home might all be considered factors in this case.

In contrast, the girl with an IQ at 18 of 139 may well have been affected in her early preschool years by the critical illnesses of her mother and brother and the resulting emotional and financial strain. As a small child she showed poor muscle tonus, had pneumonia at 6, and was shy and reserved. But from 10 on "she had many supports in her life—music, athletic success, summer camps, the honor roll at school." At 18 she went away from home to college where she found "her first completely satisfying social life, which resulted in great expansiveness." The figure shows rises in test ratings coincident with these favoring conditions. Both parents were college graduates.

The boy with marked shifts showed his lowest Binet rating at 6 when he had chronic sinus trouble and asthma and was in bed for 12 weeks and the father's tuberculosis made it necessary for the mother to work. The school at this time reported him to be restless, sensitive, and shy. The highest rating at 10 was when the father was reëmployed; the school then reported the boy to be showing "marvelous concentration." The drop to an IQ of 111 at 18 was at a time when the boy showed compulsive delinquency, overactivity, preoccupation, and poor coöperation.

Sometimes development seems to be independent of or even to go contrary to the influence of known factors. But usually, if the case history is adequate, a concomitance of reported influences explains something as to the trends in abilities. Thus, a boy who was frequently ill and came from a very poor home with little reading matter and a quarrelsome family life showed some decline in ability. In contrast, an initially sickly daughter of well-educated and prosperous parents, in a comfortable and culturally well-supplied home, gained in mental rating. She read much while home ill and had a strong desire to excel, resulting partly from jealousy of an older brother and perhaps from feelings of insecurity with other children because of her restricted contacts with them as a result of her illnesses. Another child of able parents and a stimulating home presumably had excellent constitutional capacity, but after a superior beginning, his ability appeared somewhat to decline. The family was very artistic and musical; the boy showed an early interest in music, lying awake to hear his father play the violin. At an early age he also became adept in making costumes for plays, in improvising dances, and in painting. He enjoyed performance tests but had little enthusiasm for predominantly verbal tests like the Binet and also seemed little interested in getting adult approval; hence, he would not put forth much effort unless the task appealed to him.

Analogous follow-up data past the age of 18 are largely lacking. Terman's continuing study of his gifted group may increasingly be expected to yield such information. Biographical accounts of famous people give hints as to ways in which abilities may be stimulated or hampered in the adult years, and data on the senium show something of the course and factors in later mental failing. But these last topics can be better discussed in later chapters that touch upon problems of mental health and of the work life.

Major Trends, Problems, and Applications

This chapter has attempted to sketch in broad perspective the development of abilities throughout the life span as indicated by tests and in relation to major factors influencing that development. It seems clear that through the growth years there is an upsurging growth of abilities, at maturity there is a certain cessation of the growth as there is of physical growth at about the same time, and in old age there is lessening of intellectual energies if not of abilities. It seems reasonably well evidenced also that mental as physical growth may be stimulated and perhaps even increased, or retarded and perhaps stunted, by certain favorable or unfavorable influences. At least in the adult and older years, there appear to be progressive changes with age in the composition or nature of abilities. At all ages, there are great individual differences. These findings are substantial and important. However, the writers venture the judgment that, to an extent not commonly appreciated, present evidence about the growth and change of abilities throughout the life span fails to give any real picture of the richness and variety of the phenomena of intellectual growth and change through the years.

Especially do the more recent test findings reported in this chapter raise questions and widen the scope of desirable inquiry. Do the continuing increases even up to old age, in the scores on the "concept-mastery" test made by Terman's gifted group, indicate possibilities of adult mental growth heretofore almost inconceivable? Or are these really only narrow gains in verbal skills of an intellectual élite? Yet even if this last interpretation be considered the more probable, do not able people in other segments of the population make analogous gains in their special abilities? Should not these also be measured? Anyhow, it seems quite obvious that the average person at the age of 40 is both better informed and more sagacious than at 20. Should there not be tests measuring such important trends? Recent investigators (for the most part themselves relatively young) have piled up evidence of slowing, rigidity, and circumstantiality rather than logic in the older years. But surely at least the abler mature minds may have some merits! Sundry evidence shows increases in abilities as tested, with increased education. But nature-nurture experiments regarding effects of various types of educational programs are largely negative. May programs or tests be inadequate? And how are the longitudinal findings of occasional substantial change in general ability concomitant with strong favorable or unfavorable circumstances to be interpreted? Three issues seem here of major importance.

THE INADEQUACY OF CONVENTIONAL TESTS

Sundry studies have shown the inadequacy of conventional tests for measurement of the abilities of persons in a different culture and also the substantial weighting of most tests in favor of the middle and upper socioeconomic classes. Analogous inquiries presumably would emphasize the recognized fact that current tests are practically all clerical, more or less schoolish in content or at least largely involving verbal facility and information, and otherwise weighted against adults with below-average education or in other than clerical or professional occupations. But if it were possible to devise tests without such weightings, they would not, the writers believe, be sufficient to meet the needs of fair appraisal of such persons. Tests are needed which bring out the distinctive valuable abilities of mechanics, farmers, and salesmen. Their abilities are of major importance in our culture and need more adequate measurement based on analyses not only of the skills but also of the attitudes and way of life of these groups. Unskilled workers usually have some know-how, the nature of which should be investigated. Even a miserable slum may develop social skills in survival about which more knowledge is needed. The activities of these various groups should be so empirically and understandingly investigated that the involved abilities can be appraised with materials indigenous to them and with due account of the life pattern in which they operate. Such an approach seems clearly necessary for any adequate inventory or fair measurement of the abilities of other peoples in other cultures. It seems needed also for adequate and fair appraisal of the abilities of various socioeconomic subcultures in the total American community.

A similar sympathetic empirical approach seems called for if there is to be adequate comparative appraisal of the abilities of various age groups. The tests for very young children seem reasonably well suited to take account of the experiences and life tasks of that period and to measure the simple skills and everyday knowledge involved. But by middle and later adolescence, tests seem appreciably to have lost touch with major segments of the total life experience of these young people. Certain types of vocational aptitude (mechanical aptitude as in factory or shop work or social aptitude as in service or sales work) have little opportunity to show themselves in the usual test batteries used in secondary school. And the broader social abilities, including the ability to get along with the other sex, which is very important to the typical adolescent, are simply not recognized in such measuring instruments. Also left out, even from tests designed for use with adults, are the most important and especially the most distinctive abilities of middle life and the older ages. Not only are major vocational abilities given little or no chance to show themselves, but broader abilities involving total capacity for effective living in the adult and older years may be neglected. May it not well be that each major age group has, so to speak, its own subculture with its own set of values, its own weaknesses, and its own strengths? Studies like *One Boy's Day* (6) may be needed to show adequately what life is like at 70, or 40, or 20 as compared with 7, what abilities are brought out by the total circumstances of life at each age, and what might be done so that the potentialities of each age might be yet more developed.

A simple exploratory study (25) directed by one of the writers may make clearer the above concepts, possible types of tests, and possible outcomes. Everyday adult activities were first informally surveyed, as shown by the doings of several families, news items and advertisements in a local paper, and other means. Certain colloquially simple tests were then made, covering some of these activities. For example, one test concerned use of the yellow pages of the telephone directory—as whom to call to order some DDT. Another dealt with community resources for common needs—as the person to seek to get a key made. A third involved everyday problems of tact—as appropriate conversational topics when visiting a sick friend. On such tests, indigenous to adult life, the middle-aged and older did substantially better than young adults.

Would tests for the older years be so incommensurate with tests for the younger that comparisons could not be made? Or, rather, might tests of the carefulness, broad understanding, and social perception of the older adults be especially useful in measuring the "maturity" of the younger years and be thus far more significant than tests for the younger have been in their use with older people?

NEED FOR STUDY OF INTENSIVE AND LONG-TIME INFLUENCES UPON ABILITIES

The first need is thus felt to be for empirical studies of abilities that are sufficiently broad that they might reveal differences in abilities from one culture or socioeconomic group to another, and from one period of life as compared with another, and sufficiently free from conventional concepts that distinctive features of the abilities found in different cultures, socioeconomic classes, or age groups would be found. A second need, for longitudinal studies, is generally recognized. Combined with the wide range of inquiry urged above, longitudinal studies may well substantially enlarge present concepts regarding the modifiability of abilities. What are the cumulative effects through life of the essentially very different influences affecting the two sexes to develop their mechanical or verbal or social abilities? What does retirement do to abilities? May long-continued inquiries regarding persons of more and of less (and of good or indequate) education show instances of substantial influence on abilities, and identify methods and materials of especial educational potency?

What may very favorable and challenging influences do, and not only in childhood but also in adult life? A statement by Francis Perkins regarding Franklin Roosevelt in the early years of his administration is apropos here: "I saw his mind continuing its growth in this period, as I had seen it develop in previous years and as I was to see it take on further depth and stature in the years ahead. Roosevelt's mentality was not intellectual in the sense in which that word is ordinarily used. He was a man of high intelligence, but he used *all* his faculties when he was thinking about a subject. . . . He had to have feeling as well as thought. His emotions, his intuitive understanding, his imagination, his moral and traditional bias, his sense of right and wrong—all entered into his thinking, and unless these flowed freely through his mind as he considered a subject, he was unlikely to come to any clear conclusion or even to a clear understanding."[5] Here is mental "growth" in the mature years but

[5] Francis Perkins, *The Roosevelt I Knew*, New York, Viking Press, 1946, p. 153.

as a phenomenon of the total personality, and in reaction to world events. Terman reports (87) that those most successful in career of his gifted cases were especially well-integrated in personality and abilities. May they have developed in analogous fashion, and may their increasing scores on the "concept-mastery" test be an evidence of that growth?

THE NEED FOR A BROADENED CONCEPT OF ABILITIES

The very broad concept of abilities implicit in this last quotation makes insistent a problem of definition which may well have troubled the reader throughout this chapter. The concept of a constitutional general capacity or intelligence with which each individual is genetically endowed, and which develops so much according to its own inner biological necessities that it is little affected by any except very extreme environmental circumstances, has too little place for current concepts of the interacting relationships of biological constitution and environment. This chapter has talked broadly and somewhat loosely about abilities, these being understood as demonstrable competencies of various types (to employ verbal information effectively in certain types of problem-solving, to utilize certain arithmetic skills to solve mathematical problems, to deal with certain materials exemplifying spatial and mechanical problems, etc.) which are of wide usefulness. These competencies are the result of each organism's growth *in its environment*. The investigations regarding factors related to abilities stressed the major importance of constitutional capacity but recognized the influence of such pervasive conditions as culture and socioeconomic class. The quotation in the preceding paragraph suggests a dynamic element. In his address as president of the clinical and abnormal psychology division of the American Psychological Association in 1949, Wechsler argued that "general intelligence cannot be equated with intellectual ability, but must be regarded as a manifestation of the personality as a whole" (94). Abilities then become the product of a biological constitution growing in an environment with a developmental impetus which may vary greatly in strength and perhaps in direction from person to person and perhaps from one type of circumstance to another, and at different ages. Chapter 4 will explicate this concept further.

Studies of cultural and socioeconomic influences upon the development of abilities and longitudinal case reports should yield indications that certain cultural and social factors and types of energizing or debilitating personal experience are especially potent in affecting that development. Once such information is available, substantial improvements in school programs, in adult education, in guidance, in adjustment of work to competency, in the conservation of abilities in the older years should be possible. If it is found that abilities at different ages are somewhat different in nature, then recognition of the distinctive potentialities of the man of 60 or 40 as compared with 20 should increase vocational effectiveness at each age. Would such research invalidate the findings presented earlier in this chapter? It seems well established that abilities grow during the growth years, reach something of a level thereafter, and may ultimately decline; that individual differences are great; and that constitutional factors are the basic element determining them. Research along the lines suggested above would rather make possible a more effective building upon these basic facts so that biological potentialities might be more fully realized. Again, Chapter 4 will carry these issues further.

Summary

This chapter has been concerned with a major contribution of American psychology during the first part of this century: the development of means for measuring general ability and the use of these means in furthering the understanding of the nature of abilities. In so doing, the need to broaden concepts of ability has become increasingly evident, and in that connection it has become increasingly clear that conventional tests are limited and special in nature. From work with them, the major outlines of the phenomena concerned with abilities through the life span have nevertheless emerged.

1. Conventional tests of general ability have in "cross-sectional" studies shown rapid and relatively steady increases in average score through the growth years, these increases largely ceasing around 18 or 20; the curve of growth in mental ability seems similar to the curve of growth in physical height. Individual differences appear to increase rapidly during these growth years, and longitudinal records show that most children maintain roughly the same relative standing from about the age of 5 or 6 on, though a few youngsters show considerable variation in growth rate. On conventional tests, adults have been found to average progressively lower with increasing age; however, the somewhat clerical and academic nature of these tests may make them progressively less satisfactory for older adults who are farther away from their schooling, have had less education than young adults, and are less accustomed to tests. Further,

recent longitudinal research has shown young people continuing to score better at least until 25, and able adults have shown little if any decline in certain abilities with age; instead they often show some gain!

2. Analyses indicate that different kinds of ability—as verbal, mechanical, artistic—all tend to grow throughout the growth years. However, there is some evidence to suggest stages in growth; sensorimotor abilities are central in the first year, habituation in speech and in acquaintance with home and immediate neighborhood are of prime importance in the next four or five years, habituation in use of the printed word and acquaintance with the larger environment of school and community are most important in the following six or eight years, and so on. There appear to be stages in learning—readiness for different types of learning at different ages. Through the growth years, children show increasing diversity of abilities. Age appears to bring slowness and lessened ability to learn. However, unsuitableness of materials to older persons may account in considerable part for their poorer records on tests of learning.

3. Inherited constitutional capacity is clearly a basic factor in abilities. Race differences appear to be slight or nil. But cultural and socioeconomic influences often appear to be pervasively important. Very poor environment may bring progressively less realized ability, and early improvement of a poor environment may cause a little gain. So, perhaps, may a good nursery school. Added years of schooling may add years to "adult level," and programs of adult education may perhaps lessen decline of score with age in the adult years or may even be associated with a rise. But both test materials and school programs appear to be sufficiently weighted in favor of American middle-upper class subject matter, standards of performance, and points of view that reappraisal with more richly diverse material and methods is desirable. Longitudinal studies suggest that the concomitance of special circumstances may sometimes affect the development of an individual's abilities rather markedly.

4. Broad empirical studies of the abilities of all socioeconomic classes and of adults as well as children and longitudinal studies which recognize the possibility of a certain dynamic in the growth and maintenance of abilities should do much to enrich conventional concepts of abilities. Influences especially affecting abilities should be located, and ways of using them for fostering abilities should be developed. The psychology of abilities may then at last get free from its limiting origins in child study and the schools, and appraisal, training, and guidance suitable for

all segments of society, and for adults as well as young people, may then be greatly furthered.

BIBLIOGRAPHY

1. Ammons, R. B., Shearn, C., and Larson, W. L., The full-range picture vocabulary test; results for an adult population, *J. Consult. Psychol.*, 1950, *14*:150–155.
2. Anastasi, Anne, and Foley, J. P., *Differential Psychology* (rev. ed.), New York, Macmillan, 1949.
3. Asher, E. J., The inadequacy of current intelligence tests for testing Kentucky mountain children, *J. Genet. Psychol.*, 1935, *46*:480–486.
4. Bagley, W. C., Do good schools pay? *J. Nat. Educ. Assoc.*, 1923, *12*:211–216.
5. Balinsky, B., An analysis of the mental factors of various age groups from nine to sixty, *Genet. Psychol. Monogr.*, 1941, *23*:91–234.
6. Barker, R. G., and Wright, H. F., *One Boy's Day*, New York, Harper, 1951.
7. Bayley, Nancy, Consistency and variability in the growth of intelligence from birth to 18 years, *J. Genet. Psychol.*, 1949, *75*:165–196.
8. Bayley, Nancy, On the growth of intelligence, *Amer. Psychol.*, 1955, *10*:805–818.
9. Bayley, Nancy, and Oden, Melita H., The maintenance of intellectual ability in gifted adults, *J. Gerontol.*, 1955, *10*:91–107.
10. Berkowitz, B., The Wechsler-Bellevue performance of white males past age 50, *J. Gerontol.*, 1953, *8*:76–80.
11. Bingham, W. V., Inequalities in adult capacity—from military data, *Science*, 1946, *104*:147–152.
12. Birren, J. E., and Botwinick, J., Rate of addition as a function of difficulty and age, *Psychometrika*, 1951, *16*:219–232.
13. Birren, J. E., and Botwinick, J., The relation of writing speed to age and to senile psychoses, *J. Consult. Psychol.*, 1951, *15*:243–249.
14. Botwinick, J., and Birren, J. E., Differential decline in the Wechsler-Bellevue subtests in the senile psychoses, *J. Gerontol.*, 1951, *6*:365–368.
15. Brodbeck, A. J., and Irwin, O. C., The speech behavior of infants without families, *Child Development*, 1946, *17*:145–156.
16. Burt, Cyril, *The Backward Child*, New York, Appleton-Century, 1937.
17. Burtt, H. E., An experimental study of early childhood memory: final report, *J. Genet. Psychol.*, 1941, *58*:435–439.
18. Carmichael, L. (ed.), *Manual of Child Psychology* (rev. ed.), New York, Wiley, 1954.
19. Charles, D. C., Ability and accomplishment of person earlier judged to be mentally defective, *Genet. Psychol. Monogr.*, 1953, *47*:3–71.
20. Chesrow, E. G., Wosika, P. H., and Reinitz, A. Y., A psychometric evaluation of aged white males, *Geriat.*, 1949, *4*:169–177.

21. Christian, A. M., and Paterson, D. G., Growth of vocabulary in later maturity, *J. Psychol.*, 1936, *1*:167–169.
22. Cornell, Ethel L., and Armstrong, C. M., Forms of mental growth patterns revealed by reanalysis of the Harvard growth data, *Child Development,* 1955, *26*:169–204.
23. Corsini, R. J., and Fassett, Katherine K., Intelligence and aging, *J. Genet. Psychol.*, 1953, *83*:249–264.
24. Dearborn, W. F., and Rothney, J. W., *Predicting the Child's Development,* Cambridge, Science-Art Pub., 1941.
25. Demming, J. A., and Pressey, S. L., Tests "indigenous" to the adult and older years, in *Aging and Retirement,* Gainesville, University of Florida Press, 1955, pp. 28–38.
26. Eells, K. W., *Intelligence and Cultural Differences,* Chicago, University of Chicago Press, 1951.
27. Estes, S. G., Deviations of Wechsler-Bellevue subtest scores from vocabulary level in superior adults, *J. Abnorm. and Soc. Psychol.*, 1946, *41:* 226–228.
28. Eysenck, M. P., The psychological aspects of aging and senility, *J. Ment. Sci.*, 1946, *92*:171–181.
29. Fischer, A. E., and Dolger, H., Behavior and psychological problems of young diabetic patients: a ten- to twenty-year survey, *Archives of Internal Medicine,* December, 1946, *78*:711–732.
30. Flory, C. D., Intellectual growth of college students, *J. Educ. Psychol.*, 1940, *33*:443–451.
31. Foulds, G. A., Variations in the intellectual activities of adults, *Amer. J. Psychol.*, 1949, *62*:238–246.
32. Foulds, G. A., and Raven, J. C., Normal changes in mental abilities of adults as age advances, *J. Ment. Sci.*, 1948, *94*:133–142.
33. Fox, Charlotte, The intelligence of old indigent persons residing within and without a public home for the aged, *Amer. J. Psychol.*, 1950, *63:* 110–112.
34. Fox, Charlotte, Vocabulary ability in later maturity, *J. Educ. Psychol.*, 1947, *38*:482–492.
35. Fox, Charlotte, and Birren, J. E., Some factors affecting vocabulary size in later maturity; age, education, and length of institutionalization, *J. Gerontol.*, 1948, *4*:19–26.
36. Freeman, F. N., Holzinger, K. U., and Mitchell, B. C., The influence of environment on the intelligence, school achievement and conduct of foster children, *27th Yearbook,* National Society for Study of Education, 1928, Pt. I, pp. 103–217.
37. Garrett, H. E., A developmental theory of intelligence, *Amer. Psychol.*, 1946, *1*:372–378.
38. Gilbert, J. G., Memory loss in senescence, *J. Abnorm. and Soc. Psychol.*, 1941, *36*:73–86.
39. Green, E. B., *Measurements of Human Behavior,* New York, Odyssey Press, 1941.

40. Halstead, H., A psychometric study of senility, *J. Ment. Sci.*, 1943, *89* 363–373.

41. Hamlin, R. H., An analysis of age progress curves as related to the mental growth curve: a study of vocabulary, *Archives of Psychol.*, 1944.

42. Hardy, Martha C., Improvement in educational achievement accompanying a health education program, *J. Educ. Res.*, 1936, *30:*110–123.

43. Havighurst, R. J., Child development in relation to community structure, *Child Development*, 1946, *17:*85–89.

44. Hildreth, Gertrude, Three gifted children: a developmental study, *J. Genet. Psychol.*, 1954, *85:*239–262.

45. Hilgard, E. R., *Theories of Learning*, New York, Appleton-Century-Crofts, 1948.

46. Hollingshead, A. B., *Elmtown's Youth*, New York, Wiley, 1949.

47. Honzik, M. P., Macfarlane, J. W., and Allen, L., The stability of mental test performance between 2 and 18 years, *J. Exp. Educ.*, 1948, *17:*309–324.

48. Hull, C. L., and B. I., Parallel learning curves of an infant in vocabulary and in voluntary control of the bladder, *Ped. Sem.*, 1919, *26:*272–283.

49. Jastak, J., An item analysis of the Wechsler-Bellevue tests, *J. Consult. Psychol.*, 1950, *14:*88–94.

50. Jones, H. E., and Conrad, H. S., The growth and decline of intelligence: a study of a homogeneous group between ages of 10 and 60, *Genet. Psychol. Monogr.*, 1933, *13:*223–298.

51. Kallman, F. G., and Sander, G., Twin studies in senescence, *Amer. J. Psychiat.*, 1949, *106:*29–36.

52. Kaplan, O., *Mental Disorders in Later Life* (rev. ed.), Stanford, Stanford University Press, 1956 (the aged subnormal, pp. 333–347).

53. Klineberg, O., *Negro Intelligence and Selective Migration*, New York, Columbia University Press, 1935.

54. Klineberg, O., Racial differences in speed and accuracy, *J. Abnorm. and Soc. Psychol.*, 1927, *22:*273–277.

55. Klineberg, O., A study of psychological differences between racial and national groups in Europe, *Archives of Psychol.*, 1931, *132:*58.

56. Kugelmass, Isaac N., Poull, L. S., and Samuel, E. L., Nutritional improvement of child mentality, *Amer. J. Med. Sci.*, November, 1944, *208:*631–633.

57. Kushner, Rose E., *The Relationship Between Content of an Adult Intelligence Test and Intelligence Test Score as a Function of Age*, Teachers College Contribution to Education No. 933, New York, 1947.

58. Lamson, E. E., To what extent are IQ's increased by children who participate in rich vital school curricula? *J. Educ. Psychol.*, 1933, *29:*67–70.

59. Lewinski, R. J., Vocabulary and mental measurement, *J. Genet. Psychol.*, 1948, *72:*247–281.

60. Lewis, Claudia, *Children of the Cumberland*, New York, Columbia University Press, 1946,

61. Lorge, I., The influence of the test upon the nature of mental. decline as a function of age, *J. Educ. Psychol.*, 1936, 27:100–110.

62. Lorge, I., Schooling makes a difference, *Teachers College Record*, 1945, 46:483–492.

63. Madonick, M. J., and Solomon, Marion, The Wechsler-Bellevue scale in individuals past sixty, *Geriat.*, 1947, 2:34–40.

64. McGraw, M. B., Later development of children especially trained during infancy: Johnny and Jimmy at school age, *Child Development*, 1939, 10: 1–19.

65. Miles, C. C., Influence of speed and age on intelligence scores of adults, *Ped. Sem. and J. Genet. Psychol.* 1934, 10:208–210.

66. Miles, C. C., and W. R., The correlation of intelligence scores and chronological age from early to late maturity, *Amer. J. Psychol.*, 1932, 44:44–78.

67. Myklebust, Helmer R., and Burchard, E. M. L., A study of the effects of congenital and adventitious deafness on the intelligence, personality, and social maturity of school children, *J. Educ. Psychol.*, 1945, 25:321–343.

68. National Society for the Study of Education, *39th Yearbook, Intelligence: Its Nature and Nurture*, 1940, Pt. I, Pt. II.

69. Newman, H. H., *Multiple Human Births*, New York, Doubleday, Doran, 1940.

70. Owens, W. A., Age and mental abilities: a longitudinal study, *Genet. Psychol. Monogr.*, 1953, 48:3–54.

71. Peraza, G., Mental and physical benefits of a well-balanced diet on a group of undernourished children, *J.A.M.W.A.*, November, 1946, 1:256.

72. Rabin, A. I., The relationship between vocabulary levels and levels in general intelligence in psychotic and non-psychotic individuals of a wide range, *J. Educ. Psychol.*, 1944, 35:411–422.

73. Rappaport, S. R., and Webb, W. B., An attempt to study intellectual deterioration by premorbid and psychotic testing, *J. Consult. Psychol.*, 1950, 14:95–98.

74. Raven, J. C., The comparative assessment of intellectual ability, *Brit. J. Psychol.*, 1948, 39:12–19.

75. Ruch, F. L., The differentiative effects of age upon human learning, *Ped. Sem. and J. Genet. Psychol.*, 1934, 11:261–286.

76. Sanford, R. N., Age as a factor in the recall of interrupted tasks, *Psychol. Rev.*, 1946, 53:234–240.

77. Schaie, K. W., Rosenthal, F., and Perlman, R. M., Differential mental decline of factorially "pure" functions in later maturity, *J. Gerontol.*, 1953, 8:191–196.

78. Segal, D., *Intellectual Abilities in the Adolescent Period*, Washington, D.C., Office of Education, 1948.

79. Shakow, D., Dolkart, M. B., and Godman, R., The memory function in psychoses, *Dis. Nerv. Syst.*, 1941, 2:43–48.

80. Skeels, H. M., and Fillmore, E. A., The mental development of children

from underprivileged homes, *Ped. Sem. and J. Genet. Psychol.*, 1937, 50:427–439.

81. Smith, M., University student intelligence and occupation of fathers, *Amer. Soc. Rev.*, December, 1942, 704–711.

82. Sorenson, H., Mental ability over a wide range of adult ages, *J. Appl. Psychol.*, 1933, 17:729–741.

83. Stewart, Naomi, A.G.C.T. scores of Army personnel grouped by occupation, *Occupations*, 1947, 26:5–41.

84. Stroud, J. B., and Maul, Ruth, The influence of age on learning and retention of poetry and nonsense syllables, *Ped. Sem. and J. Genet. Psychol.*, 1933, 42:242–250.

85. Sward, K., Age and mental ability in superior men, *Amer. J. Psychol.*, 1945, 58:443–479.

86. Terman, L. M., and Merrill, M. A., *Measuring Intelligence: A Guide to the Administration of the New Revised Stanford-Binet Tests of Intelligence*, Boston, Houghton Mifflin, 1937.

87. Terman, L. M., and Oden, Melita H., *The Gifted Child Grows Up: Twenty-Five Years' Follow-Up of Superior Groups*, Stanford, Stanford University Press, 1947.

88. Thompson, Clare W., Decline in limit of performance among adult morons, *Amer. J. Psychol.*, 1951, 64:203–215.

89. Thorndike, E. L., *et al.*, *Adult Learning*, New York, Macmillan, 1928.

90. Thorndike, R. L., Growth in intelligence during adolescence, *J. Genet. Psychol.*, 1948, 72:11–15.

91. Thorndike, R. L., Retest changes in IQ in certain superior schools, *39th Yearbook*, National Society for the Study of Education, 1940, Pt. II, pp. 351–361.

92. Thorndike, R. L., and Gallup, G. H., Verbal intelligence of the American adult, *J. Genet. psychol.*, 1944, 30:75–85.

93. Tuddenham, R. D., Soldier intelligence in World Wars I and II, *Amer. Psychol.*, 1948, 3:54–56.

94. Wechsler, D., Cognitive, conative and non-intellective intelligence, *Amer. Psychol.*, 1950, 5:78–83.

95. Wechsler, D., *A Measurement of Adult Intelligence* (1st ed.), Baltimore, Williams and Wilkins, 1939.

96. Wechsler, D., *The Measurement of Adult Intelligence* (3rd ed.), Baltimore, Williams and Wilkins, 1955.

97. Welford, A. T., *et al.*, *Skill and Age*, London, Oxford University Press, 1951.

98. Wheeler, L. R., A comparative study of the intelligence of East Tenn. mountain children, *J. Educ. Psychol.*, 1942, 33:321–334.

99. Wolfle, D., *America's Resources of Specialized Talent*, New York, Harper, 1954.

CHAPTER 4 •

• Development of Abilities as Indicated by Achievement and by Mental Disease: Perspective by Contrast

THE previous chapter has argued that abilities develop and change throughout life and that (more than is usually recognized) they are part of the total organism and affected by the dynamics of the individual life pattern. These conclusions, if sound, should be evidenced in material indicating competence in meeting life problems at different ages. Chapter 2 on physical growth and change used data regarding age of winning championships in sports to differentiate the years of greatest physical efficiency and statistics as to the frequency and nature of illness at various ages to show something as to the course and characteristics of physical decline. It would surely seem of interest, and possibly of great fruitfulness in terms of the broad concepts mentioned above regarding abilities, to consider the analogous questions of the ages when notable intellectual accomplishments are most frequent and the age incidence of mental disease and breakdown.

Moreover, an important contribution will indeed have been made if these broad concepts can bring any better understanding of problems of mental health and of means of fostering notable accomplishments. The great number of cases in hospitals for the mentally ill is a cause of much concern; any concept which might, for instance, suggest possible means for delaying or preventing the onset of "senile dementia" could be of great practical worth. Contributions might be made to an even more important problem. The world conflict of these times may well be decided by the comparative capacity of different countries and parts of the world to produce people of outstanding abilities in scientific discovery and in leadership. Study of the ways in which such abilities

122

develop, and influences fostering that development, thus seems especially urgent now.

Ages When Notable Achievements Are Most Commonly Made

Strangely enough, it is only in relatively recent years that careful and comprehensive investigations have been made regarding ages when men do notable work. An extensive series of papers, recently brought together in a monograph, by H. C. Lehman (25) have treated the topic exhaustively. In essence, Lehman's methods were simple and straightforward. For instance, to find the ages when poets are at their best, he first listed all poems mentioned in some fifty histories of English literature. Then, by tabulating the number of these books which mentioned each poem, he got a sort of vote as to the merit of each. When he was seeking age of doing very outstanding work, he kept only those few poems thus chosen by a considerable number of authorities. He then looked up the age of the author at the time each of those poems was produced. From his entire table, he next found that age or age group (such as 25 to 29) when most poems were written—taking account only of the authors living at that age. And he graphed his findings by considering the production at the peak or most productive age as 100 percent and expressing the productivity at all other ages as a percentage of this peak productivity.

In most of these studies, Lehman included only notable people not now living; he was thus certain that they had made all their contributions and that there was some time perspective in evaluating them. Inevitably, methods varied somewhat from one field to another. Thus, greatest operas were considered those "best-loved" but greatest chemical discoveries were those so considered by chemists. In some fields, evaluating lists (such as of "great books") were already available, but in others judgments of experts had to be solicited. Similarity in results despite the great difference in the fields considered suggests that basic phenomena, as regards development of abilities, were being found.

AGE OF IMPORTANT CREATIVE WORK

Lehman found substantial differences between age of creative work, as in literature or science, and age of accomplishments of a leadership type, as in politics or business. Further, the curves for very best creative work were different in shape from those including accomplishments less preëminent. Most striking were the findings for age of doing very out-standing creative work, as illustrated in Figure 46.

These curves are quite similar to those showing ages of winning cham-pionships in sports; the peaks for notable intellectual creativity are a little later, but there is the same rapid rise in early adult life and then a falling off, with comparatively little outstanding creative work done in later middle life or the older years. Moreover, the curve for chemistry seems to be for dates of first publication of chemical discoveries (25, p. 3). After having his brilliant idea, a chemist might spend much time

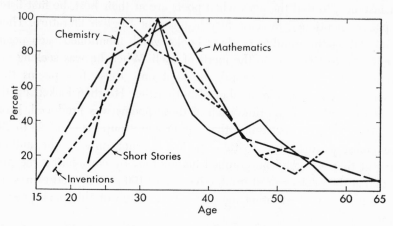

Figure 46. Age of Creative Work: Most Important Inventions of 35 Great Inventors, Finest Short Story of 38 Great Short Story Writers, Greatest Discovery of 46 Famous Chemists, Superior Contributions of 27 Mathematicians. (Adapted from H. C. Lehman, Age and Achievement, Princeton, Princeton University Press, 1953.)

in experimentation before it was verified, spend additional time in writing it up, and then wait some months more before it appeared in print. Somewhat similarly, the curve for short stories presumably shows date of publication, with the actual writing occurring earlier; it was found that for "miscellaneous poetry . . . the mean time lag between date of composition and the date of first publication was 2.65 years" (25, p. 95). For inventions, the date used may, at least in some instances, be that of obtaining patent, in which case there would be an analogous time lag. The assumption thus seems reasonable that much of the creative work with which Figure 46 deals was actually done perhaps two years earlier than it shows.

Chemistry has the earliest peak in this graph; "years of maximum productivity" of very important chemical discoveries were 26 to 30

(25, p. 20). In view of the present elaborateness of that science, notable accomplishment at such an early age seems surprising. However, a century and more ago, the frontiers of chemical knowledge were much closer, and much less training was necessary. Thus, Sir Humphry Davy moved into chemical experimentation while an apothecary's apprentice. There was no long sequence of courses and doctoral requirements then! But relatively early notable productivity seems to be continuing in chemistry—perhaps in part because a youngster may in boyhood have a chemical set or other educational toys and can begin study of the subject in secondary school, continue intensively in college, and then go directly into graduate work. In contrast, Lehman reports peak productive years in psychology to be 30 to 39 (25, p. 20)—perhaps in part because the study of philosophy used to be a prerequisite to the subject, and in more recent years psychology was not offered to students in their first year or two of college. Figure 46 shows a few outstanding inventors and mathematical discoverers in their teens and a few who did notable work in the sixties. Such extreme cases will be returned to later.

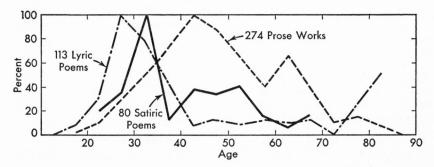

Figure 47. Age Differences in Types of Superior Literary Productivity. (Adapted from H. C. Lehman and J. B. Heidler, Chronological ages vs. quality of literary output, Amer. J. Psychol., 1949, 62:77–81.)

Age differences in productivity seem to appear within certain fields. As indicated in Figure 47, the best lyrical verse tends to be written by very young poets, some in their teens. But peak age for best prose is in the forties. There appear to be age differences in the total complex of abilities, interests, feelings, and favoring circumstances which produce outstanding writing of various types.

The previous paragraphs have reference to the very best and most outstanding creative work of distinguished people in various fields. But the very best work of an author, scientist, or inventor is presumably not his only work; and the question naturally arises as to the nature of his productivity throughout his adult career. Figure 48 is informative in this connection. The heavy line showing best painting indicates that the very best came early in life, as in the fields shown in the preceding figures. And this finding is even more interesting because the painters considered in this particular statistic were men who lived to be 70 or over. It can therefore not be said of them that they did not have an adequate and presumably reasonably healthy and vigorous older adulthood for later superior creative work. But the other lines tell the distinctive story involved in this graph. When not the one best but the three best paintings of each man are considered, more are found at a somewhat older age.

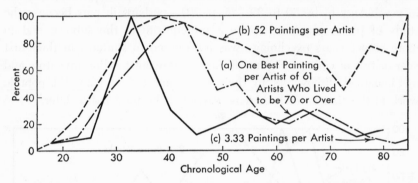

Figure 48.   Relation of Quality and Quantity: (a) Best Painting of 61 Artists Who Lived to be 70 or Over; 506 Paintings of 152 Artists; and (c) 7082 Paintings by 135 Artists. (Adapted from H. C. Lehman, The creative years: oil paintings, etchings, and architectural works, Psychol. Rev., 1942, 49:19–43.)

When many paintings for each artist are included, it appears that work of some quality was produced throughout the active professional life.

Quite similar results were obtained in a study of authors. And in the sciences the same phenomena appeared, except that in the older adult years productivity dropped more. Very likely the diversion of many good research men into administrative work may be a factor. And, of course, it should always be recognized that there are many individual differences, with some outstanding people (as, for instance, the psychologist, E. L. Thorndike) producing vigorously until almost the end of life. Such individual variations will be turned to later.

There arises in these connections the question as to possible relationships of age of beginning productivity, total number of contributions, and range of ages over which productivity continued. Figure 49 indi-

cates that those chemists who made 14 or more contributions all made
the first before they were 30; no one who made more than 2 contributions began to contribute after he was 50. Apparently, from the point
of view of both quality and quantity of work, it is desirable to begin
young.

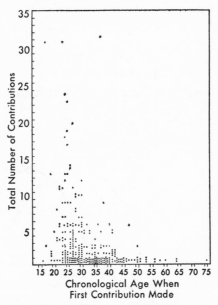

Figure 49. The Age at Which Each of 306 Chemists Made His First Important Chemistry Contribution vs. the Total Number Made by Each. From H. C. Lehman, *Age and Achievement,* Princeton University Press, 1953, p. 186.

AGE OF LEADERSHIP

The previous material has dealt with creative types of achievement.
Similar studies made with reference to age of leadership show a substantially different situation. The data, again from Lehman, were gath-
ered and handled by the methods already described. Figure 50 shows
age of army commanders at the time of important battles, age of service
of elected and appointive American officials (state governors and justices of the Supreme Court), and also years of service of British cabinet
members. As will be seen, peak age of military commanders was in the
forties which was also the peak age for state governors. But the national
positions were usually attained later, and service in these sometimes ran
into the eighties.

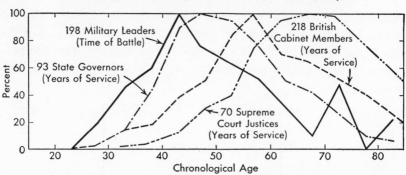

Figure 50. Age of Leadership: Years of Service of 218 British Cabinet Members, 932 State Governors, 70 U.S. Supreme Court Justices, and Age of 198 Military Leaders at Time of Battle. (Adapted from H. C. Lehman, Optimum ages for eminent leadership, *Sci. Mont.*, 1942, 54:163, 166, 168.)

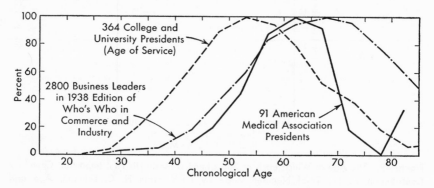

Figure 51. Age of Leadership: 91 Presidents of the American Medical Association, 364 Presidents of Colleges and Universities, and 2800 Business leaders. (Adapted from H. C. Lehman, Optimum ages for eminent leadership, *Sci. Mont.*, 1942, 54:171–172.)

The findings in Figure 50 were for governmental positions. Figure 51 shows that leaders in education, medicine, and business tend to be in later middle age or older. A few college presidents may achieve their positions while still in their twenties, but typically they are men in their fifties. The professional recognition of the presidency of the American Medical Association comes most commonly in the sixties (later than most professional groups). And business leadership shows an even slightly higher mode, though many of these cases probably are "chairman of the board" or relatively if not entirely inactive.

Why does leadership tend to come later than creative work? Possibly leadership calls for qualities of maturity and judgment which are typical of the later rather than the earlier adult years. A range of experience in leadership situations may be needed which can ordinarily be obtained only after a considerable time. Perhaps caution, willingness to suspend a decision until various factors are apprehended, and other similar traits of personality are especially important in leadership.

There may be factors of circumstance or public attitude. Thus, many years may be required simply to make the many personal contacts which ordinarily are the basis for leadership and to establish a reputation on the basis of which leadership can be carried on. The public may not have confidence in younger leaders. Perhaps such an elementary matter as the amount of room at the top plays a part. If, for instance, a considerable number of senators are over 60 and are well established in their positions, there will be that much less opportunity for younger aspirants. That such factors may be operating is suggested by the finding that men in public office average now substantially older than a hundred years ago. Thus, the average age of cabinet members was 47 in 1789–1824, but it was 60 in 1925–1945. In contrast, notable work in some sciences (not chemistry) seems to be occurring at a somewhat younger age than formerly. Thus years of maximum productivity of 80 physicists born from 1781 to 1867[1] was 30 to 34, but for 44 physicists born prior to 1785, the maximal years were 45 to 49 (25, pp. 289, 301). It has been suggested that this latter trend may be due to modern laboratories and methods which make it possible for a young man who is just getting started to have immediate access to such equipment as may be needed for scientific study. Further, research is professionalized now, but two hundred years ago, it more often tended to be the part-time interest of a gentleman.

The ever-present fact of individual differences must not be neglected, however. There have been notable young leaders—Alexander the Great, Napoleon, the younger Pitt—and leadership may appear well into old age, as instanced by Churchill in his seventies and Gladstone serving as prime minister in his eighties. Remarkable creative work may come in the teens, as evidenced by Mozart in music and Shelley in poetry, and also sometimes in old age. Potentialities for outstanding accomplishment apparently may be present at any age from the teens on. Presumably, favorable circumstances and motivations for such accom-

[1] Lehman's "now" is thus hardly contemporary! The judgment is ventured that contemporary American scientists will reach this peak at a little later age than was formerly the case and than European scientists at their peak, because of a lengthening of education in this country which may well be undesirable (38). The topic will be returned to in Chapter 5.

plishment are more likely at some ages than at others. The greater frequency of notable accomplishments of various types at certain ages might be due to more favorable influences or to more potentiality then. Conceivably, factors might be differentiated and controlled with the object of lengthening the span of years when outstanding work might be hoped for or increasing its frequency at a given age. The age range of achievement must, therefore, be given special consideration.

AGE RANGE OF GREAT ACHIEVEMENTS AND CHARACTERISTICS OF ACHIEVEMENT AT DIFFERENT AGES

It was said that notable achievement may come early or late. But is very early achievement sufficiently common that it can be considered more than the somewhat freakish display of precocity in genius? Are instances of accomplishment in old age common enough and of such nature that the lengthening of life and improvement of health in the older years may be expected to bring corresponding lengthening of highly fruitful careers?

There is abundant evidence that brilliant creative work may be done in the early twenties and even in the teens. A compilation by Lehman from a great variety of fields includes 65 instances where persons 20 or under did such work. For instance, William Cullen Bryant's masterpiece, *Thanatopsis,* was written at 18. Samuel Colt whittled out his first model of a revolver when he was 16. Walter Crane at 17 had a picture exhibited at the Royal Academy. Perkin discovered the first synthetic dye when 18, and Lord Kelvin published an important geological paper at that age. Many famous musicians were very precocious—Mozart composed at 4! Precocity in music is believed to be a somewhat special phenomenon which will be given special attention a little later.

Aside from musicians, poets appear to flower earliest—Blake, Chatterton, and Pope as early as 12, Bryant at 13, Burns at 14. Cowley was famous as a poet at 15 when he published a collection of five poems. At this same age, Milton wrote a hymn that is still widely used. Of Lehman's 65 examples of notable creative work at the age of 20 or under, 13 were poets. Why should this be? Practically all this early notable versification seems to have consisted of lyrics or other short pieces; some of it (as Keats' sonnet "On First Looking into Chapman's Homer" and Holmes' "Old Ironsides," both written at 20) was produced in one brief effort of only an hour or so under the stimulus of strong emotion. These triumphs might perhaps be described as products of the high energies and strong feelings of adolescent youth expressed in a medium (language) and, indeed, a mode long familiar—even very young children may show a delight in verbal rhythms and indulge in much juvenile versifying. At least, these seem to be reasonable hypotheses.

At first thought, it may seem hardly possible that scientific discoveries could come early; yet Lehman mentions 12 such achievements in physics and 7 in chemistry by youngsters of 20 or under. Thus, Galileo was 17 when he determined the principle of the pendulum from observations of a swinging cathedral lamp. Davy discovered the anaesthetic properties of nitrous oxide gas when he was 20. Eight important inventions in these same early ages are also listed. For instance, Pacinotti invented the slotted iron-ring armature at the age of 18 while serving as a soldier under Garibaldi. But when one remembers the delight of many boys in basement workbenches and experimental chemistry kits, such early discoveries seem a natural fruition for brilliant youngsters with such interests; and sundry famous scientists showed this interest in childhood. For instance, Newton as a boy "showed great aptitude in making kites, windmills, and other mechanical toys." Liebig spent much boyhood time repeating chemical experiments he found described in books. As a 14-year-old messenger boy for a bookstore, Faraday read scientific books which passed through his hands and "made such simple experiments in chemistry as could be defrayed in their expense by a few pence per week, and constructed an electrical machine."

Inventions and relatively simple scientific discoveries thus seem rather natural early outcomes of boyish fondness for handicraft and experiment, and lyric poetry seems to be a derivation from childish fondness for playing with words and for rhyme and of adolescent emotion. What is the amount, range, and nature of creative work in the older ages, and does any such work have relationships to major characteristics of age? A compilation of such cases, by the indefatigable Dr. Lehman, includes some 100 instances of notable work completed at the age of 70 or over, 33 of which were completed in the eighties. Most common (21 cases) were discoveries in medicine. A considerable number of these were the results of long clinical observations or were otherwise based on broad experience and previous knowledge. Second in order (16 cases), were contributions in the biological sciences, and third were 11 contributions in history. Some notable poetry was written by old men—6 instances are given, of which 2 appeared when their authors were 85. Chemists, physicists, and inventors each made five contributions at the age of 70 or over.

But in general these contributions of the older years seemed to come from experience and broad learning more than from originality and intense feeling.

The following samples of notable accomplishment appearing after the age of 80 are illustrative of both the variety and the general nature of such work. Robert Bridges "published his last great poem . . . 'a confession of philosophic faith'" at the age of 85. In the second part of *Faust*, Goethe "finished at the age of 80 the plan which he had conceived 60 years before." Friedrich Hoffman wrote a "notable treatise" on pediatrics at 81. James Martineau's "most important book, *Types of Ethical Theory*, was published when he was 80 years old, but for many years before, the content of this and his other publications had formed the material of his college lectures." Morgagni at 80 brought out his two-volume work on pathological anatomy, 20 years after it was begun. Oughtred issued the last of three mathematical treatises when 83. Tennyson's last volume of poems, of which "Crossing the Bar" was one, appeared when he was 80. Verdi "produced four beautiful sacred pieces" when he was 85. The clinician and pathologist Naunyn completed his memoirs when 86, and Wundt completed his when 88. The contributions of old men as compared with younger appear to be philosophic rather than romantic in feeling, scholarly rather than pioneering in nature, and often are the completion of earlier efforts more than a distinct product of the later years. However, as stressed by Vischer (46), a lifetime of experience may contribute to later work a rich perspective and sometimes an urbanity and a depth, if not an intensity of feeling, which gives it a distinctive worth. And vigorous minds tend to continue active, often until the very end of life.[2]

IMPLICATIONS REGARDING ABILITIES FROM DATA ON AGE OF ACHIEVEMENT

Perhaps the most striking feature of the figures showing achievement is the rather close similarity between profiles for age of outstanding cre-

[2] Thus, in his very last years, E. L. Thorndike published papers on such diverse topics as The $10,000 salary fetish, The psychology of invention in a very simple case, On the frequency of semantic changes in modern English, The organization of a person, New data on the influence of frequency and of mind set, and Opinions concerning fair prices. Part of an incomplete manuscript on "Traits of Personality and Their Intercorrelations as Shown in Biographies" was (according to his son, Robert) "certainly written during the week before he died." It contains the following moving passage: "Any one of these correlations can be explored further. . . . I intended to do this, but I cannot . . . my memories [at age seventy-five] are failing rapidly. Nor have I the strength to review the written notes I made when reading the biographies. So I leave the intercorrelations . . . and append the ratings . . . for the use of any psychologist making similar studies. I hope the weakness of my study will not discourage them." (*J. Educ. Psychol.* April, 1950, pp. 193–216.) But perhaps—as he had long ago stated regarding fatigue—he felt much more inadequate mentally than he really was; these last papers show scholarship, originality, style, and humor that are indicative of abilities that continued largely intact to the end.

ative work and of athletic championships—especially in greatly skilled but not exhausting sports like target-shooting and billiards. If allowance be made for the time lag in reporting or publishing, it appears that in most sciences, in literature, and in the arts, as well as in sports, peak is commonly reached between 25 and 35; this holds for fields as different as chemistry and poetry, for different countries, for men who live long as well as those who die early. Present-day longer life and better health do not seem to have lengthened appreciably this climax period of life. The curves mount in about the same slant from a little before or after 20 and fall off after the thirties at about the same rate. The dozen years from about 25 to about 37 or 38 are not only the years of greatest health, physical strength, and championships in all sports, but they are the "champion" years for creative intellect. The hypothesis seems inescapable that there is here exhibited a basic biological phenomenon—an organic prime —showing in psychological as well as physiological functioning.

That leadership tends to come later than creative work and that in certain fields, at least, certain types of accomplishments seem to come at somewhat different times than others suggests that there are somewhat different abilities involved in various types of accomplishments and that these develop somewhat differently. Finally, the fact that creative work may now begin earlier than formerly, and leadership climax later, suggests the operation of factors which might be used to foster major accomplishment in various ways. Major factors must next be considered.

Factors Involved in Notable Achievement

An outstanding accomplishment is presumably usually the product of an exceptional total personality whose abilities, persistence, preparation, and opportunities combine to result in an individual's writing a poem, making a scientific discovery, or attaining a position of leadership. The first question to consider is the comparative importance of such factors, next, the ways they operate together when great achievements result, and, finally, whether any reinterpretations regarding the nature of abilities come from such an approach.

MAJOR FACTORS

Occasionally rather mediocre persons seem somewhat by accident to have come upon the idea for an invention or scientific discovery or to have composed a song or written a poem of much merit. But usually, continuing achievements, and other evidence, indicate superior intellectual capacities as basic. More than 80 years ago Galton stressed the frequency with which men of exceptional achievement tended to appear in family clusters. Half the illustrious men he studied had one or more eminent relations. Moreover, accomplishments in a given family were often similar, with indications of similar intellectual traits in several members of a family. For instance, Galton traced through four generations of the Darwin family the "many instances of a love of natural history and theory, and of an aptitude for collecting facts in business-like but peculiar ways." And he mentioned, with quiet pride, the connections of the Darwins with the Wedgwoods and the Galtons (*16*, p. 34.) Such relationships were found for men of notable accomplishment in a great variety of fields—statesmen, authors, scientists, painters, and clergymen, as well as oarsmen and wrestlers. As total organisms the intellectually notable tended to be superior. Thus, the men of science usually had great energy, excellent health, and good physique. "A collection of living magnates in various branches of intellectual achievement is always a feast to my eyes; being, as they are, such massive, vigorous, capable-looking animals" (*17*, p. 332).[3]

The importance of constitutional intellectual traits in bringing about notable achievement is often considered evidenced by the extraordinary precocity which many great men have shown, especially in certain fields. Great talent has appeared in many musicians astoundingly early. Mozart was an accomplished player at 4, was composing difficult pieces by 8, and conducted the largest symphony orchestra in Europe at age 14. It will shortly be argued that other factors are of neglected importance in explaining musical precocity, however. As already mentioned, some of the poets produced verse of substantial merit while still in childhood. The careers of some poets and musicians have been feverish and tempestuous like a flame burning hot and soon out; Mozart died at 35, Schubert at 30, Shelley at 29, Keats at 25, and Chatterton at 18. However, other careers have been placid and long, as instanced by Verdi, Tennyson, Bryant, and Wordsworth. Differences in constitutional trends in development

[3] At this distance in time and after the racism of Hitler's Germany, it is indeed interesting to review Galton's very English arguments regarding the superior contributions and presumed biological potentialities of Western Europe and his doubts regarding primitive peoples. Ingenuously he argues that though their primitive conditions may prevent achievements in many fields, yet their chiefs have abundant practice in leadership, without becoming great leaders; when these chiefs are met, explorers seem almost unanimously agreed on their own superiority! But the vigor and clarity of Galton's alarmed call for eugenic, social, and educational measures to maintain the vigor of Western civilization can hardly be matched since.

might perhaps be thought of as important elements in the distinctive merits of the verse of Keats and Shelley as compared with Tennyson and Wordsworth. The abilities as well as the personalities of most poets and musicians seem to differ in quality and pattern of development from the abilities and personalities of men in other fields such as Gibbon the historian, Samuel Johnson the essayist and biographer, and Kant the philosopher.

In short, early work stressed the extent to which superior abilities seemed to appear in families and to develop in ways emphasing the importance of constitutional factors. But even the early work recognized that notable accomplishment was not primarily the product of abilities coming to their almost inevitable fruition; a favorable soil and climate is also essential. The Classical period of the ancient world produced a substantial number of great accomplishments, but the Dark Ages produced few; however, the last 200 years have seen an astounding increase in notable achievements, at least as we recognize them, which have been attained primarily (in spite of Russian claims!) in the Western world. Indeed, certain western countries have been most productive at certain times. Thus, in the last century music came especially from Germany and Italy, accomplishment in government and law from England, and practical invention from the United States. Prior to 1850, France made most contributions in mathematics and chemistry; from 1850 to 1900 Germany led; now in many fields the United States is leading.[4] Figure 52 (p. 136) shows productivity in three countries in two very different fields.

Galton showed, more specifically, that certain special areas in England had been most fruitful of highly productive men; Cattell, Visher, and Bowerman have similarly shown that some areas of this country are much more intellectually productive than others. Thus, Massachusetts has produced some 69 eminent Americans per 100,000 inhabitants of about the time when these eminent persons were born, but North Carolina produced only 2. Different areas have tended to nurture different types of ability; Virginia has produced many statesmen and military men; New England, authors and inventors; New York, capitalists and philanthropists. Productivity is moving west and somewhat south, as certain socioeconomic and cultural advances so move. These general facts are well known and are recognized as products of the stages of development and circumstances of these countries and areas. Are the gains in productivity

[4] H. C. Lehman, National differences in creativity, *Amer. J. Sociol.*, May, 1947, 52:475–488.

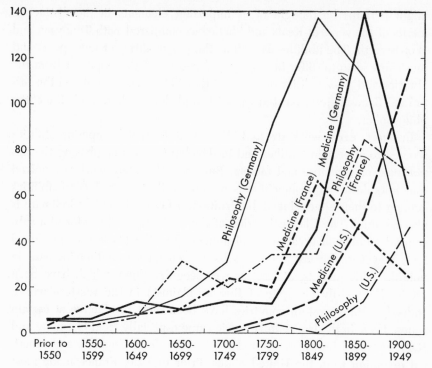

Figure 52. National Differences in Contributions to Medicine and Philosophy. (Adapted from H. C. Lehman, National differences in creativity, *Amer. J. Sociol.*, May, 1947, 52:475–488.)

simply the result of gains in opportunity? A broad, functional viewpoint may presumably see them as gains in developed ability, giving constitutional capacity the possibility of a growth not otherwise occurring. These phenomena seem worth emphasizing here as exhibiting, in terms of notable accomplishment, the effect of such influences, which many investigators only grudgingly have recognized when considering possible influences of culture and socioeconomic circumstance upon the tested abilities of children.

If, indeed, certain favorable conditions may markedly increase the number of notable accomplishments in a given place and time, then attempts to determine those conditions as clearly as possible, and to increase their influence, would seem of vital importance. And the possibility that a third world war might bring another dark age becomes indeed one more reason for every effort to avoid such a devastating outcome. In his vigorous prose, Galton made much of the need for more effective nurture of those minds which might bring forth notable accomplishment.[5] Much of what he wrote near the middle of the last century seems still very modern now—and the fact that he was largely unsuccessful (for instance, in his efforts to reduce the classical emphasis in education and to increase scholarships for able young men of limited means) is evidence of the resistive powers of established institutions to the efforts of a man, even of his capabilities and influence, in a cause which would seem to the advantage of almost everyone. A recent study by Visher of distinguished American scientists has again shown regional differences; 222 per million population were born in Massachusetts, 158 in New York, 120 in Minnesota, and so on, down to 2 in Arkansas. Further, proportionately more were born in cities or towns than in the country, and communities which were the sites of colleges or were state capitals or county seats were especially productive. Of these future scientists, 43 percent went to a college not more than 25 miles away from their home, and 68 percent had been helped by scholarship or other financial support. Universities varied much in the number of "starred" scientists they produced, and the same institution varied from one period in its history to another. Universities with vigorous young presidents who had distinctive policies and who brought in vigorous younger faculty members with fresh points of view seemed especially to have turned out such men. The above findings might perhaps be considered arguments for the community college, for federal scholarships, for a good proportion of younger men in university administrative positions as well as in faculty positions, and for willingness to venture fresh new policies.

Various other factors appeared to play a part in the development of men of notable achievement. Galton, Ellis, and Bowerman all found that travel seemed often an important element. The encouragement and interest of a parent or friend might be of great inportance. Thus, one of the geologists mentioned by Galton was initially stimulated by the fact

[5] Though his greatest eloquence was directed against the dysgenic socioeconomic and educational influences which resulted in the ablest people tending to have the fewest children, his arguments have indeed been elaborated and abundantly supported in continuing research since. Presumably, he would be pleased with present tendencies for graduate students to marry, the evidence that married students and particularly those with children did well in school, and the continuance of educational acceleration in some colleges—as against the "monastic" spirit in the English universities which he bitingly criticizes. It is also interesting, in connection with Galton's arguments against late marriages, that on Visher's 1946 questionnaire, 70 percent of the starred scientists recommended that their students marry earlier than they did, and 79 percent that they have a child sooner (48, p. 546).

that both his father and an aunt collected geological specimens. Sometimes early accident played a part; another geologist went to school in an area abounding in interesting rock formations. Decision to become a scientist had been reached by 41 percent of Visher's scientists by the age of 16; evidently important factors have often operated early. That 45 percent of the fathers of these scientists were professional men implies a type of home environment that is culturally rich, with conditions favorable to such interests. There is occasional indication of the extent to which a combination of favorable influences could be exceptionally effective. Thus, the neurologist, Herrick, has told how a boys' nature study club, in pioneer Minnesota, seemed to have stimulated a large proportion of the boys belonging to careers in some phase of biological science (19). Most of this might perhaps be taken for granted. But in total it would seem to show that those with superior abilities are very much influenced by and indeed highly sensitive to their environment, that efforts to extend and better educational and other related advantages have indeed been productive, and that more intensive study of such influences and their judicious increase might be expected greatly to increase the amount of notable achievement which the Western world so desperately needs. Now, Russia seems to be making such efforts more than we.

CHARACTERISTICS AND DEVELOPMENT OF THE INDIVIDUAL NOTABLE ACHIEVER

The material immediately preceding has implied that the development of individuals who make notable achievements might sometimes be affected by highly specific influences or circumstances (as membership in a science club for youths) and was usually, in considerable part, the product of a fortunate combination of favorable influences rather than simply the inevitable emergence of innate genius. Such a position calls for supporting evidence in terms of particular cases. The case of Mozart (10), the best-known example of extraordinary musical precocity, will be examined first, since his type of genius might at first thought seem especially difficult to explain on a more environmentalist ground.

A form of case presentation that is very simple, yet far-reaching enough to include the wide variety of factors considered important, will be used. A first paragraph will attempt to outline the important socioeconomic and cultural features of the environment in which the case lived. His career will then be briefly sketched, with special reference to the development of the abilities and the influences which brought about the notable achievements. A final paragraph will attempt an appraisal of the traits, the molding influences, and the circumstances which combined to bring it about that the individual accomplished what he did.

An Extraordinary, Precocious Musician: Mozart (1756–1791)

Social, Economic, and Cultural Circumstances. Germany in the middle of the eighteenth century was a country of many small principalities. And in each court it was the fashion to have musicians and to have special compositions composed for special occasions. Mozart's father was a violinist and composer in the service of the archbishop of Salzburg. Mozart's sister, who was five years older than he was, was already a fledgling musician. Interest in music was part of the culture of the time in Western Europe, and a career in music offered opportunities for young people that were hardly obtainable otherwise, if they were not of the privileged class. However, as entertainers they might be expected to eat with the servants and were subject to the whims of their patrons.

Development. Mozart's home was permeated with music, and at an early age he was delighted with it and was encouraged by his family and family friends. At the age of 3, he shared his sister's harpsichord lessons. A year later he played minuets and composed. At 6 he was taken by his father on a musical tour with his sister to various German courts. Everywhere he went he received much attention and was considered to be a child prodigy. At 7 he went on tour again; Mozart sang, composed, and played on the harpsichord, organ, and violin. When he was 8, his father took him to England, where he played before the court and composed a symphony. To complete his son's musical education, his father took Mozart to Italy when the boy was 13; there he exhibited further his extraordinary talent of composing, and at the age of 14 he conducted the largest orchestra in Europe and received many honors. All through his middle and later teens, Mozart continued to compose prodigally, with great versatility and maturing excellence. However, the rewards for his compositions were often niggardly, and a new archbishop at Salzburg was not interested in music.

Another tour, when Mozart was 21 and no longer a child prodigy, brought inadequate financial returns; his mother died; a love affair went sour. At 26 he married a mediocre young woman. Financial problems mounted. Tours in the Europe of his time were exhausting. He was extraordinarily prolific in composing—a total of 626 items from the age of 4 until his death from typhoid at the age of 36—and exhibited constant musical growth and remarkable versatility, many of his works being among the greatest of all musical compositions.

Back of these extraordinary, precocious accomplishments was apparently a very likable, vivacious, and relatively unspoiled child; a young man of great sociability, earthy humor, and energy who enjoyed life and his art. His wife and children were apparently devoted to him. Many other musicians, notably Haydn, were his friends.

Appraisals and Interpretations. Mozart was a very precocious, alert, likable, and intelligent child (very sensitive to music and dextrous) who was brought up in a hothouse of music, with expert guidance and stimulating musical companionship from infancy. He lived in a world which gave recognition to music as to no other field of accomplishment open to persons of his class and had a feverishly active career under pressure of chronic financial need. Lack of physical vigor plus hardships due to his career and his times led to his death in mid-career.

In further explication of the point of view of the above case report, it is to be recalled that most famous musicians of about Mozart's time were precocious—indeed, precocity seems a common characteristic of musicians up to the present time. Handel played on the clavichord "when but an infant" and was composing by the age of 11; Chopin played in public when 8; Liszt, at 9; Verdi, at 10; Schubert, at 12. Mendelssohn was playing publicly and also composing by the age of 9, as was Debussy at 11 and Dvořák at 12. Yehudi Menuhin was a child prodigy, and a recent statement about the notable Russian violinist, Oistrakh, tells of a musical father who got a small violin for his 5-year-old son, intensive training, a (racial) situation making music perhaps the one field of opportunity, and soon a series of successes which swept his career forward.[6] All these youngsters undoubtedly were constitutionally of great musical potential. They were precocious and of superior general ability, were un- usually sensitive to musical sound and to rhythm, had exceptional motor coördination and finger dexterity, and possibly had some further un- defined special musical talent. But also an extraordinary powerful con- comitance of favorable circumstances pervaded all their formative years. At an early age they were exposed to conditions which favored the development of their musical talent. They lived in musical homes and received constant encouragement from family and friends. There was ample opportunity to practice their abilities, and excellent instruction and instruments were provided. In addition, there was social facilitation: family and friends shared and nurtured musical interests, and there were cumulative, powerful success experiences.

It is further to be noted that in different countries, at different times, similar total situations have developed cases of precocious superiority in other fields—as athletics in America (37).[7] The field may be more exclu-

---

[6] *Time,* November 28, 1955.

[7] Opportunities for success in athletics are available, as in no other field, even to those who are socioeconomically or racially handicapped. Often other members of the family are athletic and encourage and help the youngster. He can continually practice in a playground or even in a vacant lot. School or playground coaches give

sively intellectual. The extraordinary precocity of John Stewart Mill developed from influences very similar in nature to those fostering Mozart's extraordinary early talents (35). Under the tutelage of his father, he began the study of Greek at 3; at 8, he was reading Plato and beginning to study geometry and algebra; at 16, he was publishing controversial articles in political economy.

Notable and Dedicated Scientist: Marie Curie (1867–1934)

Social, Economic, and Cultural Circumstances.   In the middle of the last century Russian-dominated Poland felt itself in subjugation. However, a Pole could find in scientific work a field free of political pressures and giving contacts with university work in other countries; and there was then great interest in science throughout Europe. Marie was one of four children of a poor Polish secondary school science teacher (Dr. Sklodowski) who was ill, underpaid, and insecure under the Russian government. An older sister was also ambitious and studied medicine in Paris (9).

Development.   Even as a small child Marie showed scientific interest which was nurtured by her father and his scientific books and materials. From early childhood she was brilliant, happy, healthy, sensitive, active in play. In her youth she was involved in a students' revolutionary organization, and the brother of a friend was executed for conspiring against the Russian government. This tragedy made a deep impression on her. Her older sister's desire to study medicine had priority in the family and, therefore, for four years after graduation from the Gymnasium, Marie worked as a governess. An incipient romance with the son of the family for whom she worked was blocked by his family.

Finally her turn came to enter the Sorbonne; she lived in a cold attic, half starved, absorbed in her study of mathematics and physics. After several years of this hard, relentless life, when 28, she married Pierre Curie, already known as a physicist, and began with him the long and arduous investigation which led to the discovery of radium. Their laboratory was an unheated shack in which they worked 44 months over a boiling, acrid cauldron extracting a precious decigram of the element from tons of ore. She and Pierre then became world famous and were awarded a Nobel prize, but they were nevertheless denied a laboratory in which to continue their work.

Pierre was accidentally killed in traffic, but Marie continued her research. Then the First World War broke out. With characteristic energy she devoted her skill and her invaluable radium to establishing radiological clinics for treatment of the wounded. Then she returned to her scientific investigations. By

---

expert instruction. Other youngsters admire and encourage. Frequent contests give challenge and success experiences. A special type of athletic champion appears especially to exhibit the importance of strong motivation with superior training and social facilitation—the victim of some handicap such as polio whose great effort to recover carries clear through to great superiority, as in swimming.

now she was an internationally known figure, playing a part not only in science but in public thought. Slowly her great efforts brought exhaustion; also, she was scarred from radium burns and almost blinded. She continued working practically until her death.

Appraisals and Interpretations. Marie Curie was of superior intellectual capacity and came from a professional family. From early childhood, interest in and knowledge of science was nurtured by the father's interest, instruction, library and equipment. At a later age she was stimulated by study at the Sorbonne and marriage to a scientist. She was powerfully motivated by interest, frustrations in Poland, ambition to make good in Paris, and the stimulus and opportunities resulting from the fame of discovering radium at the age of 31.

Again there is at an early age strong and continuing nurture of interest and ability; social facilitation from family, friends, and husband; ambition stemming from social class and frustration; and the powerful stimulation of great success. There were sundry possible hazards to her career on the way. Suppose the romance when tutoring had flowered, marriage in Paris had been to a man of different interests, or the long toil of the project had failed! Probably anyone experienced in graduate supervision has known a girl whose brilliant promise ended in marriage, or a compulsively hard-working young woman whose health broke, or a devoted student who put every energy for months or even years into a brilliant research idea which obstinate nature finally showed was wrong.

A Leader Whom War Rescued from Failure: General Grant (1822–1885)

Social, Economic, and Cultural Circumstances. Grant was born in pioneer Ohio in 1822; his lifetime was a period of rapid increase in population, of great economic development, of political ferment, and of two wars—with Mexico and between the states. The father was a vigorous, tight-fisted businessman who made money as a tanner and trader, was argumentative, was politically of some influence, and had ambitions to have his sons make good (29, 55).

Development. As a child, Grant was apparently somewhat precocious, shy with strangers, and an outstanding horseman. His father was proud of his adeptness with horses and assigned the boy a certain amount of haulage business which took him about more widely than most youngsters and gave him an understanding of problems of transportation in his day. After brief schooling in the locality and an academy, his father obtained for him an appointment at West Point, where he was noted for his horsemanship but was otherwise little noticed; he graduated twenty-fourth in a class of 39. Very soon thereafter he saw service in the Mexican War, where his capabilities in supply were recognized by assignment to the Quartermaster's Corps; his total record was good but not distinguished. Before going to Mexico he had become engaged to the sister of a West Point friend and married her after his return. He was next assigned to routine Army post duty in Detroit and then on the Pacific Coast.

Post life in the West was one disappointment after another. The salary was too meager to have his family with him. Business ventures aiming to supplement his income were failures. Frontier life and frustration led to increased alcoholism. After resigning from the Army and returning to his family he failed as a farmer, as a real estate salesman, and even did poorly as a clerk in the leather store of his younger brothers. At the start of the Civil War Grant at first had trouble getting back into the Army; he drilled a company but wasn't elected captain, got a job as clerk in the Illinois governor's office, finally was made colonel of a volunteer regiment because no other man with military training could be found, and then was made brigadier general because a local congressman needed to show his constituents that he could do something for somebody.

However, Grant soon demonstrated that he could quietly bring discipline in a camp of recruits, was highly competent in vital matters of transport and supplies, was energetic, and continually drove ahead. He had an obsession from childhood against ever turning back to retrace a road, and he finally led armies totaling a million men to victory. After the Civil War he was elected to the presidency. He suffered from political scandals which resulted from placing too much confidence in friends, but in other matters he made wise decisions. At a later date he went bankrupt in business, again because of too much confidence in friends; but courageously restored the family fortune by writing his memoirs while slowly dying of cancer.

Appraisals and Interpretations. Grant was a man of good though not outstanding ability (his letters for the most part are commonplace, and apparently his military campaigns were more competent than brilliant) whose boyhood experiences in the frontier, training at West Point, and service in the Mexican War were all highly relevant to the needs of the War Between the States; whose career was almost wrecked by the frustrations of the abominably disorganized between-wars Army; whose experience, personality, and willingness to learn more than brilliance won the Civil War; and who lived out his later years in a courageous prominence resulting from his military victories.

What, now, does Grant's career contribute to an understanding of abilities? It would seem to show, first, that a man who until almost 40 had shown practically no evidence of great abilities may, nevertheless, accomplish great things; second, that, pragmatically, "ability" may be more a combination of persistence with adaptability and common sense than great intellectuality; third, that great opportunity may in pragmatic fact make great abilities when otherwise there might have been progressive dilapidation.

Editor and Author: William Allen White (1868–1944)

Social, Economic and Cultural Circumstances. In the last half of the last century Kansas changed from a frontier area and moved through boom and bust episodes into a midwestern state of established communities and culture. Population was on the move, the economy was essentially prosperous, politics was lively, education was highly regarded, and a tangy journalism and literature were nascent. White's father was a restless, highly gregarious, short, fat man who after sketchy medical training had in 1868 settled in a little Kansas town as physician and storekeeper. His wife was a former teacher who had managed in the face of hard times to obtain part of a college education. Another son died in early childhood, and "Willy" remained the only child. The father was shrewd, prosperous, locally prominent, interested in politics, and elected to local offices (*21, 50*).

Development. Willy was a very healthy, plump, precocious baby who was already reading before going to school and was frequently read to by his mother from a library which included Dickens and other similar authors. He also displayed musical ability at an early age. While still a child of 3 or 4, he sang to customers in his father's store. When he was 10, he was printer's devil in a local newspaper plant for the summer. He was at that time already a small boy-about-town, known and liked by everyone, and into everything. His father died when he was 14.

At 16 he entered a struggling little church college at Emporia, Kansas, belonged to a "literary society," and made many friends who surprisingly often later became prominent. Then for some months he held a newspaper job for 12 hours a day which started at three dollars a week. At 18 he went to the University of Kansas, was class poet, wrote for the student magazine, was correspondent for newspapers, joined a fraternity, got into a minor scrape, and did not obtain a degree because he could not pass solid geometry. Thereupon he returned to newspaper work, being three years on the famous Kansas City *Star,* married a school teacher at 25, and bought the little Emporia *Gazette* because he liked small Kansas college towns and because an invitation to go to New York did not seem best for his wife's health. He also began writing magazine articles, got under way a book of verse, and in 1896 (when a stout 32) wrote the famous editorial "What's the Matter with Kansas?" which rocketed him to national fame. In that same year he published a novel, shortly issued with a friend a volume of verse, and visited Mark Hanna and other national political figures. In the next few years he turned out a succession of books, magazine articles, and continuingly lively editorials. He was *the* small-town editor of the country and became close friends with Theodore Roosevelt and other historical personages.

In World War I (when 49) he went abroad with his old friend the former governor of Kansas as a Red Cross representative and saw much of the last days of the war and very much of the peace negotiations. Returning home, he shrewdly continued in the little Kansas city and in his later years became a sage often quoted. He fought the Klu Klux Klan, wrote his autobiography, and continued active practically to the end of his long life.

Appraisals and Interpretations. White was a man of much ability and great sociability who grew up with the Midwest and was in intimate contact with its growth. He was prosperous and happy in his childhood home and the home of his adult life and was a tremendous worker who seemed to do every-thing effortlessly (in his seventies he spoke casually of dictating his autobiog-raphy every day beginning at 7:30 in the morning and then going to his office for a full day's work). In his later years he moved naturally into a position of national leadership.

Here, there does not seem to be any membership in a minority group, no long frustrations, and no special intensive training or extraordinary special gift. Rather there is zestful, overflowing expression of a very lively mind in a world that White greatly enjoyed and in which he operated easily because he felt so comfortable.

These grossly compacted attempts at biography will doubtless seem to the reader as crude and inadequate as a child's drawings. However, in part because they include only the gross features, certain characteristics seem to emerge with some clarity. The first is this: aside from their great accomplishments and traits associated therewith, these people seem much indeed like the rest of us! And this is no illusion resulting from the meagerness of the case summaries. The more one reads the extensive biographical volumes, letters, and other matter that reveal the day-by-day self, the more it becomes evident that these notable people have traits mostly like the mass of humanity. Until one gets over into the area of their great achievements, their abilities seem much the same as those of many people one knows. And one is reminded of Wechsler's argument that people really do not differ very much in height, quick-ness, sensory acuity, or (in the ages when one does such things) the time it takes to run 50 yards. Nor is the very able person so very much su-perior to the average individual in memory span or time needed to learn 30 lines of verse. To be sure, the situation may be such that a little su-periority is made very important. Running the 100-yard dash a fraction of a second faster than another man may win an Olympic crown. The general who wins a battle may have only a little more ability (or luck) than the commander who is defeated. A little more ability may some-times get a person over a threshold into an area of much enlarged po-tentialities; a dull child who can learn to read can do much more than a child who is so dull that reading is beyond him, though in most respects (and on a mental test) the differences between the two may not be very great. Somewhat similarly, a little superiority over other able people might carry a great achiever over a threshold into modes of thinking which yielded solutions to baffling problems.

However, there is another way by which a person may rise to a higher level of integrations—by persistent and intensive effort and practice. A person learning to read may first learn letters, but soon he reads words and even phrases, and not so much words as ideas. Certainly the youthful Mozart must have been very bright, auditorially sensitive, and of great dexterity. But those gifts were fostered from infancy in almost every hour, in almost every association, with almost every advantage of expert guidance, and with almost every encouragement and recognition that the Europe of his time afforded! The opinion is ventured that in his and other cases the importance of such nurture has been given too little thought.

Suppose Mozart had been born to a middle-class couple in present-day America! The kindergarten teacher would have shooed him away from the piano out onto the playground to get big-muscle exercise and socialize with the other little children. In elementary school, the parents would have been told of the grave dangers of advancing a child beyond his age group, the unhealthiness of too much association with adults, the grave risks to health and to personality of any program of public appearances. Summers at camp would have involved little opportunity for the development of musical virtuosity; the college advisor would have urged *not* majoring in music but rather getting a broad education; and other students would have regarded piano players a bit contemptuously. Might he, at 35, have been only a bright young junior executive who could be very musically entertaining at an office party!

In short, great achievers usually seem differentiated by having had exceptionally rich, sometimes intensive, preparatory experiences (not simply schooling), often from early childhood. There was strong interest that was fostered by associates and furthered by successes; social motivations became increasingly powerful. There were opportunities; the stories of these great achievers also include evidence that when opportunity is lacking there may be (as with Grant) gross failure. Interests and emotional dynamics will be systematically considered later in the text, and educational problems will be discussed in Chapter 5. But it seemed desirable at this point to emphasize that great achievements, and the great abilities which bring them about, are products of the individuals' total development—not simply or usually even primarily the result of superior intellectual endowment.

Finally, these sketches of people of great accomplishments give some intimations as to how varied abilities may be and how much broader in scope they are than narrowly intellectual capacities. Mozart's composing was not simply an intellectual exercise; there was involved exquisite auditory and kinesthetic sensitivity and deep feeling for human joys and troubles—which indeed he knew. The unrelenting drive of Grant's campaigns appeared to be partly a product of his intellectual awareness that they needed to be so, but it was also related to his boyhood conviction that one should never turn back on a road. White's abilities were more of social sensitivity and expression than of cold intellect. Does such broadening disintegrate the concept of ability? It is aimed at a correction of what is believed to be an overemphasis on the intellectual and statistical aspects of that concept.

A PROGRAM FOR THE DEVELOPMENT OF MORE, AND MORE NOTABLE ACHIEVERS

There is presently a need for more scientists and engineers, as well as for more competent leaders in almost every important field. Reports from Russia indicate that they are training more scientists and engineers than is this country. Do the materials in the preceding pages offer suggestions for helping to meet these needs?

An obvious first step is to find those having the constitutional potential for notable achievement. As mentioned in the previous chapter, able youngsters are really more numerous in the middle and lower classes[8] than in the upper; the proportion of them in the upper classes is higher, but the total population in these privileged groups is relatively small. Those who search for bright children should always keep this in mind. But it follows that the number of capable adults in the middle and lower classes must also be great. Means for finding them, including tests suitable for adults, as emphasized in the preceding chapter, would seem much needed.

But once these people of high potential are found, what is to be done with them? One of the writers has had opportunity to watch two very well-known athletic coaches build up their teams. How these coaches do not only scout for promising youngsters, but entertain them in friendly groups and make social contacts for them, get them jobs (or financial aid) if needed, take care of them if injured or ill, give them highly individualized training, give opportunities as they become ready for them, see that they have publicity, and assure them jobs when they are through! Why

[8] In spite of their less favoring circumstances, more college graduates actually appear to come from these classes. Wolfle has estimated that of 1000 children in this country the fathers of 65 are in professional or semiprofessional occupations and of these 28 graduate from college; however, the fathers of 487 are in skilled or unskilled work and of these 39 so graduate. Of youngsters from professional homes, 43 percent graduate from college, as compared to only 8 percent from homes of skilled or unskilled workers. But this last group nevertheless produces the greater number of graduates (53, p. 162).

don't people on school and college staffs do the same for potential scientists or mathematicians? The suggestion is ventured that by such means the interests and abilities mentioned in the preceding pages might be fostered (37). The idea will be returned to. But how about the superior adult who is as yet largely undiscovered? Perhaps the contrast between two able college deans (now both dead) may have some relevance. One worked almost entirely through his departmental chairmen and his executive committee made up of them; the remainder of the faculty rarely saw him. The other had various members of each department serve on the executive committee, frequently had informal groups in his office for consultation on this or that matter, often dropped in at this or that man's office, ate lunch with him at the faculty club, and had funds available to help on any research project which seemed worthy. It need hardly be said that the second dean discovered and fostered talent more effectively. How to find and develop the able man lost in mass industry is doubtless another problem. But many unions seem to do that, as will be pointed out in Chapter 6.

Mental Disease and Ill-Health as Indicative of Change and Decline with Age

The preceding pages have dealt with evidence of maximal human potentialities, as indicative of changes through the life span and also as a topic of the greatest importance for society—and for Western society in particular if it is to keep its leadership. Now the contrasting question is as to relevant phenomena in mental breakdown, again as indicative of age changes in mentality and personality and also as a major social problem. In 1950, nearly three-quarters of a million persons in this country were in hospitals for the mentally ill. Many other mild cases were not in institutions, and additional great numbers were unstable or neurotic though not mentally deranged. Obviously, mental health is a topic of great importance.

INCIDENCE OF MENTAL DISEASE THROUGH THE LIFE SPAN

Many persons mentally ill are not in institutions, and some are cared for in nursing homes or private hospitals or "retreats." However, data from state mental hospitals probably give a general picture of the frequency and types of mental disease at different ages. Figure 53 shows that the first admission rate to these institutions rises from a low of 2 per 100,000 for persons under 15 years of age to 87 in the age group 35 to 44 years, levels off between 85 and 90 for persons 45 to 64 years, and then climbs rapidly to a high of 203 at ages 65 years and over. The figure also gives information about age differences in first admissions for various disorders. For example, in the age range 15 to 54 years, schizophrenia and manic-depressive psychosis predominate. During the next decade of life

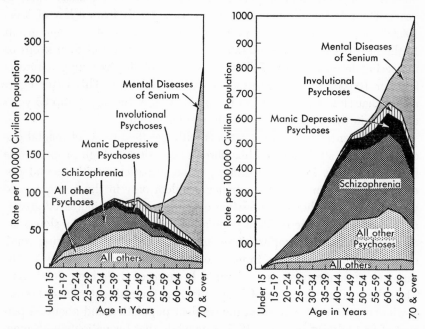

Figure 53.   First Admission Rates for Selected Diagnoses by Age, to State Hospitals for Mental Disease, United States, 1950.

Figure 54.   Resident Patient Rates for Selected Diagnoses by Age, State Hospitals for Mental Disease, California, Louisiana, Michigan, Nebraska, Ohio, Pennsylvania, Virginia, 1950. (Figures 53 and 54 were data presented by M. Kramer, Chief, Biometrics Branch, National Institute of Mental Health, Bethesda, Maryland, in "A Discussion of the Gerontological Problems of Mental Hospital Populations" at the Session on Psychological and Social Sciences of the 1955 Gerontological Society meetings.)

the involutional, syphilitic, and alcoholic psychoses attain considerable importance. In the sixties, the cerebral arteriosclerotic and senile psychoses assume prominence, and these mental diseases of the senium continue to rise in frequency until the end of the life span.

The characteristics of the resident patients (that is, the population resident in state mental hospitals on any one day) are considerably different from those of the first admissions. Although resident patient data by age, sex, diagnosis, and length of stay are not available for the United States as a whole for 1950, there are such data available for 7 states, as shown in Figure 54. The resident population consists essentially of patients hospitalized for long periods of time. Thus, one-quarter of the patients resident at the end of 1950 had been hospitalized for more than 16 years, one-half for more than 8 years, and three-quarters for more than 2½ years. The rate for all mental disorders rises steeply from a low of 3 per 100,000 population under 15 years to 70 in the 15 to 24-year age group. In the next decade of life the rate more than doubles and then keeps on increasing in each of the following decades of life, reaching a rate of 906 per 100,000 in the age group 65 years and over. This latter figure means that close to 1 percent of the population in the age group 65 years and over in these states is in a state mental hospital.

Age differences in resident patients with specified types of mental disorders are also shown. The schizophrenics constitute a high proportion of resident patients in all age groups, whereas patients with mental diseases of the senium become a major problem only in the age group 65 years and over. Although admissions of senile cases have increased greatly in the last decade, the resident population consists largely of a slowly accumulated core of schizophrenic patients, who are admitted during youth or early maturity and stay, in many cases, for the rest of their lives. The turnover of senile cases is very rapid because of their high death rate. Thus the median duration of hospitalization for resident schizophrenics —who constitute 46 percent of the resident population and about 24 percent of first admissions—was 10.5 years while that for patients with mental diseases of the senium—who constitute 11 percent of the resident population and 26 percent of the first admissions—was 2.4 years.

Since physical debilities and chronic conditions such as arteriosclerosis rapidly increase in old age, cases of senile dementia with cerebral arterial hardening and of psychoses with heart failure, kidney disease, anemia, or infections might especially be expected then (31). But sickness and death among relatives and friends, loss of job and status, loneliness, and hopelessness are also most frequent in elderly people. Involutional psychoses in women around the age of the menopause might be largely a product of organic changes then; but often this is also a time of stress because of children leaving home and other readjustments and stresses in living. Possibly surprising is the smaller total number of first admissions around 50 than either after *or* before. But is not the explanation quite probably that problems of age are not yet reached, and those of youth are largely passed? First admissions in the twenties and thirties are most commonly for the "functional" schizophrenic and manic depressive psychoses and possibly result largely from the many problems met in getting started in adult life. Perhaps, in terms of the concepts of this chapter, these mental diseases might be described as often exhibiting, and indeed often substantially caused by, great incoördination in operation of those factors which, when operating powerfully together, helped produce the individuals of great achievement considered in the first part of this chapter. But may these factors be important in age? Or are mental disturbances then presumably almost always mental declines and a result of degenerative changes in the nervous system? Again, examples may be of help in elucidating these questions.

SAMPLE CASES OF MENTAL ILLNESS

The variety of cases of mental illness and their complexity make both minimal sampling and brief summary of dubious value. But the following résumés may somewhat aid in showing age differences and developmental factors of importance for the larger issues of this volume. All are Americans and roughly of middle class, with all that these general facts may imply regarding socioeconomic and cultural backgrounds. Only their development with special reference to their illness need therefore be summarized. The crises are clearly of the total personality and so are a compound of many factors, most of them considered later, as in connection with Chapter 8 on emotional development. They are presented here because it is believed that they contribute to an understanding of broader concepts regarding development of abilities.

An Acute Manic or Excited Psychotic Episode in a College Student

Charles' father was a big, domineering, successful, and somewhat alcoholic lawyer; his mother was quiet and gentle and subject to spells of depression. A maternal great-aunt had had a number of attacks of depression for which she had been hospitalized, and a paternal great-aunt had had a manic episode following an operation.

In childhood, Charles was something of a mother's boy, and she did not send him to school until he was 8. As a boy, he was roly-poly and clumsy at sports and was much derided for this by the father. This attitude greatly disturbed the youngster, especially since he idolized his father and admired his easy confidence and physical assurance. In secondary school he was interested in dramatics, and this pleased his mother, but his father frequently criticized him for lack of athletic interests. A younger brother was athletic and became his father's favorite. And a very intelligent and attractive but moody younger sister seemed to Charles to be taking his place in his mother's affections.

Charles attended three different colleges each for one year, giving no good reason for this restlessness. In the third college he went out for football, and in his second year he made the team but was injured and was unable to continue playing. That winter and spring he was irritable and restless and could not sleep. For that summer, he had a position in a boys' summer camp. On the train going there he attracted attention by his excessive and loud talkativeness and exaggerated playfulness. In camp he was overactive. He nearly upset a boat by his horseplay, went about in the middle of the night making noise and shooting blank cartridges which set the camp in a turmoil, and otherwise carried on. The sheriff was finally called in and had him taken to a state hospital.

There he was overactive and showed flight of ideas, but gradually he calmed down. As a result of wise treatment, and his own good intelligence, he became interested in and understanding of probable causes of his difficulties. He came to feel that conflicts with his father and in his attitudes toward that parent (whom he both admired and feared), a growing feeling of being displaced in the affections of both parents, and frustration when his incipient athletic career was brought to a stop all contributed to his psychotic episode. The football injury was cleared up, and the recreational therapist maintained and extended the range of his recreational interests. It was arranged that at discharge he would go for a while to his grandmother's home, where he would be the man of the house and there would be no conflicts of authority or long-standing tensions. He returned to school and became an excellent athlete as well as a good student. (5, pp. 84–98.)

The family history suggests a cyclothymic constitution, a tendency toward unusually lively and depressed moods. Charles' own history shows a lifelong ambivalence toward his father, incompatible loyalties to both father and mother, and growing feelings of insecurity in relations with both. Then—just when athletic success seemed somewhat to mitigate the situation—the injury occurred which brought him up short. The episode —sort of a psychic fever—took its nature from his constitutional temperament and his youth and blew itself out with little damage and little likelihood of recurrence, because (in contrast to the next case) problems were largely solved and opportunities were available for a satisfactory future.

A Long-Developing Mental Illness in the Prime—Schizophrenia, Paranoid Form

Ricardo's father was a small-town businessman who was, for a while, fairly successful and well known. Ricardo was physically small during childhood and adolescence and was timid and shy, but he took many trips in the woods with his father who seemed to have been an introvert also. The boy began music lessons when 5 and became quite musical. Early in high school he planned a career in medicine and read many medical books. But when Ricardo was in secondary school, the father failed in business, the home was lost, the parents were divorced, and the mother began clerking in a store. The youth was very much upset. All plans for a medical career, or for any further education, seemed blocked. He worked for a while in a factory, then ran a music store, and also played a guitar and a saxaphone in a night club. In the meantime his height jumped from 5 feet 4 inches at 17 to 6 feet 1 inch at 20, this marked growth spurt being related to a late pubescence; he reported that in high school his smallness and immaturity had been very distressing to him and that he was not adult sexually until 20. The music store failed, and he worked for several years on the road, in the meantime playing with dance bands and eating and sleeping irregularly. At 26 he accepted the paternity of a child but did not marry the mother until after another child was born. Then, his wife became ill and was found to have multiple sclerosis.

When the Second World War began, he worked in a defense plant and did well. After a few months he was made an officer in the guard force. He now felt himself an enemy rather than a friend of his former co-workers. And following tactless reporting of some irregularities, he was disliked by some of his superiors. He became increasingly uncomfortable, developed duodenal ulcers, quit his job, left home, nostalgically returned to a town he had liked as a boy with his father, and worked briefly in a number of places. Finally, he came back to his wife and children. But now inevitably things were different. He became increasingly uncomfortable, felt his family to be hostile, the unions against him, and people spying on him. By the age of 40 he was convinced that his family had it in for him, declared his daughter not his own child, threatened to kill his wife—and was committed to a state hospital, where a diagnosis of paranoid dementia praecox was made. (5, pp. 52–70.)

Somewhat in contrast to the previous case, everything cumulatively seemed to go against Ricardo: physical inadequacy in childhood with too close association with father and little with other children, gross disruption of home life and of plans following the father's business failure and divorce, much delayed pubescence and then sex irregularity, his wife's and his own illnesses, irregularity of employment during the depression, and troubles with both other workers and superiors after a good job was finally found. Difficulties seemed inexorably closing in on him from every side; there seemed no way out on any issue. Some rationalizing delusions, and a slow dementia, seemed almost inevitable.

A Psychotic Episode in a Man of 67

Mr. M. was an American who for 27 years had been works manager in a manufacturing concern in England, in which position he had shown excellent ability and great tact in handling management-employee relationships. His general health was good, but recently he had shown some symptoms of prostatic enlargement, with occasional pus in the urine. Several days before a dinner in his honor on the occasion of his retirement, he complained of sleeping little, was restless, argumentative, and had dizzy episodes. At the dinner, the speech he was called upon to give was rambling.

A few days later, he suddenly made up his mind to return to America. On the morning of sailing he was found not yet to have a ticket nor to have packed his baggage. On the boat he became increasingly confused and drank too much. Upon landing in New York he lost his landing ticket, argued with customs officials and tried sending a cablegram about a murder he declared had been committed on the boat. The day after arrival he rode around in a taxi, was found neither to know where he wanted to go nor to have enough money to pay for his ride, and was taken to the police station by the driver. His relatives in this country were notified.

He showed increasing overactivity but was willing to enter a mental hospital, where he remained three weeks. At first he was irritable, slept poorly, had many ideas of reference; he showed generalized arteriosclerosis, high blood pressure, enlarged prostate, and pus in urine. After the first three days there, he showed marked improvement. Blood pressure dropped and illusions disappeared and came to be regarded with amusement. The diagnosis was "essential hypertension, generalized arteriosclerosis; hypertensive crisis with symptomatic psychosis of the delirious type." The patient recovered and has adjusted well in this country. (30, pp. 234–238.)

Mr. M. had a psychotic episode which might, perhaps, at first have been regarded as the beginning of an arteriosclerotic dementia; but the recovery under careful and tactful treatment makes clear that this was only a flare-up of certain chronic physical conditions of the older years brought about by emotional stress plus a minor physical crisis. As stated by the psychiatrist reporting this case, "Many patients show great mental changes thought to be due to advancing years, yet at autopsy only moderate pathological changes of the brain are noticeable, and patients actually having marked cerebral lesions often have the ability to adjust and meet environmental demands."

Senile Dementia in a Woman of 80

Mrs. X. was an elderly married woman who, until the age of 80, had been in excellent health and seemed to get along well with her husband except for some friction because of his drinking. Then, increasing financial difficulties made it necessary for her to sell the home in which she had lived all her life and which had been deeded to her by her father. Her husband was then sent to the county infirmary, and she went to live with relatives.

In the home of the relative she became increasingly upset and couldn't understand why she was there. Up to this time she had seemed younger than her years. Now she neglected her appearance, seemed to age very markedly in a short time, and became physically feeble, having several falls. She was very restless, sometimes screamed at people, and didn't recognize her relatives. Upon admission to a state hospital she showed marked impairment of memory, was disoriented and irritable, rapidly grew weaker physically, and died of pneumonia. Autopsy showed considerable but not extreme degenerative changes in the central nervous system. However, these changes must have been going on for some time—back when Mrs. X. seemed in excellent health and was getting along well. But when, after a long lifetime of established living, house and husband and independence all went at once, a dementing condition soon began and rapidly progressed. (23, p. 302.)

Onset and progress of senile dementia may be much more gradual than with Mrs. X., but relations to the burden and crises of age may still be fairly apparent. A leading geriatrician writes, "While senile psychosis is a disease, much of it seems to be a giving up to the accumulation of years" (31, p. 73). And again, "Senile dementia . . . is largely a disease of atrophy, of disuse, of giving up in despair to life and its problems. Men who cannot adjust to retirement can get it; so can . . . those who never recover from dependency brought on by an accident or illness" (31, p. 76). And dementia appears to have been averted or at least lessened by "rehabilitation back into a job" of aging people after accident or illness and by finding new areas of useful endeavor for those who are retired.

Moreover, recent very practical experiments have shown that even long-standing cases of "dementia" could be largely rehabilitated. Thus, in the Topeka State Hospital, 40 percent of the patients were aged individuals who were "silent, remote, incontinent." But of 74 in one ward 70 were gotten back on their feet, and their interest in life was somewhat revived by an intensive program of enticements, stimulations, and encouragements into social contacts and activities and by rehabilitation of physique and morale, in which psychiatrists, occupational therapists, psychologists, nurses, and attendants all worked concertedly together. Largely similar efforts in institutions in Minnesota and Pennsylvania have actually returned a few elderly cases to living in the community, and other cases have improved sufficiently to enable them to get out of bed, look after themselves, and even help around the ward (22, 54).

The four cases just summarized ranged in age from 20 to 80. In various respects, they showed age differences in reaction to stresses and in total disease picture. The activity of the youngest at the height of the psychosis was not only so excessive that it could hardly have been maintained by the two oldest cases or even the man of 40, but the 20-year-old also showed an exuberance of mood and what seemed like a juvenile jocularity that was different from the obviously anxious agitations of the older patients. The differences in these cases are partly to be ascribed to differences in the disease processes rather than to age; but different diseases are most common at different ages, and the same disease may at different ages show somewhat different characteristics. The stresses met at the different ages were very different in nature and severity. All at once, the old woman's long-established and very limiting pattern of life was destroyed, and there was nothing for her to look forward to. The young man's problems were relatively very minor. The major problem of relations with his parents was already being left behind as he moved into young manhood, and opportunities for further education and for career seemed wide open.

All this, as mentioned earlier, involves total personalities and so involves topics to be discussed later—especially, changes in motivations and in emotions through the life span. But these cases do seem to illustrate certain concepts regarding abilities—as broadly conceived in this and the preceding chapter. It would seem hardly to be doubted that the old woman's inabilities were in large part a product of degenerative changes with age in the central nervous system and more generally in the entire organism. But even though the 67-year-old man appears to have shown rather more evidence of arterial hardening and other physical change, he recovered from his psychosis. Both had had only meager education, and both seemed to have gotten along reasonably well up to the time of the crisis. But she had lived all her life in the same little community and even in the same house! He had traveled much more, even to another country. He had plans and resources for the future, but she had neither.

Somewhat similarly, the 40-year-old dementia praecox case had an unusual adolescent growth, and obscure organic pathology may have been involved in his psychosis. But his whole life was plagued with difficulties, many of them not his fault—his father's business failure and divorce, the abandonment of his plans for education and career which might at least have gone somewhat further, his vocational vicissitudes during the depression, his wife's progressing serious illness, and his difficulties with both workers and management at the defense plant. The previous chapter reported longitudinal studies indicating that vicissitudes in childhood might affect the growth of ability as measured. Cumulative vicissitudes from youth into middle life presumably might have their cumulative effects on the maintenance of ability over that time.

Regarding individuals of notable accomplishment, it was said earlier that, in most respects, they seemed very much like other people. Somewhat similarly, these people who had mental breakdowns appear very like persons one knows in everyday life who are getting along reasonably well. The derangements seem usually to have come more because of especially critical or cumulative stresses and perhaps only a little instability (which might have remained latent), rather than almost inevitably and because of gross constitutional inadequacy.

Indeed, a somewhat different approach to the problems presented by these cases would appear to lead more challengingly to essentially similar interpretations. Suppose the 80-year-old woman had had just a little more money so that she could have stayed in her old home, or a little financial and other help had permitted her to do so—might she have remained in placid sanity until death? Might some retirement counseling and arranging have prevented the older man's psychotic episode? Suppose Ricardo's father had not failed in business and the divorce had not followed, or the Great Depression not wiped out the young man's business and kept his whole life insecure and disorganized in the most determinative years of young adulthood—might he have got along after some fashion? Suppose (surely an intriguing thought) the college student had in his freshman year taken a course in psychology which wisely touched upon such problems as his, and there had been available a counselor who wisely counseled? Might his upset have been avoided? These considerations look ahead to later chapters on education, work life, emotion, and social relationships. But they have sufficient bearings at this point in the total volume that they seem worth mentioning here.

A Larger View of Abilities and Their Development

This chapter has ranged from genius to dementia; and it has treated these topics together in an effort to broaden concepts of ability. The question now is whether, after a review of all the material presented thus far, including the previous two chapters, any valuable larger concepts do emerge.

THE MAJOR CONTOUR OF GROWTH AND DECLINE OF ABILITIES THROUGH THE LIFE SPAN

The elementary fact that the first 15 to 20 years are growth years is evident from all the diverse material presented. It might even be said that these years are preëmpted by the growth processes to such an extent that neither accomplishments nor derangements occur then. But, of course, limitations of experience, motivation, and ego development, as well as of abilities, are major factors here. Almost all the material also concurs in showing decline to some degree in the later years.

However, two further major features are emphasized and somewhat reinterpreted. Data on both outstanding creative achievement and athletic championships indicated a prime from perhaps 20 to 45 and the very best decade around 25 to 35. Excellent though not top creative work was found extending into old age, as did leadership abilities which seemed greatest after 40. The prediction is ventured that improved tests will similarly show highest total score around 30 (as does the 1955 Wechsler even though it is believed to be too narrow in nature) with good levels maintained to old age and some subtests even rising. And it is believed that all these materials together have made two somewhat distinctive contributions (1) in bringing out the concept of the prime and the organic peak around 30 and (2) in providing evidence that abilities may continue at a good level thereafter even into old age.

THE DISTINCTIVENESS OF ABILITY PATTERNS AT DIFFERENT AGES

In Chapter 3 on abilities as tested, certain evidence was indicative of the fact that the pattern of abilities was somewhat different at the age of 5, for instance, as compared with 10 and that with increasing age, abilities became more diverse and less closely correlated. Tests also seemed to indicate that in the adult years certain abilities declined more rapidly than others, and that certain qualities in work, such as carefulness versus speed, changed with age. The data on notable achievements indicated differences in peak of accomplishment for creative work as compared with leadership. And different types of mental disease were found to occur most frequently at different ages. All this material considered together strongly suggests that different types of abilities grow and decline at different rates and that mentality changes as an aggregate, and perhaps more subtly in quality, at different stages of development from childhood to old age.

It has also been suggested that possibly concepts of ability may be too narrowly intellectual—that Mozart's genius, for example, involved exquisite sensitivities to sound and rhythm and also to human experiences and emotion, expressed in music, as well as extraordinary intellectual capacity in musical composition. And in contrast, the dementias mentioned a few pages back were not simply or primarily "loss of reason"; they were diseases of the entire personality, and the irrationality involved a variety of emotional and sensory and attitudinal as well as more narrowly intellectual phenomena. But if concepts of abilities were interpreted this broadly, then differences from one period of life to another would be expected even more.

THE GREAT IMPORTANCE OF NURTURE

The "classical" investigations of some 25 years ago led one to doubt the possibility of any substantial nurture of intellectual potential, but recent longitudinal studies have reported, as mentioned in Chapter 3, various instances where special circumstances in a child's growth seemed rather clearly to have affected his measured ability. And it has long been agreed that grossly unstimulating environments, as in isolated mountain districts, might slow if not stunt the development of functioning ability, but improvement of these conditions brings improvement in scores. In accord with the "classical" point of view of a quarter of a century ago, genius has been thought of as so predominately constitutional or at least mysterious that little might be done in the way of substantial programs for its nurture.

However, broad studies regarding the backgrounds, education, and other circumstances affecting people of notable accomplishment have shown certain common favoring factors, and there is a positive relationship between achievement in different areas or groups and the presence of these favorable circumstances. Intensive biographical studies of famous people have also shown how such factors may operate powerfully together. Similar studies of mental disease have increasingly shown the harmful effects of combining and continuing unfavorable influences. Clearly, if dementia can be prevented or lessened in severity, a major contribution to welfare will have been made. If judicious fostering can substantially increase the number of great achievements, the possibility is of general and, indeed, of international importance, especially now. For it would seem that much in current Russian efforts to increase the number of students in the sciences, to intensify training in these fields, and to enhance the status of both teachers and scientific workers might well make Russia preëminent in scientific achievement. If there are such possibilities, then surely the considerations mentioned above are not only important but are urgent. The topic will be returned to in Chapter 5.

Close study of life histories of both notable and psychotic individuals indicated their relatively small deviations from the average except when special influences operated to nurture either notable or disorganized abilities. And Wechsler's arguments for the relative smallness of individual differences (as compared to the greatly predominant importance often seemingly presumed) seem congruent. The comparative importance of nurture is thus stressed, and it is recognized that there is a possibility that many have sufficiently good innate capacities to develop superior abilities under favorable conditions.

Nurturing influences might be supposed to have their greatest potential in the growth years, and Mozart's childhood and youth illustrated well how powerfully they might combine to pervade the entire existence. However, when Grant was 40, the opportunities of the Civil War developed his abilities in leadership far beyond the stage they had reached up to that point. A commentator has remarked that, contrary to Lord Acton's dictum that power corrupts, the powers and responsibilities of the U.S. presidency seem sometimes to have made great men out of even relatively mediocre politicians. It is surely not minimizing the greatness of a man like Lincoln to say that he grew greatly in the presidency.[9] Curie and White seemed to have developed somewhat new capacities for international usefulness as their spreading fame and the crises of the First World War drew them out. In answer to the charge that terms are being used too loosely, as in saying that Grant's abilities grew after he was 40, it may again be replied that modern concepts of interaction between organism and environment would seem somewhat in congruence. At least it might be said that great new challenges and resources brought about remarkable, new, effective adaptations and learnings. Because of the increasing numbers of older people, it is important to give full consideration to their potentialities; perhaps new stimulations and opportunities might bring out more abilities than might be expected from many of them. The last chapter will return to these topics.

Why did the nature-nurture research of a quarter of a century ago unduly minimize the importance of nurture? Because (the writers would contend) such cumulating factors as the effects of radio and extensions of education, travel, and general mental horizon were too vast to be included in experimental designs. And intimate individual factors which emerged from the longitudinal records were missed. In addition, studies of great men have been unduly dominated by concepts of constitutional genius or special pathology.

[9] Suppose in 1860 that friends had not packed the galleries of the convention hall with Lincoln supporters, by giving them surreptitiously printed extra tickets, and he had not got the nomination. Might he have become simply what he seems initially to have desired—the junior senator from Illinois? And if not that, would he have ended simply as what he then almost was—the state's leading corporation lawyer? (44, pp. 157–212.)

Summary

Distinctive contributions to the understanding of abilities conceivably might be obtained from study of extreme manifestations of them—in notable accomplishment and in mental breakdown. And these topics are of great importance to society; consideration of them in the perspectives of development through the life span might yield somewhat new viewpoints regarding them. This chapter has thus sought to treat these topics very briefly, with the hope that interrelations may be found illuminating.

1. Data regarding notable achievements show that the best creative work tends to be done early in the prime—in the twenties and thirties—with remarkable poetry and musical compositions appearing sometimes in the teens. In general, creative workers tend to be precocious; and though they often continue productivity into old age, later work is likely to be less brilliant than that produced earlier. Also, those who produce most, usually begin early. Moreover, those who live to a good old age do not reach their creative peak later. The lengthening of life in modern times (and the increasing complexity in such fields as science) does not seem to postpone the age of best creative work or lengthen that period. Instead, it has recently tended to come earlier, perhaps because of better opportunities. Somewhat in contrast, great leadership comes at later ages —military leadership most often appearing in the forties and political and business leadership in the fifties and sixties. And leadership is now tending to come even later—perhaps because of longer life, seniority rules, and the like. Development and change in the nature of abilities through adult life seem clearly suggested. And favoring or handicapping factors in the environment are also shown to be increasingly important.

2. It was observed early that men of notable accomplishment are often related and that similar accomplishments may appear in families; the predominant importance of constitutional capacity seemed thus suggested. However, the similarly favorable environments and interests in these family groups could also be major factors in bringing about notable and similar accomplishments. There is much evidence that such accomplishments appear in those times and in those countries and localities where conditions are favorable. Intensive study of the careers of famous people emphasizes the extent to which congruent combinations of favorable factors have been important.

3. Mental disease, largely absent in childhood and early youth, grows steadily in frequency in earlier adult life, levels off in the later middle years, but mounts rapidly in frequency in old age. The functional dis-

organizations of schizophrenia and the manic-depressive extremes of mood are characteristic of earlier adulthood; anxieties and depressions are more typical of later middle life; senile deterioration is most common in old age. Constitutional inadequacy or instability appears to be a factor in some cases; identifiable physical disease is a cause in others; but it becomes increasingly evident that largely controllable stresses of life play at least a precipitating part. Study of individual cases emphasizes this last conclusion.

4. Consideration of the present along with the preceding chapter indicates that the intellectual capacities seem to grow until about 20 and are at their prime from about 20 to 45, with the peak around 30; under favorable conditions they remain good (though not quite at their prime) until old age. However, the nature and aggregate of abilities seem to change throughout life, with great leadership coming in the later adult years. For notable accomplishment, superior constitutional intellectual capacities are undoubtedly prerequisite; and constitutional weaknesses of some sort may be the major factor in mental disease. However, sundry influences seem to affect abilities more than was formerly realized. It appears that with a little more understanding of these matters and willingness to act accordingly a country might greatly increase its rate of scientific and cultural advance. It also seems that mental ill-health might, with wise effort, be much reduced. Chapter 5, Education Through the Life Span, will consider certain of these possibilities further.

BIBLIOGRAPHY

1. Anastasi, Anne, and Foley, J. P., Jr., *Differential Psychology* (rev. ed.), New York, Macmillan, 1949.
2. Anderson, Emily, *Letters of Mozart and His Family* (3 vols.), New York, Macmillan, 1938.
3. Barlow, F., *Mental Prodigies,* New York, Philosophical Library, 1952.
4. Bett, W. R., *The Infirmities of Genius,* New York, Philosophical Library, 1952.
5. Burton, A., and Harris, R. E. (eds.), *Case Histories in Clinical and Abnormal Psychology,* New York, Harper, 1947.
6. Cameron, N., *The Psychology of Behavior Disorders,* Boston, Houghton Mifflin, 1947.
7. Clow, H. E., and Allen, E. B., Manifestations of psychoneuroses occurring in later life, *Geriat.,* 1951, 6:31–39.
8. Cox, Catherine M., *The Early Mental Traits of 300 Geniuses,* Stanford, Stanford University Press, 1926.

9. Curie, Eve, *Madame Curie: A Biography* (translated by Vincent Sheean), New York, Doubleday Doran, 1938.
10. Davenport, Marcia, *Mozart*, New York, Scribner's, 1942.
11. Deford, Miriam A., *Psychologist Unretired: The Life Pattern of Lillian J. Martin*, Stanford, Stanford University Press, 1948.
12. Dysinger, R. H. (ed.), Mental health in the U.S., *Annals of the Amer. Acad. Polit. Soc. Sci.*, 1953.
13. Ellis, Havelock, *A Study of British Genius*, Boston, Houghton Mifflin, 1926.
14. Faris, R. E. L., Sociological factors in the development of talent and genius, *J. Educ. Sociol.*, 1936, 9:538–44.
15. Field, Minna, *Patients Are People*, New York, Columbia University Press, 1953.
16. Galton, Francis, *English Men of Science*, New York, Appleton, 1890.
17. Galton, Francis, *Hereditary Genius*, New York, Macmillan, 1914.
18. Greenhill, M. H. (ch.), *Evaluation in Mental Health*, Washington, D.C., National Institute of Mental Health, 1955.
19. Herrick, C. J., The young naturalists' society, *Sci. Mont.*, 1942, 66:251–258.
20. Hunt, J. McV., *Personality and the Behavior Disorders*, New York, Ronald Press, 1944.
21. Johnson, W., *William Allen White's America*, New York, Henry Holt, 1947.
22. Jones, Maxwell, *The Therapeutic Community*, New York, Basic Books, 1953.
23. Kaplan, O. J. (ed.), *Mental Disorders in Later Life* (rev. ed.), Stanford, Stanford University Press, 1956.
24. Kubie, Susan H., and Landan, Gertrude, *Group Work with the Aged*, New York, International Universal Press, 1953.
25. Lehman, H. C., *Age and Achievement*, Princeton, Princeton University Press, 1953.
26. Lehman, H. C., The exponential increase of man's cultural output, *Social Forces*, 1947, 3:281–290.
27. Lehman, H. C., Men's creative production rate in different ages and in different countries, *Sci. Mont.*, 1954, 78:321–326.
28. Lehman, H. C., The most proficient years at sports and games, *Res. Quart. Amer. Assn. Health Phy. Educ.*, 1938, 9:3–19.
29. Lewis, L., *Captain Sam Grant*, Boston, Little, Brown, 1950.
30. McGraw, R. B., Recoverable or temporary mental disturbances in the elderly, *J. Gerontol.*, 1949, 4:234–238.
31. Monroe, R. T., *Diseases in Old Age*, Cambridge, Harvard University Press, 1951.
32. Moses, Anna M., *Grandma Moses: My Life's History*, New York, Harper, 1948.
33. Mountin, J. W., Public health and the aging, *Public Health Reports*, No. 25, 1950, 65:795–802.
34. Murphy, G., *Personality: A Biosocial Approach*, New York, Harper, 1947.

35. Packe, M. St. J., *The Life of John Stuart Mill,* New York, Macmillan, 1954.
36. Pinner, M., and Miller, B. F. (eds.), *When Doctors Are Patients,* New York, W. W. Norton, 1952.
37. Pressey, S. L., Concerning the nature and nurture of genius, *Sci. Mont.,* 1955, *81:*123–129.
38. Pressey, S. L., *Educational Acceleration: Appraisals and Basic Problems,* Columbus, Ohio State University Press, 1949.
39. Schwrimmer, F., *Great Musicians as Children,* New York, Doubleday, 1930.
40. Stieglitz, E. J., Factors contributing to mental disease in the aged, *J. Gerontol.,* 1947, *4:*283–295.
41. Stump, A. J., *Champions Against Odds,* New York, Macrae Smith, 1952.
42. Terman, L. M., The discovery and encouragement of exceptional talent, *Amer. Psychol.,* 1954, *9:*221–227.
43. Terman, L., and Oden, Melita H., *The Gifted Child Grows Up: Twenty-five Years' Follow-up of a Superior Group,* Stanford, Stanford University Press, 1947.
44. Thomas, B. P., *Abraham Lincoln,* New York, Knopf, 1952.
45. Tsanoff, R. A., *The Ways of Genius,* New York, Harper, 1949.
46. Vischer, A. L., *Old Age, Its Compensations and Rewards,* London, Allen and Unwin, 1947.
47. Visher, S. S., Geography of American notables, *Indiana Univ. Studies,* 1928, *79:*15, 138.
48. Visher, S. S., *Scientists Starred in 1903–43: A Study of Collegiate Training: Birthplace, Backgrounds, Developmental Influences,* Baltimore, Johns Hopkins Press, 1948.
49. Wechsler, D., *Range of Human Capacities* (rev. ed.), Baltimore, Williams and Wilkins, 1952.
50. White, W. A., *The Autobiography of William Allen White,* New York, Macmillan, 1946.
51. Wiener, N., *Ex-prodigy,* New York, Simon and Schuster, 1953.
52. Wilson, R. C., Guilford, J. P., and Christinsen, P. R., The measurement of individual differences in originality, *Psychol. Bull.,* 1953, *50:*362–370.
53. Wolfle, D., *America's Resources of Specialized Talent,* New York, Harper, 1954.
54. Woods, W., Is there hope for the senile? *Menninger Quart.,* July, 1951, pp. 10–13.
55. Woodward, W. E., *Meet General Grant,* New York, Garden City Publishing Co., 1928.

CHAPTER 5 •

• Education Through the Life Span

TRADITIONALLY, education has been concerned with a relatively brief period in childhood and youth and has centered its efforts on acquisition of the tools of literacy and acquaintance with the local culture, with perhaps some preparation for vocation. But now the "pupils" may range from the two-year-old in nursery school to an octogenarian in a hobby class, and the tasks range from the tot's learning to put on his snowsuit and grandfather's use of the jigsaw to mother's Red Cross first-aid training and father's retraining program for defense industry. Fifty years ago, none of these last-mentioned individuals would have been "in school," and analogous instruction would have been received informally at home or in the neighborhood or a shop. This chapter will take the position that education has now become an important part of life at practically all ages, and if the education is to be effective, the development of a psychology of the life span that recognizes the potentialities and needs of each age is as essential as is a psychology of childhood for teaching in elementary school. The assertions will also be ventured, largely on the basis of certain matter in the previous two chapters, that the potentials of education are greater than usually assumed, that greater realization of its potentials is vital for this country in the cold war, and that for this purpose certain marked changes in education are called for.

The Growth of "Life-Span" Education

An increasingly complex and rapidly changing world needs more education to meet its problems. A longer life with different problems at different ages calls for continuing or recurrent education and reëducation. Gross data regarding the extent to which formal educational programs are now responding to these needs must first be considered.

LENGTHENING AND EXPANDING FULL-TIME EDUCATION

Table 14 shows for 20-year intervals, from 1890 to 1950, something of the extraordinary increase in this country of formal full-time education. In 1950, over a fifth (over 31 million) of the total population of the country was in full-time school. From 1890 to 1950 the population of the country increased over 2½ times. The number in elementary school did not keep pace because of the larger proportion of adults in the total population; the number in elementary school was not quite doubled. But the number in secondary school increased 18 times. The number of college students increased 17 times; the number of undergraduate degrees earned increased 28 times, and the number who earned graduate degrees increased 57 times. More recent figures show the postwar "baby boom" continuing and flooding the elementary schools, and expected numbers in secondary schools and colleges are far beyond educational facilities. Clearly, formal education is now an extraordinary total undertaking in this country.

TABLE 14. Numbers of Elementary, Secondary, and College Students at 20-Year Intervals from 1890 to 1950, and Numbers of Degrees Given

Enrollments	1890	1910	1930	1950
Elementary	14,181,415	18,528,535	23,717,796	22,201,505
Secondary	357,813	1,115,398	4,804,255	6,427,042
Collegiate	156,756	355,215	1,100,737	2,659,021
Degrees				
Bachelor's	15,539	37,199	122,484	432,058
Master's	1,009	3,771	15,043	58,183
Doctor's	126	420	2,216	6,633
U.S. Population	62,947,714	91,972,266	126,775,046	151,240,000

SOURCE: Adapted from U.S. Office of Education, *Statistical Survey of Education*, Washington, D.C., U.S. Government Printing Office, 1952, Chap. 1, pp. 7, 16, 35.

A different construing of largely the same material brings out a somewhat different feature of the educational picture as shown in Figure 55. In 1890 only about 7 percent of all young people of secondary school age were in secondary school, but by 1950 over 75 percent were; in the first year mentioned, some 3 percent of young people 18 to 21 were in college, but almost a fifth were in 1950. Evidently, a high school education is becoming the usual thing for American youth (though Figure 60 shows that the number who do not graduate from high school is still sufficiently large to suggest that the needs of many students are not being met), and college education is no rarity.

The figures mean not only an extraordinary increase in the amount of formal education obtained by the great mass of Americans and a great increase in the number who obtain some collegiate or technical training, but the extension

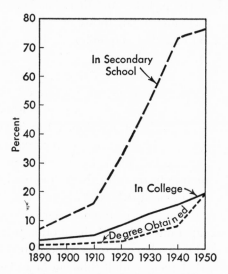

Figure 55. Percentage of Young People 14–17 Years Old in Secondary School, of Those 18–21 in Higher Education, of Those 21 Obtaining a College Degree. (Adapted from U.S. Office of Education, *Statistical Summary of Education,* Washington, D.C., U.S. Government Printing Office, 1953, Chap. 1, pp. 19, 38, 39.)

of full-time school results in postponement of full-time work and of adult responsibility. It means that a majority of American youth spend their middle and later teens in an adolescent life of school and play, a circumstance which is very different from life at this age 50 years ago in this country and today is largely unique to this country. Thus, Table 23 in Chapter 6 shows that around 1950, 83 percent of the boys and 78 percent of the girls 15 to 19 in England were at work, as compared to 45 percent and 26 percent of those at these ages in the United States. Abroad, those who are in school seem to be more a part of the adult culture, as in their concern with politics, and less a somewhat independent subculture absorbed in its own athletic and social interests.

ADULT EDUCATION AND "EDUCATION FOR AGING"

Not only have increasing proportions of young people been enrolled in established programs of secondary and higher education, but various special programs, often serving adults wholly or in part, have appeared.

Since World War II, there has been a "strong upsurge in adult enrollment in public schools. California doubled its adult enrollment in seven years" (*32*, p. 6). The number of students in federally aided vocational schools has grown from 265 in 1920 to 3,365,000 in 1950. In only the 10 years from 1940 to 1950, enrollments in evening and part-time programs in the distributive occupations (merchandizing) grew from 129,000 to 365,-000 (Statistical Abstracts, p. 131). And there has been an estimated "increase of adult participants in all forms of adult education from approximately 14 million in 1924 to 30 million in 1950 or over 100 percent increase" (*17*, p. 195).

More or less extensive vocational training may be required at almost any point in the work life. A big department store estimated that it spent $50.00 on an "orientation course" for each new employee. A change in process or machines may call for retraining. For instance, railway engineers learned about Diesels after having operated steam locomotives. During the last war, training programs were a major problem both in the services *and* in wartime industry (*21*). Now "more adults than ever before are having to change occupations at age 40, 50, or 60. Many others repeatedly have to take in-service training courses to keep up with the progress in their occupations." Methods have often been unusual—much use of instructional aids, lively conference procedures—the aim being to meet adult needs and challenge adult thinking in a vigorous manner. As mentioned in the first chapter, the return of married women to work is a major feature of the present day in this country and brings somewhat special training problems. Ewan Clague, Commissioner of Labor Statistics, has stated that "Those over 45 give the educational institutions of the country their greatest challenge. Vocational adjustments, guidance, and retraining are especially needed for those over 50" (*32*, pp. 51–52).

The adult education programs mentioned above have been predominantly for young or middle-aged adults. But there may well be significance in the fact that the longest chapter in the June, 1953 issue, on adult education, of the *Review of Educational Research* (*17*) deals with "Developments in education for later maturity." Some of these programs are in homes for the aged and others are in social centers for old people, in community recreation centers, in colleges, in public schools, and in churches. Some industries offer courses for employees who will soon retire on planning for retirement, hobbies, and making a will. A few of these various programs have been very broadly conceived, taking "the nature of action—seminars in which the students survey community needs for aging, report their findings to the community, and press for action" (*17*, p. 208). A major purpose may be rehabilitation, as in a home for the aged or a hospital. And the bibliography in the above-mentioned *Review* includes various factors—social adjustment, ability to learn, needs and interests—bearing on these various programs. Clearly, educational programs now extend over the life span, and evidently there is recognition that psychological study of development and change over the life span is of importance throughout.

Even the above extensive figures do not include all types of education. For very young children the nursery school offers a varied "curriculum." For youth, there are programs of part-time education not completely covered in the above statements. Under forms of adult education might well be included lyceums and forums and many programs of libraries, women's clubs, religious groups, and unions. Nor is the list yet finished. For instance, the number of pupils of private teachers of music is presumably large. There are courses and more informal instruction in automobile driving, flying, bridge, golf, etc. Documentary movies, TV shows (not to speak of radio and TV courses), and nonfiction books might also be considered as educational efforts. Anyhow, it seems clear that in one way or another all ages now "go to school" and that methods and materials used in such "universal" education are indeed various.

EDUCATION AND THE INTERNATIONAL CRISIS

It is generally recognized that American development of the atomic bomb—also of radar and other special devices—was of critical importance in winning the war and probably in restraining Soviet aggression in the years immediately following. Clearly, finding and training brilliant young people for such scientific and technological advances is of major importance in current international competition. In recent studies of man power much stress has been put upon the shortage in this country of engineers and scientific experts in certain areas important for defense. For instance, in 1954 Russia is said to have graduated 53,000 engineers, but the United States graduated only 24,000 (*16*, pp. 168–169).[1] It will

---

[1] "The Soviet Union graduated twice as many engineers, about 80 percent more agricultural specialists, and about three times as many physicians as the United States did," but had a "drastically small number" in "the humanities, the social sciences, and the liberal arts, which represent 65 to 70 percent of all U.S. graduates." In 1951, 50.5 percent of Soviet professionals were women (p. 241). Dodge (*U.S. News and World Report*, Sept. 16, 1955) gives data and personal observations of Russian education.

be argued shortly that the traits of the superior individual and factors involved in his development need more study and that important cues may thus be obtained for early and more effective differentiation of individuals having such talent and for their effective education.

A major handicap of Asiatic countries has been predominant illiteracy. Now, many of them are attempting some education for the masses; and in some countries, as India, distinctive programs of "fundamental" education are emergent. One distinctive feature seems to be the high degree to which these programs are close to the daily lives of the total community and part of the total tissue of human development in these communities. And these programs may reach adults as well as children. Here, too, then, there seems to be education for all ages (46, pp. 245–251).

As mentioned above, adult training and retraining programs in the war were an important factor in this country's effective participation in it. Further crises may be expected to happen more suddenly and to make rapid and effective retraining even more important (if happenings are not so catastrophically rapid that nothing can be done). Crises or not, as the tempo of total change increases, training that can quickly adapt workers to scientific and to technical change will become increasingly important.

There are still more wide-reaching educational needs. The general public should have continuing "education" regarding national and international issues and protective psychological understanding of propaganda. There should be a general understanding of the needs for adjustment and readjustment mentioned above. These are tasks largely of adult education but of education in youth also and are of increasing significance in the cold war. Needs often seem great—and results minimal—in such efforts. For example, a six months' campaign in Cincinnati to increase information about the United Nations used several mass media and left 28 percent of adults "totally unacquainted with the main purpose" of the U.N., this being a decrease of only 2 percent from six months previous (32, p. 415).

Three Major Psychoeducational Problems

As educational effort extends over the life span, and enlarges its scope at each age, three problems that seem to be poorly handled now become increasingly important: coördination with development, adjustment to increased individual differences, and recognition of enlarged complicating social problems. It will be argued that better handling of these problems could not only result in increased educational effectiveness but could also effect savings in staff and equipment of possible great importance in the face of the rising tide of young people now coming into the schools.

COÖRDINATION OF EDUCATION WITH DEVELOPMENT

In the first place, it seems evident that a stage of education cannot effectively begin until the learner has sufficiently matured so that he is

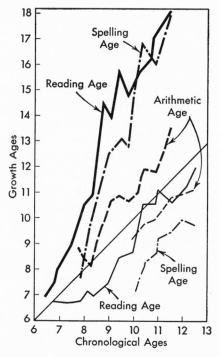

Figure 56. Growth of a Boy at a High Level of Ability (Heavy Lines) and a Boy at a Low Level of Ability (Light Lines). (Adapted from W. C. Olson, *Child Development,* Boston, D. C. Heath, 1947, pp. 178, 179.)

"ready" for it. It also seems probable that there may be boredom with tasks that are too easy, if an educational opportunity is delayed after the learner is ready and indeed waiting for it; and when the belated subjects do come, interest may be flat. Figure 56 contrasts two boys. One of them appears to have had reading readiness at six (perhaps earlier) and almost leaped forward in reading from age six on, and he also did well in spelling and better than average in arithmetic. But the second boy made almost no progress in reading or spelling until he was nine (48).

The figure is from studies by Olson and makes test scores in various subjects comparable by expressing each in relation to the average scores made by children of different chronological ages. Thus, a reading age of 10 means that the child made the score of the average 10-year-old.

It seems clear that the educational readiness of the first boy is three or four years ahead of the second. The aggregate of many such studies suggests that the "average" youngster is ready for the usual first grade program at about the age of six—as school entrance ages assume. But many children are not average; and an admission program which assumes that all are is ignoring the facts of development.

Beginning secondary school with the seventh grade or around ages 12 or 13 (the 6–3–3 plan with elementary, junior, and senior high school or 6–4–4 plan with elementary and secondary school and junior college) has been justified on the grounds that adolescence begins at this age; and a richer and more social program for adolescent needs can then more appropriately be begun than in the ninth grade, as under the older 8–4 plan. But again a set age for almost all children neglects individual differences; though the average girl first menstruates in her thirteenth year, some girls begin as early as 10 or 11 and others not until 15 or 16. And sex differences in rate of development are substantial in the early teens, boys reaching puberty about a year and a half or two years later than girls. Educational adjustments to the beginning of adolescence thus apparently should be available over a range of ages in relation to each youngster's need, rather than introduced rigidly.

There are many and more subtle ways in which stage of development is related to schooling. Table 15 shows scores made on an ingenious brief test of appreciation of poetry. Each page presented a stanza by a well-known poet and also three modified versions of it; one was made commonplace in diction, a second had the meter spoiled, and a third was made excessively sentimental. Directions were to mark the best version.

The average child in grades six and eight did barely better than chance; apparently, real appreciation for fine poetry does not usually develop in childhood. But the medians steadily rise through high school and college, and a few in secondary school score high. However, many in secondary school, and some even in the graduate classes in English, still score no better than chance. Perhaps some students major in literature who should not! And it seems strongly suggested that much English poetry is not appropriate for the great mass of high school youngsters. An analysis somewhat modifies this last sweeping conclusion, however. Figure 57 shows the percentages in each grade choosing each type of stanza from a typical set of four. Few after the sixth grade chose the metrically damaged or the matter-of-fact version of the stanza.

TABLE 15.   Number of Right Choices of "Best" Verse

Number of Right Choices	Grade School 6	8	High School 10	12	College Soph.	Jr.–Sr.	Grad.
13				1	3	9	25
12				1	5	7	29
11			1	5	6	15	26
10			3	13	10	15	35
9				13	20	29	29a
8		3	7	21	20	25a	30
7	2	13	29	36	27a	28	30
6	1	17	57	51a	22	29	27
5	9	73	76a	53	32	20	18
4	12a	78a	71	39	16	15	10
3	22	94	65	37	13	8	1
2	9	56	16	11	4	1	
1	7	19	4	3		1	1
0		3					
Total	62	356	329	284	178	202	261
Median	3.7	4.1	5.1	6.0	7.0	8.0	9.5

SOURCE: Adapted from A. Abbott and M. R. Trabue, A measure of ability to judge poetry, *Teachers Coll. Record*, 1921, pp. 101–126.

NOTE: The letter "a" indicates the median.

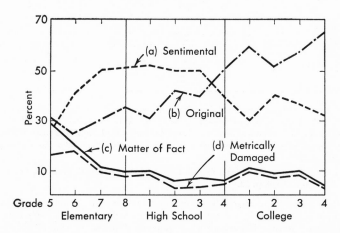

Figure 57.   Percentage of Students in Each Grade Marking as Best: (a) the Sentimental Variant of a Stanza, (b) the Original Stanza, (c) the Matter of Fact, and (d) the Metrically Damaged Variant.

The favorite, over the adolescent period from the seventh through the eleventh grade, was the sentimental version—which thereafter was less liked. An early liking for rhythm, adolescent emotionality, and gradual appearance of mature taste—all these developmental trends are displayed here. Good poetry congruent with these preferences at each age seems needed in courses in literature.

There should be coördination with development not only in starting primary and secondary school[2] but also in age of completing full-time school and beginning a career. Table 16 presents certain material on this last topic for persons who had taken advanced graduate training leading to the doctorate. The table shows American scientists before the last war receiving the doctorate at the median age of 29.5, with 3 percent receiving it at 45 or over (since the war, time out for military service or training, or related reasons, has delayed the degree still more). It will be recalled that material on age of productivity showed most brilliant scientific work tending to be done in the early thirties or even the twenties and also that best health and greatest energy was in the twenties. Presumably, taking the doctorate after 40, or indeed after 30, and so postponing beginning of full professional career until then, might both

TABLE 16.   Age of Receiving the Ph.D. in Science in the United States and in Germany

	Percents at Each Age						Number of Cases	Median Age
	20–24	25–29	30–34	35–39	40–44	45 and Up		
American	7	47	28	10	5	3	503	29.5
Starred cases	14	55	19	5	4	3	200	28.3
Germans	57	38	3	2			200	24.4

NOTE: Data on Americans were obtained from *American Men of Science,* 1938. Data on Germans were obtained from *Who's Who in Science International,* 1914. This edition was used to get results undisturbed by the First World War and following unsettled conditions in Germany. Americans in the last-mentioned volume showed median age of 30; later German data showed similar early completion of degree.

SOURCE: S. L. Pressey, *Educational Acceleration: Appraisals and Basic Problems,* Columbus, Ohio State University Press, 1949, p. 53.

[2] As to the age for entering college, numerous studies are in agreement that many young people would benefit by entering college a year (or even two) earlier than at present. One extensive inquiry found 31 percent of those entering at 16 or younger obtaining a degree in the regular time, but only 17 percent of those entering at 19 obtained the degree in the regular time. And young entrants showed good participation in activities (52, pp. 19–26, 59–63). The topic will be returned to.

shorten career and reduce the likelihood of best accomplishment. That the "starred" cases (so designated by their fellows as most notable in their field) obtained their degrees on the average a year earlier—14 percent of them were under 25—suggests some value in earlier start of career. Moreover, in the Golden Age of German Science, the doctorate was obtained (doctorate programs originated in Germany) at a median age of 24.4! All this would imply that earlier completion is possible and that at present American professional men often complete their professional training at a later age than evidence regarding development and change through the life span would suggest was desirable.

A basic reason why the German doctorate is taken earlier seems to be that general education is completed earlier; from completion of the Gymnasium around 18 to 20, the German student may go directly into his graduate work. But the American is around 23 before he receives his undergraduate degree (a median of 22.8 for men before the war). Why? Surely one factor is "the haphazard manner in which the American educational system grew. . . . Our kindergarten was first developed in Germany, the elementary school followed a Prussian model, the high school is a unique American product, the college originated in England and the graduate school was imported from Germany." This "educational system of poorly connected parts held together by the principle of the chronological lock step" holds back the abler and usually more rapidly developing college-bound youngsters to the pace of the slow to average student. "By custom, and in most communities by regulation as well, children are placed on the starting line at age six, marched along in unison one grade per year . . . and finally graduated from high school right on schedule with their age group. Then they . . . continue in the academic lock step through four years of college" (56, pp. 11–12). There is also wasteful duplication. A committee from Andover, Exeter, Lawrenceville, Harvard, Princeton, and Yale "found a striking similarity between the 12th grade course (in English literature) in all three schools and the standard freshman English course in two of the universities." In American history "the evidence of repeated reading and duplicated material is overwhelming." "The most striking evidence of sheer repetition is in the sciences. . . . The great majority of the prospective concentrators in engineering or the physical sciences spent *four* years, two in school and two in college, completing elementary chemistry; they repeated *both* subjects. Yet when we compared the grades of these repeaters with those of boys taking physics or chemistry in college for the first time, we found that the repeaters had only a negligible advantage" (6, p. 13).

If duplication is reduced, the lock step broken, or other means (shortly to be discussed) are utilized to enable students to finish college younger, what is the usual outcome? Numerous investigations have shown that they make better academic records than those who graduate at the usual age, present fewer disciplinary problems, and fit well into the student group. A sample study is summarized in Table 17. Students graduating at the age of 20 or under had clearly the highest point-hour ratio or academic record. In addition, those graduating at 21 or under were more often in activities, in more of them, and more often held office than graduates at the average age of 22. Those graduating young tested at entrance as a little brighter, but not much. And when these last differences were allowed for by pairing younger and older students on the basis of entering ability and then comparing records, the younger were still found to be doing a little better (52, p. 58).

TABLE 17.   Median Point-Hour Ratio at Graduation and Participation in Student Activities of Graduates in the School Years 1941–1942 and 1942–1943 Who Had Taken All Their College Work at Ohio State University[a]

Age at Graduation	Below 21	21	22	23	24	Over 24
PHR[b]	2.80	2.68	2.58	2.52	2.43	2.53
Percent "B" average or better	34	28	19	14	11	19
Percent in activities	90	89	80	79	80	66
Median number of activities	3.0	3.1	2.5	2.2	2.3	1.5
Percent holding office	27	28	19	14	22	10
Median percentile in test of general ability at entrance[c]	91	81	76	71	72	75

   [a] Academic records for 2055 graduates, 108 being then below 21 and 217 over 24; participation data on 1034 cases or one year's graduates, 68 being 20 or younger when graduating and 100, 25 or older.

   [b] Point-hour ratio is total points (with "A" counting 4; B, 3; C, 2; D, 1; and E, 0) divided by number of hours.

   [c] The percentiles are for all entering freshmen. Since the less capable tend to drop out (and probably since the original norms may be too low for later classes because of increasing test sophistication of students or for other causes), these medians for graduating students are all rather high.

   SOURCE: Adapted from S. L. Pressey, *Educational Acceleration: Appraisals and Basic Problems*, Columbus, Ohio State University Press, 1949, pp. 63–64.

Why do younger students do *better* than the older? It has been suggested that perhaps the growth years are especially suitable years for general learning—years of a lively, wide-ranging curiosity. As maturity is reached, around 18 to 20, there may be changes in personality, making the young men or women less "docile," less satisfied with undergraduate education, especially of the so-called "liberal arts" type which often seems to pride itself on having no vocational point, and increasingly restive of the whole school situation. The individual increasingly desires economic independence, with adult vocation either entered or in view. He wishes escape from his childhood family and is beginning to think of marriage and a family of his own. He may also be increasingly impatient of a certain intellectual dependence involved in his student status and feel that he is now ready to go forward in his own thinking and the development of his own ideology. In a notably vigorous statement made in 1913, President Lowell of Harvard summarized the situation well:

Carefully compiled statistics show that the men entering college young are on the average better, both in their studies and their conduct. . . . With the long period of special training now required in every profession, there is a universal cry that men are beginning their careers in life too old, and that the period of education is too long. Disease and death are not postponed because a man starts upon the practice of his profession a year or two later than is necessary. His period of active life, his achievements, and his usefulness are simply curtailed to that extent. . . . Boys of ordinary capacity could, by beginning young enough, be ready to enter college a year earlier than most of them do now, and they would be perfectly competent to pursue the courses even of the best colleges. The advantages, indeed, would seem to be almost wholly in favor of entering college young. Seventeen is a more appropriate age than eighteen to begin the life of college. The real pleasures are more fully and innocently enjoyed. Under a proper environment the moral dangers are in fact less. The means of education are quite within the reach of the youth who is well prepared for admission at that time; and, paradoxical as it may appear, he is in fact more likely to take advantage of them. He is at the period of life when his intellectual powers are growing rapidly, and when it is a natural process to develop those powers by exercising them without too much regard for the direct use to be made of the knowledge acquired. In short, there is a normal time for general education. A man who is too old, if a serious student, seeks to prepare directly for his career, to study his profession; or if not, is in danger of treating his studies lightly. Much has been said about maturity, but that is the result less of age than of environment and responsibility. Maturity may easily become over-ripe.[3]

Students graduating from college young (around what has been called the age of maturity or near 20) thus appear to do better in college than those graduating at the usual age of 22 or older. But may the early grad-

[3] A. Lawrence Lowell, *At War with Academic Traditions in America*, Cambridge, Harvard University Press, 1934, p. 245. Reprinted with permission of the publisher.

uates begin their careers when too immature to begin well? Rather, the younger seem to do better. Thus, 71 women who had graduated from a college of education in the school years 1926 to 1934 at the age of 19 or 20 were paired with 71 others in the same classes who graduated at 22, but who had scored at approximately the same percentile on the test of general ability given at entrance and who had the same final academic point-hour ratio at graduation. A follow-up on these cases in 1944 found that *more* of the early graduates taught after the first year, more took graduate work, and more were rated "B" or better by principal or school superintendent. Their salaries were better, and more obtained administrative positions (52, p. 72). Other evidence to the same effect is summarized in Table 18. It shows careers of Amherst graduates in the classes from 1880 to 1900 (far enough back for the careers of these men to be finished) as shown by the exceptional alumni records of this institution. Most striking is the large number of those graduating young who achieved some prominence[4] and the steady decline thereafter; after 25 there is an increase in the number of failures. Also, the youngest married earliest.

TABLE 18.   Age of Graduation and Success in Adult Life

Adult Careers of 924 American-Born Amherst Graduates Who Lived to Be 50 or Over: All Those Graduating Under 21 and Over 25 Between 1880 and 1900 and the Entire Graduating Classes of 13 of These Years

Age of Graduation	19	20	21	22	23	24	25	26	Over 26
Number of graduates	24	114	216	235	132	59	47	37	60
After college success Percent nationally known	29	22	15	12	10	3	2	3	
Percent failures	4	6	6	5	2	3	6	11	15
Median age marriage	27.7	29.7	28.9	30.0	30.1	30.9	30.9	30.1	33.6

NOTE: Outstanding success, as shown, for instance, by listing in Who's Who, is most common for young graduates; failure (as shown by poor jobs, etc.) is most common among the older.

SOURCE: Adapted from S. L. Pressey, *Educational Acceleration: Appraisals and Basic Problems,* Columbus, Ohio State University Press, 1949, p. 69.

In short, a variety of evidence indicates that completion of collegiate education closer to the time of reaching biological maturity seems to improve under-

[4] Early completion of graduate school has been found associated with productivity of social scientists (44). All this is clearly in close congruence with the data on age of productivity in the previous chapter.

graduate work, obviously permits earlier technical training, and is favorable to success in career. And in reply to any argument that more adequate college programs are needed, rather than earlier completion of them, it may be said that, perhaps, sundry topics now included in secondary and collegiate education might somewhat be postponed *until* the need arises and dealt with in programs of adult education. Thus, a person planning a trip abroad might then take intensive work in a needed foreign language. Consumer education means more to a young housewife; consideration of management of investments will mean more at an age when there are some to manage than in school. Child care means more if the child is soon to come. There is abundant and indeed startling evidence that much if not most of what is learned in school and college is soon forgotten and little applied (54). The earlier completion of full-time education may thus be facilitated by a more adequate educational program in the adult years with greater efficiency and better meeting of developmental needs throughout the life span. The topic will be returned to.

LIFE-SPAN EDUCATION AND MOUNTING INDIVIDUAL DIFFERENCES

It has already been stressed that youngsters at a given chronological age may differ in stage of development. At 6, some may and some may not be "ready" for reading. At 14, some will and some will not be pubescent. But those at a given stage of development differ greatly. In total, individuals of any one age differ very much indeed. Thus, an early survey of a school reported a child in the first grade with a mental age of 10, one fifth-grader with a mental age of 7, and another with a mental age of 15.[5] Nevertheless, schools and colleges in most respects do even less to adjust to these differences now than 25 years ago, although their student groups are now both larger and more heterogeneous. It is, therefore, first desirable to emphasize once more the greatness of these differences, with the added emphasis that cumulative divergencies in experience and aims in adult life make it then even harder to adjust educational programs thereto.

Not only may there be great differences in a grade or a class in what might be called general aptitude for school work, but there may also be differences in ability in a particular school subject—and great overlapping from grade to grade. Figure 58 deals with accomplishment in successive semesters in one subject—Spanish. An occasional student at the end of the first semester scored higher than the median for the eighth; the upper quarter of the first semester pupils was above the median for the second semester. And in spite of the

[5] L. M. Terman, Use of intelligence test in the grading of school children, *J. Educ. Res.*, 1920, 1:20–32.

fact that many had dropped out by the seventh semester, there were still then a few below the median for the first.

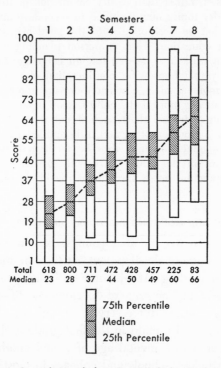

Figure 58. Scores on a Spanish Vocabulary Test Made by Students at the End of One to Eight Semesters' Study of That Language. (From V. A. C. Henman, *Achievement Tests in Modern Foreign Language*, New York, Macmillan, 1929, p. 141. Reproduced with permission from The American Council on Education.)

Overlap between secondary school and college may also be great, as shown in Figure 59 from a study (38) also rather old but unique in adequacy and range of cross-comparisons. A test battery was constructed that aimed to cover the essentials of a college education and consisted of some 1400 objective-test items requiring some eight hours of testing time. The battery may have been somewhat overfactual and placed too much emphasis on lower division subjects and content. But even if findings be substantially discounted on the above grounds, certain striking conclusions would seem nevertheless warranted. In the first place, there is substantial overlap even between the high school senior year and the college senior year; and appreciable numbers of high school seniors score, on these college tests, above the average of college seniors at graduation.

And a few college seniors score below average for the high school young-sters. In the second place, at each academic level—high school seniors, college sophomores, and college seniors—the youngest average highest and so on down in regular progression until the oldest score lowest.

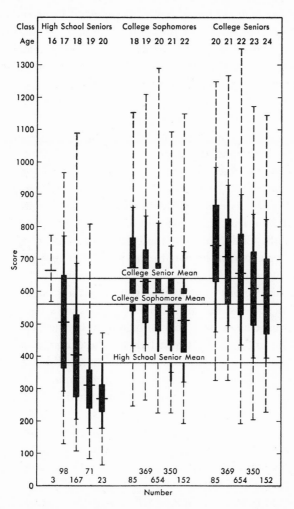

Figure 59. Scores Made on a Battery of Tests Totaling Some 1400 Questions and Re-quiring About 8 Hours, Supposed to Cover the Essentials of a College Education. The tests were given to high school seniors and college sophomores and seniors in Pennsyl-vania. Note: Heavy bars show the middle 50 percent of cases with crossbar indicating the medians; lighter bars extend to the 10 and 90 percentiles, and dashed lines to the extreme cases. (Adapted from W. S. Learned and B. D. Wood, *The Student and His Knowledge*, New York, Carnegie Foundation, 1928, p. 278.)

Clearly, from the lowest grades through college there are great individual differences in ability and accomplishment. And the higher scores of the younger might well seem an educational anomaly!

The above are findings in continuing formal education. That diversity at succeeding levels is also great, even in professional education where there has been much selection, is well recognized by every professional and graduate school. And that programs of adult education can include extraordinary diversities as regards age, socioeconomic status, previous education, experience, and purpose is indeed well known to everyone having experience with extension or evening classes.

COMPLICATING SOCIAL PROBLEMS

The potentialities of school seem largely dominated by developmental status and by individual differences in capacity to learn plus accrued learning to date. But there is one major complicating (and all too often obfuscating) problem: the effects of the school on social adjustment.

In the first place, as emphasized by Chicago studies cited in Chapter 3, the typical American school is middle and upper class in its control, ideals, and staff. Children from these socioeconomic classes may well find the teacher a person known to the parents. These parents will approve school success and deplore school failure; schooling is part of their "way of life" and serves important purposes of their class; they support their children's social status and social ambitions in "school life." In contrast, the lower classes will feel antagonism to the schools, and the schools will be antagonistic toward them; these homes will be largely without relevant cultural materials; their children will be social outsiders. All this is likely to cause poor classwork and dropping out of school. So the daughter of a prosperous farm tenant who had left school explained that when she started high school she was lost. She tried to get in with some of the other girls, but never did and overheard another call her "that hick." A daughter of a truck driver, who was snubbed because of her father's job, and also because she worked in the cafeteria, quit school the day she was 16 and legally could (28, pp. 342 ff.) The first sustained effort in the young person's career—schooling—thus ends unhappily, and adult life begins with a feeling of frustration, and limitation in vocational possibilities. In spite of the present program of more years of schooling, great numbers thus fail to complete educational plans. Figure 60 shows how progressively more youngsters drop out of school; and of those who enter college, only about 40 percent ever obtain a degree.

The above statement implies that leaving school is due to social rather than scholastic difficulties. These last may be determinative. But today schools question whether it is a desirable educational practice to fail pupils, and efforts are made to retain them. Family financial need may cause a youngster to leave school for work. But this last explanation has been found to be used as a face-saving explanation when the real reason

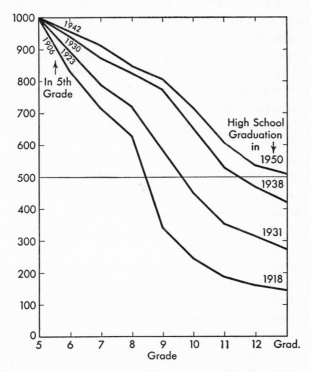

Figure 60. School Survival Rates in the United States: Number of 1000 in the Fifth Grade Who Reach Succeeding Grade and Graduate from High School. (Adapted from U.S. Office of Education, *Statistical Summary of Education*, Washington, D.C., U.S. Government Printing Office, 1953, Chap. 1, p. 8.)

was failure to "make" high school society. In recent years American families have been more prosperous than ever before. And poor grades may be more a product of social discontent than dullness or laziness. Figure 60 shows *more* who entered the ninth grade failing to graduate from high school in 1950 than in 1918. The hypothesis seems reasonable that the greater dropping out of secondary school in recent years is due in part to a larger number of pupils entering from social classes which find the school program and school life less compatible. The academic mortality in college is presumably less of this origin—but perhaps more often so than college authorities usually realize.

Much in programs for adults suffers from similar faults. Evening or extension courses may be taught as a side task by regular college or high school teachers, and they often simply repeat day offerings for employed people working toward a diploma or degree. Too often noncredit offerings for adults seem to be of the same flavor. Perhaps the retired tailor and saleswomen in classes in English literature and in poetry writing really do desire such courses. But much that is read seems uncomprehended, and the poetry is doggerel. A visitor wonders whether offerings more indigenous to these people's lives might also be found, which would serve more effectively than the verse and the great books as bases for pleasant social contacts not only with others in the adult education center but with neighbors.

In the second place, the schools have a rigidity of grouping according to chronological age and the lock step which often greatly handicaps satisfactory social adjustment. That is, the closely held-to practice of admitting children to school at the age of six and promoting them a grade a year initiates and continues social grouping on the basis of chronological age, with leadership or conflict or social isolation depending on elements of social weaknesses or strength *as of the same age group*. Thus, the boy big for his age has a playtime advantage and the small, slow developer a handicap, and the rigid age-grade system tends to restrict any escape from his age group which would tend more to put each boy with his play peers. Neighborhood play groups are not so rigidly age-based—nor are the social relationships of the one-room school. The writers venture the judgment that a major and almost completely neglected fault of the grade system—intensified by the lock step—is this tendency to restrict social relationships to the same chronological age group, when companionships would more naturally develop with older or with younger persons. Thus, a slight, prepubescent boy of 14 may be most comfortable with other boys a year or so younger, but an early-maturing girl of the same age may seek the companionship of boys a couple of years older. In fact, the average teen-age girl may prefer slightly older boys. As one mother of a pretty 16-year old put it: "You know, I hadn't realized how much difference there was in the way boys and girls grow up. These girls don't like to go out with boys their own age. They say they're so icky and gooney and they don't know how to act, they're careless about dressing, and the girls want to go around with older boys who, as they put it, know what the score is."

In short, sex and individual differences in rates of development indicate that social groupings, especially in the early and middle teens, should not be confined largely to those of the same chronological age. And individual differences in rate of development suggest the desirability of flexible and readily changing groupings, since slow developers may catch up and physiological acceleration is, after all, largely a temporary phenomenon; associates desired at one age may not be most desired at another. Further, social and academic maturity may not be the same; a grouping satisfactory for schoolwork may not be satisfactory for play contacts. A variety of groups may well often be desirable. A bright boy with a science hobby may well be a member of a science club where most of the membership is older than he; but in sports he may best associate with others who are substantially younger. Chronological age grouping, made rigid in the lock step, makes difficult all these desirable flexibilities.

Colleges, especially the smaller institutions, usually have somewhat similar rigidities in their practically universal assumption that four years *not* less, and more only as a result of academic or other handicaps) are necessary for undergraduate programs. All entering students are designated as of the class which will graduate four years later (if Smith enters in 1953 he is at once designated as Smith '57); this label will be constantly associated with his name not only throughout his undergraduate career but in alumni records and gatherings forever after. Curricula are organized on the assumption of four years. Dean's rules about participation in athletics and office holding in student organizations have the same orientation—thus, freshmen may be barred from varsity teams, and the presidents of certain organizations must be seniors. And student customs early enforce, as through freshman hazing, and constantly emphasize the four-year pattern.

The above problems appear primarily in school and college. But somewhat analogous issues may appear in adult education and involve the issue as to whether, for instance, classes planned especially for older adults should be thought of as "segregated," and the extent to which the occasional older student may be regarded somewhat out of place in the evening school class which is made up primarily of younger adults.

The previous paragraph stated that because of incongruity between the social class of a pupil and the character of an educational program, or incongruity between a student's social maturity and the school classification of him, there may be social problems which are distressing in themselves and interfere with educational effectiveness. And, of course, social difficulties may develop for yet other causes. Implied in the above discussion has been the premise that a really vital school program should take responsibility for a pupil's social as well as academic development. If this is true, then there should be means of determining the satisfactoriness of a pupil's social adjustment and of improving that adjustment where necessary. In fact, there is much validity to the argument that programs of this sort are really much more important than means for measuring and improving competence in spelling or arithmetic or Latin. Social development is considered in later chapters. Here it is necessary only to point out that there are methods for social appraisal, and methods are being developed for improving social adjustment.

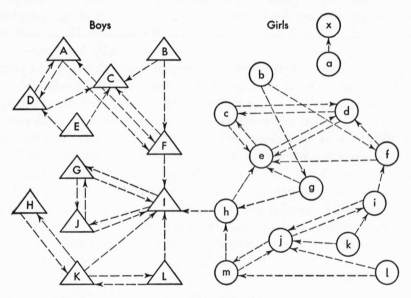

Figure 61. Social Structure of a Small Sixth-Grade Class, as Shown by Results of the Request That Each Child Name the Two Classmates Whom He Would Like Best to Have Sit Next to Him. The chart shows that Boy A chose D and F and was chosen by D and C; Boys B and E and Girls a, b, k, and l were unchosen or isolates; Boy I, Girl e were popular being chosen by six and five other children. (Method modified from J. L. Moreno, Who Shall Survive? Nerv. & Ment. Dis. Monog. 1934.)

Figure 61, which diagrams the social structure of an elementary school class, resulted from a very simple "sociometric" test; each pupil was simply asked to write on a slip of paper the names of the two other pupils he would most like to have sit next to him in a proposed rearrangement of seating. The diagram makes clear that some pupils were chosen by several others, as girl "e" by five. But girl "b" was chosen by no one; she had two choices, but they did not choose her. Girl "a" chose only "x," who was in another room. The choice by girl "h" of boy "I" is the only instance, in this preadolescent group, of heterosexual interest. The six boys in the lower left-hand part of the diagram show no interest in any other pupils. Clearly, this class presents many problems of social isolation and cleavage.

Techniques for dealing with situations like that displayed above may include such elementary steps as rearranging the two boy groups so that they are more intermingled. But this must be done shrewdly. If one group is from a poor neighborhood, and is the makings of a gang, other measures, such as utilizing its leader "I" and involving coöperation of the city's recreation department and other agencies, may be necessary. The isolate may be a small, slow learner, needing help and encouragement in both schoolwork and playground skills. But sometimes a stroke of friendly tact may transform a problem situation into strength. Thus, a shy Italian girl, from a family antagonistic to the school, was asked to bring some products of the family's home country. These were featured by the teacher and class and much admired by the other children. The girl thus became looked to and popular. And this outcome not only brought the emergence of a lively personality and the release of abilities so that schoolwork went better, but the parents were much pleased, and family-school relationships were much improved.

Clearly, sociometry and other related methods may reveal social problems which may have their roots in many causes—socioeconomic class schisms, developmental incoördinations, or difficulties more individual and personal to the particular child. And many methods may be used to deal with them. As already mentioned, problems of social development will be more fully discussed later. They are touched upon here to emphasize that they are indeed part of the total task of education, though often not so seen, and that they may both have origins in development and affect total development of personality and ability in many ways.

Educational Problems of the Handicapped and the Mentally Inadequate

It has long been recognized that the blind, the crippled, and the grossly mentally defective need not only special care but also special training.

Increasingly, it has come to be realized that children only somewhat moderately handicapped in various ways might be greatly helped by special educational programs, but in classes with average youngsters they often miss contact with what is going on and become increasingly frustrated. Because it has been difficult to obtain teachers with either the patience or the special preparation needed for such work, the tendency has been to allot special funds for extra payment of them—and for the special facilities often desirable. And sympathy has gone out to the often pathetically handicapped child. Children with either physical or mental defects may appear in fine families and of able parents who are highly sensitive to their needs. Programs for handicapped children have in consequence been very vigorously supported in many communities. Those in such work have become well organized, support publications dealing with their problems, and have texts summarizing their field (3, 14, 25). But many adults also have handicaps which present educational problems. And data on the outcome in adult life of childhood programs for the handicapped are both informing and encouraging. Education for the handicapped must therefore be given brief consideration, with emphasis on the life-span view.

TYPES OF HANDICAPPED AND INADEQUATE CHILDREN AND PROGRAMS FOR THEM

A totally blind child clearly needs special help. But needs vary according to whether blindness was from birth or a result of injury in later childhood. Children not blind may yet have gross visual handicaps of various types needing special equipment or training. Deafness may be total or of various degrees and kinds. It has been estimated that 5 percent of all school children have speech defects of one kind or another—some result from deafness or from physical deformities such as cleft palate, but most speech defects (as stuttering) have obscure psychological origins. There are children who are crippled in many ways and from various causes, such as poliomyelitis, tuberculosis of the bones or joints, cerebral palsy, or accidents. Special educational provision may be desirable for children suffering from cardiac or tuberculous conditions or epilepsy. Special programs are also needed not only for the mentally defective (perhaps as much as 2 percent of the total school population might be so considered) but for the much larger number of the "mentally retarded" and "slow-learning." The total number of handicapped children is thus large, and their educational needs are not only great but exceedingly various.

Adequate diagnosis may be very difficult. Careful medical diagnosis is obviously an essential first step. The extent of the handicap must be determined. Can a blind child see enough to avoid obstacles? Can some use of a crippled leg be regained? But may a physically handicapped child be also mentally limited? Testing a blind or deaf child is not easy, even with tests especially planned for them. Not only may communication be difficult (as with the deaf and the cerebral palsied) and much test material inapplicable (as with the blind), but the whole world of the congenitally deaf or blind is so limited that their ideas and modes of thinking presumably must be greatly affected. But may such a case nevertheless have sufficient constitutional capacity for learning that he can profit from a long and difficult program of training, as in use of Braille? In general, the evidence seems to be that more handicapped children are dull or mentally defective than children not handicapped, but that some of the handicapped are very bright. Appraisal of personality may be exceedingly difficult. Many items in personality inventories may be inapplicable. And—what *is* good adjustment for a blind or crippled child? Nevertheless, a skilled examiner can usually arrive at very shrewd appraisals (Newland, in *14*).

For many types of cases certain special types of training may obviously be desirable. A blind child may need to learn Braille, and lip reading may be needed by the deaf child. An accident victim may need help in learning the use of an artificial limb. Most will need understanding assistance in learning how to live with their handicap—to accept themselves as handicapped, find what they can do, and in what ways they can associate with other children. There may be very difficult problems in educating parents neither to reject nor to overprotect the child but to accept him as he is and help him to develop to the fullest extent of his possibilities. If given vocational training realistically with regard to both the handicap and the possibility of finding work of the type prepared for, the deaf, the crippled, and the dull may nevertheless become self-supporting. Thus, follow-ups in adult life of children diagnosed in school as dull or indeed feeble-minded have shown a majority to be earning a living and to be respected though humble members of their communities, with delinquency or crime only a little higher than for the population as a whole (*12, 13*).

For example, H. G. had a childhood Binet IQ of 50, but at age 40 he had a Wechsler-Bellevue full scale IQ of 84. He was unmarried, neat, pleasant, and employed as a factory custodian since the death of his mother several years agô. He has stayed in the clean three-room family home with his sister and her four-year-old boy. H. G. was on relief occasionally in 1941 and 1947 and had a juvenile court misdemeanor in 1928 but no further such record.

A couple live in a brick house which the husband built and owns. He had a childhood IQ of 70 and at 45 made a Wechsler IQ of 80; he has worked as a mechanic and now as a bricklayer. The wife in childhood had a Binet IQ of 59, and at the age of 43 she had a Wechsler IQ of 80. She is florid, obese, and slovenly in appearance. She had a record for sex delinquency before marriage and has been a housekeeper all her adult life. The house was dirty with old food on the table. Their five children, ages 9 to 22, all tested near 90 IQ on a group intelligence test. The youngest is still in school; the others left in the ninth or tenth grade.

Various total "ways of life" may be found reasonably satisfactory for certain types of handicapped persons. Thus, in New York City the deaf "hold numerous social events and have many clubs and organizations for varied interests" (14, p. 157), living largely within their own special world. But such companionship with people who have similar handicaps may clearly not be possible in a smaller community; ways of living with those who hear must then of necessity be sought.

PROBLEMS OF REHABILITATION AND REËDUCATION IN ADULT LIFE

Problems of retraining in industry have been mentioned and will be returned to in Chapter 6 on the work life. Reëducation of individuals who have been crippled, or have suffered a handicapping disease, is a highly special topic which deserves brief mention here. Until recently, many such cases have been regarded as hopeless, or at best greatly limited by these handicaps. But now broad programs involving retraining to adjust to the handicapping condition, occupational therapy, psycho-therapy, and perhaps psychiatric treatment may help a person with a leg amputation to regain a substantial amount of the former ability to get about through learning the use of an artificial limb. There may be an education to do only certain simple things, if such a limiting disease as a chronic cardiac condition makes this necessary. An individual may be retrained after a stroke so that he can walk again and speak largely as before. In the old person, "cerebral accidents" are relatively common. Most patients need no longer be regarded as hopeless. A psychology of the life span sees special problems of education thus sometimes assuming major importance even in old age (42).

Complications with socioeconomic status and with age are sometimes not sufficiently recognized. The mentally inadequate and the handicapped child *or* adult is most likely to be in an underprivileged home. Family resources, both material and mental, for aiding and stimulating him may be meager. As in a regular school, teachers with middle-upper social background may not really understand such homes or neighborhoods. However, if an unfortunate child is in a superior family, he may suffer from parental impatience or over-protection. An able adult may be more crushed by a greatly limiting accident or illness. A physiotherapist of 25 or even a physician of 40 may have little realization of the loneliness and hopelessness of an old person after a long illness or a stroke, or of the difficulties to which he will return if and when he leaves the hospital (67). But all these factors may greatly influence his efforts at reëducation.

A Much Fumbled and Critical Problem: Education of the Most Able

The slow-learning or mentally defective or handicapped child may be a problem demanding attention; he may be delinquent, impossible in a regular school class, or obviously in need of special care. Children of these types in families of ability and influence arouse strong efforts to obtain special educational provision for them. Special funds available for this purpose have been used to build up extensive programs for the slow learner and the handicapped. But for the gifted not only is little done, but smug rationalizations operate against doing much. Any special groups for them are slurred as undemocratic "segregation." Progress faster than the lock step is considered a hazard to health; and "enrich-ment" is too often largely some added busy work or class-conscious ad-dition like French in grade school. But in the continuing international crises, effective education of technical and professional workers and of leaders seems to be a crucial educational problem. Improvements in the education of these gifted people could be of great importance. It might be expected that able young people would respond far more than the dull or handicapped to special educational opportunity and that marked efforts along these lines might be outstandingly profitable. The previous two chapters included matter to this effect. The issue will be briefly con-sidered not only for these reasons, but also because it is believed that developmental psychology has great contributions to make in this area.

PRECOCITY AND "EARLY" BEGINNINGS OF SCHOOLING

Studies of outstanding adults almost always show that their superiority was recognized in childhood. In the relatively few instances where this was not so, closer analysis usually revealed lack of interest in humdrum school programs but lively competence in significant hobbies (like Darwin's dislike of Latin but great interest in his insect collection) rather than real lack of early evidence of superior abilities. Terman's studies of gifted children have shown that they usually walk and talk earlier than average children and learn to read earlier. Often, in spite of an effort to prevent the child from preschool reading, he learns from older children in the family and from the everyday environment of a highly literate home. In short, developmentally these children already have an important head start for schooling. Yet the usual policy is to refuse either to admit a bright and early-reading child at five or to start him in the second grade at six.

Thus, Marie was a lively six-year-old and the youngest of five children in a family of extroverts. By her fifth year she was reading. But she was no sickly bookworm; physically, she was almost as big and strong as the average child two years older. Socially, she held her own capably with her siblings and in the neighborhood. In spite of the school's protest that she would become maladjusted if put with older children, she was started in the second grade. Even there the school work was too easy for her, and she regarded the other children with a certain tolerant amusement as often "such babies." Throughout school and college she continued somewhat accelerated but was accepted by the other youngsters for what she indeed was—developmentally as old as or a bit older than they.

Also reading at five, but started in the first grade, was a bright girl so socially sensitive that she carefully concealed her literacy and pretended to stumble through reading lessons with the other children, so as not to seem different from them. There was no overt social maladjustment; instead, throughout her educational career, she was in groups so far behind her in competence that her time in school was one long polite acquiescence in boredom.

Some dozen experiments with admission of children according to mental rather than chronological age have agreed that those admitted young on this basis almost always do well in further school work and get along well with other children (52, p. 13, 75). If, as should be the case, admissions were more broadly based, not alone on mental but also on physiological and social age, early admission of the superior (really not "early" for them) should be even more successful. Other means of getting precocious, bright children off to an early start may be even better. Thus, where there are kindergartens, children may be kept in them for a longer or shorter time according to their ability to begin the first grade.

"ACCELERATION" OR OPPORTUNITY TO PROGRESS IN CONGRUENCE WITH DEVELOPMENT AND NEED

As indicated in the previous paragraphs, youngsters of superior abilities may well enter school a bit earlier than the average. In any event, they usually enter school further along in certain respects, as in ability to read, than the average youngster. As pointed out earlier, they almost invariably develop more rapidly through childhood and youth than the youngster who is average in abilities, and they usually also develop faster in physique and social adjustment. Many will go to college and many of these into professional or graduate training. But it seems desirable that mere "getting ready" should not continue so long that the period of maximal potential accomplishment in the early prime should be unduly invaded. And society needs as many of the best years of these superior persons as possible in the full usefulness of adult life. Surely there should be no educational dawdling. It would seem desirable for the educational development of the superior person to progress at a rate that is related to his pace in general development rather than at the rate of the average person. The brilliant youngster often could and should progress faster in his schoolwork than in play and social companionship—if only associations for these last purposes and for classwork might be made more independent. This possibility has already been touched upon and will be returned to.

How may bright youngsters move through a school or college program at a more rapid rate than others? It seems to be usually assumed that the only method in elementary school is occasional grade-skipping or double-promotion and that the risks of social maladjustment in moving a child into an older group and of educational handicap in allowing the child to skip topics are great. But gifted children usually are really older than their years and usually are two or three grades ahead of their class in actual achievement. If the skipping omitted some special instruction, such as in fractions, a little special help from a teacher would usually remedy the matter.

Rapid progress need not come by the crude method of grade-skipping, however. Rapid-progress sections in junior or senior high school, covering three years' work in two, have been found to work admirably; follow-ups in senior high and in college have shown pupils who were in rapid-progress sections doing as well in schoolwork as control cases originally of the same ability and school record, and also fitting well into the student group. The "multiple-track" plans of some 30 years ago, with fast sections doing the first six grades in five years, seem to have been dropped more because of difficulties in administration and public relations (as protesting parents who could not see why their average or dull children were not in the favored sections) than because bright children were not thus benefited. Adjustment rooms in elementary school where special attention is given to special cases, including youngsters needing a little help for grade-skipping, may eliminate subject-matter gaps. Or the first three grades of elementary school may be treated not as three grades, but as a "primary pool" out of which some children are moved early and some later, as they are ready to go on. And grades 4 to 6 may similarly be pooled.

Evidence that rapid progress (apparently usually made by grade-skipping) leading to early graduation from high school normally works well is notably presented by data summarized in Table 19, regarding Terman's famous gifted group as appraised when they were at an average age of around 35. Those who had accelerated the most finished high school at the decidedly early age of 14.9—the conventional or lock-step age for high school graduation is just before or after the eighteenth birthday. This most accelerated group was in childhood not very much brighter than the slowest group of the gifted: average IQ's were 158 and 149. But not only did 16 percent more of the most accelerated group graduate from college, and two years earlier at the age of 19.9 (average age for college graduation in the country generally being between 22.5 and 22.9), the youngest group also obtained most graduation honors and most often went on to graduate work. Health of the youngest group was superior. Social adjustment was about as good. About the same number married (and over a year younger), and fewer were divorced as compared to the oldest gifted group. And over twice as many of the youngest were judged by the investigators to be already outstanding vocationally. Acceleration seemed to have been a good thing for these gifted young people.

The common assumption is that acceleration in college can only be by a lengthened school year and that this endangers health and unfortunately limits experience as compared to summers on vacation or a job. Again, these hazards have been found greatly exaggerated. But they are avoided by better methods, as credit by examination. Tests at college entrance show many bright youngsters (especially if they come from a good secondary school) already able to pass certain freshman courses; if they are on that basis given credit for these courses, they have an initial head start in their program. In college, honor-section programs may facilitate progress of superior students in one or more subjects. The able student may often, with stimulation rather than fatigue, carry a bit more course work than the less able. Individual projects, sometimes involving field work or even a little research problem, may facilitate the progress

TABLE 19. Relationships of Age of High School Graduation to Ability, Adjustment, Health, Later Educational, and Vocational Success: 785 Men and 607 Women in the Stanford Gifted Child Study

Age of High School Graduation	13.6 to 15.5	15.6 to 16.5	16.6 up
Mean ages of high school graduation	14.9	16.0	17.3
Number of Students	62	332	998
General ability			
Childhood Binet IQ	158	154	149
Concept mastery score (1940)	112	98	95
Educational record			
Percentages graduated from college	83	74	67
Mean age at graduation	19.9	20.9	21.9
Percentages having			
Average grade B or better	77	82	74
One or more graduation honors	43	38	35
One or more years of graduate work	58	48	39
Social adjustment			
Percentages rated "satisfactory"			
By field worker (1928)	80	79	85
On composite all-round data (1940)	77	83	81
Health			
Mean age of puberty—men	14.2	14.5	14.8
women	12.7	12.8	13.1
Percentages having good health as			
Rated by parents in 1928	100	89	85
By self in 1940	91	81	86
Marriage			
Percentages married—men	73	68	70
women	60	74	71
Mean age at marriage—men	24.8	25.5	26.1
women	22.8	23.5	24.1
Percentages separated or divorced	5	12	12
Vocational Success			
Percentages in highest group—men	42	22	19

SOURCE: Adapted from L. M. Terman and Medita Oden, *The Gifted Child Grows Up*, Stanford, Stanford University Press, 1947, pp. 265–279.

of a superior student; and he is usually delighted at such an opportunity to work closely with a faculty member. This possibility will be returned to. As shown by Table 20, students progressing rapidly through college usually do well.

TABLE 20. A Comparison of 104 Women Who Graduated from College in 3 Calendar Years or Under and 104 Other Women Paired with Them, on the Basis of Age and Ability at Entrance and Residence Locally or Not, but Who Took the Regular 4 Calendar Years

Record at Graduation	Accelerates	Controls
Median point-hour ratio	3.10	2.87
Percent under 2.0 point-hour ratio	0	2
Percent in one or more student activities	94	94
Percent holding office	20	36
Report 10 years after[a]		
Percent considering that acceleration was		
A strain on health	7	15
Prevented best school work	12	15
Undesirably limited social life	9	16
A desirable challenge	62	40
Desirably saved time	79	34
Percent who		
Had had further schooling	51	43
Earned further degrees	24	12
Had married	85	87
Had one or more children	83	90
Employed	39	28
In at least one community activity	84	84
Median age of marriage	22.3	23.2

[a] Replies received from 86 percent of the accelerates and 68 percent of the controls.

SOURCE: Adapted from Marie A. Flesher and S. L. Pressey, War-time accelerates ten years after, *J. Educ. Psychol.*, 1955, 46; pp. 228-238.

One hundred and four women who completed an undergraduate program in three calendar years or less (several in two calender years) were paired with 104 others of the same age *and* ability at entrance but who took the conventional three years and nine months or four years for the same program. The table shows that the median point-hour ratio of those who finished in three years or less was actually higher (3.10 as compared to 2.87) than the overall academic record of those who entered college at the same age and with the same ability but who took the usual four-year period. As many of the accelerates as of the nonaccelerates participated in activities, though the accelerated were in somewhat fewer activities and held office somewhat less often.[6] Apparently, the more lively pace did little harm as regards campus life and was if anything stimulating academically. The accelerates may have

[6] A comparison of students who took five years or over for a degree with similarly paired four-year students showed those taking more than the usual time doing poorer school work and participating less in extracurricular activities.

been more highly motivated than the controls. But in any event, the figures indicate that individuals who are reasonably competent and motivated often do not need the usual four years for the undergraduate program. And the lower part of Table 20 shows that when asked 10 years later, on a questionnaire dealing ostensibly with other topics, about their schooling and their careers, responses were still favorable to rapid progress.

The accelerated students used attendance summer quarter as the chief mode of rapid progress (84 percent attended two or more summers), but 19 percent got 15 or more credit-hours by examination, and 29 percent averaged a course load of 18 or more hours for their entire time in college. A further study yielded the anomalous finding that the heavier the course load students took, the higher their total academic record and the more likely their participation in activities; the anomaly was probably the result of the great care used in college offices to assure that only those who were clearly able to do so took heavy loads. And an investigation of those obtaining credit by examination in the first course in chemistry showed them getting better grades in a second course than those who had actually taken the first course—the high standards for giving examination credit being a probable explanation.

The 104 accelerates in Table 20 had gone ahead on their own; a few might have been advised otherwise if advisement had been sought. A group of coeds carefully chosen in their freshman year as able, healthy, and well adjusted were, therefore, selected and guided in accelerated programs. And comparisons were made with others of similar ability taking the usual four years. Not only were academic record *and* participation in activities of the accelerates superior, but almost twice as many graduated from college as in the comparable group not accelerating. Again vigor of personality may have been a major factor. Opportunity to move rapidly so as to get into advanced training and into career presumably was a motivating influence. For some, as those of limited finances or planning early marriage, a three-year program seemed feasible, but four years did not. But the writers venture the hypothesis that these bright accelerates did well also because progress that was faster than average was their pace and carried them more and more quickly into work at their level, and all this was stimulating to them.

This last factor should, it is believed, be stressed. Surely it is stimulating to an entering student if he is told that he has done so well on freshman-week tests that he is to be given credit for two college courses, or it is stimulating for a student to be invited into an honors course or to be allowed a desired extra course because of a superior record. It is believed to be especially stimulating if a student makes the astounding discovery that he *can* "get ahead." In almost every college in the country four-year curricula are so firmly established that such a possibility simply never occurs to most students—and is decried by almost every faculty member. The quip has been made that a certain state penitentiary has this advantage over the state university in the same community: *from the pen,* one can get out sooner for good behavior!

Able, attractive Viola, entering college in 1944 at the age of 17, was pleased to be told that high scores on freshman-week tests gave her credit for certain freshman courses and to be invited to attempt an "accelerated" program, in which her petitions for extra work and outstanding accomplishment brought her many and favorable faculty contacts. Her attractiveness, energy, and shrewdness made her popular with students; she was a leader in her sorority. She obtained the A.B. degree with high honors in two calendar years. In her third year she obtained the master's degree, in the meantime holding a part-time teaching assistantship, and married. The couple then went to an eastern university where by the end of the fourth year she had completed most of the work for the doctorate, which she received shortly thereafter. He is now on a university faculty; she cares for their two children, is active in the community, and carries on some research with her husband. Abilities which would ordinarily have been dissipated in the diffuse inanities of undergraduate life were thus channeled into a rapid-moving career, still only in its beginning (52, p. 107). For a man, for whom his profession would have been more of his life, such rapid progress might have facilitated accomplishment even more.

"ENRICHMENT" OR OPPORTUNITIES ENCOURAGING SPECIAL INTERESTS AND TALENTS

"Enrichment" of the school program rather than rapid progress is most generally advocated in the public schools for superior youngsters. It is maintained that they should all read more widely in history or literature or take French! Recently, less class-conscious, more discriminating, and more dynamic types of enlarged opportunity have been increasingly discussed. For instance, talented students interested in science may find the school's laboratories open to them at noon and after classes in the afternoon, with teachers there available at these times to help and encourage them (7). Field trips to local industries, possibly opportunities to assist during summers in the laboratories maintained by some of them, membership in a science club, and attendance at a junior academy meeting may yet further feed these interests. Books and magazines appropriate to these interests may be made available. The previous chapter has emphasized how such personalized, dynamic "enrichment" at home and in school has been important in the careers of notable people. These possibilities will be returned to in the last pages of this chapter.

THE MUCH STRESSED PROBLEM OF SOCIAL ADJUSTMENT

It has often been assumed that the superior student was usually an odd personality. However, the investigations of Terman, Hollingworth, and others indicate that on the average the gifted are physically taller and heavier than the average youngster, reach puberty a little earlier, and are socially well adjusted—often leaders. It is true that their social interests around adolescence may be less advanced than either their general level of intellectual interest or their academic potentiality. Clearly, there is a problem here; the lock step retains them in groups too young for them in all ways—the bright students kept in their age group may show more social maladjustment than those somewhat accelerated (33). But a spread between general intellectual interests and capability and social maturity is likely still to remain. Flexibility seems clearly to be called for so that a bright youngster may, as has been mentioned, be in a science club where most others are somewhat older than he, but also be in a sports group of those about the same physical age. This happens to a certain extent in large high schools. Large universities and an occasional college may minimize the four-year convention; thus at Antioch, where there is much coming and going to field projects, examination credit, and no set length of time for the degree, students do not think of themselves as sophomores or juniors or seniors but simply as students going forward in the program. Secondary school rapid-progress sections minimize these problems, since the bright groups largely form their own society.

In the childhood and youth of many famous individuals, their great abilities (usually prococious) often seem to have been especially nourished and brought to flower when they were members of small groups with similar interests and superior capacities. These groups gave continuing encouragement and constructive guidance and often furnished the occasion for notable accomplishment; they also provided social contacts which for these persons were highly satisfying. Mozart's early associations with other musicians have already been mentioned. The little group with which Keats associated, reading Chapman's Homer, stimulated his famous sonnet on that experience. Shelley and Byron had their companionships with other feverish young intellectuals. In renaissance Italy, the studios were hotbeds for fostering artistic interests and abilities. In the best university graduate programs, many student groups or "teams" so operate under the leadership of vigorous faculty personalities. A boyhood club or other group may be notably stimulating; as mentioned earlier, a high school nature study group in rural Minnesota made contributions to the biology of the region and led to scientific careers for a number of the members. If anything like the financial resources and special staff now commonly devoted to slow learners and the handicapped were put into the education of the gifted, the statement is ventured that notably profitable special means for serving them could be developed, and that included in the program there might be provision for continuing companionship with others of like minds, such as in the above examples, which would be a healthy development of an intellectual elite but would still not be unfortunately segregating or undemocratic.

In short, the assertion is ventured that most difficulties in social adjustment of bright students, and especially difficulty when they are academically accelerated, are products of a socioeducational lock step and conventionality in school social groupings, which greater flexibility in all types of grouping in school and a little social imagination and enterprise should largely take care of. Higher valuation, by both students and community, of superior accomplishment may also help solve this problem. The last section of this chapter, on motivation and community valuation, will bear on this topic.

Major Developmental Needs and Problems in Education

The previous pages have stressed the great numbers of students, the extending age range of American education, and the extent to which developmental problems are thereby increased. Three issues seem outstanding.

DEVELOPMENT TASKS AND TIMING

In a recent vigorous book (22) the position has been taken that the concept of "developmental tasks" may well be of major orienting value in educational planning. The infant and small child have their elementary developmental tasks of learning to walk and to talk. At school entrance, around six or shortly after, come the well-recognized tasks of learning use of symbols, as in reading; learning social skills, such as learning to adjust to age mates and, more broadly, to children beyond the family and immediate neighborhood; and also learning physical skills that are appropriate to the age group, such as throwing and catching, swimming, and use of simple tools. Gradually, in middle childhood, there is the task of finding status and role in peer groups. Then, in later childhood the individual develops social values and independence. In adolescence come tasks of achieving a masculine or feminine role and planning and moving toward economic independence. The school recognizes many of these developmental tasks of childhood and youth, though usually not the full breadth of them. But after that, the broad developmental tasks are all too little recognized as calling for educational guidance.

Of all the periods of life, early adulthood is the fullest of teachable moments and the emptiest of efforts to teach. It is a time of special sensitivity and unusual readiness of the person to learn. Early adulthood, the period from eighteen to thirty, usually contains marriage, the first pregnancy, the first serious full-time job, the first illnesses of children, the first experience of furnishing or buying or building a house, and the first venturing of the child off to school. If ever people are motivated to learn and to learn quickly, it is at times such as these. Yet the amount of educative effort expended by society on people is probably less during this period than during any other period except old age —if we make the proper exception of college and university education, which are really an extension of the schools, and seldom deal with the developmental tasks and problems of young adults. It makes one wonder what education is about, after all, if it is not directly concerned with helping the individual to meet such problems as these. (22, p. 257.)

The failures of educational programs to meet developmental needs are dramatically displayed in an inquiry (19) regarding problems mentioned by women college graduates as troubling them at different ages and subjects studied more or less concurrently. The problems—as of relations with parents, vocational choice, marriage, finding one's place in a new community, raising a family—were indeed common. And the courses in college—algebra, medieval history, rhetoric, geology—were of little or no help to these women in meeting these problems! The largest group of problems was found to be psychological. Yet the blunt statement is made that "psychology, which is supposed to be the science of human behavior, had little functional value for these women in their own personality development" (19, p. 260).

Developmental tasks of middle age may need perspectives which adult education could give as regarding changing parent-child relations and readjustment of leisure to this time of life and to middle-age circumstances. It is increasingly being recognized that the older years also have their developmental tasks.

The fact that man learns his way through life is made radically clear by consideration of the learning tasks of older people. They still have new experiences ahead of them, and new situations to meet. At age sixty-five when a man often retires from his occupation, his chances are better than ever of living another ten years. During this time the man or his wife very likely will experience several of the following things: decreased income, moving to a smaller house, loss of spouse by death, a crippling illness or accident, a turn in the business cycle with a consequent change of the cost of living. After any of these events the situation may be so changed that the old person must learn new ways of living. (22, p. 277.)

In short, the concept of developmental tasks in education gives perspectives and breadths which are very healthy and stimulating for educational programming. The concept also emphasizes timing. There is some evidence that delays past the "normal" time in developing an ability may permanently limit its full development.

[If a task] is not achieved at the proper time it will not be achieved well, and failure in this task will cause partial or complete failure in the achievement of other tasks yet to come . . . there is some evidence, from the few cases on record of children who were denied human companionship during the first few years of life and therefore did not learn to talk, that the task of learning to talk is extremely difficult and may never be accomplished well if it is not achieved in the second year of life. This is the crucial period for this particular task. (22, p. 3.)

Certainly, as mentioned earlier, there is wasted effort to attempt learning before the organism is ready for it; but it is unfortunate also to delay the opportunity after readiness has come. Not only interest but also total suitability and setting play a part here, as indeed is evident with reference to the educational tasks of young adulthood and of approaching old age.

THE PROBLEM OF FLEXIBILITY IN MASS EDUCATION

The beginning of this chapter stressed the enormous number (more than 30 million) in full-time school in this country, plus the great numbers in part-time and adult education. But also stressed was the range of individual differences—plus differences in each individual in abilities of different types and in developmental status in various respects. As a matter of actual practice, can these various differences be taken account of, and can we still at the same time deal with the enormous number of individuals in all these groups seeking or at least needing some type of education? The stock answer is that there should be many more teachers (similar to present teachers except that they presumably should be somewhat better, but in the same old ways) and more schools and equipment (better but of the same general type as before). There should be *smaller* classes! There should be more people and more buildings and equipment to continue essentially the same kind of unscientific "handicraft" education that was found in the better schools of 50 years and more ago! The wearisome old cliché may be repeated that the essential need is simply for Mark Hopkins at one end of a log and a student at the other![7] More

---

[7] As a matter of fact, there is some question as to whether Hopkins really was an especially good teacher. The father of one of the writers, who knew him, said no.

teachers and buildings and equipment *are* needed. But surely the American way, when faced with such problems, is to consider whether ingenuity and practical science might aid in dealing with such a vast and complex problem. Data already presented in this volume have, it is believed, several applications here.

The writers would contend that experiments with "accelerated" programs in school and college, and data regarding individual differences and numbers of the superior, warrant the estimate that a good tenth of all youngsters could save at least a year of schooling, and a considerable number could save two. A reduction in enrollments each year of perhaps three hundred thousand, by earlier completion of schooling, would involve substantial savings in number of teachers and rooms and equipment—thus released for better teaching of the remaining pupils.

The two preceding chapters have presented evidence regarding the matured abilities of the middle and older years. Chapter 6 will emphasize the value of the mature and the older person in various types of work and also show that *the* major change in the composition of the labor force in recent years has been the increasing numbers of employed women, and especially married women, of these ages. The war brought return of former teachers to the schools; and increasingly, married women are kept in, or are returning to, teaching. Since the war, shortages of teachers have stimulated campaigns for such return of former teachers to the profession. Also, training programs have appeared which may be of a much larger significance than usually recognized. Intensive programs have been instituted to train graduates of colleges of arts or commerce, or even those in other fields, for teaching. One of the writers has for some years been teaching courses in such a program. A large portion of the students are married; many have children, some grown. Their maturity and understanding interest are a delightful contrast to the adolescent shallowness, and preoccupation with the trivialities of campus life, of the typical teen-age undergraduate in the college of education. As will be pointed out in the next chapter, there is much need for more and varied occupational opportunities for women entering or reëntering employment in the middle or even older years. Surely, teaching is a profession where the maturity and experience of many of them could be of especial value. Perhaps teacher-training programs for such people should become a major and established source of teacher supply.[8]

[8] One advantage of these older teachers may be that, in fact, they stay in the profession longer; the typical girl graduate of a teacher-training institution remains in teaching only about five years.

The above comments are made with special reference to means of augmenting (and improving) the supply of teachers for the public schools. But older persons may be educationally useful in a variety of other places. Increasingly, colleges are using retired faculty members from other institutions for fill-in or even brief, regular staff positions. Industrial training tasks and many classes in adult education can best be handled by a mature person with relevant job experience—and a knack for teaching or willingness to learn. Classes or conferences on "education for aging" and preparation for retirement are in many respects most appropriately handled by older and perhaps retired people. Many of these people may need some training for such work. But might "teacher-training" programs, wisely adapted to their needs, be set up for them? If such programs are developed, it may well be that great numbers of persons coming into teaching from a great variety of other occupations (including homemaking) may become a major resource not only for staffing such various educational efforts as mentioned above but also for making them more realistic and fostering good public relations.

The writers believe that much more could be done than is realized even by most professional educators by various means which might be grouped under the term "efficiency engineering in education." Now, there are gross inefficiencies. Most school and many college plants are largely idle three months of the year, though they might be used for various special educational purposes, and almost all of the considerable evidence regarding summer sessions for children and lengthened school year for college students is favorable.[9] Curricular deadwood and overlap (especially of secondary school and college curricula, as mentioned earlier) and unnecessary prerequisites and admission requirements waste student and faculty time.[10] Much may be learned outside of school; the most out-

[9] A good school may be a better place for children in summer than the streets of a city slum. Many college students may need other-than-school experience, as in work, but for others an occasional "four-quarter" year is a desirable continuity of education. Really, four quarters, or two semesters and a summer session, total to only about ten months actually in school (52).

[10] Through an inadvertence, a well-known college of engineering once admitted about 20 students without an admission requirement in geometry and did not discover this gross omission until their records were being finally appraised with reference to graduation. The records of all of them were excellent, and careful scanning, also inquiry of the faculty, turned up no evidence of handicap because of this "gap" in preparation. One of the writers once arranged for a brilliant college senior majoring in psychology (now nationally known in that field) secretly to take the final written comprehensive examinations for the doctorate, and then slipped her papers in with some dozen written by doctoral candidates—all papers being numbered and not identifiable as to writer. The reading committee unanimously passed

standing student found in the Pennsylvania survey (38) scored highest in subjects she had never studied in school—and dropped out of college apparently from disgust at being taught things she already knew. Youngsters with hobbies, as in radio or aviation, may, on their own, go far in technology. Now, there is an extraordinary richness of means for out-of-school education—through reading, radio, television, travel, and sundry extracurricular and extra-school activities (15). Educational "efficiency engineering" would require that such learnings be taken account of (probably by tests) and coördinated with more formal educational efforts. Back in the twenties, experiments showed that even first-grade children could largely teach themselves to read, by use of clever practice exercises (59). By similar means, college students have taught themselves the mathematics needed in dairy technology (20). One of the writers has found that self-scoring instructional tests[11] may greatly facilitate instruction; in fact, a class of mature students was "taught" an entire course by this means (51). Perhaps before long, various such special materials and devices may become accepted aids in schools and colleges, somewhat as bookkeeping machines are used in offices and movies and closed-circuit television are now beginning to be used. In short, the opinion is ventured that what might be called educational technology could both greatly facilitate and greatly improve the efficiency of schools and colleges and perhaps be especially helpful in dealing with some of the newer problems, as of adult education and industrial training.[12]

---

her. But because of this and that requirement, she only received her Ph.D. after five years of graduate study. A well-known Clark alumnus states that some 40 years ago a very capable young businessman sought admission there, to undertake some special study. Finding that he had never even attended high school, the college brusquely turned him away. Instead, he went to see President G. Stanley Hall, who sensed his ability and interest and said, "Young man, the College acted rightly, since it has a rule requiring a high school diploma for admission. But the Graduate School has no such rule, and to it I will admit you." The man did excellent work there and obtained the master's degree! Such freedoms are not advocated here. But American education seems to have become so enormous and stuffily institutionalized that it has lost flexibility and common sense (and humor)—traits especially needed in these times of great growth and rapid change.

[11] Perhaps the simplest form involved chemically treated test answer sheets and fountain pens filled with a special pink ink: when the student marked the right answer to a question, the pink mark immediately turned gray, and he was required to keep marking the various answers until he did thus find the correct answer. A mechanical test device not only provided for testing and instruction in analogous fashion but automatically presented the student with a piece of candy if he made a good score!

[12] As with every advance, the big difficulty is conservative opposition from the great majority of those most involved. One of the writers was very close to efforts to adapt educational programs to the emergency during the Second World War. Most science teachers immediately rejected any suggestion that scientific methods might be used

MOTIVATIONS AND COMMUNITY VALUATIONS

Table 21 summarizes replies of over 2000 children in grades one through twelve when asked what they enjoyed most, both in and out of school, and what they would like to learn more about. The table shows, for example, that both sexes showed increases with age in interest in sports. Boys gained interest in science, and girls in high school gained interest in self-improvement and vocation. The social studies and current affairs were little favored. In general, interest in schoolwork and education seems to wane as children pass through the school system. The investigators make the following statement in summary:

TABLE 21.   Percentages of Pupils of Various Grade Levels Who Mentioned Various Subjects or Activities, in Answer to a "Free Response" Question Regarding Things Liked Best in School

| | Boys-Grades | | | | Girls-Grades | | | |
Area	1–3	4–6	7–9	10–12	1–3	4–6	7–9	10–12
Sports, gym	11	13	31	35	8	9	33	34
Arithmetic, mathematics	28	24	24	14	21	26	19	8
English usage, reading, etc.	32	19	10	11	36	28	20	28
Nature study, science	0	3	7	21	1	4	9	9
Local and world affairs	1	9	7	8	1	11	10	6
Art, music, dramatics, etc.	13	11	10	16	17	15	16	14
Self-improvement, vocations	0	0	0	5	0	0	0	15
Number of cases	363	309	282	159	331	343	290	171

NOTE: When asked about "one of the happiest days of my life," no group mentioned areas of subject matter by as many as 1 percent.

SOURCE: Adapted from A. T. Jersild and Ruth Tasch, *Children's Interests and What They Suggest for Education,* New York, Teachers College Bureau of Publications, Columbia University, 1949, pp. 138–141.

The typical first or second grader is interested in school and what the school represents. More likely than not he likes his teacher, too. The life of a scholar appeals to him. He is challenged by what there is to learn. He may say, as one

---

toward improvement of their own teaching. Engineering faculty members would speak proudly of their methods of increasing industrial efficiency, and in the next sentence, they would reject with irritation the notion that analogous steps might be taken to eliminate unnecessary topics and streamline instructional methods. And in 1956 an extensive form being used by a committee, to survey all the institutions of higher education in a large state regarding their adequacy for dealing with mounting enrollments, asks much about number of rooms and staff members and books in libraries—but there is not one question about any experiments in instructional methods, educational research, or new ideas!

child in this study said, that one of the happiest days in his life was the day he learned "to take away." When he tells what he likes about school he mentions things that distinctly belong to school much more frequently than he mentions things that school shares with life outside, such as games and outdoor play.

The young child's friendly feeling about school appears not only when he talks about school as such but also when he happens to mention school in describing his likes and wishes. When describing what he dislikes most in life outside school, the young child is likely to make very few unfavorable references to any burdens or discomforts which the school had placed on his out-of-school life.

As the average child moves up through the grades he seems to become less eager about things that distinctly belong to school and scholarliness, more inclined to complain, more interested in the things that go along with school rather than with work in the classroom. He becomes relatively more interested in recess periods than in class periods. He mentions play and sports more often. There is a greater hiatus between his wishes and what the school offers. (*31*, pp. 41–42.)

Some of the decreases in interest may well be the result of failure to relate topics to developmental needs, as mentioned earlier. For instance, an analysis showed decrease with age in interest in such health topics as digestion but increased interest in causes of pimples, in grooming, and in boy-girl relations. Cumulative boredom because of inadequate adjustment to mounting individual differences and out-of-school learning, as mentioned in the preceding pages, may be a factor. But the contrast remains to be explained of relatively little and usually decreasing interest in schoolwork at the same time that interest in athletics increases, and is probably greater than Table 21 shows, since spectator interest may not be fully included. Why should this be?

A blatantly evident factor is the great publicity given to athletics. Not only do major athletic events get headlines, and coverage in newspaper and radio and TV that is greater than that given to all but the most outstanding other news, but local papers and radio stations increasingly give similar prominence to local high school teams. And in the school, rallies and other devices whip up excitement. But less obvious factors are also believed to be important. A father's encouragement of his son's basketball playing is likely to be more hearty than of his son's current events class. It may build up from very early beginnings. For instance, a former college athlete bought a small plastic football for his infant son to play with in his crib! Interest in sports can be maintained elsewhere than at school—on community playgrounds or vacant lots, after school, week ends, and during vacations. There is great social support and facilitation: sports *are* social, companionships are found in sports and associations they bring about, and they are a prime topic of talk. The coach gives individualized instruction *for excellence*, not class instruction for passing. The competitions of sports give frequent appraisals and hearty, generally acclaimed successes, beside which the triumphs of the classroom are pallid and of dubious social worth. Clearly, many influences work together to build up sports interests—and to develop excellence in sports. But could such factors, in such powerful concert, similarly support other phases of schooling?

An issue of *Time* with a cover portrait of the 1955 "Star Farmer of America," and a full four pages about him, illustrates that something similar is possible.[13] Twenty-one-year-old Joe Moore's winning of this honor not only received national attention in the press and on the radio and as high point of a national convention attended by 10,000 other "Future Farmers of America," but it was shrewdly featured in his state and locally. Its origins went back to his joining the 4-H Club in grade school. At the suggestion of his 4-H supervisor, Joe "bought a black steer, fed it for five months, and took it to the Nashville Fat Cattle Show." And through their teachings (not only at school but on the home farm and throughout the year), their competitions, and their organizational orders of ascendancy, these organizations continued to stimulate, guide, and give prestige locally, regionally, and nationally, in somewhat the same broad and pervasive fashion as does athletics. Somewhat similarly, though less adequately, science fairs and junior academies foster interest in science, and junior achievement clubs foster interest in business. The judgment is ventured that in programs such as those offered by the Future Farmers and the 4-H are to be found the most effective ideas for stimulating interest and more generally for increasing educational effectiveness, rather than in more classroom-bound and conventional efforts to "improve teaching."

One of the writers (as mentioned earlier) has suggested that a person on the staff of a school or college, somewhat analogous to the athletic coach, who would seek out, guide, foster, and publicize the able students in such fields as science might analogously build up interest and status in these fields (50). In certain respects programs of the vocational agriculture teacher and the F.F.A. work even more pervasively and effectively. The reader should note that the total combination of influences described as operating to develop athletes and "star farmers" has many similarities to the influences described in the previous

13 *Time*, October 24, 1955, *66*:16–19.

chapter as developing "genius" in music and science—and urged for the education of the gifted student earlier in this chapter. The Russians seem somewhat similarly to be focusing interests and resources on the training of their scientists. As suggested in the preceding chapter, genius may be made by such factors more than is usually supposed.

A degree with distinction in a college of education, which one of the writers was largely instrumental in setting up, may serve as an example of a program at the college level with some evidence of outcome. Superior students (not only in academic record but also in participation in worth-while activities and employment) were usually admitted in their sophomore year. These students had certain privileges—upon petition, they might be excused from certain required courses, be admitted to a desired course for which they did not have a prerequisite, etc. They did a field project under the supervision of a faculty member—many of the reports were worthy of publication. They associated together. They were continually in close contact with their faculty advisor, somewhat as is a graduate student. The commencement program carried their names as receiving their degrees "with distinction," and the student placement office emphasized this honor and its significance to superintendents seeking teachers. The program was also publicized in a college publication sent throughout the state and stressed in releases to newspapers. Evidence of the program's decided stimulating values may be found by the fact that it doubled the number of young men in the program who later obtained the doctorate. Several may already be called distinguished in their fields.[14]

What about interest in adult education? Table 22 exhibits a situation

TABLE 22. Percentage of Various Age Groups Enrolled in a Home Study Program Who Took Courses for Specific Reasons

Purpose	Age						
	15–19	20–24	25–29	30–39	40–49	50–59	60 up
To complete school requirement	37	17	14	11	6	4	
For personal need	7	10	16	19	20	23	18
For vocational major	10	27	28	28	25	23	14
For vocational minor	28	25	22	20	22	15	19
For cultural interests	19	21	21	22	26	36	50
Percent completing course	17	18	16	18	24	20	32
Number of cases	281	914	1167	1775	889	319	101

SOURCE: Adapted from G. B. Smith, *Purposes and Conditions Affecting the Nature and the Extent of Participation of Adults in the Time Study Department of Columbia University, 1925–1932*, Teachers College Contributions to Education, No. 633, New York, Teachers College, Columbia University, 1935.

[14] S. L. Pressey, The new program for the degree with distinction in education at the Ohio State University, *School and Society*, August 27, 1932, and Outcomes of a special "honors" program, 20 years later, *School and Society*, 1955, 82:58–59.

which is believed to be still largely current. Much adult education is a belated effort to complete school requirements, or a vocational major or minor probably similarly part of an earlier full-time educational program. Only gradually is there any considerable interest in programs for personal need or cultural interests. And relatively few adults—more than a quarter only in the small group 60 years old or more—complete a course.

Greater attention to the developmental needs of adults should bring greater and more general interest in adult education. The adult programs in some public school systems are fascinatingly rich, including courses for vocational up-grading as in accounting and business law, discussion courses on current events including local issues, and a variety of leisure interests like choral singing and decoy-duck making! Programs are appearing not only in schools and colleges but in various other places, as city recreation programs and golden age centers. Results are getting recognition and publicity in hobby shows and concerts by musical groups. Adult education programs are increasingly becoming part of the tissue of adult life and are rewarding in multiple ways. It is believed that development of these wider relationships and programs is especially needed. For example, a widow took up hand-weaving in a city recreation department class. There she made friends with similar interests who were in somewhat similar circumstances, joined a weavers' guild, found a market for handicraft through a gift shop, and soon had so much business that she took on a friend to live and work with her. Her widowhood was transformed, and she was made self-supporting by the "hobby" class.

Summary

The chapter has attempted an overview of education, as seen in the prospective of development through the life span, the hypothesis being that such a perspective might somewhat reinterpret educational programs and perhaps offer cues for their reorientation and improvement.

1. A survey of current educational programs shows that they are indeed substantial. Not only are there now over 30 million young people in full-time school, with numbers in secondary and collegiate education increasing with extraordinary rapidity, but part-time and adult education are becoming increasingly important. Increases in length of life and numbers of adults, as well as technological change, increase educational tasks and numbers to be served. Education extending essentially throughout the life span needs guidance from study of life-span development.

2. In this situation, three major psychoeducational problems seem es-

pecially important. (1) There should be better coördination of education with development so that work is not assigned before an individual is ready for it, full-time education does not extend unduly far into the adult years when the individual is ready for the independent responsibilities of adult life, and (as in education for retirement) developmental needs and readinesses throughout the life span are recognized. (2) Extensions to include both greater numbers of individuals and individuals over a wider age range make increasingly acute the already serious problem of individual differences in a system of mass education structured by the educational lock step according to chronological age. Individuals at a given age differ greatly in abilities, interests, and stage of maturity. They differ throughout life in rates of maturing and decline. Especially around such change times as puberty, maturity, and the menopause, they differ at a given age in developmental status. (3) The school is a social as well as an educational institution. It usually fails to recognize problems of socioeconomic class. There is often incoördination between educational and social development, inadequate recognition of individual differences in position in school "society" and of problems of social adjustment, and little consideration of problems of "social psychology" in adult education.

3. As the world becomes more complex and changes more rapidly, handicapped or inadequate persons have more difficulty preparing for it in youth and adjusting to it in adulthood. A variety of educational programs for handicapped and inadequate children have been devised that try to help them, and programs for adults having similar needs are developing.

4. Superior or gifted individuals are the students of greatest potentialities but are now the most neglected of all special groups. They are usually precocious. Yet early school entrance is usually questioned as is rapid progress, recognizing their usual rapid development. The gifted usually have both special needs and special potentialities socially, but conventional school social structures handicap them. "Enrichment" tends to be class-conscious "extras" rather than enlarged opportunities suitable to each youngster's potentials. The need for an individualized developmental approach in education is especially exemplified in the case of the gifted person.

5. In review, three major needs are seen. The concept of broad "developmental tasks" seems of value in relating educational thinking to knowledge of life-span development and to broad, lifelong educational needs. The present greatly expanding and lengthening programs in edu-

cation make necessary educational "efficiency engineering," if these needs are to be adequately met; no unfortunate "factory" methods need result, but rather a freeing of teaching from drudgery and application of scientific methods to education. Lacks in both student interest in and public regard for education suggest major problems of motivation and public attitudes; these might perhaps well be dealt with in considerable part by methods suggested by the prestige of athletics and by such programs as the F.F.A. and 4-H clubs in vocational agriculture.

The above summary is with reference to education in this country. But the chapter has attempted to give some larger, world-wide perspectives. These should be emphasized. This country, with its lengthening life span plus its rapid change, especially needs educational programming throughout life. Rigidity and inflexibility become dangers especially where the educational effort is so huge. American vigor tends to unhealthy bigness of cities, automobiles, industrial concerns, and perhaps government. Has there also been overgrowth of full-time education? But in times of a hot *or* cold war, it is especially important to keep in mind the major importance of education—all the means of education from public school to the mass media of communication. So seen, all the educational problems discussed in the preceding pages take on urgency. In the long view, it is as important that educational programs keep up with current progress and changing needs as that the national defense does. Instead, American education seems clumsily big and slow and defensive, rather than alert and adaptive in this changing world.

BIBLIOGRAPHY

1. Anastasi, Anne, and Foley, J. P., Jr., *Differential Psychology* (rev. ed.), New York, Macmillan, 1949.
2. Anderson, R. H., Ungraded primary classes, *Understanding the Child*, 1955, 24:66–72.
3. Baker, Harry J., *Introduction to Exceptional Children* (rev. ed.), New York, Macmillan, 1954.
4. Barker, R. G., and Wright, H. F., *One Boy's Day*, New York, Harper, 1951.
5. Biber, B., Murphy, L., Woodcock, L., and Black, I., *Child Life in School*, New York, Dutton, 1942.
6. Blackmer, A. R., *et al.*, *General Education in School and College*, Cambridge, Harvard University Press, 1952.
7. Brandwein, P. F., *The Gifted Student as Future Scientist*, New York, Harcourt, Brace, 1955.

8. Bray, D. W., *Issues in the Study of Talent*, New York, Columbia University, 1954.
9. Bruno, H., *Wings over America*, New York, Stratford Press, 1942.
10. Bugenthal, James, Clinical approach to the guidance of superior students, *Peabody J. Educ.*, 1948, 25:268–282.
11. Carmichael, L. (ed.), *Manual of Child Psychology* (rev. ed.), New York, Wiley, 1954.
12. Cassidy, Viola M., and Phelps, H. R., *Postschool Adjustment of Slow Learning Children*, Ohio State University, Bureau of Special and Adult Education, 1955.
13. Charles, D. C., Ability and accomplishment of persons earlier judged mentally deficient, *Genet. Psychol. Monogr.*, 1953, 47:3–71.
14. Cruickshank, W. (ed.), *Psychology of Exceptional Children and Youth*, New York, Prentice-Hall, 1955.
15. Dale, Edgar, *Audio Visual Methods in Teaching* (rev. ed.), New York, Dryden Press, 1954.
16. De Witt, N., *Soviet Professional Manpower*, Washington, D.C., National Science Foundation, 1955.
17. Essert, P. L., *et al.*, Adult education, *Rev. Educ. Res.*, June, 1953, 23:191–293.
18. Flesher, Marie A., and Pressey, S. L., War-time accelerates ten years after, *J. educ. Psychol.*, 1955, 46:228–238.
19. Foster, R. G. and Wilson, P. D., *Women After College*, New York, Columbia University Press, 1942.
20. Frutchey, F. P., Removal of deficiencies by practice exercises, *Junior College J.*, 1934, 4:403–409.
21. Grace, A. G., *et al.*, *Educational Lessons from Wartime Training*, Washington, D.C., American Council on Education, 1948.
22. Havighurst, R. J., *Human Development and Education*, New York, Longmans, Green, 1953.
23. Havighurst, R. J., *Who Shall Be Educated?* New York, Harper, 1944.
24. Havighurst, R. J., Stivers, E., and DeHaan, R. F., *A Survey of the Education of Gifted Children*, Chicago, University of Chicago Press, 1955.
25. Heck, A. O., *Education of Exceptional Children* (2nd ed.), New York, McGraw-Hill, 1953.
26. Heisher, R., Meeting the challenge of intellectual youth, *Ed. Outl.*, 1952, 27:2–11.
27. Hildreth, Gertrude H., *Educating Gifted Children*, New York, Harper, 1952.
28. Hollingshead, A. B., *Elmtown's Youth*, New York, Wiley, 1949.
29. Ivins, W. H., and Runge, W. B., *Work Experience in High School*, New York, Ronald Press, 1953.
30. Jennings, Helen H., *Leadership and Isolation*, New York, Longmans, Green, 1943.
31. Jersild, A. T., and Tasch, Ruth, *Children's Interests and What They*

Suggest for Education, New York, Teachers College, Bureau of Publications, 1949.

32. Kempfer, H., *Adult Education,* New York, McGraw-Hill, 1955.
33. Keys, N., *The Underage Student in High School and College,* Berkeley, University of California Press, 1938.
34. King, H. F., The response of older rural craftsmen to individual training, *J. Gerontol.,* 1955, *10*:207–211.
35. Klein, A. J. (ed.), *Adventures in the Reconstruction of Education,* Columbus, Ohio State University Press, 1940.
36. Kuhlen, R. G., *The Psychology of Adolescent Behavior,* New York, Harper, 1952.
37. Kuhlen, R. G., and Thompson, G., *Psychological Studies of Human Development,* New York, Appleton-Century, 1952.
38. Learned, W. S., and Wood, B. D., *The Student and His Knowledge,* New York, Carnegie Foundation, 1928.
39. Lehman, H. C., *Age and Achievement,* Princeton, Princeton University Press, 1953.
40. Lewis, Claudia, *Children of the Cumberland,* New York, Columbia University Press, 1946.
41. Lynd, Helen M., *Field Work in College Education,* New York, Columbia University Press, 1946.
42. McCoy, Georgia F., and Rush, H. A., *An Evaluation of Rehabilitation,* New York, Institute of Physical Medicine and Rehabilitation, 1953.
43. Melcher, G., *An Evaluation of the Northeast Accelerated Junior College Experiment with Superior Students,* Kansas City (Missouri), Board of Education, 1953.
44. Meltzer, B. N., The productivity of social scientists, *Amer. J. Sociol.,* 1949–1950, *55*:25–30.
45. Moore, E. H., Preparation for retirement, *J. Gerontol.,* 1946, *1*:202–212.
46. Murphy, G., *In the Minds of Men,* New York, Basic Books, 1953.
47. Olsen, E. G., *School and Community Programs: A Casebook of Successful Practice from Kindergarten Through College and Adult Education,* New York, Prentice-Hall, 1949.
48. Olson, W. C., *Child Development,* Boston, D. C. Heath, 1949.
49. Passow, A. H., *et al., Planning for Talented Youth,* New York, Teachers College, Bureau of Publications, 1955.
50. Pressey, S. L., Concerning the nature and nurture of genius, *Sci. Mont.,* 1955, *81*:123–129.
51. Pressey, S. L., Development and appraisal of devices providing immediate automatic scoring of objective tests and concomitant self-instruction, *J. Psychol.,* 1950, *29*:417–447.
52. Pressey, S. L., *Educational Acceleration: Appraisals and Basic Problems,* Columbus, Ohio State University Press, 1949.
53. Pressey, S. L., The place and function of psychology in undergraduate programs, *Amer. Psychol.,* 1949, *4*:148–150.
54. Pressey, S. L., and Robinson, F. P., *Psychology and the New Education,* New York, Harper, 1944.

55. Ravner, Pearl C., *Training Mature Women for Employment*, U.S. Department of Labor, Woman's Bureau, Bulletin 256, Washington, D.C., U.S. Government Printing Office, 1955.

56. Research Division of the Fund, *Bridging the Gap Between School and College*, New York, Fund for the Advancement of Education, 1953.

57. Riecken, H. W., *The Volunteer Work Camp: A Psychological Evaluation*, Cambridge, Addison-Wesley, 1952.

58. Smith, G. B., *Purposes and Conditions Affecting the Nature and Extent of Participation of Adults in the Time Study Department of Columbia University, 1925–1932*, Teachers College Contributions to Education, No. 633, New York, Teachers College, Columbia University, 1935.

59. Smith, Nila B., An experiment to determine the effectiveness of practice tests in teaching beginning reading, *J. Educ. Res.*, 1923, 7:213–228.

60. Sumner, F. B., *The Life History of an American Naturalist*, Lancaster, Jacques Cattell Press, 1945.

61. Terman, L. M., The discovery and encouragement of exceptional talent, *Amer. Psychol.*, 1954, 9:221–230.

62. Terman, L. M., and Oden, Medita, *The Gifted Child Grows Up*, Stanford, Stanford University Press, 1947.

63. U.S. Office of Education, *Statistical Summary of Education*, Washington, D.C., U.S. Government Printing Office, 1953.

64. Van Til, W., *et al.*, Research in human relations and programs of action, *Rev. of Educ. Res.*, 1953, 23:287–385.

65. Visher, S. S., *Scientists Starred in 1903–43, A Study of Collegiate Training*, Baltimore, Johns Hopkins Press, 1948.

66. Wagner, Mazie E., *Anticipatory Examinations for College Credit: Twenty Years Experience*, New York, University of Buffalo Studies, 1952.

67. Warren, Marjorie W., Retraining the elderly hemiplegic, *Geriat.*, 1953, 8:198–203.

68. White, L., *Educating Our Daughters*, New York, Harper, 1950.

69. Williamson, B. L. and Feder, D. D., Scholarship winners; how they rate on campus and in class, *Personnel and Guidance J.*, 1953, 31:236–240.

70. Wilson, F. T., A survey of educational provisions for young gifted children in the U.S. and studies and problems related thereto, *J. Genet. Psychol.*, 1949, 75:3–9.

71. Witty, P. A., *The Gifted Child*, Boston, D. C. Heath, 1951.

72. Witty, P. A., *Helping the Gifted Child*, Chicago, Science Research Associates, 1952.

73. Wolfle, D., *America's Resources of Specialized Talent*, New York, Harper, 1954.

74. Woodbury, D. O., *Beloved Scientist: Elihu Thomson*, New York, Whittlesey House, 1944.

75. Worcester, D. A., *The Education of Children of Above-Average Ability*, Lincoln, University of Nebraska, 1955.

CHAPTER 6 •

• The Work Life

LITERALLY and figuratively work is at the center of life. It is the prime concern of most people through their best years. In these years, it is the major factor determining their income, their associates, their status in their community, and their way of life. The work of the head of a family is thus largely determinative of the associates, community status, and opportunities of his wife and children. The gross facts regarding work, and also some of the implications and derivatives of work as affecting the nature of life, must therefore be carefully considered.

Gross Data Regarding Workers and Jobs

Certain gross facts regarding workers and jobs seem necessary as background material. Once these are in mind, sundry associated psychological phenomena and problems can be seen with a greater sense of their importance and their complexity.

SIZE AND COMPOSITION OF THE LABOR FORCE

Figure 62 gives some of the major data regarding employment in this country over the approximately quarter-century period from just before the Great Depression through the Second World War into the nineteen fifties.

Obviously, the total labor force (total number of people either working or seeking work) grew steadily over this period, as would be expected from the growth in total population. However, inclusion of the armed forces made a bulge during the war in the otherwise very steady increase. Evidently, reserves outside the usual labor force make possible its expansion in an emergency; the nature of that reserve will be noted shortly. The fact that in 1950 the total labor force was 40 percent of the total population and 41 percent in 1930 suggests that the total,

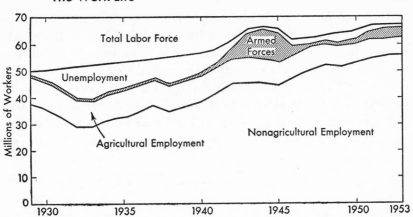

Figure 62. Labor Force, Employment, and Unemployment—Annual Averages. (From U.S. Department of Labor, Bureau of Labor Statistics, *Fact Book on Manpower*, Washington, D.C., U.S. Government Printing Office, 1954.)

massive complex of influences putting people into the labor force had been relatively constant over this 20-year period. Figure 62 also shows that the persistent economic disease of unemployment was a major phenomenon for over a decade, from the beginning of the depression into the war. It is very evident that the growth in the labor force over this period has been in nonagricultural types of employment. Clearly, these must be differentiated.

It must first be noted, however, that in sundry respects the composition of the work force has been changing. The proportion of women increased from about 17 percent in 1890 to 27 percent in 1950. During the war, women made up about a third of the total number employed. And though by 1950 the number of women in the labor force had dropped, the proportion of employed women who were over 45 increased—from about 15 percent in 1890 to about 30 percent in 1950. And the proportion of women 14 to 24 dropped from 52 percent to 24 percent in these same 60 years. Apparently, women are not only coming into the labor force more, but they are coming in older and staying longer. The proportion of males 14 to 24 in the labor force has also decreased over the last 60 years—from about 27 percent to 16 percent. As was seen in the preceding chapter, American youngsters are now staying in school longer.

The situation is explicated still further by Figure 63 which shows the proportion of the total population of each sex that was in the labor force in 1890 and in 1953. Clearly, people now are tending to go to work later than they did then; in 1890 a large portion of boys in their middle teens were already at work—9.2 percent of those were 10 to 13! About the same proportion of men in the age group 20 to 50 were in the labor force in 1953 as in 1890. But after the age of 50, the recent curve begins to drop; now, fewer older men are working—68.2 percent in 1890 but 41.6 percent in 1950 of those aged 65 and over were in the labor force. In 1890, over a quarter of the young women worked; but many soon

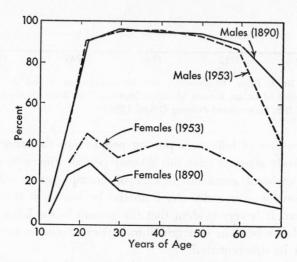

Figure 63. Labor Force as a Percentage of the Total Population of Each Age Group, 1890 and 1953. (Data for 1890 are from J. D. Durand, *The Labor Force in the United States*, New York, Social Science Research, 1948, p. 208, and are estimates comparable to 1940 census data, adjusted to include persons of unknown age. Data for 1953 are from U.S. Department of Labor, Bureau of Labor Statistics, *Fact Book on Manpower*, Washington, D.C., U.S. Government Printing Office, 1954.)

dropped out of the labor force, presumably because of marriage and childbearing, and after 30 the number employed continued to fall slowly. In 1953 not only did more young women work, but after leaving the labor force around 30, some returned. After 50, however, the curve drops more rapidly than in 1890. Though the number of older people is increasing, the proportion employed is decreasing. Of the population 10 years of age and older, 75.5 percent of males were in the labor force in 1890, as compared to 72.8 percent in 1950; for females the corresponding figures were 16.6 and 26.5 percent. The work of the country is increasingly being done by that portion of the population from about 20 to about 65—a portion of the population which is proportionately decreasing in view of the growing numbers of children and of older people.

The above statistics may indeed seem to be cold, economic data—not matter for psychology. But these figures concern people, and they paint, in sweeping strokes, major changes in the way of life in this country. As will be seen shortly (and as everyone who lived through the Great Depression well knows), unemployment is indeed an economic disease which can have festering psychological effects in the destruction of self-confidence, of status with family and associates, and of personal and group morale. As will also be stressed later, such effects were not only pandemic during the depression: except in boom times, unemployment is relatively frequent among young workers, and psychological consequences may be very debilitating to morale at the beginning of a career. The great and growing mass of unemployed oldsters is an increasingly important problem. The increasing proportion of women employed (when considered in connection with the increasing tendency of women to marry, and to marry younger) certainly involves changes in the socioeconomic status of women and presumably in their total personalities. Changes also occur in the nature of family life and in the place of women both in the work world and the home.[1]

TABLE 23. Percentage of Population Economically Active According to Age Group (Selected Countries)

	Males			Females		
	15–19	20–64	65+	15–19	20–64	65+
U.S. (1950)	44.9	90.0	41.4	26.3	33.0	7.8
Italy (1951)	87.3	95.3	35.4	47.4	27.4	5.0
France (1946)	75.6	93.2	54.4	58.6	50.0	22.3
Belgium (1947)	66.8	90.3	24.7	41.8	24.7	5.4
United Kingdom (1951)	82.9	96.8	32.0	78.2	36.0	5.3
Yugoslavia (1948)	90.0	98.6	82.8	86.7	81.5	59.0
New Zealand (1945)	71.3	92.6	30.7	62.5	25.2	2.8
Japan (1952)	58.7	99.4	55.3	53.8	54.4	22.0

SOURCE: Adapted from the International Labor Office, *Year Book of Labor Statistics*, 1954, p. 8.

[1] Being a woman or being a wife or even being a mother is no longer a separate kind of existence; or is the work world a separate man's world. Existence for everyone, including children. is different in consequence.

Viewed with reference to the larger complications as to the nature of living indicated above, comparative data from other countries are relevant. Table 23 shows that 82.9 percent of English boys 15 to 19 were at work and 78.2 percent of English girls of the same ages worked, as compared to 44.9 percent of American boys and 26.3 percent of American girls of these ages. Obviously, later adolescence is a different period of life for most young people in Britain, Italy, and Yugoslavia than it is here. In mid-life, women are employed most in Yugoslavia and Japan and least in Italy and New Zealand. After 65, only 24.7 percent of men are "economically active" in Belgium but 88.8 percent are in Yugoslavia; 7.8 percent of women these ages in the United States work, but 22.3 percent do in France. Presumably, old age is lived differently in different countries.

TYPES OF WORK

Figure 62 showed about the same number of people employed in agriculture from 1929 to 1950, though the total labor force *and* total population grew greatly over this period. Table 24 exhibits this phenomenon as a long-time decrease in proportion of workers in agriculture —31.0 percent in 1910 (almost two-thirds in 1850) on the farms but only 12.1 percent in 1950. Yet the country has more than supported itself agriculturally. As a result of increasing efficiency in agriculture, a larger and larger nonfarm population has been supported by a given number of workers on the farm. The table shows a drop also, in the 40-year period, in number of nonfarm laborers. Biggest gains are in numbers of clerks and semiskilled workers—and these are the two biggest groups in 1950. Whether automation may bring decreases in these last groups

TABLE 24.   Percent of Total Workers Engaged in Each Field

	1910	1950
Farmers	16.5	7.5
Farm laborers	14.5[a]	4.6[a]
Laborers	14.7	7.8[a]
Skilled workers	11.7	13.8[a]
Semiskilled workers	14.7	22.4[a]
Clerks	10.02	20.02[a]
Professions	4.4	7.5[a]

[a] Estimated.

SOURCE: Adapted from the U.S. Department of Labor, Bureau of Labor Statistics, *The Workers' Story, 1913–1953,* Washington, D.C., U.S. Government Printing Office, 1953.

and increases in numbers of skilled workers and engineers remains to be seen. But three trends seem clear: decreased numbers on the farms, decreased numbers of unskilled workers, and continuing rapid change in the nature of work in almost every field and numbers in each.

These may seem economic rather than psychological materials; but certainly work on a farm and on a semiskilled factory job are two very different experiences and involve two very different total ways of life. The different types of work and rapid changes also involve problems of selection, training, and retraining; possible transfer or advancement; and supervision, all of which are important to industrial psychologists. School psychologists or counselors should take account of such facts in guidance. The total situation is of importance to every young person planning his career.

INCOME

Comparison of occupations as to income involves many various difficulties. High hourly rates in seasonal or irregular occupations may not add up to as much yearly income as is earned in other work seemingly more modestly paid. Table 25 shows average annual earnings for certain types of work. The rises in dollar income over the 21 years, and sub-

TABLE 25. Average Annual Earnings (in Dollars Without Correction for Changing Purchasing Power) per Full-Time Employee by Industry, 1932 and 1953

	1932	1953
Agriculture, forestry, and fisheries	247	1653
Mining	1016	4364
Contract construction	907	4244
Manufacturing	1150	4051
Wholesale and retail trade	1315	3476
Finance, insurance, and real estate	1652	3761
Transportation	1373	4441
Comm. and public utilities	1438	4034
Services	918	2650
Government and government enterprise	1477	3351

SOURCE: Adapted from the U.S. Department of Commerce, Office of Business Economics, National Income, 1954 Edition, Washington, D.C., U.S. Government Printing Office, 1954, pp. 200–201.

stantial increases to 1953, do not, of course, mean that much increase in purchasing power. Real increases in different occupations have been very different. For instance, the average year's wage of a railway engineer in 1953 was $7352, a gain of 57 percent in purchasing power from 1904. But the 1953 salary of $7000 of a university professor was a decrease of 2 percent in purchasing power from the earlier data. In purchasing power, the yearly 1953 income of an auto worker ($4947) was up 140 percent and a grade school teacher's salary at $4817 was up 60 percent from 1904; high school teachers at $5526 were down 1 percent in actual purchasing power from 50 years earlier.[2] Net income of physicians (total fees less office expenses) has been reported as $4870 in 1930 and $13,432 in 1951. Similar figures for lawyers were $5194 and $8730 (97).

In 1953, out of about 50 million "consumer units" (families or unattached individuals) some 3 percent had incomes of $15,000 or more (perhaps a twelfth of these had incomes of $50,000 or more), and in contrast, 5.7 percent had incomes under $1000; most common was an income of $3000–$3999 (97). The average person appears to reach peak income in the forties, as indicated in Chapter 7.

Once again, it may be felt that the above material is economic rather than psychological. But income indicates capacity for satisfying wants; it is a major indication of status; to the extent that income is secure, the individual feels secure about his place in life and can plan for his future. Lack or uncertainty breeds discontent; and affluence may produce self-complacency or smugness or arrogance. All this is true not only for the wage earner but for his family. An older worker's status with family, neighbors, and associates may suffer when income starts down. It might rather be said that to omit such considerations from any realistic study of human life would make that treatment inadequate.

The Course of the Work Life

The gross classifications of the preceding pages suggest very inadequately the enormous variety of work in this country—the *Dictionary of Occupations* includes 22,028 defined jobs. Further, the course of the work life varies from one field to another. But certain large features are common.

[2] *U.S. News and World Report*, November 25, 1955, data from the Ruml-Tickton study.

In childhood certain vocational interests are a passing product of a stage of development, as small boys' thoughts of being cowboys. In high school, such interests become more immediate and serious, but they may still be unrealistic. For example, in 1937, 53 percent of high school senior boys in Canton, Ohio, stated that they were interested in the professions, but only 14 percent of the graduates of that high school six years earlier actually were in such work. Of the girls, 46 percent sought clerical work, but only 23 percent had obtained such positions; 43 percent landed in domestic and personal service jobs (65, p. 591). These data are for a prewar date when opportunities were presumably limited—but interests should have been more realistic. Recent data are similar. Of 4700 high school seniors in Philadelphia and New Haven in 1952, 91 percent considered that they had reached a decision regarding career. And 4 out of 10 chose a profession though only 19 percent of workers 25 years of age or older in those areas, with a four-year high school education or more, were in professional or semiprofessional work. Of the boys, 6 out of 10 sought a profession (79). A 1948 Indiana survey showed no senior girl in a large high school planning or expecting to do such work as waiting on table, maid service, or cleaning; but one year later, 20 percent were doing such work (41, p. 83). However, when pupils have been asked to differentiate desires and actual expectations, they have been more realistic (86). And evidence cited in Chapter 7 on motivation will show marked differences between socioeconomic classes in age of appearance of vocational interests and hope for vocational up-grading.

In childhood, a boy may have "work" responsibilities in the care of the lawn, and a girl may have certain tasks in the house. There may be more or less formal set chores, which may or may not be paid for. School requires regular attendance at regular times and tasks to be done at particular times and in particular ways. A trade school may include work experience. Certain other high schools may recognize work experience as sufficiently significant educationally to be allowed for and perhaps given credit. A few colleges, such as Antioch, may have full-time work experience as an established (indeed featured) part of their program. But more commonly, first employment is in a part-time or summer job. Of a group of high school boys, 38 percent had paper routes, 33 percent were sales clerks, and 5 percent were filling station attendants. Of the girls, 33 percent were sales clerks, 32 percent were housemaids, and 33 percent were nursemaids. Summer jobs were more complete as full-time work experiences. Table 26 summarizes such work done by high school and college students in a medium-sized city and shows relations to work in the labor force in general.

TABLE 26.   Types of Male Initial Work Period Jobs: (1) High School Summer Jobs in an Industrial City, (2) College Summer Jobs, 1946, and (3) Ohio Male Labor Force, 1940

Occupational Classification	High School	College FS[a]	College JS[a]	Labor Force
Professional	1		12	6
Owner, manager		4	11	20
Clerical	30	17	27	14
Skilled		10	3	19
Semiskilled	15	42	28	26
Unskilled	4	22	14	15
Domestic	50	5	5	
Total	100	100	100	100

[a] Freshmen-sophomores and juniors-seniors.

NOTE: As mentioned in the previous chapter, a high school may have programs of work experience which constructively utilize such experience for vocational training and more or less broadly for vocational orientation (41). A few colleges, notably Antioch, have work experience as a feature of their programs.

SOURCE: Adapted from D. C. Miller and W. H. Form, *Industrial Sociology*, New York, Harper, 1951, p. 552.

UNEMPLOYMENT

A distressing anomaly is the fact that at the beginning of the work life, lack of work is especially common. For example, in 1950 (a relatively prosperous year) the percentages of persons of different ages in the labor market who were seeking work but did not have any were as follows: 14 to 19, 9.7 percent; 20 to 24, 6.8 percent; 25 to 44, 4.1 percent; 45 to 64, 4.2 percent; 65 and older, 5.1 percent. Doubtless many of the unemployed who were 19 and younger were relatively incompetent; most of the people at these ages were in school and not in the labor market. But even a dull 18-year-old boy may be much distressed by continuing failure to find work; his home situation may suffer, and delinquency may follow. And the percentage 65 and over desiring work and not finding it was undoubtedly more than 5 percent; many discouraged oldsters dropped out of the labor market. In 1950, urban unemployment was 5.5 percent but unemployment in farming areas only 1.8 percent; 8.3 percent of nonwhites but 4.5 percent of whites were unemployed; the sexes were about the same—4.9 percent of men and 4.7 percent of women were seeking work but not finding it (95). In recessions or depressions, unemployment hits especially the younger workers (51 percent of the unemployed in 1937 were from 15 to 34 years of age), the oldest, and such marginal groups as married women (65, p. 691).

Some unemployment is presumably inevitable, as in seasonal or irregular types of work, or as "time out" when a person is changing jobs or an industry is making some change. But long-continued unemployment or employment involving mounting financial distress and uncertainty regarding career is a different matter. Everyone having contact with young people during the Great Depression knows how demoralizing it can be for them to come into the labor market, often with high hopes of financial and familial independence, of career and perhaps early marriage, only to find these hopes frustrated and themselves vocationally unwanted. In certain respects the older person may be even more injured; he loses status he had, and the older he gets, the less likely he is to obtain any work. As pointed out earlier, the proportion of older people who are now not working as compared with 50 years ago is decidedly larger. For example in 1947, a man of 60 could hope to live one year longer than in 1900 (and probably in somewhat better health), but he might expect to be dropped from his job about two years earlier—and spend twice as long in retirement (5.6 years as compared to 2.8 years in 1900). For some, retirement might be desired or necessary because of ill-health or incomptence; but for many others it might be resented, hopeless unemployment simply because of age. The topic will be returned to.

CAREER PATTERNS

The question now is as to the patterns of work lives after they have definitely been embarked upon. Figure 64 summarizes a study of a variety of careers, the lines indicating modal patterns for persons in different types of occupation. The figure indicates that the father of the typical professional man in this inquiry had an eleventh-grade education and was himself in a proprietary-managerial or official position. While in school, the son probably had a variety of initial work experiences, part-time or summers, as indicated in an earlier table. But once professional training has been completed, trial positions are at the professional level, and stable positions at this level are attained relatively soon thereafter. The fathers of those who become managers or officials are likely themselves to be such; traditionally, they begin with office or other jobs lower down and "work up" again to stable jobs. The fathers of clerical workers are typically themselves in skilled or clerical work; education includes presumably some business school or college training,

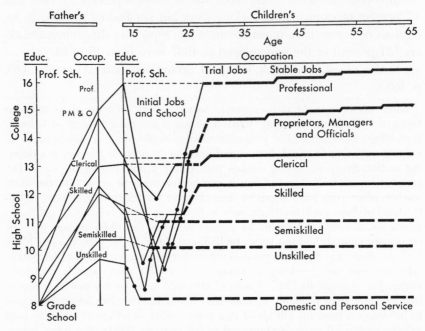

Figure 64. Career Patterns of Different Occupation Levels. Note: The chart shows that the typical professional man's father went through the eleventh grade (first vertical line), was a proprietor, manager, or official (second vertical line); the son went to professional school (third vertical line), but during the long time in school (top dotted line) had various summer and part-time service, semiskilled, skilled, and clerical jobs (fine line with dots at these levels), two trial jobs, then a stable professional position and some advance in rank or status (rising professional line). The service worker's father went only to the eighth grade, was unskilled; the child went to the ninth grade, had a couple of summer unskilled or service jobs, then a series of service jobs. (Adapted from D. C. Miller and W. H. Form, *Industrial Sociology*, New York, Harper, 1951, pp. 741–742.)

and then trial clerical jobs soon lead to stable jobs of the same type. At their level, the picture is the same for skilled workers; the father was a skilled worker, and after an apprenticeship period, the son becomes one. However, the semiskilled, unskilled, and domestic and personal service workers typically start and continue a series of jobs, none attaining stability.

Four features are important in the above patterns. (1) The individual's education may lead into the occupation, or lack of it may greatly limit choice of occupation. However, upward vocational "mobility through the schools in slowing up and (2) the higher positions tend to be filled in each succeeding generation by the sons and daughters of families who already enjoy high positions" (*111*, p. 185). In 1928 Taussig and Joslyn found that 58 percent of the fathers of American business leaders had been business executives or owners. In 1937 Davidson and Anderson reported that 60 to 73 percent of sons were in or adjacent to the fathers' occupations, and in 1945 71 percent of sons were found to have fathers at occupational levels relatively similar to their own. (Centers in *65*, p. 721). Further (3) because young people who go into professional and managerial work usually come from homes in which the parent was of similar occupational status and had a relatively good education, the part-time and summer jobs obtained while in school may well be the one great opportunity for the future business executive or professional man to obtain an easy and intimate first-hand contact with and understanding of the various groups of wage earners. The boy who has a part-time job as helper at a filling station and summer work in a factory and the girl who waits table while in school and in summer works in an office get contacts, points of view, and work experiences hardly to be had later—perhaps making the difference between an understanding and a bigoted upper-class adult.

A final feature of Figure 64 (4) is the distinct upward slant in a section of the two top lines only. Certain professions have a built-in stairway for advancement; the young college teacher may expect to advance in rank to a professorship and perhaps to administrative work. In law and medicine an expanding clientele and reputation in the community and among associates may be hoped for, and "proprietors, managers, and officials" hope for advancement in position and status. But even the skilled worker may have little chance of becoming foreman, and the semiskilled and unskilled have even less of a chance. For example, in the Middletown of the nineteen twenties there were only 10 vacancies for foremen in plants employing over 4000 workers; the wife of a machinist said that her husband had "been doing the same thing over and over for fifteen years, hoping he'd get ahead, and he's never had a chance; I don't suppose he ever will" (*57*, pp. 65–67). And more recently Lynd has stated that "The business man still tends to point his life up the long slope of the future to a relatively distant goal; whereas the working man and many white collar workers are accepting themselves as stuck where they are and forced to wrest such meaning as they can out of life on a dead-level" (R. S. Lynd, *Knowledge for What?* pp. 92–93, quoted in 65, p. 677).

Thumbnail sketches of a type of person at each occupational level may make clearer how different in almost every important respect these persons are. The modal professional worker is a man born into an upper-middle- or upper-class family; his father is a businessman of above-average education, who encourages his son to go to college and gives him financial aid. While in school he may hold miscellaneous short jobs, but after completion of professional training he goes directly into professional work, changes jobs twice in the first four years to find the one he wants, then settles down. When about 28 or 29 he marries a girl who is of his own social class and a college graduate, has one child (who in turn goes into professional work), lives in a good neighborhood, votes Republican, and "Toward the end of his life, he looks back on a long career and a healthy life, satisfied that his contribution to society was substantial and that the future is safe in the hands of men like his son."[3]

The father of the typical businessman (merchant, manager, manufacturer, government official) was a businessman or farmer—owned or managed property. The father had some high school education but wished he had more, and he encourages his son to go to college. The boy stays there two years, then starts in business, tries three different jobs in five years, then settles in a minor executive position obtained with the help of his father. He marries a college girl of similar background, has two children, lives in the best neighborhood, joins the best clubs, votes Republican, belongs to the Episcopalian or Presbyterian church, and looks forward to passing on his estate to his children and grandchildren.

The father of the typical clerk (salesman, bookkeeper) was himself a clerk or a skilled worker who encouraged his son to finish high school and take a year or two of college or business training. After two changes in the first five years, he settles down in a clerical position. At 25 or 26 he marries a girl who is also a clerk in one of the offices, rents a house in a middle-class neighborhood, has a daughter whom he encourages to get a college education so that she may have a better opportunity than he has had. He continues in his clerical job.

The skilled worker's father was himself an artisan or farmer with an eighth-grade education who encourages his son's high school attendance but is proud when the boy shows interest in skilled work—and drops out of secondary school. The father arranges through a foreman friend for the son to be taken on as an apprentice in semiskilled work; after six or seven years the young man is promoted to a skilled job, where he remains most of his working life. When 25, he marries a girl from a foreman's family, and they have two children. He starts to buy a home in a middle-class neighborhood, is loyal to his union, votes Democratic, feels that his kind are the aristocracy of labor—his son follows him in his trade.

[3] The sketches are condensed from 65, pp. 742–747.

The father of the semiskilled worker was a farmer or skilled worker whose children dropped out of high school before finishing. After a year as a truck driver, the son goes into a factory as a drill press operator. At 25 he marries a girl in his neighborhood, rents a home in a poorer part of town, and has two children. The family has a good deal of sickness and is almost always in debt; the children are occasionally delinquent. A layoff or unemployment may come any time. He sees a strong union as his only hope.

The unskilled worker's father was semiskilled and had a grammar school education. The boy leaves school at 15 to work as an unskilled laborer, marries at 23, lives in a poor section, has three children; the family has much sickness and is usually in debt. The wife and children work when they can. He cannot find a steady job. When there are layoffs, they live on unemployment insurance and then go on relief.

Evidently the different occupational levels are different groups, largely self-perpetuating and involving different total ways of life. The manifoldness and pervasiveness of these differences will be returned to. Moreover, upward mobility is, contrary to American tradition, relatively rare and becoming more so; the unskilled young worker practically never rises to become president of the company. If anything, he hopes for a better lot for his child, as a result of more education. Or he finds an opportunity in the union. This possibility also will be returned to.

The above paragraphs give types of cases, not individuals, and do not include any women or domestic and personal service workers. An actual case of this last type will also illustrate something of the many factors involved in a particular career. Mrs. Armand was born on an Iowa farm, went to a country school, worked in a country store, married a dull farm laborer, worked for a telephone company for a while and as a maid and housekeeper for various people—none more than two years, went to Chicago to get away from her husband and because an acquaintance working as a cleaning woman in a hospital said there would be an opening there for her. She kept the hospital job until she retired on a pension at 65, since which time she has for eleven years managed to get along in very cheap rooming houses. In good weather she sits in a park, goes to church meetings, and does nothing (37, pp. 10–21).

Nor must it be thought that even professional careers are as straightforward as the typical case suggests. Clark Hull's autobiography tells a fascinatingly different story, surely of interest at least to every student of psychology. Born in a log cabin of an almost illiterate father ("my mother completed teaching him to read after their marriage" when she was fifteen), Hull grew up on a backwoods Michigan farm and attended a one-room country school; thereupon, without further education, he taught in such a school for a year. Meanwhile, when 11 or 12 years of age he had been "converted" at a "violent" religious revival but "became very doubtful regarding the whole religious hypothesis. I announced my conclusions in open meeting and withdrew my affiliation!" After a year in a small-town high school, doing work around the place in exchange for living with the school superintendent (but refusing to kneel with the family in morning prayers) and two years in an "academy" (meanwhile working in a small hotel), he completed his secondary school education. But an almost fatal attack of typhoid fever invalided him for the next year. Next, two years were spent in the "narrow provincialism" of a little Presbyterian college, preparing to be a mining engineer—meanwhile working for board and room in a sanitarium. However, after only two months on a chemical job at a mine, he was invalided again, this time with poliomyelitis which left him with one leg paralyzed and health enfeebled.

Now he considered preparing for the Unitarian ministry, believing that faith to be "a form of free godless religion," but finally decided on a career in psychology as more fully including his interests without involving him in activities not to his liking. He then married and, with his own and his wife's meager savings from more country school teaching, entered the University of Michigan as a junior, finding the "free atmosphere . . . like entering a new life." Because of the elective system, he was able to concentrate in psychology much as in a graduate school, found vigorous teachers, after graduation taught a year in a Kentucky normal school, returned to graduate work with an assistantship at the University of Wisconsin, and finally obtained his doctorate at 34—and his notable career there and at Yale was under way. Clearly, this is a life much affected by handicap and misfortune, gradually emerging as a career dedicated to the stubborn insistence on thinking clearly and objectively about mind and personality—a dedication which was perhaps nascent when the 12-year-old boy courageously stood up in the little country church and "in open meeting" renounced a "conversion" which he felt violated his intellectual integrity (Hull in 51).[4]

The two preceding cases may illustrate the marked differences in the extent to which the occupation may take possession of life. For a man like Hull his work may, indeed, be central in his life—his devotion to science his major life purpose. The charwoman's work presumably was little more than a daily task, put aside when the hours of work were done. But sometimes her work involved more; she became so friendly with one woman for whom she kept house that she was invited back there for a several days' visit in her old age. And when working in the

[4] Both these lives began humbly; the second, perhaps, was humble more in circumstances and much burdened by illness. Probably a key difference in careers was in motivation and the meaning their work had for them. A certain amusement is now commonly expressed for the "puritanical aphorisms" regarding work as "the main goal in life." Presumably, Hull's career was a product of his dedication to a scientific search for truth. Could the former maid and charwoman (considering her sex, origins, and career opportunities) have been much more than she was? She seems to have been conscientious and competent in her humble tasks. Is not one major need of such as she to make possible some career recognition, some advancement, and some membership in a society of people similiar to her? These topics will be returned to.

hospital, she lived there. Later in this chapter there will be consideration of the meaning of work to the worker. Clearly, the meaning of their work is different in various ways for these two people. Relatively lowly work can, to the worker, mean much. For instance, an immigrant woman, grateful for the position as housekeeper for a kindly couple which she obtained soon after entering this country, shyly lived and spent most of her leisure in their home, became with the years a bit of a privileged character, and liked to feel that she was indispensable. Her distress was great when, in illness and old age, her employers (themselves now old) found it impossible to care for her, and her last few months had to be lived in a nursing home where she felt bewildered and abandoned. A job may be disliked in itself and as a symbol. A New York woman taxi-cab driver angrily resented the great city from which she had been trying to escape for many years. But she seemed bound to it by her husband's job, her children's schooling, and their combined debts.

As indicated, an occupation involves its particular way of life and associations, including those which lead to marriage; and marriage further binds the person into the situation. As Bacon's epigram put it, "A wife and children are hostages to fortune." And soon the individual is locked into a type of life, for life. These larger commitments of the job usually seem to be entered upon with little awareness of either their pervasiveness or their permanence.

That instability of employment is part of the lives of the great mass of American workers is indicated by a 1951 report by the Bureau of the Census (95). Workers between the ages of 55 and 64 had been on their current job only 8.0 years. A job was defined as a continuous period of employment with a single employer even though the person may have worked at several different occupations while with that employer. Workers 45 to 54 had been with the same employer, as defined above, for only an average of 6.3 years; those 35 to 44, only 3.2 years; those 25 to 34, 2.6 years. When all ages were thrown together, it appeared (the youngest workers, of course, inevitably having had relatively brief employment) that the average length of time with one employer was 1.4 years in construction, 2.0 in trade, 3.6 in manufacturing, 5.1 in transportation, and 6.3 in agriculture. The disruptions of the Second World War and Korean conflict presumably caused much shifting about. Also, special groups, such as married women, moved in and out of the labor market. But it seems reasonable to expect that, with industrial and other changes, instability in employment will continue. In certain types of work it may be a major characteristic; so, migratory workers may "follow the fruits around" for years. At a higher level, construction workers move with the job. Obviously, such workers and their families can hardly become assured members of a community, nor can their children have consistent schooling or companionships. And in proportion to the general instability, adaptability and perhaps readiness in retraining need to be characteristics of the worker, and his wife and also his children need to be adaptable and resourceful.

VOCATIONAL VALUE AND AGE

If age affects vocational usefulness in important ways, these should be known in planning labor policy and in the everyday operations of a company's personnel office. Table 27 summarizes certain findings of an investigation bearing on this last issue. In an industry in which the

TABLE 27.   Causes of Leaving Employment in a Manufacturing Company, and Appraisals by Foremen at Leaving—Percentages of Men in Each Age Group

	Age at Leaving			
Causes of Leaving	16–30	31–45	46–60	61 Up
Discharges	11	15	11	2
Layoffs	5	3	4	7
Quits for better jobs	19	26	20	7
Quits for physical reasons	3	8	14	28
Quits for family reasons	9	6	3	1
Dissatisfaction	12	11	8	7
Failure to report	41	3î	34	38
Deceased	—	—	6	10
Rated by foreman as excellent or good in:				
Ability	67	65	57	62
Attendance	53	56	58	65
Attitude	58	61	57	67
Considered worthy of rehire	50	42	36	52
Number of cases	685	413	437	163

NOTE: Not all these cases were included in the appraisals or the ratings, but the number in each instance was believed sufficient to give some indication as to the trends.

SOURCE: Adapted from M. W. Smith, Evidences of potentialities of older workers in a manufacturing company, Personnel Psychol. 1952, 5:11–18.

workers moved about from one company to another and often came
back for rehire, the factory studied had its foremen carefully appraise
every worker who left, as a basis for any later possible employment.
The personnel office was dubious about reëmployment of workers over
45 and would not take on new workers over 30. The table gives certain
pertinent data from the company's files regarding "separations" at different ages.

The table shows decrease with age in frequency of discharges (presumably because work was unsatisfactory in some way). Even a few of
those in the sixties left for better jobs. Percentages rated excellent or
good in ability changed relatively little with age, while attendance and
attitude seemed to improve a little, and number considered worthy of
rehire was as high over 60 as under 30. It was recommended that (with
reasonable care in selection as to competence and physical condition)

TABLE 28. Percentages of Employees with over Two Years' Service Mentioned
by Foremen as Having Certain Traits

Trait	Men				Women			
	18–29	30–44	45–59	60 Up	18–29	30–44	45–59	60 Up
Efficiency	49	41	40	40	41	37	41	48
Job knowledge	15	13	12	11	8	12	12	8
Accuracy	8	7	4	3	34	15	22	20
Initiative	6	7	5	5	11	5	16	4
Dependability	27	26	22	26	26	19	30	24
Tactfulness	15	11	11	6	16	14	12	20
Instability	—	2	3	2	4	6	12	4
Attendance[a]	5	10	13	15	3	5	12	24
Steadiness[a]	10	14	19	19	8	13	27	28
Conscientiousness[a]	10	8	10	14	8	6	17	20
Coöperativeness	32	28	25	24	24	19	29	24
Ability to learn[b]	12	7	2	3	17	6	11	4
Slowness[b]	−1	−2	3	12	−9	−5	2	4
N =	280	644	538	316	115	242	165	25

[b] Traits showing a difference of more than 5 in favor of the first two as compared to the last two
age groups.

[a] Traits showing a similar superiority for the last two age groups.

NOTE: The following items were omitted as showing no net percentage in any age group for
either sex of more than 10: thoroughness, job satisfaction, supervisory ability, work without supervision, physical difficulties, and overtalkativeness. Thus, the highest mention of physical difficulties
was 6 for men 60 and over.

SOURCE: From W. H. Bowers, An appraisal of worker characteristics as related to age, J. Appl.
Psychol., 1952, 36:296–300.

older workers might be rehired with confidence and that the age limit for new workers might be dropped.

That certain abilities and traits tend to change somewhat with age is indicated by Table 28. A large enterprise employing workers in various tasks, mostly of a semiskilled nature, had foremen make informal appraisals from time to time. These records were gone over, consolidated as reporting on certain basic abilities and traits, and expressed as percentages of employees in different age groups considered to have these characteristics. Table 28 summarizes certain of these materials, showing, for instance, that 49 percent of men 18 to 29 were mentioned as efficient as compared to 40 percent of those 60 and over; of the small group of women that old, 48 percent were so appraised. The older people of both sexes were somewhat more often considered slow and not quick in learning but were more often considered steady and of good attendance.

The question naturally comes up, however, as to the extent to which different individuals may show a piling up of favorable or unfavorable characteristics at different ages. In order to get some indication regarding this question, the total number of favorable and unfavorable comments regarding each worker was added into a net total (in which each favorable or unfavorable comment counted plus or minus 1, except that for efficiency, a statement that a person was very efficient counted 2 whereas not efficient or very inefficient counted minus 1 or minus 2 respectively). The distributions of these net totals, for each age group, are displayed in Table 29.

The table shows that the means (indicated by the letter "a") changed little with age for men who had been employed two or more years by the organization and who thus presumably could be appraised rather accurately (data for women, not included in the table, were similar). The number rated distinctly favorably (for instance, the proportion rated 3 plus or more in each age group) fell off little with age, while the number rated distinctly unfavorably (as with a net minus 3 or more) also changed little. Further, the men 60 and over included 54 aged 65 to 69 and 17 who were 70 to 76, yet these last two groups showed means of 3. And none of the 70-year-olds had a minus total. The four columns to the right, showing the appraisals for workers hired within the past two years, are of especial interest in that those 45 and over must have been at least 42 when hired, and those 60 and up at least 58—yet this last group shows the highest mean and only one minus case, and the

TABLE 29. Distributions of Net Appraisals for Men with Over Two Years' Service and Under Two Years

Net Appraisal	Men Over 2 Years				Men Under 2 Years			
	18–29	30–44	45–59	60 up	18–29	30–44	45–59	60 up
13		1						
12		1	1					
11		4	2			1		
10	1	5	2				2	
9	4	12	10	5			3	1
8	9	11	7	5	1	3		
7	10	27	24	9	5	5	2	
6	18	48	32	25	7	12	8	1
5	30	44	26	20	25	28	14	5
4	37	60	40	22	29	40	15	4
3	28a	69a	73a	21	30	40	14	6a
2	20	51	39	27a	32	36a	15a	2
1	18	52	31	27	32a	22	13	1
0	12	23	32	20	27	21	9	5
−1	18	24	13	19	17	20	7	
−2	6	14	7	6	16	7	3	1
−3	5	12	5	6	3	6		
−4	1	3	2	1	2	3	1	
−5		3	1		2	1	1	
−6				1				
−7								
—								
Total	217	465	347	214	228	245	107	26
Mean	3.2	3.2	3.2	2.7	1.9	2.4	2.8	3.0
Percent over 3	50	47	42	40	30	36	41	42
Percent under 3	0	2	1	1	2	2	2	0

NOTE: The letter "a" indicates means of net appraisals in each age group.

SOURCE: From W. H. Bowers, An appraisal of worker characteristics as related to age, J. Appl. Psychol., 1952, 36:296–300.

45 to 59 mean is higher than that for those 18 to 29. In short, even workers first hired when 58 or over were almost all doing well.

The above cases were primarily semiskilled or skilled workers. An investigation of salesmen for a large company showed a correlation of age with sales of .28, with number of calls made .29, with customer relations .30, with overall sales ability as appraised by superiors .28, with knowledge of products .59; the only minus correlations were −.23 with physical stamina and −.22 with supervision required! Apparently the older salesman were the best. In fact, those 60 and over were outselling those in their thirties by over 50 percent per man per year (58). Further,

TABLE 30.   Number of Part-Time Saleswomen Hired at Different Ages, Workdays Available, and Percentages Receiving One or More Wage Increases

Age When Hired	Number of Women	Work Days Available	Percent Receiving Wage Increase
14–30	300	103	11
31–45	192	196	21
46–60	98	305	23
61 up	7	412	57

SOURCE: Adapted from J. E. Stanton, Part-time employment for older women, J. Appl. Psychol., 1951, 35:418–421.

turnover was much more rapid in the younger groups. It was strongly recommended that the company's rigid retirement age of 65 for salesmen be dropped. Table 30 shows that older saleswomen are especially useful for part-time work.

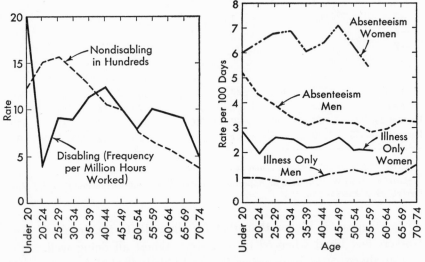

Figure 65.   Injury Frequency Rate in Relation to Age. (From U.S. Department of Labor, Bureau of Employment Security, *Joint Committee on Railroad Retirement Legislation,* Washington, D.C., U.S. Government Printing Office, 1953.)

Figure 66.   Absenteeism Rates for Men and Women. (From U.S. Department of Labor, Bureau of Employment Security, *Joint Committee on Railroad Retirement Legislation,* Washington, D.C., U.S. Government Printing Office, 1953.)

A further important consideration, especially in appraisal of older workers, is likelihood of accident or illness. Different investigators in different industries and over a period of time have found quite consistent results, as indicated by Figures 65 and 66. Frequency of accidents and also of illnesses tends to decrease with age, though time out for recovery tends to increase.

Figure 65 showed data without reference to type of accident, and with the possibility that older workers might have been on somewhat different, perhaps somewhat protected work. Table 31 indicates that, on farm work that is probably about the same for all ages, older workers tended to fall more and were slower to get out of the way, but all in all they got along about as well as the younger workers.

TABLE 31.   Frequency of Different Types of Farm Accidents by Ages

Cause	Number of Cases	Percent of Each Kind of Accident by Age			
		15–20	21–30	51–60	61–80
Increases with age					
Falls	252	7.6	8.4	19.2	16.4
Slipping or tripping	201	3.8	6.3	11.0	16.4
Hit by moving object	339	14.0	15.7	21.4	21.3
Decreases with age					
Caught in machine	202	13.4	11.8	7.9	6.6
Injured by own tool	184	13.4	11.8	6.6	9.3
Starting an engine	98	12.7	7.9	1.3	1.1
No significant change with age					
Moving heavy objects	103	3.2	4.8	7.5	1.6
Hit or trod on object	90	6.4	3.6	3.4	3.8
Action of animals	79	1.3	3.9	5.3	2.7

SOURCE: Adapted from H. F. King, An age analysis of some agricultural accidents, Occup. Psychol., 1955, 29:1–8.

In total, the preceding data suggest that the general run of business and industrial workers show some slowing down and loss of ready adaptability and of physical vigor with age, but they show an increase in dependability and consistency of work. Furthermore, though the percent of workers judged by foremen to be slow increased with age, not all older workers were so characterized. Adjustments in a job to make it less active or less speedy might continue the usefulness of an older man on that task. And when some change in process or job is called for, a little extra patience and encouragement with older workers might well largely eliminate any age differential in this respect. During the Second World War, older workers in a number of plants have been reported to have made such shifts with little difficulty. A statement by an English investigator is of interest in this connection:

Older people appear to waste less time than the younger and to have fewer accidents attributable to carelessness. There are certain jobs from which people tend to move away as they get older, but it seems that they will often carry on under an ever-increasing strain, almost to the breaking point, before they will make a change. When they do have to change, they often have difficulty in learning a new job, partly it would seem (although evidence here is not as full as we should like), because they lack the necessary confidence to try their hand at something unfamiliar. The most difficult work for older people, whether to do or to learn, seems to be that which lays emphasis on speed in some form. Where they have an opportunity to display care and accuracy to advantage, and speed is of secondary importance, older people get on much better and are often the most valuable workers in the factory. (114.)

Figure 23 in Chapter 2 summarized results to this effect of a very practical test requiring the sorting of small metal blocks according to the size they appeared to be and whether or not certain holes were drilled in required places. Each person could proceed at his own preferred rate. The graph showed that the oldest testees initially took most time, but after getting well started the next to the oldest group tended to do best.

Data presented earlier regarding age of leadership, as well as the above material on salesmen, would suggest that work that is supervisory, technical, or policy-making in nature, or otherwise involving accumulated knowledge and judgment, might be especially well done by older people. Various instances are to this effect. Not only have Churchill and Adenauer at 80, and several senators over 75, demonstrated notable leadership, but an inquiry by one of the writers located various everyday instances of work done well or even *best* by older persons (71). For instance, a physician of 84 continued to see only patients of long standing who were themselves elderly; his long acquaintance with them and personal feeling for the problems of age, plus some specialization in geriatrics, made him able to serve them admirably. A lawyer, also 84, specialized in wills and settlement of estates, keeping only long-standing clients. A 72-year-old mechanic, too old for his former highly skilled work, was put in charge of the tool cage, where his acquaintance with both the shop's work and its workers, and his loyalty to the company for thus being kept on, made him more valuable than ever before. A big department store used older sales people for part-time work; they came about 10:00 A.M., after the morning transportation rush, and left about 3:30 P.M. before the crush in the buses at the end of the day, worked through the noon hour, served especially older customers—and made some of the highest sales records in the company.

In short, persons even past 65 may be distinctively useful. Also, the increasing number of people past 65 creates a growing market for goods and services which older persons might best understand and provide. At present, the greatest numbers proportionally of workers in these ages appear to be farmers and farm managers, "charwomen" (a term used by the census to include men as well as women doing janitorial and cleaning work), and guards and watchmen (56). Emphasis on other types of work, as mentioned above, surely is to be desired.

RETIREMENT: WHEN—HOW?

From early in the work life, there is some dropping out of the labor force because of accident or illness, mental inadequacy, gross temperamental difficulty, or mental disease. Some are victims of economic circumstance—their firm goes out of business or their special skill becomes out of date, when they are too old to find other work. Some are in work so demanding that they drop out of it—but too late to start another career; for instance, house-to-house salesmen for a bakery usually found the work too taxing to continue after 60, but new jobs were hard to obtain then (16). As workers get over into the beginnings of old age, some show its infirmities early, or an employer anticipates they may soon do so and eliminates them. But the great majority of workers do not in any of these ways suffer an early termination of their life work. Some continue even into old age, as described above. However, a large proportion find their careers terminated by reaching a set retirement age. And by a combination of circumstances, 65 has been widely assumed, in this country, to be the desirable age for retirement. The most important influence seems to have been the emphasis on that age in the government's provision for old age and survivor's insurance. This insurance was a depression measure and aimed to give some support to individuals often permanently out of work at that age or before. Business firms also found such an age convenient in a period when they had no difficulty in finding employees, and so this policy worked to the advantage of management in eliminating the less productive old people. There were even tendencies to retire earlier, as at 60 for women in some companies[5] and 60 also for men in certain types of work, such as overseas jobs. Work that is especially responsible and demanding might also call for early retirement, such as pilot service for transport planes or commissioned personnel in the armed services (63). There was also the tendency of labor unions to name 65 as a time when pension systems might begin, though the unions usually opposed compulsory retirement.

However, statistics show that a man who has reached the age of 65 may be expected to live on the average of 12 years more and a woman 14 years more—substantial periods to live in idleness and which require a substantial outlay of pension or other funds to support these people over this time. And it has become evident that a large percent of individuals at 65 did not wish to retire—partly because pensions or other sources of income were inadequate but more because idleness after the first few months became a burden rather than a rest. In fact, as mentioned earlier, the effect of the 65-year retirement trend was to reduce an amount of wage-earning after this age which heretofore had been substantial; in 1900, 63 percent of men 65 and over were gainfully employed as compared with 42 percent in 1950. The loss in productivity from the enforced idleness of pensioners desiring to work has become increasingly substantial. It has been estimated as some five billion dollars a year or more (80). And data reported in the previous section make clear that, although many older workers may be slow and adapt less readily to new procedures, they have merits of steadiness, carefulness, and good attendance which may in total be of great practical value. Retention according to effectiveness as a worker, not according to age, seems clearly called for. The efficient work done during World War II by older workers has emphasized these possibilities. Certain business firms have long retained employees even into their seventies.

For instance, the Ithaca Gun Company had a director who continued interest in company affairs until his death at 104. A considerable proportion of its skilled workers have been with the firm many years and remained with it after 65. These facts, widely publicized in connection with the New York

[5] As for instance Standard Oil of New Jersey. And when a shareholder argued that it would "be an economic benefit to the Company to retain trained women personnel for five years more. . . thereby saving the cost of training replacements, or paying pensions" the president replied that most oil companies had a 60-year retirement for women and that this was "desirable and satisfactory" (70th Annual Meeting, 1952).

Joint Committee on Aging and a related newsreel film, brought much favorable (and profitable) publicity. The manager of a restaurant chain found older workers so much more reliable than younger that he advertised for persons over 60 and declared that his best worker was an 80-year-old woman who "could slice meat thinner than any other person he knew." As already mentioned, a large department store found that older persons were superior to younger as extra workers in sales and similar emergencies, being more willing to remain on call for such occasional work and more conscientious in it. A small dress shop found that older saleswomen made more sales than younger. And many professional men and self-employed skilled workers continue active in old age. For instance, a tailor in his eighties exhibited a special clothing design in a New York fashion show. A retired faculty member of 96 published a history of his science.

The tendency seems to be toward some relaxation of a rigid retirement at 65, with much interest in possible procedures by which retirement may equitably be made flexible. Thus, a state teachers' system makes retirement possible after attaining the age of 55 with 30 or more years of service credit, but maximal benefits are given only after age 65 or 40 years of service, and mandatory retirement is at 70. A civil service system permits continuance in a job even after this last age, if continuation is necessary to obtain a certain minimal number of years in the service for minimal benefits. Certain firms are trying systems whereby, for example, a worker who so desires may retire after 60, "normally" does so at 65, but may then continue each year, if he so desires, up to 70 if yearly medical examinations show him able and his foreman approves. If a worker wishes to continue but health officer or foreman says no, the matter is referred to a board or arbitrating committee. However, a rigid retirement age seems to remain the most common arrangement. Though 65 appears to be the most common retirement age, there seems to be some tendency toward a later date. Thus, a January 12, 1956, news item tells of a large insurance company (Mutual Benefit Life) changing the retirement age to 68. In times of short labor supply, capable older workers may be quietly continued. When pensions become available at 65 but the worker can continue, substantial numbers do (84).

Instead of abrupt retirement from full-time work to none, a tapering off may sometimes be possible; as mentioned earlier, a physician or lawyer or operator of a small business may gradually withdraw from his profession or business, usually turning over more and more of his work to a younger associate. A large concern may have some older employees long on its payroll who are quietly allowed sundry privileges such as coming to work later, leaving earlier, or longer or more frequent vacations and a relaxation of expectations regarding amount of work done. As will be stressed shortly, such gradual reduction in the amount or requirements of work would seem most in accord with the gradual reduction in energies and some abilities which seem usual with increasing age. But most companies appear to feel that any express and general policy in this direction would be difficult to administer and uneconomic except in a very tight labor market where somewhat marginal workers had to be turned to.

Though retirement rigidities are being relaxed somewhat, a common sequence of events still is that through his sixty-fourth year a man is fully employed at a full-time wage, in a concern with which he has long been and where he has many friends; he has status with family and neighbors which an established job gives. But on or shortly after his sixty-fifth birthday all this suddenly ceases—no work whatever, none of the daily routine associated with the work, no regular contacts with fellow workers, probably a much reduced income, and the status in family and neighborhood of a man who is "through." The change may well be the most drastic and complete in the man's life. Often he may be almost wholly at a loss as to how to meet the situation. It is assumed that now he will wish only to sit and rest, or divert himself with fishing or gossip with others of his kind. But soon he becomes restless and weary of such amusement. At home he feels in the way. The neighbors and his former fellow workers all, he feels, regard him as a has-been.

In a large industrial area thousands of men go through this experience every year and join a growing mass of idle, restless, unhappy older people who often become problems to their grown children and in neighborhood stores, recreation centers, union offices, and other places where they seek diversion and companionship. To prepare people somewhat for "retirement shock" and help them in retirement, big concerns have carried discussions of these problems in their company papers and set up offices for preretirement counseling. Informal courses have been offered by college extension divisions or other agencies for discussion of such problems, and radio programs have considered them. Excellent recordings of such programs, and movies vividly dramatizing these issues, are now available. Such programs usually try to forewarn that retirement does need to be planned for, to suggest the comparative merits and faults of various other parts of the country as compared with one's own home town as a retirement locality, to inform as to health in the older years and as to wise management of lessened income, and to make suggestions regarding both recreation and possible occupations in retirement. Certain of these topics are touched upon elsewhere. Regarding earning money in retirement, it need only be said that sundry books and pamphlets are now available that describe possible profitable hobbies and both part- and full-time work suitable for old people. Often older people make tragic mistakes; a person without relevant experience may lose all his savings in a neighborhood store or little place in the country for which he had high hopes. But some continuing work or service activity, as in a church or community enterprise, appears to be usually best for healthy, retired old people.[6]

The "Way of Life" and Work

As already intimated, not only the tasks themselves but the total "way of life" may vary greatly from one occupation to another. Everyone recognizes the many differences between the lives of a railway engineer and a haberdashery clerk, a nurse and a stenographer. But the variety of the differences between different occupations must be stressed.

OCCUPATIONAL HAZARDS, UNCERTAINTIES, AND CIRCUMSTANCES

Great differences exist between occupations as regards liability to accident, a circumstance affecting way of life for worker and family. In industrial towns the word goes from mouth to mouth of the "slaughter house" reputation of certain plants. A heavy materials manufacturing concern in one large city was known for years as the "finger-a-day" plant. Table 32 shows that accidents vary much according to the nature of the work. Construction people work in risk of falling objects and in high places. They have the most frequent and most severe accidents. Firemen don't always sleep or play checkers. On their runs they are exposed to many hazards of both heat and cold, smoke, falls, and burns. Various special types of work have special risks. A supervisor noted on his job analysis of a window-washer's work that "he doesn't have many accidents, but when he does, they're bad!" Possibilities of accidents can be a continuing element in the lives of a group of workers and their families,

[6] The following may be mentioned as brief, popular treatments of the above topic: Federal Security Agency, *Looking Forward to the Later Years,* Washington, D.C., U.S. Government Printing Office, 1952; Norman D. Ford, *Where to Retire on a Small Income,* Greenlawn (New York), Harian Publications, 1950; Ray Giles, *Begin Now to Enjoy Tomorrow,* Newark (New Jersey), The Mutual Benefit Life Insurance Co., 1951; George Lawton and Maxwell S. Stewart, *When You Grow Older,* Public Affairs Pamphlet No. 131, New York, Public Affairs Committee, 1947; The Mutual Benefit Life Insurance Co., *Helping Employees Get Ready to Retire,* Newark (New Jersey), The Mutual Benefit Life Insurance Co., undated.

as in a mining town; and lack of special hazards is part of the comfortableness of office work.

Agricultural work is seasonal. Itinerant agricultural workers follow the seasons and the crops. Resort workers follow the tourists—as from Michigan in summer to Florida in winter. Construction work may be both seasonal and episodic; a big job may bring large numbers of workers and their families flooding into a dizzied community for a couple of years and then release them as quickly. The children of such families

TABLE 32.   Injury Frequency and Severity Rates in Various
Occupations, 1949

Occupation	Injuries per Million Employee Hours Worked	Days Lost from Injuries per Thousand Employee Hours Worked
Construction	39.9	3.9
Fire departments	32.1	2.5
Police departments	27.5	2.4
Waterworks	27.5	1.1
Heat, light and power	16.0	2.3
Manufacturing	14.5	1.4
Trade	12.7	.6
Personal service	8.9	.5
Education service	7.6	.4
Business service	3.9	.3

SOURCE: Adapted from U.S. Department of Commerce, Bureau of the Census, *Statistical Abstract of the United States, 1955*, Washington, D.C., U.S. Government Printing Office, 1955, p. 194.

may be always in schools which are crowded with children in similar circumstances and which tend to resent them somewhat. Most of these people may live in buildings or trailers that are grossly inadequate and in an isolated area; neither children nor parents have a feeling of belonging or of community responsibility. Slack periods with layoffs and then overtime episodes are chronic in some industries. In the manufacture of women's shoes, "When an order is received, the factory must push production so that the order may be completed before the style changes. With the changing styles, there is a decreasing demand for standardized types of shoes. The result is alternation between rush work and lay-offs" (111, p. 62).

In any sizeable company, different groups of employees may work not only under very different conditions but with sundry concomitant circumstances often causing resentments. Clerical personnel usually have not only better workrooms but more conveniences, more sick leave, more holidays, and more nonscheduled rest periods. A survey of 199 companies regarding time allowed for lunch showed 68 percent restricting hourly workers to 30 minutes or less, but 90 percent giving salaried employees (usually both clerical and supervisory) more time; only 8 percent gave hourly workers 60 minutes or more, but 69 percent gave those on salary that much time. Differences in lunch time between departments were not nearly as great as between hourly and salaried personnel. When different groups eat in the same place, such differences may be a chronic irritation to those less privileged. In any event, there will be status groupings—as was well illustrated by a study of those eating together in a plant cafeteria. Higher management went to the most pleasant table near a window, and back from them in order were supervisors, office workers, and finally plant workers, some in cramped areas behind a post, with colored workers in the darkest corner. (*65*, p. 353, from E. C. Hughes, The knitting of racial groups in industry, *Amer. Sociol. Rev.*, October, 1946, p. 514.)

Different companies in the same industry and same city may differ in many pervasive ways. For instance, Company A in a metropolitan area is known as a good place to work, but competing Company B in the same city has a poor reputation among workers. Company A has a nice building and pays good wages. You get an hour for lunch and can get away to do some shopping; you don't have to punch a time clock. There are 10 paid holidays. Though located undesirably in the center of the city, Company A is thus able to attract "desirable" employees from the good suburbs. Company B is located in a pleasant suburb, but not only are its wages less, but its policy is more rigid and morale lower. In consequence, it must hire workers who live in the tenement districts, near the center of town. In consequence, workers from this last area take transportation to the good suburb, while girls living there pass them on the way to work in the favorably known factory in the slum neighborhood. But within the favored company, jobs differ enormously. Hilda reports at 6:00 P.M. in the evening and works until 2:00 A.M. She is one of the horde of cleaners who swarm through the rooms every night. Actually in Company B the night cleaning job is a little better. It has not been "efficiency engineered," and Mary, the scrubwoman there, gets a chance to gossip with Herman, the night porter. In great contrast with her work is that of chemist Jones, who does research during convenient daylight hours in an air-conditioned laboratory because controlled temperature and humidity are necessary. But operator Smith works in a hot, steamy room, all day long, making up the market mixtures that have come out of Dr. Jones' research. Extensive data from some

50,000 workers in various industries in various parts of the country have shown greater differences in attitudes from one department to another in the same company than from one company to another.

HOURS OF WORK

As mentioned above, the workday also shows important variations from one job to another. The northern resort concessionaire, in an attempt to get all the trade he can in the summer months, may open his stand early in the morning and not close until after midnight. Often it is the owner of an establishment or the head of a department who will put in the longest hours. The independent cab driver may put in 10 hours a day 7 days a week, while the hired hand in the factory is virtually shot out of the door after 8 hours, in order to eliminate overtime and keep the payroll straight.

In considering what life may be like in a given occupation it is always important to note not only how many hours one works but at what hours one works. In every big city thousands of people—scrubwomen, street cleaners, bus and taxi operators, policeman, as well as night shifts in factories—work at night. Associations with family and friends, recreation, and the whole way of life are obviously dominated by such hours. That night work is not the extreme exception is shown by some National Industrial Conference Board data. Of 199 plants, 79 percent had second shifts (usually about 4:00 P.M. until midnight), and 52 percent had third shifts (midnight until 8:00 A.M.). These data are not adequate for all industry, large and small, but they do suggest appreciable numbers of nighttime workers.

Unusual hours may be liked or detested, according to circumstances. Thus, the split shift in a seaside resort restaurant was liked by the majority of workers in that afternoons from one to four could be spent on the beach and evenings after eight with family and friends. Bank adding-machine operators, however, almost without exception hated their graveyard shift hours, because they seldom had adequate opportunity for contact with friends and never seemed to sleep well enough during daylight hours.

Hours of work have sundry effects on almost every phase of life. An overland truck driver's wife divorces him because of his "neglect" of her in the hours spent away from home. The overworked executive's wife grows suspicious of his overtime. The coupon-clipper's wife, on the other hand, grows tired of him because he is around the house too much. The night bank workers mentioned above tried to solve their recreation problems by having parties after work, at 9:00 in the morning. But one of them described it as "too much like getting drunk before breakfast."

Even on the normal daylight shifts, there are differences between the hours of factory and clerical people. The workman who is due on the job at 7:30 in the morning is still set apart, in important ways, from the business and professional groups. He must have his breakfast before the children need to have theirs to get to school. On the streetcar he sees only those in similar occupations, since the white collar people are not yet abroad. Through the day, the clock sets him apart as a separate class. He has another lunch hour, and probably the policy manual will even dictate his rest pauses. And the late commuters—what satisfaction these people take in the fact that *they* are among the few whose morning begins late. Some have been known to report at such a late hour that they have had time to exercise their hunting horses before boarding the train![7]

STATUS, ROLE, AND GROUP FEELING

Workers at tasks and in circumstances as various as have been described would be expected to have very diverse attitudes toward their work. Table 33 shows not only that they do, but that various attitudes

TABLE 33. Meanings of Work in Five Occupational Groups for Older Workers; Relative Percentages, Assuming Each Group to Have Given One Response per Person

	Steel-workers	Coal Miners	Skilled Craftsmen	Sales People	Physicians
Money only	28	18	11	0	0
Routine	28	19	15	21	15
Self-respect, prestige	16	18	24	11	13
Associations	15	19	20	20	19
Self-expression	13	11	30	26	15
Service to others	[a]	16[b]	[a]	10	32
Continued work past 65 or wanted to	32	42	49	65	67
Number of respondents	128	153	208	74	39

[a] Not covered in the questionnaire or interview.

[b] The responses from the miners classified here were to the effect that work gave them a chance to be useful.

NOTE: The steelworkers were unskilled and semiskilled and 55 or older, the coal miners were 50 or over, and the skilled craftsmen and the physicians were over 65.

SOURCE: Adapted from E. A. Friedmann, R. J. Havighurst, and W. H. Harlan, *The Meaning of Work and Retirement*, Chicago, University of Chicago Press, 1954, pp. 173, 183.

and feelings may be intermixed. The inquiry dealt with older workers, some of whom were retired, and thus may be presumed to report attitudes well established in these work groups and resulting from long experience with whatever satisfactions the work might bring. In none

[7] The writers are indebted for certain of the above detail, and some other matter in this chapter, to certain former graduate students with industrial personnel experience who prefer to remain anonymous.

of these occupational groups did a majority of the workers report money income to be the only meaning of their work; except for the steelworkers, less than a fifth declare that attitude. As might be hoped, physicians most commonly reported service to others as the major meaning of their work, but only 32 percent of the 39 included in the inquiry so replied. Physicians most commonly worked past 65, or wanted to—but so did at least 32 percent in the other occupations. Most mentioned by both skilled craftsmen and sales people was what is summarized in the table as "self-expression." Clearly, almost every person's work means several things to him. A similar inquiry of young workers would undoubtedly show different complexes of meanings, but almost certainly the meanings of their work even then would be complex.

As earlier recognized in discussion of work choice, different types of work have different status or prestige. In general, professional and managerial work has high status, and unskilled and service work is low in status. Within any field and within any work group, there are differentiations. For instance, in a large restaurant, a rather elaborate status order may run from owner, chef, hostess, waitresses, countermen, cook, down to runners, dishwashers, and charwomen. Each worker is expected to defer to those above him in status and to receive the respect of those below him. Deviations from these expectations are likely to be sharply dealt with. For instance, a runner who tried to get a cook to prepare food faster was bluntly told to mind his own business (*115*). Also, a status group may be further subdivided. Thus, the older, more professional waitresses may differentiate themselves from those temporarily in that work. One of them remarked that even in the rest room "when the girls are all mixed up, sitting on different sides of the room, you'll have two conversations going right across the room; the two groups will talk right across each other, and they just don't mix in" (Whyte, quoted in *65*, p. 448).

A worker's status may be a product of circumstances long past and of which he may be unaware. For instance, in the plants of a shoe manufacturing town, operators of edge-setting and trimming machines were found to have comparatively high status, this being exhibited by their being the one class of machine operators who wore their shirts and neckties under their work aprons. This superior status of the edgers and trimmers seemed to stem from the fact that their machines had been introduced early, when shoemaking had a higher prestige. An historical circumstance occurring 50 years previously, and not known by these workers, thus affected their standing with their fellows and their habits of work. And as often occurs, a feature of dress was a status symbol. Status situations may become complicated and incoördinate. Janitors tend to have low status, this being caused or at least symbolized in part by their having to handle garbage and waste. But in part because of knowledge (sometimes intimate and often derived from telltale waste) about tenants, plus sometimes both wages and accommodations superior to them, janitors may be something of a threat to the status of their tenants, and chronic, uneasy relationships may result (32).

As has been mentioned, status may be evidenced in a great variety of ways—in dress, hours of work, place and conditions of work. Status within a group may be shown in sundry ways, some primarily symbolic; thus, the importance of an official may be indicated by the size of his office and his desk and whether or not he has his own carafe! The status of a city school teacher is affected and indicated in part by the school in which she teaches (1). And all these differentiations emphasize and foster similarities in the types of persons with whom each individual associates, and a group feeling builds up. Furthermore, persons in a given type of work are likely to have had fathers in work of the same general status and to have grown up in the same general socioeconomic group as their work places them—as already indicated. Table 34 indicates some-

TABLE 34. Percentage in Various Occupational Levels Reporting (1) Work Associates of the Same Social Background, (2) Various Mean Social Participation Scores

Occupational Levels	Same Social Background	Mean Social Participation Scores
Professionals	84	28
Owners, managers	60	28
Clerical, sales	63	21
Skilled workers	70	20
Semiskilled workers	65	17
Unskilled workers	58	10

SOURCE: Adapted from D. C. Miller and W. H. Form, *Industrial Sociology*, Harper, 1951, pp. 344, 352.

thing as to how, in consequence, the majority of work associates at every occupational level tend to be of similar social background. This was especially true for the professional; less so for the managers, because their work usually involved a range of contacts; less so for the unskilled, perhaps because being managed and rendering services involved contacts with those of a higher status. The limited nature of the contacts of this last group is made clearer by the last column; the unskilled workers "bowl with the boys" or otherwise associate with their immediate work groups but participate relatively little in formal organizations outside the work plant. In contrast, the professional and managerial people are very active in community, professional, or trade organizations, and other larger groups.

Age is a factor in status in almost every group. The young beginner has little and may be hazed. The old worker may be called "Dad" and treated with a certain condescension. Somewhat the same attitudes appear in professional and managerial groups—but expressed in ways and with reference to circumstances specific to each group. The young college instructor tends to be regarded critically by both students and older colleagues. Elderly faculty members may be considered out of date and in the way of younger men's advancements in rank. That professional organizations most commonly elect as presidents men in their forties and fifties (median for the American Psychological Association is 46) would seem one bit of evidence that these years have highest status in these fields (55).

With different types of jobs go different roles—often pervasively different folkways. So, a carpenter will wear a certain kind of work clothes, have a vocabulary and way of talk and fund of dirty stories like other carpenters, eat with them (probably from a lunch pail) and with similar manners. A supervisor should not eat with the workers he supervises, etc. A person's facility in fitting into the work role may be much more important than his ability to do the work. Age affects role. The older skilled craftsman has traditionally played the role of mentor to apprentices who were less skilled in their craft. But the older semiskilled worker in mass industry would seem to have no distinctive role. To develop roles and to increase status for older persons would seem a major need, in most fields of work, which will be returned to.

Differences between different occupational groups are thus almost all-pervasive. Moreover, "it seems probable that our class system is becoming less open, and mobility increasingly difficult for those at the bottom of the social heap" (111, p. 185). The great cleavage between the mass of unskilled and semiskilled workers and the managerial group in big industry tends to increase class feeling and status sensitivities. But within a particular occupational group and particular plant there are usually subgroups and informal groupings and contacts, as is well indicated by Figure 67. It shows that the president and vice-president golf and lunch together, and these two have luncheon contacts with managers and superintendents. A threesome of clerical workers is close-knit with lunch, car pool, and recreation, and a foursome of three office workers and a supervisor is often together. However, Clerk 16 has only the contact of lunch. In the groupings there are at least the potentials of real or fancied favoritisms. Informal communication is clearly easier between certain individuals and certain groups than others. All this is in considerable part independent of the formal organization of business relations.

In addition, most of these individuals presumably had sundry contacts outside the plant. Management may belong to Rotary or Kiwanis, Shrine, a country club and a golf or bridge crowd, attend an Episcopal church,

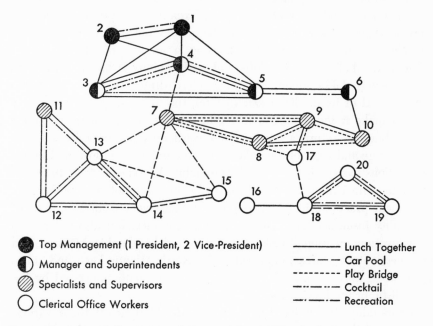

Figure 67. Informal Associations of Managerial and Office Staff of a Midwest Manufacturing Concern. (From D. C. Miller and W. H. Form, *Industrial Sociology*, New York, Harper, 1951, p. 219.)

and occasionally visit a night club. Workers may drop in at a beer garden or a corner "tavern," belong to a bowling crowd, and attend a Catholic or Baptist church. They probably belong to a union. In almost every social respect, management and labor tend to be separate.

THE LABOR UNION AND WAY OF LIFE

A major phenomenon of recent times has been the great growth of labor unions and of their power and paramount significance for the workers. No longer ago than 1932, labor union membership in this country totaled only a little more than 3 million; by 1950 the number had grown to 15 million. Not only did the unions serve to increase wages, decrease hours, and improve working conditions, but increasingly, "the union served as a composite symbol of protection for all those social values which were in themselves unexpressible as well as for the protection of reasonable wages. To the worker, the union represented a medium through which his work within the factory would be better integrated with his life outside the factory" (*111*, p. 131).

The miners' pension and welfare programs illustrate union accomplishments for the protection of the worker. Even more broad are the services rendered by the garment workers' union: they not only include security in old age but also coöperative housing, a summer resort for vacation rest, medical clinics, social clubs, and credit unions. It has been said that "the modern labor union, like the modern drugstore, caters to almost every need of its public" (*49*). In total, the union may render services which make it *the* dominant factor in the lives of its members, and it may obtain in return a loyalty felt toward no other organization. The great range and vigor of the policies of some unions are illustrated by the resolutions passed by the United Automobile Workers at their 1949 convention. The Union declared itself to be in favor not only of fair employment practices, increased old age and survivor's insurance, national disability insurance, and national health insurance, but also federal aid to education; creation of valley authorities in the Columbia, Missouri, and Connecticut river areas; approval of the North Atlantic Pact; and aid to Indonesia, Korea, "and other democratic governments oppressed by imperialistic or totalitarian forces."

Presumably, the union leaders were interested in all these various topics, and they were more or less remotely of concern to the membership. But certain "psychological" factors might well also be involved. Both leaders and members might find a satisfaction in the feeling that, through the union, they could have more of a share than otherwise possible in affecting policy on such matters. On these and also more immediate labor policies, the individual may sense his unimportance but gain much in satisfaction if not in power by identifying himself with a vigorous organization which speaks out strongly as he wishes he might do. As an individual he probably feels insecure and, indeed, an insignificant, helpless nonentity who is simply an employee of some huge corporation, but as a union member he becomes again a person who may have some voice in meetings and gain some sense of security and means of action. If he feels that he has been overlooked or pushed around by management, union activity may give him an opportunity to express his hostility and aggression. An ambitious man finding no outlet for his energies in his job may see ready at hand in his union interesting and challenging things to do, opportunities for leadership, and possibilities of attaining national recognition and power (54).

For instance, William Green rose from miner to district president of the United Mine Workers at 27, to secretary-treasurer of the AFL at 39, to president at 51. George Meany at 16 was a plumber's apprentice, at 40 he was president of the New York AFL, at 46 he was secretary-treasurer of the AFL, and at 60 he was president of the combined AFL-CIO. Walter Reuther at 17 was an apprentice tool and die maker, at 28 he was a labor organizer, at 35 he was vice-president of the international UAW-CIO, and at 40 he was president of the CIO.

Major Needs Indicated from a "Developmental" Study of Work

The preceding pages have brought together a great variety of material in an effort to see work in relation to development and change through the life span and as related to life as a whole at different ages. Certain needs and problems emerge from this approach which must now be emphasized.

VOCATIONAL PLANNING AND COÖRDINATION WITH DEVELOPMENT

Already stressed is the need for young people to plan not only more realistically but with a longer forward look than many do. And this holds not only for the youngster who drops out of school as soon as the law allows, but for the college student, who can be almost unbelievably unrealistic, and the faculty, who may be unknowing or irresponsible. The following are some examples of unrealistic plans: the dullish boy who earns his way but is determined to enter medicine; the bright little freshman girl, made much of by the professor of classical languages (whose students were few), who decides to major in Greek; the retired Army noncom with a family of four who uses his GI benefits to major in English literature with the expectation of teaching that subject in high school, simply because he liked to read—but never a query from his advisor as to his meeting requirements for teaching or likelihood of getting such a job; the 50-year-old, not-too-capable former county school superintendent who struggles for the doctorate with the hope of a professorship in some college of education. These are extreme cases. But many students get into vocational problems because they drift along with the common assumption that they should "follow their interests" rather than make clear-eyed plans—or obtain a "liberal" education which seems to take a perverse pride in graduating them without any vocational orientations. In these times of delay in completing education because of national emergencies, and of earlier marriage, realism in vocational preparation and planning seems increasingly necessary.

An essentially vocational problem was the situation of the coed who was happily engaged to an Air Force officer and happily majoring in Shakespearian drama. But she had no interest in courses in child care and homemaking that were available in the department of home economics, no interest in courses in current events or problems of the Near East with which in fact her fiancé was already involved, and no thought of a possible career for herself if she were widowed.

A student should not only plan his education with consideration of vocation, but vacation and part-time jobs can also be used for vocational exploration, at the same time that they are sources of earnings. A boy so enjoyed summer work in a state forest that he made forestry his career. After two weeks as assistant to a high school principal before the college year began, a girl decided that she did *not* want to teach. Not only the immediate appeal of a job should be considered. An able young man found an offer from a big corporation very intriguing, until he discovered that it involved a marginal venture which would quickly be dropped if there was any business recession. And what are the possiblities for the more remote as well as the immediate future? This last issue may be of immediate importance for a young person in understanding a family crisis. For instance, the daughter of a very well-paid buyer for a big department store was greatly distressed and indeed humiliated to discover that her father had been made elevator-starter on the main floor— where her friends frequently saw him. At 55, the frequent trips of the buyer's job had become a health hazard, and the store had found his judgment slipping as to fashions and the customer-appeal of goods. Really, he deserved his daughter's admiration for taking this best-paying alternative the store had offered him, and his down-grading illustrated the exigencies to which many types of work are subject in later adulthood.

Even in these days of pension plans and old age and survivor's insurance there are still some persons who have missed coverage or have special needs and are desperate for work in old age. A vivid, anonymous magazine article tells of the plight of a former advertising man and free-lance writer, unable to find any work or sell any of his recent efforts, who finally, near 70, took a job as a messenger "boy" in a publishing house where 30 years before he had had a good position and where many of his younger friends now worked. They pitied or ignored him and gossiped about him for awhile; but he at least had some regular wage and regular day's routine and some companionship with others in somewhat similar straits.[8]

The preceding matter has stressed difficulties and maladjustments in relation of work to development. And material earlier in the chapter may have seemed largely defensive—though older workers were slower, at least they came on time! But might there be more positive steps toward utilization of the distinctive merits of each age? A previous chapter has presented evidence that capacity for creative work came early, capacity for leadership came later, and matured scholarship and a relaxed mellowing came still later. What might be done, congruent with these findings, for earlier creativity and utilized age in a science, for instance? At first glance relevant is the Social Science Research Council plan for "undergraduate research training"[9] which provides funds for a summer of research work between junior and senior year for selected students. But on further reading it appears that this opportunity is intended more as a lure into professional study than as an early beginning of research. Faculty research fellowships are "designed to enable young social scientists . . . to devote one half or more of their time to self-directed research."[10] But most postdoctoral fellowships are for further study rather than creative work! One retired faculty member, a retired colonel, and a retired rear admiral were given grants for research more of a scholarly than a creative nature. The suggestion is ventured that foundations might well explicitly try to support and encourage the distinctive potentialities of each age. It would seem that schools and universities and business concerns might more rapidly open up opportunities appropriate to the energies of the younger years and at the same time still foster and feature the opportunities more suited and increasingly adjusted to the older years. These opportunities would be tapered to the energies of older peo-

[8] Anonymous, An old man finds a job, *The Reporter*, February 23, 1956, pp. 38–40. It is evident from the account that he was motivated not alone from financial need, but from "the tragic realization of no longer *belonging*, of being no part of a group, of being no use. Hobbies don't seem to fill the void, time killers and diversions merely postpone the day of reckoning. You are alone with yourself, and that does not seem to be enough."

[9] Annual report of the Council for 1954–1955, p. 47.

[10] *Ibid.*, p. 26.

ple and would be recognized with appropriate prestige. As has been illustrated, there are types of work which even the old can do well and even sometimes best. And as a person plans and goes forward in his own career, it should be possible for him to accommodate himself at least a little to the weaknesses and utilize the strengths of each age. As illustrated by Lillian Martin in her initiation of old age counseling in her retirement, a distinctive and notable career may sometimes begin in old age!

MEANS OF REINTEGRATING WORK WITH COMMUNITY

A major problem in the social psychology of work is now so general as to be often neglected or even not recognized. Contrast of an earlier and psychologically more healthy work situation with the present should make the problem clearer. Some 75 years ago the grandfather of one of the writers owned a little sawmill and box factory, on a small stream in the little New Hampshire village where he had been born, and operated the little establishment with the help of three or four neighborhood men. Not only did they all work together but they and their families were all neighbors together, and everyone in the little community, including the children, knew what each man did and how the business was going. Everyday talk included such matters as naturally as it did the weather. In contrast, management in modern big business is not only remote from the workers in origins, socioeconomic status, education, place and mode of living, place and conditions and hours of work, recreation, manners, and friends, but a worker's job is probably not understood—may not even be known—in other groups to which he belongs or with which he has some association. Even his family may know little about what he does. To many people with whom he has some contact—in the supermarket, on the bus, walking in the park on Sunday afternoon—he is a nameless, almost faceless figure, seen only in that one relation. "Though the urban structures are massively organized in terms of specialized functions, they are dispersive in terms of human nature. They fragment life. . . . Anonymous contacts characterize many if not most of the associations of people with one another" (*10*, p. 81).

Under such circumstances, the union, as intimated earlier, may be not only an organization for bargaining with management but also a means by which the workers collectively get back into contact with community leaders and obtain the attention and respect of the general public. Union locals may make this an important part of their policy. For instance, union strength and membership allegiance in a steel town were not satisfactory, apparently in part because collective bargaining was going on in a distant city on a national basis. Local union leaders thereupon initiated a vigorous program for union participation in community affairs, and union action became "decisive in shifting community control in municipal and education fields from high community status groups, including management, to the labor group" (64).

Various means may be used to increase community interest in and understanding of local businesses. Guided tours of a plant may be available on certain days or at the request of any community groups. In one large city, 16 industries combined to hold "open house," and articles and pictures in the newspapers featured workers, machines, and processes; emphasis was put on family visiting. A big plant in another city sponsors guided tours for workers' families, with stops at key points for illustrated talks by supervisory personnel, opportunity to observe what the workers do, and emphasis on the role and importance of the different workers in the total operations of the company. Yet another big concern put on a television program, after advance notices to employees, stockholders, and customers; operations of the company were shown and explained, and employees were commended for safety records and contributions to company success (92).

An industrial information institute supported by local business in another city not only provides material about local industries to the schools of the area, but it also provides speakers and films for any groups desiring them. The plant-community relations program of General Motors includes giving local newspapers information about production, work force, promotions, awards, retirements. Company magazines are distributed on a community-wide basis (50). The company magazine of another huge company, also very widely distributed, ran a series of articles on places to go and things to do in retirement, and union representatives in another city helped sponsor clubs for old people.

Both labor and management may courageously lead desirable community action against opposition. A union leader proudly told one of the writers of his getting management to accept colored workers—and then of his difficulties in getting his own members to accept them. An industry in a small city, having brought in a group of Puerto Rican laborers, found good lodging for them and arranged special classes in English for them. Then, when race antagonism appeared, the company enlisted the aid of city officials, church groups, and the union in a plan of community education involving public recognition of the Puerto Ricans as good workers and the finding of new job opportunities for them (67). In short, by various means, even in big industry in big cities, workers can be restored to some status in the community, and both workers and management can participate in community affairs.

PSYCHOLOGICAL SERVICES INVOLVING WORK THROUGH THE LIFE SPAN

A life-span view enlarges the possibilities of service which a psychologist may render to the work world. The need for realistic vocational counseling in the last year of school has already been stressed. Vocational planning should, of course, begin earlier, may use summer and part-time work in exploratory as well as money-earning fashion, and may even make work an integral part of the educational program in high school (41) or in college, as is done at Antioch. Wise placement in the first career job, by school or college, may be of major importance in career success. It may solve both an educational and a vocational problem. For instance, a dull college student failing in journalism was "sold" on a job in a newspaper pressroom; modest success there replaced probable college *and* career failure.

The psychologist in an employment office may demonstrably aid selection and placement. For instance, all those rated unusually promising on a systematic initial interview of factory applicants were found later to be above average in on-the-job ratings, but only 1 out of 31 who were initially rated unpromising but were nevertheless hired (McMurry and Johnson in 54, p. 100) was so rated. Industrial change and labor mobility bring in applicants of a wide age range, and many married women are returning to the labor market. Employment offices should know the merits and proper placement of the older worker and even sometimes campaign for him—while eliminating or finding more suitable jobs for the incompetent.[11]

Industrial psychologists should be alert to conditions of work. For instance, girls on a seemingly easy inspection job complained of aching backs and shoulders. New chairs that steadied the spine and work fixtures adjustable to height eliminated the aches and increased production (54, p. 207). Older workers may need certain adjustments, such as brighter lighting; as many slow down, they may need transfer to work that is less

---

[11] For instance, a survey in a large Ohio city in April, 1950 found age restrictions on 80 percent of clerical and sales openings, 73 percent of professional and managerial jobs, 70 percent of semiskilled jobs, and 43 percent of skilled jobs. And of those vainly seeking work for over 20 weeks, 24 percent were over 65, 23 percent were 45 to 64, 12 percent were under 20, and 10 percent were 20 to 24.

demanding of speed. They may exhibit sundry changes, such as a decrease in liking for active and outside work (well displayed in Figure 68); and adjustments to age should be a regular part of personnel policy and handled with studied considerateness. For instance, the buyer, mentioned earlier, who was transferred to elevator starter was told of the great importance of the starter's work in directing customers and facilitat-

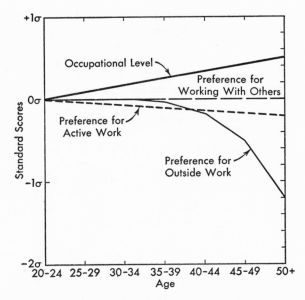

Figure 68. Age and Interest Inventory Scores for Semiskilled Workers. (Adapted from C. W. Brown and E. E. Ghiselli, Age of semiskilled workers in relation to abilities and interests, *Personnel Psychol.*, 1949, 2:497–511.)

ing their movement through the store—unfortunately, these explanations did not reach his family. There should be sensitiveness to retirement problems, probably preretirement counselling. In firms where retirement age is flexible, it would be desirable to have tactful consideration of when retirement might best come. Motivations (the topic of Chapter 7) must always be considered. The most famous investigation in industrial psychology showed that wages, conditions, and hours were less important than recognition and status (73).

Almost always, a job requires some training, and changes in jobs or processes require retraining. The hesitations, misgivings, and slowness of older workers should be allowed for (45). And the marked gains made possible by effective training should be recognized (54).

There should always be sensitiveness to workers' larger human problems, often outside the work situation but nevertheless determinative of efficiency there. A special counselor for such work may be needed. Sample notes from the files of a woman counselor during World War II will show something as to the variety of problems and help which may be given.[12]

The case of a girl from a poor section of the city who was just out of school and beginning work was essentially simple. She was bewildered and not very bright. She did not know how to get along with fellow workers. They complained that she was always frowsy and often smelled unpleasant. The counselor talked with the girl and tried to give her some elementary suggestions regarding her appearance and hygiene and her relationships with her associates.

Somewhat the same type of problem, but with greater complications, was presented by a married couple who recently came up from the South and were both employed. City life was strange to them; they literally did not know their way about. They were often uncouth in manner and dress. Moreover, they had five small children who, left by themselves in the run-down rented dwelling while the parents were at work, were so ill-cared-for that the neighbors complained. The problem involved local welfare agencies and health authorities, and it illustrated the ramifications an employment problem may have in a community.

A not uncommon case of a different character involved a girl who drove to work with a fellow worker who was a married man; before long she had an affair with him. The attempt was made to break off this relationship—but then, how would she get to work! In this particular instance it was found that the young woman could live with an aunt in a different part of the city and closer to the plant. This arrangement at least somewhat alleviated the situation.

Another case was also typical of rather numerous instances during the war. A married woman in her middle forties whose children were grown, and whose husband was ill, took a job because of both financial need and a feeling that she should do her part. The combination of the swirl of traffic about the plant when shifts were changing, the hurry and noise in the plant, and the routines to which she was supposed to conform almost dizzied her. She was a problem to herself and her supervisor. A friendly counseling to give some explanation of certain of the procedures she did not understand and some support to her confidence, a conference aiming at better understanding of her relations with her superviser, and arrangements by which a fellow worker went with her to lunch two or three times and showed both friendliness and unobtrusive advise in her getting about all gradually helped her to adjust.

[12] The writer is indebted to Miss Cynthia Ware for the opportunity to look over certain of her very keen case notations and for her perceptive comments about her work.

Indeed deserving of help was the young woman in her late twenties whose parents were both ill at home. Her two brothers were in the service, and one was invalided and about to be sent back from the front. She was on the night shift. Transfer to a day shift, housekeeping care for the incapacitated parents, and arrangements for the injured brother all needed to be planned.

Evidently such a counselor or personnel officer can somewhat replace the personal contact which in early days could readily exist between employer and employee. Problems to be dealt with may range all the way from difficulties in beginning work to planning for retirement and may involve a host of issues from personal cleanliness and morality to parental responsibilities and relations to the community.

Summary

The chapter deals with a topic that is central in the adult lives of most people and is most broadly determinative of the success and happiness of those years—work.

1. Over the past half a century the composition of the labor force has changed very substantially; most marked has been the increase in number of women working, and continuing to work (or returning to work) through middle age. The work world has "gone coeducational"! Fewer youth now work, and a smaller proportion of those over 65 work. The percentage of workers has decreased markedly in agriculture and increased in clerical and semiskilled work. Income in some types of work has increased greatly; real income in certain salaried types has actually decreased. In short, types of work, rewards therefor, and composition of the labor force have all changed markedly even in the last 25 years and may change more rapidly in the near future, as a result of such innovations as automation and atomic power.

2. Career patterns in different occupations differ very greatly indeed. The father of the typical professional man was himself in business or a profession and had a fair to good education; he encouraged and helped support his son in college and professional training. After some miscellaneous summer and part-time jobs while in school, and three or four years of trial experience in his profession (meanwhile marrying a girl of his own socioeconomic class and a college graduate), the son obtains a stable job, gradually moves up in his profession, and feels that on the whole it's a good world. In contrast, the unskilled worker comes from a family of that socioeconomic class and leaves school as soon as the law allows. At an early age he marries a girl of his own class and soon has a

family which is often ill. He never has a stable job or one much better than when he started, is chronically in debt—and chronically dissatisfied. Careers may begin with disappointment, as when a professional career is hoped for when neither ability nor resources are sufficient. As he grows older, a worker may suffer because of an age limit in hiring (usually unjustified) or because of failure to take account of either the weaknesses or the strengths of the older years (as slowing but increased accuracy). He may be retired at an arbitrary age while still able and desiring to work. In short, at every stage of the work career, problems of selection or adjustment are frequent.

3. Different types of work not only are typically done by people of different socioeconomic backgrounds and education, but differences in hours, places and conditions of work, and privileges and associates will be involved which in total make different ways of life. Differences in the status and role associated with different jobs, and their values to the worker, may be enormous. Great groups of workers, feeling circumscribed in status, role, and possibility of advancement, turn to their unions not only for aid but to provide enlargements of their lives; they may find in a union a worker's society with its own opportunities and possibilities of prestige.

4. A developmental consideration of the work life suggests for the individual more realistic and informed planning while in school and use of summer jobs for vocational exploring; alertness throughout one's career so as to adjust or change work (insofar as is possible) in accordance with age changes in abilities or liabilities; planning for retirement. Particularly in cities, special efforts may usually be needed to assure that the community understands and appreciates the worth of the many different groups. In the long developmental view of the life span the guidance of a psychologist may be helpful from first vocational planning in school, through choice of a job, adjustment to employment, possible advancement or transfer in mid-career, to planning for and living in retirement. The nature, conditions, and motivations of work may need to be adjusted to the young worker and readjusted to the older worker; at different ages there may be different problems of training or retraining, and at all ages there are diverse problems of living regarding which a wise counselor can be of much help.

In short, it is believed that the long developmental dimension *should be* a major consideration in vocational and industrial psychology; now, "age" is not even in the index of some books in these fields!

BIBLIOGRAPHY

1. Becker, H. S., The career of the Chicago public school teacher, *Amer. J. Sociol.*, 1952, 57:470–477.
2. Belbin, R. M., Older people and heavy work, *Brit. J. of Industrial Medicine*, 1955, 12:309–319.
3. Berlin, H., The community occupational survey and studies of occupation choice, *Personnel and Guidance J.*, 1953, 31:455–457.
4. Bowers, W. H., An appraisal of worker characteristcis as related to age, *J. Appl. Psychol.*, 1952, 36:296–300.
5. Brayfield, A. H., and Crockett, W. H., Employee attitudes and employee performance, *Psychol. Bull.*, 1955, 52:396–424.
6. Breckenridge, Elizabeth L., *Effective Use of Older Workers*, Chicago, Wilcox and Follett, 1953.
7. Britton, J. H. and J. O., Work and retirement for older university alumni, *J. Gerontol.*, 1954, 9:468–474.
8. Brower, F. Beatrice, *Handbook on Pensions*, New York, National Industrial Conference Board, 1950.
9. Brown, C. W., and Ghiselli, E. E., Age of semiskilled workers in relation to abilities and interests, *Personnel Psychol.*, 1949, 2:497–511.
10. Brownell, B., *The Human Community*, New York, Harper, 1950.
11. Burns, R. K., and Brown, L. B., The older worker in industry, A. I. Lansing (ed.), *Problems of Aging*, Baltimore, Williams and Wilkins, 1952.
12. Chamberlain, N. W., *The Union Challenge to Management Control*, New York, Harper, 1948.
13. Chinoy, B., Social mobility trends in the United States, *Amer. Sociol. Rev.*, 1955, 20:180–186.
14. Clague, E., The working life span of American workers, *J. Gerontol.*, 1949, 4:285–289.
15. Cook, P. H., and Syndham, A. J., Patterns of eating behavior; a study of industrial workers, *Human Relations*, 1953, 6:141–159.
16. Cover, C. B., and Pressey, S. L., Age and route sales efficiency, *J. Appl. Psychol.*, 1950, 34:229–231.
17. Covner, B. J., and Smith, M., Times absent vs. days absent as a measure of absenteeism, *Personnel*, 1951, 28:23–27.
18. Davis, N. M., Attitudes toward work among building operatives, *Occup. Psychol.*, 1948, 22:56–62.
19. Davis, N. M., The hope of industrial workers for their children, *Occup. Psychol.*, 1953, 27:11–22.
20. Dean, Lois, Union activity and dual loyalty, *Industrial and Labor Relations Rev.*, 1954, 7:526–536.
21. DeFord, Miriam Allen, *Psychologist Unretired: The Life Pattern of Lillian J. Martin*, Stanford, Stanford University Press, 1948.
22. Desmond, T. C., *Making the Years Count*, New York, New York State Joint Legislative Committee on Problems of the Aging, 1955.

23. Dewey, R., and Humber, W. J., *The Development of Human Behavior*, New York, Macmillan, 1951.

24. Drucker, P. F., The employee society, *Amer. J. Sociol.*, 1953, *58*: 358–363.

25. Dublin, L. I., and Lotka, A. J., *The Money Value of a Man*, New York, Ronald Press, 1946.

26. Durand, J. D., *The Labor Force in the United States*, New York, Social Science Research, 1948.

27. Federal Security Agency, Committee on Aging and Geriatrics, *Fact Book on Aging*, Washington, D.C., U.S. Government Printing Office, 1952.

28. Fox, Harland, Lindbom, T. R., and Stone, C. H., After 65—what? *Personnel J.*, 1951, *30*:5, 181–187.

29. Friedman, G., Technological change and human relations, *British J. of Sociol.*, 1952, *3*:95–116.

30. Friedmann, E. A., Havighurst, R. J., and Harlan, W. H., *The Meaning of Work and Retirement*, Chicago, University of Chicago Press, 1954.

31. Gardner, B. B., and Moore, D. G., *Human Relations in Industry*, Homewood (Illinois), Richard D. Irwin, 1950.

32. Gold, R., Janitors versus tenants: a status-income dilemma, *Amer. J. Sociol.*, 1952, *57*:5, 486–493.

33. Hall, H. R., *Some Observations of Executive Retirement*, Cambridge, Harvard University Press, 1953.

34. Harrison, E. C., One year later: vocational choices and reality, *Personnel and Guidance J.*, 1953, *32*:144–146.

35. Harrison, E. C., See what they choose, *Occupations*, 1952, *30*:277–279.

36. Hartmann, G. W., and Newcomb, T. M. (eds.) *Industrial Conflict, A Psychological Interpretation*, New York, Gordon Co., 1939.

37. Havighurst, R. H., and Albrecht, Ruth, *Older People*, New York, Longmans, Green, 1953.

38. Heron, A. R., *Why Men Work*, Stanford, Stanford University Press, 1948.

39. Imberman, A. A., Personalities in labor-management conflict, *Advanced Management*, 1950, *15*:19–22.

40. International Labor Office, *Year Book of Labor Statistics*, 1954.

41. Ivins, W. H., and Runge, W. B., *Work Experience in High School*, New York, Ronald Press, 1951.

42. Jaques, E., *The Changing Culture of a Factory*. New York, Dryden Press, 1952.

43. Jucius, M. J., *Personnel Management*, Homewood (Illinois), Richard D. Irwin, 1955.

44. King, H. F., An age analysis of some agricultural accidents, *Occup. Psychol.*, 1955, *29*:1–8.

45. King, H. F., The response of older rural craftsmen to individual training, *J. Gerontol.* 1955, *10*:207–211.

46. Kiochner, W., Lindbom, T., and Paterson, D. G., Attitudes toward the employment of older people, *J. Appl. Psychol.*, 1952, *36*:154–156.

47. Kornhauser, A. (ed.), *Psychology of Labor-Management Relations,* New York, Industrial Relations Research Association, 1949.

48. Kossoris, M. D., Absenteeism and injury experience of older workers, *Monthly Labor Rev.* 1948, 67:16–19.

49. Krech, D., and Crutchfield, R. S., *Theory and Problems of Social Psychology,* New York, McGraw-Hill, 1948.

50. Kurtz, L., Industry's stake in public relations, *Advanced Management,* August, 1950, 7–9.

51. Langfeld, H. S. (ed.), *A History of Psychology in Autobiography,* Worcester, Clark University Press, 1952, IV.

52. Latham, A. J., Job appropriateness: a one year follow-up of high school graduates, *J. Soc. Psychol.,* 1951, 34:55–68.

53. Lauer, A. R., Age and sex in relation to accidents, *Highway Research Board Bull.,* 1952, 60:25–35.

54. Lawshe, C. H., *et al., Psychology of Industrial Relations,* New York, McGraw-Hill, 1953.

55. Lehman, H. C., Ages at time of first election of presidents of professional organizations, *Sci. Mont.,* 1955, 80:293–298.

56. Lehman, H. C., Jobs for those over 65, *J. Gerontol.,* 1955, 10:345–357.

57. Lynd, R. S., and H. M., *Middletown,* New York, Harcourt, Brace, 1929.

58. Maher, H., Age and performance of two work groups, *J. Gerontol.,* 1955, 10:448–451.

59. Manis, J. G., and Meltzer, B. N., Attitudes of textile workers to class structure, *Amer. J. Sociol.,* 1954, 60:30–35.

60. Mason, W. S., and Grass, W., Intra-occupational prestige differentiation: the school superintendency, *Amer. Sociol. Rev.,* 1955, 20:326–331.

61. Mathiasen, Geneva (ed.), *Criteria for Retirement,* New York, G. P. Putnam's, 1953.

62. McFarland, R. A., *Human Factors in Air Transportation,* New York, McGraw-Hill, 1953.

63. McFarland, R. A., Psycho-physiological problems of aging in air transport pilots, *J. Aviat. Med.,* 1954, 25:210–228.

64. McKee, J. B., Status and power in the industrial community: a comment on Drucker's theses, *Amer. J. Sociol.,* 1953, 58:364–370.

65. Miller, D. C., and Form, W. H., *Industrial Sociology,* New York, Harper, 1951.

66. Mills, C. W., *White Collar, the American Middle Classes,* New York, Oxford University Press, 1951.

67. Monserrat, J., Industry and community—A profitable partnership, *J. Educ. Sociol.,* 1953, 27:171–181.

68. Morse, N. C., and Weiss, R. S., The function and meaning of work and the job, *Amer. Sociol. Rev.,* 1955, 20:191–198.

69. New York Joint Legislative Committee on Problems of the Aging, *Memo to Mature Workers RE How to Get a Job,* New York, New York Joint Legislative Committee on Problems of the Aging, 1950.

70. Owen, W. V., The dynamics of employee status, *Personnel*, 1952, *28*: 456–461.
71. Pressey, S. L., Certain findings and proposals regarding professional retirement, *AAUP. Bull.*, 1955, *41*:503–509.
72. Reynolds, L. G., and Shister, J., *Job Horizons*, New York, Harper, 1949.
73. Roethlisberger, F. J., and Dickson, W. J., *Management and the Worker*, Cambridge, Harvard University Press, 1942.
74. Rose, A. W., How Negro workers feel about their jobs, *Personnel J.*, 1951, *29*:292–296.
75. Rowntree, B. S. (ch.), *Old People*, Nuffield Foundation, Oxford, England, 1947.
76. Roy, D., Quota restriction and gold bricking in a machine shop, *Amer. J. Sociol.* 1952, *57*:427–442.
77. Schwarztrauber, E. E., Education in industrial and labor relations, *Industrial and Labor Relations Rev.*, 1950, *3*:542–547.
78. Sheppard, H. L., Approaches to conflict in American industrial sociology, *Brit. J. Sociol.* 1954, *5*:324–341.
79. Shosteck, How well are we putting across occupational information? *Personnel and Guidance J.*, 1955, *33*:265–269.
80. Slichter, S. H., Retirement age and social policy, pp. 106–114 in *The Aged and Society*. Champaign, Illinois, 1950.
81. Smith, M. W., Evidences of potentialities of older workers in a manufacturing company, *Personnel Psychol.*, 1952, *5*:11–18.
82. Stagner, R., *Psychology of Personality* (2nd ed.), New York, McGraw-Hill, 1948.
83. Stanton, J. E., Part-time employment for the older worker, *J. Appl. Psychol.*, 1951, *35*:418–421.
84. Stecker, Margaret L., Beneficiaries prefer to work, *Social Security Bull.*, 1951, Vol. 14, No. 1.
85. Stephenson, R., Status achievement and occupational pyramid, *Social Forces*, 1952, *31*:75–77.
86. Stephenson, R. M., Occupational aspirations and plans of 443 ninth graders, *J. Educ. Res.*, 1955, *49*:27–35.
87. Strong, E. K., Interest scores while in college of occupations engaged in 20 years later, *Educ. Psychol. Meas.*, 1951, *11*:335–348.
88. Strow, C. W., A survey of employee benefit plans, *Personnel J.*, 1949, *28*:3, 98–101.
89. Taylor, G. R., *Are Workers Human?* Boston, Houghton Mifflin, 1952.
90. Tiffin, J., *Industrial Psychology* (3rd ed.), New York, Prentice-Hall, 1952.
91. Tuckman, J., and Lorge, I., Retirement practices in business and industry, *J. Gerontol.*, 1952, *7*:77–86.
92. T-V—a new employee communications medium, *Management Rev.*, 1952.
93. United Automobile, Aircraft and Agricultural Implement Workers of America, CIO, *Proceedings Twelfth Constitutional Convention*, United Automobile, Aircraft and Agricultural Implement Workers of America, CIO, 1949.

94. United Nations, *Yearbook of the United Nations*, New York, Columbia University Press, 1951.

95. U.S. Department of Commerce, Bureau of the Census, Experience of workers on their current jobs, *Current Population Reports Series*, 1951, 36.

96. U.S. Department of Commerce, Bureau of the Census, *Historical Statistics of the United States, 1789–1945, A supplement to the Statistical Abstract of the United States*, U.S. Government Printing Office, Washington, D.C., 1949.

97. U.S. Department of Commerce, Bureau of the Census, *Statistical Abstract of the United States, 1955*, Washington, D.C., U.S. Government Printing Office, 1955.

98. U.S. Department of Commerce, Office of Business Economics, *National Income, 1954 Edition*, Washington, D.C., U.S. Government Printing Office, 1954.

99. U.S. Department of Labor, Bureau of Labor Statistics, *Employment and Economic Status of Older Men and Women*, Bulletin No. 1092, Washington, D.C., U.S. Government Printing Office, 1952.

100. U.S. Department of Labor, Bureau of Labor Statistics, *Fact Book on the Employment Problems of Older Workers*, Washington, D.C., U.S. Government Printing Office, 1950.

101. U.S. Department of Labor, Bureau of Labor Statistics, *Fact Book on Manpower*, Washington, D.C., U.S. Government Printing Office, 1954.

102. U.S. Department of Labor, Bureau of Labor Statistics, *Monthly Labor Review*, Washington, D.C., U.S. Government Printing Office, 1955.

103. U.S. Department of Labor, Bureau of Labor Statistics, *The Workers' Story, 1913–1953*, Washington, D.C., U.S. Government Printing Office, 1953.

104. U.S. Department of Labor, Bureau of Employment Security, *Older Workers at the Public Employment Office*, Washington, D.C., The Bureau, 1950.

105. U.S. Department of Labor, Bureau of Employment Security, *Joint Committee on Railroad Retirement Legislation*, 1953.

106. Viteles, M. S., *Motivation and Morale in Industry*, New York, W. W. Norton, 1953.

107. Walker, C. R., *Steeltown*, New York, Harper, 1950.

108. Walker, C. R., and Gues, R. H., *The Man on the Assembly Line*, Cambridge, Harvard University Press, 1952.

109. Walker, J., and Marriott, R., A study of some attitudes to factory work, *Occup. Psychol.*, 1951, 25:181–191.

110. Warner, W. L., *American Life*, Chicago, University of Chicago Press, 1953.

111. Warner, W. L., and Low, J. O., *The Social System of the Modern Factory*, New Haven, Yale University Press, 1947.

112. Warner, W. L., and Lunt, P. S., *The Status System of a Modern Community*, New Haven, Yale University Press, 1942.

113. Weinberg, S. K., and Arond, H., The occupational culture of the boxer, *Amer. J. Sociol.*, 1952, 57:460–469.

114. Welford, A. T., *Skill and Age, An Experimental Approach*, London, Oxford University Press, 1951.

115. Whyte, W. F., *Human Relations in the Restaurant Industry*, New York, McGraw-Hill, 1948.

116. Williams, H. F., Jr., The town tells teens about jobs, *Personnel and Guidance J.*, 1954, 32:266–269.

PART TWO .

. Dynamic and Social Development

CHAPTER 7.

• Changing Motivation During the Life Span

HARDLY any problem is as fascinating and as puzzling as that of trying to discover the "why" of someone's behavior. To achieve some explanation, such concepts as "drive," "motive," and "need" have been formulated and now stand among the major explanatory concepts in psychology. They have proved fruitful not only in providing a certain unity to the diversity of human personality at any point in time, but also in contributing to an understanding of developmental changes. The emphasis of the chapter will be upon *general* features of motivation, on broad age changes, on the "organizing" role of motivational tendencies in providing unity to an individual life and to the individual's reactions to the complex features of the external world. Subsequent chapters will provide information regarding many specifics—changes in worries and anxieties, in interests and recreational patterns, in values and attitudes, in social life, and in marriage. Indeed, almost all of the chapters in this volume concern, in one way or another, directly or indirectly, the changes in motivational orientation, drives, and purposes that people experience as they pass through the successive phases of infancy into childhood, into adulthood, and finally into old age.

Constitutional Factors in Motivation

Physiological pressures and innate equipment making for pleasurable sensations represent the original motivating conditions with which the child is born. What kinds of constitutional factors are most significant for understanding human urges and needs? What relative weight may be assigned these urges at different points in the life span?

PHYSIOLOGICAL TENSIONS, URGES, DISCOMFORTS

The newborn infant is a dynamic organism exhibiting cycles of quietude and activity. When in a state of relative equilibrium physiologically, he is likely to sleep or doze. He becomes active when this comfortable equilibrium is disturbed by cyclic development of discomforts, such as those caused by deficits of food or water or by pressures as in bladder or rectum. External conditions, such as extreme, sudden, or painful stimuli—loud, sudden noises, brilliant flashes of light (such as a flash bulb), uncomfortable heat or cold, pin pricks, sudden loss of support— will also cause discomfort and produce essentially the same activity pattern as that resulting from the internal stimuli, though a typical "startle pattern" initiates the activity in the instance of sudden, strong stimuli.

The activity pattern initiated by discomforts is at first essentially random and undirected, involving the total limited response repertoire of the infant—waving arms and legs, wiggling, and crying. When the behavior is observed in the absence of knowledge of the stimulus, it is not possible to identify with any certainty the source of the tension or discomfort. The young mother with a crying, disturbed infant knows from his behavior only that *something* is wrong. Just *what* this is, since the infant cannot tell her and his behavior gives no specific identifying cues, must be discovered by checking off various possibilities. Is he hungry? Wet and cold? Clothes uncomfortable? A pin pricking him? Infants show the rather direct working of biological drives, relatively uninfluenced by learning, producing a random, mass behavior. Behavior at this age seems dominated almost exclusively by physiological pressures.

The physiological discomforts which seem to characterize the human animal are, of course, numerous and, through learning, produce different behavior tendencies. Some tensions are reduced by intakes, some by outputs, some by retractions (54). Biological pressures cause the organism to be active. Gradually, as certain behaviors rather consistently remove the discomforts, the infant learns to seek some objects and conditions and to avoid or move away from others. In the course of time and experience, the child learns to anticipate a change in feeling tone contingent upon certain acts, and thus these directional tendencies become well learned. Among the commonly recognized biological drives are the needs for food, water, and oxygen, for the elimination of excretions, for sleep and rest, for relief from pressures of sex, for avoidance of pain and noxious stimuli, and for the avoidance of such discomforts as those arising from postural or other fatigues or from temperature variations. Some drives are stronger than others. In animal studies,[1] thirst and sex seem

---

[1] The relative priority of these drives has been studied in animals by ascertaining the number of times deprived animals will cross an obstruction (in many studies, a

more important than hunger in the early phases of deprivation (i. e., up to one day) but over longer periods the hunger drive takes precedence. Studies of semistarvation conducted on human subjects (35) also show hunger needs, after long deprivation, to be stronger than sex, yet in the American society sex seems much stronger and more pervasive in its influence, probably because hunger for food is fairly readily satisfied, whereas the taboos of society prevent free satisfaction of sexual needs.

INNATELY PLEASURABLE SENSATIONS

The influence of physiologically produced discomforts upon behavior is fairly obvious. But there also seem to be certain innately pleasurable experiences. Animals seem to have a constitutional liking for certain sensations of taste and smell and feel. Rats learn with saccharine as a reward —even though it has no nutritive value to reduce discomforts due to hunger (65). Salty water is preferred to ordinary water (80). Sexual stimulation is pleasurable even though sexual tensions may not be reduced (66), and stroking seems an innately pleasurable experience. Through experimentation an organism may learn which of a wide array of experiences are directly pleasurable.

Especially interesting is the characteristic tendency of organisms to be active and their apparently innate curiosity regarding new features of the environment. The "need" for activity of one sort or another is apparent in the exuberant running and playing of a child or a puppy, the activity seeming almost a simple "going off" of the organism. Activity may be sheer, undirected activity enjoyed for its own sake, or it may be exploratory activity prompted by the presence of *new* objects, ideas, or conditions. The capacity of a stimulating environment to motivate behavior has been emphasized in a vigorous paper by Harlow (31). The very presence of puzzles stimulated monkeys, in his studies, to manipulate them and to work them through to a solution. And other research with rats has shown their persistent tendency to explore new situations, independently of other primary drive conditions, and has led some investigators to conclude that a primary exploratory or "curiosity" drive exists, a drive which is evoked by novel stimulation (51).

---

grill administering electric shock) in a given unit of time to get to the appropriate goal object—food, water, a sexually receptive female, a litter of young. The maternal drive has not been adequately investigated, but present evidence (79) suggests that *at its maximum* the urge of a mother rat to get to its litter is stronger than any of the other drives yet studied, with thirst, hunger, and sex following in that order when at their maximum.

The possession of physical structures (neural-sensory-muscular) that permit certain activities seems to result in a "need" to utilize those structures by pursuing appropriate activities. A large part of the infant's play involves a seeking out of new experiences. Maturing motor and intellectual capacity results in shifts to increasingly complex and stimulating play and interests during childhood and adolescence. On the adult level it is well recognized by competent industrial and business personnel workers, for example, that an applicant can be not only too dull for a particular job, but he may indeed be *too bright*. Having the capacity for more complex activity and response, the bright person *needs* opportunities for complex and varied activity to be happy and satisfied.

The specific drives—for food, for sex, for activity—do not, of course, exert their influence upon behavior independently. They do not operate as discrete tension systems. Instead, motivation typically involves a continuing interaction of internal and external stimuli and adjustments; never does the organism achieve a state of perfect equilibrium. As Murphy has pointed out:

Motivation . . . never "starts" or "stops." There are rapid or slow rises in tension level, and rapid or slow transmissions of the tension. The level in a given region is a function of local chemical reaction and depends on food, temperature, the blood stream, and much besides. But the essential fact about motivation seems to be the continuous instability or restlessness, and the consequent inter-stimulation which characterizes all living systems. If energy changes resulting from inner and outer impulses converging upon a given region pass slowly or swiftly from one region to another, a time comes when a *manifest* change with reference to the environment forces our attention upon a given muscle group; then, as we look back, a "motive" for the act is artificially designated. But in reality the cycle of internal stimulation goes on ceaselessly. (53, p. 88.)

INDIVIDUAL AND AGE DIFFERENCES

Major differences exist among individuals in the importance of various constitutional factors. Some people, perhaps because of inherited glandular conditions, are essentially sluggish and inactive, whereas others have a high energy level, are hyperactive, and have to be "doing something" most of the time. Some people are especially sensitive to tone—have pure tone sensitivity—while others seem almost innately insensitive. Biochemical differences may create marked differences in "craving" for different substances—salt, sugar. Some people have high and others have low sex drives (36, 37). Some require more and some less food intake. However, such differences are not due entirely to innate differences in strength of drive. High sexual drive may be a learned neurotic compulsion, and apparent low or declining sexual drive may be due to inadequate stimulus. The same may be true of apparent strong activity or hunger drives.

It was suggested earlier that physiological urges and pressures seemed to dominate the behavior of the newborn child. This state of affairs changes as the child begins to associate other people, especially the mother, with the satisfaction of his biological needs. Gradually, through conditioning, social needs emerge, and, gradually, through interaction with the broader environment, a whole array of derived needs come to influence behavior.[2] Thus, physiological pressures and urges are likely to become relatively less important in the total motivational complex as the infant matures into childhood and on into adulthood. During adult years complex changes in endocrine function, metabolism, and general bodily tonus will likely result in a certain sluggishness and further subordination of biological drives.

What about the later years? Do physiological pressures assume greater importance again in old age? In some cases there does seem to be general concern about and preoccupation with physiological functioning, but how general this may be is uncertain. But if so, the psychological context is very different. In early infancy social needs have not yet developed. In old age the difficulties of physiological function, of digestion and elimination, for example, and greater susceptibility to fatigue and illness may require greater attention to diet and general regimen and result in overattention to physiological needs. Or the decline in efficiency of the body's homeostatic mechanisms in later years may produce substantial changes in awareness of external factors such as heat or cold. The young person has greater capacity to adjust to heat and cold by maintaining a constant internal temperature, whereas the oldster must adjust by avoiding extremes.

Most of the evidence on age changes in particular biological urges and pressures is, in the case of human beings, of a quite indirect sort, based largely on everyday observation, but there is also evidence of the types that have been or will be summarized elsewhere in this volume. Thus, the rapid acceleration of physical growth just prior to pubescence,

---

[2] It is of some interest that in the human species, in comparison with lower animals, behavior seems less dependent upon biological factors and more upon environmental influences. In lower animals, for example, sex behavior conforms closely to cycles of underlying endocrine changes whereas among human beings sex behavior shows no such close dependence upon endocrine changes (6). The importance in human motivation of environmental stimulation in contrast to biological urges has also been emphasized by Harlow (31).

described in an earlier chapter, and the greater metabolic rate at this age involve a greater tissue need and a greater hunger drive. It has been shown that very young rats possess a stronger hunger drive than do post-pubescent rats when deprived of food for the same length of time, and adult rats show somewhat less hunger drive than do postpubescents (44). The advent of pubescence, occurring at different ages in the two sexes, likely gives impetus to the sex drive—but at an earlier age in the case of girls.[3] Glandular changes resulting in decline in the sex drive are likely responsible, in part at least, for the decline in sexual activity noted in Chapter 2, though habit, satiation, inadequate stimulus, and other factors besides waning of the sex drive per se may be in part responsible.

Freudian theory stresses the importance of sex as a motivating force in early childhood and the relative freedom of the child from sexual pressures during the latency period (from about five to prepubescence), with sex being a strong diffuse force in behavior generally during ado-lescence until the youngster learns how to manage and direct it toward an appropriate sex object. At menopause some writers see a resurgence of sex as a diffuse drive and as an energy source which may be directed into many activities, such as organizational activities in the case of women (7). While such views are widely held, they do not appear to be consistent at every point with the facts and interpretations of those facts that are presented in this volume.

A pervasive factor in changing motivation with age, evident in di-verse activities of life, is the changing need for activity. Clear age trends in activity drive have been demonstrated for rats, as shown in Figure 69, activity being measured by revolutions of a revolving drum in which the rats were placed or in movements made within a specially mounted cage. With pubescence, which occurs at about 60 days of age, a marked increase of activity was noted. Activity reaches a peak somewhere be-tween the hundredth and two hundredth and seventieth day of a life span which is roughly 900 days long, and declines thereafter (62, 67, 70);[4] all studies show the very old and the very young to be least ac-

[3] Kinsey (36) has noted that women typically do not experience orgasm at as early an age as men and has thus concluded that females mature sexually later than do males. The present writers interpret the later achievement of complete sex response as due to inhibitions prompted by cultural taboos against free expression of sexuality by females rather than due to their later biological maturation.

[4] Superimposed upon these gradual age trends in activity are various short-term cycles reflecting changes in other drive conditions. In female rats regular four-day cycles in activity parallel the four-day sex cycle, and cycles of activity parallel cy-cles of hunger and satiation.

tive, though they disagree on the specific age of greatest activity. Although objective data bearing directly on age trends in level of human activity are not available, it is almost self-evident that trends paralleling those in Figure 69 also characterize human beings. Older people, for example, are likely to need more sleep, one survey showing that only 56 percent of 20-year-olds retire by 11:00 P.M. compared with 86 percent of those over 60.[5] The trend toward inactivity with increasing adult age will also be clearly apparent in later discussions of changing interest patterns.

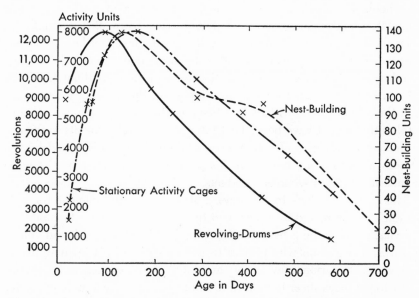

Figure 69.   Curves Showing the Relation of Activity to Age in Laboratory Rats. (From C. P. Richter, A behavioristic study of the activity of the rat, Comp. Psychol. Monogr., 1922, Nos. 1 and 2.)

What, now, of the seeking of new and pleasurable experiences, of the "curiosity" drive? It is possible, and probable, that changes occur in the nervous system with increasing adult ages which make it more difficult to learn new and different things. And sensory losses decrease susceptibility to environmental stimulation. These and other changes, especially declining energy and activity level, may be partially responsible for the decline in curiosity and exploratory tendencies and for the increasing desire for "sameness" and stability noted in subsequent chapters. But what appears to be a decline in curiosity drive with age may be in part (as

[5] Public Opinion Quart., 1945, 9:97.

was suggested above in the case of sex) a result of stimulus failure rather than drive failure. By the time a child has reached adulthood he has become pretty well acquainted with his environment, with the result that he may experience relatively little that is new—unless he seeks it out. Curiosity and desire for stimulation seem, almost, to be a predisposition on which society—and individuals—has failed to capitalize. Indeed, social institutions seem to stultify this tendency (and the resulting intellectual stimulation) very early in life. As noted in Chapter 5 on education, Jersild and Tasch, after making an extensive survey of children's interests in school, concluded that the typical first or second grader is eager, stimulated, and challenged by what there is to learn. But gradually he loses this eagerness, and by the time he is in high school he is more interested in what happens outside the classroom than in (33). While this trend may be interpreted simply as the result of the subordination of one type of need when another becomes dominant, the possibility also exists that the school programs have not been as challenging, stimulating, and vital as they might have been. That interesting, novel elements in the environment do demand attention, even in adulthood, is illustrated by the father's all-consuming interest in his son's electric train or by the wide popularity of "do-it-yourself" gadgets.

This general failure to maintain a stimulating environment for self, for one's children, and for others and the consequent failure to capitalize on what seems to be a basic tendency of people may have broad consequences. The person who refuses to get in a rut, who tries new foods, and who seeks various new sensory and intellectual experiences is not only likely to get more sheer fun out of life but is likely to be a more effective, better-adjusted person with a better chance of withstanding many of the typical impacts of increasing adult age.

Changing Social Motives

As the child grows, biological pressures and predispositions rapidly become subject to a complex overlay of culturally imposed patterns of expression. New motivations arise, apparently learned in the course of satisfying biological urges and pressures in a social context, but often appearing to have only a remote, if any, connection with biological drives. Major insights into individual personalities are best achieved through efforts to understand not their biological predispositions—important as these are—but the motivations they have learned primarily through social interaction.

THE DIVERSITY AND COMPLEXITY OF SOCIAL MOTIVES

That there should be a great diversity of social motives is almost inevitable, since growing children are exposed to a heterogeneous set of social values, are given opportunity for a broad range of pleasurable as well as unpleasurable experiences, and come under the influence of varying patterns of reward and punishment. In the course of living and in the process of adjustment to internal and external pressures, countless habits develop which are relatively peculiar in many instances to the individual and which may become so strongly established that they tend to function as motives in their own right. People who regularly read the paper before dinner, for example, develop a "need" to read the paper before dinner, and disruption of this habit is likely not only to be unpleasant but also to induce the various reaction tendencies associated with the frustration of any motive. Thus, any list of the social motives of an individual could, in theory, become as extensive as his repertoire of habits (2), or his range of values, likes and dislikes, whereas biological drives are few in number.

Although it is often convenient to speak of specific motives, as though motives operate separately and can be readily identified, the motivational structure of an individual is a complex of interrelated strivings, urges, and pressures that are difficult to fathom. A variety of motives prompt an individual to attend church or a movie, to go shopping, or to read the newspaper, and a variety of satisfactions result. A long-term course of action, such as a vocational choice and subsequent career, may involve not only one or more long-term goals which give overall direction but also short-term "subsidiary" needs which have subeffects and are satisfied along the way. And just as some biological needs take precedence over others (and generally over social needs), some social needs are more basic than others.

Psychological needs are manifest in a great variety of ways, and it is extremely difficult to infer from the behavior of a person the motivations that lie behind it. The same motive may, in different people or in the same person at different times, give rise to different behavior, and yet essentially similar behavior may be the product of quite different motives. The manner of expression of needs ranges from direct, overt dealing with actual objects or situations, through expression in fantasy which though indirect may be obvious in meaning, to marked distortions of expression either in fantasy or in overt behavior.

Identification and study of motives are made even more difficult by the circumstance that most of the psychological needs and motives of people are "unconscious" in the sense that even the individual concerned is unable to recognize and report the reasons for much of his own behavior. Feelings of guilt may result in the repression of certain tendencies and give rise to overt behavior that is quite the opposite of what might be expected, knowing the underlying feelings. A mother who strongly rejects an unwanted child may, for example, submerge and deny these feelings through a strong surge of overt affectional behavior and over-protection. A person may feel attracted to older people without knowing why or feel insecure, restless, and anxious in certain kinds of situations without being able to identify a reason. Unhappy childhood relations with parents may be forgotten (repressed) even though the emotional predispositions engendered at the time may remain and have an important influence in adult life upon relationships with other adults—teachers, spouse, employer.

It is because of the extreme degree to which motivations are "unconscious" that attempts to evaluate the motivational dynamics of an individual case require drawing the most subtle inferences from a wide variety of case material and behavior. And it probably requires a long-term program of self-study under special conditions—as in psychotherapy, perhaps psychoanalysis—to enable a person to appreciate the diversity, the complexity, the obscurity, and the curious manner of expression of many of his own psychological needs. It is little wonder that specialists in the study of human behavior evidence little agreement as to the number of social motives that exist or the labels which should be applied to them.

COMMONLY OBSERVED MOTIVES AND GOALS AMONG VARIOUS GROUPS

Despite such obscurity and complexity, many needs are translated into rather specific objectives and goals which are recognized by the individual and observable by others. Even here, much diversity is to be noted. But since people do, after all, come under many common cultural influences, they do share many goals and motives. In Table 35 are listed goals which are commonly found among adolescents. In this particular study, the goals of high school students were judged by counselors who based their inferences upon observations of overt behavior, on the direct statement of students, and upon indirect evidence accumulated in student folders. Of 287 goals identified for 105 individuals, 54 percent were classified as long-term goals, and the remainder were classified as goals possible of achievement in the relatively near future. The table lists these specific goals in order of frequency of occurrence. In the main, they relate to economic and vocational considerations and social and family relationships. With respect to certain goals (e. g., sex and religion) the counselors felt their information to be inadequate. The latter are, of

TABLE 35. Categories into Which 287 Goals of 105 High School Students Were Classified

Goal	Boys	Girls	Total
To enter certain definite vocations	26	44	70
To marry	8	29	37
To participate in school activities	18	14	32
To obtain economic independence in the future, but with no expressed vocational field in which to earn money	14	8	22
To follow a profession, but with no definite profession or one of several in mind	15	6	21
To gain status as an individual	13	3	16
To gain recognition for achievement	9	3	12
To gain personal prestige as a leader	9	3	12
To improve present social status (to be accepted by a group to which he aspired to belong)	4	6	10
To go to college for social prestige	2	7	9
To follow a leisure-time interest or hobby	7	1	8
To obtain economic security in the present	3	4	7
To ameliorate family conditions	3	3	6
To conform to the family pattern	6	0	6
To become independent of family supervision	2	3	5
To go to college to conform to family pattern	1	3	4
To improve physical condition	4	0	4
To gain economic independence until marriage	0	2	2
To have a "best friend" of same sex	0	2	2
To have a "best friend" of opposite sex	0	2	2
	144	143	287

SOURCE: Adapted from M. Brown and V. Martin (directors), The University High School study of adolescents: characteristics of high school students, *University High School J.,* 1941, 19:177–219.

course, the types of motivations which are likely to be less open to observation and less well recognized by the youngsters themselves.

A comparison of the relative frequency with which certain of these goals characterized girls as compared with boys illustrates the obvious but important point that social motivations will reflect particular sub-cultures. Girls more often indicate marriage as a basic goal, in part because the predominant feminine role involves marriage and family, but partly too because convention does not grant women full prerogatives when it comes to initiating marriage proposals. Girls, too, more frequently had *specific* occupational goals, a fact that might be expected in view of the clearer cultural definition of women's occupations.

Another study which illustrates the differences between subcultures dealt with work motivations in different occupational groups. Detailed histories were taken of the development of vocational interests and work life from earliest recollections for three groups, male and female teachers and male factory workers. These three groups represent three different subcultures—the male and female subcultures at one occupational level and two occupational levels within the male subculture. The interview records were judged as to the extent to which the various types of motivations were involved. Some of the results are shown in Table 36.

Among the teachers, the most common motivations included needs for self-expression, for status, and for association with people. Although desire for money and security was also frequently noted among male teachers (actually more frequently than among any others of the group), this was the most frequently noted motivation among the factory workers. It is apparent within the table that, at least in the vocational sphere of life, at the middle-class level men show more varied and generally stronger occupational motivation than women. Factory workers, on the other hand, seemed to show little in the way of career motivation, and their life histories during childhood and adolescence seemed to reflect much less pressure and stimulation from family or school. The data also indicated the multiplicity of needs operating in a complex area such as vocational life. At least 25 percent of the group gave evidence of all 6 needs or motives in their *vocational* histories, and over 50 percent had 10 or more major influences or needs evident in their interview record (56).

It is in part from such differential pressures, stimulations, and examples that differences in motivation among various groups develop, and it is precisely these differences that represent some of the more significant differences psychologically among various social classes and other groups. Sex differences in motivation are far more general and pervasive than the data in Tables 35 and 36 suggest. For example, a test recently devised to measure psychological needs has shown college women to have stronger needs to defer to others, to have close affiliation with others, to introspect regarding own personality and motives, to help others

TABLE 36. Percentage of Cases in Which Various Needs or Motives Played Some Role or a Major Role in the Evolving Vocational History

	Played Some Role[a]			Played Important Role[a]		
	Women Teachers	Men Teachers	Factory Workers	Women Teachers	Men Teachers	Factory Workers
Motivations (desire for)						
Self-expression	96	95	77	25	61	19
Status	93	96	74	37	51	9
Association with people	99	95	51	28	52	0
Money and security	85	92	95	9	47	30
Variety	72	68	86	8	13	7
Helping others	59	71	26	7	17	2
Influences						
Family	100	100	84	45	67	21
Financial need or lack	67	81	98	19	40	51
School	88	87	42	44	51	0
Early extended contact	80	84	51	39	40	7
Own work experience	56	87	84	9	17	26
Friends	80	68	70	13	27	14
Lack of stimulation	52	49	79	17	12	30
Talent	57	53	44	5	5	0
Other relatives	52	36	30	15	4	0
Opportunity	27	28	37	5	3	2
Health	12	19	39	0	3	5
Number of histories	75	75	43	75	75	43

[a] Histories were rated on a zero-to-four scale, depending on degree to which various motives and influences seemed to enter into the shaping of the vocational career. "Played some role" means that a rating of at least one was assigned by the raters. "Played important role" means a rating of three or four was assigned.

SOURCE: Based on J. C. Norton, General Motives and Influences in Vocational Choice, J. Genet Psychol., 1953, 82:235–262.

and to be dependent (i. e., accept help), and to be self-abasing. College men, on the other hand, have stronger achievement needs, stronger needs to dominate and to be autonomously self-directing, stronger needs to be aggressive, and stronger heterosexual needs (21). These differences between the sexes in motivational patterns will be apparent at numerous points throughout this volume. Mainly a product of sex-patterning of cultural influences, these differences will be important determiners of sex differences in behavior in most spheres of living.

Cultural pressures and influences tend also to be somewhat "age-graded." Just as there are changes in biological urges and pressures with age, so there are also changes in cultural roles, demands, and pressures. Certain behaviors are permitted, indeed are expected, in a teen-ager but are frowned upon in a person of 40. But the 40-year-old may be accorded certain privileges denied the 70-year-old or the 15-year-old. The middle-class culture places a premium upon success in school during the school years, but academic goals give way to vocational goals in the twenties and thirties. As time passes and an individual moves from one age bracket to another, appropriate changes in his motivations will normally occur.

THE NEED FOR SOCIAL ACCEPTANCE AND SECURITY

It was noted in Table 36 that the desire to associate with other people and the desire for status were among the strong motivating factors in many vocational histories. Here is reflected an extremely pervasive need —the desire to be with others, to be accepted by them, to have their affection, respect, and regard, to have a feeling of status in their eyes, and to have the feeling that these relations are enduring and secure. People will vary greatly in the extent to which such needs are evident in their behavior, in their views as to *who* the significant people are in whose eyes they want status, and in the ways in which the need is translated into behavior. The fawning sychophant, the clinging vine, the scheming social climber, the domineering boss, the defensive, irritating colleague, the shy, tentative Casper Milquetoast are all, but in quite diverse ways, revealing their need for status and acceptance—some by overly eager striving or catering, others by defiantly rejecting what they most want, others by quiet withdrawal. Although from its inception, the American culture has emphasized, in statute and in philosophy, the integrity and worth of the individual and his equality among others, only in recent decades has the basic importance of social acceptance needs gained recognition and been translated into programs and policies in home, school, and business personnel operations. The emergence of what might be called a "mental hygiene" point of view is one of the striking features of the last half-century of cultural change.

Evidence of the importance of social motives is contained in numerous

research reports which show that providing opportunities for social gratification pays off in better production in the case of school-age children
as well as in the case of adults on the job. It has long been recognized,
for example, that "praise" is an extremely effective incentive (32). In
Figure 70 are charted the findings from one study which demonstrates
the effectiveness of praise over blame, but which shows also that its
effectiveness will depend upon the urgency of the social needs of the
individuals involved and their typical patterns of social behavior. Fifth-
grade subjects in the study were selected as "introverts" or "extroverts"
on the basis of a personality test and were asked to perform, under conditions of praise and blame, the task of canceling out the 7's on a test
sheet made up of lists of numbers. Presumably, youngsters who are
blamed will work harder to gain the social approval which is withheld,
whereas those who are praised will work harder because they are in this
way gaining approval. But socially insecure individuals may withdraw
and fail to extend themselves if reprimanded, whereas socially secure individuals who get adequate approval may not really exert themselves
until their status is threatened by blame. It is likely that introverts and
extroverts differ in this regard, and, as Figure 70 shows, they differed
in their response to praise and blame.

At the adult level, one interesting study of the production of workmen
erecting standardized houses in a housing development revealed that
workers produced reliably more when they were assigned to work in
groups of their own preferences. Indeed, the production engineer reported to management that:

. . . savings due to this psychological procedure have exceeded those of any
previous work saving device or any combination of five previous work saving
methods. Financial benefits are such that we are now constructing every 29th
building entirely free from labor and materials costs. Even greater financial
gains would occur were it possible to evaluate monetary savings due to the
great reduction in turnover. (78.)

Developmental patterns with respect to social interaction are described in detail in a later chapter. In general, changes occur as regards
the group in which acceptance is desired and in the traits that seem to
make for acceptability. At very early ages the crucial importance of acceptance by parents is evident in the bizarre reactions that a first-born
child of two years of age may display when a newborn sibling diverts
parental attention. Acceptance among peers begins to become important
at an early age, increases when entrance to school broadens social con-

tacts, and is accentuated at adolescence when status in the eyes of the opposite sex and status as an adult are much desired. Social acceptance needs may be expected to wane in the adult years as a secure niche is carved out or as present situation, though inadequate, is adjusted to. Discontinuities, such as change of job and residence, which disrupt estab-

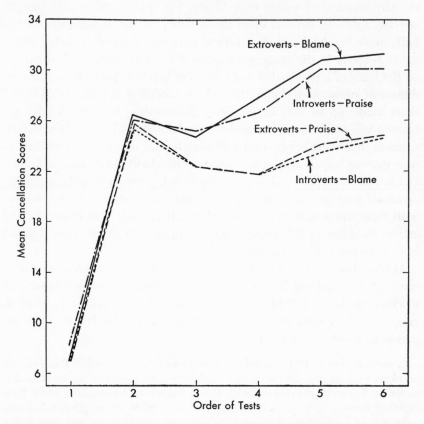

Figure 70. The Differential Response of Introverts and Extroverts to Repeated Praise and Blame. (From G. G. Thompson and C. W. Hunnicutt, The effect of repeated praise or blame on the work achievement of "introverts" and "extroverts," J. Educ. Psychol., 1944, 35:257–266.)

lished ties, or threats to status, such as loss of family fortune or reputation, may reactivate status needs. The status losses associated with aging, and especially the "rejection" occasioned by retirement, may so accentuate the social needs then that, as has been frequently pointed out, "the need to be needed" may become one of the most important of all in old age.

THE NEED TO ACHIEVE

Just as a need for general social acceptance or affiliation might grow out of the universal fact that infants and children are dependent upon others for comfort, protection, food, and care, a general need to achieve might be expected to grow out of the rather universal requirement that youngsters master certain skills, such as learning to talk and walk, if they are to obtain continued gratification of their needs. The winning of approval for accomplishments in basic skills, an experience common to many if not to most or all children, presumably further fosters the desire to achieve or to master, and this desire may later be reflected in a wide range of activities in various spheres of life. No matter what the endeavor, some people are not satisfied unless their performance is of top quality, and they may even refuse to participate in an activity in which they cannot do better than most. Others are quite satisfied with a passable performance. Some people have a strong drive for vocational success; some are satisfied with "a living."

The degree to which a person may be characterized as having high or low achievement motives has been determined, in most of the recent research, by ascertaining the frequency with which individuals express competition with a standard in stories they make up about pictures shown to them (46). They may, for example, have a person in a story trying to do better in some respect—to get a better job, to get ahead in the world. People who thus indirectly reveal themselves as having high achievement needs also reveal these needs in more concrete ways. They tend to show more learning when asked to do complex tasks than do those with low achievement needs, and on simple tasks where learning is not required they tend to produce more (43). They tend to be positively and constructively oriented toward success (49), to have higher levels of aspiration, and to be better at remembering incompleted tasks, possibly regarding them as challenges (4). Those with moderate achievement needs tended to be more on the defensive, to "forget" incompleted tasks, to show decreased sensitivity to "failure" words in word perception experiments, and, in short, to be more oriented toward the *avoidance* of failure. As McClelland, the investigator who has most intensively pursued research in this area, has pointed out, such studies "strongly suggest that there are at least two kinds of achievement motivation, one of which appears to be oriented around avoiding failure and the other around the more positive goal of attaining success. It cannot be stated, of course, which type of motivation is more efficient, since an excessive concern with either success or avoiding failure may be maladaptive, depending upon the requirements of the situation" (47, p. 410).

Although comparable types of data regarding achievement needs are not available for different age groups, such needs seem to develop early in some subcultures and to show striking differences in development and in adult age patterns in different subgroups of the population. If competitiveness in social situations may be interpreted as indicating achievement needs, they do indeed develop early. For example, in one study of children in certain Viennese kindergartens, none of the children between two and three years of age seemed to show unequivocal competitiveness, but by ages six to seven, 86 percent exhibited competition (29). The development of strong achievement needs seems to depend upon the extent to which the particular culture emphasizes independence training in children. In a study of several cultures, the age at which independence training was instituted and the severity of that training was found to correlate with the achievement need scores for those cultures, the latter being based on an analysis of the folk literature (48). General differences seem to exist among groups of various educational levels and religious backgrounds in the degree to which they stress independence training in their children (50).

In another study of 29 8-to-10-year-old boys, those who had highest achievement scores had mothers who more frequently "demanded" before age 8 such behavior as knowing one's own way around the city, trying new things for oneself, doing well in competition, and making own friends. Mothers of boys with high and low achievement needs did not differ in their demands regarding such behavior as looking after own possessions, going to bed by oneself, or doing tasks around the house (46, p. 303). It is further interesting that those mothers who bestowed primary physical affection (kissing and hugging) for fulfilling an achievement demand had sons who at 8 or 10 showed stronger achievement needs on the average than did the sons of mothers not reporting such physical rewards. The investigators sum up thus: The boy with strong achievement needs "is of a parent who urges her child to master a skill early (e. g., 'to know his way around the city'), restricts him until he does (e. g., 'not play away from home'), and then lets him alone. In short, she has faith in her son's ability to master something and do it on his own, whereas the mother of a son with low [achievement needs]

tends not to have that faith and to continue restricting her child to playing around the house" (*46*, p. 303).

To the extent that differences in incidence of vocational interests or
plans may reflect differences among groups in achievement needs, the
data in Figure 71 show differences in development during childhood and
adolescence and different patterns in early adult years between factory
workers and teachers. The latter apparently began thinking about such
matters earlier; by the late teens, expressions of specific vocational interests were almost universal and continued at this level after these in-

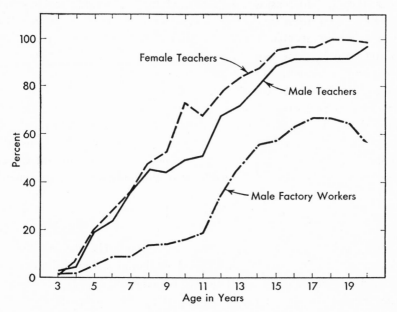

Figure 71. Percentage of 75 Male and 75 Female Teachers and 43 Factory Workers
Whose Vocational Histories Indicated the Existence of Vocational Interests at Various
Ages. (Based on J. L. Norton, Patterns of vocational interest development and actual
job choice, J. Genet. Psychol., 1953, 83:235–262.)

dividuals had begun their actual work lives (i. e., up to 28 years of age
in this study). Factory workers, on the other hand, were slower in development of vocational interests, and a substantial proportion (about a
third) expressed no particular interest even in the late teens. After the
teens, when jobs were obtained, the expression of vocational interests
declined.

It has been suggested that the achievement need decreases with age during the adult years (46) as people gradually achieve their goals or become reconciled to their failure. In one study of the likes and dislikes of professional men, for example, there was a steady decline with age in "liking" for "opportunity for promotion" (74), and a group of younger eminent scientists had higher achievement need scores than did a similar group of older scientists (46). But the matter is complex. The younger scientists may have achieved eminence at a younger age because they were more highly motivated to begin with. And although the professional men seemed less interested in opportunity for promotion as they got older, they did increasingly believe that they were able to "put drive into the organization" and to stimulate the ambition of associates (74). The latter suggests that although personal striving may become less important with age, one values this trait no less and sees his role as stimulating its development in others.

Figure 72 presents certain other facts relevant to age changes in achievement motivation and contrasts married males with single and married females in this regard. In this study a substantial number of teachers had been asked, among other things, to indicate what they would most like to be doing 10 years hence. Striking age and sex differences appear in these verbalized goals, though it is not clear whether the responses represent personal desires or a certain adjustment to reality and expectation. But in part the data would seem to reflect what these people hoped to achieve. For women, even employed women, this seems to be primarily marriage and own home. The vast majority of young single women hope to be married, while the vast majority of young married women employed as teachers hoped to have a home and be a housewife. Achievement for men appears to mean primarily vocational achievement. Getting a different (presumably a better) job or getting a promotion in the same place taken together constituted, up until 50, the most frequently mentioned goal. For married women occupational advancement as an avenue of achievement appears to be definitely secondary throughout life, but for women who have not married by age 30, occupation seems to have replaced marriage as the area in which achievement is sought.

Although the data presented in Figure 72 suggest, in the main, that desire for occupational advancement declines rather steadily with age, it is likely that the drive for achievement may in many cases be intensified at around 40 years of age. It is to be noted that approximately one-quarter of the 40- to 44-year-olds in this study hoped to get into another type of work. For many, occupational frustrations may be building up as a result of gradual recognition that vocational progress has not reached the level of earlier aspirations and that time is running out. A certain urgency may thus be created regarding achievement of goals, and possibly there is a desire to seek greener pastures as a hopeful means

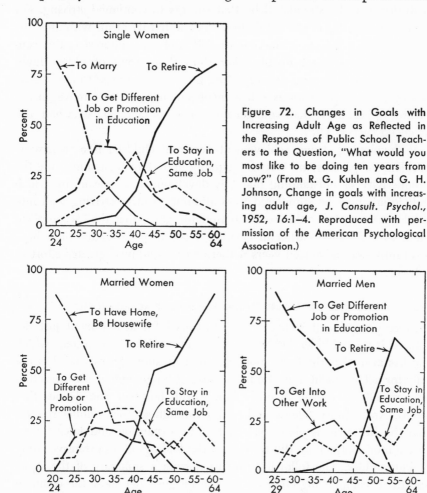

Figure 72. Changes in Goals with Increasing Adult Age as Reflected in the Responses of Public School Teachers to the Question, "What would you most like to be doing ten years from now?" (From R. G. Kuhlen and G. H. Johnson, Change in goals with increasing adult age, J. Consult. Psychol., 1952, 16:1–4. Reproduced with permission of the American Psychological Association.)

of escaping blocks in the present situation. Other investigators (11, 25) have also concluded, as the result of analyses of life histories, that at around 40 there is a certain stock-taking of progress with respect to goals and an upsurge of new effort if the results of this evaluation are not satisfactory.

Such findings argue against the view that achievement needs decline steadily with adult age and instead stress the likelihood that accumulating frustration may rather accentuate this need at certain ages as compared with earlier years. Or some people, instead of becoming complacent and relaxed as a result of success that has come with increased maturity, may be stimulated by that success to continued striving. For these cases, achievement needs may decline hardly at all with age; the drive to achieve may become habitual. It is of some interest in this connection that a recent investigation showed a group of older "high-achievers" (average age, 56) reporting greater willingness to move their homes and accept various other inconveniences, if this move meant greater opportunity, than younger men (average age, 36) who had also achieved success (61).

If developing strong achievement needs in children is a worrisome problem for parents and teachers, equally important for maintaining the productivity of outstanding talent is development of means by which individuals may be stimulated to continuing positive striving well into the later years. It would seem a reasonable guess that the "accomplishment curves" noted earlier in Chapter 4 would be extended on a high level into more advanced years if there were continued greater effort to achieve.

THE CHANGING NEED FOR EXPANSION AND FOR DEFENSE AGAINST LOSSES

More general and inclusive than the need for achievement just described is what Buhler (12) has called the need for "expansion," which she has argued is the basic motive of life. Presumably, this need is not only for achievement, but also for a sense of on-goingness, for a position as a significant person in one's own world, however one defines that world. And sundry figures and tables throughout this volume suggest that the life span is characterized first by expansion and later by restriction or contraction. Illustrative are the findings of an extensive study of biographies. The following quotation from a summary of the study and the accompanying chart of one life (Figure 73) show the common pattern:

Up to a certain point we can observe that new spheres and new fields of activity are added. In all fields of life, expansion, ascent and increase, can be noticed. The period in the middle of life, called the culmination period, includes the largest and most complete number of dimensions. In this period we find stability also, since losses are replaced by new acquisitions. Beginning with a certain age (around the fiftieth year), certain activities are given up and external losses, such as a case of death, are not compensated for anymore. One can observe a decline, a form of retirement from life. If we at first only take those data which relate to the behavior of the individual and present them graphically, we will find here also the ascent and descent in the curve as it is clearly shown in the upper part of Figure [73]. It should be emphasized that other lives, even those of simple working men, would show a very similar general distribution. (25.)

Evidences of continued *gains* are satisfying and sought after; *losses* tend to be threatening and to evoke defensive reactions. Assuming the existence of these two opposed needs—the first more dominant in younger adult years, the latter increasingly important as age increases—helps to

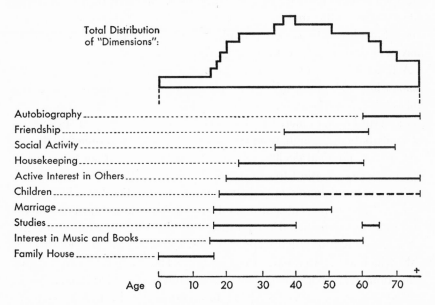

Figure 73. Expansion and Restriction in Life Activities as Illustrated in the Life of Elizabeth Textor-Goethe, 1731–1808. (From E. Frenkel-Brunswik, Motivation and behavior, Genet. Psychol. Monogr. 1942, 26:121–265.)

relate in a meaningful way a variety of behavior and personality changes during the adult years and also to suggest steps which society and/or individuals might take to combat "psychological aging."

A whole succession of goals, interest and activity areas, identifications, beliefs, and values tend to reflect the need for expansion. The primary avenues by which this need is satisfied in the adult years are through marriage and family and through occupation. These (or other) avenues may be pursued until success removes the possibility of further satisfaction along those particular lines or until chronic frustration forces the individual to seek other avenues. Thus, it has been noted in Figure 72 that single women at around the age of 30 change from "marriage" to occupational advance as their major goal. When children leave home, married women may find opportunities for continued expansion in community activities. Later, identification with children and their "expansions" in marriage, family, and job are to be noted (38). Still later, there may be a return to religion, particularly an increasing belief in immortality (15). And interest in genealogy—often noted among oldsters—may be a means of achieving a sense of on-goingness through seeing one's own life span as one in a sequence of generations. Many of the age trends in interests, social life, and values described in later chapters document the foregoing observations and provide further suggestions of how people may achieve a sense of continued growth.

A time in life comes, however, when utilization of basic avenues of "expansion" (children, job) is no longer possible, when losses begin to outweigh gains to such a degree that the need *to conserve and to protect* one's status becomes increasingly dominant. The possibility of "expansion" or contribution through reproduction is irrevocably terminated by the menopause; physical decline sets certain limits—lower than previously—upon capacity to adjust to external demands and to achieve usual gratifications; cultural biases operate to limit opportunities for advancement and to threaten present status; and accumulated investments of money and time in occupational preparation and seniority, as well as accumulated family and financial responsibilities and ties, limit freedom to take risks which are often a part of opportunity. The gradual increase in such limitations with increasing adult age is likely to produce insecurity and anxiety which may serve to generate a certain handicapping defensiveness. Such defensiveness may become evident in a wide variety of behavior and constitute a basic cause of some of the more general personality changes with age.

The point at which "expansion" ceases and losses begin—and presumably any attendant sense of threat and insecurity—will vary a great deal among individuals and among groups representative of different cultures. Figure 74 shows contrasting age trends for the proportion of various occupational groups employed. It will be noted that at a time of less than full employment (1940) the threat of unemployment was felt earliest for the labor group, whereas the professional group was not so greatly threatened by age. To a degree, different patterns of expansion and restriction would be revealed in age curves for income of different groups. In a society where economic values are important, inability to gain salary increases and/or actual decrease in earning capacity presumably would represent important personal indications of shifts from "expansion" to "restriction" in life phase. According to one analysis (20), the man who earns a low peak income typically experiences decline early in adult years whereas the high-income man experiences expansion, as evidenced by increased financial rewards, well into middle age. It is likely that motivational changes which are dependent upon the age of onset of basic losses will, in a similar way, vary greatly from culture to culture.

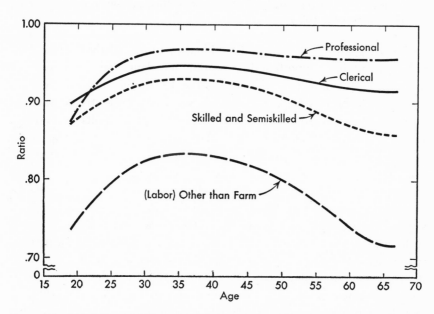

Figure 74. The Differential Threat of Aging for Various Economic Groups as Reflected in Age Trends in the Percentage Employed in Different Categories at Different Ages. Data are for 1940, a time when cultural discrimination would likely be better reflected than in times of peak employment. (From L. I. Dublin and A. J. Lotka, *The Money Value of a Man*, revised ed., New York, Ronald Press, 1946.)

The emphasis upon protection and conservation in the motivational patterns of older people is apparently widespread and characterizes many cultures. One investigator who has studied the role of the aged in various primitive cultures, has hypothesized that the following five basic interests (or goals) are rather generally held by old people:

1. To live as long as possible, at least until life satisfaction no longer compensates for its privation, or until the advantages of death seem to outweigh the burden of life.

2. To get more rest, relief from the necessity of wearisome exertion at humdrum tasks and protection from too great exposure to physical hazards—opportunities, in other words, to safeguard and preserve the waning energies of a physical existence.

3. To remain active participants in personal and group affairs in either operational or supervisory roles—any participation, in fact, being preferable to complete idleness and indifference.

4. To safeguard or even strengthen any prerogatives acquired in a long life, i. e., skills, possessions, rights, authorities, prestige, etc.

5. Finally, to withdraw from life, when necessity requires it, as honorably as possible, without too much suffering, and with maximum prospects for an attractive hereafter. (69.)

Clearly, goals change as the individual matures and then moves into old age. But it is important in assessing the data, and the inferences drawn from them, to raise the question as to whether the situation described *need* be this way. Some trends seem inevitable, trends such as declining physical capacities which necessarily place limits on activity. But even here medical science is making progress. The major question is as to whether old age need be characterized by so much planlessness and resignation as seems the case now, whether efforts to conserve and to defend against losses are not self-defeating. One study of oldsters on old age assistance, for example, revealed that 78 percent made no plans whatsoever, even for the morrow (52). There are some striking examples that such need not and should not be the case. Lillian Martin, a pioneer in old age counseling and a notably active oldster herself, together with her co-worker Clare de Guchy, has demonstrated the value of a counseling program which seeks to help older individuals recapture old motives and develop new purposes. Lives which seemed clearly on the decline developed new orientation toward the future and entered upon a new phase of "expansion" with resulting improvements in adjustment, happiness, and, it seemed, in abilities as well (17). New vistas have been similarly opened for a group of older people (average age, 64) who enrolled at the Cold Spring Institute.[6] A 65-year-old retired school teacher learned to paint. A 73-year-old former university art teacher reported: "I had found I had lost all interest in art. After retiring, my life came to consist of just going to church and rocking in a chair on the front porch."

[6] See *Time*, July 4, 1955, p. 34, for a brief report of this program.

At the Institute she discovered a new talent of writing TV scripts. The maintenance of interests and activities, the development of new purposes, the active participation in life, rather than retreat and withdrawal, represent major methods of combating many of the psychological trends characteristic of aging.

Pressures of Time and Money: Major Factors in Human Motivation

The discussion thus far has neglected the fact that people have only 24 hours per day, a rather clearly defined life expectancy, and a finite amount of money to utilize in satisfying their needs and desires. The tremendous influence of these requirements of living—pressures of work, whether on the job or in the house, and financial pressures—in the changing motivational picture is clearly evident in any broad age survey of human activities. In modern life, they seem almost as important as physiological pressures.

AGE CHANGES IN PROPORTIONING OF TIME AMONG VARIOUS NEEDS AND DEMANDS

How completely the newborn child's day is dominated by his physiological needs is illustrated by the fact that in the first 10 days of life more than three-quarters of the 24 hours are spent in sleep. At five months only about 12 of the 24 hours are so spent, and this proportion is maintained (though there is less "dozing") until at least one year of age. On the other hand, positive movements of expression and experimentation increase rapidly, especially during the second half of the first year, as the child reacts with active interest to all sense perceptions. At one year of age, about 8 hours daily are spent in "experimentation." Reflected in these trends, based on round-the-clock observations of a group of infants (13), are a clear decrease in time spent in meeting physiological demands and a clear increase in the "need" for activity and exploratory behavior growing out of maturing capacities.

Gradually, *external demands* upon time and energy begin. Although during his first five years the child's activities are largely limited to home and immediate neighborhood, he is not left entirely to his own pursuits. Demands are constantly being made with respect to the establishment of fundamental habits and "desirable" behavior patterns. At five or six, at school entrance, formalized demands upon time are met, and for the next dozen or more years, school requirements will constitute the largest single demand (other than sleep) upon youngsters' time. And as school demands increase, especially in high school, college, and professional training, many other "desired" activities must be curtailed or eliminated completely.

Certain facts, showing changes in use of time during adolescence, are presented in Table 37. The present writers have classified the data from an interview study (*19*) to give some indication of the relative amount of time spent in meeting physiological and environmental demands and in "free-choice" activities. There are probably some errors in this classification. Time spent in "routine" may be mainly bodily care and thus be classifiable under "physiological demands." Time spent in "music" might

TABLE 37.   Distribution of the Hours in a Week Among Physiological Demands, Environmental Demands, and Free-Choice Activities for 12- and 16-Year-Old Boys

Activity	12-Year-Olds	16-Year-Olds
Physiological demands		
Sleep	74.1	69.2
Eating	8.8	6.8
Total	82.9	76.0
Environmental demands		
School (classes and study)	25.4	31.1
Travel	9.6	12.5
Work and chores	6.0	7.7
Routine	2.6	2.8
Total	43.6	54.1
Free choice		
Physical play (participation)	10.5	6.7
Physical play (spectator)	.7	2.0
Entertainment and amusement	12.2	12.5
Music (in home and elsewhere)	10.2	11.5
Reading	6.2	5.0
Club	2.0	.2
Total	41.8	37.9
Overall Total	168.3	168.0

SOURCE: Adapted from H. S. Dimock, A research in adolescence: the social world of the adolescent, *Child Development*, 1935, 6:285–302.

be free-choice listening to phonograph records or time spent in study—at parental insistence. Nonetheless, over this four-year period (from 12 to 16 years of age) the increase in time spent meeting environmental demands increases by 10.5 hours—more than one and a quarter full working days! This increase has been about equally at the expense of time in eating and sleeping and time in recreation. In these changes are to be noted growing responsibility, broader geographic horizons (increase in travel time), and declining interest in sheer physical activity.

The adult years are, of course, characterized by even more emphasis upon work and environmental demands. Some years ago E. L. Thorndike, utilizing the data of another investigator (53), computed the time spent in various activities by 500 young businesswomen. He concluded that:

"Forty-eight hours a week are used to get a living (including time of transportation to and from work), 56 hours for sleep and 3½ hours for responsibilities to the home where one lives. Twenty-four hours are spent in eating, personal care and shopping. The remaining 36½ hours include: church activities, 1½; outdoor games and sports, 3¼; automobile rides and trips, 4½; reading, including the newspaper, 7; studies and lectures, 1; sewing, painting, arts and crafts, 1; parties, dances, picnics, club activities, dates with men and entertaining in the home, 9." (77, p. 121.)

In another analysis of time usage, schedules provided by 103 adults (22 males, 81 females)—most of whom were between 20 and 30 years of age with only a few as young as 18 or over 30—were analyzed. From this investigation it appeared that some 18 hours and 16 minutes per day were spent in activities satisfying physical and economic needs. As the investigator points out: "If in and through these activities other more refined needs are simultaneously satisfied—and often they are—then all is well. If they are not, there remains only some six hours per twenty-four hours for the satisfaction of these other needs taken together" (72, p. 47). Even within this rather narrow young adult age range, age changes in environmental demands occurred. The older subjects (who were married in the majority of instances) spent more time in chore-type activities, whereas the younger individuals participated more in recreational or pleasurable activities.

In Figure 75 data from the United States census are presented to give a certain overall picture of major activities at different ages—the percentage of people who are in school (reflected in curve for those "out of school"), in the labor force, actually employed, and who are married or head of a household. In such facts may be sensed changing demands upon time, changing responsibilities, and changing roles over the broad sweep of the life span. The first and perhaps most striking fact to be noted in this chart is the importance of the period between 15 and 25 as

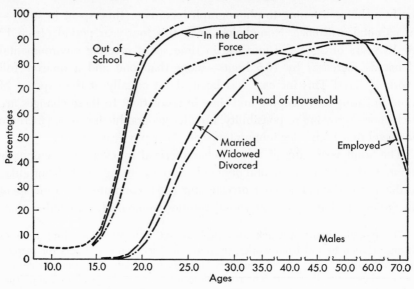

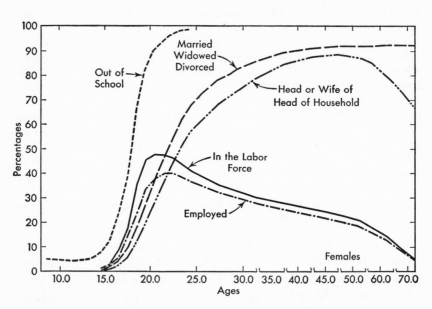

Figure 75. Age Trends in Major Activities and Roles as Evidenced by United States Census Data, Reflecting the Various Pressures and Responsibilities Present at different ages for the two sexes. (Adapted from F. K. Shuttleworth, The adolescent period: a graphic atlas, Monogr. of the Society for Research in Child Development, 1949, Vol. 14.)

a transition period. "Adolescence" has often been so defined—a transition period between childhood and adulthood, a period of uncertain role and status. The transition from school to work, from single freedom to married bliss and responsibility, is evident in the chart. A second major contrast relates to a sex difference. In the lower chart (for women), the relatively secondary role of employment and the major role of marriage are again implied. Many fewer women than men enter paid employment, and in the case of women the decline in percentage employed begins in the middle twenties. Many more men work, and the percentage employed is maintained at a high level until approximately 60 years of age.

A third feature of the charts in Figure 75 relates to the lessening demands upon time of "required" activities as age increases, another transition period. If it be assumed that amount of sleep is fairly constant with age, then data indicating the extent to which work (i. e., paid employment) is important at various ages should reflect the amount of "free time" available for activities other than those forced upon one by circumstances of life or physical demands. It might reasonably be inferred that as the family unit size increases, more and more demands are made upon a housewife's time, that such demands are greater when family size is at a peak—at about 40 to 45 according to available surveys (39)—and that more time becomes available as children leave home and the family shrinks in size. For the average man great increases in amount of free time do not usually (it might be inferred) occur until retirement. Thus, it might be anticipated that women will begin to experience increasing free time earlier in life than will men, an expectation which was confirmed in an unpublished study, some results from which are charted in Figure 76. It is of some interest to note, from another study (15), that 11 percent of men in their early sixties had all day free to do as they pleased, with the percentage increasing with increasing age to the point where 81 percent of those between 85 and 89 and all of those in their nineties had all day free. Among women, 34 percent of those in their early sixties and 80 percent of those over 80 had all day free.

A marked increase in leisure time at all ages has been a notable achievement in recent decades, and the trend is continuing. In 1890, blast furnaces kept men 12 hours a day, 7 days a week, for a total of 84 hours. Today the typical work week is less than half that, often permitting two-day weekends and special holidays and vacations with pay. These trends change the picture of time consumption from what has been cited above, reducing somewhat the environmental demands upon time and

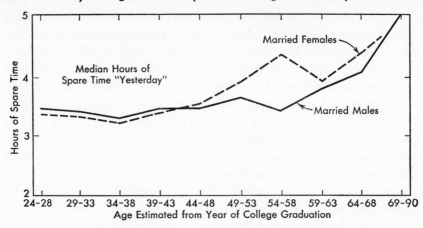

Figure 76. Age Changes in Amount of Leisure Time as Shown by Estimates of a National Sample of College Graduates. (Unpublished data from R. G. Kuhlen, Age trends in adjustment during the adult years as reflected in happiness ratings, Paper read at a meeting of the American Psychological Association, Boston, 1948.)

increasing time available for recreation, study, travel, and hobbies. Here lies one of the important results of technological developments, a contribution to the possibilities for enriched living.

Although the foregoing discussion has emphasized the "enforced" character of many activities and their demands upon time, the facts summarized in these charts have important other meanings. Though school is in a sense "forced" upon the individual (the child *has* to attend whether he wants to or not), consumes much time, and thus limits his other activities, it provides many opportunities for satisfaction of such fundamental needs as needs for social activity and for achievement. It would be unrealistic, too, to assume that work is merely time-consuming, engaged in only for purposes of "earning a living," or that housework and caring for children are devoid of intrinsic satisfaction. Actually, work has many meanings and provides a source of satisfaction of social needs, needs to be creative and to serve others, needs for status and prestige (*16, 27*). And marriage and rearing of family provide some of the major and deepest satisfactions of life. In cases where these intrinsic values are high (and intrinsic values likely vary in degree from person to person, and from social class to social class), termination of school, of work, and of family responsibilities represent not so much a *gain* of time and new freedom for desired activities as an undesired *loss* of a satisfying role. But perhaps the most significant loss in later years is loss of spouse through death and the resulting breakup of the household. Due to the younger age at marriage of women and the shorter average length of life of men, this problem is more frequently faced by women, as a comparison of the two charts in Figure 75 will indicate. Such losses—whether of children, of spouse, of employment—necessarily affect the motivational make-up of the individual. A whole structure of responsibilities, affections, and time-consuming activities is suddenly without foundation. Unless new goals and purposes are found, this structure—which, psychologically, is life itself—may crumble into despair and apathy.

CHANGING TIME PERSPECTIVES

Although the problem of finding enough time in the available 24 hours per day is a major factor in human motivation, especially as family and job demands build up, even more important is the time limitation upon the achievement of long-term goals and upon life—time measured in blocks of years. Changing time perspective represents one of the major variables in developmental psychology (23, 42). Lewin has argued that in early childhood the psychological future is vague, undifferentiated, and extends only slightly ahead, but that in adolescence there occurs a rapid increase in the psychological future (42). At this age, the future is infinite and though not well defined holds rosy promises, anticipated on a fantasy level. Perhaps in the thirties, the typical adult probably becomes conscious of the fact that time is finite, that progress or lack of progress, as well as other matters, must be viewed with reference to time. Goals may become specific; activities toward those goals become more significant in terms of day-by-day importance; orientations and self-evaluations become more realistic (8). It makes a great deal of difference in one's orientations and goals whether the "future" *lies ahead* as it does for the 20-year-old, is *here* as the 40-year-old may sense it, or is in the past (or ahead not in one's own life but in one's children's) as the reminiscing oldster may view it.

Perhaps more important than the recognition that the average life has just so many years in it is the realization that there are "sublimits" within the overall time perspective. The particular age ranges that, in this sense, represent critical periods are to some degree determined by biological factors. Time is a crucial matter for the woman who marries late but wants children or for the champion professional athlete seeking a fortune before he is too old. But, in the main, cultural factors are likely to be more significant in determining these sublimits. Age roles of young adulthood, middle age, old age, although only vaguely defined in the minds of people in general, nonetheless imply certain expectations, privileges, and limitations. The single woman of 30 who desires to marry feels that time is running out; the 35-year-old clerk with aspirations to become an executive senses a serious time limit; the 64-year-old professor who wants to finish a book before retirement finds time short. The shortness of time in all of these situations is due to the fact that, in a sense, and often quite specifically, the culture has established certain deadlines.

But whether the deadline is imposed by biology or by culture, the result is that the time variable likely becomes more significant and more threatening at some ages than at others. Such sublimits in time perspectives may heighten existing motivation in an already established direction, may be crucial in the reorientation of goals, or may have the effect of concentrating frustration and attendant symptoms of maladjustment at certain ages. Long-term planning for personal achievement, while feasible at an early age, may be viewed as patently unrealistic in later years. In old age, with time short, apathy and futile resignation may more readily take over. In total, changing time perspectives may well be one of the important factors distinguishing the "psychology" of old age from that of the middle years and the psychology of the middle years from that of early adulthood and adolescence.

Sensitivity to the time variable likely varies a great deal from one social level to another. One investigator, summarizing varied sociological and anthropological evidence, concluded tentatively that:

In the lower-lower class, the orientation is one of quick sequences of tension and release. One does not frustrate one's self for long periods or plan action with goals far in the future. The future generally is an indefinite, vague, diffuse region and its rewards and punishments are too uncertain to have much motivative value. In this social class, one eats when he is hungry; there are no regular meal hours and each member of the family takes food when he feels like it if food is available.

In the upper-lower, middle, and lower-upper classes, orientation is one of much longer tension-release sequences. As the individual grows older, he plans further and further into the future and acts on these plans. As an adult, he may start planning for retirement when he is in his twenties. In these classes, one eats at regular "clock" hours. One quickly learns to inhibit activity leading to the release of a basic tension (food-getting behavior) until a watch shows that it is time to eat.

In the upper-upper class, the individual sees himself as part of a sequence of several or more generations, and the orientation is backward to the past. One eats at traditional hours and lives out the tradition set up in the past. (41.)

In order to check the correctness of these conclusions, the investigator asked children from middle-class and lower-class homes simply to "tell a story." He hypothesized that if his analyses were correct, the middle-class children would tell stories involving a longer time episode than would the lower-class children, a prediction borne out by the analysis of the stories told. Other studies (63) seem to confirm the view that middle-class youngsters are better able than those of lower classes to work toward long-deferred goals.

MONEY INCOME AND USES MADE OF IT

Money has value only to the degree to which it can be used to satisfy human wants. Time is translated into money at different rates by different people, the rate depending upon factors such as occupational level, sex, and age. How far available money extends beyond the *requirements* of living becomes, as does the availability of time, an important factor in motivation. Depending upon the amount available, money can be a seriously limiting factor (thus, for example, shaping careers by preventing the completion of educational plans) or a resource permitting wide and varied free-choice activities. Lack of economic security can be a tremendous motivating force, as was noted in the case histories of outstanding individuals in Chapter 4.

The proportion of families earning or receiving various annual incomes was commented upon in an earlier chapter. The average family, it will be recalled, earned $4460 per year in 1950. If the reader of this volume be a college student, supported by his parents, he need only ponder his own annual expenses to appreciate the extent to which the average family income represents a limiting factor. How money resources are distributed among *requirements* of food, shelter, and clothing and among other expenditures is shown in Table 38. Here are gross figures indicating the number of dollars spent in the country at large for various services and commodities. Although there is substantial stability in the percentage distribution of expenditures from year to year,[7] a number of factors will influence gross expenditures, with the result that the figures for any one year will be only illustrative.

Again, as in the case of time, the requirements or demands of living are seen to take the major share. Food, housing, household operation, clothing (plus accessories and jewelry), medical care and death expense. and personal care total some 79.2 percent of total expenditures. And other items, such as the 11.7 percent for transportation, are at least par-

[7] A U.S. Bureau of Labor Statistics survey of consumer expenditures in 1948 suggested that major expenditures took about the same percentage of income in that year as in 1934–1936. About 32 percent was spent for food and about 11 percent for clothing. Shelter in 1948 took only about 16 percent of income compared with 23 percent in 1934–1936. Rent controls in the postwar period resulted in this last difference. ("Consumer Spending: Denver, Detroit and Houston, 1948," U.S. Bureau of Labor Statistics, Washington, D.C., 1949.)

tially chargeable to necessity, as transportation to work. To be sure, all of the foregoing expenditures do not qualify as *necessities*. "Housing," "food," and "clothing" may represent in many cases mainly luxury. But it is a good guess that for the average family, these expenditures—on a minimal comfort level—constitute the major uses of income. Actually, as level

TABLE 38.   Expenditures for Personal Consumption, United States, 1950

	In Millions of Dollars	Percent of Total
Food	52,838	27.3
Housing	19,894	10.3
Household operations	26,439	13.7
Total	99,171	51.3
Clothing, accessories, jewelry	22,909	11.8
Personal care	2,291	1.2
Medical care and death expenses	9,531	4.9
Personal business	8,519	4.4
Transportation	22,667	11.7
Total	65,917	34.0
Recreation	11,290	5.8
Tobacco	4,409	2.3
Alcoholic beverages	8,100	4.2
Total	23,799	12.3
Private education and research	1,773	.9
Religious and welfare activities	1,822	.9
Foreign travel and remittances	1,086	.6
Total	4,681	2.4
Durable commodities	29,157	15.1
Nondurable commodities	102,310	52.8
Services	62,101	32.1
Total	193,568	100.0

SOURCE: Adapted from U.S. Department of Commerce, National income and product of the U.S., 1929–1950, 1951 *National Income*, Supplement to the Survey of Current Business, Washington, D.C., 1951, pp. 195–199.

of income *increases,* the proportion chargeable to such necessities (even at a more "luxurious" level, if such an inconsistent use of terms may be permitted) decreases.

Some years ago E. L. Thorndike obtained estimates from a jury of psychologists and a jury made up of people of other backgrounds as to how money might be apportioned in meeting various human needs, recognizing, for example, that money spent for food may be properly related to diverse needs. It was estimated by the psychologist jury that some 1700 units spent for food might be chargeable thusly: 876 to satisfy hunger, 275 for pleasures of taste and smell, 122 for social entertainment and companionship, 53 for welfare of others, 50 for protection against disease, 45 for sex entertainment, with the other 279 units spread among some 15 other needs! In a general summing up, after translating dollar expenditures into estimates of time expenditures, Thorndike concluded that time—the 16 hours of the waking day— is used in the indicated proportions to meet the following needs: 25 percent for subsistence and perpetuation, 30 percent for entertainment, 10 percent for companionship and affection, 10 percent for approval, 8 percent for welfare of others, 7 percent for security, 4 percent for intellectual activity, 2 percent for dominance over others, 2 percent to avoid or reduce sensory pain, 2 percent for other wants (77, p. 135).

Obviously, demands upon money change with age—but so also does income. In Table 39 are shown average income figures for employed

TABLE 39. Age Changes in Earnings by Level of Income and by Sex, United States, 1951

	Under 25	25–34	35–44	45–54	55–64	65 and Over
Males						
First decile	$ 175	$1380	$1385	$1070	$ 585	$ 185
Median	1827	3299	3621	3299	3036	2031
Ninth decile	4350	5360	6300	6180	5780	4700
Females						
First decile	130	225	320	215	170	85
Median	1382	1949	1807	1793	1551	690
Ninth decile	2425	3150	3745	3325	3315	2040

SOURCE: Based on Bureau of Census data as presented by M. W. Reder, Age and income, *J. Amer. Econ. Assoc.,* 1954, 44:661–670.

Americans in 1951. Peak income occurs between the ages of 35 and 44. The close correspondence of peak income with peak family size is a fortunate coincidence, but it will be noted that beyond this peak, income for lower paid individuals drops much more rapidly than does income for higher paid people. The bad feature of these trends, from the point of view of sheer security and enjoyment of life, is the fact that income is least at an age when time is most plentiful for participation in nonwork activities. Actually, for many old people the major resources are Social Security checks supplemented by meager savings. Money at this age is often a seriously limiting factor, and thus economic needs rank high among the wants of old age.

Table 40 contains certain information regarding financial status and feeling of financial pressure in a group for whom (in contrast to the gen-

TABLE 40. Age Differences in Financial Pressures as Indicated by Percentage of Married Men Teachers (MM), Married Women Teachers (MW), and Single Women Teachers (SW) of Different Ages Who Answered Selected Questions

		Age Groups				
		20–29	30–39	40–49	50–59	60–69
Is your income sufficient	MM	44	56[a]	51	27	14
to meet your financial	MW	15	19	26	22	30[a]
obligations and support your family? (No)	SW	17	31[a]	26	23	26
Are you kept from dress-	MM	44	59[a]	52	30	14
ing as you would like	MW	30	19	26	27	40[a]
because of insufficient income? (Yes)	SW	32	44[a]	35	29	24
Are you kept from living	MM	44	65[a]	60	45	43
as you would like be-	MW	35	28	30	30	60[a]
cause of insufficient income? (Yes)	SW	29	48[a]	42	43	47
Percentage reporting ex-	MM	56	62[a]	57	27	57
tracontractual em-	MW	13[a]	2	4	5	0
ployment	SW	11	13[a]	7	1	5
Median income from pri-	MM	$3359	$3954	$4354	$4500	$4850
mary employment	MW	$2583	$2829	$3232	$3358	$3286
	SW	$2551	$3178	$3373	$3471	$3475
Number of cases	MM	9	69	94	40	7
	MW	46	47	106	73	10
	SW	83	96	127	133	38

[a] Indicates decade of peak pressure as indicated by that item. Note that the number of cases in the twenties and sixties for married men and in the sixties for married women is extremely small.

SOURCE: The data are adapted from G. H. Johnson, Differences in the job satisfaction of urban teachers as related to age and other factors, unpublished Ph.D. dissertation, Syracuse University, 1951.

erality noted in Table 39) income tended to rise steadily with age, a group of teachers. Here is to be noted the feeling of financial pressure in the thirties on the part of individuals whose responsibilities and requirements have increased more rapidly than income. A variety of pressures—own children, dependent older relatives, needs for graduate training for vocational advancement—all seem to become greatest in the young adult and middle years while income peak is still years off. For this group of professional people, it will be noted, not only were financial limitations most frequently felt in the thirties, but the need was sufficiently great to require extracontractual employment of the majority of married men, especially in the thirties. These trends characterized those two groups who were dependent upon their own resources alone. Married women, a special group, showed a different peak of financial pressure—in the late years.

Broad Significance of Adjustment to Basic Needs

The broad significance of motivation as an organizing factor in life and behavior and of adjustment to basic needs as a key to understanding human personality and changes therein during the course of life deserves emphasis in the concluding section of this chapter.

PERSONALITY AS ADJUSTMENT TO NEEDS

It is readily apparent that many characteristics of people, such as their personality traits and their attitudes, are, to a large extent, to be understood in terms of the underlying dynamics; that is, in terms of their meaning as adjustive mechanisms utilized in connection with the needs, frustrations, and conflicts of the person involved. Many of the special characteristics of adolescence—at least to the extent that the existence of special personality characteristics can be objectively documented—may be explainable largely in dynamic terms (73). This is also true of many reactions commonly associated with the menopause (7, 18). It has been suggested that the frequently observed ability of old people to recall in detail events of years gone by and their inability to recall immediate events may be explained in terms of current frustration and resulting regression (64). Increasing insecurity resulting from increasing threats to status may explain the generally observed increase in rigidity with increasing adult age which, in turn, may explain a variety of changes in personal traits with age. Already threatened and insecure because of organic and cultural losses, new experiences and new demands and challenges are likely to threaten older people still more (3), with the result that they may cling to established ways of behaving and "protect" themselves by not venturing forth. Having a reduced status, one more rigidly controls that aspect of his environment still under his control. This need to protect against losses, and the resulting defensive behavior, was stressed earlier in the chapter as one of the major changes with age in motivation, and it will be emphasized again in Chapter 8 where age trends in anxiety are described and in Chapter 10 on values where conservatism is discussed. Unless guarded against, such changes may counterbalance, to a degree, the advantage of experience that comes with age in the constructive dealing with frustration.

Perhaps more than any other writer, Freud emphasized the importance of dynamic factors in long-term personality development. He believed that certain adult personality types were the outgrowth of very early experiences of success or frustration. Such trait syndromes as an all-pervasive optimistic viewing of the world as a warm, friendly place where everything will work out all right, on the one hand, and orderliness, parsimony, and obstinacy, on the other hand, were considered different personality types growing out of frustration or success experiences in first feeding situations or in toilet training. The important feature of this view lies not so much in the assertions regarding origin of specific traits as in its insistence upon long-term personality development depending upon frustration or success, security or insecurity, existing in earliest childhood.

Such emphasis upon early years neglects the possibility that basic frustrations or satisfactions even in adult life can substantially alter personality and color outlook on life and the world at large. The following quotation illustrates the pervasive influence of frustration and sense of failure:

I am a single woman and forty. . . . I know, like scores of other women, what I need in order to live. To me life is a trinity of needs—money, a mission, and a man. At twenty there was a possibility that I might find all three. At forty I haven't even a sporting chance at any of them. I find myself doomed to exist on makeshifts—a salary, a job, and other women's husbands. And no matter how sublime the courage she feigns, no woman has ever lived the more abundant life on substitutions. What scope is there at forty for the satisfying of these needs? . . . At forty, one is able to develop a protective stoicism—thank God for that! . . . A cynicism is now mine that is not despair. It is rather the virtue of a calm courage retained by one disappointed in life and the world. (71.)

In contrast, one can cite numerous examples of individuals who, shy and insecure in childhood, largely because of threats and frustrations within the family, achieved a high degree of security in adulthood through vocational success and a happy, secure marriage, with the result that the shy tenseness of youth was replaced by a relaxed tolerance and easy, out-going attitude in middle age. While increasing adult years seem generally to bring a decrease in carefree attitude (*30*), it does seem to bring, for some groups at least (if not for the majority), and up to middle years, an increase in self-confidence (*9*).[8]

In general, the long-term cumulative effects of success or frustration of motives are reflected in the development of broad interest patterns and patterns of emotional reactions. The successful fulfillment of needs or the satisfaction of motives may result in the development of extensive interest in those conditions or activities which satisfied the need or which were present when the need was satisfied. One continues to do those things or to seek those conditions. On the other hand, frustration, punishment, and failure tend to result in dislike and avoidance of the conditions both directly and indirectly involved in the frustration and in the development of certain fears and anxieties. Various studies (*22, 28*) have documented the fact that success experiences or expectations of success make particular activities and goal objects more attractive, whereas failure or expectation of failure decreases their attractiveness.

SUCCESSES, FAILURES, AND EVALUATIONS IN BROAD AGE CHANGES IN MOTIVATION

It is one advantage of the long view of human development that life can be seen in broad perspective and larger organization in contrast to the momentary motivation and the specific isolated behavior studied so frequently in the laboratory. Such a broad view of motivational changes was obtained by one investigator (*11*) in extensive analyses of autobiographical and biographical material, wherein general changes in motivation and related behavior seemed apparent. In this analysis, the adolescent period was seen as a period of diverse, nonspecified activities, essentially exploratory and orienting in nature. The twenties and thirties represent the period of life when decisions as to mate and job have been made and energies are fairly well directed toward the achievement of basic goals as determined by these decisions. At about 45, according to

[8] This finding may seem inconsistent with comments elsewhere in this volume. In general, as pointed out in the next chapter, security and self-confidence with respect to normal spheres of living may increase with age, at the same time that people are becoming more susceptible to the threat of *change* and *stress*.

this analysis, there is apt to occur a period of evaluation when life progress is assessed with reference to achievement of goals and motives. For those who are not satisfied with their progress, this period is frequently followed by renewed striving to achieve, or perhaps by general restlessness and unhappiness. And, finally, there may be a period of review and looking back.

As was noted in Chapter 4, success or failure, outstanding or moderate, is the product of capacities, drives, and total circumstances of opportunity (or its lack) and stimulation. The following quotation illustrates, in the practical context of life, how goals and progress may be continuously evaluated and aspirations altered in such a way that at least partial satisfaction of life goals may be achieved:

There is hardly a member of the Philharmonic who did not aspire at one time to become a virtuoso. My own dream was to conduct opera. Most of us have had to give up aspirations of that kind because of the time and expense involved. [Notice that he attributes failure to unfavorable conditions and not so to limited talent. It is less damaging to one's conception of himself!] Faced with the problem of making a living, we did the next best thing for ourselves artistically—we took jobs with the Philharmonic-Symphony. Eventually all of us become realistic enough to know that we will never reach the pinnacle. We become reconciled to our status. After that it becomes a matter of trying to advance to the first desk in our section. That is only a matter of prestige—it does not affect our salaries—but it helps our egos a bit. (71.)

More generally, and as the life span is viewed, the ebb and flow of various motivations can be partially explained in terms of the principle that the satisfaction of motives reduces their importance (though in some instances it may instead whet the need), that frustration heightens the strength of the drive, but that chronic or too strong frustration may tend to eliminate a motive or at least reduce it to a latent state. Motives may be viewed as arranged in a hierarchy of importance in which lower-level motives take precedence (45). That is, those motives lower in the hierarchy must be relatively well satisfied before higher-level (less basic) motives become operative. Biological needs, being more "basic," tend to take precedence, for example, over social needs. Thus, the sex drive, an example of a basic biological drive, has pervasive importance because of the degree to which it is frustrated by society. In adolescence and in young adulthood when this need is strongest and most generally frustrated, personal desires and "sex-social" interests are very strongly in evidence. Later, as sex needs are satisfied in marriage and decline somewhat in biological strength, the way is paved for other needs to achieve prominence. (The decline in sex-social interests, as will be noted later, is a major characteristic of interest changes in adulthood.) Such a sequence of frustration and later satisfaction of a basic need may underlie the observation of Frenkel-Brunswik (26) that a major change in values during adult years is the change from "personal desires" in young adulthood to "a sense of duty" and cultural responsibility in middle age. The dominance of achievement motives over family satisfaction is often observed in young adulthood. But with achievement of success, interests may turn to family—a trend reinforced by a certain urgency with children growing up. The reorientation of the goals of single women—from marriage to occupation—at around 30 years of age may, on the other hand, be explained by the chronic frustration of desire to marry and a consequent shifting of goals and life plan. The time of such reorientation may represent a period of considerable stress (40).

THE ORGANIZING ROLE OF MOTIVES AND NEEDS

A careful examination of an individual's behavior, either in a particular short-term situation or over a broad span of years, will reveal the degree to which needs give a certain unity to diverse features of the behavior observed. Thus, as previously noted, McClelland and Liberman (49) have shown the effect of an individual's need for achievement on the speed with which he could recognize need-related words. Individuals who had high achievement needs were able to recognize more quickly words relating to achievement which were presented for very brief exposures, thus revealing their greater sensitivity to such matters. Subjects who had success or failure experiences in an experimental setting were similarly differentially sensitive to stimulus words relating to goals and deprivation (58). In another experiment, subjects who were hungry gave more food responses in an ambiguous test situation than did those who were not hungry (5). And in still another study (59), subjects with different sets of values tended to show differences in the ease with which they recognized words related to their cherished values. In short, how the world looks to an individual and the significance of various stimuli present will depend to no small degree upon the strength and nature of his current needs.

Motives similarly give certain organization to what on the surface may appear to be quite inconsistent and unrelated behavior. Thus, Frenkel-Brunswik (24) has demonstrated that such seemingly diverse behavior as that described as "exuberance" or as "irritability" may both be manifestations of the same drive, in this instance, aggression. She states: "Adolescents whose ratings on the aggressive drive cluster are high are likely to be either maladjusted, tense, and anxious, or else successful in their overt social activity, say as leaders; or they may even display both manifestations" (*24*, p. 362).

In turning now to the longer-term view, it is to be noted that Murray, who gives the concept of needs a central place in his theory of personality, has argued that "because of the meaningful connection of sequences the life cycle of a single individual should be taken as a unit, the long unit for psychology (*54*, p. 39).[9] And the editors of a recent volume containing the autobiographies of some 15 psychologists, all of whom were over 60 years of age, call attention (in the preface to the volume) to the great differences that existed among these autobiographers with respect to the degree with which they found unity in their lives. The editors write as follows:

Perhaps they differ most in the degree with which they find unity in their lives. Presumably everyone of them would like to see his intellectual history as the evolution of a single purpose, where integrity is good and simplicity is elegant. No one, of course, fully succeeds in this undertaking, where the story of every life is constrained by the exigencies of its owner's environment.

Some of these accounts are more intellectualistic than others, and it may be that they show the greater unity, either because some irrelevancies are omitted from the life history or because irrelevancies are actually, at least to a certain degree, omitted from the actual living. Other accounts are more environmentalistic, because social and institutional events and accidents have figured so largely in them. The environmentalistic autobiographer may have had a chief long-term goal, have pursued it, have achieved it with some fair degree of success, yet he may feel that the unforseeable accidents of living have determined much of his life and have perhaps even altered his goal. The intellectualist, if such we may call him, may, on the other hand, have suffered disruption of plans less than his colleagues, but it is probable that he has also been less interested in the effect of external forces upon himself. (*1*.)

But even lives that on the surface seem heterogeneously determined by environmental forces may have a certain inner motivational unity. The distinguished E. L. Thorndike was very frank to admit that he had been "pushed about" by environmental demands. In his sixties, some years before his death, he wrote:

[9] Attention should be called to a recent effort to study lives in their totality and to sense the basic unity and purposiveness in lives over a relatively long period of time. The reader in this connection is referred to the stimulating book by R. W. White (*81*).

I have recorded my beginning as a psychologist in detail because it illustrates what is perhaps the most general fact about my entire career as a psychologist later; namely, its responsiveness to outer pressures or opportunities rather than to inner needs. . . . Obviously I have not "carved out my career," as the biographers say. Rather it has been a conglomerate, amassed under the pressure of varied opportunities and demands. Probably it would have been wiser to plan a more consistent and unified life work in accord with interests and capacities, but I am not sure. (76.)

But perhaps Thorndike was too harsh with himself—or too modest. Perhaps the basic unity to be found in his life was the dominating need to be realistic and practical, to seek truth, to satisfy curiosity. But another need, to promote human welfare, may have made his intellectual curiosity responsive to the many practical demands that were made upon him by his classes, by administrative offices of his university, and by foundations with money to spend for research on important psychological problems. If space permitted the detailed description of other cases, it could likely be demonstrated to the satisfaction of most readers that viewing behavior from the vantage point of the "deeper" motivations involved may, in similar fashion and in a wide variety of individuals, give a certain meaningful unity to acts which on the surface seem quite unrelated and even inconsistent.

Summary

Of the psychological concepts that have been developed to help in the explanation of human behavior, few have proved more fruitful than those relating to motivation. This chapter, which has attempted to describe some features of changing motivation over the life span, is now summarized in a few paragraphs.

1. Biological drives with which the child is born and constitutional predispositions to experience certain sensations as pleasurable and others as unpleasant represent the initial sources of motivation. The strength of these various drives varies somewhat with age during the developmental period, the hunger and sex drive, for example, probably being accentuated in the early teens as a result of the prepubescent growth spurt and the advent of pubescence. Changes in the drive for activity and in the sex drive, which reach a peak apparently in the teens and then decline, have an impact upon a wide range of activities and probably underlie many of the adult age changes detailed in subsequent chapters. Biological drives, of major significance in infancy, soon become subject to a variety of culturally imposed patterns of expression and tend to become

subordinated to derived social motives during much of the life span, but they may reassert their importance in later years as physical losses impose notable limits upon behavior, making satisfaction of these needs more difficult and hence more evident.

2. Beginning almost at birth, a complex structure of learned social motives emerge, as a result of the child's experiencing the satisfaction of biological drives through the ministration of other people (parents, siblings), experiencing various sensations as pleasant and unpleasant, being exposed to a broad range of human values, and being influenced in the direction of certain values by a system of social rewards and punishments. These social motives (hopes, desires, aspirations), so learned through interaction with others, are to a marked degree a reproduction of the values of a particular subculture, but are at the same time highly personalized and somewhat unique to the person, since they include various individualized habits of living and reflect the relatively unique meanings various experiences have to the person. Although the list of social motives may be conceived of as being as extensive as one's repertoire of habits, a few learned "needs" are general and of basic importance in understanding people. Basic social needs include the need for social affiliation and acceptance, the need for achievement, and the contrasting needs for "expansion" and for defenses against losses.

3. Age changes in these social needs come about partly because cultural values and expectations are somewhat "age-graded," but also as a result of the satisfaction or chronic (or acute) frustration of basic motives or goals. The satisfaction of basic motives—e. g., social affiliation, achievement—may reduce those needs to a latent state, and thus their effective strength may normally decline with increasing adult age (since satisfaction is typically achieved) unless there should occur some threat to this satisfaction (loss of job, family scandal that threatens status), resulting in a resurgence of these needs. New goals may emerge as achievement of early goals removes them as avenues of achievement and satisfaction. On the other hand, chronic frustration may also subordinate and for practical purposes eliminate a particular need with the result that the way is paved for the emergence of other motives and goals. Thus, the need to achieve may decline with age either because success makes further striving unnecessary or because chronic failure makes it futile. In either case, other motives will likely assume new prominence.

4. Pressures of time and money are probably just as important in the changing motivations of people in modern society as are biological pres-

sures. Increasing pressures of school, job, and family-rearing force aside other desired activities. New-found leisure at retirement or when children are grown up, or as a result of reduction of the work week, may create problems because appropriate motives and goals necessary to fill the void have long since dropped out. The person with varied interests, desires, and goals is more likely to meet these periods of increased freedom with greater ease. Of special importance in developmental changes in motivation are the changing time perspectives—time pressures measured in larger blocks of years. The limitless future filled with rosy promises of adolescence gives way, possibly in the 30's, to an awareness of the finiteness and realities of life and their implications for goal achievements, and in old age to an awareness of the shortness of the remaining years. This realization of the finiteness of life and the awareness of time limits within the overall life span imposed both by biology and culture are major factors in changing motivation. They may heighten drive in a given direction at particular ages, may concentrate frustration and attendant symptoms of anxiety and unhappiness at particular points, and may be crucial in the reorientation of goals and motives.

5. Many changes in behavior and personality with age, as well as behavior characteristic of such periods as adolescence and menopause, may be understood partly in dynamic terms, i. e., in terms of reactions to the frustrations occurring at these times. Such dynamic explanations have been proposed for the increased rigidity observed with increasing adult age, the attendant personality changes, and even for inability to remember recent events in old age in contrast to vivid recall of early events. Patterns of adjustment to frustration and conflict, whether constructive or maladaptive, tend to become habitual, even lifelong, modes of reacting and thus determine the long-term course of personality development. A basic unity of a lifetime or of diverse behavior at any point in life is often discernible when viewed from the perspective provided by an understanding of the basic motivations of the individual.

BIBLIOGRAPHY

1. *A History of Psychology in Autobiography*, Worcester, Clark University Press, Vol. IV, 1952.
2. Allport, G. W., *Personality: A Psychological Interpretation*, New York, Henry Holt, 1937.
3. Atkin, S., Discussion of the paper by M. R. Kaufman, Old age and aging: the psychoanalytic point of view, *Amer. J. Orthopsychiat.*, 1940, *10*: 79–83.

4. Atkinson, J. W., The projective measurement of achievement motivation, Unpublished Ph.D. dissertation, University of Michigan, 1950.

5. Atkinson, J. W., and McClelland, D., The projective expression of needs, II. The effect of different intensities of the hunger drive on thematic apperception, *J. Exper. Psychol.*, 1948, *38*:643–658.

6. Beach, F. A., Evolutionary changes in the physiological control of mating behavior in mammals, *Psychol. Rev.*, 1947, *54*:297–315.

7. Benedek, Therese, Climacterium: a developmental phase, *Psychoanal. Quart.*, 1950, *19*:1–27.

8. Billings, E. G., The clinical importance of some normal attitudinal and ideological transitions of mid-life, *Amer. J. Psychiat.*, 1949, *105*:615–618.

9. Brown, M., and Martin, V. (directors), The University High School study of adolescents: characteristics of high school students, *University High School J.*, 1941, *19*:177–219.

10. Brozek, J., Personality of young and middle-aged normal men: item analysis of a psychosomatic inventory, *J. Gerontol.*, 1952, *7*:410–418.

11. Buhler, C., *Der Menschliche Lebenslauf als Psychologisches Problem*, Leipzig, Verlag von S. Hirzel, 1933.

12. Buhler, Charlotte, Maturation and motivation, *Personality*, 1951, *1*:184–211.

13. Buhler, Charlotte, *The First Year of Life*, New York, John Day, 1930.

14. Cartwright, D., The effect of interruption, completion, and failure upon the attractiveness of activities, *J. Exper. Psychol.*, 1942, *31*:1–16.

15. Cavan, Ruth S., Burgess, E. W., Havighurst, R. J., and Goldhamer, H., *Personal Adjustment in Old Age*, Chicago, Science Research Associates, 1949.

16. Centers, R., Motivational aspects of occupational stratification, *J. Soc. Psychol.*, 1948, *28*:187–217.

17. de Gruchy, Clare, *Creative Old Age*, San Francisco, Old Age Counseling Center, 1946.

18. Deutsch, Helene, *The Psychology of Women: A Psychoanalytic Interpretation*, New York, Grune and Stratton, 1945, Vol. II.

19. Dimock, H. S., A research in adolescence: the social world of the adolescent, *Child Development*, 1935, *6*:285–302.

20. Dublin, L. I., and Lotka, A. J., *The Money Value of a Man*, New York, Ronald Press, 1946.

21. Edwards, A. L., *Manual of the Edwards Personal Preference Schedule*, New York, Psychological Corporation, 1953.

22. Filer, R. J., Frustration, satisfaction, and other factors affecting the attractiveness of goal objects, *J. Abnorm. and Soc. Psychol.*, 1952, *47*:203–212.

23. Frank, L. K., Time perspectives, *J. Soc. Philos.*, 1939, *4*:293–321.

24. Frenkel-Brunswik, Else, Motivation and behavior, *Genet. Psychol. Monogr.*, 1942, *26*:121–265.

25. Frenkel-Brunswik, Else, Studies in biographical psychology, *Character and Personality*, 1936, *5*:1–34.

26. Frenkel-Brunswik, Else, Wishes and feelings of duty in the course of human life, in Jones, H. E. (ed.), *Research in Aging,* Proceedings of a Conference held on August 7–10, 1950, at the University of California, Berkeley. Social Science Research Council, 1951 (mimeographed), pp. 116–122.

27. Friedmann, E. A., and Havighurst, R. J., *The Meaning of Work and Retirement,* Chicago, University of Chicago Press, 1954.

28. Gebhard, Mildred E., The effect of success and failure upon the attractiveness of activities as a function of experience, expectation, and need, *J. Exper. Psychol.,* 1948, *38*:371–378.

29. Greenberg, Pearl J., Competition in children: an experimental study, *Amer. J. Psychol.,* 1932, *44*:221–248.

30. Guilford, J. P., and Martin, H., Age differences and sex differences in some introvertive and emotional traits, *J. Gen. Psychol.,* 1944, *31*:219–229.

31. Harlow, H. F., Mice, monkeys, men and motives, *Psychol. Rev.,* 1953, *60*:23–32.

32. Hurlock, E. B., An evaluation of certain incentives used in school work, *J. Educ. Psychol.,* 1925, *16*:145–149.

33. Jersild, A. T., and Tasch, R. J., *Children's Interests and What They Suggest for Education,* New York, Teachers College, Columbia University, 1949.

34. Johnson, G. H., Differences in the job satisfaction of urban teachers as related to age and other factors, Unpublished Ph.D. dissertation, Syracuse University, 1951.

35. Keys, Ancel, *et al., The Biology of Human Starvation* (2 vols.), Minneapolis, University of Minnesota Press, 1950.

36. Kinsey, A. C., *et al., Sexual Behavior in the Human Female,* Philadelphia, W. B. Saunders, 1953.

37. Kinsey, A. C., *et al., Sexual Behavior in the Human Male,* Philadelphia, W. B. Saunders, 1948.

38. Kuhlen, R. G., Age trends in adjustment during the adult years as reflected in happiness ratings, Paper read at a meeting of the American Psychological Association, Boston, 1948.

39. Kuhlen, R. G., Expansion and constriction of activities during the adult life span as reflected in organizational, civic, and political participation, Paper read at the Second International Gerontological Congress, St. Louis, 1951.

40. Kuhlen, R. G., and Johnson, G. H., Change in goals with increasing adult age, *J. Consult. Psychol.,* 1952, *16*:1–4.

41. LeShan, L., Time orientation and social class, *J. Abnorm. and Soc. Psychol.,* 1952, *47*:589–592.

42. Lewin, K., Field theory and experiment in social psychology: concepts and methods, *Amer. J. of Sociol.,* 1939, *44*:868–896.

43. Lowell, E. L., A methodological study of projectively measured achievement motivation, Unpublished M.A. thesis, Wesleyan University, 1950.

44. Margolin, S. E., and Bunch, M. E., The relationship between age and the strength of hunger motivation, *Comp. Psychol. Monogr.,* 1940, Vol. 16.

45. Maslow, A. H., A theory of human motivation, *Psychol. Rev.*, 1943, *50:* 370–396.
46. McClelland, D. C., *The Achievement Motive*, New York, Appleton-Century-Crofts, 1953.
47. McClelland, D. C., Measuring motivation in phantasy: the achievement motive, in McClelland, D. C. (ed.), *Studies in Motivation*, New York, Appleton-Century-Crofts, 1955, pp. 401–413.
48. McClelland, D. C., and Friedman, G. A., A cross-cultural study of the relationship between child-rearing practices and achievement motivation appearing in folk tales, in Swanson, G. E., *et al.* (eds.), *Readings in Social Psychology*, New York, Henry Holt, 1953, pp. 243–248.
49. McClelland, D. C., and Liberman, A. M., The effect of need for achievement on need-related words, *J. Personal.*, 1949, *18:*236–251.
50. McClelland, D. C., Rindlisbacher, A., and deCharms, R., Religious and other sources of parental attitudes toward independence training, in McClelland, D. C. (ed.), *Studies in Motivation*, New York, Appleton-Century-Crofts, 1955, pp. 389–397.
51. Montgomery, K. C., The role of the exploratory drive in learning, *J. Comp. and Physiol. Psychol.*, 1954, *47:*60–64.
52. Morgan, Christine M., The attitudes and adjustments of recipients of old age assistance in upstate and metropolitan New York, *Archives of Psychol.*, 1937, No. *214.*
53. Murphy, G., *Personality: A Biosocial Approach to Origins and Structure*, New York, Harper, 1947.
54. Murray, H. A., *Explorations in Personality*, New York, Oxford University Press, 1938.
55. Nelson, J. F., *Leisure-time Interests and Activities of Business Girls*, New York, Woman's Press (Not dated, but about 1934).
56. Norton, J. L., General motives and influences in vocational choice, *J. Genet. Psychol.*, 1953, *82:*263–278.
57. Norton, J. L., Patterns of vocational interest development and actual job choice, *J. Genet. Psychol.*, 1953, *82:*235–262.
58. Postman, L., and Brown, D. R., The perceptual consequence of success and failure, *J. Abnorm. and Soc. Psychol.*, 1952, *47:*213–221.
59. Postman, L., Bruner, J. S., and McGinnis, E., Personal values as selective factors in perception, *J. Abnorm. and Soc. Psychol.*, 1948, *43:*142–154.
60. Reder, M. W., Age and income, *J. Amer. Econ. Assoc.*, 1954, *44:*661–670.
61. Reissman, L., Levels of aspiration and social class, *Amer. Sociol. Rev.*, 1953, *18:*233–242.
62. Richter, C. P., A behavioristic study of the activity of the rat, *Comp. Psychol. Monogr.*, 1922, Nos. 1 and 2.
63. Schneider, L., and Lysgaard, S., The deferred gratification pattern: a preliminary study. *Amer. Sociol. Rev.*, 1953, *18:*142–149.
64. Schuster, D. B., A psychological study of a 106-year-old man: A contribution to dynamic concepts of aging and dementia, *Amer. J. Psychiat.*, 1952, *109:*112–119.

65. Sheffield, F. D., and Roby, T. B., Reward value of a non-nutritive sweet taste, *J. Comp. and Physiol. Psychol.*, 1950, *43*:471–481.

66. Sheffield, F. D., Wulff, J. J., and Backer, R., Reward value of copulation without sex drive reduction, *J. Comp. and Physiol. Psychol.*, 1951, *48*:3–8.

67. Shirley, M., Studies in activity. II activity rhythms; age and activity; activity after rest, *J. Comp. Psychol.*, 1928, *8*:159–186.

68. Shuttleworth, F. K., The adolescent period: a graphic atlas. *Monogr. of the Society for Research in Child Development*, 1949, Vol. 14.

69. Simmons, L. W., Attitudes toward aging and the aged: primitive societies, *J. Gerontol.*, 1946, *1*:72–95.

70. Slonaker, J. R., The normal activity of the albino rat from birth to natural death, its rate of growth and the duration of life, *J. Animal Behavior*, 1912, *2*:20–42.

71. Slotkin, J. S., Life course in middle life, *Social Forces*, 1952, *33*:171–177.

72. Sorokin, P. A., and Berger, C. Q., *Time-Budgets of Human Behavior*, Cambridge, Harvard University Press, 1939.

73. Spiegel, L. A., A review of contributions to a psychoanalytic theory of adolescence: individual aspects, *The Psychoanalytic Study of the Child*, International University Press, 1951, Vol. IV, pp. 353–393.

74. Strong, E. K., Jr., *Change of Interests with Age*, Stanford, Stanford University Press, 1931.

75. Thompson, G. G., and Hunnicutt, C. W., The effect of repeated praise or blame on the work achievement of "introverts" and "extroverts," *J. Educ. Psychol.*, 1944, *35*:257–266.

76. Thorndike, E. L., Edward Lee Thorndike, in *A History of Psychology in Autobiography*, Vol. III, Worcester, Clark University Press, 1936, pp. 263–270.

77. Thorndike, E. L., *Human Nature and the Social Order*, New York, Macmillan, 1940.

78. Van Zelst, R. H., Validation of a sociometric regrouping procedure, *J. Abnorm. and Soc. Psychol.*, 1952, *47*:299–301.

79. Warden, C. J., *Animal Motivation Studies: The Albino Rat*, New York, Columbia University Press, 1931.

80. Weiner, I. H., and Stellar, E., Salt preference of the rat determined by a single stimulus method, *J. Comp. and Physiol. Psychol.*, 1951, *44*:394–401.

81. White, R. W., *Lives in Progress*, New York, Dryden Press, 1952.

CHAPTER 8 •

• Emotional Development: Unresolved Tensions, Aggressions, Fears, and Anxieties

THROUGH interaction with his physical and social environment a person learns to enjoy and seek many different objects and activities which have in one way or another (and perhaps one or more times removed) been associated with the satisfaction of his primary drives and motives, or which have directly provided pleasurable sensations. In the complex scene of the modern world a whole host of stimuli thus become "interesting," "enjoyable," and "satisfying." Developmental trends in many of these satisfying interests and activities will be detailed in the next chapter. The present chapter, in contrast, will consider the kinds of situations in which people encounter frustration or threat of frustration, situations that create tensions, producing distress and dissatisfaction, instead of *reducing* tensions as do satisfying activities. The chapter will discuss emotional development and motivational changes as they are reflected in the fears, worries, anxieties, and problems that people typically face at various ages.

It should be emphasized at the outset that consideration of what may seem essentially negative aspects of human development may pave the way for constructive action. There is considerable merit in knowing the kinds of conditions which, in the present culture, create fears and anxieties and the areas of adjustment which cause concern at different ages. Here lie direct points of attack for the improvement of human welfare and happiness through programs in fields such as education, social security, and medicine.

Nature and Nurture in Emotional Development

EARLY EMOTIONAL DEVELOPMENT

It is the popular conception that a number of basic emotions are in-born and present at birth. This view, once held by eminent psychologists (85), has been largely discredited through subsequent research (65, 72, 80). It was once thought, for example, that it was possible to distinguish "rage" in the newborn child when movement was restrained, "fear" when support was suddenly removed, and "love" when the infant was fondled (85). Later investigations indicated, however, that such judgments could be made and such labels applied only when the stimulating conditions were observed. When only the behavior was seen, without knowledge of what had been done to the child, it was impossible to distinguish one "emotion" from another.

Thus, it seemed doubtful if more than one undifferentiated emotional reaction was present at birth. Other types of emotional behavior, so apparent in the adult, appeared to develop later—possibly because of innate changes but in any event greatly enriched by environmental experience and stimulation. In Figure 77 a diagram is presented illustrating one investigator's conception of how emotional development proceeds from birth through the months immediately following. This figure is based on observations over three or four months of some 62 infants in a "foundling" hospital. In the newborn child, and for some days thereafter, emotional reaction to highly stimulating conditions was an undifferentiated reaction of general agitation or excitement. But by as early as three weeks of age it was possible to identify a differentiated response (distress) to conditions causing pain or discomfort and to hunger. By about three months evidence of "delight," keen interest, and pleasure—reflected in such behavior as cooing, smiling, and watching seemingly with interest—could be observed.

Two generalized types of emotional response thus seem early established. The ages at which other types of emotional responses are differentiated from these two earlier patterns in this group of infants may be noted in the figure. It is not important here *exactly* when these various emotional responses appear, nor is it important how an observer might distinguish between "elation" and "delight" or whether "affection for children" and "affection for adults" are *different* emotions. The main point is that at birth emotional responses are generalized and un-

differentiated—a conclusion supported by other investigators (72, 80)—
and that with increasing age, and as a result of either maturation or
environmental experience or both, various other emotional behaviors become distinguishable. "It seems," as this investigator pointed out, "that
in the course of development, emotional behavior becomes more and

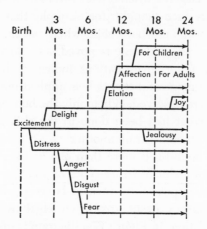

Figure 77. Approximate Ages of the Differentiation of Various Emotions During the
First Two Years of Life. (Adapted from K. M. B. Bridges, Emotional development in early
infancy, *Child Development*, 1932, 3:324–334.)

more specific, both as regards arousing stimuli and form of response.
Distress, though more readily aroused, comes to find adequate expression in a variety of actions, and delight becomes sensitive appreciation
and joy in numerous pursuits. The emotions evolve slowly, and the exact age of differentiation is difficult to determine" (9). The emerging
tendencies to react negatively to a wide variety of stimuli and pleasur-
ably to a wide variety of other stimuli represent, of course, exceedingly
important changes in motivational dispositions.

"INNATE" FACTORS IN EMOTIONAL DEVELOPMENT AND BEHAVIOR

A basic question regarding developmental changes in behavior is the
extent to which those changes are innately determined or are learned
modifications. What are the findings with respect to emotional development? That there are important *inherited* differences among organisms
with respect to temperamental make-up or predisposition has been demonstrated in studies of animals. By selective breeding, over several generations, of calm, placid animals it is possible to obtain offspring much

different "emotionally" from the offspring resulting from selective breeding of "high-strung," "nervous" animals (26). Different breeds of dogs appear to show important differences in predispositions for different types of "emotional" behavior (77). In view of such results, it seems reasonable to conclude that differences in heredity likely account for a portion of the observed differences among organisms in emotional predispositions.

Patterns of emotional expression also appear to have an innate basis. The startle pattern, for example, not only is a highly consistent response from person to person but varies little with increased age (47). And observations of a deaf, blind girl of 10, who would have had no opportunity to observe the emotional behavior of others except through the cutaneous senses, nonetheless revealed emotional behavior (smiling, laughing, frowning) of a typical sort (23). However, the marked differences that have been observed among cultures, as well as basic similarities, suggest that native and cultural factors interact in the determination of emotional response (44).

Since certain types of emotional response (e.g., fear and anxiety, discussed below) arise in situations with which the individual is unable to cope, gross maturational changes which result in increased or diminished ability to deal effectively with particular situations may be expected to play an indirect but no less important role in developmental changes in emotional reactions. As intellectual maturity and size and strength increase in childhood and adolescence, fears may drop out simply because the maturing child becomes able to understand and handle situations that previously provoked fear. Declining physical or intellectual capacities during maturity and old age may give rise to anxiety or fear. For example, anxiety regarding sexual competence may afflict the male sensitive to declining capacity. And anxiety regarding falling in the dark and on slippery streets may characterize the old person preoccupied with the infirmities of old age and a deteriorating sense of balance. It might be hypothesized, in passing, that such anxieties are accentuated at the ages when such decline (and failure) is first noted rather than after the trend has become established and appropriate attitudinal and behavior adjustments made to the decline. Only slight evidence exists at present in support of this view. One physician, for example, reports more consultations regarding loss of sexual capacity among men in their thirties than among those of more advanced ages where actual loss is notably greater (28).

ROLE OF LEARNING IN EMOTIONAL DEVELOPMENT

Inherited predispositions and constitutional changes are thus important in emotional development, but, as already noted, experience also plays a vital role—to those interested in influencing development, perhaps it plays the more important role. Many studies demonstrate that through learning, a great variety of stimuli become capable of producing emotional reactions which initially were produced by only a limited range of stimuli.

In one early study of emotional conditioning (86), a healthy 11-month-old child who had a history of marked emotional stability, including almost complete freedom from fear responses, was "taught" to fear a white rat by means of the following treatment. Although the child had not previously been known to show fear, he gave a typical fear response, including startle and crying, when a suspended steel bar was struck with a hammer behind the child when his attention was diverted. It had been ascertained in previous test situations that the child was unafraid of a white rat, a rabbit, a dog, a monkey, masks with and without hair, cotton wool, etc. But now, in the conditioning phase of the experiment, the child was presented with the white rat and reached for it. Just as his hand touched the rat, the steel bar was struck. The child jumped violently and fell forward; on the second stimulation the same response plus whimpering occurred. A week later when the rat was again presented there was evidence of hesitancy in touching the rat (hand was suddenly withdrawn before contact), thus indicating the effect of the two joint stimulations of the previous week. Five more joint stimulations were given this same day and at the conclusion the rat was presented *alone*. A violent fear reaction resulted including crying and flight (crawling rapidly away). Five days later an attempt was made to discover whether this fear response, conditioned to one object, would transfer to other objects. It was demonstrated that such transfer did occur—to a rabbit, a dog, a fur coat, a Santa Claus mask. A follow-up revealed that fear responses to these objects, though reduced in intensity, were still evident a month later.

Such conditioning and its generalization illustrate how many emotional reactions (involving both pleasure and displeasure) to all sorts of stimuli—popular songs, perfumes, foods, odors, colors—may develop.

Learning also plays a role in emotional development by producing growth in knowledge and understanding which results both in increasing sensitivity to potentially "dangerous" situations and in increasing understanding of means to deal with them. Illustrative of such growth is a study reported some years ago of the development of fear of a snake. Under properly controlled conditions a fierce-looking but actually harmless snake was presented to children of various ages and to adults. Children up to two years of age showed no fear; by three or four and a half, reactions of caution were common; definite fear behavior occurred more often after four years of age, but was much more pronounced in adults. These investigators (38) offered three possible interpretations of this "maturing" of a specific fear: "(1) as the result of conditioning, (2) as the result of a ripening of an innate fear of snakes, (3) as the result of a general maturation of behavior, which leads to greater sensitiveness and more discriminatory responses." The first two of these possibilities were rejected. In accepting the third explanation, the investigators wrote as follows:

Fear may be regarded as a response to certain changes in a total situation— changes requiring a sudden new adjustment which the individual is unprepared to make. The arousal of fear depends not only upon situational changes, but also upon the individual's *general* level of development. With a young infant, perhaps the only changes which are fear-producing are those which substitute loud sounds for quiet, pain for comfort, or loss of support for a previous state of bodily balance. As a child develops, his intelligence innately matures, and his perceptions become enriched through experience. New things startle him because of his keener perception of the fact that they *are* new and unusual. We have an old saying, "They who know nothing fear nothing." It would be equally true to say, "They who know everything fear nothing." *Fear arises when we know enough to recognize the potential danger in a stimulus, but have not advanced to the point of a complete comprehension and control of the changing situation.* (38.)

Thus, it may be expected that specific fears, worries, and anxieties will wax and wane as the life span is negotiated. At any age, increasing experience may result in increasing sensitivity to certain situations; shifts in role or changes in other situational factors may produce "problems" for which established habits are inadequate. Thus, fears and anxieties may arise at any age from childhood to old age, only to wane in significance as familiarity, understanding, and skill in dealing with them are developed. Such waxing and waning will be illustrated later in the chapter.

THE "CRITICAL PERIOD" HYPOTHESIS

Does it make much difference *when* threatening or satisfying experiences occur in determining their impact upon emotional development? The emphasis upon general growth and understanding in the immediately preceding paragraphs may well lead to the conclusion that early experiences (before experience and maturation have provided much understanding and insight) will be more serious and far-reaching in their outcome. The view that habit patterns and personality, including patterns of emotional response, become more rigid and harder to change with increasing age would also lead to the view that experiences having emotional impacts are psychologically important in inverse proportion to the age of the subject; i. e., the younger the person, the more constructive or damaging the experience may be. The family disruption and uncertainty caused by a divorce, for example, would, over the long term, presumably create more problems for a young child than for an adolescent. This point of view is, within broad limits, widely held and finds much support in the clinical experience of those engaged in psychotherapy with malad-justed adults. Students of parent-child relations similarly find that fam-ily disruptions and insecurities have greater effect upon young children than upon those older. Precise research related to this problem is, of course, difficult to conduct in human subjects.

In contrast to this position, other investigators hold that certain periods of life may be more *critical* as regards emotional experience and its effect upon future emotional predisposition. One group of writers (69), who have experimented mainly with dogs and other animals, have found some periods of life more crucial than others as regards the psychological impact of various stressful experiences. Though they had no relevant human evidence, they hypothesized that among human beings critical periods might exist for the infant at the time of weaning, for the toddler establishing new relations with others, for the child starting to school for the first time, and for the adult at the advent of first sexual behavior and at its decline. Presumably also, critical periods might exist at the start of vocational or marital life, at the time of leaving home and enter-ing college or the military service, and at the time of retirement. At such times particular experience of either a positive or negative sort may assume special importance.

Although evidence is at present lacking regarding such extensions of the animal studies, such extensions do not seem unreasonable. For example, one of the present writers has been somewhat startled on a number of occasions at the recollections of graduating seniors regarding conversations they had had with him during "Freshman Week." Certain suggestions given them (and which they were able to repeat almost verbatim, they claimed) were asserted to have been most influential. Perhaps the almost complete change in environ-ment and in social relationships rendered them especially vulnerable or sus-ceptible to influence at this "critical" time. Less impressionistic than the fore-going observation is the finding, reported from a military study of the influence of brief bits of advice (given after extremely brief psychological sizing-up of each selectee) upon early military adjustment. An experimental group receiving such advice rated reliably better on adjustment during their initial training than did a control group who did not receive advice (14). Perhaps even brief advice, much maligned as a clinical procedure, has genuine and important therapeutic value at such a critical period in the lives of young people.

There seems to the present writers no essential disagreement, for practical purposes, between the two views presented above. *In general,* early emotional experiences may be of greater total significance than those occurring later in life, but other critical periods may exist and should be identified. Certainly, there should be more intensive study of such periods as adolescence and the climacteric, both long thought (though with little evidence) to represent critical periods, as well as more research seeking to identify and explore other possible "danger" periods. As Scott and his associates comment, "the possibility exists that critical or danger periods in human development may eventually be delineated in such detail that parents and educators may know when to be especially careful to avoid psychologically damaging experiences" (69).

Anger and Aggressive Tendencies

Anger, an emotionalized reaction to frustration, involves visceral responses not unlike those in fear and other disorganizing types of emotions, but unlike fear, anger involves aggressive behavior, usually directed toward the frustrating agent. In some instances, the aggression may be "displaced" and directed toward other agents or objects or even toward oneself. Aggressive behavior, involving varying degrees of "anger" from slight irritation to rage, is such a characteristic reaction to frustration that one group of writers (19) proposed a general "frustration-aggression" hypothesis which asserts that aggression is the "natural" reaction to frustration and is aimed at hurting the frustrating agent. Since aggression is generally disapproved, the aggression may be displaced and directed toward objects or people other than the frustrating agent, or aggressive tendencies may in the course of time (i. e., as age increases) become modified or suppressed, and other adjustive behaviors may become more prominent. This concept of frustration leading to aggression is tremendously important. It is helpful in understanding irritabilities and hostilities that may attend a particular phase of life or a particular group of people or a person on a particular occasion. This issue will be returned to with constructive suggestions after a variety of material dealing with frustration has been presented.

AGE TRENDS IN ANGER RESPONSES

How frequently do people of different ages become angry? How and toward whom (or what) do they express their anger? Some evidence on these issues is available, especially at the early childhood level. In Figure 78 is presented information regarding the frequency of occurrence of anger episodes in the preschool years. It will be noted that anger responses become more frequent up to about 18 months of age, with a

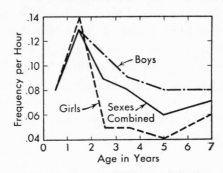

Figure 78. Age Changes in Frequency of Anger Outbursts During the Preschool Years. (From F. L. Goodenough, *Anger in Young Children,* Minneapolis, University of Minnesota Press, 1931.)

sharp decline thereafter. Evidence from college students suggests that this decline in frequency of anger episodes continues with increasing age.[1] Comparable data on the adult years are not available, but it is noteworthy that crimes of violence decline with age also; although such data are of quite a different type, the direction of the trend is consistent with the view that with increasing age there is less overt anger and aggression.

Though the general age trend appears to be toward reduction of aggression, certain periods may be expected to show temporary increases

[1] A study of college girls (1) suggests that they experience what they report as anger on the average of perhaps twice a day (15.7 times per week), when they included angry reactions not only to present situations but to recalled and anticipated situations as well. This frequency is higher than that reported by Meltzer (56) and by Gates (21) (these writers reported respectively 4.02 and 2.84 anger responses per week), a difference presumably due to their insistence on more detailed description of each anger response and limiting of description to anger in relation to present situations.

in stress and hence in frequency of anger and aggressive behavior. That adolescence is so characterized has been argued by certain writers (*19*), but the evidence is inconclusive. One investigator has presented evidence based on 10 cases to the effect that those boys whose male hormone content was *just beginning* to increase showed more aggressiveness and more antisocial conduct. And he speculated that: "This observed lessening in aggression with increasing distance in time from the original increase in sex instigation might be partially explained as the result of learning socially approved activities (such as competitive sports) in which the aggressive tendencies would find an outlet" (*75*). Little, if any, evidence is available regarding increase in aggressive behavior at the menopause[2] or at retirement. Such transitions presumably involve greater frustration which might be expected to increase the tendency toward delinquency and aggression. Indeed, such data as are available suggest that from maturity into old age there is a reduction in aggressiveness and an increased tendency toward tolerance and submissiveness. This trend will be the subject for comment later in this chapter.

As will be noted in the figure dealing with young children, sex differences in frequency of outbursts are not apparent until about two years of age; from that time through the age range of the study, boys evidence greater frequency of anger responses than girls. Data on college students and adults give similar results regarding sex differences, and related data show that in the American culture males are, by and large, the more independent, aggressive, and self-sufficient sex. Why such sex differences exist is a matter for some speculation. There is little doubt that the cultural stereotype has been, and is, for girls to be more submissive and quiet and boys to be more aggressive and boisterous. Some supporting evidence, for example, indicates that parents prefer submissive girls to submissive boys (*67*). And it is likely that parental treatment is such as to foster differential personality development along these lines. Of some interest in this connection are wartime studies of the aggressiveness of preschool children in experimental doll-play situations; differences were found between boys whose fathers had been absent and those whose fathers were not away from home which suggested that

___

[2] Pollak (*62*) has suggested, on the basis of rather old data regarding crime in Germany, that there may be an increase among women at menopause in the frequency of arrests for assault, disorderly conduct, and the like. He interpreted these findings as indicative of increased stress and increased aggressiveness at this presumably stressful period of life. The present writers have been unable to confirm this finding in more recent American crime reports.

the father plays an important role in the sex-typing of boys with respect to aggressiveness (70).

Whether there is a partial biological base for sex differences in aggressiveness is difficult to determine. One writer, after reviewing the literature on animals showing a relationship between sex hormones and aggression, is cautious in extending generalizations to the human species, though certain published studies are positive. He writes: "In man, aggressive tendencies may find direct or indirect expression in so many forms, and are obviously stimulated, modified, or inhibited by such a wide variety of complex cultural and social conditions, that even if this type of behavior were basically correlated with hormonal conditions the relationship would be extremely difficult to demonstrate. Furthermore, human patients under surgical treatment or hormone therapy are notoriously prone to report, and actually experience, marked psychic changes which have apparently been induced by suggestion, and are totally unrelated to the physiologic consequences of the medical procedure." (5, p. 102.)

As regards age changes in types of anger responses, some data for the early years of life are presented in Table 41. Certain clear trends are apparent, in this case, up to the beginning of the school years. There is

TABLE 41. Percentage of Children of Various Ages Who Showed Various Types of Behavior During Outbursts of Anger

		Age			
		1 Yr.–	2 Yrs.–	3 Yrs.–	4 Yrs.
	Under	1 Yr.	2 Yrs.	3 Yrs.	and
Type of Behavior	1 Yr.	11 Mos.	11 Mos.	11 Mos.	Over
Display of undirected energy					
Boys	100	78	73	65	45
Girls	87	79	83	30	29
Motor or verbal resistance					
Boys	27	71	40	39	60
Girls	12	43	21	56	61
Retaliative behavior					
Boys	0	9	10	26	30
Girls	1	4	11	25	26

SOURCE: Adapted from Florence L. Goodenough, *Anger in Young Children*, Minneapolis, University of Minnesota Press, 1931.

a marked decrease in behavior involving display of undirected energy. It would seem that in infancy the child becomes angry, but has not yet learned to identify the source of his frustration or know how or where to direct his energies. Motor or verbal resistance builds up during the second year, declines the third year, and builds up during the fourth and fifth years of life. But most interesting is the slow increase in the proportion of anger outbursts involving retaliative behavior. A change also occurs, with increasing age, in the *nature* of the retaliative behavior. There is an increase in "persisting generalized reactions toward a single person, and more attempts to retaliate by means of indirect attacks designed to hurt the feelings rather than to injure the body of the offender" (22, p. 295). Further, the percentage of after-reactions (particularly resentfulness and sulkiness) showed a steady increase during the age range studied.

In adulthood, the most frequent responses in anger are verbal, and frequently they are not obviously "directed" toward a particular person but expressed in excited talking or exclamation. Various types of restless behavior—pacing, tossing in bed, shifting in chair—are also prominent. It would seem that while the young child "learns" to direct his anger toward the frustrating agent, further maturity results in the additional learning that such "directed" aggression is socially unacceptable, and generalized irritability, hostility, or sheer undirected energy expenditure again characterize the response.

A number of studies agree that there are significant sex differences from an early age onward, not only in the frequency of anger episodes (as already noted above) but also in manner of response. Boys react with more overt violence. Girls more frequently manifest their aggressiveness verbally, in disparagement, scolding, bossing. These differences are apparent at an early age both in the actual life behavior of children[3] and in their expressions in experimental situations involving play with dolls (70). In the latter study of doll play, it was apparent that there are clear sex differences in the *frequency,* in the *direction,* and in the *kind* of aggression.

It would be anticipated from such findings regarding sex differences that there would be significant differences among other subgroups of the general population, as, for example, those from different social classes. It has been noted in interview investigations, for example, that upper-middle-class mothers, compared with upper-lower-class mothers, are less restrictive, more permissive, and more acceptant of aggressive behavior directed by their children toward them or toward other children (51).

---

[3] Among studies of actual life behavior are those by Green (24), Caille (11), and Muste and Sharpe (61).

Such different patterns of training for aggression control should be apparent in the youngsters' behavior.

As the human organism matures from the moment of birth, it presumably becomes increasingly susceptible to certain anger-provoking frustrations in its environment and less susceptible to others. Thus, in the early months of life, the child is likely to be little influenced by verbal stimuli, but "angered" by restriction of bodily movement. Later, he will encounter frustrations in the establishment of routine physical habits, but these disappear as those habits are established. In one study of young children (mainly of preschool years), some two-thirds of the anger episodes reported stemmed from three types of sources: (1) objection to routine habits (toilet, going to bed, eating, grooming), (2) direct conflict with authority, and (3) problems of social relationships (22). Less important (in descending order of importance) were problems of self-help, minor physical discomforts or fear, changes in routine, and restriction of movement.

Studies at the adult level, mainly of college students, are in essential agreement (1, 21, 56) as to "causes" of anger, emphasizing the role of other people. In an investigation (1) involving college girls, for example, the most frequent cause of anger (in 52 percent of the episodes) was thwarting of plans. Other anger-producing situations involved inferiority and loss of prestige (21 percent), schoolwork (13 percent), family relationships (10 percent), and abstract problems (4 percent). It is of some interest that in all of these situations, people were the chief frustrating agent. Combining all anger-producing situations, *people* were responsible 46 percent of the time; *institutional factors*, 23 percent; *personal inadequacies*, 16 percent; *accidents and chance factors*, 15 percent. "It is an interesting reflection on modern life," the original investigator points out, "that nearly one-fourth of all the anger-arousing situations consisted of such institutional factors as regimentation, rules and regulations, railroad schedules, 'red tape,' organizational inefficiencies, social customs, governmental actions, and the like" (1). In short, *other* people, either personally or through institutions, represent the main source of frustration leading to anger. Such findings provide insight into how to reduce the frequency of anger, a topic which will be returned to a few paragraphs later.

As already noted, available age trend data are largely limited to the very young ages, though some data are available in special areas of adjustment. As will be shown in a later chapter, for example, friction with parents increases in adolescence. Some further suggestion of adolescent and adult age trends may, however, be gleaned from studies of "annoyances." Although the term "annoyance" implies irritation and vexation (anger at a low intensity, perhaps), it likely also includes reactions which might be termed "disgust" (or something else) rather than anger. During adolescence, according to the findings of a longitudinal study covering grades 6 through 12 (15), no significant age change in sources or relative frequency of annoyance was evident. However, in a study involving people from the teens to old age (12), age trends were apparent, both with respect to the relative extent of annoyances in general and with respect to the particular circumstances found to be annoying. The data in this study were classified into four age groups (10 to 25, 25 to 40, 40 to 60 and 60 to 90), of which the 40-to-60-year age group had the highest "annoyability" score. The scores increased gradually over the first three of these groups and declined in the last (60 to 90 years). The increase in annoyance may seem somewhat contrary to the earlier statement suggesting that aggressiveness declines in the adult years; perhaps what happens is that adults have fairly well learned to control expressions of aggression but nonetheless *feel* irritation.

As might be expected, some annoyances tend to drop out while others are acquired, and on some items opposite trends characterize the two sexes. Items such as the following were checked as annoyances more frequently by the older groups: to see suggestive dancing at a social dance, to walk on ice-covered slippery sidewalks, to hear a person refer to a sex subject in a conversation, to see a woman smoking a cigarette in public, very noticeable powder on a woman's face, the odor of liquor on a person's breath. The following are typical of those checked less frequently by the older groups: a person with a gushing manner, to hear a person make bad grammatical errors, to have to get up in the morning, to hear a person scratch his fingernails on the blackboard, to see a woman wearing high heels, to see a person wearing clothes which are not appropriate for the occasion. In general, borderline moral wrongs are more annoying to older people, yet at the same time they seem increasingly tolerant of many ordinary annoyances. Some of the trends seem to grow out of age differences in cultural backgrounds (e. g., seeing a woman smoke); others to be the result of changed values with age (e. g., appropriateness of dress); some to be due to increasing infirmities (e. g., slippery sidewalks) and others due to the fact that items were being judged in the light of experience which as age increases becomes less common or has receded farther into the background (e. g., scratching fingernails on blackboards).

It will be noted that a number of these "annoyances" relate to "attitudes." It may be said that for many people, and particularly the less tolerant ones, the observance or experiencing of behavior in conflict with one's own values is found to be irritating and annoying. In many instances (as in discussions of politics or religious views), the conflict may become so threatening that more intense forms of anger arise.

THE MANAGEMENT OF ANGER AND AGGRESSION

A consideration of the causes and conditions related to anger and aggression lead to several concrete suggestions regarding their management.

In the first place, recognition and appreciation of the fact that anger and aggression are likely to result when needs or desires are frustrated, or when activities are interrupted, should permit the mature adult to accept and tolerate more readily the aggressive behavior, especially when it is recognized that children are especially susceptible to frustration, and hence prone to anger, when other conditions are also creating tensions. Thus, more anger episodes occur in children when they become hungry (i. e., just before lunch and dinner), when they are ill (colds, constipated), or when they are unduly fatigued, as at bedtime (22). Parents or other adults who are cognizant of the genesis of anger should be more able to view the behavior objectively as a *symptom of other conditions* that should be dealt with, rather than as a behavior toward which punitive action must be taken.

In the second place, a reduction in anger and aggression might be accomplished by the simple expedient of reducing the number of frustrations that a child experiences. Convincing personal evidence that many home or school environments are excessively restrictive can be obtained by simply counting the number of times during the day when a child is told "no"—when actually it mattered little whether he did or did not engage in the activity in question. A variety of evidence exists indicating the advantages of a relatively free environment. In one series of studies, done under the direction of Lewin (49), greater aggression and hostility on the part of children occurred in groups under autocratic as contrasted with democratic leadership. Another study has revealed that the curtailment of combative behavior among children in school by teachers during one year apparently resulted in an increase in such behavior the next year, whereas children subjected to less restriction showed a slight decline (but not enough to be conclusive) in combative behavior the next year

(36). In total, the evidence points to the adoption of a less restrictive policy as a concrete means of reducing aggression.

Thirdly, standards should be set within the potential grasp of the child. It is obvious that a child can experience nothing but frustration if *too much* is expected of him; yet many parents insist on certain behavior (as in the establishment of excretory habits) before the child is sufficiently mature or before he has learned adequate skills for dealing with the situation. Certain investigators (41) have studied the tendency toward anger when children are required to perform impossible or very difficult tasks. It has also been demonstrated that such tendencies toward anger, crying, sulking, or destructive behavior can be reduced or largely eliminated if the child receives greater opportunity to achieve skill in the performance of the task, perhaps by individual guidance through a series of tasks of increasing difficulty (40, 41).

A fourth suggestion relates to the commonly observed fact that children often *learn* to attain ends by anger because parents or others yield the issue when faced with anger, a temper tantrum, or other aggressive behavior. In order for the child to learn that such behavior is unacceptable it must not be permitted to achieve its purpose. Learning can be most effective if the child is *consistently* treated rather than being permitted to achieve his ends through anger on one occasion while on another he is completely quelled. Although any one individual is likely to be inconsistent (some more so than others), obviously the more adults there are within a home, the greater the possibilities are of inconsistency in the treatment which a child receives. There is, interestingly enough, evidence in this connection of a positive relationship between the frequency of anger episodes in children and the number of adults in the home (22).

Children, of course, learn how to react in a frustrating situation not only through the kind of reception their behavior receives (e. g., whether a temper tantrum achieves an end) but also through their observation of how adults behave when frustrated. Thus, a mother who achieves her own ends through anger or sulking will find difficulty in preventing her child from doing likewise. A child growing up in a lower-class family and neighborhood where overt expressions of anger and aggression are commonly accepted will become prone to react in the same way, whereas an upper-class child will very likely have learned to behave differently, in particular, to suppress overt aggressive tantrums.

Although the discussion thus far has dealt mainly with the management of anger in young children, the same suggestions apply to the management of anger in adults, though possibly less directly. The final suggestion—the adoption of a nonthreatening attitude in human relations —finds more general application in the relationships among adults. In discussing this question one writer observes: "One difficulty in dealing with anger is that it frequently involves the disposition to assign blame to somebody or something other than oneself, and that a show of anger is likely to arouse a response in kind. Sometimes it is possible to break this by reducing the area of friction through yielding points except those directly at issue, by seeking ways in which the angry person's feelings may be assuaged through praise, successful achievement, and friendly attention in matters not directly concerned with the issue that is under dispute" (33, p. 772). The maintenance of a calm, friendly, objective manner in discussions and in dealing with situations is one guarantee of calm relationships. A threatening, angry approach, in the nature of an attack on a person, his attitudes, or his views, is likely to generate anger. Behavior that signifies respect for the other person and which promotes *his* status will reduce aggression. But, unfortunately, such formulas are difficult to follow. How a person behaves is likely to be more a function of the *kind of person* he is (how secure, how well adjusted) than a product of what he *knows* intellectually to be desirable. However, the mature, emotionally well-adjusted person can by analyzing and correcting his own behavior learn to manage anger and aggression with some success.

Age Changes in Fears and Anxieties

An examination of the specific fears and worries that beset people at various ages should be particularly helpful in identifying areas of difficulty. Once such areas are identified it becomes possible to develop means of dealing with them. And often, even when such means are not available, the simple knowledge that certain fears, anxieties, and concerns are not unique but are widely shared—and typically only relatively temporary—provides a relaxing perspective!

FEARS AND WORRIES OF CHILDHOOD

A series of studies (35, 37) conducted at Columbia University some years ago sought to determine developmental changes in fear-producing situations by (1) asking children, in interview, to report their fears, (2) having parents keep records of the fear manifestations of their offspring, and (3) placing children in situations (involving such stimuli as being left alone, a strange person, a high place) which presumably would produce fear. The various methods revealed essentially the same trends, some of which are illustrated in Figure 79. A large proportion of the fears of very young children relate to noise, strange objects, situations and persons, pain, falling, and sudden, unexpected movement, plus lights, flash, shadows, etc. These fears are rapidly eliminated during the first six years of life. Indeed, in the experimental phase of the study, where children were actually put in fear-producing situations, none of the children age 60 to 70 months of age reacted with fear to such stimuli as a high place, being left alone, a strange person—yet between 12 and 36 percent of children age 24 to 36 months had responded with fear to these same situations.

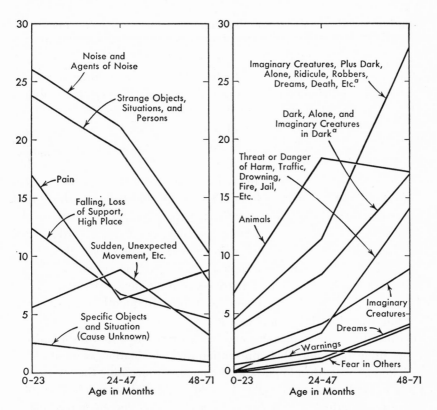

Figure 79. Relative Frequency of Various Fear Situations During the First Six Years. Entries followed by the letter "a" include a combination of categories some of which are also shown separately. (From A. T. Jersild, "Emotional development," in L. Carmichael (ed.), *Manual of Child Psychology* (2nd ed.), Wiley, 1954, pp. 833–917, after A. T. Jersild and F. B. Holmes, *Children's Fears*, New York, Teachers College, Columbia University, 1935.)

Figure 79 also shows fears that are increasing in the early years. Fears of improbable events and situations, largely imaginary, predominate as the child gets older, up to at least six years of age, the highest age shown in the figure. It is likely that such increases are at least partially influenced by increasing intellectual ability—ability to discriminate, think, imagine—coupled with increasing experience, but not enough experience to discount the probability of the event's actually happening or to deal with the event if it did occur. Certain fear-producing stimuli ("animals"; in an experimental situation, a snake) seem to gain in their capacity to evoke fear during the first three or four years and to evidence definite decline by six. Apparently with broadened experience, even young children learn that animals are usually harmless.

During childhood there are also important changes in the manifestations of fear, as of other emotional reactions. An important identifying response in young children to a fear-producing situation is withdrawal, getting away from or out of the situation. Along with withdrawal, various vocal, motor, and visceral responses are likely to occur—crying, trembling, paling, increased heartbeat, and the like. Some of these behaviors are voluntary—subject to control—and some are involuntary. Since modern society attaches a certain stigma to fear, as age increases there is gradual elimination of the more overt aspects of the total response. Older children and adults are less likely to cry frequently, to withdraw overtly from the feared situation, or even to admit verbally that they are afraid. But since society condones freer emotional expression on the part of the feminine sex, one would anticipate that age trends such as described above would be more pronounced in the case of boys than girls. Thus, as Jersild (33) has noted, one investigator found no sex differences in the tendency of young children to cry during dental treatment (6), whereas at the adult level women cried more frequently than did men in trying experimental situations (46).

Because fears are unpleasant and have a restrictive and disorganizing impact upon behavior, their prevention and elimination are matters of much importance. Most important, of course, is preventing the occurrence of fear in the first place, a goal to be achieved mainly through the avoidance of fear-producing stimulation. To a surprising degree, adults almost deliberately instill fears in their offspring by gesture, noises, and the like. In addition, many unwitting remarks ("You won't be afraid while I'm gone?") may suggest that the child should be afraid or may suggest to him that certain things may be harmful—even though remote and personally not experienced. Display of own fears to a child is common and tends to breed the same fears in him. Such introduction of fear-producing stimulation is often inadvertent and unintentional; consistent attention to the problem on the part of adults can probably substantially reduce the incidence of fear. Actually, of course, some parents deliberately attempt to develop specific fears and anxieties in their children as a means of controlling their behavior. While often effective, the possibility of long-term limiting effects of such procedures should not be overlooked.

Elimination of fears, according to reports of adults describing their own experiences (35), seemed to occur mainly through the normal course of development of increased experience and capacity to understand and deal with the feared situation. Experience in and habituation to the situation is an important answer to the problem. The decline of timidity with passage of time (which implies, of course, both increased age and increased *experience*) in a new situation has been demonstrated in one study in the day-by-day reduction of fear and uneasiness apparent in school children attending nursery school for the first time (73) and in another study which noted that some 59 percent of the emotional disturbances in five- and six-year-old school children were responses of "timidity" (7), a percentage which was reduced to 3 percent by ages seven and eight.

Providing reassurance by the presence of a known adult in the fear-producing situation can be helpful. Thus, in an experimental study of insecurity in children, each of 16 children, ages 11 to 30 months, were left alone in a strange room for a period of five minutes on alternate days. Each of a second group of 8 children were left in the room with a familiar adult (in three cases the child's mother) who sat near the entrance to the room and remained as "impassive as possible." Over 11 "trial" periods, the "alone" group showed gains in "security" but still showed considerable insecurity. The "mother-present" group, on the other hand, was quite secure from the outset, and by the sixth trial received maximum security ratings. The study focuses attention upon *experience* as a significant factor in reducing insecurity, either experience in the strange situation itself or familiarity (experience) introduced into the strange situation through the presence of a known person. The investigator concluded: "The most certain provision that can be made for the security of young children faced with unstructured environments appears to be the presence of a familiar adult whose protective power *is known*. Even a *familiar object* may lessen in some degree the insecurity of children in strange situations" (2).[4] The same principle holds for other ages as well. Many an adolescent (and even an adult) who would not venture into a situation alone will do so if a friend goes along.

Anticipation of typical fears and providing prior favorable experiences (as with one's own dog) will be helpful as a preventative measure, just as providing favorable experiences in a secure environment serves as a remedial measure. According to one study (25), verbal explanation alone was better than nothing as a remedy, but it often failed. Explanation was best when the child was also exposed to the situation. Casual, matter-of-fact conversation between parents (planned to be overheard by the youngster) may counteract the lurid but garbled tales of a current crime presented by playmates. The utilization of attractive stimuli, as toys in a physician's office, may entice the youngster into favorable experience with a feared situation and eliminate the fear. In general, efforts aimed at eliminating fears involve efforts to recondition, to provide understanding of the situation, and to develop skills for dealing with the feared situation.[5]

FEARS AND ANXIETIES OF ADOLESCENCE

A number of studies of the worries, fears, and anxieties of adolescents (8, 54, 59, 63) have served to emphasize the importance of vocational, social, and educational problems and physical inadequacies. Three studies will be cited here to highlight certain features of the developmental trends in fear- and anxiety-producing situations during the teens. The first study involved the administration of the Pressey Interest-Attitude test to a large group of children and young people from the sixth grade through college. A section of this test consists of 90 items which the subjects are asked to check once if they worry about them or twice if they worry very much. Certain results, in terms of the number of checks assigned an item per 100 subjects, are presented in Figure 80.

A most significant finding of the study was the marked decline in worry about remote, improbable events (murder, hold-ups, fire, death, etc.) which was shown in a study described above to be increasing during the first six years of life. As mentioned earlier, certain fears are likely to increase as the child matures intellectually or experientially (in many instances the "experience" is vicarious and incomplete) to the point where he recognizes a situation as

---

[4] Italics not as in original.

[5] An excellent discussion of methods of handling emotional behavior can be found in papers by Jersild (33–37). These papers have been most helpful in the preparation of the present chapter.

potentially dangerous. Such fears and anxieties are reduced when he further matures to the point where he can comprehend and master the situation. Once the latter occurs (as illustrated in improbable fears), the fears and anxieties drop out. It is of some interest that, even so, in some people these childhood fears persist into adulthood—fears relating to animals, the dark and imaginary dangers associated with the dark, personal failure and inadequacy, and dangers of accident or injury through drowning, collision, fire (35). Extensive fears of this type at the adult level are evidence of neuroticism.

The curves in Figure 80 focus upon typical adolescent fears and anxieties. In adolescence there is increasing worry or concern about educational, social, and economic matters. Thus, there is increasing worry about

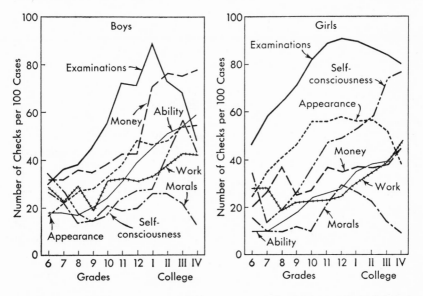

Figure 80. Age Trends in Worries and Anxieties During the Adolescent Period. Indexes are number of checks assigned per 100 cases when respondents were asked to check on a check list of worries those things about which they worried or felt anxious, and to check items twice if they worried much about them. (Based on unpublished data of S. L. Pressey.)

ability, money, work, appearance, morals, and school examinations. Differences between the sexes in pubescent status and in cultural backgrounds and role are also apparent in the figure. Social concerns (clothes, appearance, self-consciousness, morals) begin to emerge earlier, to be more frequent, and to drop off earlier among girls. In the economic and related spheres (ability, money, work), the concerns of boys are more frequent and tend to emerge earlier than is true of girls. It is a reasonable inference that those worries which show a decline do so because young people gradually learn to handle the situation effectively.

In a second study, a group of boys and girls were asked repeatedly, as they progressed through school from the sixth grade, to record on a checklist those situations which they feared. Certain results are presented in Table

TABLE 42. Sex and Grade Differences in Frequency of Various Fears

Specific Fears	Grade 6	7	8	9	10	11	12
Going down a dark street							
Boys			11	6	3	3	3
Girls			19	15	17	24	31
Being followed on the street							
Boys			23	11	14	15	10
Girls			60	47	39	61	49
Noises in the night							
Boys	31	11	7	4	6	3	3
Girls	35	25	22	18	18	24	17
Being alone in the house at night							
Boys			10	7	6	3	0
Girls			26	26	12	15	18
Walking along the edge of a cliff							
Boys	35	35	32	20	23	18	23
Girls	47	33	43	33	33	43	33
Snakes							
Boys	38	27	21	18	24	24	18
Girls	64	58	50	56	51	49	53
Thunder and lightning							
Boys	6	4	4	0	1	3	1
Girls	14	22	14	11	8	18	10
Singing by myself in music class							
Boys			8	8	11	13	14
Girls			15	15	24	22	28
Nightmares							
Boys			11	3	3	4	8
Girls			21	17	8	17	12
Earthquakes							
Boys			13	10	11	11	6
Girls			49	31	28	42	47

NOTE: Figures represent the percentage of a group of boys and girls who were asked to indicate (on a check list) their fears; data were collected on these same pupils for each of seven years.

SOURCE: Adapted from C. M. Tryon, *UC Inventory I, Social and Emotional Adjustment. Revised Form for Presentation of the Cumulative Record for an Individual, with Group Norms for a Seven-Year Period*, University of California, Institute of Child Welfare, 1939.

42. Aside from the specific fears noted there (which the reader can examine for himself), certain more general facts are to be observed. It will be noted, in the first place, that all of these fears characterize girls more than boys. Second, with increased age, these fears decreased more rapidly for boys than for girls. Indeed, in some instances (in this study, for example, in the case of fear of "going down a dark street") a decrease in fear occurs for boys while an *increase* occurred for girls with increased age. Thus is illustrated the role played by adults in the genesis of fear in children and adolescents, as well as the differential treatment accorded the two sexes as they develop.

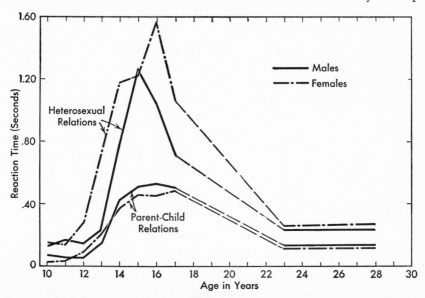

Figure 81. Waxing and Waning of Conflict in Selected Areas of Adolescent Adjustment as Reflected in Reaction Time to Key Words. (Adapted from M. Powell, Age and sex differences in degree of conflict within certain areas of psychological adjustment, *Psychol. Monogr.*, 1955, Vol. 69, No. 387.)

Still a third study of areas of adolescent conflict is noteworthy because of the difference in technique of investigation and in the fact that groups of adults were included to give developmental perspective. In this study, subjects were shown various stimulus words and asked to give the first response (word) that came to mind. Since individuals tend to "block" on conflict or emotionally toned words, reaction time was taken as a measure of conflict, the time required for the critical words being at every age compared with time required to respond to a series of neutral words. The first two of the following sets of stimulus words represent the adjustment areas graphed in Figure 81. Others are illustrative of other areas:

Parent-Child Relations: Father, Children, Home, Mother, Parents.
Heterosexual Relations: Dance, Kissing, Marriage, Dates, Hugging.
Religion: Church, God, Heaven, Worship, Prayer.
Vocational Outlook: Wages, Money, Employed, Hire, Job.
Sample Neutral Words: Apple, Window, Minnow, Piano, Tree.

It will be noted in the figure that, as measured in this way, conflicts in the area of heterosexual relations are especially pronounced in adolescence (also in the case of social acceptability which is not charted), and especially so for girls. Parent-child conflicts seem to be a less serious area of adjustment according to this study, and little sex difference is noted. These two areas of adjustment (and others such as religion, physical appearance, and social acceptance) may be viewed as typically adolescent, since adults in their twenties gave little evidence of conflict, nor did children as young as 10 or 11. In contrast, the area of "vocational outlook" (not graphed) built up as an adolescent problem, *but continued* as an area of conflict throughout the adult age range studied, namely until 30 at least. In instances where there are sex differences in age of emergence of conflict in these areas, as in the case of heterosexual relations as shown in the figure, the conflict occurs earlier in girls. This would generally be expected in view of their earlier maturity.

These findings are at variance with certain other studies utilizing paper-and-pencil techniques and thus warrant caution in interpretation. The number of stimulus words in any area was small, and the adult subjects available to the investigator were likely not as representative of their age groups as were the adolescents. Nonetheless, the study suggests clearly the waxing and waning of certain conflict areas in adolescence. It is noteworthy that an earlier investigation of adolescent problems (71), utilizing "objective" measures, also gave results at variance with questionnaire or check-list techniques. Greater use of such objective methods is much needed in the study of changing problem areas.

THE ANXIETIES OF MATURITY AND OLD AGE

The fears and anxieties of adults (other than college students) have received little research attention, but such data as do exist confirm expectations, growing out of the data on childhood and adolescence, that various phases of adult life have their own typical worries and anxieties. Changes with adult age in worries have been demonstrated by a series of studies in which members of different adult groups were asked to note on a sheet listing various worries the age at which each "worry" had been most prominent in their lives. Responses were collected from psycholo-

gists, labor leaders, businessmen, and from a group of psychological cas-
ualties from skid row (*20, 42, 84*). A summary of the findings is contained
in Table 43 where are shown the percentage of subjects (businessmen
and psychologists) reporting particular worries, the median age, and the
range of ages at which these "worries" occurred. Appearance, sexual morality, and lack of confidence in making a good impression in meeting
people were problems of early adult years, the twenties. Problems of the
late thirties and early forties, on the average, included worries regarding
political convictions, health, marital difficulties, and giving up of important hopes and ambitions.

As was suggested in previous paragraphs in this chapter (in the case
of childhood and adolescent worries), some of these problems are placed

TABLE 43.   Reported Ages at Which Various Types of Worries Characterized a Group of
Businessmen and a Group of Psychologists

Source of Worry	Percent Expressing Worry		Median Age		Interquartile Range	
	Business-men	Psychol-ogists	Business-men	Psychol-ogists	Business-men	Psychol-ogists
Appearance	59	52	27	20	18–38	16–31
Sexual morality	34	54	26	23	19–39	18–30
Lack of confidence of making a good per- sonal impression in meeting people	40	65	25	26	19–35	19–39
Religious or philosoph- ical convictions	37	88	33	26	22–40	21–41
Economic worries	80	91	35	30	26–47	23–38
Lack of confidence of business success	—	63	—	31	—	26–38
Job security	74	75	39	32	28–45	26–38
Peace of mind	—	67	—	35	—	26–47
Political convictions	56	82	44	38	36–53	29–48
Health	69	57	39	38	21–49	28–50
Giving up important hopes and ambi- tions	35	56	30	40	24–45	28–45
Marital difficulties	44	42	39	41	31–47	34–48

NOTE: Absence of data in certain spaces above results from the fact that certain items were not
included in all phases of the investigations.

SOURCE: Adapted from R. A. Dykman, E. K. Heimann, and W. A. Kerr, Lifetime worry patterns
of three diverse adult cultural groups, *J. Soc. Psychol.*, 1952, 35:91–100.

as they are chronologically because new demands (e. g., need for good social or business appearance) raise concerns which are eliminated once skill and self-confidence in these regards are obtained. Other worries have a particular chronological placement because of changing time perspective; e. g., "time is running out," with respect to the achievement of certain ambitions or the continuation of highly valued activities. The latter factor would seem involved in certain problems of middle age, such as the marital difficulties and giving up of ambitions noted in Table 43 as occurring around 40. Some illustrations from data obtained by one of the present writers as "free response" answers to questions regarding personal anxieties and worries are quoted relating to these two problems:

Married Woman, Age 40: I think women my age dread middle age—I did myself—until I thought the idea out and realized that maturity has a great many opportunities for usefulness—so now I don't even think about growing old. I'm much too busy.

Married Man, Age 43: People of my age are apt to have domestic troubles. Husbands at my age are apt to feel that, on account of advanced years, the romance of life is slipping away from them and they try to cling to it by plunging themselves into illegitimate love affairs.

Married Man, Age 46: So many men of my age seem to realize that their marriage is empty and lacking in the depth and richness that it could have. Apparently romance at home has ceased to exist, if it ever really did, and they are emotionally starved.

Male, Age 40: Job quite satisfactory, but personal annoyance with self for unwillingness to break away from social surroundings for advancement professionally.

Male, Age 43: Job dissatisfaction. Have not reached the point I had hoped for by this time in life. Many people experience a general restlessness if an evaluation of one's life, half-lived, gives negative results.

Male, Age 40: Feeling that I might have accomplished more during last 20 years and impatience with self in that respect for known traits of passivity.

In still older ages, problems of declining ability, actual or threatened, may give rise to anxiety. Thus, in a study of the worries of trade union leaders (84), it was noted that beginning with about age 50 the worries are those of declining years. At ages 50 to 55 the two most common worries reported pertained to loss of work efficiency and death, with health worries being quite common. In still later years, after employment has ceased, other problems may come to the fore. Thus, in one study of recipients of old age pensions, reported worries were distributed as follows: financial worries and dependence, 48 percent; concern for spouse and family, 21 percent; poor health and physical dependence, 18 percent;

unable to work, 6 percent; family relationships, estrangements, etc., 5 percent; death, 1.3 percent (60). Such problems in extreme old age may engender feelings of futility, since solutions are limited because of declining capacities, lack of opportunity due to cultural bias, and lack of future because time is running out. It seems that many old people would have reason to be apathetic. But large numbers of older people have refused to admit these limitations as crucial and have managed to fix their sights on future accomplishments and to live vigorously and effectively.

Developmental Trends in Anxiety and Emotional Stress

Up to this point consideration has been of rather specific emotional reactions—fears, anger episodes, anxieties. How, now, do all of these tensions total up? What is the *gross* amount of anxiety or stress at different ages *regardless* of the source? It has already been demonstrated that different areas of living—different types of problems—give rise to stress at different ages. Are specific problems, fears, and anxieties scattered rather evenly over life so that the overall adjustment is about the same? Or are they so concentrated that particular periods (e. g., adolescence, change of life) stand out as especially stressful?

In attempting to answer such questions, it is necessary to examine the symptoms or manifestation of stress, regardless of the circumstances that have produced it. Generally, such evidence is in the form of rather direct indications of somatic involvement, general psychological consequences (neuroses, psychoses) or overt symptoms (fingernail biting, hair twisting) that may be symptomatic of stress arising from different sources, or verbal statements regarding tension, happiness, or unhappiness, such as "nervousness" and the like. Such self-evaluations as the latter, tend to be "overall" evaluations. And sometimes general level of adjustment, tension, or anxiety may be judged by studying summated responses to comprehensive lists of worries, fears, or anxieties, using total frequency as an overall index.

STRESS IN CHILDHOOD AND ADOLESCENCE

Childhood is often viewed nostalgically as the happy, carefree period of life. Actually, as already suggested, the lack of understanding of many natural phenomena as well as lack of ability to deal effectively with many of the situations encountered results in the occurrence of fears that later are eliminated. An overall view of changing tension and changing adjustment during at least part of the childhood years is presented in Figure 82. The chart on the left provides a gross index of worry and anxiety at different ages. The score plotted represents the total number of "checks" used per 100 cases when individuals in different school grades were asked to check once those items on a list of 90 about which they worried or felt anxious and to check twice those that were especially anxiety-producing. Although this particular chart starts with the sixth

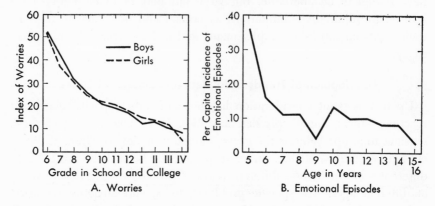

Figure 82. Age Trends During Childhood and Adolescence in Frequency of Worries and Emotional Episodes. (Chart A unpublished data of S. L. Pressey; Chart B from data of W. E. Blatz, S. N. F. Chant, and M. D. Salter, Emotional episodes in the child of school age, *University of Toronto Studies in Child Development*, 1937, Series No. 9.)

grade (thus, does not extend back into early childhood), the picture from this age onward appears to be one of decreasing anxiety and tension. In total, it would seem, more of the situations in which young children find themselves tend to generate anxiety than is true of the situations encountered at a later age.

The same conclusion may be drawn from the data portrayed in the right-hand chart of this figure. Here are shown relative frequencies of emotional episodes occurring among children in school. In contrast to the study cited in the above paragraph, these data were obtained by actual observation, by teachers, in the classrooms. The similarity of this trend, established by quite different procedures, to that obtained by means of a check list of worries is striking. Again, there is a steady decline in frequency of emotional episodes as age increases.

What about the situation in adolescence? Here is a period traditionally considered to be fraught with stress and disturbance. G. Stanley Hall (27), over a half-century ago, stressed the rapid change and the emotional upheaval of adolescence, placing the responsibility for these disturbances and change upon biological developments. Psychoanalytic writers of today (76) similarly emphasize the stressfulness of the period and also attribute this "upheaval" to biological developments, notably to the inability of the adolescent to master and properly direct his sexual urges which have surged forth at pubescence after the sexually quiescent years of the latency period. A recent textbook in adolescence emphasizes the essential discontinuity of development (primarily biological change) in adolescence and the essential stressfulness of the period (3). Lewin (48), writing some years ago, also believed adolescence to be stressful but attributed this not so much to discontinuity in biological developments as to discontinuity in social change, notably to the rapidly expanding social world of the adolescent, which creates for him a great deal of uncertainty and ambiguity with attendant anxiety and stress. Specialists and popular opinion appear to agree on the stressfulness of this period.

The evidence is not, however, so convincing. Reference again to Figure 82 reveals no upsurge of symptoms of stress at this period. Studies of adolescence by means of the Rorschach test (29) have revealed no special indications of emotional upheaval. In a follow-up study of the same children from sixth grade through the twelfth, the vast majority denied the existence of various nervous symptoms, and age trends among the minority reporting symptoms showed no regular peak at pubescence (83). Age incidence figures for suicides and mental illness show marked increases from the early to the late teens, but there are even greater increases in the adult years. There is no adolescent peak. Another study, based on observation of the incidence of nervous symptoms at various ages, revealed no general relationship with age over the range 6 to 13 (66).

The evidence is not all one-sided, however. Some evidence is compatible with the view that adolescence is stressful, or at least has more than its share of frustration. Thus, certain Rorschach studies (30, 31) suggest that adolescents may be "more introversive and concerned with their inner urges and experience" than those younger (30). And various studies suggest that there may be more daydreaming in adolescence.[6] One investigator (82) reports observing in girls at about age 13 "behavior suggestive of emotional upheaval characterized by desultory interest in the objective environment; unorganized, unoriented activity; excessive response in the form of screaming and giggling to mild, ordinarily ineffective stimuli; and

[6] Unpublished (except in mimeographed form) item-analysis data on interests by S. L. Pressey and on personal problems by Ross L. Mooney suggest growing incidence of daydreaming in adolescence, whereas a study by Willoughby (90) suggests dropping incidence in adulthood.

excessive, egocentric interest in their own persons." Similar behavior was not observed in boys, though they were observed over the age range from 11 to 17. An early study of fingernail biting (a nervous symptom) suggested peak incidence just prior to pubescence, at about 11 for girls and 13 for boys (87) with a decline thereafter. Although this was interpreted as evidence of pubertal stress, with relaxation of strain as this period receded, a later study (52) shows no such neat relationship of fingernail biting with pubescence. The age of peak nail biting in this study occurred at about 10 years of age. Girls began to stop biting their nails at 9 years of age, the boys at 10. The present writers interpret the decline in nail biting in the years beyond 9 or 10 mainly as the elimination of an undesirable symptom of poor grooming as social interests emerge. Another investigator (79) has reported more indications of unhappiness in stories told about stimulus pictures among 20 children 15 years of age and older than among 20 children 14 years of age and under. And still another paper (81) reports that ninth- and twelfth-graders have more unpleasant and fewer pleasant experiences than do sixth-graders. In a recent investigation (64) utilizing reaction time to stimulus work, a sharp increase in reaction time to the words, "worry," "afraid," "unhappy," "restless," and "anxious," occurred at age 13 for girls and 14 for boys and stayed high until 17 (the last age sampled). Adults in the twenties showed a marked decline in reaction time. Such results suggest greater stress in the teen years.

The inconsistency of these data, as well as certain inadequacies in the studies[7] calls into question the conception of adolescence as a period of *generalized* storm and stress. Increase in anxiety and stress in adolescence seems instead to be relatively specific to certain areas of adjustment typical of the teens—family relations, ideological developments, heterosexual relations, vocational orientations. The existing data do suggest the possibility that girls may experience more generalized stress and anxiety at adolescence than do boys, a finding which would seem reasonable in view of the greater control that is maintained over their development and their resulting lag in self-reliance.

Quite aside from the generality emphasized in the last few paragraphs,

[7] Among major criticisms of these studies are the following: (1) too few cases to provide reliable normative trends, (2) failure to report adequately (or at all) data on which conclusions are based, (3) lack of comparable data on adult years necessary to provide age perspective for the adolescent findings, (4) use of stimulus materials, e. g., fantasy pictures, prepared to highlight problems of a particular age group. Actually, few if any studies have been designed specifically to test the storm and stress hypotheses.

there are undoubtedly many individual cases which are characterized by much adolescent stress. One investigator (29), who found no evidence for emotional upheaval to be associated with adolescence, did suggest that individuals who were very early or very late in reaching pubescence might be disturbed. And surely those individuals who have been over-protected and dominated to such a degree in childhood that their social life space is suddenly expanded at adolescence are likely to be disturbed by their lack of acquaintance with the broader environment and their lack of social know-how.

The whole question of adolescence obviously needs further study. In addition to research designed to measure the stressfulness of these years, investigation of the degree to which the social life space suddenly widens or sex drive suddenly increases is much needed. These are major causes of adolescent problems, according to most writers. Present evidence suggests that, on the average, social horizons widen *gradually* during childhood and adolescence (4) and that sex urges have emerged over a period of years and are not suddenly characteristic of the adolescent (43). Adjustments seem, on the average, also to be made gradually. The wide popular acceptance of the view that adolescence is especially stressful may well be due to the stress experienced by adults in their relationships with adolescent offspring. Threats to parental authority and to moral codes are likely more disturbing to parents than to the adolescent. It is a reasonable hypothesis that "adolescent stress" is to be found mainly in parents rather than in adolescents but is projected by parents into their conceptions of adolescence!

ANXIETY AND ADJUSTMENT IN MATURITY AND OLD AGE

Figure 83 summarizes data from two studies which have provided evidence relating to age trends during the adult years in adjustment. In the right-hand chart are presented the results of administering a paper-and-pencil test of "neuroticism" to adults of various ages. In this case low scores reflect better adjustment. The evidence seems to suggest an initial rise in emotional disturbance as the adjustment problems of early adult years are encountered, an improvement as these problems are solved, with a later increase in "neuroticism" as old age and its problems are approached. The left-hand chart shows the age incidence of "nervousness" as reported by a large number of adults in medical examinations. No special age trends are evident; in fact, the incidence is about the same for various age groups. This same finding was reported in another study of the age distribution of women seeking medical help for "nervousness" (28). A study of later maturity, ages 60 to over 100, revealed a slight trend over this age range toward poorer adjustment (13).

It is noteworthy that these studies were made under what might be called "typical conditions" of living. At the time of taking these tests the subjects were, presumably, exposed only to the ordinary stresses of living;

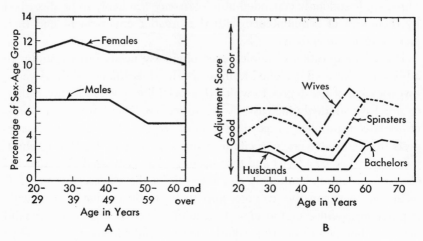

Figure 83.   The Relationship Between Age and General Adjustment as Shown by (A) The age incidence of "nervousness" revealed by medical examinations and (B) scores made by different age groups on a psychological test of adjustment. (Curves for "nervousness" adapted from R. H. Britten, Sex differences in physical impairment in adult life, Amer. J. Hygiene, 1931, 13:741–770. Curves for psychological test scores adapted from R. R. Willoughby, The relationship to emotionality of age, sex, and conjugal condition, Amer. J. Sociol., 1938, 43:920–931. By permission of the University of Chicago Press.)

presumably, things were going along reasonably well. Under such conditions relationships of adjustment with age were inconsistent from study to study, and no general statement seems warranted, at least over much of the adult age range. Three conclusions are, however, compatible with several sets of findings. First, in the later years of life, perhaps beyond 50, there does seem to be decreasing happiness and increasing symptoms of anxiety and/or maladjustment. Second, women appear to be more prone to "nervousness" and anxiety than do men. Third, the studies quite consistently dispute the frequently encountered view that the menopause is characterized by much emotional disturbance. While some individuals may experience stress because of physiological changes, psychological reasons, or both, this seems not to be the typical experience. Or at least if stress occurs, it is not sufficient to be reflected in measures such as these.

It is noteworthy that of a thousand women interviewed after the menopause was over, 90 percent had lost no time from work (16). This matter certainly warrants the attention of more carefully designed research, but at least existing data call into serious question any dogmatic assertion to the effect that the menopause (or the forties) is sufficiently stressful to cause an upsurge of anxiety.

It could well be, of course, that the impact of age upon adjustment is more evident under conditions of stress than under normal circumstances of living. This, it will be recalled, is the typical situation in physiological aging: age effects are most noticeable when the organ system is subjected to stressful loads. Psychologically, also, an older person may get along well enough in day-to-day living but evidence much anxiety and disorganization if he should lose his job or if his spouse should die. Hints that older adults might indeed be more susceptible to threat and frustration are to be found in a number of studies of personality changes with adult age. Data from the Stanford later maturity studies (57) suggested that older adults were more submissive than younger ones. Another study from the same series (78) revealed important losses in self-concept with age. A group of older professors made twice as many self-belittling comments (which were surreptitiously recorded by the investigator) than did a group of younger professors when asked to take an intelligence test during the course of an experiment. Such insecurities, probably engendered by the losses (biological and cultural) attendant upon aging, imply that if environmental stresses should increase, resulting anxiety would be greater at an older age than at a younger adult age.

This conclusion appears to be supported by other data. A British investigator (89) reported that he had difficulty persuading individuals beyond 30 to participate in a skill-learning study and that once they had participated, they showed considerable concern about the adequacy of their performance. In a study of military personnel, ages 17 to 35, conducted by one of the present writers (45) at a preëmbarkation center, the number of reported nervous symptoms increased with age to a greater degree for those men who had previously been in combat than for those whose previous military experience had been confined to the United States. It is assumed that embarkation for combat areas represents a much more stressful situation for the first group than for the second. Data for suicides and for mental illness might be interpreted as reflecting susceptibility to stress, and it is of interest that both types of data show much greater incidence of psychopathology as adult age increases. Data for suicides are available for various sex, race, social, and economic groups, and it appears that the suicide rate is greatest in those groups and at those ages where, because of external or personal pressures, the stresses of living are greatest (88). Suicide rates fluctuate with economic trends; they were higher, for example, in 1930 than in 1940, and they dropped markedly in the period after Pearl Harbor (December 7, 1941), particularly among men in the older brackets (39). This latter trend was possibly due to improved employment opportunities for the old because of war industry demands.

In total, then, the evidence suggests that increasing adult age brings with it certain losses in self-concept, in self-confidence, and in security and that under conditions of stress, increases in anxiety accompany increases in age. As will be emphasized again a few pages later, these findings lend support to the view, ventured earlier, that with increasing age there is an increasing "need" to erect defenses against the anxieties generated by losses.

EFFECTS OF EMOTIONAL STRESS AND ANXIETY

Emotional stress and anxiety have a number of effects, three of which will be discussed here. In the first place, as psychosomatic events, emotional stress and anxiety involve characteristic physiological reactions, which if long continued will have adverse effects upon physical well-being. Second, anxiety and stress will often have adverse effects upon performance and general efficiency. And third, emotional stress and anxiety, being unpleasant, will serve as a "drive" which may give rise to various types of defensive behavior or may result in constructive efforts of considerable personal, and perhaps social, significance. These types of outcome are symptomatic of the presence of anxiety or emotional stress and thus of the existence of frustration or conflict.

In the first place, when a person is reacting emotionally, a number of physiological changes occur: the heart rate increases; adrenalin is secreted into the blood stream; blood sugar is released, permitting greater energy expenditure; blood is pumped to the skeletal muscles rather than to the internal organs; the digestive processes are slowed or stopped; perspiration, especially in the palms, is apt to occur; a general state of excitement develops, and muscular tension increases. Such changes reflect an exceedingly complex state which may have far-reaching effects, particularly if they persist over any considerable time. And, unfortunately, some people continue in such a state (and wear themselves down) because of their inability either to solve a problem directly, to escape it, or to develop substitute solutions. Some people become so conditioned that they are constantly anticipating difficulties and thus keep themselves in an almost continuous state of apprehension or anxiety with the accompanying physiological disturbances.

Continued emotional stress will have important effects upon health. If digestion is slowed or stopped for any length of time, digestive disturbances will obviously ensue. In fact, gastrointestinal disturbances (vomiting, lack of appetite, diarrhea, constipation) are major symptoms of emotional tenseness. Stomach ulcers appear more frequently among tense, nervous individuals, and cure is hastened by the solution of the tension-causing problem (as making a decision or getting out of the tension-producing situation instead of worrying). Headaches may result from stress, and muscular tenseness coupled with sleeplessness may produce marked fatigue. The person under chronic frustration and emotional stress is very apt to become "run down." While these physiological consequences of continued tension (headaches, digestive disturbances) may have adjustive value for the individual—that is, they may be capitalized on as a means of attention-getting or escape from an undesirable situation—they may be thought of as almost *direct* end results of the physiological tensions created by continued anxiety or emotion.

Emotional stress and anxiety will also show themselves in inefficiency and flightiness. Shifts in moods, instability, and unpredictability are apt to characterize the individual under stress. In work records in business and industry these reactions show up in inconsistency of performance and lowered efficiency (17, 55). Anxious subjects or subjects under stress do less well on such tasks commonly found on intelligence tests as digit-symbol substitution (53) and digit recall (58). In one interesting study, the impact of mounting failure experiences on the performance of insecure, maladjusted children on intelligence tests was demonstrated. Two pairs of matched groups, one pair poorly adjusted, one well adjusted, were studied. One group of each pair responded to the Stanford-Binet scale under standard conditions where the tasks get increasingly difficult, and frustration and stress presumably mount, and the other group responded under "adjusted conditions" in which tasks of different degrees of difficulty were interspersed so as to yield occasional success experiences. The results, shown in Table 44, indicated that the maladjusted group (presumably more anxious) which performed under the more stressful condition was substantially handicapped compared with its control, whereas the well-adjusted groups did equally well under both conditions.

As previously noted, anxiety and emotional stress are unpleasant, often actually painful, and are to be avoided. These conditions thus serve as a strong motive force or drive. Much of the striving for achievement and the general drive for social learning probably derive from culturally engendered anxieties or fears—fear of "failure," of being "looked down

TABLE 44.   IQ Ratings of Matched Groups Compared for "Adaptive" and "Consecutive" Methods of Testing

Type of Group	Consecutive Method		Adaptive Method	
	N	Mean	N	Mean
Very well adjusted	33	109.6	33	110.4
Very poorly adjusted	24	91.7	24	102.7

SOURCE: Adapted from M. L. Hutt, A clinical study of "consecutive" and "adaptive" testing, J. Consult. Psychol., 1947, 11:93–103.

on," of doing an inappropriate act, of incurring the displeasure of parents or others through violation of cultural taboos.[8] Anxiety may be the source of important constructive efforts leading to such ends as the achievement of educational goals and notable vocational accomplishments. Important developments in personality improvement may result because a high degree of anxiety stemming from maladjustment may lead (or force) the person to seek counseling or therapeutic help, and thus anxiety may give rise to constructive efforts to achieve better adjustment. Such efforts are constructive in the sense that they alter the conditions (either in the individual or in the external environment) which create the emotional stress or the anxiety. Anxiety may also give rise to adjustive behavior that serves mainly as ego defenses which operate only to reduce, or partially reduce, the anxiety, but which do little or nothing to alter or eliminate the objective causes of the anxiety. Thus, anxious individuals seem to take extreme positions when asked to make judgments (50), as though in ambiguous situations they achieve a degree of security by overstructuring the situation. Under stress designed to create anxiety, according to another study (74), subjects prematurely structured a series of ambiguous pictures. In general, anxious subjects or subjects under stress appear to be more rigid, perhaps achieving a certain security by inflexible behavior.

The similarities between differences in behavior between anxious and

[8] For an excellent discussion of the role of anxiety in personality development and socialization of the adolescent, see Davis (18).

nonanxious subjects, of the types noted above, and differences in behavior and personality between young and old adults are too great, it seems to the present writers, to be dismissed as a coincidence. As noted a few pages ago, older and younger adults are also differentiated in terms of the degree of anxiety or insecurity generated by stress. Such findings support further the hypothesis advanced at several points in this book that many of the adult age differences in personality and performance may be due in part to the increasing anxiety growing out of the threats posed by social and physical losses.

Constructive Adjustments Reduce Stress

At several points in this chapter, certain constructive suggestions were given as to how to deal with the particular emotional reactions under consideration. But mainly, the chapter thus far has been concerned with general age patterns—through childhood, adolescence, and adult years—in the extent of various types of emotional reactions, the manner of their expression, and the particular types of situations which seemed to generate emotional reactions at different ages. The emotional reactions discussed have been those that have grown out of frustration or threat. It is suggested, in concluding the chapter, that recognition of the types of frustrating conditions that generate anxiety and stress and awareness of general constructive modes of adjustment may enable an individual to reduce somewhat his own tensions and stresses or arrange things to help other people to do so.

CONDITIONS THAT TYPICALLY FRUSTRATE

Consideration of the various difficulties people have in meeting their needs leads to the conclusion that the conditions which thwart them are often of four types: (1) biological or organic deficiencies, whether innate or environmentally induced—deficiencies such as dullness of intellect and physical or health shortcomings, (2) inadequate or inappropriate habits and skills, (3) environmental lacks or hazards, and (4) conflicts between opposing or incompatible motives. Identification of the need being frustrated and the frustrating circumstance is an obvious first step in the elimination of the accompanying emotional stress.

In the first place, biological deficiencies represent a source of difficulty: it frequently happens that people have aspirations beyond their intellectual or physical ability or are handicapped in their efforts by physical conditions or appearances that either constitute disabling limitations in themselves or are evaluated by others (employers or social associates) in such a way as to represent very real limitations. Such factors are important at all ages. In childhood, the weak or undersized individual is apt to be frustrated in normal childhood play, a competitive means to social acceptance. In adolescence, physical unattractiveness may handicap in heterosexual relationships, or inadequate intellectual capacity may result in failure to be admitted to a professional school of one's choice. During young adult years, sterility may prevent fulfillment of a strong desire for children. As age increases, a slowing down and loss of physical resiliency, a decline in sensory acuities, or declining sexual capacity may necessitate the giving up of highly valued activities, or at least a reduction in capacity to perform as adequately as one might wish. Indeed, one of the major readjustments that must be made in aging is that of accepting the limitations (and appropriately adjusting expectations and aspirations) of physical changes which begin to impose limits.

Second, inadequate habits and skills may be as real a handicap (though often more subject to remediations) as are physical shortcomings. Examples can be drawn from all phases of life. The first-grader who has not developed habits of self-reliance is overwhelmed by the complex social situations in which he finds himself. The physics student with inadequate mathematics background is handicapped by that fact. Adolescence is often defined as a transition period of many "firsts." This means simply that the adolescent is finding himself in situations for which the skills and habits already in his possession fail to equip him. The naïve college girl who is overwhelmed because she has been kissed and the naïve bride who knows nothing about sex are both frustrated by their naïveté. The middle-aged housewife whose children have left home may not have the resources in habit and skills (interests, hobbies, and the like) to enable her to fill her new leisure, and the retired 65-year-old man may find himself in exactly the same situation.

The fact of rapid cultural change, described in an earlier chapter, poses special problems in adult years. It is apparent that a rapidly changing culture, economic and otherwise, means that the adult cannot find for himself a niche and expect to remain there for the rest of his life. He will almost of necessity meet situations for which he is not equipped and will be required to learn appropriate methods of dealing with them. Moreover, and especially is this true in professional areas, development of theory, factual knowledge, and techniques may have been so rapid that the average 40- or 50-year-old specialist may find himself overshadowed in quality of training and general competence by the young man recently finished with his professional training. This difference in training and knowledge imposes a very real threat not only psychologically but actually, for example, when it comes to changes in employment.

In the third place, a great many environmental circumstances make the satisfaction of motives difficult or impossible, thus constituting frustrating circumstances. Such sources of frustration may be material, spatial, or social. Lack of funds for an adolescent date, for a college education, for an appropriate house for one's children, for support of aged parents, or indeed for one's own economic security in old age represent types of frustration due to environmental circumstances. Parents' refusal to grant freedom of decision to the adolescent, a teacher's sarcastic reprimand, a spouse's display of temper, or society's economic chaos represent social aspects of the environment that are frustrating to individuals. Some are broadly cultural in origin. Indeed, some of the most frustrating circumstances that exist in human development are those imposed by the culture. It has been said that the major frustrations of adolescence are those resulting from the taboos of society upon sexual behavior and from the failure of society to grant adolescents the status of adults. Cultural norms and cultural biases may be similarly frustrating in adult years, as in the case of single women who find most recreation requiring a male escort, or the 45-year-old job-seeker who is considered too old by potential employers, or the vigorous, intellectually competent scientist who finds himself retired at 65. All are experiencing frustration growing out of environmental conditions.

Fourth, and finally, adjustment problems may result because of the incompatability of simultaneously operating motives. A typical adolescent conflict is that between his desire to be a "good fellow" and to follow the crowd, on one hand, and a desire, on the other hand, to adhere to the standards of conduct learned at home which may declare drinking, smoking, and petting to be moral wrongs. Or the case of the 40-year-old man who is dissatisfied with his work and wants to get into a new field before it is too late, but who, on the other hand, is afraid to risk economic security which he now possesses in order to protect the welfare of his children. Oftentimes, choices must be made between two opposing, or at least mutually exclusive, goals. The college student may be faced with the decision as to whether to be married or to complete his education, both goals representing positive attraction. Or the decison may lie between two negative "musts" or risks, as in the case of a child who must take punishment or perform an unpleasant chore. Or the problem of choice lies in a decision that has both positive and negative features. Thus, a particular job adds security but little opportunity for advancement. Almost any major life decision involves to some degree a conflict of goals, purposes, or values. The difficulty becomes more intense when the opposing motives are strong and nearly equal in strength.

CONSTRUCTIVE HANDLING OF FRUSTRATION

Fortunately, a rather direct attack upon these various categories of frustrating conditions offers much hope for the reduction of human frustration and the promotion of greater happiness and better adjustment. Many social institutions and agencies, as well as individuals, are devoting time, money, and energy to this purpose. The substantial contributions of medical science and practice to the reduction of health and physical handicaps are noteworthy. "Human engineering" efforts can adapt machinery to people in such a way that declining physical capacity or various physical handicaps become less important in work efficiency. Educational efforts—formal and informal—promote the development of skills and understandings which permit easier adjustment and also help reduce biases in the culture which handicap various groups, such as older age groups. Specially planned "refresher courses" can assist the older professional man whose training has become outdated.

Guidance and counseling programs, in schools and in various non-school agencies, help in making job choices and plans which are better related to abilities, thus reducing frustrations due to inadequate ability. Psychological and psychiatric therapy facilities are becoming increasingly available for more difficult cases of adjustment and offer help especially in reconciling conflicting motives and values and providing means of emotional reëducation as a means of reducing anxiety and maladjustive behavior. There seems to be an increasing realistic attitude in society toward the satisfaction of basic needs. For example, career training and marriage are no longer viewed as completely incompatible. Colleges instead of terminating the enrollment of students who marry, as was true relatively few years ago, now often provide apartments for married students in the college housing program. In short, once types of frustrating conditions are identified, much can be done by a realistic society and by individuals to reduce their seriousness.

Constructive dealing with frustration on the part of individuals (in contrast to social efforts outlined above) requires first the development of a certain tolerance of bothersome and thwarting circumstances and, secondly, a degree of skill in intelligent solution of problems. By "frustration tolerance" is meant the individual's capacity to withstand frustration without resorting to inadequate modes of adjustment (68), p. 385). *Below* a particular point, an individual may be inadequate because tensions do not build up sufficiently to motivate him to do anything about a situation, i. e., initiate appropriate behavior, whereas *above* his particular range of tolerance of stress, inadequacy may manifest itself in disorganization and anxiety. Ability to tolerate frustration is one of the marks of maturity.

Developmental changes in ability to tolerate frustration have not been studied over the life span. As the gain in the ability to handle aggression already mentioned suggests, positive advances are likely made through childhood and adolescence in tolerance of frustration, and probably there are further gains well into the middle years. Gradual achievement of status and security in adult years, together with increasing experience with human behavior and with the inevitability of certain frustrations, likely results in a certain mellowing and acceptance in middle and later years. In still later years, when threats to status increase and energies ebb, there may be a decline in ability to tolerate conditions that earlier would be taken in stride.

Constructive adjustments available to the individual are of two types. First are those responses that adequately alter the environment in such a way as better to fit the capacities, interests, and personality of the person. Changing a course or a job or finding a more congenial social group are examples of fitting the environment to the individual. Second are those alterations in the individual himself which have the effect of voiding the frustrating circumstances by, for example, the establishment of substitute goals, reduced level of aspiration, or changed values which permit the person psychologically to accept his situation or to develop the skills and knowledge which permit successful dealing with the frustrating situation.

Although psychotherapy, counseling, or other types of attitude-changing experiences may be the means of accomplishing such changes in the individual, many constructive adjustments (such as discovery of alternate methods of reaching a goal or working out of substitute goals) are achieved through objective consideration of the problem in an effort to discover solutions. It is likely that in the case of most people, the intellectual solution of problems is anything but systematic, partly because of lack of knowledge as to *how* to think and partly because of insufficient experience in objective thinking. But thoughtful problem solving is further handicapped by habits of thinking in already established patterns or within already established limits or by emotional biases and prejudices that obscure important aspects of the problem and blind one to some of the possible solutions. Educational programs have largely neglected the task of teaching youngsters *to think;* yet they have much to offer in developing skill in this fundamental method of constructively dealing with frustration.

Summary

Objective consideration of developmental trends in disorganizing types of emotions, notably anger and fear, is mainly useful as a means of identifying possibly "critical" phases of the life course for more detailed research and analysis and as a means of spotting the particular types of problems that characterize succeeding ages—all of this to the end that constructive measures may be taken by society (through means of education, for example) or by individuals to reduce some of the stresses of living. Oftentimes, too, examination of developmental trends in anxieties and fears and overall tensions may yield negative findings, an important first step in dispelling popular misconceptions of "ages of crisis." It is commonplace that people are more likely to experience problems if they *expect* them to occur! What, in summary, has the material of this chapter shown?

1. During the very early years of life various types of emotional reactions become differentiated out of the generalized state of excitement which characterizes the "emotional expression" of the very young infant. Maturational changes and broadening experience contribute to emotional growth and widen the range of stimuli capable of eliciting emotional reactions and the types of responses available. As youngsters learn how to manage the situations they encounter and/or to control overt expression in conformity with social expectation, the incidence of emotional reactions declines. Further maturational changes during the middle and later adult years may reduce capacity to deal effectively with one's environment and thus generate new fears.

2. Anger is an emotionalized reaction to frustration that usually involves aggression, either directed toward the frustrating agent or displaced onto some other person or object. In general, evidence suggests that, at least insofar as overt behavior is concerned, aggressive tendencies come under increasingly better control as the child matures and as the adult accumulates years. Presumably, such a trend results from increasing ability to handle frustrating situations successfully, partly by learning to avoid them or by "outgrowing" them, and as a result of the development of a certain frustration tolerance as the person becomes more sophisticated and recognizes the inevitability of certain frustrations and the futility and personal expense of anger reaction. Means of "control" of anger include reducing the degree of restrictions imposed upon others; tolerance and acceptance of anger responses in others, partly through understanding of the dynamics of anger; setting standards for others that lie within their potential grasp; and meeting anger situations not with anger, which leads mainly to mounting reciprocal aggression, but with a calm, objective attitude. Teaching of skills which permit successful mastery of a situation reduces frustration and hence anger. It is of some interest that "other people," either personally or through institutions, represent the most frequent cause of anger episodes.

3. An analysis of the fears and anxieties of various ages reveals that each age tends to have its own set of "adjustment areas," in the sense that certain types of situations tend to generate more fears, worry, or anxiety at some ages than at others. Thus, early childhood is characterized by fear

of many remote and improbable events; worries and anxieties are generated in adolescence with special reference to heterosexual relations; the thirties and forties bring health problems and frustration of hopes and ambitions. Here lie focal points for action planned to ease these adjustments. Parents and schools might well take cognizance of such data in planning the kinds of experiences they will provide for children, and farsighted individuals might well take their own precautions by eliminating in advance, insofar as is possible, the conditions or personal deficiencies that make those situations anxiety laden.

4. Attempts to evaluate the overall stressfulness of various age periods have agreed mainly in showing women to be more prone to anxiety than men and the years of early childhood and the later years of life to involve more worry and concerns than the earlier or middle adult years. Strangely enough—in view of theoretical expectations, clinical experience, and popular opinion—neither adolescence nor menopause stands out as a period of high anxiety or stress. Mainly, the data are inadequate for sound conclusions, and more research is clearly called for; in the meantime, dogmatic assertions, with all the attendant dangers of engendering anxiety where perhaps none or little need be, regarding the stressfulness of these periods are not warranted.

5. But the data underlying the last summary point have mainly been collected under normal circumstances of living, conditions under which anxiety is usually well controlled. Evidence is beginning to accumulate which rather consistently suggests that *under stress* individuals from perhaps 30 onward become increasingly prone to anxiety and increasingly show evidences of insecurity. This general insecurity which possibly is generated by the threats of aging (physical and social losses) may well be responsible, in part, for a variety of adult age changes in personality and performance, a hypothesis which gains some support from studies which show anxious and nonanxious subjects to differ in many of the same ways in which younger and older adults differ.

6. Again and again, the literature relating to the disorganizing emotions emphasizes the importance of learning how to deal effectively with frustrating situations as a means of eliminating the accompanying emotional stress. In this connection, efforts to identify the typical kinds of frustrating circumstances may be a helpful first step. It has been suggested that, in general, frustrating circumstances may be grouped in four categories: (1) organic deficiencies, (2) inadequate or inappropriate habits and skills, (3) environmental lacks and hazards, and (4) conflicts

among motives or desires. Correction of health and physical shortcomings may alleviate the first; appropriate educational programs, both formal and informal, may help solve the second; objective consideration of the total situation may suggest means of solving environmental lacks and blocks; weighing of one's own purposes and values may help in arriving at decisions which reduce the conflicts between desires. Often, mature, reasonably well-adjusted individuals have the capacity to work out such problems through their own resources. But, increasingly, services are being provided which can assist the individual in this process, and even well-adjusted individuals may find those services helpful. Basically, better adjustments are made by seeking a situation (job, marriage) suited to one's capacities and personality or by altering oneself in such a way as to better fit and more effectively deal with the situation as it is. The latter may involve learning new skills, altering (often lowering) one's goals and aspirations, and, more complexly and in more difficult instances, taking steps to alter in more fundamental ways basic personality make-up. Increasingly, psychological and psychiatric services are becoming available to aid in thus dealing with basic personality issues.

BIBLIOGRAPHY

1. Anastasi, Anne, Cohen, N., and Spatz, D., A study of fear and anger in college students through the controlled diary method, *J. Genet. Psychol.* 1948, 73:243–249.
2. Arsenian, Jean M., Young children in an insecure situation, *J. Abnorm. and Soc. Psychol.*, 1943, 38:225–249.
3. Ausubel, D. P., *Theory and Problems of Adolescent Development,* New York, Grune and Stratton, 1954.
4. Barker, R. G., and Wright, H. F., *Midwest and Its Children: The Psychological Ecology of an American Town,* Evanston (Illinois), Row, Peterson, 1955.
5. Beach, F. A., *Hormones and Behavior,* New York, Hoeber, 1948.
6. Bell, J., Psychological aspects of dental treatment of children. Unpublished Ph.D. dissertation, Teachers College, Columbia University, 1940.
7. Blatz, W. E., Chant, S. N. F., and Salter, M. D., Emotional episodes in the child of school age, *University of Toronto Studies in Child Development,* 1937, Series No. 9.
8. Bonar, H. S., High school pupils list their anxieties, *School Rev., 1942,* 50:512–515.
9. Bridges, K. M. B., Emotional development in early infancy, *Child Development,* 1932, 3:324–334.
10. Britten, R. H., Sex differences in physical impairment in adult life, *Amer. J. Hygiene,* 1931, 13:741–770.

11. Caille, R. K., Resistant behavior of preschool children, *Child Development Monogr.*, 1933, No. 11.

12. Cason, H., Common annoyances: a psychological study of every-day aversions and annoyances. *Psychol. Monogr.*, 1930, Vol. 40, No. 2.

13. Cavan, R. S., Burgess, E. W., Havighurst, R. J., and Goldhammer, H., *Personal Adjustment in Old Age*, Chicago, Science Research Associates, 1949.

14. Closson, J. H., and Hildreth, H. M., Experiment in psychotherapy during selection examination, *U.S. Naval Medical Bull.*, 1944, 43:39–43.

15. Conrad, H. S., and Jones, H. E., Some results from an "Annoyance Inventory" in a cumulative study of adolescents, *Psychol. Bull.*, 1942, 39:475.

16. Council of Medical Women's Federation, Committee Report, An investigation of the menopause in one thousand women, *Lancet*, 1933 (1), 224: 106–108.

17. Culpin, M., and Smith, M., The nervous temperament, *Brit. Industrial Health Research Board, Report No. 61*, 1930.

18. Davis, A., Socialization and adolescent personality, in National Society for the Study of Education, *43rd Yearbook, Adolescence*, Pt. I, 1944. Chap. 11, pp. 198–216.

19. Dollard, J., *et al.*, *Frustration and Aggression*, New Haven, Yale University Press, 1939.

20. Dykman, R. A., Heimann, E. K., and Kerr, W. A., Lifetime worry patterns of three diverse adult cultural groups, *J. Soc. Psychol.* 1952, 35:91–100.

21. Gates, G. S., An observational study of anger, *J. Exper. Psychol.*, 1926, 9:325–336.

22. Goodenough, Florence L., *Anger in Young Children*, Minneapolis, University of Minnesota Press, 1931.

23. Goodenough, Florence L., Expression of the emotions in a blind-deaf child, *J. Abnorm. and Soc. Psychol.*, 1932, 27:328–333.

24. Green, E. H., Friendships and quarrels among pre-school children. *Child Development*, 1937, 8:343–350.

25. Hagman, R. R., A study of fears of children of preschool age, *J. Exper. Educ.*, 1932, 1:110–130.

26. Hall, C. S., Temperament: a survey of animal studies, *Psychol. Bull.*, 1941, 38:909–943.

27. Hall, G. S., *Adolescence* (2 vols.), New York, Appleton-Century-Crofts, 1904.

28. Hamilton, G. V., Changes in personality and psychosexual phenomena with age, in Cowdry, E. V. (ed.), *Problems of Ageing* (2nd ed.), Baltimore, Williams and Wilkins, 1942, Chap. 30, pp. 810–831.

29. Hertz, Marguerite R., Evaluation of the Rorschach method in its application to normal childhood and adolescence, *Character and Personal.*, 1941–1942, 10:151–162.

30. Hertz, Marguerite R., and Baker, Elizabeth, Personality patterns in

adolescence as portrayed by the Rorschach ink-blot method: II. The color factors, *J. Gen. Psychol.*, 1943, 28:3–61.

31. Hertzman, M., and Margulies, H., Developmental changes as reflected in Rorschach Test responses, *J. Genet. Psychol.*, 1943, 62:189–215.

32. Hutt, M. L., A clinical study of "consecutive" and "adaptive" testing, *J. Consult. Psychol.*, 1947, 11:93–103.

33. Jersild, A. T., Emotional development, in Carmichael, L. (ed.), *Manual of Child Psychology* (1st ed.), Wiley, 1946, Chap. 15, pp. 752–790.

34. Jersild, A. T., Emotional development, in Carmichael, L. (ed.), *Manual of Child Psychology* (2nd ed.), Wiley, 1954, Chap. 14, pp. 833–917.

35. Jersild, A. T., and Holmes, F. B. *Children's Fears*, New York, Teachers College, Columbia University, 1935.

36. Jersild, A. T., and Markey, F. V., Conflicts between pre-school children, *Child Development Monogr.*, 1935, No. 21.

37. Jersild, A. T., Markey, F. V., and Jersild, C. L., Children's fears, dreams, wishes, daydreams, likes, dislikes, pleasant and unpleasant memories, New York, Teachers College, Columbia University, *Child Development Monogr.*, 1933, No. 12.

38. Jones, H. E., and Mary C., A study of fear, *Childhood Education*, 1928, 5:136–143.

39. Jones, H. E., and Kaplan, O. J., Psychological aspects of mental disorders in later life, in Kaplan, O. J. (ed.), *Mental Disorders in Later Life*, Stanford University Press, 1945, Chap. 4, pp. 69–115.

40. Keister, M. E., The behavior of young children in failure: an experimental attempt to discover and to modify undesirable responses of preschool children to failure, *University of Iowa Studies in Child Welfare*, 1938, 14: 27–82.

41. Keister, M. E., and Updegraff, R. A., Study of children's reactions to failure and an experimental attempt to modify them, *Child Development*, 1937, 8:241–248.

42. Kerr, W. A., Newman, H. L., and Sadewic, A. R., Lifetime worry patterns of American psychologists, *J. Consult. Psychol.*, 1949, 13:377–380.

43. Kinsey, A. C., *et al.*, *Sexual Behavior in the Human Female*, Philadelphia, W. B. Saunders, 1953.

44. Klineberg, O., *Social Psychology*, New York, Henry Holt, 1940.

45. Kuhlen, R. G., Nervous symptoms among military personnel as related to age, combat experience, and marital status, *J. Consult. Psychol.*, 1951, 15:320–324.

46. Landis, C., Studies of emotional reactions: II. General behavior and facial expression in emotions, *J. Gen. Psychol.*, 1924, 2:59–72.

47. Landis, C., and Hunt, W., *The Startle Pattern*, New York, Farrar and Rinehart, 1939.

48. Lewin, K., Field theory and experiment in social psychology, *Amer. J. Sociol.*, 1939, 44:868–896.

49. Lewin, K., Lippitt, R., and White, R. K., Patterns of aggressive behavior

in experimentally created "social climates," *J. Soc. Psychol.*, 1939, *10*:271–299.

50. Lewis, Nan A., and Taylor, Janet A., Anxiety and extreme response preference, *Educ. and Psychol. Meas.*, 1955, *15*:111–116.

51. Maccoby, Eleanor E., and Gibbs, Patricia K., Methods of child-rearing in two social classes, in Coladarci, A. P. (ed.), *Educational Psychology: A Book of Readings*, New York, Dryden Press, 1955, pp. 97–121.

52. Malone, A. J., and Massler, M., Index of nailbiting in children, *J. Abnorm. and Soc. Psychol.*, 1952, *47*:193–202.

53. Mandler, G., and Sarason, S. B., A study of anxiety and learning, *J. Abnorm. and Soc. Psychol.*, 1952, *47*:166–173.

54. Marsh, C. J., The worries of college women, *J. Soc. Psychol.*, 1942, *15*:335–339.

55. Mayo, E., *The Human Problems of an Industrial Civilization*, New York, Macmillan, 1933.

56. Meltzer, H., Students' adjustments in anger, *J. Soc. Psychol.*, 1933, *4*: 285–309.

57. Miles, W. R., Age and human society, in Murchison, Carl (ed.), *Handbook of Social Psychology*, Worcester, Clark University Press, 1935, Chap. 15, pp. 596–682.

58. Moldawsky, S., and P. C., Digit span as an anxiety indicator, *J. Consult. Psychol.*, 1952, *16*:115–118.

59. Mooney, R., Surveying high-school students' problems by means of a problem check list, *Educ. Res. Bull.*, 1942, *21*:57–69.

60. Morgan, Christine M., The attitudes and adjustments of recipients of old age assistance in upstate and metropolitan New York, *Archives of Psychol.*, 1937, No. 214.

61. Muste, Myra J., and Sharpe, Doris F., Some influential factors in the determination of aggressive behavior in preschool children, *Child Development*, 1947, *18*:11–28.

62. Pollak, O., *Criminality of Women*, Philadelphia, University of Pennsylvania Press, 1950.

63. Pope, Charlotte, Personal problems of high school pupils, *School and Society*, 1943, *57*:443–448.

64. Powell, M., Age and sex differences in degree of conflict within certain areas of psychological adjustment, *Psychol. Monogr.*, 1955, Vol. 69, No. 387.

65. Pratt, K. C., Nelson, A. K., and Sun, K. H., The behavior of the newborn infant, *Ohio State University Studies, Contributions to Psychology*, 1930, No. 10.

66. Olson, W. C., *The Measurement of Nervous Habits in Normal Children*, Minneapolis, University of Minnesota Press, 1929.

67. Radke, Marian J., The relation of parental authority to children's behavior and attitudes, *University of Minnesota, Institute of Child Welfare Monogr.*, 1946, No. 22.

68. Rosenzweig, S., An outline of frustration theory, in Hunt, J. McV. (ed.), *Personality and the Behavior Disorders,* New York, Ronald Press, 1944, Vol. I, Chap. 11, pp. 378–388.

69. Scott, J. P., Fredericson, E., and Fuller, J. L., Experimental exploration of the critical period hypothesis, *Personal.,* 1951, *1*:162–183.

70. Sears, Pauline S., Doll play aggression in normal young children: influence of sex, age, sibling status, father's absence, *Psychol. Monogr.,* 1951, Vol. 65, No. 323.

71. Sharp, Delia L., Group and individual profiles in the Association-Motor test, Pt. III, pp. 97–196, in *Studies in Emotional Development, University of Iowa Studies in Child Welfare,* 1938, Vol. 15, No. 1.

72. Sherman, M., The differentiation of emotional responses in infants: I. Judgments of emotional responses from motion picture views and from actual observation, *J. Com. Psychol.,* 1927, *7*:265–284.

73. Slater, E., Beckwith, R., and Behnke, L., Studies from the center for Research in Child Health and Development, School of Public Health, Harvard University: II. Types, levels, and irregularities of response to a nursery school situation of forty children observed with special reference to the home environment, *Monogr. of the Society for Research in Child Development,* 1939, No. 4.

74. Smock, C. D., The influence of psychological stress on the "intolerance of ambiguity," *J. Abnorm. and Soc. Psychol.,* 1955, *50*:177–182.

75. Sollenberger, R. T., Some relationships between the urinary excretion of male hormone by maturing boys and their expressed interests and attitudes, *J. Psychol.,* 1940, *9*:179–189.

76. Spiegel, L. A., A review of contributions to a psychoanalytic theory of adolescence, pp. 375–393 in Vol. 6, *Psychoanalytic Studies of the Child,* New York, International Universities Press, 1951.

77. Stockard, C. R., Genetic and endocrinic bases for differences in form and behavior as elucidated by studies of contrasted pure-line dog breeds and their hybrids, *American Anatomical Memoirs,* 1941, No. 19.

78. Sward, K., Age and mental ability in superior men, *Amer. J. Psychol.,* 1945, *58*:443–479.

79. Symonds, P. M., Inventory of themes in adolescent fantasy, *Amer. J. Orthopsychiat.,* 1945, *15*:318–328.

80. Taylor, J. H., Innate emotional responses in infants, *Ohio State University Studies, Contributions to Psychology,* 1934, *12*:69–81.

81. Thompson, G. G., and Kepler, M. O., A study of the production of pleasant and unpleasant items as related to adolescent development, *J. Educ. Psychol.,* 1945, *36*:535–542.

82. Tryon, C. M., Evaluations of adolescent personality by adolescents, *Monogr. of the Society for Research in Child Development,* 1939, Vol. 4, No. 4.

83. Tryon, C. M., *U C Inventory I, Social and Emotional Adjustment. Revised form for Presentation of the Cumulative Record for an Individual,*

with *Group Norms for a Seven-Year Period,* Berkeley, University of California, Institute of Child Welfare, 1939.

84. Van Zelst, R. H., and Kerr, W. A., Reported lifetime worry experiences of Illinois building trades union leaders, *Personnel Psychol.,* 1951, 4:151–159.

85. Watson, J. B., *Psychology from the Standpoint of a Behaviorist,* Philadelphia, Lippincott, 1919.

86. Watson, J. B., and Rayner, R., Conditioned emotional reactions, *J. Exper. Psychol.,* 1920, 3:1–14.

87. Wechsler, D., The incidence and significance of fingernail biting, *Psychoanal. Rev.,* 1931, 18:201–209.

88. Weiss, J. M. A., Suicide: an epidemiologic analysis, *Psychiat. Quart.,* 1954, 28:225–252.

89. Welford, A. T., *Skill and Age,* London, Oxford University Press, 1951.

90. Willoughby, R. R., The relationship to emotionality of age, sex, and conjugal condition, *Amer. J. Sociol.,* 1938, 43:920–931.

CHAPTER 9 .

. Satisfactions in Life Activities: General Interests and Recreation

THE last chapter concerned various unpleasant tensions. What, now, of pleasures and satisfactions, trends in happiness and zest for living, and sources of greatest happiness experiences and deepest satisfactions? As will be noted shortly, the more basic satisfactions are found in social relationships, in marriage and family living, and in work life. These topics thus warrant special attention, and separate chapters have been devoted to them.

But during nonwork hours and in the course of family and social relations people engage in a wide variety of recreational and other activities. Understanding of such activities will enhance understanding of psychological development and adjustment, and perhaps suggest points of improvement. In the things people do *because they want to,* they reveal themselves, their personality, their motives, and their modes of adjustment. Moreover, since interests (e. g., movies, radio, TV) indicate stimuli to which people of different ages habitually expose themselves, they suggest media of communication best suited for reaching and influencing various groups and types of appeals that may be helpful as first steps in attracting interest to new activities, as, for example, in school. But perhaps most important are the implications that broad and constructive interest and activity patterns have for individuals themselves in their continuing good adjustment. Not only do varied interests add zest to life, but they provide alternative avenues of satisfaction and fulfillment when the usual avenues (such as job) are no longer available. And as leisure time increases, it is probable that basic satisfactions will, more and more, have to be found in nonwork activities.

372

Happiness and Basic Satisfactions in Life: Overall Perspective

A first question concerns general age trends in happiness. Although, at best, ratings of own happiness are but crude measures of general adjustment and satisfaction in living, they do provide a certain overall judgment, necessarily subjective because happiness *is* subjective. When adults are asked to look back over their lives and indicate the happiest period of several possible choices, they most frequently select young adulthood (ages 25 to 40), as Table 45 shows. In another study, the results of which are not shown in this table, adult subjects were asked to rate their happiness at all ages by charting happiness on an age line. Their ratings agreed essentially with the findings in Table 45, highest

TABLE 45. Percentages of Individuals Over 65 Who, in Retrospect, Designated Various Periods of Life as Happiest

	New York Sample (Morgan)	Iowa Sample (Landis)[a]
Childhood (5–15 years)	14.5	11.1
Youth (15–25 years)	18.9	19.3
Young adulthood (25–45 years)	49.1	51.4
Middle age (45–60 years)	12.4	5.8
Later life (60 and up)	5.1	4.7
Undecided or no data	—	7.7
Number of cases	370	450

[a] Exact figures were provided by Dr. Landis in a personal communication.

SOURCE: The data are from the following two studies: J. T. Landis, What is the happiest period of life? *School and Society*, 1942, 55:643–645; M. Morgan, The attitudes and adjustments of recipients of old age assistance in upstate and metropolitan New York, *Archives of Psychol.*, 1937, No. 214, 30:131.

average ratings being assigned to the 25 to 29 age range (*46*). The status of young adulthood as the period of highest average happiness in all of these studies probably derives from the fact that two events (frequently the happiest events of life)—marriage and birth of children—tend to be concentrated in these years. According to still another study, beyond the age of 60 the average trend in zest for living is steadily downward, with increasing proportions showing a lack of interest in life (*13*).

Differences among individuals are, of course, great. Thus, in Table 45, about a third indicated that childhood or youth had been happiest, and 5 percent indicated that, for them, the years beyond 60 were the happiest. Various groups may also be expected to vary in significant ways. In one of the studies summarized in Table 45, about two-thirds of the single individuals reported "youth" to be the happiest years, though only about a third of the total group thought these years most outstanding (52). In one of the other studies, highest happiness was not reached by single women until after the peak for married individuals, though they rated childhood and youth as happier than did the married individuals (46). Apparently having missed the happy experiences in marriage and birth of children, they did not achieve highest happiness until they became re-oriented in life purpose and found satisfactions in occupation. Presumably, other broad categories of individuals (economic groups) might experience greatest happiness and fruition at various periods. One investigator has noted that the psychological curve of life in the case of "mental" workers reaches a high point later than the curve of those whose success depends mainly on physical factors (10). Presumably, average happiness trends, too, may vary between those groups who differ in age of peak success.

What are the major sources of happiness? Presumably, they are those conditions which satisfy basic motives. When people are asked this question, in one way or other, they are likely to identify and describe not general persisting conditions, but outstanding events and episodes. Such facts nonetheless provide some insight, especially when contrasts are made between age, sex, and other groups. Table 46 contains facts relative to childhood and adolescence. In this study, youngsters were asked to describe "one of the happiest days" of their lives. Younger children more frequently mentioned a holiday or festive occasion, probably because at these times they received special attention or gifts. Older children placed more emphasis upon pleasure connected with self-discovery and self-realization, upon occasions when they were made aware of favorable aspects of their own qualities and achievements. They seemed to get more pleasure from self-improvement experience. Girls, as might be expected in view of their greater affiliation needs, more frequently than boys stressed pleasures from relationships with people—friends, companionship, relatives. Boys, especially older boys, more frequently emphasized travel—going to camps, resorts, parks—as major happy times. Jersild concludes: "Throughout life, satisfactions will arise from unimpeded activity, successful achievement, and ventures into new activities which give a person a broadened conception of himself" (39, p. 902).

Table 47 contains data relevant mainly to the adult years from one of the investigations dealing with happiness that has already been referred

TABLE 46. Frequency of Responses in Various Categories When Children Described "One of the Happiest Days in My Life"

		Grades 1–3 Ages 6–9	Grades 4–6 Ages 9–12	Grades 7–9 Ages 12–15	Grades 10–12 Ages 15–18
Receiving or having or otherwise enjoying material things, gifts, toys, money, living quarters	Boys	9	10	10	6
	Girls	8	7	4	3
Holidays, festive occasions, birthdays, Christmas, etc.	Boys	39	32	6	1
	Girls	40	39	10	6
Sports, games, hiking, hunting, bicycling, etc.	Boys	10	9	12	13
	Girls	6	5	6	7
Going to miscellaneous places of recreation, camps, resorts, parks, traveling	Boys	10	10	10	30
	Girls	9	11	14	7
Self-improvement, success in school, educational opportunity, evidence of vocational competence, getting a job	Boys	2	3	5	14
	Girls	2	2	4	16
Happenings connected with school, including last day, end of school, going to a certain school	Boys	4	5	14	7
	Girls	3	4	11	5
Relationships with people (explicitly described), companionship, being with certain friend, return home of relatives, etc.	Boys	8	8	10	9
	Girls	16	16	22	20
Residing in, moving to a certain city or community	Boys	1	1	1	1
	Girls	1	3	3	5
Benefits befalling others, or mankind in general, including end of war	Boys	1	3	2	8
	Girls	1	3	3	10
Number of cases	Boys	363	309	282	159
	Girls	331	343	290	171

NOTE: The values represent percentage of children giving one or more responses in each category

SOURCE: Adapted from A. T. Jersild, Emotional development, in L. Carmichael (ed.), *Manual of Child Psychology* (2nd ed.), New York, Wiley, 1954, Chap. 14, pp. 833–917; after A. T. Jersild and R. J. Tasch, *Children's Interests and What They Suggest for Education*, New York, Teachers College, Columbia University, 1949.

to. Adults of varying ages were asked to draw, on a specially prepared chart, a curve that represented their happiness at various ages. Such charts typically involved ups and downs, happy and unhappy episodes. Since

TABLE 47. Percentage Distribution of Reasons Given for Major Happy Episodes When Subjects Were Requested to Draw a "Curve of Happiness" Characterizing Their Lives Thus Far and Were Then Interviewed Regarding Causes of "Upswings" in Happiness

	Married Men	Married Women	Single Women
Love and family			
Love and romance	4.2	8.3	3.6
Marriage	10.6	13.4	0
Birth of children	5.6	7.3	0
Family and home life	8.1	8.9	0
Satisfactions in presence or success of children	1.9	3.5	0
Family relationships (parents, siblings)	0	0	7.0
	30.4	41.4	10.6
Occupational life and academic achievement			
Occupation	20.2	7.2	27.9
Occupational training	1.7	.6	4.2
Success in school or college	3.5	1.0	2.0
Graduation from school or college	2.7	1.0	1.7
	28.1	9.8	35.8
School and social life			
Happy or normal childhood	3.3	2.3	4.2
Going to school or college	4.2	6.9	11.2
Social life in school or college	4.9	1.9	7.0
Social life, good times, friends	2.4	4.5	7.8
	14.8	15.6	30.2
No data (apparently adjusted to previous unhappy circumstance)	4.9	7.0	8.9
No data (no reason apparent)	.7	1.9	2.0
Other reasons	21.1	24.3	2.5
Number of individuals	100	106	63
Number of happy episodes (base for above percentages)	838	684	358

SOURCE: Data from R. G. Kuhlen, Age trends in adult adjustment as reflected in happiness ratings, unpublished paper presented at the Boston meeting of the American Psychological Association, 1948.

the numbers of such fluctuations were relatively few, even over a life span, they presumably were produced by major satisfactions and dissatisfactions. Subjects were then interviewed as to the cause of these happiness changes. Table 47 summarizes the responses regarding happy episodes for three groups: married men and single and married women. First to be noted is the major role that love, marriage, and family relationships play in the lives of married individuals, both men and women, but especially women, and how devoid of such experiences is the life of single women. It is perhaps because of such emptiness that, as already noted, so many unmarried oldsters said they were happiest in childhood and youth (52). As Table 47 shows, single women seemed to get major satisfactions from occupation, mentioning this area even more than did men, but also (and this again is perhaps a reflection of the emptiness of their adult life) they recalled more frequently than did the married groups the happy incidents and social relationships of childhood and adolescence. These results are in essential agreement with other studies (52, 62, 96). The table also suggests that single women do not have the range of possibilities of satisfaction open to them. Only 2.5 percent of their reasons for happy episodes fell in the "other reason" category compared with 21 and 24 percent of those of married men and women respectively.

Although the data in the study under discussion were not extensive enough to warrant detailed treatment with respect to age differences in sources of happiness, age tabulations did indicate that various age groups have their particular joys and pleasures. Thus, in the family setting a clear age progression occurred: love and romance in the late teens and early twenties; marriage in the twenties; a little later, but still in the twenties, birth of children; and still later, in the late forties and fifties came pleasures from the success of one's children.

As has been pointed out, striking differences are found among individuals in the way they view their happiness and their lives in retrospect. Each life has its own special circumstances, its unique character, its own pattern of satisfactions and disruptions. An inspection of individual records[1] reveals the extent to which basic fulfillments and satisfactions, though perhaps different in kind, are possible at any age.

Here, for example, is the history of a 73-year-old man. Born of poor parents, in a moderate-sized eastern city, Mr. Donaline's early years were rated as somewhat average or below in happiness. He didn't get along well with his

[1] The following life histories are from the records of one of the writers (46), and have been modified so as not to reveal identity. Names and many details are fictitious.

father, nor did he do well in school. He quit school at 12 years of age and began work as a delivery boy for a grocery store. At 17 he became the regular driver, and, as he worked hard, saved money, and advanced with the company, his general happiness and life satisfaction improved. Married at 20, his happiness reached its highest level (rated +14 on a scale from −15 to +15) at 22 when his first child, a son, was born. A daughter was born two years later. He began making real estate investments in a small way. At age 35, he established his own grocery, sold real estate "on the side," had a few minor downward dips in happiness occasioned by "hard times." "But we really enjoyed them . . . real estate investments paying off . . . children were married." From 22 to 47 his "happiness curve" was at the top level with only minor fluctuations in the forties. When Mr. Donaline was 47, the depression of the early nineteen-thirties hit and at the same time his wife died. His happiness rating hit its all-time low of −14. Gradually, he adjusted and his happiness edged upward, but with important downward fluctuations, during the next six years. At 53 he married a woman he had known "for years"; his happiness was rated at the old level (+14) and has continued at this level to the present. He is now retired and has moved to the city where his children are living. Both he and his wife like the new environment very much. "Enjoy our own home, our children's families, our friends, and church activities." He hopes for continued good health, economic security and independence, success for his children (who "are doing all right"), and for world peace. Mr. Donaline, quite properly, views his life as a happy one. He had his rough times, but he was a resilient hard-working person who found basic satisfaction in home and family, vocational success, and in later years in contacts with friends, church, and family. There is, in this case, no old-age depression; zest for living continues high. When asked what he would like to be doing 10 years hence, he replied: "Enjoying life as I am enjoying it now."

Miss Knight, a 58-year-old teacher, had a childhood of only average happiness. She went to college at 17, but was dominated by a sister who was also at that school, was unable to make friends, and was bothered by ill-health. A year later she changed schools, and, away from her sister, "I found myself." She was out of school a year, taking care of her ill mother. The peak of happiness (+10) for her early adult years was reached at about 25. "Had an enjoyable teaching job, on my own, was more independent, enjoyed social times, dates, etc." But a love affair didn't work out and a broken engagement resulted in a very low period in her early thirties. The highest happiness ratings of her life (+15) were assigned to the years of 35 to 45. "I established a home with a friend, had a small shop, a summer home in the country, liked the teaching I was doing. . . . I was really very happy." The death of this friend left her completely alone again, and happiness ratings plunged to a low of −10. Within a three-year period her mother, father, and two sisters died; home was broken up completely. "I was very nervous and upset . . . a period of about 10 years when I was not at all well or happy." Now "kind of getting along again, getting used to it . . . you get over everything after awhile." She rates her present happiness as "average," expects to retire in a year and is looking forward to it. If income allows, she expects to do volunteer service work, possibly work part time. Asked if she viewed her life as successful she replied "I don't know . . . should have had a family . . . lot of good maternity wasted. But with circumstances as they have been, I think I've made a reasonably good job of it."

Mrs. Jones, a 64-year-old widow, was born in the rural Midwest. She recalls an unhappy childhood which, even at 64, she attributes to being "bullied" by an older girl in a country school. Not until entry to high school did she reach what she considered average happiness. In college, she was only moderately happy. A combination of first teaching job, falling in love and marriage, and, shortly after, the birth of a daughter resulted in the years from 20 to 25 being assigned the highest possible happiness rating (+15). A serious illness of her daughter plus financial insecurity plunged her into a five-year period of unhappiness which was only temporarily relieved when the family moved back to her home town. Between the ages of 23 and 40 she bore seven children. Not until her early forties did the combination of happy home life and financial security lift her above the "average" rating for any sustained period, but even here the rating was only +5. This period of relative happiness was abruptly terminated by the death of her husband when she was 47, and the next year or or two were rated at the lowest possible point of happiness on the scale. Then she returned to teaching, achieved average happiness. In her late fifties she was promoted to a major administrative job, thoroughly enjoys her work, and for the first time since her early twenties she views her life as extremely happy, rating her happiness over the last four years at +15. In total, this life shows early and rather complete fulfillment in marriage and family, with this high level of happiness tempered and disrupted by the vicissitudes of work, finances, and child-rearing and then climaxed by bereavement. But all of this in the instance of a person of sufficient strength and stability, who, at a mature age and after children were grown, was able to move ahead to a new kind of self-realization through vocational achievement.

In total, these illustrative case histories, as well as the tabulations of Tables 46 and 47, emphasize the degree to which basis satisfactions are found in social relationships, marriage and family life, and in work—an important reason for consideration of these areas of life adjustment in separate chapters. The remainder of the present chapter is devoted to an overview of general activities and recreation and to a general evaluation of the contributions of interests to good living.

Play, Recreation, and General Interests

Research regarding the interests and recreations of people has shown in striking fashion that an unbelievably wide variety of specific activities can and do become satisfying. Indeed, such studies have provided so much richness of detail that the reader must be cautioned not to become lost in the welter of specific information available. As consideration shifts from general recreational interests and activities to radio and television, to movies, to reading, it will be noted that the same basic patterns become apparent again and again. In fact, a major purpose in presenting facts regarding the broad range of interests is to emphasize that basic developments reveal themselves in diverse activities.

PLAY IN EARLY CHILDHOOD

In very early childhood, play and pleasure seem mainly to involve a pattern of exploratory behavior, of getting acquainted with one's own body and its capacities and seeking new sensory experiences. Playing with hands and feet (and seriously contemplating them) is common at four months, and at this age the youngster is just beginning to play with objects. For the first time now he begins to express his pleasure by laughing (previously he could only smile). By about six months he begins to pat the table with his hands and to bang on furniture with a spoon or rattle; by about nine months he has learned that objects fall when brushed aside—and seems to delight in hearing them fall (29).

At about one year of age activities of types more commonly spoken of as play begin to appear. Manipulation of blocks, use of such materials to construct "houses," and dramatic imitation of elders, as in playing house or store, soon are to be observed. Sand boxes, tricycles, toy wagons, dolls, and the multitude of other objects produced commercially to tempt children (and parents) come to have an important place in the child's life. Without them, however, he is not lost. He will take advantage of his surroundings and play happily with whatever is available, and he will play contentedly by himself. Even when small children are together, the play is often simply in the presence of rather than with the other children—and talk is monologue (38). Attention span increases with age (6, 92), one study showing an average attention span of 6.9 minutes at two years, 8.9 minutes at three, 11.4 minutes at four, and 12.6 minutes at five (92). And changes in interests are to be noted even in the four- to six-year range; for example, interest in toy animals declines whereas interest in plastic materials for play increases (93). Interest in being read to gradually emerges.

More than anything else, changes in play in early years reflect emerging abilities, physical and mental. As the child matures, he becomes able, in terms of motor ability or intellect, to play with rattles, to ride tricycles, to skate, and to understand and enjoy simple stories and, later, complex ones. Increased physical size and motor abilities open the possibility of ranging over a wider area, out of the crib, out of the playpen, out of the yard. Obviously, of course, there must also be opportunity. And in these early years, as later, opportunity differs tremendously for children. The isolated farm family, the apartment dweller, the family living on a busy corner, and the family in a child-centered, open-spaced suburb all likely impose differing degrees of restriction on the play of their offspring. Parents differ, too, in the extent to which they provide stimulating play material and the degree to which they participate with children in their play activities. Evidence seems to suggest that although developing abilities will effect developing play interests, the opportunities and stimulation characterizing the child's environment will, in turn, determine the degree to which these abilities receive nurture. Thus, in early years, play is more than recreation; it is life. Various studies, some already cited in the earlier chapter on abilities, have shown that early stimulation may have important long-term effects.

CHANGES IN PLAY THROUGH THE SCHOOL YEARS

Soon comes the school with its new surroundings and new companions. Potentialities increase even more with physical and mental growth, and horizons widen well beyond the home and immediate neighborhood. What are the findings regarding the development and change in play and recreational interests during the school years?

An overview of such developments is contained in Figure 84. In this study youngsters from the sixth grade through college were asked to indicate, on a check list, various activities (and other items) that appealed to them, to check the item once if they liked it, and to double check it if they liked it very much. Clearly, the later school years represent a period involving many shifts in interest. Liking for some activities prominent in the sixth grade has practically disappeared by the last years of college, whereas other activities which were of only minor importance at the early age have become important. At the sixth-grade level, horseback riding, hunting, shooting, and fishing have great appeal for boys (it must be remembered that this study did not involve actual participation), as do bicycling and roller skating. By the late teens, interests in dancing, social affairs, and clothes have assumed new importance, while

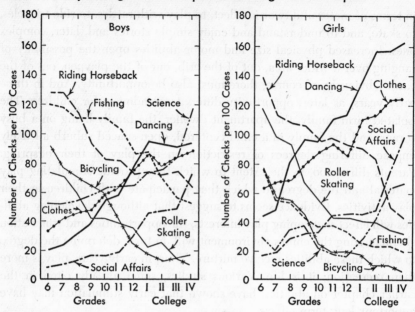

Figure 84. Changing Behavior Patterns Through Adolescence as Shown by Interests Prevalent at Various Grade Levels. (Based on unpublished data of S. L. Pressey.)

interest in the foregoing activities was dropping out. Much the same trend is to be noted for girls, except there is less emphasis upon very active types of interest and more emphasis upon social activities.

The manner in which these changes are evidenced in the actual day-by-day activities of children is illustrated by the following contrast between 12- and 16-year-old boys.[2]

The 16-year-old boy gets up a little earlier than the younger boy, chiefly because he has further to go to school. Like the 12-year-old he arrives at school early enough to play, watch others play, chat, or study for a while before classes begin. At recess, he is more likely than the younger boy to be found around the halls or outside talking or "fooling around" with some girls along with some other boys. After school he is a little more likely than the 12-year-old to have some remunerative job such as selling or delivering papers. If not, he may stay around school to play football, basketball, or baseball, or to practice for track athletics, but unless he is "trying out for the team," he is more likely to be found watching the team practice or play. Quite a large number of boys spend some time during the afternoon at home reading or listening to the radio.

Two or three new tendencies are apparent in the evening program of the 16-year-old. He is more likely to do something outside of the home, play or

[2] Modified slightly from Dimock (22).

visit with friends, go to a movie, or go riding in the car. He is much less likely to attend any organized club activity. Unless he is a patrol leader the chances are slight that he will still be a member of the Scout troop. Neither is he likely to attend club meetings at the church or Y.M.C.A. Many boys generally spend the evening at home, listening to the radio, reading, perhaps playing pool, checkers or ping-pong, and quite often studying.

The activities of the 16-year-old boy on Saturday or Sunday are not substantially different from those of the preadolescent. On Saturday morning he enjoys a late sleep unless he has a paper route or similar responsibility, does a few chores or errands, and plays or reads for a short time. His afternoon program varies in detail with the season, but its general motif is athletic participation for a few, the spectator role for many more, and the spectator role via the radio for a large number, especially in the football season. Attending movies, usually with one or more boy friends, is also a common Saturday afternoon event. One new feature is occasionally included in the week-end program. That is the "mixed party" which occurs most frequently on Friday or Saturday night. The mixed party, on anything like a regular basis, is still an affair for the minority, however. For the majority, Saturday night means a show; or just hanging around with the crowd; or reading, playing cards or other games, or listening to the radio, at home.

The 16-year-old is less likely to attend Sunday school than the younger boy, but somewhat more likely to attend adult church services. The rest of the day is used for reading, car riding, a "date" for a few boys, movies for many, listening to radio programs, a little study, and visiting or being visited by friends or relatives.

The items selected for graphing in Figure 84 and the descriptive picture just presented illustrate the two dominant patterns of change during the child-adolescent period. First is the decline in those types of activities which demand considerable activity and energy output and in the relatively simple, unchallenging types of interests. Second is the strong upsurge of what might be called "sex-social" interests, the most notable characteristic of adolescent recreational interests. This strong heterosexual orientation, understandable in young people with strong biological attractions in a culture that delays marriage and restricts intimate physical relations between the sexes, is often misunderstood and unappreciated by adults—for example, their parents—whose own situation with respect to such basic satisfactions is much different indeed.

The importance and pervasiveness of this new orientation, and the extent to which this may be hidden from observation, is apparent in the case of a 15-year-old boy whose diary one of the writers has in his possession. This lad was a vigorous, out-of-door boy, and his daily jottings were replete with mention of such activities as hiking, ice-skating, Boy Scout meetings, "plinking" with his .22, playing basketball, football, and all the rest. In terms of sheer frequency of mention, these items predominate and would superficially appear to represent the center of his interests. But, occasionally, throughout the year's diary are brief records in code—the dot-dash code used by Boy Scouts in signaling. When transcribed, the event and the reason for the secrecy were both evident—"Saw Mary. Got a kiss." Occasionally, on a particularly successful night, the number would be recorded—"Got 6 kisses," or whatever the score! And at the end of the year, on the final page of the diary, a longer sentence *in code* summarized what in this adolescent's mind was apparently the theme and essence of the year: "Saw Mary 82 times this year." This was his summing up, and it leaves little doubt as to the importance of this new interest in his scheme of things.

In addition to illustrating the important qualitative changes in the interests of young people, Figure 84 emphasizes another important feature of interest development: there is a gradualness of change and a continuity of development. No one age group is distinctly different from the adjoining ages. Kites and marbles and dolls and jumping ropes are only gradually discarded and are frequently sandwiched in between first dates. Even the impact of pubescence, of pervasive importance over a long period, is not sufficient to produce sharp, immediate changes. Relationship of the maturity of interests to pubescent status is positive (76, 79), but changes are in no sense dramatic or even marked.

A wide variety of studies, some 30 years old at the present writing, some quite recent, confirm these trends. Thus in the famous Lehman and Witty studies of a generation ago (55), 10-year-old girls reported most frequent participation in playing the piano, going to movies, looking at comics, playing with dolls, and roller-skating, whereas 20-year-old girls most frequently engaged in social dancing, playing the piano, having dates, going to entertainments, just "hiking" or strolling. Boys showed similar patterns. In a recent investigation (60), reading and radio increased for both sexes as home activities, and dancing, movies, and sports increased as evening away-from-home activities. At the third-grade level boys and girls spent an average of 1.4 and 1.7 evenings respectively away from home, an average which increased to 3.5 and 3.2 by the eleventh grade. Even in counts made of "collections" children make (and here reference is again to a study over 25 years old!) the emerging sex-social interest of adolescence is apparent (97). For both sexes, the teens brought increasing frequency of collecting photographs and letters! The same patterns will be noted later with reference to specific radio, reading, and movie interests. Such versatility of expression and such stability from the last generation to the present emphasizes the basic nature of these interest changes.

The foregoing description, which has emphasized age changes, has neglected a basic fact about interests—a fact which people (such as teachers, youth leaders, and playground supervisors) need to recognize in planning programs and dealing with young people. Interests and recreational practices are, within broad limits, a product of the culture in which the individual matures. And where the *same* activity is involved, the setting may be such as to make the total activity quite different from place to place. Thus, although all groups of adolescents seem interested in dancing, *where* a person dances and the general atmosphere varies with social class.

The lower class boys and girls do not have access to the Country Club, and, in large part, they cannot attend lodge dances, because few of their parents belong. They could participate in the high school dances, but they are not "comfortable" there. This self-feeling is very important in the determination of where an adolescent goes and what he does. If his friends go to a certain place and do a given thing, he feels "comfortable." If his friends are not there and the activity is outside his action pattern, he feels "uncomfortable." The boys and girls in classes IV and V who attend the dances at Morrow's Hall or Scrugg's Tavern would be uncomfortable at the Country Club, because experience has not prepared them to go to the Country Club in any capacity other than as caddy, waitress, janitor, garbage collector, or workman. Conversely, the "Country Club crowd" would be morally outraged to be invited to a dance at Scrugg's. The net effect is the segregation of the young people along class lines at the private, semi-public, and public dances. The corrected coefficient of contingency of 0.62 demonstrates that there is a very real relationship between a high school boy's or girl's class position and his or her attendance at private, semi-private, or public dances. (37, pp. 306–307.)

Unlike dancing, which though prominent at all levels occurs in varying settings, some types of activities are definitely class associated. School activities—dances, club memberships, game attendance—are participated in only to a slight degree by lower-class youngsters,[3] and, depending somewhat on the community, the extent of participation in specific out-of-school recreational activities, such as bowling and skating, varies from one cultural level to another.[4]

These students look upon roller-skating as "low-class stuff," "a cheap sport." Skating is a much cheaper sport than bowling, a fact which appeals to youngsters who have little money, and it is not coincidence that these young people come disproportionately from classes IV and V. . . . Such persons have more fun at the skating rink where they skate to the music of an electric gramophone with an oversized loudspeaker. There they may waltz, fox trot, speed-skate, crack the whip, or skate with a date and neck in the corners, for hours on end, cheaply. The high school authorities frown upon students' skating, except Tues-

[3] See Chapter 11 for evidence on this point.
[4] The following passages have been adapted from A. B. Hollingshead, *Elmtown's Youth* (37), pp. 310–313.

day afternoon and evening, when all other patrons are barred. Young people in classes II and III, particularly the girls, if they do not want to be suspected of loose morals, avoid the skating rink, for many young men go there to pick up dates; and frequent quarrels, which end in fights, are common.

Hunting, fishing, and trapping are strictly male activities. All the boys report that they fish some time during the spring and summer in Indian River or a tributary creek. . . . Trapping is a "low-class" and a "young-boy" trait; 16 of the 23 trappers are freshmen, the remaining 7 are sophomores. These boys are also nondaters. . . . By the time a boy reaches the sophomore year, he is usually ready to date, and, through subtle controls exerted by his peers, he learns that a trapper is a marked man. . . . Rearing rabbits, guinea pigs, pigeons, and pups is another younger boy pastime found in all strata, but with greater frequency in classes III and IV than in classes II or V. Rearing of pets, like trapping, fades out when a boy grows old enough to start dating.

RECREATIONAL PARTICIPATION IN ADULT LIFE

What happens to interests and recreations as the individual moves from the opportunities and leisure of school or college and passes through the readjustments immediately following school into the efforts and time-consuming routines of earning a living? As might be guessed, participation in recreational activities drops off. Several studies covering various age periods are in agreement. The older of two groups of college graduates, averaging 25 and 31 years, participated less frequently in leisure pursuits (65). A survey of recreational activities done some 20 years ago revealed that people in the age range of 46 to 60 participated in some 42 percent fewer activities than those in the 21 to 26 age range (63). In a recent 20-year follow-up study, 176 men and 192 women, first tested in their mid-twenties, rated themselves as having narrower interests at the older age (44). And a recent study of teachers revealed the younger adults to have a more varied recreational program than those older (42).

Something of the character of this change during the early adult years is shown in Table 48 which reports relative frequency of participation in various activities on the part of women elementary school teachers, mostly single. Almost all activities decreased in frequency of participation—dancing, horseback riding, swimming, active games. Of the activities listed, only concert-going and reading nonfiction appeared to increase with age, the former evidenced by a drop in the proportion "never attending." Of especial interest is the increase with age in "resting" and "retiring early," presumably due to increased fatigue or work pressure,

TABLE 48.   Adult Age Changes in Leisure-Time Activities as Illustrated by the Percentage of Women Elementary School Teachers Participating in Various Activities

Activity	Age 20–29 N 265	Age 30–39 N 171	Age 40 and Over N 49
Daily			
Listening to the radio	82.7%	73.1%	61.2%
Reading fiction	19.2	12.9	10.2
Reading nonfiction	10.9	18.1	24.5
Retiring early	5.8	17.5	26.5
Weekly			
Resting	17.0	17.0	26.5
Cultural courses	20.7	15.2	6.1
Professional courses	29.1	36.3	14.3
Playing instrumental music	18.5	11.7	8.2
Playing bridge	30.6	20.5	8.2
Daily and weekly			
Dancing	18.5	7.0	0.0
Swimming	25.7	18.7	14.3
Active games	17.0	5.8	2.0
Resting	35.9	33.4	46.9
Movies	39.2	33.4	16.3
Cultural courses	22.6	17.5	6.1
Professional courses	31.0	39.2	16.3
Never			
Dancing	6.8	26.9	55.1
Swimming	26.0	43.9	49.0
Skating	40.0	55.0	61.2
Active games	38.1	56.7	71.4
Horseback riding	63.3	70.2	77.6
Golf	74.3	72.0	81.7
Resting	41.5	32.7	30.3
Watching athletics	25.3	42.1	49.0
Concerts	20.7	17.5	8.2
Group singing	68.3	65.5	49.0
Professional courses	38.5	26.3	42.9
Playing bridge	13.9	18.7	38.8

SOURCE: From Lucille Allard, A Study of the Leisure Activities of Certain Elementary School Teachers of Long Island, Teachers College Contributions to Education, No. 799, New York, Teachers College, Columbia University, 1939.

possibly to boredom. Other studies show much the same trends (45). In a statewide survey in Missouri some years ago, decreases with age in participation in sports, in card playing, in dancing, and in entertaining were evident (8). Liking for music apparently resists age effects; other studies (8, 63) agree with the facts presented in Table 48 in showing concert-going as either relatively unaffected by increasing age or positively influenced.

A major trend noted in surveys of adult recreational activities is a marked decrease in the sex-social activities so prominent in the lives of adolescents. A number of factors may account for this: less time, less energy, more vital uses for available funds. But probably also influential is the fact that sexual needs, which though at a biological peak were frustrated in adolescence, are in adult years satisfied in marriage. Much premarital social activity and recreation is probably engaged in (though not necessarily consciously so) as a secondary source of satisfaction of sexual needs when primary satisfactions are taboo.

Detailed quantitative contrasts in general recreational interests between different subcultures are not available for the adult years, but that there are important differences is obvious. Interests will certainly vary according to the companionship available. A small city with an enthusiastic fisherman's club, a new suburb with a booster's club and a choral society, a community with a planned program of activities of varied types for all ages may be contrasted with a slum area where boys find their companionship in gangs and men in saloons, or an isolated farming district where there is little companionship outside the family. The middle-aged laborer's wife who is shy in a new neighborhood, the child or old person who happens to be the only one of his age in the block, the girl all of whose friends have married—all of these people present problems of recreation and interests. Hours and circumstance of work, the day or night shift, inevitably affect recreation.

Marked are the contrasts in use of the usual two weeks' vacation. Some stay at home, fixing up a little, overeating a little, saving. Some take trips—and what contrasts here! The ungrammatical, middle-aged factory worker at the Grand Canyon, who plans all year for his treasured fortnight in one of the national parks, exquisitely sensitive to beauty, pitifully anxious to find companionship among those similarly sensitive. The two clerks with the two prostitutes, drunk all the time on their Great Lakes cruise. The family in the crowded cottage wearing themselves out to make the most of their meager time by a real lake! And what of those with more time? There are the wealthy New York women, contentious and bored on their South American trip. Why did they come? They'd been everywhere else—what else was there to do! There is the careful school teacher, going to inexpensive places but with this one rule, not to go to the same place twice, and so through her life steadily broadening knowledge and acquaintance. And there is the family which has been to the same resort for the past 20 years, fishing the same shallows, sailing the same bay, talking with the same friends, rocking on the same porch.

And in the use of leisure moments—again, what contrasts! Middle-aged adolescents in a fever of parties and going out, middle-aged sports on hand at every game. Those for whom life is bridge. Those for whom life is their family. Those for whom life is their dog. Those for whom life is simply sitting and reading the paper. The old person who simply sits. And the old person who finds in increased leisure manifold opportunities for culture, usefulness, and enjoyment.

Interesting contrasts between income groups are shown in Table 49 with respect to number of activities participated in and the degree to which these groups were satisfied with their respective recreational programs. *Both* the high- and low-income groups reported relatively few activities, and fewer of their numbers were satisfied. Greatest participa-

TABLE 49. Variations According to Income in Mean Number of Activities in Which Families Participate and in the Percentage Judging Their Recreation Program to Be Satisfactory

| Income Level | Mean Number of Activities Participated In | | Percentage Believing Program Satisfactory | |
	N	Mean	N	%
Under $3000	152	20	143	38
3000–4000	115	26	108	39
4000–5000	75	27	62	48
5000–6000	51	32	47	53
6000–7000	20	32	19	50
7000–8000	19	29	16	44
8000–10,000	21	27	51	33
Over $10,000	51	26	—	—
Total	504	25	466	42

SOURCE: Adapted from J. A. Wylie, Survey of 504 families to determine the relationships between certain factors and the nature of the family recreation program, *Res. Quart.*, 1953, 24:229–243.

tion and most frequent satisfaction were among those in the $5000 to $7000 brackets. One can only speculate as to the cause of these differences, but the opinion is ventured that the low-income families were handicapped by lack of funds, possibly by lack of initiative or imagination, while the upper-income groups (probably largely busy professional or business men) may have been handicapped by lack of time. In support of this interpretation is the further finding in this study that insufficient

income and insufficient time for participation were the two most frequently mentioned types of restrictions, with "not available nearby" a
close third. The latter would likely be more restrictive in the case of
low-income groups.

What about the later years of life? Do active recreational patterns
narrow still further? The data on this question are not clear cut. One
study of people beyond 60 showed steady decreases in the proportion
showing a "high degree" of participation while the proportion showing a
low degree increased (*13*). But, for a national sample of college graduates, increased participation in leisure activities appeared to accompany
increased amounts of leisure in old age, earlier in the case of women
than men because (apparently) increased time becomes available earlier
for them as children leave home and family unit size shrinks (*47*).

Up to a certain point, hobby participation also increases with age.
Hobbies presumably differ from "interests" in the sense that hobby interests are more intense, and the activity is likely to be one with sufficient complexity and challenge as to offer especially rich opportunities
for enjoyment. Hobbies, thus, are more likely to offer possibilities for
satisfying basic needs when other modes of satisfaction (such as job)
are no longer available. Something of the age trends in hobby participa-

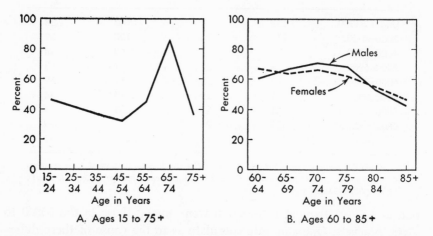

Figure 85.   Age Trends in Hobby Participation, as Shown by Two Studies. Chart A
shows trends from age 15 to over 75 as determined by interviews of adults in Missouri.
Chart B, based mainly on replies to a mailed questionnaire widely distributed in the
United States, shows trends from age 60 to over 85. (Chart A adapted from E. S.
Briggs, How adults in Missouri use their leisure time, *School and Society*, 1938, *47*:
805–808; Chart B adapted from R. Cavan *et al.*, *Personal Adjustment in Old Age*,
Chicago, Science Research Associates, 1949.)

tion is shown in Figure 85. The left-hand chart of this figure, from a Missouri survey of adult leisure, gives the proportion of adults in various age groups who reported a hobby. From the teens up to 50 years the number so reporting regularly decreased, presumably as pressures of family and job increased, but at 50 the trend is strikingly reversed until in the decade 65 to 74, 95 percent reported hobbies. The drop thereafter might well be expected on the basis of physical decline, e. g., of sensory functions. But in the right-hand chart (from another study of the older age brackets), the decline is seen to be not so sharp as it appears when *all* of those over 74 are lumped together. The trends for males and females are quite similar, and in this latter study 40 percent of the 85 and over group reported hobbies.

The type of hobby followed varies with age. Thus, one investigator (85) found that, when selected independently of age, 50 model engineers averaged 33 years of age, 50 amateur musicians averaged 37, photographers averaged 41, and stamp collectors averaged 43 years of age. Another investigator (64) found that constructional activities (preparing and cooking food, furniture making, painting, taking motion pictures) are found more frequently among men aged 25 to 35 than among those 18 to 25 or 45 to 55.

In view of the potential importance of hobbies, once work has ceased, it is noteworthy that those who have hobbies in childhood and youth are more likely to have hobbies in adult years (64). Presumably, also, those who develop hobbies in mature years will be more likely to pursue them in old age. And hobbies might well be developed with a view to their future usefulness and practicability. One writer (50) suggests that men have greater difficulty than women in adjusting to old age because their hobbies (in contrast to those of women) are too demanding physically to be continued into old age. Thus, when old age is reached men frequently must give up not only their jobs but their hobbies as well.

What, beyond hobbies, do people do in their later years when more time is available? The studies on hobby and activity expansion in older years mentioned above did not provide data on this point sufficiently refined to permit conclusions. But some facts are available from other sources. In Table 50 are some findings from a study of 381 oldsters (recipients of old age pensions, age 70 and over) who listed some 875 items in response to the question, "How do you spend your days now? What kind of things do you do?" Approximately a third of these items related to working around the house; but hobbies, games, and intellectual pursuits also accounted for about a third of the responses. But 10 percent of the responses indicated nothing was done! Another group of 199 out of a group of 782 laborers indicated that an average of 13 hours per week was spent "doing nothing at home" (30). This single item— just loafing—was the largest single item in use of leisure by this group. It need hardly be said that such a group presents a serious problem of provision for use of leisure and, in the schools, of education for leisure. Higher economic groups report less inactivity. According to another study (28) inactivity in elderly people was six times greater among the lower economic group than among the higher.

TABLE 50.   Type of Daily Activities Participated in by 381 People
Over 70 Years of Age (875 Items Mentioned)

Type of Daily Activity	Percent of Total Items Mentioned
Housekeeping, housework, helping with housework and care of grandchildren, caring for invalid	32.9%
Hobbies, games, and intellectual pursuits, reading, studying, writing letters, games, music	31.5
Walking, seeing and calling on friends, club and churchwork	13.6
Resting, sitting in the sun, watching out of the window, "not much of anything"	9.6
Gardening, flowers, pets, livestock, chores	8.1
Employment, small jobs	4.3

SOURCE: From M. Morgan, The attitudes and adjustments of recipients of old age assistance in upstate and metropolitan New York, Archives of Psychol., 1937, No. 214, 30:131. By permission of the American Psychological Association.

This whole matter of how time is used when employment is ended has tremendous implications for adequacy of adjustment, whether this be in old age or at times of prolonged unemployment at younger years. This question will be returned to later.

CHANGING "INTERESTS" IN ADULT YEARS

The foregoing has emphasized *participation*. A much broader variety of data regarding adult interests is available relating to *liking for* things and activities, regardless of actual participation. Such facts may be deceptive: liking for an activity may well persist long beyond the point where actual participation has ceased (63). Thus, data on "interests" or "liking for" activities may obscure lack of participation. Men "like to fish," for example, who have not fished for years! But, more positively, even though expressed interest may not reflect actual participation, information regarding "liking" for activities may identify areas worth exploring on the part of those who suddenly, perhaps at retirement, have more time on their hands. And, in any event, such expressions of interest probably reflect important personality changes.

The most extensive data on liking for various activities has been collected by Professor E. K. Strong, Jr., in connection with studies with his Vocational Interest Blank, a questionnaire containing some 400 items

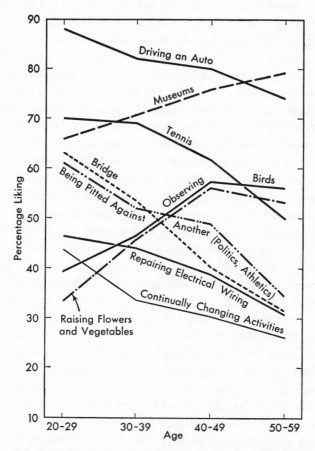

Figure 86. Changes with Age in Percentage of Men Liking Certain More Active or Competitive, as Compared with More Sedentary and Noncompetitive Diversions. (Adapted from E. K. Strong, *Change of Interests with Age*, Stanford, Stanford University Press, 1931.)

dealing with a wide variety of matters. The facts presented here are drawn from two populations he studied: one, a sample of 2340 men from 8 professions, ranging in age from 20 to 60; the second, a sample of 472 15-year-old boys, 215 men between 23 and 27 years of age, and 151 men between 50 and 59 years of age, these three groups being carefully selected so as to be representative of the population at large. Figure 86 shows selected trends with age for the professional men.

Three important changes were apparent in both sets of data for the age range 25 to 55. The greatest change related to a decrease in liking for activities involving physical skill and daring. As age increases, decreases are noted in interest in such activities as driving an automobile, being pitted against another, climbing along the edge of a precipice, performing sleight-of-hand tricks, auto racing. In contrast, interest increases with age in such relatively sedentary and relaxed activities as bird watching, gardening, visiting museums and art galleries, reading a book rather than going to a movie. (As data presented in a later chapter on social interaction will show, there is a general decrease in liking for social activities.) A second change is a decline of interest in linguistic activities involving writing. Older men express much less interest in such occupations as reporter of sporting pages, advertiser, foreign correspondent, author of a technical book, poet, and the like. These are diverse items, to be sure—some implying physical exertion and daring—but they have the element of writing in common, and all show interest losses with age.

A third and especially interesting change with age is the decrease in liking for changing activities. Older men express greater dislike for changing activities, prefer work in one place rather than change, prefer methodical work and methodical people, dislike studying latest hobby, like regular work hours, like cautious and conservative people. This change was first attributed by Strong (81, p. 74) to the fact that doing new things usually requires the development of new habits, usually at the expense of older ones, an accomplishment that is easier in youth because habits are not so engrained and surplus energy is available for the purpose. But, surprisingly enough, a later study showed 15-year-olds and 55-year-olds to be relatively alike in unwillingness to change habits (84). The 25-year-olds seemed most flexible. Thus, the above explanation seemed not completely adequate. It may be, for example, that a degree of uncertainty and insecurity may characterize *both* adolescents and oldsters so that they hesitate to venture into new situations demanding change, preferring the security of the known. But in the present writers' opinion, the matter of habit rigidity and energy loss is likely also involved in the oldsters' resistance to change. Though the difference between 15- and 55-year-olds was not reliable, the oldsters did dislike change more, a circumstance that might be expected if several factors were contributing to their condition in adult years and fewer in adolescence.

This particular change in interests has important implications. It may be argued, for example, that oldsters may compensate for slow-down in mental functions by greater motivation to learn. But this evidence suggests that such decline in ability as may exist is coupled with a parallel decline in desire to change or to learn. Educators thus have a special problem of motivation in programs planned for oldsters. And individuals interested in developing a constructive "style of life" that may serve to retard many aspects of psychological decline with age must guard against this common trend toward complacency that normally accompanies increasing age.

Recreation and Entertainment via the Media of Mass Communication

A striking feature of modern life is the degree to which people are surrounded by almost limitless opportunities to engage vicariously in activities that they could not, or would not dare to, engage in in real life. The tremendous growth of the media of mass communication is a development of major psychological significance. The spending of a few cents or the turning of a knob opens a world of ready-made fantasy, a vast resource of education, entertainment, amusement. And subtly, but just as really as in the overt participation described above, people reveal themselves in their preferences among this vast array of choices.

EXTENT OF READING, LISTENING, VIEWING

A first question: How much time is devoted daily to the mass media? And how many people, on a typical day, engage in reading, listening, viewing? One study, done before the days of widespread television, gives a partial answer. As Table 51 shows, of 4000 people interviewed, 21 percent said they read a book "yesterday"; 85 percent read newspapers; 40 percent read magazines; 74 percent listened to newspapers; and 12 percent went to a movie. For the total group, an average of 170 minutes—almost 3 hours—were so spent! What other recreational activity could claim so great an amount of daily time?

This time was, of course, not equally distributed among the media, nor did all age groups show the same interest. Radio listening (perhaps

TABLE 51. Age Changes in Reading, Radio, and Movie Interests in Terms of Percentage of Various Age Groups Participating and Time Spent

	Age Groups						
	15–19	20–29	30–39	40–49	50–59	60 and Over	Total
Books							
Read a book yesterday	34%	27%	19%	17%	16%	18%	21%
Average time spent in minutes	22	19	12	10	8	12	13
Newspapers							
Read a newspaper yesterday	84%	85%	84%	87%	86%	83%	85%
Average time spent in minutes	22	31	33	39	43	44	35
Magazines							
Read a magazine yesterday	51%	44%	38%	36%	35%	35%	40%
Average time spent in minutes	20	22	18	19	17	20	19
Radio							
Listened to radio yesterday	77%	74%	71%	74%	77%	75%	74%
Average time spent in minutes	91	98	80	78	83	87	85
Movies							
Went to movies yesterday	27%	18%	11%	8%	9%	6%	12%
Average time spent in minutes	44	24	15	12	15	9	18
Total time spent in minutes	199	194	158	158	166	172	170
Total interviews	425	746	831	791	586	621	4,000

SOURCE: From H. C. Link and H. A. Hopf, *People and Books*, New York, New York Book Industry Committee, Book Manufacturers Institute, 1946.

while doing other things) claimed most time, almost an hour and a half, with newspaper reading second, with about a half an hour. Newspaper reading steadily increased with age in terms of time so spent; movie attendance declined. Middle-aged folk seemed to do less reading and radio listening than either the young or the old. The overall figures indicated that the teen-agers and those in their twenties spent most time on the mass media; those in their thirties and forties spent least; the total time spent increased in the fifties and sixties.

But all of this, though rather recent, was *before* television! With the advent of TV things changed. Table 52 gives the results of a study showing the nature of this change and the phenomenal success of this new medium in capturing time and attention. In this study, two surveys were conducted in Fort Wayne, Indiana, with the changes being noted in the instance of those families who had obtained TV sets in the meantime. Although those who had not purchased sets spent virtually the same amounts of time on the various media at the two surveys, the new TV owners had markedly reduced their radio listening and their magazine reading and, to a lesser degree, their newspaper reading. But they had added almost an hour and a half to the total time devoted to the mass media! Surprisingly enough, this high level of interest in TV is not simply a function of novelty. A study of viewing patterns in four-year histories of families owning sets during the entire period showed gains of from 68 to 77 percent viewing on an average evening during the period from 1951 through 1954, with the total weekly hours per person increasing from 10.7 to 12.6 over this period (*18*).

TABLE 52.   Changes in Time Spent on Each Medium After Purchase of TV Set

	Minutes per Person "Yesterday"		
	Before TV	After TV	Percent Change
Magazines	17	10	−41
Newspapers	39	32	−18
Radio	122	52	−57
Television	12[a]	173	—
Total time	190	267	+41

[a] "Guest viewing."

SOURCE: From T. E. Coffin, Television's impact on society, *Amer. Psychol.*, 1955, 10:630–641, after T. E. Coffin, J. B. Landis, and M. W. Baiman, *Strangers into Customers*, New York, National Broadcasting Co., 1955. By permission of the American Psychological Association.

Evidence suggests that concurrent with the new TV interest—probably in part as a result of it—significant changes have occurred in the *pattern* of radio listening, which, being a parallel activity, had suffered most at the hands of television. The shift seems to be from *family* to *individual* listening. In homes that have TV, there are increasing numbers of multiple radio-set homes, increasing sales of portable and personal radios, and a strong trend toward placing radio sets in rooms other than the living rooms (*18, 68*). There are other *re*adjustments to television as well. A recent study (*18*) shows that *without decreasing the time spent on TV,* people are rearranging their time—their housework, their reading, their radio listening—and the manner of doing these things so as to include both *these* activities (which have then increased in time so spent) and television. The MC on a morning TV show refers to his viewers as the "ironing-board brigade," and the teen-age daughter of one of the writers not infrequently *watches* TV while *listening* to an exciting basketball game through a portable radio placed close to her ear!

The total increase in mass media "recreation" has undoubtedly had a profound effect on other recreational activities and on life in general. Evidence regarding the impact of television recalls to the writers' minds similar effects in the mid-twenties of radio.

The TV family reports the acquisition of new acquaintances, renewed friendliness on the part of old acquaintances, and a general increase in evenings *at* home and decline in evenings *away* from home. Out-of-home attendance at commercial entertainments, however, seems to be affected more than noncommercial activities such as parties, organizational meetings, and church attendance. Within the home, the routine of meals and bedtime is often disturbed, and hobbies may be somewhat neglected, but new interests may be aroused as well.

Just as it brings visitors in, so does television bring the family back to the home. Observers have remarked, however, that the increased family unity is "passive" rather than "active." TV is both credited with increasing the family's fund of common experience and shared interests, and blamed for decreasing its conversation and face-to-face interaction.[5]

So much for the overall picture of the role of mass media as reflected in time devoted to listening, reading, and watching. What, next, is the character of the interest in the various *offerings*, in reading material, in radio and television, in movies? And, later, what are the psychological effects of such media on individuals?

---

[5] This quotation, from a paper by Thomas E. Coffin (*15*), is based on findings from a number of studies. The present discussion of television viewing is based largely on Dr. Coffin's excellent review of "Television's Impact on Society," even though in some instances citation in the text is, for convenience of the reader, made to the original source.

READING INTERESTS

As noted above, more people read the daily newspaper than any other reading material. An early study (41) of newspaper reading interest during the school years showed gains in interest in almost all sections of the paper, the exceptions being the "children's page," which dropped rapidly, and the comics, which showed little change but continued high at all ages. Something of the changes in reader interest during the adult years is shown in Table 53, where it is to be noted, first, that the

TABLE 53. Percentage of Various Items in Newspapers Read by Members of Various Age Groups

Item or Topic	Age Group					
	10–19	20–29	30–39	40–49	50–59	60+
Comics						
Men	76	66	60	59	32	36
Women	71	54	43	35	22	12
Crime and disaster news						
Men	12	21	34	26	32	31
Women	14	23	36	39	33	31
News pictures						
Men	47	61	65	68	47	52
Women	45	60	62	59	52	41
Sports news						
Men	17	32	22	25	18	14
Women	4	4	5	4	7	5
Public affairs news						
Men	7	25	31	31	26	38
Women	8	19	26	27	25	27
Editorials						
Men	2	26	43	44	48	36
Women	8	23	36	36	33	32
Society news						
Men	4	7	11	9	11	11
Women	8	14	20	21	20	15
Number of cases						
Men	37	84	60	60	67	35
Women	61	91	74	86	59	32

SOURCE: Adapted from W. Schramm and D. M. White, Age, education, economic status: factors in newspaper reading, *Journalism Quart.*, 1949, 26:149–159.

"lighter" portions of the paper—comics and news pictures—seem to have greatest appeal, though the comics lose readers as the age of the reader group increases. Men are attracted to the sports page, especially in their twenties, and women to the society page, but this latter interest grows in adult years and is maintained at about the same level through the fifties. Interest in editorials, in public affairs news, and in crime and disaster news shows a somewhat slower growth but is well maintained during the adult years.

These findings illustrate how sex roles are reflected in reading interests but, more important, suggest the greater concern of more mature adults with broad social matters. Indeed, one of the investigators from whose study the facts in Table 53 were taken suggests that in this age pattern of reading interest are to be found important contrasts between needs for immediate versus delayed gratification (somewhat akin to the Freudian "Pleasure" versus "Reality" principles). Younger individuals will seek immediate rewards or vicarious experiences, whereas reading for delayed reward would be a later and more sophisticated form of learned behavior. "If that is so," this investigator argues, "we should expect this kind of reading to increase with education, start later and come to a peak at a later age than immediate reward reading, and increase more rapidly with economic status (which makes possible wider experience). We should expect the readership of comics to follow the reading pattern of immediate reward news, and the readership of editorials to follow the pattern of delayed reward news. This is exactly what [our] data do show." (74.)

Magazines represent the second most popular source of reading material. In this medium, both sexes and all ages agree in liking short stories best and show high interest in humor and continued stories. New articles, editorials, and political articles all show increases in popularity for both sexes during adolescence. Males show increasing interest in scientific articles through the school years, but this interest lags in adult years (41). Although the writers are not aware of relevant data, it would be anticipated, in the light of other findings relating to interests, that the young to middle-aged homeowner would evidence marked interest in do-it-yourself publications, whereas the middle-aged and older male might find greater appeal in gardening magazines and articles.

In a study of women's interest in magazines done at Syracuse University, "women's magazines" (e. g., *Woman's Home Companion*) were quite popular at all ages, but especially in the forties. *Reader's Digest*, on the other hand, was read by a larger proportion of the 60-year-olds than any other age group. Movie magazines were read mainly by the younger members of this adult group. Interesting effects of the interaction among generations were also apparent in this study. Children's magazines were most frequently read by those in their thirties, and *Seventeen* (the most widely read fashion magazine among the adult group, in this study) was most frequently read by women in their forties. It is a reasonable guess that such reading was stimulated by the presence of children or adolescent offspring in the home (77).

What about that special, much maligned "magazine," the ubiquitous comic book? That such materials are widely read there is no doubt. According to surveys (99), children in grades four through six read about 13 different comic books on the average; ninth graders read an average of 6; and twelfth graders an average of 3. Table 54 shows comic book readership in somewhat different terms (percentage regularly reading) and calls attention to what is likely a little known fact: a great many adults regularly read comic books. In addition to the "regular" readers over 31, another 13 percent of men and 10 percent of women were occasional readers! Here, one might say, is low-level, immediate reward reading with a vengeance!

TABLE 54. Percentage of People of Various Ages Who Reported That They Regularly Read Comic Books

	Age in Years			
	6–11	12–17	18–30	31 and Over
Males	95	87	41	16
Females	91	81	28	12

SOURCE: Survey conducted by the Market Research Company of America cited by P. A. Witty and R. A. Sizemore, Reading the comics: a summary of studies and an evaluation, I., *Elementary English*, 1954, 31:501–506.

Do comic books have the deleterious effects often attributed to them by anxious parents? Although undesirable comic books exist, and occasionally get into youngsters hands, the more popular ones (11)—*True, Sports, Crime Does Not Pay, Donald Duck, Patsy Walker, A Date with Judy*—are hardly threatening on this score. Others argue that the too unrealistic comics crowd out better reading materials and develop overdependence on pictures (and inferior pictures, at that) for the plot and, in addition, that there is little opportunity for progression of reading experience. But, argue others, comic books represent a type of modern folklore, provide a source of mental catharsis and vicarious experience, help build vocabulary, and give reading pleasure to children of limited reading ability.[6]

It would be indeed difficult to prove or disprove these contentions, and appropriate studies of such effects are lacking. However, studies have shown that the typical comic book does have a substantial amount of reading material

[6] These arguments are summarized by Strang (80).

(about 10,000 words each), that the difficulty level is about at the upper elementary or even junior high level, and that there is a minimum of slang and word distortions (*35, 36, 91*). Such findings would argue against fears that comics may unduly harm growth in vocabulary and reading.

And now what is the development of interests in books? Before 9, children show special delight in short, profusely illustrated, rather fanciful stories about animals or fairies or other children, such as Peter Rabbit stories and the Thornton Burgess series (*43*). The adventure stories later become absorbing to boys, and gradually their interests shift to adult fiction and to a wide range of miscellaneous topics (especially science, invention, and history). Girls, curiously enough, maintain interest in juvenile fiction longer and yet shift earlier than do boys to adult fiction (*43*). Their earlier and greater interest in adult (usually romantic) fiction again suggests both earlier maturing of girls and the greater importance for women of sex-social relationships. The following grouping of titles from one study (*90*) gives a general picture of changes during the age range of 9 to 15 and illustrates the similarity between reading interests and general psychological-social development.

Titles Showing Decreases in Interest
> Realistic animal stories (*Lonesome Laddie Finds a Friend, Woof-Woof the Terrier*).
> Talking animal stories (*Buster Bear's Birthday, Bob the Beaver Builds a Dam*).
> Stories of rather mild child adventures (*Cowboy Billie, Pollie and Peter in the Prairie*).
> Child life in other lands.
> Magic and fantasy (*The Magic Wand, Doll Island*).
> Boy outdoor adventure (*Boy Rangers in the Great Smokies*).

Titles Showing Little Change in Interest
> Stories of adult adventure (*Men from Mars, Call in the G-Men*).
> Travel stories (*Up and Down South America, Life Among the Head-Hunters*).
> Sports (*Making a Big-Leaguer, Camping Hints*).
> Biography and biographical adventures (*Born an Inventor, King Richard the Lion-Hearted*).
> War (*Must America Fight?*).

Titles Showing Growing Interest
> Stories of occupations (*Don't Be an Actress, Is There a Doctor in the House?*).
> Money-making and practical (*Me and My Job, Money-Making Ideas, Self-Support in College*).

Love and romance (*Cupid Takes a Holiday, Her Night of Love, Mary Mitchell's Sweetheart*).

In the study just mentioned, sex differences were larger even than age differences within this age range. Girls tend to read boys' books more frequently than boys read girls' books, and (curiously enough) those boys who do transgress into the domain of the girls are the duller ones, while the bright girls' interests most frequently overlap those of the boys (53, pp. 76–78).

Such detailed information regarding book reading is not available for adult ages, but it does seem clear that nonfiction is increasingly read with increasing adult age and fiction less frequently read (*1, 81*). "Quality" of reading appears to increase with age (*31*). Fiction is much more read by adult women than men, one investigation showing women's reading to be about 65 percent fiction while men read less than 50 percent fiction (*59*). But two points must be kept in mind about adult book reading. In the first place, many adults do not (as already mentioned) read books. In one survey 29 percent had not read a book for a year or more, (some had never read a book), and such nonreading characterized most (56 percent) of those of grade school education as contrasted with 25 percent of adults of high school education and 10 percent of college-educated adults (*59*).

In the second place, adult reading interests are often of a special nature, and these special interests are very diverse. The title most frequently mentioned as the "last book read" by nearly two thousand "active readers" in 1945 was read by only 95 people—and that was the Bible. The next title in frequency, a long, sex-laden historical novel—a best seller—was read by only 84. Fifty-eight percent of all titles were fiction and 37 percent nonfiction (the rest were both or not remembered). College-educated adults read a larger proportion of nonfiction than did those with less education.

The book reading of old people has not been adequately studied, but it is likely that the older man who is developing new hobbies, the mother whose children have grown up, or the individual who has retired may show marked shifts. Romantic fiction seems hardly appropriate for such individuals. Do they call for fiction of a special type, providing vicarious satisfaction of frustrated desires of their age? The large and increasing group of people over 65 may present special characteristics as regards reading interests: magazines, books, and special library service for them may appear. Special format may be helpful. Thus, when, in 1955, the

Saturday Evening Post introduced a new format with larger type and more spacing, "letters to the editor" from older people congratulated them on its greater readability for older people who are more susceptible to visual fatigue.

Although age differences have been emphasized above, reading interests—as other types of predispositions and behavior—are to a large degree products of one's subculture. Those of lower educational level showed less preference for novels in general, for biography, and for books related to social problems; they preferred adventure and mysteries and read more on religion (59). Those of lower social classes, according to another study, bought more copies of *True Story* and *True Romances;* those of the middle classes consumed most copies of *Ladies' Home Journal, Better Homes and Gardens,* and *Physical Culture;* and those in the top social classes read more in *Fortune* and *Time* (95). Lower socioeconomic groups were, in newspapers, somewhat more likely to read comics than upper economic groups, but the latter were more likely to read almost any other portion—editorials, public affairs, sports, society news (74). Not only are there important differences in the nature of the reading, but higher educational and cultural groups have more reading material—newspapers, magazines, books—available and read more (61, 95).

CHANGING LISTENING AND VIEWING INTERESTS

Radio and television, it will be recalled, claim more time than any other medium. Almost everyone has radio available; many homes have several sets and an additional one in the car. In the beginning of 1955, two out of every three homes in the United States were equipped with TV sets (15). Even when relatively new (in 1952–1953 when there were about half as many TV sets as at the present writing), TV often claimed a larger audience than radio. "An average broadcast of the most popular radio program (Jack Benny) was heard by 18 million persons aged 10 and over; an average issue of the most popular magazine (*Life*) was seen by 26 million; an average broadcast of the most popular TV program ('Comedy Hour') was seen by 28 million."[7] Since radio and television are thus so accessible to all or most, make little demand upon physical energy, and offer such a wide variety of programs, it might be anticipated that expressed program preferences would be rather sensitive indicators of changing interests, needs, and orientations.

Table 55 shows certain trends during the school years in preferences for radio programs. Most striking, perhaps, is the strong emergence of interest in popular dance music for both sexes, but at a much earlier age for the girls. Here is another reflection of the dominant adolescent sex-

[7] This quotation is from Coffin (15), based on a study by Politz (69).

social interest noted earlier. Interest in mystery plays drops off with age, especially for girls, whereas boys (but not girls) lose interest in dramatic plays. Semiclassical music, popular in the early grades, has been largely crowded out by the twelfth grade. Boys, much more than girls, show increasing interest with age in political speeches and news. Interest in the offerings of the radio clearly parallels the interests expressed in newspapers and books in general recreation.

TABLE 55. Percentage of Pupils in Various Grades Who Indicated Preferences for Various Types of Radio Programs

Type of Program	Boys (Grades)				Girls (Grades)			
	5	8	10	12	5	8	10	12
Mystery plays	94	94	85	67	97	95	76	39
Comic dialogues and skits	86	92	88	77	96	98	93	78
Dramatic plays	88	83	67	55	90	85	86	90
Popular dance music	47	63	83	94	70	81	95	99
Orchestra, and band (semi-classical)	44	78	61	17	60	81	57	32
News (including sports)	12	47	55	55	46	31	53	26
Political speeches	7	46	51	45	2	20	33	18
Classical music	6	16	12	11	10	25	23	20

SOURCE: From F. J. Brown, *The Sociology of Childhood*, Englewood Cliffs, N.J. Prentice-Hall, 1939. Reproduced by permission of the publisher.

The changes in program appeal during the adult years—again for radio—are shown in Table 56. Facts are presented for three cultural levels—those with grade school, high school, and college education. In general, *trends* in the same direction characterized those of college or grade school education, though level of interest was not always the same. First to be noted is the increased "seriousness" of listening with increasing age. Increasing interest in the affairs of world and locality is suggested in the larger percentages among older groups who listen to news and to discussions of public issues. Interest in religious programs and in classical and semiclassical music also increases. Second, there is decreasing interest in comedy, in popular dance music, in complete dramas, in mystery programs, in sports programs.

These facts describing radio interests were obtained prior to the widespread development of television and thus may not correctly represent actual radio preferences today. But even though the advent of TV has reduced radio listening, it is not likely that it has markedly altered the

TABLE 56. Percentage of Various Age and Educational Status Groups Who Indicated Preferences for Different Types of Radio Programs[a]

	College			High School			Grade School		
	21–29	30–49	50 and Over	21–29	30–49	50 and Over	21–29	30–49	50 and Over
News broadcasts	75%	78%	83%	72%	75%	79%	61%	70%	74%
Comedy programs	70	59	49	72	64	57	55	52	51
Quiz and audience participation	51	56	57	60	61	62	46	53	47
Popular and dance music	66	56	29	68	56	32	56	46	29
Complete dramas	61	55	46	51	39	43	44	42	32
Discussions of public issues	59	63	67	33	45	54	21	37	36
Mystery programs	56	41	21	53	45	32	59	42	27
Semiclassical music	55	48	50	28	36	36	14	20	25
Sports programs	47	37	35	41	35	34	25	32	3
Classical music	53	50	61	21	27	36	15	31	24
Hillbilly and western music	10	8	19	24	22	20	42	39	38
Religious programs	11	14	28	9	17	29	11	25	36

[a] Percentages do not add to 100 percent in any of these columns because more than one answer was permitted each respondent.

SOURCE: From P. F. Lazarsfeld and P. L. Kendall, *Radio Listening in America*, Englewood Cliffs, N.J. Prentice-Hall, 1948. Reproduced by permission of the publisher.

relative rank or age patterning of program preferences. What about TV program preferences? In a 1953 survey, "I Love Lucy" was at the top of the list of favorites for elementary school children, for high school pupils, and for parents as well (98). Other program preferences (top five) for several groups follow (98):

Elementary School Children: "I Love Lucy," "Superman," "Red Buttons," "Dragnet," "Roy Rogers Show."

High School Pupils: "I Love Lucy," "Dragnet," "Colgate Comedy Hour," "Arthur Godfrey," "Red Buttons."

Parents: "I Love Lucy," "What's My Line?" "Omnibus," "Arthur Godfrey," "Mr. Peepers."

Teachers: "Meet the Press," "Omnibus," "News," "What's My Line?" "Mr. Peepers."

Dropping out of childhood adventure programs ("Superman," "Roy Rogers") and emergence of the adolescent interest in variety programs and humor are evident here, as is also the more serious and intellectual interest of the adult years, though the latter trend is only slightly evident in this listing.

These trends would be anticipated on the basis of other interest trends in radio and movies discussed earlier. So similar are the trends, in fact, that little is to be gained by detailing them again for TV. It might be expected, however, that certain adult age trends in television interests might differ from trends in, for example, movie interests. It is suggested below that movie attendance declines in part because of declining physical energy. Does interest in movies and plays persist with increased adult age when they can be viewed in one's own home without expenditure of effort in getting dressed and going out? One age analysis of TV viewing (77) suggests that the decline of interest in plays and movies is still evident though perhaps not so sharp in the case of TV. But this trend might again be explained on the basis of declining energy, since such plays and movies are often presented on TV late at night. A second contrast between radio listening and TV viewing appeared in this study. Whereas with increasing adult age there was a decline of interest in radio programs involving variety shows and popular music, TV viewers reported no decline of interest in programs featuring popular music and an actual increase in interest in variety programs (77). Perhaps the richer presentation of TV, involving both visual and auditory stimuli, is responsible for the reversal of this age trend.

What now of movie interests? This medium clearly resembles television except that choice of program (a particular movie) represents more of a commitment, more of a decision, since it involves the inconvenience of dressing and travel and the price of admission. But once in the movie theater, the viewer is a relatively passive spectator as in TV. Perhaps it is these very differences that make movie-going behavior so much different from behavior with respect to the other communication media. If TV is a family activity, movie-going is largely a nonfamily social activity. The most striking aspects of the change in movie behavior are the changes in the extent of attendance and with whom! The gradual emancipation from home is reflected in attendance in childhood. According to a study now some years old, early attendance, particularly for girls, is primarily with parents, but in the teens attendance is mainly with one's own friends. At all ages boys attended alone more than girls did (19). Movie attendance is a major dating activity in the teens (37). But movie attendance begins to decline in the late teens, probably because of the competition of other activities (27). And this decline continues into the adult years (8, 54).

In the twenties only 19 percent never attend, but in the "over 60" group, 73 percent never attend (54). In fact, the investigators in a recent study refer to the decline in movie attendance in adult years as one of the most spectacular findings in the entire field of communication behavior. In explanation they write as follows:

It is not difficult to account for the fact that the movie fans are found among the young people. The teens and twenties are age periods of relatively few personal and social responsibilities, and therefore those people have more "free evenings." And since few young people have as yet developed definite intellectual goals, a free evening might just as well be spent at the movies as in any other type of activity. Furthermore, movie going is a social activity (more than magazine reading, for example) through which the young people make social contacts which are important to them. Movie going is thus much more than mere entertainment. Whatever the content of the film, the experience of attending a movie probably plays an important role in the daily lives of young people.

As people grow older, however, they find their evenings filled with duties and plans, either imposed or self-assigned. In addition, movie going becomes more and more of an effort with increasing age. Having to travel to a theater, perhaps stand in line, and not return home until late are considerations which make movie going less enjoyable. Finally, older people, married and with a circle of friends of long standing, have less need for the kind of social activity represented by movie going.

There are additional data in our study to indicate the social context of movie attendance. We find, for example, that single people, whatever their age, are more likely to be movie fans than married people. Furthermore, there is a marked sex difference in this respect. The single men in each age group, those who initiate social contacts, are more frequent moviegoers than are single women. Among the married people there is no such sex difference. Further evidence is contained in the radio program preferences expressed by different segments of the movie audience. The movie fans, no matter what their age, choose popular and dance music, the kind of program suitable for social gatherings, much more frequently than do either the occasional or rare moviegoers.[8]

What types of movies do people like best at different ages? First, in the school years comes an interest in active, swashbuckling tales; then, at adolescence there is an interest in the romantic (25). During the school years there is a decline with increased age in attendance at crime, juvenile, and especially western movies but a slight increase in movies dealing with romance, musical comedy, historical drama, and comedy and

[8] Quoted from Lazarsfeld and Kendall, *Radio Listening in America*, New York, Prentice-Hall, 1948, pp. 11–12.

farce. But, in the main, for pupils of all grade levels and for adults attendance follows very closely the availability of any given type of picture, though there are certain exceptions (25). For adults, attendance at movies dramatizing novels or dealing with historical or social drama or with romance was, in one study, greater than would be expected on the basis of availability. On the other hand, adults tended to neglect showings of westerns, comedy and farce, and character drama (25).

EFFECTS OF THE MASS MEDIA

Because of the amount of time devoted to the mass media by children, adults have frequently expressed much concern about their effects upon the younger generation. And, of course, the alarmists—who frequently are those who most vigorously express their views—have tended to focus upon alleged harmful effects and have neglected positive contributions. The contributions of these media to the enrichment of modern life are, in fact, almost beyond comprehension. In almost all spheres—political, economic, educational, recreational, spiritual—the mass media are among the very potent agents. And while criticisms may be advanced, it is not surprising that parents as a group view television, for example, in a most favorable light and see more advantages than disadvantages. Its great educational contribution is widely recognized, with the chief criticism relating to the frequent portrayal of horror and violence (15).

A first approach to assessing the effects of the mass media is to determine objectively what sorts of "content" are being beamed, in one way or another, upon the presumably susceptible youth. Such analyses, when done, have often seemed to support those who are fearful of the effects. Thus, in studies of movie content some years ago, innumerable scenes of drinking, crime, and love-making were noted (20). And a more recent analysis of TV programs presented in New York City during one week in January, 1951, disclosed a dearth of really constructive programs for children in contrast to many westerns and thrillers.[9] Those who examine comic books can readily identify many which would hardly be viewed as wholesome.

Some of the most direct efforts to evaluate the effects of such media are to be found in the excellent Payne Fund studies of the effects of movies. These studies were done some years ago but are still pertinent. It was shown, for example, that children are measurably stirred emotionally by the movies. Apparatus much like a "lie detector" was used ("emo-

[9] A survey discussed by Witty and Bricker (99).

tion detector" it might be called) to give records of pulse, breathing, and electrical changes in the body while certain moving pictures were being watched. Melodramatic danger scenes strongly affected the 9-year-old children, but older persons apparently sensed the unreality. Erotic scenes affect a few children as early as 9 years, have greatest effect around 16 to 18, and thereafter have less, probably because of adult "discount" or the greater possibility of direct rather than vicarious satisfaction (24). A device under children's beds which recorded every movement showed youngsters frequently to be more restless in sleep after seeing a moving picture (as restless as two cups of coffee made them) (72).

Moving pictures were found to affect young people's attitudes on important questions, and these changes in attitude continued as long as a year and a half after the picture was seen (66). Conduct was affected. Autobiographies written by young people, anonymous answers to questions, interviews, conversations at high school parties, and similar evidence from delinquents and criminals all agreed that this was often so.

Of considerable importance is the cumulative effect on manners and mannerisms and on both the details and direction of social life. Here is the common case of the girl who "kept my hair just like" the admired actress, "plucked my eyebrows in her way," imitated ways of holding her hands, glancing down. Others "learned to put on make-up . . . to make love, to smoke, and to wear swell clothes . . ." "what to do when in a crowd . . ." "how to act with boys," "how to make a good appearance." Desires stirred: "When I see movies that show snappy clothes and wealth I . . . want these things also," . . . and "passionate love pictures . . . make me . . . want to be loved." (5, p. 85f.) And antisocial behaviors may occur. A 12-year-old slum boy said, "I feel brave when I see an exciting picture, and go home and lick my little nephew." A young burglar told how "When we came out of the show a couple of the boys suggested that we try to rob a store, the way we had seen in the picture. . . . We . . . bought a crowbar and screw driver and went to a clothing store and sprung the lock." (5, pp. 19, 51.)

Although there is little doubt that radio and television also have temporary emotional effects upon children, it is of some interest that when habitual listeners to crime dramas were compared with nonlisteners in respect to such general behavior as nervous habits, fears, and daydreaming differences were of little or no significance (73). And analysis of contrasts between those who listened and those who did not listen to such programs as anticrime, daily adventure, modern music, and soap operas suggested that "while they do not seem to contribute anything positive to the listening groups, neither are they very harmful to children in general"

(73, p. 139). The most significant differences between listeners and nonlisteners, according to this study, were found in the case of such program categories as educational, drama, quiz, and comedy-variety. Listeners in general exceeded nonlisteners in such positive traits as intelligence and school achievement.

Differences between those who read many comic books and those who read few have also been shown to be negligible (57), and a recent reviewer of the research literature on television concludes that TV has little effect on academic attainment (15). Differences between movie-goers and nonmovie-goers among public school children were also negligible in one study (34), as were differences between those who attended movies, read comic books, and listened to radio serial programs to excess compared with those who seldom or never indulged (33). Studies are not in entire agreement on these issues, but they are sufficiently consistent to indicate that the mass media do not have a generally disruptive effect (4, 15).

The broader effects of such fantasy opportunities as those provided by TV, radio, and reading upon the modern personality have not yet been adequately evaluated. The average individual is now provided with pseudoexperiences in such profusion that over a period of time there must be important cumulative effects. Various collections of evidence provided in this chapter indicate that ideas are acquired, emotions stirred, manners and customs modified, interests redirected or accentuated, and conduct affected. In the aggregate, psychological experience has been added to. It seems almost inevitable that in certain respects emotional development must be accelerated and the imagination stimulated. Thus, a total personality is evolved which is stimulated and enriched and perhaps at the same time made wishful and impractical. Psychologically, experience has perhaps, escaped the limitations of reality. And those who partake of one fare tend also to partake of others, i. e., the radio fan tends also to be a frequent movie-goer and a regular magazine reader (54). Whether, with all such reënforcing experiences, conduct can nonetheless be kept responsible and interest congruent with reality is not yet clear.

But, as already suggested, the total effects may not be as directly harmful as they seem. It is likely that much of the psychological influence of movies, radio, television, and reading may be secondary rather than primary. That is, while such stimuli may reënforce or arouse tendencies already present, it is unlikely that they are frequently a primary cause of delinquency or other behavior. The child frightened by various programs is likely already an insecure child made that way by other influences in his social environment. Nor is it the fault of the movie that some people find "escape" there. The need for "escape" has a deeper source and would likely be fulfilled, perhaps by unsupported fantasy, in the absence of movies and other media of mass communication. The youngsters mentioned above who put to use a burglary technique shown in a movie were likely already well on the road to delinquency if not previously delinquent. For every child already predisposed to delinquency who has a delinquent act suggested by the movies, there are hundreds of others who were exposed to the same movie but, lacking a predisposition in this direction, were not so influenced.

Developments and Contrasts in Interest Patterns

Participation in a *particular* recreational activity, liking a *particular* radio or television program, or enjoying a *particular* comic strip seldom has much psychological significance. It is only as these specific interests are found to be part of a general *pattern* of similar interests that they reveal much about motivation or personality or become useful as predictors of later patterns of behavior, such as vocational choice. It will thus be instructive to examine developmental trends in interest patterns. Also, examination of a variety of contrasts in general patterns—as between occupational and sex groups—may be corrective of the common tendency when studying human development of focusing attention upon *specific* instances of age differences (as in particular preferences) at the neglect of essential similarities. Often, as will be noted below, differences between educational, sex, and occupational groups are greater than those between age groups.

AGE DIFFERENCES IN RATE OF CHANGE

How rapidly do interests change or mature, considering the total picture and disregarding specific interests? One analysis seemed to indicate that between the fifth grade and the fourth year of college growth toward maturity was rapid, with girls showing earlier maturity of interests than boys, a difference especially noticeable at about the age when pubescence occurs (70). These trends for grades 5 through 12 are shown in Figure 87. Analysis of the data of the Strong Vocational Interest Blank shows similar rapid change during the teens. A scale of "Interest-Maturity" (the score of which is indicative of the degree to which the interest of an individual more closely resembles those of a 15-year-old or a 25-

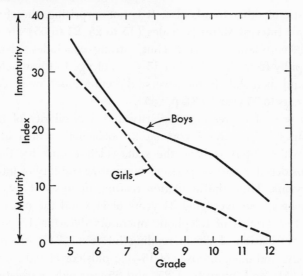

Figure 87. Progress of the Two Sexes Toward Maturity of Interests as Shown by Grade Indexes Based on Interest Subtest of the Pressey Interest Attitude Text. (Adapted form S. L. and C. L. Pressey, Development of the Interest-Attitude tests, *J. Appl. Psychol.*, 1933, 17:1–16.)

year-old) showed very rapid change between the ages of 15 to 23, with little change thereafter (*84*, p. 260), but, as will be noted below, interests have apparently stabilized enough by the junior or senior year in high school to permit good prediction of patterns well into adult years.

The rate of change during the adult years has been studied by means of a second Interest-Maturity scale[10] which was developed to show change between 25 and 55. A steady but much slower change in interest patterns occurred over this adult age range than was true in childhood and adolescence, year-to-year changes being quite uniform in adult life.[11] It will be recalled in this connection that a dominant feature of interest change in the teens is the emergence of sex-social interests and that in adult life a striking feature is declining social interest. This reversal is

[10] Two Interest-Maturity scales (one ages 15 to 25, the other ages 25 to 50) were necessary because age curves for individuals were not consistently increasing or decreasing. About two-fifths of the items increased or decreased from age 15 to age 25, at which point their directions were reversed to age 55.

[11] This finding reported by Strong in 1943 differs from his report in 1931 (*81*) that 50 percent of the change that occurs between ages 25 and 55 occurs between 25 and 35. It should be noted, however, that Strong is discussing changes in "liking," not changes in participation. Other research already mentioned in this chapter indicates that actual participation drops our earlier in adult years than does "liking" for the activity.

characteristic of other trends also. It is not surprising, therefore, to find that the two Interest-Maturity scales (15 to 25, 25 to 55) are negatively correlated (correlation, −.41). Thus, Strong concludes "that interests change rapidly from those held at 15 years of age to those held at about 25 years, and then shift in the reverse direction much more slowly from about 25 years to 55 years" (*84*, p. 285).

Another way of expressing similarity and dissimilarity of interests at different ages is by way of correlation coefficients which indicate the extent to which interests have the same relative rank for the two age groups considered. Such comparisons emphasize stability of interests during adult years. Thus, the nonfiction reading interests of two groups of school teachers, one averaging 24 years of age and the other 41, correlated .81; two groups of telephone operators differing 12 years in age showed a correlation of .85 in reading interests (*94*). Among Strong's group of boys and men, interests of 15-year-olds correlated .73 with those of 55-year-olds, and interests of 25- and 55-year-olds correlated .88. According to Strong, the "primary conclusion regarding interests of men between 25 and 55 years of age is that they change very little. When these slight differences over 30 years are contrasted with the differences to be found among occupational groups, or between men and women, or between unskilled and professional men, it must be realized that age and the experience that goes with age change an adult man's interests very little. At 25 years of age he is largely what he is going to be, and even at 20 years of age he has acquired pretty much the interests that he will have throughout life" (*84*, p. 313). The present writers, nonetheless, venture the opinion that despite these high correlations between overall patterns, those age differences that do exist are very important in understanding the older as compared with the younger man.

CONTRASTS OF THE SEXES

Sex and the factors associated with sex play a profound role in the formation of interest patterns and personality generally. Indeed, sex differences in interests are as marked as any other type of contrast that can be made, a fact which has been evident in the preceding discussion but which is even more striking when "pattern" comparisons are made.[12] In

[12] R. L. Thorndike (*90*) in a study of reading interests has shown sex differences to be more pronounced than differences between age groups (within the age range of 9 to 15) and between high and low intelligence groups. And one of the present writers has shown Oriental adolescents in Hawaii to be more similar to whites of the same sex in America than to members of their own race of opposite sex (*49*).

a major study of sex differences, a "masculinity-femininity" test consisting of several hundred items (a substantial portion involved interests) which had been shown to differentiate the two sexes was administered to a large number of people from high school age on through the seventies. Disregarding age, the general contrasts between the sexes in adult years were described by the investigators as follows:

From whatever angle we have examined them the males included in the standardization groups evinced a distinctive interest in exploit and adventure, in outdoor and physically strenuous occupations, in machinery and tools, in science, physical phenomena, and inventions; and, from rather occasional evidence, in business and commerce. On the other hand, the females of our groups have evinced a distinctive interest in domestic affairs and in aesthetic objects and occupations; they have distinctively preferred more sedentary and indoor occupations, and occupations more directly ministrative, particularly to the young, the helpless, the distressed. Supporting and supplementing these are the more subjective differences—those in emotional disposition and direction. The males directly or indirectly manifest the greater self-assertion and aggressiveness; they express more hardihood and fearlessness, and more roughness of manners, language, and sentiments. The females express themselves as more compassionate and sympathetic, more timid, more fastidious and aesthetically sensitive, more emotional in general (or at least more expressive of the four emotions considered), severer moralists, yet admit in themselves more weaknesses in emotional control and (less noticeably) in physique.

But we must define some of our terms more precisely, for instance, "aggressiveness" and "self-assertion." The evidence is for initiative, enterprise, vigorous activity, outdoor adventure; "aggressiveness" need not imply selfishness or tyranny or unfair attack. The compassion and sympathy of the female, again, appears from the evidence personal rather than abstract, less a principled humanitarianism than an active sympathy for palpable misfortune or distress. In disgust, in aesthetic judgment, and in moral censure, the evidence is rather for the influence of fashion and of feeling than of principle or reason. Our evidence need not imply the possession of a "truer" taste or a more discerning conscience (88, pp. 447–448).

Although certain activities are thus characteristically "feminine" and others characteristically "masculine," the sexes appear to differ in the consistency with which they adhere to their sex roles. Boys apparently resent being called a "sissy" more than girls resent being called a "tomboy"—perhaps because of the relative status the two sexes have in the culture at large. In any event studies contrasting the activities of boys and girls typically show more girls to participate in boys' activities than boys in girls'. As previously noted, for example, girls are much more likely to read "boys' books" than vice versa. In total, analysis of sex differences in interests show much the same contrasts as do sex contrasts in motives and needs described in the earlier chapter on motivation. This perhaps is to be expected since information as to liking for various activities versus disliking constitutes basic data from which motives or needs may be inferred and by which they may then be measured.

How early do sex differences in interests appear? And are differences maintained to the same degree throughout life? Various lines of evidence suggest that sex differences appear quite early and are greatest somewhere between 9 or 10 years of age and 20. Lehman and Witty (55) found greatest differences in boys' and girls' play at around 9 or 10 years of age, the play interests becoming more similar thereafter. Others believe the differences to be greatest at pubescence. Symonds (86) suggested that this age (the "mating age") is the age when girls are most feminine and boys most masculine; that is, the age at which they most closely conform to the sex role ideal set up by the culture—when sex drive is likely strongest and differences in interests greatest.

Figure 88 shows trends during the adult years indicating that older men are somewhat more feminine in interests and older women slightly more feminine. This finding is confirmed by another study (84), also cross-sectional in plan,[13] but, interestingly enough, in a recent *longitudinal* study, both men and women became reliably more masculine in their interests between their twenties and forties (44). A suggested explanation is that the culture is tending increasingly to emphasize masculine types of interests, and thus these individuals changed in this direction. It might be expected that this change would be greatest for women (though the findings did not support this) in view of the much more general acceptance of women into what have traditionally been men's activities and pursuits—factory work, professions, smoking, sports, household chores of typically masculine responsibility. But it is clear from research on interests that although the sexes tend to rank items of interest similarly [correlations of .61 at high school and .71 in adulthood (84)] important differences exist throughout life.

OCCUPATIONAL CONTRASTS

The differences that exist among the interest patterns of members of various occupational groups have received a great deal of attention and

[13] The trends during high school and college years shown in the chart were not commented upon because they were not confirmed by the other study (84, pp. 232–233) and because these findings are likely greatly influenced by selective factors operating between high school and college.

study because of their practical significance for vocational guidance purposes. If it is possible to steer an adolescent into a congenial occupation, in the sense that *his* interests are like the interests of others actually working in that field, it is more likely that he will be happy in that work and more highly motivated to capitalize his aptitudes.

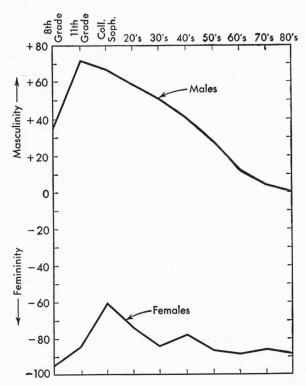

Figure 88.   Adult Age Trends in Masculinity and Femininity of Interests and Attitudes. (By permission from *Sex and Personality: Studies in Masculinity and Femininity*, by L. M. Terman and C. C. Miles, New York, McGraw-Hill, 1936.)

That occupations actually do differ markedly in the interest patterns characterizing their members is shown in Figure 89. This figure based on data obtained by the Kuder Preference Record shows the percentile ranks of the mean scores earned by members of various occupational groups on the several types of interest patterns measured by that test. Accountants and auditors all seem to be exceptionally high in computational interests, but low in mechanical, artistic, and social service inter-

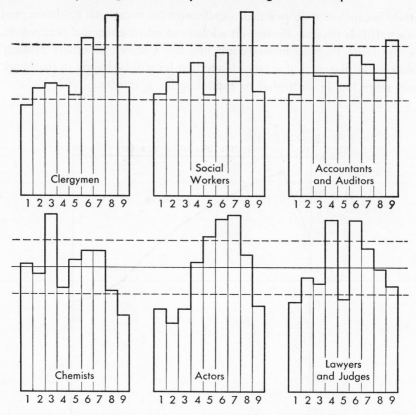

Figure 89. Interest Profiles for Men in Selected Occupations. The key to the scales is as follows: 1—Mechanical, 2—Computational, 3—Scientific, 4—Persuasive, 5—Artistic, 6—Literary, 7—Musical, 8—Social Service, 9—Clerical. The solid line across the charts is the 50th percentile; the dotted lines represent the 25th and 75th percentiles. (From G. F. Kuder, *Revised Manual for the Kuder Preference Record*, Chicago, Science Research Associates, 1946.)

ests. The three highest areas of interests for clergymen are literature, music, and social service. Such differences (the reader can note other contrasts in the chart) are striking and persistent over the years, as they would have to be if prediction into adult years is to be accomplished. A number of studies (83, 84) with the Strong Vocational Interest blank have shown measured interests to be predictive of occupation actually entered, to be related to vocational achievement (as amount of life insurance sold), and to bear a relationship to job satisfaction—though not a high relationship—18 years later.

In his extensive analysis of interest patterns, Strong observes that differences in interests among the occupational groups on his Vocational Interest blank far outweigh the differences between age groups (*81*, p. 24). And individuals who show interests characteristic of a particular occupational group at high school or college age persist in that pattern. Thus, on retesting the same individuals, test-retest correlations averaged as follows: .84 for 5 years; .82 for 10 years; and .75 for 22 years after college senior status. Thus, "those who had interests most similar to engineer, lawyer, or minister on the first occasion were the ones who had scores most similar to those same criterion groups on the second occasion, and vice-versa" (*82*).

PATTERNING OF INTERESTS IN TERMS OF ABILITIES AND NEEDS

The pervasive role of cultural factors in the development of interests has already been abundantly illustrated in this chapter. Contrasting patterns of interests between sociocultural groups, sex groups, occupational groups, and even age groups—and differences among individuals—are undoubtedly very largely a product of cultural opportunity and expectation. But individual and group differences in interests, and differences among people of varying ages, may also be attributed in part to differences in abilities and needs.

First the matter of abilities. It seems almost self-evident that of all the things a person has the opportunity to do, he will select those things which he is *capable* of doing. An infant does not play with a rattle until he is capable of grasping or manipulating it. Playing marbles, dressing a doll, riding a bicycle must all await the prior development of requisite motor capacity. Where special orthopedic, sensory, or health handicaps or special limitations of strength or motor capacities are present, the range of activities in which a person can participate is limited. The energy level of the individual—his total capacity for exertion, his resiliency—is also a major factor underlying interest development and change. High energy level seems to exert a pressure for activity and, when decreased, forces the abandonment of those activities making greater energy demands. The decline in energy, the slowing down of the organism, the increased fatigability of the individual with increasing adult age would seem to be a major factor of importance in producing the downward trend in a whole pattern of energy-demanding activities noted earlier and prompting an increase with age in the more sedentary, less demanding activities.

Mental abilities, like motor abilities, also influence interest development. Neither a 4-year-old child nor a moron will be interested in chess, nor is an 80-year-old likely to be. Bright children read more and read material of better quality and a more realistic nature (53, 87) and have more diverse interests than dull children. Bright children (who by definition are capable of more complex behavior) show a greater variation in their activities (55), choose a wider variety of radio programs (26), and tend toward greater diversification in their hobbies (7, 58). Bright children tend to participate in more activities involving thinking or intellectual activity (56, 87), to value humor content in radio programs (14), and to make collections of things requiring a high degree of classification (23). Similar differences will be found on the adult level. A keen 35-year-old man will find interest in a difficult profession, a difficult game, a complex and highly intellectual hobby. As capacity matures in childhood and adolescence, new interests will open up, and decline in capacity will likely make certain activity, for example, those calling for reorganization of behavior, less interesting.

It was suggested in the chapter on motivation that motives and needs play an important organizing role in human behavior, and it has been suggested several times in the present chapter that certain patterns of change in interests may be attributed to changes in motivation. The strong upsurge in sex-social interest in adolescence may be largely attributed to sexual maturation and increased sex drive, and the decline in such interest after 25 (as already noted) may be indicative of the lessened importance of sex drive due to both actual biological decline and to satisfaction of the drive in marriage. The increasing drive, as adult age increases, for *sameness* of activity and the dislike of change may be partially attributed to energy decline or to decreased capacity to change (either because of habit rigidity or intellectual decline), as already noted, but this important change in adult interests may also be viewed as *motivated* by a need to achieve security, in the face of losses with age, by clinging to old, established habits and by avoiding new activities.

In total, interests represent activities that are *satisfying* to the individual. The interrelationships among an individual's interests should reflect his major needs, and studies of the interrelationships among interests may reveal their meanings as expressions of needs. Thus, intercorrelations among general interests (such as sports, outdoor games, dancing, reading fiction, playing a musical instrument) computed by Thorndike some 20 years ago (89) showed certain interests to go together and others to be unrelated or even antagonistic. High interest in one's regular job, for example, tended to be associated with low interest in recreation, especially sedentary games, dancing, theater, and movies.

TABLE 57. Interrelationships Among Interests and Attitudes and Their Patterning with Respect to Certain Drives, as Revealed by a Factor Analysis Study

Factor and Items	Factor Loading
Factor 2 "Mating Drive"[a]	
I like to go to a good movie every week or so.	.54
I want to make love to a woman I find beautiful.	.41
I want to see those responsible for the present inflation (market manipulators and others) severely punished.	.38
I want America to get more protection against the atom bomb.	.37
I want to see more good restaurants serving attractive meals around this town.	.34
I like a novel with a love interest concerning a ravishingly attractive heroine.	.33
I want to travel and explore unknown corners of the earth.	.33
I do not want to get my wife the clothes she likes and to save her from the more toilsome household drudgeries.	−.30
I want to see birth control made available to and practiced by all people who need to control the size of their families.	.29
Factor 3 "Gregarious Drive"	
I like to take an active part in athletics and get exercise.	.69
I want to attend football games and follow the fate of teams.	.42
In matters of reasoning (e.g., philosophical and moral issues) I do not want to fight authority if my opinions conflict.	−.40
I like to enjoy the spirit of comradeship that exists among my fellow students at the University of Illinois.	.32
I like playing indoors, sociable games, such as card games.	.32
Factor 5 "Curiosity Drive"	
I want to listen to music.	.52
I do not want to be smartly dressed, with a personal appearance that commands admiration.	−.52
I want to know more about science.	.50
I want to see fine paintings, sculpture, art exhibits.	.44
I should like to spend more time learning about and controlling mechanical things, engines, electrical gadgets.	.33

[a] The present writers have substituted the more commonly used term "drive," for the word "erg" used by Dr. Cattell.

SOURCE: Adapted from R. B. Cattell, The discovery of ergic structure in man in terms of common attitudes, J. Abnorm. and Soc. Psychol., 1950, 45:598–618.

A more recent study utilized a factor analysis technique to study the interrelationships among some 50 statements of interest or attitude. The findings suggested that seemingly quite different activities might well be expressions of the same drive. In Table 57 are presented the items that had highest factor loadings for three selected drives, "mating," "gregarious", and "curiosity" drives. Among the "interests" which have high "loadings" for the "mating drive" were frequent movie attendance, desire for more good restaurants in town, wish to travel and explore, and liking for novels with a strong love interest and a beautiful heroine.

It will be noted in the instance of this drive that some curious items are grouped together. And this raises an important point about interests: they may be rather direct expressions of needs, or they may be obscure substitutes. Thus, the investigator suggests that the inclusion in Table 57 under "mating drive" of two items reflecting anxiety and the items relating to food-seeking and exploration may have loadings for this factor (essentially sex drive) "because, as Freud and other clinicians have argued, these are the most common sublimations and transformations of the sex drive" (12). Radio, television, reading, or sheer unsupported fantasy may provide satisfaction where direct satisfactions are impossible. In one study of conversations (78), it was found that a group of girls who had less opportunity for heterosexual social experiences *talked* more about sex than did those who had opportunities! Thus, in utilizing interests as a means of understanding people, it is necessary to see the specific activity in terms of its *psychological* meaning. Often this is not the "obvious" meaning! The major advance in the psychological study of play and interests in recent years has grown out of recognition that such activities fulfill or reflect basic biological or psychological needs of people. Studies have investigated the projection of personality into play activities (as, for example, with dolls) and the use of play activities as a means of therapy for improving personality and adjustments (3, 75).

Interests and Adjustment: Problems and Potentials

As leisure time becomes increasingly more plentiful, and as automation reduces even further opportunities for intrinsic satisfaction in work, basic satisfactions will, to a greater degree, have to be found in interests and hobbies, in nonwork activities. What, now, is the relationship between interests and adjustment at various ages? What are the potentials and the problems in the utilization of interests as a source of basic satisfactions?

RELATION OF INTERESTS TO ADJUSTMENT

One of the most striking contrasts between well- and poorly adjusted individuals lies in the extent to which they get pleasure from a wide variety of activities. This is well illustrated in a study done at the University of Minnesota.

All of the school children from 9 to 18 years of age in Noble County, Minnesota, some 3200 children in all, were assessed as to their general adjustment on the combined basis of personality measures filled out by the children and ratings by teachers. Each youngster also filled out an incomplete sentence test

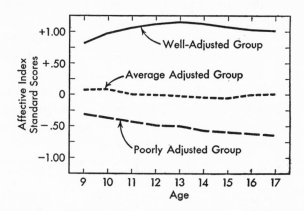

Figure 90. Trends with Age for Well-, Average, and Poorly Adjusted Youngsters with Respect to Their tendency to View Experiences and Activities Positively or Negatively. (Adapted from J. E. Anderson, The relation of attitude to adjustment, *Education*, 1952, 73:210–218.)

(e. g., When I go home from school, I . . .) and indicated on an extensive list of chores and tasks which ones he had done and whether or not he liked or disliked them. The incomplete sentences test was scored by determining the ratio of pleasant responses ("When I go home from school, I have a good time.") to unpleasant responses ("When I go home from school, the boys tease me."). This was termed the "affective index." In the case of the chores, a ratio of likes to dislikes was ascertained.

Figure 90 shows the affective index based on the incomplete sentences test for well-adjusted children, those of average adjustment, and those deemed poorly adjusted over the 9 to 18 age range. At all ages, it will be noted, the well-adjusted children showed a much more positive attitude toward experience. The poorly adjusted children, especially the older ones, tended to have more unpleasant experiences. The same relationships held in the case of liking for chores and tasks: the well-adjusted children had higher ratios of liked to disliked tasks. It is important to note, in the chart, that the general pattern of orientation is laid down early. As early as 9 years of age, there is clear separation between the groups.

Although extensive data of this kind are not available for adults, the findings that are available are just as consistent. Thus, in a study of the adjustment of school teachers, who ranged from 20 to 50 years of age, those who had active, outdoor, and social hobbies were predominantly well adjusted whereas those who had work-type and teaching hobbies were predominantly poorly adjusted (67). Another writer who studied the adaptation of 50 men and women to old age concluded that of three factors (broad interests, economic security, freedom from physical handicap) that seemed especially significant, *most* important was strong or varied interests and activities (17). A case study analysis (71) and two comprehensive studies of old age also demonstrated that having plenty to do each day is related to happiness and adjustment (51, 62). A vigorous, full, happy life at 73 years of age is illustrated in the following excerpt from a letter written by a widow:

This is no time to mope. I find no time for it. I bake my own bread, do my washing and ironing and make preserves. I made over the place that I moved to that was a mess of weeds and is now blooming profusely. I make my own clothes, grow vegetables and share with neighbors and friends, read the paper morning and evening, take an interest in civic affairs, never lose a vote. . . .

I am never unhappy; far too busy to even think of it. I have my radio and can go out and see or hear interesting things if I am not too busy at home. I can go to bed when I like, get up when I please, eat what I want (if I can meet the price), go to see loved friends or relatives near enough to reach, read or do anything I like anytime of the day. If I want to make a pie or cake at 10:00 P.M. no one is here to tell me I can't.

Many times when I want to relax I play solitaire. Some knit, but I can think better with cards as they make my mind more active. Mentally and physically I am no older than 50. Some are older at that age because they think AGE. I never do, that is one of the things that makes life sour for them—why not go out and grow a lovely plant, bake a nice batch of bread and give it to someone who has no time to do so or make a pretty apron for a friend's birthday? (32, pp. 134–135.)

The generalization that good adjustment and satisfying interests go together thus seems well supported at all ages. But the question raised by Dr. J. E. Anderson in the Minnesota study of children is most pertinent: "Are children [or is anyone?] more pleasantly oriented because they are well-adjusted or are they well-adjusted because they are pleasantly oriented?" (2). The causal relationship probably operates, to a degree, in both directions. Attempts to develop in oneself or others varied interests as a source of pleasure may effectively improve adjustment. Also, improvement of adjustment through counseling or psychotherapy or through reduction of environmental stress may well improve the subject's enjoyment of a variety of activities.

RECREATION AND BASIC NEEDS

Good adjustment is promoted by interests and recreation to the degree that basic needs are satisfied by such activities. Activity needs in childhood are met by running games; heterosexual needs in adolescence by dancing and dating; achievement needs in retirement, as one old gentleman commented, "by growing the best roses in the block." But, often, one must *learn* that basic satisfactions are thus possible in recreation; a reorientation of values may be necessary.

As certain writers (32) have pointed out, the dichotomy between work and play has lost much of its meaning. Play may be a source of recognition by others, a means of social participation, a means of creative self-expression, an escape from boredom, a service to others. All of these are frequently listed as meanings of work. "Play is not a heavy and unpleasant burden, but this meaning of work is one that men would be content to do without. Play is not easily made the basis for self-respect and a sense of worth for people reared in a work-centered society, but it may become so for the adults of the future, reared in a leisure-centered society. The one value of work which, by definition, can never be achieved by play is that of earning a living. But some ways of earning a living are so pleasant that a person can truthfully say, 'My work is my play'" (32, p. 130). And in many cases, hobbies originally started for sheer pleasure and relaxation may, at retirement or before, be turned to income-producing ends. Even here, then, the distinction between work and play is not clear cut.

Indeed, there is need to view play as not merely amusement and time-filling in contrast to work, but as useful, constructive, and worthwhile in its own right. Leisure-time interests too often seem innocuous, so empty as to provide little opportunity for significant satisfactions. They tend to be useless, even wasteful, snobbish, a means for display of socio-economic status. Thus, the tycoons of Middletown introduced fox hunting into central Indiana, golf having become too "common." And the horse comes back for leisure as a means by which some may look down upon others. To find interest in constructive and worth-while endeavor seems a major need. Sundry fraternal and community organizations, also groups of the Junior League and the Rotary type, are tending to do this. A recreational policy frankly having a broadly utilitarian character might well receive more consideration. And schools *are* becoming more interesting to young people. In some types of work, the old craftsman's spirit seems to be returning. To be interested in study and work may again come into fashion. Nor does play need be as competitive as often it is. The coöperative working together on do-it-yourself, home-making projects in young suburbia is in desirable contrast to the keen competitiveness of the golf course, or the tenseness of the bridge game or bowling match dominated by a person who always plays to win. The writers would suggest that competition need not and should not play so large a part in social recreation—and that there is now a healthy tendency away from this overemphasis.

But, whether coöperative or competitive, the need is not for a single recreational interest, satisfying though that may be, but for *broad and varied interests.* Not only does breadth in interests and recreation mean richer enjoyment of life at any time, but breadth also means that other avenues of need satisfaction are available when such developments as retirement or ill-health block usual sources of satisfaction. To the overly circumscribed, "one-track" life, such blocks to usual satisfactions can be disastrous. The busy industrialist whose *one* hobby is hunting may find that both job and hobby must be given up or seriously curtailed when a heart attack hits or that waning energies force him to give up hunting in addition to surrendering his job, and for the same reason. The person with broad interests can turn *to* still other things, other patterns already established and operating.

DEVELOPING INTERESTS FOR RICHER LIVING

If broad and varied interests are as important as has just been urged, how can they be developed in children and by the adult who sees his own living as overly narrow?

The importance of the early development of broad interests and enthusiasms is suggested not only by data already presented in Figure 90 indicating that basic orientations toward experience are established early, but also by other studies emphasizing that failure to establish interests in childhood and youth often results in significant "gaps" persisting throughout life. "Never learned," "lack of opportunity when young," "parents disapproved" have been noted in various studies as reasons for not participating as an adult in particular activities (*1, 40, 101*). Jersild and Tasch decry the tendency of children not to develop as many interests as they might, interests which would add joy and usefulness to their lives. Parents, they felt, have a limited conception of their role in the development of interests. "The typical father thinks of the leisure hours he has to spend with his children not as a time to build or to create or to learn new activities, but as a time for going through familiar motions, such as playing ball . . . " (*40*).

Five principles for promoting interest development in childhood, principles set down by Professor John E. Anderson, are well worth quoting:

1. *Bring the child to see his experiences in a different light by reorganizing his point of view.* Slight modifications in attitude produce enormous changes in the manner in which we view things—witness the manner in which the boy expends energy in playing baseball as contrasted with his lagging steps behind the lawnmower. Activities that are interesting are viewed as pleasant.

2. *Develop specific skills that enable the child to master particular demands.* It is a commonplace of experience that with skill we often come to enjoy doing what previously has seemed unpleasant. Far too often we confuse motivation with product; many a person under pressure to carry through in the early stages of an activity comes later to enjoy doing it as he builds skill. Unawareness of the implications of the activity may lead to avoidance or rejection when some acquaintance, no matter how motivated, may give insight into its possibilities as a source of happiness.

3. *Attach pleasant outcomes, through secondary devices (verbal and otherwise), to various activities.* This involves complimenting children when they do well or "celebrating their successes" as we used to say. But care must be taken not to overdo by attaching rewards to every experience. Some attention must also go to seeing that desirable conduct is reinforced and undesirable behavior is not reinforced, in order that the relation between good and poor performance may become tangible to the child.

4. *Give the child good models of behavior by showing interest and enthusiasm for activities.* Attitudes are readily communicable and apparently much more so through indirect rather than direct stimulation. If persons about the child are interested and enjoy activities, the child readily falls into the pattern, whereas if persons are half-hearted, listless, uninterested, and look upon their activities as invasions of their rights, the likelihood of interest on the part of children is much lessened. When children are approached from the point of view, "You should, must, ought to, be interested," instead of the point of view, "What fun it is to do this," "Isn't this interesting?" positive orientation is destroyed.

5. *Watch particularly the incidental, casual and indirect evaluations which,*

though almost automatic, may have great effects on the behavior of children. While these are particularly common in the family, they also arise in the schoolroom. Such comments as "I didn't like arithmetic when I was in school," "What a bore so and so is," "That is too hard for you," "Go away, I'm too busy now to look at what you are doing," etc. (2.)

What about developing interests in the adult years? If childhood opportunities have been so sparse as to leave mainly "gaps" in one's recreational repertoire, or if pressures of family-rearing or bread-winning have, for all practical purposes, caused one to "forget" how to play, is it reasonable to believe that skills can be developed, old interests revived, new interests created? Although data presented in this volume do indicate that there is a basic continuity in human development, the facts also indicate that the potential for development and change is present at all ages and that continuous growth and "expansion" are characteristic of much of the adult years. Thus, although "successful" people at one age are likely to have been the "successful" ones at a younger age, and, contrariwise, old, maladjusted people are likely to have once been young, maladjusted people, the psychological literature abounds with cases of people who even after retirement were able to defeat this pattern and develop a rich and satisfying life (21).

The earlier a person initiates the new interests, the more likely will patterns be developed that may serve currently as sources of relaxation and pleasure and later as resources to draw upon at, say, retirement. There should be recognition that individual interest histories are essentially unique, growing as they do out of the interaction of unique patterning of abilities and personality and a unique array of experiences and opportunities. Thus, one need not be overwhelmed by cultural expectation as to the appropriateness of a hobby or a leisure pursuit for a given age or sex. Indeed, one of the most enthusiastic hobbyists known to the writer is a grandmother who received a power saw as a Christmas gift! A person may revive early interests, give expression to long-held secret yearnings—perhaps to paint—or seek out totally new interests. But whether one has intelligently started early or carelessly delayed, perhaps right up to retirement, the important thing is to *do*. Actually, as was implied above in principles applicable to children, there seems to be a strong tendency for people to learn to like the things they do.

The foregoing has stressed *individual* potential and initiative. But community efforts are also greatly needed. Welfare legislation, community recreation centers, company recreational programs in industry, libraries, and adult education centers can greatly influence the trend of interests in community or nation. And the urgent need for such programs is in the adult years and old age. Communities have long been geared to the welfare of youth. Recently, needs for the aged have commanded attention. The years between young adulthood and middle age may well become the focus of broadened community programs. As more and more hours of the day become available for leisure, such programs will be of increasing importance.

Summary

What, in review, has this chapter emphasized regarding the life-span pattern of interests and recreation and their value in total life adjustment and readjustment?

1. The changing pattern of interests over the life span reflects in striking fashion the changes in abilities, in energy, in sex orientation, in personality, and in cultural expectation that are typically experienced as youngsters mature through adolescence into adulthood, become middle-aged, and aged. First, in infancy, are the rich and fascinating explorations of sight and sound and taste; then, the vigorous activity of childhood followed by the heterosexual emphasis in adolescent recreation; then, gradually, over the years, a settling back into more sedentary, less competitive and vigorous, less social, yet more serious and "cultural" activities of adult years and old age. When time and energy demands of family-rearing and bread-winning are lessened, some increase in leisure pursuits occurs, but for many, increased leisure in later years means simply more loafing, more unfilled time, more apathy.

2. The largest single block of leisure time is claimed by the media of mass communication. Program preferences in radio and TV, reading interests, and movie selections all reflect the changing pattern of interests noted above. Such media seem powerful agents in determining the modern mind, though many of the alleged harmful effects are not well demonstrated; response to mass media appears mainly to represent a symptom of personality trends already established. Interests are both stimulated and given certain partial satisfactions in the vicarious experiences provided by a ready-made fantasy world. What, in total, this extraordinary increase in ready-made daydreaming may do to the modern personality is a major problem for both psychology and psychiatry.

3. Interests are largely a product of society, of cultural expectations, influences, and opportunities, though they are also determined by physi-

cal and mental capabilities. Above all, they reflect motives and needs, representing basic avenues of satisfaction, either directly or by vicarious substitute. Tremendous differences exist among the interest histories of individuals, each with his own unique patterning of person-environment interaction. Differences among groups—the sexes, occupational groups, cultural classes—are striking, so striking as to outweigh differences due to age.

4. The relative consistency of interest patterns from year to year is noteworthy. To be sure, change is rapid in the years of childhood and adolescence, but nonetheless general orientations toward liking or disliking a wide variety of activities become established very early, by nine or earlier. By the late teens, the junior and senior years in high school, interests have become sufficiently stabilized to permit their measurement and use in vocational guidance. Measures of interests of college freshmen show substantial correlation, in recent research, to measures of the same individuals 18 to 20 years later.

5. Increasing leisure and increasing automation (with further reduction of the possibility of intrinsic satisfactions in work) mean that to an even greater degree basic satisfactions in living will need to be found in leisure-time pursuits. The fundamental relationship between broad and varied interests and good adjustment at all ages has been amply demonstrated. Interests, recreations, and hobbies do indeed offer rich potential for basic need satisfaction but this potential will be greatly increased if interests, which are often superficial and futile, merely time killers, can be made more creative and constructive and less competitive. Wise parents will accept responsibility for the development of a positive orientation toward life experiences on the part of their children (and some principles applicable to this purpose have been noted), and the wise adult (whether parent or not) will develop a personal style of life involving sufficient breadth and scope of activity so that such events as ill-health or retirement will find the individual with varied resources to draw upon for satisfaction of basic needs. So important is this whole matter of interests and their relation to human adjustment that, appropriately, they have become a matter of public concern and responsibility.

BIBLIOGRAPHY

1. Allard, Lucile, *A Study of the Leisure Activities of Certain Elementary School Teachers of Long Island,* Teachers College Contributions to Edu-

46. Kuhlen, R. G., Age trends in adult adjustment as reflected in happiness ratings, Unpublished paper presented at the Boston meeting of the American Psychological Association, 1948.

47. Kuhlen, R. G., Expansion and constriction of life activities during the adult life span, Unpublished paper read at the Second International Gerontological Congress, St. Louis, 1951.

48. Kuhlen, R. G., Interests and attitudes of Japanese, Chinese, and white adolescents: a study in culture and personality, *J. Soc. Psychol.*, 1945, *21*:121–133.

49. Kuder, G. F., *Revised manual for the Kuder Preference Record*, Chicago, Science Research Associates, 1946.

50. Landis, J. T., Hobbies and happiness in old age, *Recreation*, 1942, 35:607.

51. Landis, J. T., Social-psychological factors of aging, *Social Forces*, 1942, *20*:468–470.

52. Landis, J. T., What is the happiest period of life? *School and Society*, 1942, *55*:643–645.

53. Lazar, M., *Reading Interests, Activities, and Opportunities of Bright, Average and Dull Children*, Teachers College Contributions to Education, No. 707, New York, Teachers College, Columbia University, 1937.

54. Lazarsfeld, P. F., and Kendall, P. L., *Radio Listening in America*, New York, Prentice-Hall, 1948.

55. Lehman, H. C., and Witty, P. A., *The Psychology of Play Activities*, Barnes, 1927.

56. Lehman, H. C., and Witty, P. A., A study of play in relation to intelligence, *J. Appl. Psychol.*, 1928, *12*:369–397.

57. Lewin, H. S., Facts and fears about the comics, *Nations Schools*, 1953, *52*:46–48.

58. Lewis, W. D., and McGehee, W., A comparison of the interests of mentally superior and retarded children, *School and Society*, 1940, 52:597–600.

59. Link, H. C., and Hopf, H. A., *People and Books*, New York, New York Book Industry Committee, Book Manufacturers Institute, 1946.

60. Lyness, P. I., The place of the mass media in the lives of boys and girls, *Journalism Quart.*, 1952, *29*:43–54.

61. Miller, R. A., The relation of reading characteristics to social indices, *Amer. J. Sociol.*, 1936, *41*:738–756.

62. Morgan, C. M., The attitudes and adjustments of recipients of old age assistance in upstate and metropolitan New York, *Archives of Psychol.*, 1937, No. 214, *30*:131.

63. National Recreation Association, *The Leisure Hours of 5000 People*, New York, National Recreation Association, 1935 (mimeographed).

64. Nestrick, W. V., *Constructional Activities of Adult Males*, Teachers College Contributions to Education, No. 780, New York, Teachers College, Columbia University, 1939.

65. Pace, C. R., *They Went to College: A Study of 951 Former University Students*, Minneapolis, University of Minnesota Press, 1941.

66. Peterson, R. C., and Thurstone, L. L., *The Effect of Motion Pictures on*

the Social Attitudes of High School Children, Ann Arbor, Edward Bros., 1932.

67. Phillips, W. S., and Greene, J. E., A preliminary study of the relationship of age, hobbies, and civil status to neuroticism among women teachers, *J. Educ. Psychol.,* 1939, *30:*440–444.

68. Politz, Alfred, Research, Inc., *National Survey of Radio and Television Sets Associated with U.S. Households, May, 1954,* New York, Advertising Research Foundation, 1954.

69. Politz, Alfred, Research, Inc., *A Study of Four Media—Their Accumulative and Repeat Audiences,* New York, Time, Inc., 1953.

70. Pressey, S. L., and L. C., Development of the Interest-Attitude tests, *J. Appl. Psychol.,* 1933, *17:*1–16.

71. Pressey, S. L., and Simcoe, Elizabeth, Case study comparisons of successful and problem old people, *J. Gerontol.,* 1950, *5:*168–175.

72. Renshaw, S., Miller, V. L., and Marquis, D. P., *Children's Sleep,* New York, Macmillan, 1933.

73. Riccivti, P. A., Children and radio: a study of listeners and non-listeners to various types of radio programs in terms of selected ability, attitude and behavior measures, *Genet. Psychol. Monogr.,* 1951, *44:*69–143.

74. Schramm, W., and White, D. M., Age, education, economic status: factors in newspaper reading, *Journalism Quart.,* 1949, *26:*149–159.

75. Sears, Pauline S., Doll play aggression in normal young children: influence of sex, age, sibling status, father's absence, *Psychol. Monog.,* 1951, Vol. 65, No. 6.

76. Sollenberger, R. T., Some relationships between the urinary excretion of male hormone by maturing boys and their expressed interests and attitudes, *J. Psychol.,* 1940, *9:*179–189.

77. Starr, Doris, Adult age trends in some leisure time interests, Unpublished master's thesis, Syracuse University, 1952.

78. Stoke, S. M., and West, E. D., Sex differences in conversational interests, *J. Soc. Psychol.,* 1931, *2:*120–126.

79. Stone, C. P., and Barker, R. G., The attitudes and interests of premenarcheal and post menarcheal girls, *J. Genet. Psychol.,* 1939, *54:*27–71.

80. Strang, Ruth, Why children read comics, *Elementary School J.,* 1942–43, *43:*336–342.

81. Strong, E. K., Jr., *Change of Interests with Age,* Stanford, Stanford University Press, 1931.

82. Strong, E. K., Jr., Permanence of interest scores over 22 years, *J. Appl. Psychol.,* 1951, *35:*89–91.

83. Strong, E. K., Jr., Vocational interests 18 years after college, Minneapolis, University of Minnesota Press, 1955.

84. Strong, E. K., Jr., *Vocational Interests of Men and Women,* Stanford, Stanford University Press, 1943.

85. Super, D. E., *Avocational Interest Patterns,* Stanford, Stanford University Press, 1940.

86. Symonds, P. M., Change in sex differences in problems and interests of adolescents with increasing age, *J. Genet. Psychol.,* 1937, *50:*83–98.

87. Terman, L. M., *et al., Mental and Physical Traits of a Thousand Gifted Children, Genetic Studies of Genius,* Vol. I, Stanford, Stanford University Press, 1925.
88. Terman, L. M., and Miles, C. C., *Sex and Personality: Studies in Masculinity and Femininity.* New York, McGraw-Hill, 1936.
89. Thorndike, E. L., The interests of adults: II. The interrelations of adult interests, *J. Educ. Psychol.,* 1935, *26:*497–507.
90. Thorndike, R. L., *Children's Reading Interests: A Study Based on a Fictitious Annotated Titles Questionnaire,* New York, Teachers College, Columbia University, 1941.
91. Thorndike, R. L., Words and the comics, *J. Exper. Educ.,* 1941, *10:* 110–113.
92. Van Alstyne, D., *Play Behavior and Choice of Play Materials of Preschool Children,* Chicago, University of Chicago Press, 1932.
93. Vance, T. F., and McCall, L. T., Children's preferences among play materials as determined by the method of paired-comparisons of pictures, *Child Development,* 1934, 5:267–277.
94. Waples, Douglas, and Tyler, Ralph W., *What People Want to Read About; a Study of Group Interests and a Survey of Problems in Adult Reading,* Chicago, American Library Association and The University of Chicago Press, 1931.
95. Warner, W. L., and Lunt, P. S., *The Social Life of a Modern Community,* New Haven, Yale University Press, 1941.
96. Watson, G., Happiness among adult students of education, *J. Educ. Psychol.,* 1930, *21:*79–109.
97. Whitley, M. T., Children's interest in collecting, *J. Educ. Psychol.,* 1929, *20:*249–261.
98. Witty, P., Comparative studies of interest in TV, *Educ. Administration and Supervision,* 1954, *40:*321–335.
99. Witty, P., and Bricker, H., *Your Child and Radio, TV, Comics and Movies,* Chicago, Science Research Associates, 1952.
100. Witty, P. A., and Sizemore, R. A., Reading the comics: a summary of studies and an evaluation I. *Elementary English,* 1954, *31:*501–506.
101. Wylie, J. A., Survey of 504 families to determine the relationships between certain factors and the nature of the family recreation program. *Res. Quart.,* 1953, *24:*229–43.

CHAPTER 10 •

• Moral, Sociopolitical, and Religious Values and Behavior

VALUES and beliefs of one kind or another represent a major aspect of the motivational make-up of the individual. Parents attempt to inculcate in their children certain predispositions or attitudes which they hope will play a dominant role in determining the youngster's behavior not only as a child but throughout life. Often these values are expected to influence behavior in positive directions toward such predetermined goals as helping others or voting in primary elections. These are the things that are *right*. Often, on the other hand, the values taught are expected to serve mainly as deterrents to the expression of other motives or needs (such as sex), direct satisfaction of which (or satisfaction in particular ways) is considered *wrong*. Values become attached to an infinite variety of objects, people, and issues. Individuals "value" certain types of food, certain types of restaurants and entertainment, certain customs, certain political parties; they have biases toward certain groups of people, aversions to certain points of view, dislikes for certain activities. How major groups of values—moral, sociopolitical, religious—develop and change during the course of life is the subject of this chapter.

Moral Values and Behavior

First is the matter of morals and ideals. By what age do children learn what is right or wrong? What about the reconstruction of values in adolescence and modifications during adulthood and old age? Enough evidence is available on these questions to identify certain trends and to raise provocative questions about such diverse matters as the teaching of values and the interaction between generations.

GRADATIONS AND INCONSISTENCY IN CHARACTER

Traditionally, character is thought of as a peculiar quality that some people possess and others lack—some people are said to have "strong" characters and others have weak characters, some boys are good and others bad, some men honest and others dishonest. But other traits considered in this book have shown no such dichotomies. Both height and intelligence distribute themselves on a continuum and fall into a normal distribution. There is no separate group of geniuses, nor are the feeble-minded a group apart, and most people are intermediate between these extremes. So it is with such moral qualities as honesty, tact, helpfulness. The curves of Figure 91 are similar to those in earlier chapters exhibit-

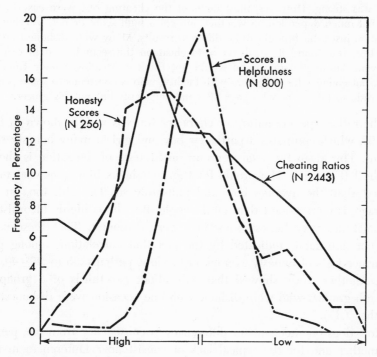

Figure 91. Distribution of Scores on Tests of Honesty, Cheating, and Helpfulness. (Adapted from H. Hartshorne and M. A. May, *Studies in the Nature of Character, I. Studies in Deceit,* New York, Macmillan, 1928.)

ing the distribution of heights, abilities, and intelligence; the scores on several tests of character traits also distribute themselves in approximately a "normal" curve. There are no separate groups of saints and sinners. Most people are sometimes honest, sometimes not, sometimes helpful, sometimes not—average in virtue as in other traits.

In view of the very practical nature of many of the tests used in investigation of character traits, the results may be thought of as having exceptional genuineness as indicators of probable conduct in everyday affairs. Usually the children did not know they were being tested. They were given an opportunity to cheat in grading their own papers, to disregard a time limit, or to steal a dime—but the investigator had ways of finding out when they were dishonest. Coöperation and helpfulness were measured by finding which children would come to school early to help make toys for hospital children or do work for someone else instead of for themselves. Such tests are bits of real life.

The graph shows a slight difference between the curves for honesty and cheating. This is because the tests were different and were given under different circumstances. The honesty test had many hard items, and motivation to do well was strong. However, most items of the cheating test were easy to get, and not much depended on whether one got a high score or not. Varying the situation just a bit brought quite different results. Many were dishonest on the first test; few found it worth while to cheat on the second. And in real life everyone knows the man who would not think of stealing money from his bank but changes his golf score with facility, who is courteous to some people and rude to others, or who pays his gambling debts but not his grocer.

The rather specific nature of character traits is vividly shown in Figure 92, which compares a particular boy and girl in many honesty situations. The mean for a large group on 21 tests of deception is shown in the left margin. The profile for the boy shows him somewhat more honest than the average boy, and uniformly so. The girl, too, on the average, is more honest than most people. But she is highly inconsistent —sometimes very honest, sometimes very dishonest. That these cases are not unusual is indicated by the fact that correlations among performance tests of honesty average rather low, perhaps .35 to .40 (*40, 39, 53*). Another study showed that only about two-thirds of a group of seventh graders who were dishonest on one occasion were dishonest on another (*35*).

How does one account for differences in consistency from one person to another and for the typical lack of consistency? Differences in maturity and level of character development are factors. Some children have thus been taught (by parents, teachers, other children) more effectively and more consistently than others. Presumably some children gradually generalize experiences involving moral issues (probably with the help of parents and teachers) into ideals of conduct and integrate their behavior, while others remain more at the level of the small child who only senses that there are certain specific things he must not do. The boy in the graph apparently had integrated his conduct much more than the girl—or the influences which had formed his habits of conduct had been more consistent. One would expect increasing consistency with age, and it is of some interest that one study has shown that children in a school in a good neighborhood became more *consistently* honest with age whereas those in a school in a poor neighborhood became more consistently dishonest (*41*)!

Inconsistency in honesty situations need not reflect a lack of organization. There may be greater consistency than is apparent to the ob-

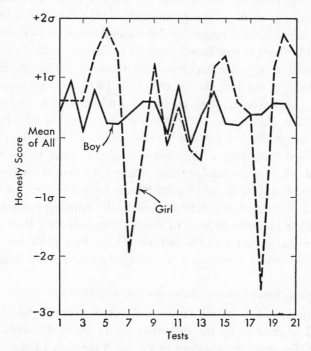

Figure 92. Honesty Profiles, Showing Consistency of One Boy and Inconsistency of One Girl. (From H. Hartshorne and M. A. May, *Studies in the Nature of Character, I. Studies in Deceit,* New York, Macmillan, 1928.)

server unless he takes the trouble to view the various situations through the eyes of the child or other person being observed. Apparent inconsistency in honesty may result from some general attitudes occasionally interfering, as timidity or desire to appear well in the eyes of others (2). Values may differ in relative priority or importance; rigorously honest behavior may be evident in one situation but not in another where some "higher" value, as being kind and generous, may take precedence.

Another cause of inconsistency in behavior, and a serious handicap to the successful teaching of moral behavior and values, is to be found in the great and often curious variations among groups as to what is desirable or forbidden. Women differ in important ways from men in moral values (*88*); children who cheat in one classroom are honest in another (*35*); many college students condone "cribbing"; in a slum area special codes governed sexual behavior with respect to various categories of girls (*110*); according to their statements, marked differences exist among college students with respect to their reactions to a friend revealing to them a theft or sexual promiscuity (*101*). Standards of conduct are not absolute but are culturally determined and vary to such a degree that a child reared in one family may be inculcated with a set of standards different at significant points from those of the family next door. And standards of conduct change with time (*80*), creating gaps between generations and even creating conflicts for adults who were emotionally conditioned as children to one pattern of behavior but who have intellectually accepted other patterns as times changed or as their own mobility has led them into a different subculture. Data to be presented later in this chapter emphasize these changes. Under such circumstances some inconsistency of behavior might be anticipated; perhaps more important, adults will have a difficult time in determining just *what* values to teach their children or *how* to teach them, and thus they are likely to be inconsistent and variable in their efforts. In a static homogeneous society there would be much less ambiguity about such matters.

DEVELOPMENTAL TRENDS DURING CHILDHOOD AND ADOLESCENCE

The general values of the American culture seem to be rather well inculcated in children by the time they are in about the sixth grade. In one study, for example, children in grades 6 through 12 were asked to write down behaviors for which they would be blamed or praised by their age mates. Their replies were categorized, and general descriptive statements representing these categories were presented in paired comparison fashion for further judgments of the praise- or blameworthiness of these behaviors. Scale scores could then be computed for each type of conduct. The results for girls are shown in Figure 93. It is to be noted that the scale scores assigned by sixth-graders are much like those assigned at other grade levels. Honesty, politeness, kindness, coöperativeness, and friendliness were highest at this grade (and in this order) while dishonesty, "have a bad character," carelessness, and disloyalty were most blameworthy. The fact that there was somewhat greater "spread" among the scale values at the twelfth grade level suggested

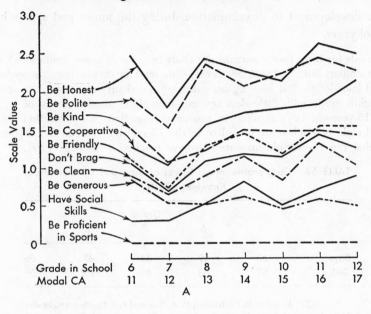

Scale Values (A): Be Honest, Be Polite, Be Kind, Be Cooperative, Be Friendly, Don't Brag, Be Clean, Be Generous, Have Social Skills, Be Proficient in Sports

Grade in School: 6 7 8 9 10 11 12
Modal CA: 11 12 13 14 15 16 17

A

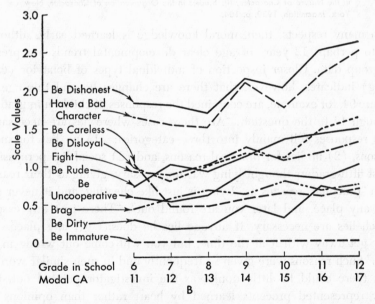

Scale Values (B): Be Dishonest, Have a Bad Character, Be Careless, Be Disloyal, Fight, Be Rude, Be Uncooperative, Brag, Be Dirty, Be Immature

Grade in School: 6 7 8 9 10 11 12
Modal CA: 11 12 13 14 15 16 17

B

Figure 93. Age Trends in Basic Values in the American Culture as Reflected in the Extent to Which Various Behaviors are Considered Praiseworthy (A) or Blameworthy (B) by Girls in Different Grades. High-scale scores indicate praiseworthiness or greatest blameworthiness. (From G. G. Thompson, Age trends in social values during the adolescent years, Amer. Psychol., 1949, 4:250.)

some development in discrimination during the junior and senior high-school years.

Trends for boys (not shown in the chart because of space limitations) were quite similar, but, as Table 58 shows, girls tend to exceed boys somewhat in moral knowledge. But here again, gains are noted up until about the seventh or eighth grade with little development thereafter. Another study of 9-, 12-, and 15-year-old boys resulted in the conclusion that "interiorization" of the moral code is much more complete in the 12-year-old than in the 9-year-old, but that the 15-year-old appeared to have reached a "ceiling" (10).

TABLE 58.   Comparative Mean Scores of Boys and Girls on Moral Knowledge Tests

	Grade				
	5	6	7	8	9
Boys	53	59	65	67	66
Girls	57	63	68	69	69

SOURCE: Based on H. Hartshorne, M. A. May and F. K. Shuttleworth, *Studies in the Nature of Character, III. Studies in the Organization of Character*, New York, Macmillan, 1930, p. 104.

In many respects, then, moral knowledge is learned early, although up to perhaps 12 years of age clear developmental trends are present in group data. Closer inspection of individual types of behavior (e. g., lying) indicates, however, that there are changes beyond this age. In Figure 94, for example, are contained the responses of children in grades 5 through 12 to the question: "Are there cases where lies are necessary?" The responses fell mainly into three categories: (1) no lies for moral reasons, (2) no lies for practical reasons, and (3) social lies permissible. Most fifth-graders thought lying was unnecessary, giving as their reasons such "practical" reasons as "Lying is just like cheating, and it never gets you any place, and later you are found out"; "There isn't any case in which lies are necessary. If anyone lies he doesn't get any place. You may get away with it at the time, but you will come out wrong in the end." Such reasons were given so frequently and in such similar wording that there could be little doubt, as the investigator pointed out, that they represented precepts learned by heart rather than opinions developed by themselves. It is especially to be noted in the chart that this type of reason drops off steadily up until the eleventh grade. Broadened experience and greater sophistication are shown in a contrasting trend—the increasing acceptance of social lies (e. g., "When your friend has got on a new dress which you find perfectly horrid really, you must tell her you think it is cute so as not to hurt her feelings.").

The findings just described seem to reflect a pattern of development in which moral teachings at a young age are accepted without question on the authority of the adult who expresses them and who is in a position to enforce them. Later, as the child grows older, gradually escapes adult domination, and comes increasingly under the influence of peer

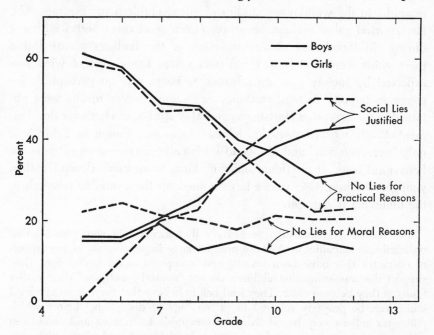

Figure 94. Percentage of Children, Grade 5 Through 12 Who Gave Various Answers to the Question, "Are there cases in which lies are necessary?" (Adapted from B. E. Tudor-Hart, Are there cases in which lies are necessary? *J. Genet. Psychol.*, 1926, 33:586–641.)

groups, he observes discrepancies between the strict and specific rules laid down by adults and actual behavior and gains broader experience which results in more generalized moral views derived largely from peers. As another writer (54) has noted, younger children have not faced the conflict between certain virtues (as honesty) and other virtues (as loyalty) in some questions as squarely as have older children. This is the pattern of development noted by Piaget (76) in his studies of children as well as by others (66).

Successful maturing in society requires not only that the child learn what is "good" and "desirable" but that he accept these values emotionally and act accordingly. Moral knowledge is a necessary but not sufficient condition for moral behavior. It is likely that these two aspects of moral development (the cognitive and the emotional) represent quite distinct processes, show different developmental trends, and are influenced in their development by different conditions (70). The contrasting developmental trends of knowledge and behavior are apparent, for example, in the well-known studies of gifted children by Terman (97). He reported gains in character scores (average of seven tests) with age during childhood, but closer inspection of the findings revealed that these gains were mainly in those tests where knowledge of what was expected by society gave an advantage. There was no perceptible increase in honesty or trustworthiness with age. Similar results were obtained in the extensive Hartshorne and May studies of character development. While moral knowledge increased (as was shown in Table 58), only "perseveration" and ability to inhibit distractions showed gains on behavioral tests. If anything, older children were more deceptive than younger children. One writer has summed up the available research in the following paragraph:

The results . . . indicate conclusively that increase in age, plus all that ordinarily accompanies it, does not produce large improvements in any aspects of character that have been investigated, except in moral knowledge. They support the conclusion that children do not "naturally outgrow" their earlier faults as they become older. They lead one to believe that there is no age level which can be properly referred to as the "age of discretion," before which children's actions may be relatively unsusceptible to training and considered unimportant or unsignificant for character development, and after which conduct rather suddenly begins to yield to education and the conditioning of the culture. (54.)

Much has been said of the reorganization of values in adolescence and the importance of "ideology" generally as a teen-age "developmental task." Actually, many of the changes commonly attributed to adolescence are changes that have been occurring gradually throughout previous development. Three lines of development are worthy of note. In the first place, the child's social world has increasingly broadened until in adolescence the youngster has come into close contact with views contrary to those taught in his home, has embarked on a social life much of which is relatively independent of adult (especially parental) supervision, and has come increasingly under the influence of peer groups and friends. In the second place, there has been a steady and gradual increase in the child's intellectual capacity and a broadening of his intellectual world. The ability to generalize and to deal with abstractions has increased, and both independent reading and formal studies have introduced him to new ideas and concepts, at least some of which likely differ in significant ways from, or even conflict with, concepts taught in home or church. In the third place, the changes of pubescence have given impetus to the sex drive and have produced bodily changes creating sexual attractiveness, with the result that codes of sexual conduct are less academic than previously. Such changes require modification of values and the acceptance of personal responsibility for moral decisions, but they are not factors that have suddenly arisen at adolescence.

The influence of the peer culture is especially potent. Large numbers of adolescents drink, and most indulge in petting. The total climate of opinion and behavior is apt to be more liberal. There is a marked drop in total number of disapprovals and, as Figure 95 shows, an increase in some. But the total climate, though more liberal, is one of heterogeneity rather than homogeneity. The conflicting pressures are aptly illustrated in the following statement of an adolescent girl:

> Sometimes I wonder if it pays to behave myself. There are naturally times when I do, and then again there are times when I don't. I have my own code of morals, somewhat affected by my parents' views, but on the whole established by myself. For instance, I don't smoke. I have been both complimented and embarrassed for that. Since most every girl I run around with smokes, and that excessively, they kid me, although for some reason, I feel that some of them admire me for refraining from it. . . . Once in a while when I'm out with a crowd of kids who are in the mood for drinking, I am rather puzzled as to what to do. If I refuse they think I'm a prig and a wet blanket; if I do, it hurts me because I hate the stuff and I know it isn't doing me any good. . . . That also goes for this business of necking and petting. (63.)

A danger in the teaching of ideals and values is that indoctrination may be so complete and literal that they may not become properly modified by reality or properly integrated with other values. Extreme, rigid idealism is likely a greater handicap to good adjustment than it is a promoter of desirable behavior. The person to whom the admonition never to tell a lie means literally that, almost inevitably encounters conflict in his relations with others, because an equally important or greater value is that of being kind to and considerate of others. The person who idealizes marriage and firmly believes that true love leaves no room for ambivalence is likely doomed to disappointment. One writer has argued that the de-

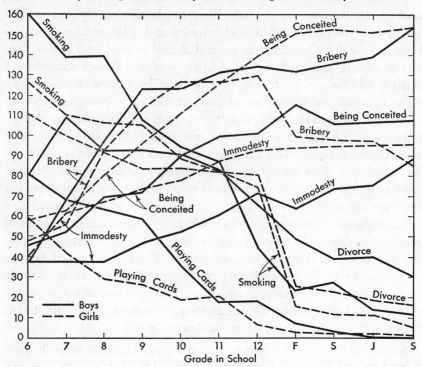

Figure 95. Changes from Grade Six to Senior Year in College in Things Thought Wrong. (From unpublished data of S. L. Pressey.)

velopment of maladjustment follows a three-step sequence: from idealism to frustration to demoralization (52). The mature set of values represents a well-integrated complex of attitudes that has certain congruence with the realities of life. There should exist some possibility of attaining one's ideals, at least the possibility of coming sufficiently close, so that an overwhelming sense of frustration, guilt, and futility is avoided. It is of some interest that in one recent study a positive correlation of .70 was found to exist between personal adjustment (as measured by the California Test of Personality) and the degree of congruence between evaluations of self and judgments as to self-ideals of a group of high school boys. Those who evidenced greater discrepancies between their judgments of self and their ideals were more poorly adjusted.

It is probably desirable that youngsters develop greater realism and become less worshipful of particular idealized "heroes" as they become older. The facts in Table 59 show something of the changes with age in the models after whom children pattern themselves. Such models represent an important source of ideals, as children identify with and imitate

others—usually their elders. It will be noted in the table that the "ideal"
of the 10-, 11-, and 12-year-old is most likely to be attractive and successful young adults whom the child knows. Composite or imaginary
characters are next in importance, and glamorous adults (movie stars,
etc.) rank third. By the 16- and 17-year level in both sexes, glamorous
adults have nearly dropped out of the picture, and "attractive and successful young adults" are less frequently mentioned as ideals. The great
increase is in composite or imaginary characters. As children grow older,
then, they appear to break away from a "flesh-and-blood hero" and turn
to a more generalized and abstract characterization of the ideal self.

TABLE 59.   The Percentage Frequency with Which 100 Ten-, Eleven-, and Twelve-Year-
Olds and 48 Sixteen- and Seventeen-Year-Olds in a Small Midwestern Community Mentioned Various Types of People as Their "Ideals"

| | Girls | | Boys | |
| | 10- 11- 12- | 16- 17- | 10- 11- 12- | 16- 17- |
Ideal	Year-Olds	Year-Olds	Year-Olds	Year-Olds
Parents and other relatives of parental or grandparental generation	6	3	7	6
Parent surrogates; teacher, neighbor of parental generation	2	1	0	11
Glamorous adults (movie actors, actresses, etc.)	16	1	12	6
Heroes (Florence Nightingale, Lincoln, etc.)	2	4	3	2
Attractive and successful young adults	36	28	53	25
Composite or imaginary character	33	61	25	48
Age mates, 2–3 years older	3	2	0	2

SOURCE: Adapted from R. J. Havighurst, Myra Robinson, and Mildred Dorr, The development
of the ideal self in childhood and adolescence, J. Educ. Res., 1946, 40:241–257.

Further studies (43) by the same investigator have inquired into the question of *who* in the community is "visible" to adolescents, whom adolescents
report to be friendly, admired, helpful, or responsible people. Of all mentions, 7 percent were family members, 21 percent teachers, and 72 percent
other adults. Mainly it is the upper- and upper-middle-class adults who were
most frequently mentioned by the 16-year-olds studied. On items requiring a
statement of admiration or emotional attachment, young adults (age 20 to
29) were most frequently named, whereas on items requiring appraisal in less
personal terms of service to the community (responsible, helpful), adults in
the thirties and forties were most frequently mentioned.

These, then, are the individuals admired. The importance of teachers in the total picture is significant. Of some 1328 mentions, 25 percent went to the top 10 people, and 34 percent to the top 20 adults. Of the top 10, 4 were teachers; of the top 20, 7 were teachers. Clearly, teachers have potentially greater influence upon youth than mere teaching of subject matter!

It is of interest that, with increased age, different traits (as well as different people) are admired. In one extensive study,[1] young people from the sixth grade through college were asked to indicate which of a list of traits they admired in people. In the sixth grade traits such as "brave," "lively," "daring," and "good looking" stood out. Older individuals gave more weight to traits like "reliable," "broad-minded," "coöperative," "dependable," "having initiative," and "sincerity." Developmental trends were gradual and steady over the broad age range, showing important and desirable changes through the entire span of adolescence.

AGE DIFFERENCES DURING MATURITY AND OLD AGE

It might be expected that once adulthood is reached, matters of morals and ideals would have been settled and little or no further change would occur. But, as a matter of fact, changes do occur during maturity and old age, and other differences exist which are likely not so much a product of aging, as such, as of differences in cultural background of those in different age brackets. The tendency of older people to be annoyed by commission of borderline moral wrongs (17) was noted in a previous chapter. And a substantial amount of public opinion poll data has confirmed this earlier finding. Although some of the findings date back as early as 1937, it has been found that older adults more frequently give a conservative (more moralistic) answer to questions such as the following: "Do you think it is indecent for women to wear shorts for street wear?" "In view of the shortage of silk would you approve of women going without stockings?" "Do you approve of the view that sex problems should be scientifically and frankly discussed in daily newspapers?" "Do you think government lotteries would produce an unwholesome gambling spirit in this country?" . . . In fact, if one examines the published results of opinion polls there is hardly a moral issue raised on which regular age trends are not observed. The top portion of Table 60 gives the actual responses for three age groups to some of the questions just noted.[2]

---

[1] Unpublished data of S. L. Pressey.
[2] See, for example, the section "The Quarters Polls" by Mildred Strunk in the quarterly issues of the *Public Opinion Quarterly*, or the large volume of poll results compiled by Cantril and Strunk (16).

TABLE 60. Adult Age Differences in Moral Attitudes and Behavior as Indicated by Percentage Expressing Particular Views or Reporting Particular Behavior[a]

	Age Group		
	18–30	31–47	48 Over
I. Moral Attitudes			
Think it is indecent for women to wear shorts on street (1939)	55	60	67
Would approve women going without hose in view of shortage of silk (1941)	62	56	44
Percentage objecting to women drinking in public[b] (1948)	42	51	76
Percentage of abstainers who disapprove of others drinking (1939)[c]	30	42	56
Approve of sex education in high schools (1943)	78	69	61
Think government lotteries would produce unwholesome gambling spirit (1938)	44	47	56
Think radio stations might broadcast discussions of social disease	73	61	52
Percentage who think it is good to have Kinsey information available (1948)[b]	70	58	46
II. Moral Behavior			
Percentage who smoke at all (about 1939)			
Men	77	80	74
Women	48	34	13
Percentage who drink at all (about 1939)			
Men	75	75	62
Women	59	47	27
Percentage who gamble at all (about 1939)			
Men	76	65	40
Women	68	50	35

[a] Unless noted in other footnotes, data are from R. P. Hinshaw, The Relationship of information and opinion to age, Unpublished Ph.D. dissertation, Princeton University, 1944.

[b] From M. Strunk The quarter's polls, Public Opinion Quart., 1948, 12:163. Age groups are 21–29, 30–49, 50 and over.

[c] From H. Cantril (ed.), Public Opinion, 1935–1946, Princeton, Princeton University Press, 1951, p. 419. Age groups are Under 30, 30–49, 50 and over.

Surprisingly enough, these same age trends in the direction of more conventional morality on the part of older groups seem to characterize even specialists in clinical psychology—individuals who might ordinarily be expected to be less moralistic than the population at large. The question was asked: "Do you think the Kinsey research findings should be freely available to all who are interested, or do you think its circulation should be censored for some groups?" Seventy-nine percent of those under 50 thought it should be freely available, but only 55 percent of those over 50 agreed. A finer break-down of the data revealed a steady trend, decade by decade, in this direction (81).

To what extent do verbal expressions of behavior correspond with actual behavior? It is unfortunate that in the case of adults one must be satisfied with *reported* behavior rather than with observations of actual behavior in carefully constructed test situations. But if reports can be trusted, age trends in behavior tend to follow age trends in opinion. Thus, the facts presented in the lower portion of Table 60 show less drinking, smoking, and gambling on the part of older individuals, especially women. On the other hand, Kinsey's data on male sex activity show contrasting trends at different cultural levels. For those with eighth-grade education or less, extramarital intercourse was most frequent in the young groups and declined steadily with age. Among males of 13 years of education, the active incidence of extramarital coitus increased with age. But considering the *total* group studied, the active incidence remained relatively stable for males, increasing from 24 percent in the early twenties to 28 percent in the thirties and declining to 22 percent in the fifties. Among married women, the active incidence increased from about 9 percent in the early twenties to 17 percent in the thirties and declined to about 6 percent in the early fifties. By age 40, about 50 percent of married males and 26 percent of married females had had extramarital intercourse at some time. These figures must, of course, be evaluated in the light of criticisms that have been made of Kinsey's procedures, especially criticisms of the representativeness of the population he interviewed (96). But, if taken at face value, they do suggest that adult trends in at least certain types of moral behavior do not follow the trends of expressed opinion.

One important characteristic of the moral judgment of older adults deserves special mention because of the role adults play in enforcing conventional standards upon adolescents and young adults—their tendency to make decisions on absolute moral bases, to see things in relatively sharp blacks or whites. Two studies have shown this tendency to exist. In one study (4) a group of college students, a group of adults the age of their parents (all of whom were parents), and a group of adults (all of whom were grandparents) the age of the grandparents of the college students responded to a series of 15 conduct situations similar to the following:

If you were at a party where everyone else was drinking, which of the following things would you do?: (1) refuse absolutely because you believed it wrong; (2) drink with the crowd; (3) refuse because the actions resulting from intoxication would be distasteful to you; (4) refuse because you believed it unwise or unhealthful to drink alcohol?

Choices in each situation were devised so that they represented (1) a right or wrong moral standard, (2) a standard of prudence or intelligent judgment, (3) a standard of public opinion, or (4) an aesthetic standard. The results of the study are shown in Figure 96, where it is to be noted that grandparents (especially) and parents tended to make decisions primarily on an absolute standard of right or wrong, whereas the college

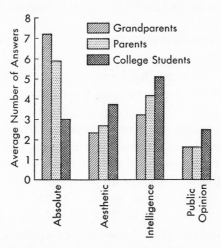

Figure 96. Combined Averages of Answers Obtained from Various Age Groups: Contrasts Between Three Generations in Their Reliance on Various Types of Moral Standards. (From A. Anderson and B. Dvorak, Differences between college students and their elders in standards of conduct, J. Abnorm. and Soc. Psychol., 1928, 23:286–292. Reproduced with permission of the American Psychological Association.)

students tended more frequently to make moral decisions in terms of whether it was the intelligent or aesthetic thing to do.

A second study (56) also involved the verbal (printed) presentation of "moral situations" with various proposed courses of action, each of which was to be evaluated by the respondents (a group of teachers) as "right," "wrong," or "excusable." The tendency of older adults to be less tolerant and to make absolute judgments was again demonstrated. The older teachers considered fewer courses of action as "excusable." Two other findings from a related study (55) are relevant here. Teachers were also asked to indicate not only their personal views but also what they thought to be the "views of society." The discrepancy between the *per-*

sonal judgments of the older teachers and their judgments of society's view was greater than was true of younger teachers, but, perhaps more significant, individual differences were greater when teachers expressed judgments of society's views than when they were expressing *personal* opinions. The suggestion here is that if adults attempt to "depersonalize" the situation when discussing moral issues with adolescents and to talk instead about "what others would think," a more *inconsistent* picture might be presented to the youngster by different adults than if personal opinions were expressed. It is indeed difficult, if not impossible, to escape the heterogeneity and ambiguity of the American culture.

FACTORS RELATED TO CHARACTER DEVELOPMENT

What conditions seem most conducive to good moral development and what circumstances appear to hinder it? Although in this area of development, as in others, biological factors play a general role in determining predispositions and setting limits (e. g., intellectual limits on seeing the consequences of an act), the more significant factors are found in the sociocultural context in which development occurs. The type of example set by others and the quality of the interpersonal relationships within the family, with other adults, and with peers (individually and in groups) appear to be the significant influential factors. This is also true when the focus of attention is upon such institutional influences as the school, the church, or "character-building" agencies. In these contexts, also, the nature of the interpersonal relations appears to be the influential element.

Table 61 summarizes a variety of data from the Character Education Inquiry showing the importance of home and neighborhood factors in character development. Case history information was obtained by home visits on approximately 50 children who gave little or no evidence of cheating or lying, 50 who not only cheated but lied about it afterwards, and a somewhat smaller number who cheated but admitted it. The figures in the table show the percentage of each group whose records revealed the presence of various handicaps, and they indicate that (like delinquency, to be discussed later in this chapter) dishonest behavior tends to grow out of bad family relations and parental examples, low-level neighborhoods, and inferior personal achievement. Those children who are dishonest seem not to have had adequate home training or are motivated by their frustrations to attempt to achieve a degree of status and satisfaction of other frustrated needs through dishonest behavior. Those who cheat in exams are those who need to raise their grades (*24*),

TABLE 61.   Percentage Prevalence of Various Handicaps, Characteristics and Conditions Among Groups of Youngsters Who Were Honest, Dishonest, or Dishonest but Confessed

Characteristic or Condition Considered a Handicap	Honest	Dishonest	Confession
I. Personal relations within family			
Parental example dishonest	2	15	11
Personality of father	15	27	26
Relations between parents	18	29	35
Discipline of child	18	25	31
Divided	22	29	44
Severe	22	31	41
Spoiling	22	27	19
Lacking supervision	4	13	19
Attitude of mother	13	27	42
Attitude of father	13	22	50
Presence of more favored child	8	10	11
Pressure on schoolwork	2	10	11
II. Cultural status of family			
Community rating	29	44	63
Home background level	43	60	70
Nationality or race	29	58	67
Economic or social level changing	37	53	26
Rising	27	38	4
Falling	10	15	22
Ambition higher than attainment	10	17	7
III. Personal characteristics			
Intelligence	36	62	63
Health	18	17	22
Age-grade displacement	20	31	19
More than 1 year overage	0	12	0
More than 1 year underage	20	19	19
School deportment	23	30	77
Maladjustment index	29	39	70

NOTE.   The table provides only a general contrast; what constitutes a "handicap" is detailed in the original source. It is noteworthy that those who confessed their dishonesties were, as a group, suffering under more handicaps—personal, cultural, and family-wise—than were those who were consistently dishonest. But the more important differences are those between the honest group, on one hand, and the two dishonest groups on the other.

SOURCE: Adapted from H. Hartshorne and M. A. May, *Studies in the Nature of Character, I. Studies in Deceit*, New York, Macmillan, 1928, p. 294.

and much lying is for the definite purpose of attention-getting, status-getting, or face-saving. Obviously the motivations in a particular case are to be found only through study of that individual in an effort to ferret out the meaning his behavior has for him.

What suggestions can be offered for helping the child in his moral development? Three very general suggestions may be ventured.[3] In the first place, the evidence suggests the importance of early, continuous, and consistent training in moral and character development. There is no particular age when moral sensitivity or reason suddenly occurs; rather, the process is gradual and continuous. If instruction is delayed too long, inappropriate values may be attached to particular behavior. Thus, cheating is not an ethical issue, but an intriguing effort to put something over on the teacher. Often, too, there is inconsistency among institutions concerned with character training and among the various behaviors of a parent himself. A child learns as much from observation of the parent's actual behavior as from the verbal instructions he receives, and often the two are incompatible.

Second, it is important to recognize that moral values and character are learned in response to the same kinds of motivational principles as are other types of behavior. Responses which meet with satisfaction are learned, while those which produce annoyance tend not to be learned. Much research on human motivation, and with special reference to the early years, emphasizes the value of positive incentives of social acceptance and approval in contrast to punitive measures. The long-term goal should, of course, be the eventual development of an *interiorized* set of norms so that behavior is governed not by external approval or disapproval (though such factors will likely be important throughout life) but rather by satisfaction when an act is consistent with one's value system or by dissatisfaction and annoyance when inconsistency becomes apparent.

Finally, there is the problem of teaching the child to generalize his experiences and to develop ethical principles based on the significant element of the various concrete experiences involved. Only thus can "transfer of training" to a new situation be expected. There needs to be training in a wide variety of situations involving the moral concept and assistance in identifying the important element in the various situations.

The dynamics of moral development and of parent-child interaction are, of course, complex. And emotionalized frictions may eliminate the

---

[3] These are the practical suggestions offered by Jones (54) at the conclusion of his detailed integration of the research on character development.

parent psychologically from a significant role in helping the child or adolescent to develop a consistent, socially acceptable ideology. The parent who has failed to establish and maintain good rapport with his offspring will hardly be the person the adolescent (for example) turns to when ethical issues arise. Indeed, the rebellion against an overrestrictive parent may take the form of rejecting the very values the parent holds important.

Sociopolitical Attitudes and Behavior and Law Observance

A second broad set of values to be considered in this chapter relates to the sociopolitical world of the individual. In a democratic society, individual citizens should hold appropriate values regarding their responsibilities and roles in organized society, evidence proper attitudes and behavior with regard to rights of others, and have respect for law and order. Here are some of the basic problems of modern America. Problems of freedom of speech, protection of basic values while guaranteeing the security of the country, and personal responsibility in time of war—these are typical of many current vexing problems of values, national as well as personal. Delinquency and crime represent another type of social problem suggesting a breakdown of personal controls upon behavior. Consideration of the development of attitudes, values, and civic and political behavior and crime may point up some of the issues and give further insight into moral development.

CIVIC ATTITUDES AND UNDERSTANDINGS

The previous section showed that the basic values of the culture become inculcated very early in life. For example, a study of the development of attitudes toward property rights (27) found that by age six, rankings of the relative seriousness of various offenses[4] correlated .75 with adult rankings. Progress toward adult norms was regular and orderly, with much progress being made between grades one and three. The complexity of what seem to be simple attitudes was evidenced by the bases of the judgments—the relationship of the owner to the offender, the possibility of punishment, the kind and value of the property involved. The younger subjects more often gave fear of punishment as a reason for their ranking. The greater maturity of the older raters' attitudes was evi-

[4] Types of offenses rated included: "to swipe flowers from a park," "to take a wheel from a wagon you find in the alley," "to help yourself to chocolates from a box in your sister's room."

denced not only by their greater variety of reasons but by their greater sensitivity to such social considerations as the extent to which others would be injured and to such personal considerations as the offender's motives.

In short, from a very early age, there is evidence of growth toward a desirable recognition of the rights of others. But the total picture is not so favorable. An extensive study some years ago in the state of New York regarding other types of knowledge and attitude presumably necessary for assuming a responsible role in society led to the conclusion that young people, at the time they left the public schools, were ill equipped to understand facts and issues and to discharge their broader social responsibilities. The report declared that:

Among the boys and girls leaving school every year are a considerable number whom the schools themselves are unwilling to recommend for responsible citizenship. . . .

Irrespective of the schools' judgment of their readiness for citizenship, the leaving pupils as a group are seriously deficient in their knowledge of the problems, the issues, and the present-day facts with which American citizens should be informed. . . .

The boys and girls leaving school are fundamentally conservative in their outlook on social problems. . . .

The results of tests indicate that most boys and girls on the point of leaving school are ready to give at least verbal allegiance to the principles of democratic living and democratic government. . . .

. . . whatever they may think about the desirability of certain kinds of action, they are reluctant to assume responsibility for civic cooperation, or to commit themselves to action which will involve personal sacrifice. . . .

Interviews . . . suggest that once he is out of school, the ordinary boy or girl does practically nothing to add to his readiness for citizenship, nor does he keep alive the knowledge of civic affairs or the interest in social problems which he may have had when he finished his schooling. (89, pp. 17–27.)[5]

The conclusion last quoted is especially significant because it emphasizes a motivational lack of desire to become more competent in civic matters. This raises another question: To what extent are young people willing to participate actively in self-government? The broad study from which the above conclusions were drawn investigated this matter by asking youngsters from grades 7 through 12 such questions as: "Should a student volunteer to help clean up the school yard, if so doing would in-

---

[5] Data supporting these conclusions are presented and discussed in two other volumes of the Regents' report: Ruth E. Eckert and T. O. Marshall (28) and H. E. Wilson (112).

volve part of his lunch hour?" "Should a student accept nomination as President of the Student Council if he is the best qualified student, if such acceptance would mean a serious curtailment in his other activities?" The percentage responding "yes" to questions of this type declines steadily with age. In contrast, answers to other questions suggested a regular increase in sensitivity to individual rights. The general picture seems to be not only one of inadequate knowledge and understanding regarding the types of issues on which people are expected to cast intelligent votes, but also a certain reluctance to accept personal responsibility for civic action.

Such civic and political ignorance and apathy seem also to characterize a large portion of the adult population. It is of some interest in this connection that of 662 eligible voters interviewed before and after the 1948 presidential election, 32 percent voted for Truman, 27 percent for Dewey, *but the largest proportion (36 percent) did not vote at all (14)*. What about age differences during the adult years? Various public opinion polls —presumably based on a reasonably representative sample of the population—and other studies have turned up facts which give some insight into (1) the degree to which younger and older adults are well informed on public matters, (2) the extent to which they might be considered to differ in political conservatism, and (3) differences in their views on specific political or civic issues. Such differences become important in any attempt to evaluate the political consequences of the observed shifts toward an older population in America.

The amount of information possessed by potential voters of various ages appears to vary from group to group and from issue to issue. In one occupational group (teachers), those over 45 were better informed on public issues than were those under 30, as indicated by the top row of figures in Table 62. However, further data in this table, from a more representative and less well-educated sample of the population, suggest that at least on certain matters older adults are less well informed than their younger associates.

Although older people tend to view themselves as being more liberal than they were in their college years[6], the older people tend to classify themselves more frequently as "conservative" than do those younger. So the middle portion of the table shows that people over 50, compared to those under 30, more often (1) regard themselves as conservative, (2) state that if only two political parties were available they would join

[6] Unpublished data of R. G. Kuhlen.

TABLE 62.   Adult Age Differences in (1) Amount of Information Relative to Social and Political Issues, (2) Political Liberalism or Conservatism, and (3) Attitudes on Specific Social and Political Issues. Unless Otherwise Noted, Figures Represent Percentage of the Respondents[a]

	Age Group		
	18–30	31–47	48+
I. How Well Informed?			
Mean score on social information test (teachers)[b]	35	40	45
Know meaning of "conservatism" in politics (1943)	53	52	44
Understood meaning of the term, "free enterprise" (1943)	27	30	24
Understood meaning of the term, "inflation" (1943)	68	67	56
Well or moderately informed with respect to war progress (1941)	72	74	65
Had never heard of the German Gestapo (1942)	11	18	24
II. Conservative or Liberal in Politics?			
In politics (1937) regards self as			
Liberal	41	40	34
Conservative	31	37	45
If only two parties (1938), would join			
Liberal	43	39	34
Conservative	34	42	46
In politics today (1950) considers self[c]			
Republican	21	30	40
Democrat	46	45	40
Independent	26	21	16
III. Attitudes on or Toward Specific Issues?			
Approve of Roosevelt's handling of job (1943)	81	78	50
Believe in one year military training for non-veterans[d] (1945)	74	75	73
Approve colleges permitting Communist leaders to address study groups (1939)	31	25	18
Favor law prohibiting membership in Communist party (1940)	61	67	74
Favor trend to give Federal Government greater power to regulate business, industry, and agriculture (1937)	45	40	36

[a] Unless noted in other footnotes data in this table are from R. P. Hinshaw, The relationship of information and opinion to age, Unpublished Ph.D. dissertation, Princeton University, 1944.

[b] Based on J. C. Sullivan, A Study of the Social Attitudes and Information on Public Problems of Women Teachers in Secondary Schools, New York, Teachers College, Columbia University, 1940. In this instance age groups are: Below 30, 30–45, 45 and over.

[c] From M. Strunk, The quarter's polls, Public Opinion Quart., 1950, 14:606. In this instance age groups are 21–29, 30–49, 50 and over.

[d] From M. Strunk, The quarter's polls, Public Opinion Quart., 1947, 11:486. In this instance age groups are 21–29, 30–49, 50 and over.

the conservative, and (3) identify themselves with the Republican party. More of those under 30, compared to those over 50, regarded themselves as Democrats or Independents in political affiliation.

As the lower portion of Table 62 indicates, on some issues (e. g., universal military training for nonveterans) the several age groups studied were of the same mind. On other issues, clear age trends were apparent. But the figures presented in the table illustrate another basic fact. In general, although age differences may exist, they are not usually striking enough to affect materially decisions based on majority vote.[7] But on some issues, the age differences may be substantial and highly important politically. Note, for example, the differences in party preference at different ages.

POLITICAL AND CIVIC BEHAVIOR

Evidence cited above has suggested a certain apathy in attitudes and lack of social understanding in the late adolescent years. Data on actual participation in community activities suggest that substantial growth in social responsibility comes later. One might expect that young people having reached voting age would rush to the polls to exercise this new right and responsibility, but evidence indicates that they are the least politically active of any age group, even in the simple act of voting.

An extensive questionnaire from a national sample of college graduates of all ages has indicated substantial increases in both civic and political participation well into middle age. Sample data from this study are contained in Tables 63 and 64. In Table 63 are facts relative to political participation, especially with respect to national politics. The proportion voting increases up to about 50 years of age for both sexes and continues at that level until rather old age is reached. Interest in political matters as reflected in newspaper reading and informal conversations similarly increases with age up to about the forties and fifties and then continues high for the rest of life. Also, adults up to middle age increasingly participate actively in the sense of making contributions, circulating petitions, and even becoming candidates for public office.

Table 64 shows a general increase in interest in local politics as evidenced in reading about and discussing local issues. Participation in local activities increases up to about 45 or 50; however, from that age onward, people begin to drop out of such activities. The present writers interpret this not so much as a decline in interest as in energy for time- and energy-

---

[7] Pollak (77) also reached this conclusion in his study of conservatism in older years.

TABLE 63.   Percentage of Married Male and Female College Graduates of Various Ages Who Participated in Specified Political Activities

Approximate Age:	24–28	34–38	44–48	54–58	64–68[a]	74–90[a]
Discussed politics with friends						
Males	89	90	89	88	90	83
Females	85	87	75	86	76	—
Listened at least once a month to political speeches, discussions						
Males	73	71	76	84	82	79
Females	77	68	73	81	86	—
Voted in last primary or local election						
Males	55	72	82	87	82	83
Females	51	68	83	90	81	—
Read one or more books about politics						
Males	25	18	10	17	15	28
Females	9	16	4	15	17	—
Signed a petition for or against some legislation						
Males	16	33	29	27	24	17
Females	24	31	40	27	43	—
Sent letter or telegram to public official						
Males	14	26	28	29	31	24
Females	12	15	29	29	31	—
Contributed money to some political cause						
Males	5	17	24	32	26	17
Females	12	15	19	27	21	—
Number of cases						
Males	45	161	108	193	90	32
Females	86	76	53	60	42	—

[a] Age was estimated from year of college graduation, assuming graduation at age 22. The final "age" group for females is actually made up of the graduating classes of 1879 to 1905. There were more male respondents at the upper ages, permitting the carrying of the age breakdown to a later age for males. To condense the table, figures for ages 29 to 33, 39 to 43, etc., have been omitted, also certain responses.

SOURCE: From R. G. Kuhlen, Expansion and constriction of activities during the adult years as reflected in organizational, civic, and political participation, Paper read at Second International Gerontological Congress, St. Louis, 1951.

TABLE 64.   Percentage of Married Male and Female College Graduates of Various Ages Who Participated in Specified Civic Activities

Approximate Age	24–28	34–38	44–48	54–58	64–68[a]	74–90[a]
Followed local events in newspaper						
Males	76	90	97	94	96	87
Females	82	97	98	97	93	—
Talked with neighbors re bettering neighborhood						
Males	39	53	55	62	66	43
Females	52	62	67	57	58	—
Attended meetings of civic groups						
Males	35	55	60	55	42	33
Females	35	50	73	60	63	—
Contact with local official about a civic problem						
Males	26	36	39	44	42	23
Females	18	35	27	23	19	—
On a volunteer committee for community service						
Males	15	39	46	43	30	20
Females	28	41	63	53	30	—
Collected money or carried petition for local cause						
Males	15	25	32	34	21	17
Females	20	30	43	43	19	—
Helped a group such as Scouts						
Males	17	28	34	24	22	20
Females	21	27	35	30	19	—
Number of cases						
Males	45	161	108	193	90	32
Females	86	76	53	60	42	—

[a] Age was estimated from year of college graduation, assuming graduation at age 22. The final women's "age" group is actually made up of the graduating classes of 1879 to 1905. More male respondents at the upper ages permitted carrying of the men's breakdown to a later age. To condense the table, figures for ages 29 to 33, 39 to 43, etc., have been omitted, also certain responses.

SOURCE: From R. G. Kuhlen, Expansion and constriction of activities during the adult years as reflected in organizational, civic, and political participation, Paper read at Second International Gerontological Congress, St. Louis, 1951.

consuming local affairs. It will be recalled that interest in reading, talking about, and voting on local matters stays up well into old age.

These facts have significant implications not only for understanding of political and civic behavior but also in demonstrating that significant social growth and expansion is occurring well into the adult years. The acceptance of social responsibilities as adult age increases by larger and larger numbers of people—a trend that will be confirmed by other data presented in the next chapter—is a significant symptom that life does not become stagnant in the adult and older years, at least for the better-educated groups; nor is there a decline of interest in broad social matters. Under such circumstances, it is reasonable to expect that civic competence, as well as civic influence, increases beyond the relatively unhappy state apparent at late adolescence. It might be recalled at this point that evidence in an earlier chapter indicated outstanding scientific, literary, and artistic contributions to be most frequently made in the thirties, but outstanding political leadership occurred later (65).

FACTORS RELATED TO SOCIOPOLITICAL ATTITUDES AND BEHAVIOR

A first question in considering the background of political attitudes and behavior is whether or not more constructive educational efforts might make positive contributions. One outstanding example, from a study done some years ago, will serve to illustrate that much can indeed be done by a well-planned school program to influence not only students but their parents as well.[8] The experimental school program was essentially a democratic program of teachers and pupils working together in groups to solve local problems. A case of typhoid in the community (one of a series of such cases) was the point of departure for the study of the causes of typhoid fever, and the study included the seeking of information from government sources, a survey of the conditions under which the immediate case developed, and the development of means to eliminate the unsanitary conditions on the particular farm. Considerable choice was given the pupils as to projects to be undertaken, a vote being taken to determine

[8] For scope of vision and tangibleness of data this study surpasses many current attempts at assessing the outcome of education. It seems strange that educational practice has been so little influenced (despite the well-known cultural lag) and that researchers have not ordinarily gone to the effort of obtaining the homely, but exceedingly important, information that Collings sought. While the present table concerns data related to community activities, a variety of other information (number of acres planted to legumes, the pounds of pork produced per sow, number of farmers participating in coöperative marketing programs, etc.) is given in the original publication to show the outcome of the "activity" program.

group activities. Not only was it discovered that such practical beginnings and procedures led to enhanced outcome along academic lines, but there was much evidence of changed practices in living habits and community participation. Table 65 shows the contrast between the children and parents associated with the democratically operated "experimental" school and the conventional school. More parents of children in the experimental school participated in community meetings, voted for school improvements, read more newspapers, and generally showed a sensitivity to community issues that previously had provoked no special concern.

TABLE 65. The Effect of Participation in a School Program upon Community Behavior of Children and Parents, as Shown by Percentage of Children and Parents of an Activity School and a Conventional School Who Participated in Various Community Activities

	Conventional School	Experimental School
Percent of children reading one or more newspapers during the year	11	66
Percent of children of district participating in children's community activities	0	100
Percent of children engaging in activities of one or more clubs	10	71
Percent of parents visiting the school during the school year	10	92
Percent of voters attending the annual school meeting	41	98
Percent of voters voting at the annual school meeting for the extra school-improvement levy	33	87
Percent of parents violating the compulsory-school-attendance law during the year	22	2
Percent of parents reading one or more daily newspapers	32	79
Percent of parents regularly attending the night community meetings	47	96
Percent of parents participating in one or more of the children's community activities	0	91

SOURCE: Adapted from E. Collings, *An Experiment with a Project Curriculum*, New York, Macmillan, 1929, pp. 265–275.

The possibilities, inherent in such programs, for more meaningful civic participation on the part of greater numbers of people need more general exploitation.

The "control group" in the table reflects what likely exists under typical school procedures. How, under usual school conditions, do the better students, those of high "intelligence," compare with the average in their social knowledge and attitudes? In general, they turned out to be better with respect to factual knowledge, comprehension of social terms, and knowledge of history, but they differed little from the average in their insight or concern about social problems of community or nation or in their knowledge of or attitudes toward such community issues as relief, health, and recreation (89, 112). Terman (97) found somewhat similar results in his investigation of gifted children. They differed from the average to a greater degree in traits and values related to self-success than in traits and values related to social responsibility and service. Those who are most competent and able thus seem no more willing than the average to put their capacities and knowledge to work for human betterment.

Aside from such "action programs" as school programs, what factors determine sociopolitical attitudes and behavior on the young adult and general adult level? In earlier considerations of moral values, strong emphasis was placed upon home backgrounds and family relations. The same kinds of relationships seem to hold in the present instance. Indeed, a number of investigators have found parents and high school students so similar in social values (including political party preference) that they concluded that sampling the attitudes of one group gave a fair picture of the other.[9] There was no indication of "the frequently assumed antithesis between 'crabbed age and youth'" (108, p. 18).

A more recent study (69) has attempted to show the relationship between the political orientation of first voters (youth between the ages of 21 and 24 at the 1952 election) and that of their parents. Agreement with party choice of parents was high: 74 percent of those who could report their fathers' party preferences preferred the same party, and 76 percent preferred the same party as their mothers. In 86 percent of the cases where both parents chose the same party, the son or daughter also chose that party. Thus, here, also, children are like parents. But just as interesting are the *differences* between children and their parents and the

[9] This has not been consistently reported, however. A recent study (68) shows relatively low correlations between parents' attitudes and those of their adolescent offspring with respect to Russia, Marshall Plan, war. Newcomb and Svehla (75) showed a tendency for parent-offspring similarity in attitudes to decrease with increasing age of the offspring, presumably as other extra-home influences became operative.

reasons therefor. Is change from parents' views a matter of rebellion against parents or a matter of influence by extra-home influences? Rebellion against parents seems to be responsible for change in the lower socio-economic group but not in the highest. Those who were subjected to a great deal of control changed most frequently; those who were subject to moderate control changed least; and those who were left pretty much on their own by their parents changed with a frequency between the other two groups. "Thus we see that maximum conformity by the younger person to the political values of his family occurs when his parents have been neither laissez faire nor authoritarian with him,—when they have taken an interest in him and attempted to guide him, but have used moderate pressure via persuasion rather than strong pressure by command or force" (69).

Though numbers of cases were too small to make a definitive test, these investigators pointed out an interesting trend: the effects of parental training method on political conformity seemed to be greatest when the parents have a high interest in politics. "Presumably, when parents do not consider politics important, their children will choose some other area of values in which to signify their loyalty or register their protest" (69).

Presumably, due to the greater opportunity for extra-home stimulation and influence among those attending college, the better-educated young people tended to change away from the orientation of their parents more frequently than did the poorly educated young adults. This was an important source of change in the upper socioeconomic groups. Upwardly mobile young people (i. e., those having better jobs than parents) tended to adopt the political behavior (voting) of the group into which they moved while retaining many of the values of the group of origin. On the other hand, those who were downwardly mobile tended to retain the voting pattern of the group of origin while accepting some of the ideology of the new group. In short, this investigation reveals the development of political orientation to be substantially influenced by parental influence and the quality of parental relationships but also to be determined by a complex psychology of group and educational influences.[10]

[10] The role of personality factors in sociopolitical attitudes should not be overlooked. A recent study (45) proposes the hypothesis that when social pressures with regard to an attitude are strong, the effect of personality factors are overruled; but when social pressures with regard to an attitude are not strong, the attitude held is likely to be more consistent with the person's characteristic way of reacting, e. g., with hostility.

The role of socioeconomic status (hinted at in the preceding paragraphs) appears to be a most significant factor in the determination of political attitudes and behavior. This conclusion is strikingly documented in Table 66 wherein are shown something of the attitudes held by members of various urban occupational levels. Clear trends from upper to lower strata are evident. Over half in the "large business" group are ultraconservative, and less than 2 percent are radical or ultraradical (the "2 percent" in the table is a rounding of 1.9 percent). The laboring groups are notably nonconservative. They are the most radical of all the groups, but many show such marked inconsistency of allegiance or opposition to the existing order that they could be classified only as "indeterminant." The bottom portion of the table shows attitudes toward a central issue in today's politico-economic strife: that between two opposed philosophies of government—the individualistic view and the collectivistic view. Clearly there are marked "class" differences in these attitudes. Apparently those who are at the top, who dominate the social order, who have been treated well by the present nature of things, who have security and status, are satisfied with things as they are and wish to protect the way of life that gives status and security. Those who lack these assets are more willing to change, are more likely to be opposed to the status quo.

TABLE 66.   Relationship Between Urban Occupational Strata and Politico-Economic Attitudes as Shown by Percentages of Various Groups Taking Various Positions

Attitude	Urban Occupational Strata						
	Large Business	Pro-fessional	Small Business	White Collar	Skilled Manual	Semi-skilled Manual	Unskilled Manual
Ultraconservative	55	30	46	24	12	5	2
Conservative	31	40	28	31	26	16	21
Indeterminate	11	19	18	28	34	29	39
Radical	0	4	7	10	17	29	21
Ultraradical	2	7	1	5	10	21	17
For private owner-ship	93	81	82	81	77	53	52
For individualism	91	77	76	68	52	30	32
Against more power for working people	74	65	64	46	31	25	29
Number of cases	54	73	131	172	163	174	77

SOURCE: Adapted from R. Centers, The Psychology of Social Classes, Princeton, Princeton University Press, 1949.

Earlier in the chapter, the discussion of developmental (age) trends in political attitudes, and particularly in political behavior, was limited at many points because of the nature of the data, to those of high educational status, namely, college graduates. To provide a better perspective (though not with respect to age trends), certain demographic characteristics of a sample of 662 adults eligible to vote are presented in Table 67. More males, it will be noted, vote than females; more whites vote than Negroes; more older people vote than younger ones; more people vote in the upper income and occupational groups; more people vote in metropolitan areas than in rural areas; more Catholics vote than Protestants (though the difference is likely determined by some of the other factors noted); more union members vote than nonunion members. These facts not only reflect again the role of social context in determining political behavior, but they also show to what extent the values represented by these various groups will be represented at the polls. Thus, in assessing the political influence of older groups it

TABLE 67. Percentage of a Sample of 662 Adults of Various Groups Who Voted in the 1948 Presidential Election

Sex		Occupation of family head	
Male	69%	Professional and managerial	75
Female	60	White collar	82
Race		Skilled and semiskilled	71
White	66	Unskilled	50
Negro	36	Farmers	42
Age		Type of community	
21–34	55	Metropolitan area	83
35–44	66	Towns and cities	61
45–54	75	Rural areas	40
55 and over	63	Religion	
Education		Protestant	57
Grade school	56	Catholic	79
High school	67	Trade union affiliation	
College	80	Member	73
Income		Nonmember	62
Under $2000	47		
$2000–2999	61		
$3000–3999	74		
$4000 and over	80		

SOURCE: Adapted from A. Campbell and R. L. Kahn, *The People Elect a President*, Ann Arbor, Survey Research Center, University of Michigan, 1952.

must be noted not only that they are more conservative but that *more of them* vote. From such data it would appear that methods that are effective in getting people out to vote might be more important determiners of election outcome than effective methods of influencing the opinions of those who normally vote.

JUVENILE DELINQUENCY

The preceding pages have been concerned with the degree to which people contribute to their own government and make positive contributions to the common welfare. What now of the negative side? To what extent are legal restrictions violated? From what backgrounds do delinquents and criminals come? And what are their personal characteristics? From such information, especially when interpreted for its causal significance, should grow further insight into the origins of moral behavior.

If the total incidence of law violation were to be ascertained, almost everyone would be involved. A survey of college students, for example, revealed a substantial incidence of such crimes as carrying concealed weapons, possession of stolen goods, petty theft, burglary, drunkenness (79). Kinsey points out that almost everyone violates, at some time, various legal restrictions on sexual behavior. Delinquency and crime are legal terms. Most studies on incidence of delinquency and crime are concerned only with those individuals who have been apprehended and often only with those who have been convicted. Studies restricted to these groups will give a limited, though not unmeaningful, psychological picture.

Actual delinquency rates as reported by 41 courts for boys and girls, Negroes and whites, are shown in the curves presented in Figure 97. Although the incidence curves begin to rise at 7 or 8 years of age, early delinquencies are likely much more frequent. In one study, for example (29), 57 percent of a group of delinquents began delinquencies at 10 years or before, and another study (32) found 64 percent beginning before 10. It is to be noted that there is no "pubescent spurt" in these curves, and, if data presented later in the chapter (Table 70) are examined, it will be noted that delinquency and crime (as evident in legal statistics) are primarily products of the late teens and early twenties rather than products of the stresses of pubescence. Striking sex and race differences in delinquency rates are apparent in the chart. Boys begin their delinquencies earlier than do girls (104), and over the whole age range boys outnumber girls perhaps four to one (103). Differential treatment of

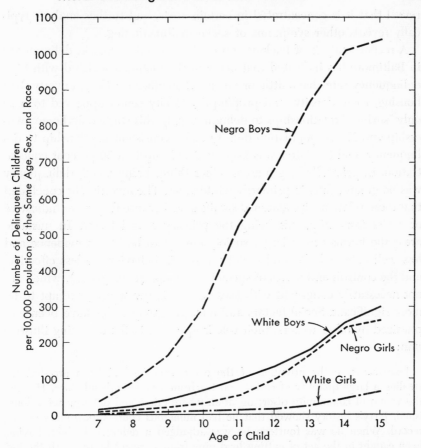

Figure 97. Juvenile Deliquency Rates at Each Year of Age per 10,000 White and Negro Boys and Girls 7 to 15 Years of Age Dealt With by 41 Courts Reporting During the Years 1932–1934. (From U. S. Department of Labor, Children's Bureau, *Juvenile Court Statistics*, Washington, D.C., U.S. Government Printing Office, 1934, p. 18.)

girls by parents, society, and the courts is likely responsible for these differences.

What kinds of youngsters get into trouble with the law? Mainly they are children from socially blighted neighborhoods. The delinquency-infested areas of Chicago, for example, are also areas with decreasing populations, high relief rates, low rentals, high alien and Negro population, high truancy rates, high infant mortality, tuberculosis, and insanity rates (86). Almost any plotting of delinquency cases on a city map will reveal that it is concentrated in certain areas, and further analysis typically reveals other symptoms of social malfunctioning.

A recent analysis of background environmental factors in delinquency in Baltimore has indicated that many of the factors associated with high delinquency rates have little or no causal significance (62). Poverty, bad housing, room density, and propinquity to city center appeared to bear only "surface" relationships to delinquency. In this study only home ownership and Negro population density had a consistent relationship to delinquency, and the latter was important only up to a 50 percent concentration. In *primarily* Negro areas, other things being equal, delinquency was no greater than in primarily white areas. The investigator concluded that these relationships assumed significance because they were indicative of *social instability*, this being the primary causal factor. In unstable areas the norms of the larger society are apt to be less in evidence and less well enforced. General social controls in behavior are less effective, and the controls and mores of special subgroups (e. g., gangs), which are not necessarily congruent with those of the larger society, are apt to be more significant. Social factors and minority group codes have been emphasized by other writers; their role is apparent in the following illustration:

Jerry came to the attention of the court after he had been arrested for stealing a large quantity of coffee and tea from a neighborhood store. He was the victim of community disorganization where crime and delinquencies flourished. Jerry's history showed that he had numerous court appearances on his record. When he was fourteen he was adjudged a delinquent child, having been caught in the act of cutting lead pipe from a vacant house, with the aid of two other boys. This was a regular gang activity of the group with which he hung out. He was placed on probation, and during the time he was under supervison, he was caught with a cigarette vending machine which he and a group of boys had stolen from a cafeteria. They planned to divide the cigarettes and the money in the machine and to go to their cellar clubroom to have a party. As a result of this violation of probation, Jerry was sentenced to a reformatory.

After he had served his term, he returned to the same community, and again fell in with the same group of boys. There were few organized activities available, and Jerry spent his spare time in a neighborhood pool-room. Here he listened to the talk of easy money and learned to plan real burglaries. Upon investigation it was found that guns could be stored in this pool-room, and that it was the headquarters for numerous delinquent and criminal gangs. It was a focal point of delinquency.

Asked about his latest offense, Jerry said that he had been playing pool, and that he and another boy—one who had been sent away with him to the reformatory on the charge of stealing the cigarettes—decided they wanted money to attend a moving-picture show the following day. The boys had been gathering firewood and discovered that it would be an easy matter to gain admittance to a building where a large quantity of coffee and tea was stored. With the encouragement they received from other friends in the pool-room, they set out to accomplish their burglary. One of the boys acted as look-out while Jerry entered the building. He picked up a few boxes of coffee and tea. But as he left the building he was apprehended with the result that he was brought into court on a new charge. (13, pp. 116–117.)

The "interiorization" of social norms—the making of society's standards one's own—occurs primarily within the home and family setting in which the child matures. That delinquents, when compared with nondelinquents of same intelligence and ethnic, and neighborhood backgrounds, have a poor biosocial heritage is evident in some of the facts presented in Table 68. It is to be noted, first, that delinquents in contrast to nondelinquents have poor ties and relationships with their parents and thus are not so likely to achieve the type of identification that will result in establishment of society's norms. But, second, even if they did have close ties, they would in a greater number of instances find a poor model to emulate. The parents themselves (and even their parents' parents) had higher rates of criminality and personal maladjustment. It would seem, then, that not only the neighborhood but often the family itself fails to provide stable and socially acceptable norms and controls upon conduct.

But all children in a "delinquent home" do not end up delinquent, and it is reasonable to suspect that those who become delinquent differ in certain personal characteristics from those who do not. In a study made some years ago, 105 delinquents were compared with 105 nondelinquent siblings (44). The delinquents turned out to be of about the same intelligence, but they were more active and socially assertive and evidenced more symptoms of emotional instability. Facts from a more recent study, presented in Table 69, confirm these findings and add other information. Delinquents differed in body type (more "mesomorphs" among them), and other evidence confirmed findings from other studies (20, 44) to the effect that they likely were more physically active and had higher energy levels. Delinquents were restlessly energetic; more impulsive; more aggressive and destructive; more extroverted and socially assertive; more defiant, hostile, suspicious, and adventurous; and more ambivalent toward and resistive of authority. In contrast, nondelinquents were more submissive and conventional and more coöperative, but they

TABLE 68.   Contrasts Between 500 Delinquents and 500 Nondelinquents with Respects to Percentage Evidencing Certain Family Characteristics and Relationships

Characteristic	Delinquents	Nondelinquents
Mother mentally retarded	33	9
Father mentally retarded	18	6
Mother emotionally disturbed	40	18
Father emotionally disturbed	44	18
Drunkenness in mother	23	7
Drunkenness in father	63	39
Criminality in mother	45	18
Criminality in father	66	32
Haphazard routine of household	30	16
No family self-respect	43	10
Poor conduct standards in home	90	54
Unsuitable supervision of children by mother	64	13
No family group recreation	67	38
No cohesiveness in family	25	1
Indifferent, hostile or rejective attitudes of father toward boy	60	19
Indifferent, hostile or rejective attitudes of mother toward boy	28	4
Boy attached to mother	65	90
Boy attached to father	32	65
Father unacceptable for emulation by boy	31	7
Number of family moves (8 or more)	53	18
Boy has left home at some time	71	9

SOURCE: Selected from S. and Eleanor Glueck, *Unraveling Juvenile Delinquency,* New York, Commonwealth Fund, 1950.

had more generalized anxiety, were less sure of themselves, and more frequently had marked feelings of helplessness and fear of failure and defeat. In short, the overall picture of the delinquent is that of a person who has failed to become adequately socialized, has failed to develop a "conscience," and is thus lacking in personal control over conduct, but he is nonetheless aggressive enough to strike out and socially assertive enough to seek out companions, even though companions of the wrong kind. It is noteworthy that a number of studies have indicated that delinquents *know* right from wrong as well as do nondelinquents (*44, 87, 106*), but they do not behave in conformity with their knowledge. Not

TABLE 69.   Contrasts Between 500 Delinquents and 500 Nondelinquents with Respect to the Percentage Evidencing Certain Personal Characteristics, Attitudes, and Habits

Characteristic	Delinquents	Nondelinquents
Wechsler-Bellevue: total verbal weighted score	36	38
Wechsler-Bellevue: total performance weighted score	46	46
Retarded in school	68	44
Index of reading ability	81	86
Wishes to stop school or only vague school plans	59	15
Truant from school	95	11
After school employment in street trades	58	37
Adventurous recreational preference	48	9
Movie attendance 3 or more times per week	45	11
Gang companions	56	1
Companions predominately older	45	10
Regular church attendance	39	67
Body build—Mesomorphic component dominant	60	31
Marked social assertion	17	5
Marked defiance	16	1
Marked feelings of resentment	50	31
Marked submissiveness	27	79
Marked ambivalence to authority	38	14
Marked feeling of helplessness or powerlessness	23	36
Marked fear of failure and defeat	23	35
Marked coöperation	71	97
Marked conventionality in ideas, feelings, behavior	8	32
Marked self-control	18	37
Marked vivacity	36	19

SOURCE: Selected from S. and Eleanor Glueck, *Unraveling Juvenile Delinquency,* New York, Commonwealth Fund, 1950.

only is there a failure of personal control, but social controls through family and neighborhood are also inadequate (82, 83).

Detailed studies of the delinquent behavior of youngsters in the setting of their own personalities reveal something of the psychological dynamics involved. Delinquent behavior may be viewed as *adjustive* behavior, albeit socially unacceptable, with the delinquency bearing a meaningful relationship to the psychological needs and frustrations of the individual. Careful psychological and psychiatric studies of a substantial group of delinquents suggested that the delinquencies studied might be interpreted as follows:

1. Attempt to avoid, even as a temporary measure, the unpleasant situation by *escape* or *flight* from it.

2. Attempt to achieve substitutive *compensatory satisfactions* through delinquent activities. These satisfactions include the thrill of delinquent adventure and the gratification at obtaining special recognition or attention, perhaps even notoriety, as a delinquent. In some instances material gains figure as compensation for deprivation.

3. Attempt to strengthen or *bolster up the ego* wounded by feelings of inadequacy or inferiority. The aim then is to obtain *recognition and status* with the delinquent crowd; or, if the offender is more solitary in tendencies, by the individual proving to himself that he really is courageous and can in some way play a spirited role. This "masculine protest" we found to be a not uncommon reaction with some previously effeminate or feminized boys. Said one such lad, "They thought I was no good so I went out to show a cock-eyed world that I was a regular guy."

4. Attempt to get certain ego-satisfactions through direct and conscious or even unconscious expression of *revenge attitudes*—perhaps through hidden desire to punish parents or others by conduct that will make life difficult for them.

5. Attempt to gain a *maximum of self-satisfaction,* to inflate the ego, by generally aggressive, antisocial attitudes, that is, by the exhibition of definite hostilities and antagonisms to authority.

6. *Response to instinctual urges* felt to be thwarted. While this response may be exhibited in sexual misbehavior, more notably in our delinquents, we have discovered the attempt to satisfy the urge for independence and emancipation which normally flares up as an adolescent phenomenon.

7. The wish for punishment was clearly discernible in a few instances and suspected in others. This *seeking punishment*—delinquent behavior possibly offering an opportunity for being punished—was always a response to a conscious or unconscious sense of guilt. (*44.*)

CRIME DURING MATURITY AND OLD AGE

In turning now to the matter of adult crime, it is noted first that after the twenties crime rates decline steadily into old age. Relevant figures are carried in Table 70. To some extent these rates are the product of continued criminal activity on the part of juvenile delinquents. But to a considerable degree they reflect the crimes of people who committed their first offenses at an adult age.

It is, of course, exceedingly difficult to estimate either the extent or nature of adult crime. As was earlier pointed out, "delinquency" and "crime" are legal terms and thus studies must start with court decisions. This circumstance makes it extremely difficult to determine with any high degree of confidence either the overall crime rate age for age, or the rates for specific crimes. It is likely, in the first place, that there are significant age differences in the ability to escape detection. But, in the second place, from the lodging of complaints, through arrests, jury trials, and court actions, favoritism (of a type) may occur that seriously biases the facts of final disposition. It is likely that girls and women, and the very young and the very old males are less frequently complained against, are less frequently arrested, less vigorously prosecuted, may be permitted to plead guilty to lesser charges, may be given suspended sentences or fail to be convicted. And a great many "crimes" of particular groups may be difficult of detection, as those of fraud in business or politics or those of women who may aid and abet male criminals. Regarding the latter, J. Edgar Hoover once wrote: "In practically every outstanding instance, it was found that gangs lived because of their women. The feminine members of the gang arranged hideouts; they looked over the scene of the robbery, thus allowing its careful planning by the masculine members; they made getaway charts for easy escape; they hired lawyers; they acted as go-betweens—in fact they performed almost every highly necessary duty in the commission of a crime except the actual perpetration of the offense itself."[11]

Despite these difficulties, it is of interest to note that the pattern of crime changes with age. The median ages of those arrested for auto theft, burglary, and robbery fall in the early twenties. Those arrested for embezzlement and fraud, for receiving stolen property, for "other sex offenses" (excluding rape, prostitution, and commercialized vice), and for assault and homicide have median ages in the early thirties. And those arrested for driving while intoxicated, for drunkenness, and for gambling have median ages in the middle or late thirties (102, 105). Regarding careers of habitual criminals, one writer points out that:

Habitual criminals . . . had juvenile court records in their childhood. Something like a process of maturation appears in these cases. Delinquencies begin at an early age and increase in frequency and seriousness. Delinquencies start as a recreational incident and become an integrated pattern of life. Criminal maturity is reached in early middle age, about thirty or thirty-five. Some criminals then abandon their crimes abruptly, others adopt less strenuous types

[11] Quoted from J. Edgar Hoover, "The Women in Crime," in *This Week*, the Magazine Section of the Detroit *News*, October 17, 1937, as quoted by A. E. Wood and J. B. Waite (*113*).

of crimes, others engage in quasi-criminal activities in connection with politics, gambling, prostitution, and the liquor business, while others become vagrants. This process, however, is only roughly characteristic of the careers, and exceptions may be found regarding the age of beginning criminality and the age at leaving the profession. Especially, the burglars and robbers abandon those careers at a relatively early age, the pickpockets and confidence men at a much later age. According to the gossip of the underworld a man ninety years of age is picking pockets today, having started . . . at the age of sixteen (93, p. 97).

Table 70 shows something of the nature of age trends with respect to total criminal behavior terminating in prison (bottom rows) and with respect to specific types of crimes. In this instance, the facts relate to prisoners received from courts and thus represent the residual after all the biases of the type noted earlier have had a chance to operate. Attention has already been called to certain of the trends in the previous comment

TABLE 70.   Percentage Distribution of Certain Offenses Within Age Groups, Male Felony Prisoners Received from State and Federal Courts, 1946

Type of Offense	Median Age	15–19 Years	25–29 Years	35–39 Years	45–54 Years	65 and Over
Murder	30.5	1.76	3.59	4.84	5.05	7.61
Robbery	24.0	11.58	10.50	5.95	3.15	1.09
Aggravated assault	28.7	3.78	6.86	7.82	6.72	11.41
Burglary	23.9	30.52	16.80	13.85	10.57	6.79
Auto theft	22.7	16.98	9.10	3.91	1.45	.27
Embezzlement and fraud	33.8	.74	2.57	3.81	5.83	7.61
Forgery	29.3	3.13	8.16	8.22	9.68	5.98
Rape	26.6	2.93	4.88	4.09	4.02	6.25
Other sex offenses	37.1	.79	1.77	3.10	6.31	15.49
Violating drug laws	34.5	.46	2.17	3.75	5.58	2.45
Nonsupport or neglect	33.8	.08	1.58	2.70	2.12	—
Violating liquor laws	36.4	.40	2.81	5.99	8.62	11.41
Total	26.6	100.02	100.04	100.01	99.99	99.99
Rate per 100,000 population		148.50	176.34	99.01	43.42	7.58
Number (excludes 34 under age 15)		8748	9830	4962	3584	368

NOTE: Certain offenses have not been included in this condensed table because they are relatively rare at every age (as carrying and possessing weapons) or involve trends better indicated by other offenses (so aggravated assault and murder more clearly indicate age trends in crimes of violence than manslaughter, which was omitted). Median age and totals are for all felonies in the original tables, however. The highest crime rate occurs in the age group 20 to 24 (rate of 245.27 per 100,000) according to this analysis.

SOURCE: Computed from U.S. Bureau of the Census, *Prisoners in State and Federal Prisons and Reformatories, 1946*, Washington, D.C., U.S. Government Printing Office, 1948, Table 33, p. 46 and United Nations, *Demographic Yearbook 1948*, Lake Success (New York), United Nations, 1949.

regarding age of arrest, but the reader may wish to examine the table for items in which he may be interested.

Only one trend will be singled out here for further comment—that of sex crimes. A number of writers in criminology have stressed sex offenses as a dominant characteristic of the crimes of old age (46, 93). In a sense this is true. Fifteen percent of those over 65 who were committed to prison in 1951 were committed for "other sex offenses," a classification that excludes rape and commercialized vice, in contrast to only 1 percent of those aged 20 to 24 who were committed to prison for this crime. Actually, though if one computes the *rate* of sex offenses from this table by multiplying the overall rate of admission for the age group by the proportion of sex crimes, it turns out that the highest rate for "other sex crimes" is in the 40- to 44-year age group. From this point on, the *rate* declines and is lowest (of all ages) in the 65 plus group. Undoubtedly, physiological aspects of aging play a role in the fact that such crimes as rape decline with age more rapidly than do the more indirect attempts at sex gratification which would be found in the "other sex offenses" category. But the gross figures do not lend support to the often asserted view that there is a moral degeneration in old age.

Sex differences in crime rates are apparent in available data, though, as noted a few paragraphs ago, the actual incidence of feminine crime is likely much greater than arrest and conviction data suggest. Yet there are many reasons—seclusion of women, their greater preoccupation with domestic affairs, and their protection from competition of commercial life—which would tend to produce an actual lower crime rate on the part of women, even though there is no evidence that they are inherently less disposed to crime than men (113, p. 238). In an extensive survey of the criminality of women, Pollak (78) notes that women show a relatively greater proportion of arrests over a given age, say 35, than do men. In New York in 1940, 35 percent of all women arrested gave their age as over 35 whereas only 29 percent of the men arrested gave their ages as over 35. (The actual difference may be greater if women have a greater tendency to understate their ages!) Pollak believes that the physiological stresses of females (menstruation, menopause, pregnancy) are reflected in their criminal proclivities—citing European crime statistics in support of his view—and offers this as one of two hypotheses explaining the later emergence of crime in women. He suggests, in the second place, that "because of the greater protection of girls in our culture, maturity brings to women a more spectacular broadening of their life sphere and a corresponding greater increase in criminal opportunities and temptations than it brings to men" (78, p. 104).

Why does the pattern of crime vary with age and the total amount decline? In one follow-up study of a group of delinquents and criminals, the relationship to improvement of some 63 factors was studied. Age emerged as *the* one significant factor. No other factor—family background, reformatory or parole history, family relationships, industrial history—appeared to have a significant influence upon reformation. With increased age or maturation seemed to come a certain "settling down" which was accompanied by improvement in all aspects of the activities of the men. This proceeded until about 36. The process of improvement tended to cease at about this age, and if a man had not "reformed" by then, he was unlikely to do so. Among the greatest impediments to improvement with the passage of time were mental and personality deviations (33).

A variety of general factors are, of course, correlated with age and may be significant in producing age differences in kind and amount of crime. There are, first of all, age variations in strength and energy level. As one writer has noted, "children and middle-aged persons refrain from robbery and burglary for the same reasons they do not play professional baseball" (93, p. 98). A second explanation of age differences in crime relates to what might be called personality change—a decline in recklessness once maturity is reached and experience and foresight have caught up with the physical strength and freedom of the individual. This change is also reflected in auto accident rates and preferred open road driving speed. And a third explanation is to be found in the changing personal and social relations and responsibilities that accompany age. Business experience and responsibilities bring opportunities for fraud. Changes in personal sexual attractiveness, which make it more difficult to obtain desirable sex partners, and loss of spouse may predispose to attempts to obtain sexual gratification in ways that result in arrest and prosecution. Experience with penalties for crime may lead to the abandonment of a criminal career or the persistence of those types of crime for which the punishment is less severe.[12]

Religion and Philosophy of Life

Religious values, the third general set of values to be considered in this chapter, play a powerful role in the lives of people the world over. Motivations for interest in religion are many and complex; they are different for the child, for the young adult, and for the older person ap-

---

[12] These are among the explanations advanced by Sutherland (93, pp. 98–99) and are consistent with interpretations of aging advanced elsewhere in the present volume.

proaching the last years of life. In the first place, a religion or life philosophy provides a certain unification of the diverse values and activities of living. As an intelligent being, man feels the need for answers to complex questions about the world and himself, and religion provides certain answers to many such questions—though many people work out concepts more in scientific or philosophical terms. Second, religion provides a certain safety and security. The ordering of the universe and life into a meaningful pattern makes a contribution in this direction (73, p. 26), but perhaps more important is recognition on the part of religious people of a greater power outside themselves that may be drawn upon as a source of strength. Third, cultural conformity plays an important role in religious motivation. The church is an established institution. Through parents, and directly, it trains the young to a particular set of religious beliefs. Many diverse elements in the culture—in law, morality, art, music, literature—owe much of their form and richness to a religious heritage and are influential in determining the general values of the individual.

Many other needs are, in fact, satisfied by religious belief and practice. Prayer, church-going, and Bible-reading, for example, may have many different meanings for different individuals. Attendance at church may satisfy needs for aesthetic experience, for social interaction, for status-seeking—and in different degrees for different people. Nevertheless, certain general patterns of development and change are apparent when groups of different ages are studied.

EARLY RELIGIOUS DEVELOPMENT

What influences operative on the child lead him into the religious life of the group? What is the nature of his concepts at different ages, and how effectively is his conduct modified by these influences? Piaget, noted for his study of "children's philosophies," pointed out that though there is no codified philosophy in childhood (and but infrequently in adult life, for that matter) there is evidence of a fairly consistent tendency in the child's effort at reflection. According to Piaget and other investigators, the child's thoughts are concrete though picturesque.

The most abstract things are made concrete by the child—his dreams are perceived by him as actual objects in his room; even his thoughts are conceived as residing in his breath. He is apt to be concerned over the origin of things. What parent has not been perplexed by such questions as "Mother, where was I before I was born?" or "Who makes the sun?"—questions to which adults frequently give religious answers. But Piaget asked these questions of children. The answers indicated what might be expected—an interpretation by the child of phenomena new to him in terms of things with which he is already familiar. He has seen things made by hand; therefore, babies are made by hand; and the sun was made by hand and thrown like a ball into the air. The active imagination of the child easily accepts the traditional teachings of the church, revised by his own experience. God is a man, only more powerful than other men; and heaven is a specific place—on the roof of the house, on top of a mountain, behind a cloud (76). Bose (11) found that children at a very early age learned these concepts, but with varying degrees of understanding. Such terms as "Christmas" and "church," words which had actually played a part in the experience of the child, were understood. But most of the frequently employed religious terms, such as "Christian" and "conversion," conveyed only vague and nebulous impressions. Another study of religious ideas, attitudes, and factual knowledge at the junior high school level has shown much less knowledge of religious concepts among nonchurch children than among church children as well as important differences among denominations and between sections of the country—though to what degree such differences might be due to differences in education or intellect was not ascertained (109).

In a more recent study (37) of religious development, children were asked to try to imagine how God would look to them and then to picture on paper what had come to mind. Though youngsters of all ages were somewhat astonished by the request, the preschool and public school children went promptly to work, depicting their image of God in concrete terms—though often patterned after fairy tales. Older youngsters encountered greater difficulty, and many post adolescents flatly refused and asked permission to offer a more adequate expression of their religious beliefs. Examination of the pictures produced led this investigator to hypothesize a three-stage pattern of religious development: a fairy tale stage from 3 to 6, a realistic stage of religion from 7 to 12, and an individualistic stage in adolescence.

The formal religious training of the child usually comes from two sources, the parents and the Sunday school. The instruction of the former is by far the more effective, and the close relationship between child and parent is peculiarly conducive to the ready acceptance of Christian religious teachings. The child early recognizes in his parents the sources of comfort and protection, and he easily attributes to them superhuman powers. The transfer of these ideas from parents to God is not at all difficult, especially when the transfer is aided both by the parents and by the content of the religious teachings (12). The Sunday school, when measured by its effect on conduct, is relatively inefficient. Hartshorne and May found that children who attend Sunday school cheat and deceive as frequently as those who do not and that the slight difference in favor of the former is explained better as a result of economic status than influence of the church (39). And Hightower (47), studying 3316

young people, demonstrated that there is no relationship of any consequence between Biblical information and various phases of conduct.

RELIGION IN ADOLESCENCE

The religious values, concepts, and experiences of adolescents have
been more extensively studied than those of younger children because
their greater verbal facility permits the use of questionnaires. The
results of one such study are presented in Table 71 which shows the
percentages of sixth-, ninth-, and twelfth-graders who indicated belief,
disbelief, or uncertainty with respect to certain statements of religious belief and practice. Three developmental trends may be noted. First of all,
with increasing age in adolescence there is a shift from concrete beliefs
to more general and abstract concepts, a trend likely due in part to increasing abstract ability and experience. This aspect of religious development is illustrated by the decrease in agreement with the statement "God
is someone who watches over you to see that you behave yourself and
who punishes you if you are not good" and the increase in agreement
with the statement "God is a strange power working for good, rather than
a person." In this connection it has also been pointed out (1, p. 120)
that "as time goes on, the specific content of a religious service means less
to [people], while the service as a whole means more." A study of prayer
revealed that with increase in religious practice there is an increased
preference for prayers containing beauty and dignity and a decrease in
preference for prayers containing single ideas or subject matter (107).
This trend toward greater generality and abstraction with increased age
is also apparent, it will be recalled, in other moral values and concepts
—as honesty.

A second trend observable in Table 71 is an increasing tolerance with
age with respect to religious belief and practice. It is increasingly recognized, for example, that Catholics, Jews, and Protestants are equally good,
that it is not necessary to attend church to be a Christian, that people
who go to church are not necessarily better than people who do not go
to church. To be sure, these are verbal expressions of attitude and may
not jibe with actual behavior. But other studies, still of verbally expressed
attitudes, have shown much the same trend, one study, for example, showing that the attitudes of Jewish children become more liberal with increasing age. Older children tended to accept fewer traditional beliefs
(31).

There is widespread interest in what happens to religious beliefs when
young people go to college. Does the trend toward liberality of views just

TABLE 71. Changes in Specific Religious Beliefs During Adolescence as Shown by the Percentage of 174 Sixth-, 243 Ninth-, and 130 Twelfth-Grade Children Who Checked Various Statements Indicating Belief, Disbelief, or Uncertainty (Wonder)

Statement	"Believe"			"Not Believe"			"Wonder About"		
	6	9	12	6	9	12	6	9	12
God is a strange power working for good, rather than a person.	46	49	57	31	33	21	20	14	15
God is someone who watches you to see that you behave yourself, and who punishes you if you are not good.	70	49	33	18	37	48	11	13	18
I know there is a God.	94	80	79	3	5	2	2	14	16
Catholics, Jews, and Protestants are equally good.	67	79	86	9	9	7	24	11	7
There is a heaven.	82	78	74	4	5	5	13	16	20
Only good people go to heaven.	72	45	33	15	27	32	13	27	34
Hell is a place where you are punished for your sins on earth.	70	49	35	16	21	30	13	27	34
Heaven is here on earth.	12	13	14	69	57	52	18	28	32
People who go to church are better than people who do not go to church.	46	26	15	37	53	74	17	21	11
Young people should belong to the same church as their parents.	77	56	43	13	33	46	10	11	11
The main reason for going to church is to worship God.	88	80	79	6	12	15	4	7	6
It is not necessary to attend church to be a Christian.	42	62	67	38	23	24	18	15	8
Only our soul lives after death.	72	63	61	9	11	6	18	25	31
Good people say prayers regularly.	78	57	47	9	29	26	13	13	27
Prayers are answered.	76	69	65	3	5	8	21	25	27
Prayers are a source of help in times of trouble.	74	80	83	11	8	7	15	10	9
Prayers are to make up for something that you have done that is wrong.	47	24	21	35	58	69	18	17	9
Every word in the Bible is true.	79	51	34	6	16	23	15	31	43
It is sinful to doubt the Bible.	62	42	27	18	31	44	20	26	28

SOURCE: From R. G. Kuhlen and Martha Arnold, Age differences in religious beliefs and problems during adolescence, J. Genet. Psychol., 1944, 65:291–300. By permission of the American Psychological Association.

noted suggest that later in college traditional, conventional beliefs are to be completely overthrown? Or what happens? A study at Syracuse University some years ago (57) revealed some change, but not a striking one, in religious beliefs during college. The trend was in the liberal direction, a continuation of trends noted in the preceding paragraphs for precollege ages. When inquiry was made as to the causes of these changes, students checked the following reasons: 72 percent checked "influence of teachings of certain courses"; 46 percent, contact with fellow students; 30 percent, the general process of maturing; 21 percent, personal influence of professors in courses; 20 percent, other influences outside of college. The changes that did occur seemed, on the whole, constructive and desirable and were considered by the students to contribute to a more satisfactory philosophy of life. Only a small minority felt they had lost something essential. It is noteworthy that in another study of the current religious practices of college students (Harvard and Radcliffe undergraduates) it was learned that 35 percent of all women students and 15 percent of men students say prayers daily, and an additional 40 percent of women and 50 percent of men students prayed occasionally but not every day. Although only 38 percent of women and 17 percent of men students attended church weekly, the majority did attend occasionally. And about 80 percent of the women and 60 percent of the men students reported at least occasional experiences of reverence, devotion, or dependence on a Supreme Being (1). By and large, no striking change in religious belief or practice characterizes college years; rather, there is a continuation of developmental trends apparent earlier.

A third trend, of some interest, apparent in Table 71 is the increasing *uncertainty* regarding certain issues. Although this is especially notable in regard to the statement, "Every word in the Bible is true," the more interesting fact is that this trend characterized all items relating to the hereafter. Another phase of the study suggested that this issue increasingly becomes a "problem" during the teens. And another study has suggested "reassurance of immortality" as a reason for going to church to be higher in youth than in people 25 to 50 (58). This general concern and uncertainty about the question of immortality and the hereafter seem to characterize youth more than the early and middle adult years, but a favorable resolution of this issue becomes, as evidence presented later will show, a characteristic of the later years.

There is substantial evidence that for large numbers adolescence represents a period of some increase in religious awareness and marks the occurrence of the formal acceptance of personal responsibility and membership in church groups.[13] Often this is precipitated or accompanied by a marked emotional experience, but, in any event, it is sufficiently clear cut that the event of "religious awakening" can be recalled and dated.

[13] According to a study by one of the present writers, there seemed to be no great general increase in either religious problems or doubts in adolescence (61).

Figure 98 presents age trends for conversion experiences from a group of studies done around the turn of the century and from one published in 1929. It will be noted, first, that there is a clear teen-age peak in the incidence of such experiences and, second, that the more recent study shows a peak some four or five years earlier than the older studies. This difference is significant since the interpretation, around 1900, was that conversion was biologically generated, resulting from the maturation of a religious instinct. This point of view cannot be strongly held if a generation brings such a marked age change. In addition, there is evidence

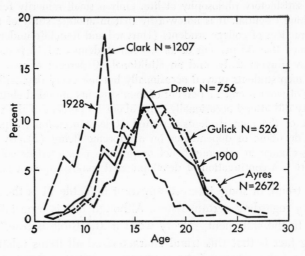

Figure 98. Percentage Distribution of Religious Conversions According to Age, Showing Age of Most Frequent Occurrence and Change of Age, from 1900 to 1928. (Data of Clark, Drew, Gulick, and Ayers from E. T. Clark, *The Psychology of Religious Awakening,* New York, Macmillan, 1929, pp. 55, 63.)

showing no difference in the religious experiences of pre- and postpubescent girls of the same chronological age (48).

The bulk of modern research tends to place emphasis upon social and cultural factors in determining not only the timing but the nature of religious experiences of various types. It has been shown, for example, that children from "Christian homes" experience conversion at a modal age of 13 whereas those from non-Christian homes who are converted have this experience at a modal age of 16 (73). Presumably, they came under the influence of Christian teachings later than did those reared in Christian families. As Table 72 shows, most people (about two-thirds of the group studied) have a rather gradual religious awakening, with about

27 percent reporting an emotional experience and 7 percent a "crisis" type of experience. Other data in the table indicate that the type of experience had will depend upon social factors. The person growing up in the city is likely to have a gradual religious awakening, but in the country, in an older group or a group with a stern theology, an emotional turning or a crisis awakening is more common.

TABLE 72. Types of Religious "Awakening" Experienced by People of Different Social and Religious Backgrounds

	No. of Cases	Type of Experience		
		Gradual	Emotional	Crisis
Persons having stern theology	176	30.7	34.7	34.6
Members of confirmation churches	133	92.3	5.5	2.2
Rural residents	423	53.0	34.0	13.0
Urban residents	571	77.4	18.4	4.2
Persons over 40 years of age	81	30.9	33.3	35.8
Total group[a]	2174	66.1	27.2	6.7

[a] Includes categories in addition to those selected for presentation in this table.

SOURCE: Adapted from E. T. Clark, The Psychology of Religious Awakening, New York, Macmillan, 1929.

By late adolescence important changes have occurred in religious concepts and attitudes. There exists in late adolescence a strong sense of need for religion (1) and for help on religious problems (61). Yet most studies agree that there is increasing dissatisfaction during adolescence with conventional church programs and practice (3, 8, 57, 61). In view of the latter, it is not surprising to find that there occurs a clear decrease in church attendance as children move through their teens (84). To some extent this may be due to dissatisfaction with what the church has to offer, to lessened parental control (or rebellion against it), or perhaps merely to the encroachment of other activities which results in a wish to "sleep in" on Sunday morning rather than to get out to church. One study of decreasing interest in church suggests that the greatest number discontinue church attendance during school grades 10 to 12, and the next largest group quit at the freshman year of college (50). Another investigator (5) noted that 89 percent of a group studied attended church sometimes; only 40 percent attended regularly. According to both the ministers and the young people, a major reason for this difference lay in the fact that little had been done to make church membership meaningful after these young people were enrolled as members. Here indeed is a challenge for those interested in religious education.

If adolescence ends with decreasing church attendance, coupled with increasing dissatisfactions with the formal religious institutions,[14] the adult years bring with them new demands on time and energy to such an extent that the dominant activities (such as occupation) seem to constitute the "meaning" of life and leave little time or need for religious speculation or observance. It is, perhaps, for this reason—the priority of other needs and pressures—that religious thinking and practice appears to be at a low ebb in the early adult years.

In Table 73 certain facts with respect to the religious practices of Catholics in a southern city are given. This particular church spells out quite explicitly many of the practices incumbent upon members, and deviations from required or expected practice are thus possibly more significant than in other churches. According to the investigator, of the three practices reported on in Table 73, two—performance of Easter duties and weekly attendance at Sunday Mass— are obligatory; the third—receiving communion once a month or oftener—is not obligatory.

It is to be noted that, despite the explicit requirement, these external observances become less frequent as age increases from the teens to the thirties and then increase into the older years. In explanation of these trends, the investigator suggested that the high observance in the teens was due to pressure from home and school regardless of individual initiative. The twenties are characterized by emancipation from these influences and include more social distractions in parties and weekends away from home. The thirties—the low point in the age profile of religious observance—probably introduce three other factors: (1) the pressure for job success, an interest that likely has a pervasive effect upon many urban behavior patterns; (2) the demand on time of young children in the home; and (3) the desire to limit the family size through birth control, a point emphasized by experienced priests in the parish. This third factor is important because the church teaches that the Catholic cannot practice birth control and also receive the sacraments. Here, then, is a rather specific conflict between purposes—and church observance suffers.

The forties and fifties bring a reversal of the age trend. By this age people "have achieved a regularity of living, assumed the responsibility of giving example to their growing children, and are not so greatly affected by recreational and occupational demands as previously" (30). The sixties bring religious ob-

---

[14] It should be emphasized, however, that the majority of adolescents in America believe in the fundamental tenets of religious teaching, attend church, engage in such personal practices as prayer, and, according to a *Fortune* survey, would be extremely loath to give up freedom of religion (*Fortune,* Vol. 26, Dec., 1942, p. 8).

servance equal to that of the teens, except for monthly communion. The failure of this aspect of observance to increase, it was thought, was due to the different view taken by the church at the turn of the century when these oldsters were developing their religious habits.

TABLE 73. Religious Practices of Catholics in a Southern City, as Shown by Percentage of Various Sex and Age Groups Who Made Easter Duties, Attended Mass Every Sunday, and Received Monthly Communion

Age	Number of Cases		Percent Making Easter Duties		Percent Attending Mass Every Sunday		Percent Receiving Monthly Communion	
	M	F	M	F	M	F	M	F
10–19	835	833	91	93	91	95	63	79
20–29	930	1064	84	86	73	78	41	41
30–39	924	1063	57	69	62	75	24	38
40–49	745	717	67	83	68	83	30	48
50–59	365	372	72	82	71	82	30	47
60 plus	216	299	75	95	83	96	17	32

SOURCE: Adapted from J. H. Fichter, The profile of Catholic religious life, Amer. J. Sociol., 1952, 58:145–150.

The trends apparent in this study (which is the best study of adult religious practices now available) are illustrative of the findings of other research showing age developments and changes. Other studies of more general populations (in contrast to the Catholic study just described) show church attendance to be maintained at a fairly constant level of frequency during the adult years. When contrasted with a steady decrease in other out-of-home activities, this fact may be interpreted as an *increase* in interest sufficient to counter the increasing tendency to stay put. And sedentary, home religious practices which do not require great energy expenditure (e. g., Bible-reading, listening to religious programs on the radio) increase during the adult years. This is in contrast to the teen-age decline noted earlier.

The adult age trends noted appear to be due to age variations in institutional and family pressures, on one hand, and to conflicts between needs and roles, on the other. The nature of the developmental trends in various types of values noted in a number of the studies cited in this chapter suggests that the moral and religious values of the culture are taught to and forced upon young children in rather verbatim, stereotyped fashion. Gradually, with broadened experience and the emergence of contrary personal drives, these values are modified and often subordinated. But later, as the individual makes adjustments to conflicting needs and/or passes through the age phase where such conflicting needs are dominant, he becomes a representative of the culture and adopts, at least externally, a rather conventional version of values and religion which he then transmits to his children. Regarding this latter, Allport has said:

In the early twenties the youth, as a rule, has not yet married a wife who, by the law of averages, will be more religious than he. Nor has he yet undertaken the training of children. When he does so he will probably want them to have the benefit of religious influence which is part of the cultural heritage. Nor, in the early and middle twenties, has he yet developed sufficient perspective upon his own upbringing to appreciate the sincerity and piety that may have marked his parents' attitudes. It is often in the thirties that people first decide the parental model is, after all, not a bad one to follow. The old folks now seem to have been acting as wisely as they could have done in the face of life's mysteries and difficulties.[15] (*1*, pp. 37–38.)

Changes in religious values in old age are of special interest, since it would be expected that at this age conflicting pressures and needs would be at a minimum, and there would exist an increasing awareness of the limited time available, a circumstance which presumably would raise in more vital fashion than earlier questions regarding the meaning of this life and the possibility of a next life. Information regarding religious attitudes and activities for an age group from 60 to over 100 years of age is presented in Table 74. If one disregards the last column of the table, where the number of cases is extremely small, it is to be noted that although church attendance shows no increase (it would be surprising if it did increase in view of increasing frailty at these ages), there is a clear increase beyond 60 in the more sedentary observances of Bible-reading and listening to religious programs on the radio. There was also evidence of an increasingly favorable attitude toward religion.

The age trend from 60 onward in certainty of belief in an afterlife is especially interesting. In the early sixties, 71 percent of the men and 83 percent of the women expressed this belief. But of the 28 cases of people who were 90 years of age or over (10 men, 18 women), there was not a single person who failed to indicate certainty of belief.[16] Can it be that at these advanced ages, when time has all but run out, there is need to view oneself as continuing on in a further life? Does the view that death marks the end, the absolute

---

[15] It is pertinent here to note that an early study suggested that "to encourage family attendance" grew rapidly in prominence as a reason for going to church during the age range 25 to 50 (*58*).

[16] The difference between the 60 to 64 group and the 90 plus group in this respect is highly reliable statistically when the sexes are combined.

TABLE 74. Changes in Religious Attitudes and Activities in Later Maturity

Religious Attitude Indicated	Age Period and Percentage with Given Religious Attitude						
	60–64	65–69	70–74	75–79	80–84	85–89	90 and Over
Males							
Favorable attitudes toward religion[a]	38	41	42	39	53	55	40
Certain of an afterlife	71	64	69	67	72	81	100
Attend services at least once a week	45	41	46	45	50	45	20
Listen to church services regularly on radio	16	21	19	26	33	37	30
Read Bible at least once a week	25	29	33	41	48	45	30
Total cases	74	92	118	121	63	21	10
Females							
Favorable attitudes toward religion[a]	51	56	57	64	69	81	94
Certain of an afterlife	83	78	86	77	91	90	100
Attend services at least once a week	60	53	52	53	56	33	45
Listen to services regularly on radio	22	27	37	30	46	59	78
Read Bible at least once a week	50	60	64	62	61	76	62
Total cases	152	163	185	135	72	34	18

[a] A score of 6 or 7 on an attitude scale, obtainable only by checking most favorable statements.

SOURCE: From Ruth Cavan, et al., Personal Adjustment in Old Age, Chicago, Science Research Associates, 1949.

end, of the person become inadmissible at advanced ages? Perhaps here, in the special circumstances of extreme old age, the basic human need for continued expansion of self finds expression in religion and in the idea of a hereafter. A very early study of religious beliefs (but one which did not extend into extreme old age) has suggested that the question of immortality is one that thrusts itself forward increasingly with increased age during the adult years and has to be resolved (90). And another study, previously mentioned, suggested that for the age group 50 and over, going to church more often involved reassurance of immortality than it did during the younger adult years (58). These studies suggest that belief in or concern about immortality increases during the adult years and is not confined to the most advanced years, though in these last years the urgency may be greater and the belief more universal. Here is a fascinating problem for more definitive research.

FACTORS RELATED TO RELIGIOUS BELIEFS AND VALUES

The preceding discussion has emphasized developmental age trends in religious values almost exclusively. What types of variations are encountered when factors other than age are studied? In the first place, it is obvious that differences in values, in strength of belief, in age trends, will exist among various religious groups. Catholics show more implicit beliefs in various religious concepts than do non-Catholics (26), have fewer religious problems and doubts (61), and defect less frequently from childhood teaching (3). Presumably, differences of varying degree would be found among other groups of like ages, and differences in age trends would be apparent—but such quantitative studies of comparative religion have not yet been made. Religious beliefs also differ with section of the country and with degree of urbanization. For example, in one opinion poll[17] only 63 percent of a West Coast sample replied in the affirmative to the question, "Do you personally believe in God?" whereas 91 percent of a southern population responded the same way. Eighty-five percent of the farmers interviewed, but only 69 percent of those in urban areas of 100,000 population and over, said "yes." Liberality of religious views has been shown to vary with economic and educational status (31). And beliefs change with the passage of time; e. g., college students in 1949 had beliefs somewhat different (though not greatly different) from those held by college students in 1930 (26).

Apparent in data already presented (see Tables 73 and 74) is another important difference—that between males and females. In practically all studies, girls and women appear to be more religious in personal values and more steadfast in external religious observance than are males. Even in extreme old age (Table 74) important sex differences are evident. It has been suggested (30) that the greater religiosity of women is more compatible with their roles in the family and as culture-bearers in the American society, whereas the secular roles of the male (occupational, recreational, political) are more likely to be in conflict with his religious role. It is noteworthy that various studies (9, 51) have shown mothers to have greater influence on the religious views and values of the offspring than have fathers.

[17] Data collected by the American Institute of Public Opinion in December, 1944, and reported in "The Quarters Polls," *Public Opinion Quarterly*, 1944, 8:579.

Early studies of religious conversion as well as modern clinical evidence has suggested that fervent adoption of religious values, or violent rejection, may often be explained in terms of the dynamics of the adjustment process, i. e., represent a reaction to the frustrations and conflicts the individual is experiencing. Are there any general relationships between personality, adjustment, and other personal characteristics, on one hand, and religious beliefs and values on the other?

One study of those who were at the extremes with respect to the acceptance or the rejection of religious authority showed those who rejected religious authority to be more intelligent and to do better in school, while those who accepted religious authority to an extreme degree were more suggestible (51). A negative relationship between intelligence and the acceptance of religious dogma was also found in a study of Jewish children mentioned earlier (31). Neither investigation revealed any evidence for a relationship between emotional stability and the acceptance of religious authority or belief. Although several studies (94, 111, 114) have suggested that religious liberals are more "emotionally mature" than religious conservatives, a more recent study using projective tests yielded little evidence of differences; the religious conservatives appeared to have slightly stronger dependence needs (25). And a study of the relationship between religiosity and humanitarianism yielded a correlation of −.24 for a sample of 215 cases, a finding that was interpreted as not supporting the common assumption of religion as the source of humanitarianism (59). In commenting upon certain studies, one writer notes that recent investigations "have uncovered the fact that among people with strong religious sentiments race prejudice is often marked. Closer analysis indicates that the religious sentiment in these cases is blindly institutional, exclusionist, and related to self-centered values. Among people with reflective and highly differentiated sentiments race prejudice is rarely found" (1, p. 59).

Studies of personality characteristics and religious values—of which the foregoing are reasonably representative—have thus not as yet established marked relationships between the two. But this may well be because more penetrating analyses were not made. Few studies have attempted to assess the meaning of religion *for the individual* when attempting to determine the relationship between personality and religion. As Maslow has recently pointed out: "a person who goes to church regularly may actually be rated as *less* religious than one who does not go to church at all, because (1) he goes to avoid social isolation, or (2) he goes to please his mother, or (3) religion represents for him not humbleness but a weapon of domination over others, or (4) it marks him as a member of a superior group, or (5) as in Clarence Day's father, 'It is good for the ignorant masses and I must play along,' or . . . and so on.

He may in a dynamic sense be not at all religious and still behave as though he were" (72, p. 25).

CONCERN WITH GENERAL PHILOSOPHY OF LIFE

Concern with the development of a general frame of reference in which to view one's self and one's world need not be couched in religious terms. Indeed, one's religious life may be highly institutionalized and compartmentalized and play little part in determining the broad general meanings a person seeks in his world or the ethical concepts and moral guideposts which he establishes. Such problems, as earlier suggested, may be worked out in more general philosophical or scientific terms or—as is more likely the case for the average person—in a quite vague and unverbalized fashion. Because of the paucity of research on this general question, the present discussion can do little more than suggest the ages when such matters seem most important and something of the direction changes in general values seem to take.

The establishment of a "philosophy of life" is often considered to be one of the major developmental tasks of adolescence. An occasional personal document has been published (64) which serves to illustrate the seeking process of adolescence but which does not establish the generality of this need. Some evidence of a more quantitative sort suggests that the younger people are indeed active in the groups who get sufficiently fired by an ideology to take definite and sometimes violent action to attain their ends. Thus, as the left-hand chart of Figure 99 shows, the peak age of joining the revolutionary party and of first revolutionary activity of a group of about 150 Russian Communist party members was between 16 and 20. New religious movements are more frequently launched by young men; long-established religious groups are headed by old men (65). Though such data relate to special groups, it may well be that these efforts represent efforts to establish a role when society has failed to provide one.

A rather interesting set of facts bearing on interest in philosophy of life is presented in the right-hand chart of Figure 99. There it is shown that interest in philosophy of life, although present to an average degree in adolescence compared to other life areas, actually increases from 15 to 50. The subjects studied were a special group—graduate students in education—and care must be taken in generalizing to a broader population. But the results are nonetheless interesting and suggestive.

The present writers would speculate that increased interest in the meaning or philosophy of life will occur at those ages or points in life where major changes in roles are occurring or when major reorientations in life goals are necessary because of successful achievement of earlier goals, because failure to achieve has forced abandonment of those goals, or because achievement has been seriously threatened. The mother whose life has been dominated by the rearing of children may well wonder "how things add up" once they have left home. The unmarried woman

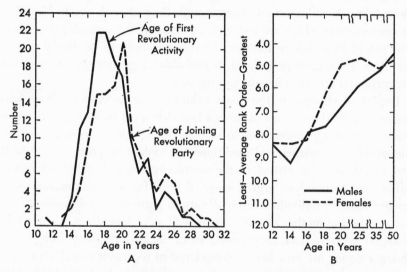

Figure 99. Age Trends in Importance of Ideology and Philosophy of Life. Chart A Suggests Ages at Which Ideologies Are Effective in Producing Action, as Reflected in Ages of Joining Revolutionary Activity; Chart B Shows Age Trend in Interest in Philosophy of Life. (Chart A after J. Davis, A study of one hundred and sixty-three outstanding communist leaders, Amer. Sociol. Soc., Papers and Proceedings, 1929, 24:42–53; Chart B from F. K. Shuttleworth, The adolescent period: a graphic and pictorial atlas, Monogr. of the Society for Research in Child Development, 1938, Vol. 3, No. 3.)

of 35 may be unhappy and see little meaning in life until she reorients her goals, perhaps toward occupational achievement. The hard-driving business or professional man who has achieved success in his late thirties —or is convinced by then that he will not achieve his goals—may find himself pondering the meaning of his efforts and his life. And so, also, may the man who has just been retired. The death of a loved one—or one's own threatened death due to illness or old age—may cause specu-lation and a need "to think things through." Although the timing of such events will vary from one individual to another, it is likely that the major frustrations, successes, and role changes that result in a need for a revised frame of reference occur most frequently at adolescence, in the forties, and in old age.

Age Trends in Conservatism: Cause and Possible Remedy

From the considerations thus far of developmental changes in moral, sociopolitical, and religious values, can any generalization be arrived at regarding the intensity or the rigidity with which people hold to their views? Are there important changes with time or with age in liberalism or conservatism which are reflected in many of the attitudes described? The extent to which an individual tends *generally* to be liberal or conservative, tolerant or prejudiced, is probably of greater significance than his particular attitudes toward specific issues.

Important changes in the many values of the American culture have occurred with the passage of time, a fact that must be recognized in any assessment of age differences in values. Realignments among countries, the gradual ascendance and sometimes the violent eruption of new political issues, and the arrival of the atomic age have highlighted certain values and fostered an urgent sense of need for internationalism and a greater sense of individual responsibility to participate politically. Necessity can be the mother of attitudes as well as of inventions. Values have changed with respect to personal moral behavior; many things once thought wrong are now hardly considered to represent moral issues. For example, a long-term follow-up of an early study in 1923, 1933, 1943, and 1953 has shown a marked reduction in the total number of "things thought wrong" in a list of some 125 items presented to public school and college students (80). A general change in the climate of opinion with time will tend to carry all or most subgroups of the population along with it and so produce changes which appear to be due to age. A population of college graduates studied in 1950, 14 years after college, were shown to be more liberal in their views than when in college in 1936. But 1950 college students differed from 1936 students in the same direction and to about the same degree. Thus, social change, not age, appeared to produce the increase in liberality (74).

What now of changes with age? Findings regarding changes through the growth years, summarized in almost every textbook on childhood and adolescence, are well known. In general, over these years opinion becomes more liberal as rigid precepts learned by rote are modified by reality or as youngsters "escape" from the moral code of the past generation into the present. Analogous studies of the adult and older years are both fewer and less known. Popular opinion asserts that older people are more generally conservative. Research somewhat supports popular opinion but emphasizes that many factors are involved and that the differences between young and old are not so great as often supposed and in certain groups are practically nonexistent.

Certain further evidence may be briefly mentioned to show the variety of information available as well as the degree to which it is consistent. The 1923–1953 follow-up cited above included in the 1953 testing a sampling of adults, from young to over 60, and showed that number of "things thought wrong" declined during high school and college and increased as adults grew older. As already noted, the innovators of new religious movements were very young men, whereas the leaders of established religious groups (presumably more interested in maintaining the status quo) were older men (65). There is evidence that older individuals tend to hold their attitudes with greater intensity than do younger ones (16, 95), do not change their attitudes so readily with the passage of time (67), even when specific efforts are made to influence them (71), and express preference for sameness and aversion to change (7, 91).

Though studies are quite consistent in showing increased conservatism with increased age, the differences between means of age groups are frequently so slight and individual differences so great that these age trends may have little practical significance. This point has already been made with respect to political attitudes. Older educators, according to one study (38), were only slightly less liberal than younger educators, and negligible correlations between age and sociopolitical attitudes have been reported for teachers (92) and for a group of parents of a somewhat restricted age range (68).

To what can the increased conservatism (and other attitude changes) of the older adult be attributed? As already mentioned, older individuals, reared when values were less liberal than today, may simply be carrying those values into their middle and later years. Although cultural change is most certainly a factor, recent data (99) have been interpreted as showing that it is not an entirely adequate explanation of adult age differences in attitudes. A second possible cause, but one also involving cultural change, is the reduced learning effectiveness of older adults. As noted in an earlier chapter, they have special difficulty in learning material in conflict with established habits and thus presumably would have difficulty in learning new values and points of view. One investigator (85) has accordingly attributed the conservatism of old age to loss of "neural plasticity," a factor he thought responsible for their lowered learning efficiency. The fact that older people do learn more slowly—whether this be attributed to loss of neural plasticity, to strength of established habits which are more difficult to alter, or to some other cause—might be expected *in changing times* to result in their having viewpoints that lag behind those of younger individuals who learn more readily and thus can adopt new viewpoints more easily.

But it is also probable that social change touches older adults less intimately. They have a more restricted social life, read less, attend fewer movies and, possibly (though this has not been demonstrated), choose their friends, books, and movies to conform to their own bias more than do younger people. This restriction of the "social matrix" may in itself be a result of reduced ease of learning, but this restriction would also tend to reduce further the probability of achieving up-to-date values and viewpoints since older adults would thus have less to stimulate them to change.

Further, changes in role with increased age may result in changes in attitudes. In carefree youth, what have been described as *private* attitudes may prevail but, upon assumption of family responsibilities, the more conventional, public attitudes may dominate behavior and expressed attitudes. Earlier in this chapter, it was pointed out that occupational status was related to conservatism and radicalism. An investigator of this matter has observed that there can be "little doubt that peoples' politico-economic orientations are closely associated with their statuses and roles in the economic order. Persons who stand at the top and dominate that order are clearly its staunchest supporters" (*19*). Thus, one might expect that increases in conservatism might accompany the increased economic status and security that often accompany increased age. The struggling youth finds little to defend in the status quo and has little reason to be conservative. But once fortune smiles on him, his status *and* his attitudes may change. The *present* scheme of things, he *now* thinks, offers endless opportunity!

Still another factor that might result in increased conservatism involves the biological and social losses that accompany age. One writer (*6*) points out that with organic losses, and status losses which occur with age, the individual is apt to react with hostility and irritability and to cling to habitual patterns of behavior and tested ego defenses against anxiety. "We may look upon the usual conservatism and rigid traditionalism of aging people as manifestations of this psychic rigidity and as expressions of the need to cling to a world in which the individual has achieved his maximum instinctual gratification and his nearest approach to a mastery of his environment" (6). In short, a person may cling to the old habits of thinking because with them he feels more comfortable, finding the new and uncertain threatening. If people become less secure with increasing age, as was shown likely to be the case in an earlier chapter, then it might be expected that they would cling with even greater tenacity to the securities of the past. Further, insecurity may lead to defensive reactions in which people, unable to tolerate ambiguity, structure their world rigidly and see things in sharp blacks and whites, ignoring the in-between. It is recalled here that older people made these kinds of responses more frequently than did younger adults in evaluating moral behavior.

There are, then, a variety of sound reasons why people might be expected to become actually more conservative as age increases. Obviously, these "explanations" will not apply equally well to all groups or all individuals. Some successful people may become conservative not because of status losses but because of complacency and a tendency to favor those conditions that brought about their success. Or, their success may enable them to view situations with personal detachment and with a tolerance or understanding brought about by broader experience. Moreover, dogmatism might conceivably be the product of greater conviction brought about by broader experience and longer time for thinking matters through.

If the analysis presented in the foregoing pages is correct, then certain suggestions for combating undesirable conservatism would seem to follow. Can one continue "expansion" of life in ways that extend beyond family and job so that continued success and stimulation are experienced? Can programs of broad reading, active participation in discussion groups, and getting about break the commonly encountered trend with age toward a comfortable, stable, but unchallenging point of view? An active and continuing "taking hold of life" instead of a passive settling back should go far in promoting flexibility of habits, an up-to-date point of view, and avoidance of rigidity.

A second suggestion is that steps should be taken which will reduce the social threat to aging. A reassessment of industry's attitudes toward older workers, resulting in more favorable views based on the facts of aging rather than on current, popular, unfavorable stereotypes, may reduce the threat of aging and give the individual greater psychological security. Biases against employment of new workers after 40 and the convention of a fixed retirement age represent present threats. If educational agencies could dispel or reduce the incorrect stereotypes of aging and produce a new social climate which gives people of all ages a sense of importance and worth, then it might be expected that many of the age differences in attitudes detailed in this chapter would be reduced. Recent emphasis in psychological research upon attitudes as a reflection of the dynamics of personality and the security or insecurity of the individual argue for the essential soundness of such interpretations.

Summary

The essential feature of human ideology as described in the present chapter is its dynamic quality. The developmental picture of attitudes reveals their sensitivity to the inevitable reality testing that comes as experience broadens and intellectual capacity to gauge that experience deepens; to the pressure of conflicting needs and values (honesty vs. loyalty, religious values vs. occupational demands); to the pressure of social groups of which one is a member or to which one aspires; to the changes in security, roles, and status that accompany increasing age; to cultural change; to changes in physiological pressures and satisfactions (such as sex); to the needs of the person to gain status, to assert his individuality, or to protect himself against threats. Though attitudes and values are thus highly personal, certain typical developmental changes occur during the course of life.

1. The fundamental values of the American culture appear to be inculcated in children at a very early age. By 10 or 12 years of age youngsters have an essentially adult grasp of what, in the broad sense, is "right" and what is "wrong." In contrast to early and steady gains in moral knowledge, there is little change in moral behavior; no particular age can be designated as the "age of discretion." Typically, there is inconsistency in moral behavior in the case of a particular person, and when individuals are compared they vary from one extreme to the other, with most being in the central range, e. g., sometimes honest, sometimes not.

2. There are, nonetheless, certain changes and reorientations during childhood and adolescence. Views seemingly learned by rote in childhood are modified with increasing experience, particularly as a result of contact with values held by other groups and brought to bear on the young person through peer group relations and as the child, in a sense, "escapes" from the views held by the older generation. In general, moral values become more realistic and liberal as youngsters mature.

3. Changes in values during the adult years are slower than in the

years before. Older adults appear more "old fashioned" and conventional, perhaps because cultural change has passed them by, perhaps because as parents they have assumed roles as representatives of the culture with responsibility for teaching the young, perhaps because the basic values of society seem essentially sound, after all, now that they have become established and find regular outlets and satisfaction for needs which had been chronically frustrated in adolescence. Older adults appear to make value judgments more clearly and in absolute terms, as "right" or "wrong," whereas younger adults see more reason to excuse certain acts and show greater tendency to evaluate behavior in terms of whether it is aesthetic or intelligent.

4. With respect to adjustment to organized society, clear age trends are apparent. During childhood and youth there appears to be increasing sensitivity to individual rights but a decreasing sense of personal responsibility for civic or social action. In addition, young people leaving school appear ill prepared in terms of social knowledge and understanding for mature citizenship. Adults, too, are often apathetic and poorly informed. Political and civic responsibility and participation increase steadily until about 50 years of age, after which civic activities requiring active participation and energy expenditure decline. Voting and political interest, as in reading and discussion, remain at the highest level reached until quite old age.

5. Antisocial behavior serious enough to be classed as delinquency or crime becomes strongly evident during the teens and reaches a peak in the early twenties. Such behavior flourishes in blighted areas and is a product of frustration and conflict in the setting of poor family backgrounds and relationships and in situations where criminal examples are plentiful. Beyond the twenties, crime rates decline steadily and rapidly, though at different rates for different crimes. There is no evidence, when actual rates are examined, for the often asserted moral degeneration in old age.

6. Religious understandings and values change during childhood and adolescence from the concrete concepts and literal views of early childhood to more abstract concepts and more liberal and tolerant views of religious belief and practice. There are, however, in adolescence certain issues that seem increasingly perplexing; young people appear to have pressing needs and problems in the area of religion; but they seem to find conventional church services increasingly unsatisfactory. After a low point of religious observance is reached in young adulthood, there appears

to be a steady increase in interest in religion reflected in increasing religious observance. Such interest seems to be highest in extreme old age, perhaps because religion holds greatest hope for those nearing the end of life and with limited resources for other types of gratifications.

7. There appears to be a steady increase in conservatism during the adult years. It is suggested that such changes, involving restriction of the social world, avoidance of change and new experience, and clinging to the past, are likely self-limiting and handicapping to most effective use of capacities and opportunities. If individuals would maintain active participation in living, expose themselves to varied stimulation and challenges, and if some of the biases in society with respect to aging could be reduced so that aging would be less threatening, it is suggested that some of the negative features of value changes during the adult years might be avoided.

BIBLIOGRAPHY

1. Allport, G. W., *The Individual and His Religion,* New York, Macmillan, 1950.
2. Allport, G. W., *Personality,* New York, Henry Holt, 1937.
3. Allport, G. W., Gillespie, J. M., and Young, J., The religion of the post-war college student, *J. Psychol.,* 1948, 25:3–33.
4. Anderson, A., and Dvorak, B., Differences between college students and their elders in standards of conduct, *J. Abnorm. and Soc. Psychol.,* 1928, 23:286–292.
5. Anderson, Leila, The attitude of rural young people toward the church, *Religious Educ.,* 1942, 37:34–40.
6. Atkin, S., "Discussion" of the paper by Kaufman, M. R., Old age and aging: the psychoanalytic point of view, *Amer. J. Orthopsychiat.,* 1940, 10:79–83.
7. Bean, C. H., The psychology of adherence to the old and of acceptance of the new, *J. Soc. Psychol.,* 1933, 4:340–352.
8. Bean, R. A., Young men—old church, *Religious Educ.,* 1938, 33:9–13.
9. Bell, H. M., *Youth Tell Their Story,* Washington, D.C., American Council on Education, 1938.
10. Beller, E. K., Two attitude components in younger boys, *J. Soc. Psychol.,* 1949, 29:137–151.
11. Bose, R. G., Religious concepts of children, *Religious Educ.,* 1929, 24: 831–837.
12. Bovet, P., Le sentiment religieux et la psychologie de l'enfant, Neuchatel and Paris, Delachauz and Niestle, 1925.
13. Brill, Jeanette G., and Payne, E. G., *The Adolescent Court and Crime Conviction,* New York, Pitman, 1938.

14. Campbell, A., and Kahn, R. L., *The People Elect a President*, Ann Arbor, Survey Research Center, University of Michigan, 1952.

15. Cantril, H., The intensity of an attitude, *J. Abnorm. and Soc. Psychol.*, 1946, *41*:129–135.

16. Cantril, H. (ed.), *Public Opinion, 1935–1946*, Princeton, Princeton University Press, 1951.

17. Cason, H., Common annoyances: a psychological study of everyday aversions and annoyances, *Psychol. Monogr.*, 1930, Vol. 40, No. 2.

18. Cavan, Ruth, *et al.*, *Personal Adjustment in Old Age*, Chicago, Science Research Associates, 1949.

19. Centers, R., *The Psychology of Social Classes*, Princeton, Princeton University Press, 1949.

20. Childers, A. T., Hyper-activity in children having behavior disorders, *Amer. J. Orthopsychiat.*, 1935, 5:227–243.

21. Clark, E. T., *The Psychology of Religious Awakening*, New York, Macmillan, 1929.

22. Collings, E., *An Experiment with a Project Curriculum*, New York, Macmillan, 1929.

23. Davis, J., A study of one hundred and sixty-three outstanding communist leaders, *Amer. Sociol. Soc., Papers and Proceedings*, 1929, 24:42–55.

24. Drake, C. A., Why students cheat, *J. Higher Educ.*, 1941, *12*:418–20.

25. Dreger, R. M., Some personality correlates of religious attitudes as determined by projective techniques, *Psychol. Monogr.*, 1952, Vol. 66, No. 3.

26. Dudycha, G. J., Religious beliefs of college freshmen in 1930 and 1949, *Religious Educ.*, 1950, 45:165–169.

27. Eberhart, J. C., Attitudes toward property: a genetic study by the paired-comparison rating of offenses, *J. Genet. Psychol.*, 1942, 60:3–35.

28. Eckert, Ruth E., and Marshall, T. O., *When Youth Leaves School*, New York, McGraw-Hill, 1938.

29. Fenton, N., *The Delinquent Boy and the Correctional School*, Claremont (California), Claremont College, 1935.

30. Fichter, J. H., The profile of Catholic religious life, *Amer. J. Sociol.*, 1952, 58:145–150.

31. Franzblau, A. N., *Religious Belief and Character Among Jewish Adolescents*, New York, Teachers College, Columbia University, 1934.

32. Glueck, S., and Eleanor, *Five Hundred Criminal Careers*, New York, Knopf, 1933.

33. Glueck, S., and Eleanor, *Later Criminal Careers*, New York, Commonwealth Fund, 1937.

34. Glueck, S., and Eleanor, *Unraveling Juvenile Delinquency*, New York, Commonwealth Fund, 1950.

35. Gross, M. M., The effect of certain types of motivation on the "honesty" of children, *J. Educ. Res.*, 1946, *40*:133–140.

36. Hanlon, T. E., Hofstatter, P. R., and O'Connor, J. P., Congruence of self

and ideal self in relation to personality adjustment, *J. Consult. Psychol.*, 1954, *18*:215–218.

37. Harms, E., The development of religious experience in children, *Amer. J. Sociol.*, 1944, *50*:112–122.

38. Harper, M. H., *Social Beliefs and Attitudes of American Educators*, New York, Teachers College, Columbia University, 1927.

39. Hartshorne, H., and May, M. A., *Studies in the Nature of Character, I. Studies in Deceit*, New York, Macmillan, 1928.

40. Hartshorne, H., May, M. A., and Maller, J. B., *Studies in the Nature of Character, II. Studies in Service and Self-Control*, New York, Macmillan, 1929.

41. Hartshorne, H., May, M. A., and Shuttleworth, F. K., *Studies in the Nature of Character, III. Studies in the Organization of Character*, New York, Macmillan, 1930.

42. Havighurst, R. J., Robinson, Myra, and Dorr, Mildred, The development of the ideal self in childhood and adolescence, *J. Educ. Res.*, 1946, *40*:241–257.

43. Havighurst, R. J., and Taba, H., *Adolescent Character and Personality*, New York, Wiley, 1949.

44. Healy, W., and Bronner, A. F., *New Light on Delinquency and Its Treatment*, New Haven, Yale University Press, 1936.

45. Helfant, K., Parents' attitudes vs. adolescent hostility in the determination of adolescent sociopolitical attitudes, *Psychol. Monogr.*, 1952, Vol. 66, No. 13.

46. Hentig, Hans von, *Crime: Causes and Conditions*, New York, McGraw-Hill, 1947.

47. Hightower, P. R., Biblical information in relation to character and conduct, *Studies in Character*, Iowa City, State University of Iowa, 1930, Vol. 3, No. 2.

48. Hillery, M. P., *The Religious Life of Adolescent Girls*, Washington, D.C., Catholic University of America, 1937.

49. Hinshaw, R. P., The relationship of information and opinion to age, Unpublished Ph.D. dissertation, Princeton University, 1944.

50. Horton, P. B., Student interest in the church, *Religious Educ.*, 1940, *35*:215–219.

51. Howells, T. H., A comparative study of those who accept as against those who reject religious authority, *Studies in Character*, Iowa City, State University of Iowa, 1928, Vol. 2, No. 2.

52. Johnson, W., The semantics of maladjustment, in Pennington, L. A., and Berg, I. A. (eds.), *An Introduction to Clinical Psychology* (1st edition), New York, Ronald Press, 1948, Chap. 20, pp. 298–516.

53. Jones, V., *Character and Citizenship Training in the Public School*, Chicago, University of Chicago Press, 1936.

54. Jones, V., Character development in children—an objective approach, in Carmichael, L. (ed.), *Manual of Child Psychology* (2nd edition), New York, Wiley, 1954, Chap. 13, pp. 781–832.

55. Jones, V., Disagreement among teachers as to right and wrong, *Teachers College Record*, 1929, *31*:24–36.

56. Jones, V., Ideas on right and wrong among teachers and children, *Teachers College Record*, 1929, *30*:529–541.

57. Katz, D., and Allport, F. H., *Students' Attitudes*, Syracuse, Craftsman Press, 1931.

58. Kingsbury, F. A., Why do people go to church? *Religious Educ.*, 1937, *32*:50–54.

59. Kirkpatrick, C., Religion and humantarianism: a study of institutional implications, *Psychol. Monogr.*, 1949, Vol. 63, No. 9.

60. Kuhlen, R. G., Expansion and constriction of activities during the adult years as reflected in organizational, civic, and political participation, Paper read at Second International Gerontological Congress, St. Louis, 1951.

61. Kuhlen, R. G., and Arnold, Martha, Age differences in religious beliefs and problems during adolescence, *J. Genet. Psychol.*, 1944, *65*:291–300.

62. Lander, B., *Towards an Understanding of Juvenile Delinquency: A Study of 8,464 Cases of Juvenile Delinquency in Baltimore*, New York, Columbia University Press, 1954.

63. Landis, P. H., Points of stress in adolescent morality, *School and Society*, 1940, *51*:612–616.

64. *Larry, Thoughts of Youth*, New York, Association Press, 1936.

65. Lehman, H. C., *Age and Achievement*, Princeton, Princeton University Press, 1953.

66. Lerner, E., *Constraint Areas and the Moral Judgment of Children*, Menasha (Wisconsin), Banta, 1937.

67. Lorge, I., The Thurstone Attitude scales: II. The reliability and consistency of younger and older intellectual peers, *J. Soc. Psychol.*, 1939, *10*:199–208.

68. Lorge, I., and Helfant, K., The independence of chronological age and sociopolitical attitudes, *J. Abnorm. and Soc. Psychol.*, 1953, *48*:598.

69. Maccoby, Eleanor E., Matthews, R. E., and Morton, A. S., Youth and political change, *Public Opinion Quart.*, 1954, *18*:23–39.

70. MacRae, D., Jr., A test of Piaget's theories of moral development, *J. Abnorm. and Soc. Psychol.*, 1954, *49*:14–18.

71. Marple, C. H., The comparative susceptibility of three age levels to the suggestion of group versus expert opinion, *J. Soc. Psychol.*, 1933, *4*:176–186.

72. Maslow, A. H., *Motivation and Personality*, New York, Harper, 1954.

73. McQuilkin, J. R., Born of the spirit, *Christian Life*, 1954, *15*:26–27.

74. Nelson, E. N. P., Persistence of attitudes of college students fourteen years later, *Psychol. Monogr.*, 1954, Vol. 68, No. 2.

75. Newcomb, T. M., and Svehla, G., Intra-family relationships in attitudes, *Sociometry*, 1937, *1*:180–205.

76. Piaget, J., *The Moral Judgment of the Child*, Glencoe (Illinois), Free Press, 1948.

77. Pollak, O., Conservatism in later maturity and old age, *Amer. Sociol. Rev.*, 1943, 8:175–179.
78. Pollak, O., *The Criminality of Women*, Philadelphia, University of Pennsylvania Press, 1950.
79. Porterfield, A. L., Delinquency and its outcome in court and college, *Amer. J. Sociol.*, 1943, 49:199–208.
80. Pressey, S. L., and Jones, A. W., 1923–1953 and 20 to 60 age changes in moral codes, anxieties, and interests, as shown by the "X-O Tests," *J. Psychol.*, 1955, 39:485–502.
81. Ramsey, G. V., and Varley, Mary, Censorship and the Kinsey Report, *J. Soc. Psychol.*, 1951, 33:279–288.
82. Reiss, A. J., Jr., Delinquency as the failure of personal and social controls, *Amer. Sociol. Rev.*, 1951, 16:196–208.
83. Reiss, A. J., Jr., Social correlates of psychological types of delinquency, *Amer. Sociol. Rev.*, 1952, 17:710–718.
84. Rosander, A. C., Age and sex patterns of social attitudes, *J. Educ. Psychol.*, 1939, 30:481–496.
85. Ruch, F. L., The differential decline of learning ability in the aged as a possible explanation of their conservatism, *J. Soc. Psychol.*, 1934, 5:329–337.
86. Shaw, C. R., and McKay, H. D., *Juvenile Delinquency and Urban Areas*, Chicago, University of Chicago Press, 1942.
87. Simpson, R. M., Attitudes of teachers and prisoners toward seriousness of criminal acts, *J. Criminal Law and Criminology*, 1934, 25:76–83.
88. Skaggs, E. B., Sex differences in moral attitudes, *J. Soc. Psychol.*, 1940, 11:3–10.
89. Spaulding, F. T., *High School and Life*, New York, McGraw-Hill, 1938.
90. Starbuck, E. D., *The Psychology of Religion*, New York, Scribner's, 1900.
91. Strong, E. K., Jr., *Change of Interests with Age*, Stanford, Stanford University Press, 1931.
92. Sullivan, J. C., *A Study of the Social Attitudes and Information on Public Problems of Women Teachers in Secondary Schools*, New York, Teachers College, Columbia University, 1940.
93. Sutherland, E. H., *Principles of Criminology*, New York, Lippincott, 1947.
94. Symington, T. A., *Religious Liberals and Conservatives*, New York, Teachers College, Columbia University, 1935.
95. Taylor, C., Age differences in rigidity as revealed in attitude scale responses, Unpublished Ph.D. thesis, Syracuse University, 1955.
96. Terman, L. M., Kinsey's "Sexual Behavior in the Human Male": some comments and criticisms, *Psychol. Bull.*, 1948, 45:443–459.
97. Terman, L. M., *et al.*, *Genetic Studies of Genius*. Vol. I. *Mental and Physical Traits of a Thousand Gifted Children*, Stanford, Stanford University Press, 1925.
98. Thompson, G. G., Age trends in social values during the adolescent years, *Amer. Psychol.*, 1949, 4:250.

99. Toch, H., Attitudes of the "fifty plus" age group: preliminary considerations toward a longitudinal survey, *Public Opinion Quart.*, 1953, *17*: 391–394.

100. Tudor-Hart, B. E., Are there cases in which lies are necessary? *J. Genet. Psychol.*, 1926, 33:586–641.

101. Turner, R. H., Moral judgment: a study in roles, *Amer. Sociol. Rev.*, 1952, *17*:70–77.

102. U.S. Bureau of the Census, *Prisoners in State and Federal Prisons and Reformatories, 1946,* Washington, D.C., U.S. Government Printing Office, 1948.

103. U.S. Children's Bureau, Federal Security Agency, *Juvenile-Court Statistics, 1944 and 1945,* Supplement to Volume II of *The Child,* Washington, D.C., U.S. Government Printing Office, 1946.

104. U.S. Department of Labor, Children's Bureau, "Children in the Courts," *Juvenile-Court Statistics,* two-year period ended December 31, 1939, Publication No. 280, Washington, D.C., U.S. Government Printing Office, 1942.

105. U.S. Federal Bureau of Investigation, *Uniform Crime Reports for the United States and Its Possessions,* Washington, D.C., U.S. Government Printing Office, 1951, Vol. 22, No. 2.

106. Weber, C. O., Moral judgments of female delinquents, *J. Appl. Psychol.*, 1926, *10*:89–91.

107. Welford, A. T., An attempt at an experimental approach to the psychology of religion, *Brit. J. Psychol.*, 1946, *36*:55–73.

108. Weltman, Naomi, and Remmers, H. H., Pupils', parents', and teachers' attitudes—similarities and differences, Purdue University, *Studies in Higher Education,* 1946, Vol. 56.

109. Wheeler, L. R., and Viola D., Differences in religious ideas and attitudes of children who go to church and those who never attend, *Religious Educ.*, 1945, *40*:149–161.

110. Whyte, W. F., A slum sex code, *Amer. J. Sociol.*, 1943, *49*:21–31.

111. Willoughby, R. R., Emotional maturity of some religious attitudes, *J. Soc. Psychol.*, 1930, *1*:532–536.

112. Wilson, H. E., *Education for Citizenship,* New York, McGraw-Hill, 1938.

113. Wood, A. E., and Waite, J. B., *Crime and Its Treatment,* New York, American Book Company, 1941.

114. Woodward, L. E., *Relations of Religious Training and Life Patterns to the Adult Religious Life,* New York, Teachers College, Columbia University, 1932.

CHAPTER 11 •

• Social Interaction: Developmental Trends in Interpersonal and Group Relations

THERE is little doubt that the status and degree of acceptance one has among his peers play a fundamental role in the quality of a person's adjustment. Ability to get along with people is a prime asset in job success and life effectiveness. In close, warm, secure relationships with other people, individually and in groups, are to be found many of the most satisfying experiences of life and the major sources of psychological security. Losses of such relationships and ties or rejection by others represent some of the most disturbing and shattering episodes people of any age encounter. In this chapter, changes in social relationships throughout the life span will be described. And, since attitudes toward people—those of different race, religion, ethnic background, or social class—constitute some of the more important aspects of personal value syndromes (phases of which were discussed in the preceding chapter), attention will be given to the patterns of development of social attitudes in childhood and adolescence, to changes in adult years, and to procedures that might be effective in combating the extensive prejudices that exist.

Interpersonal Relations in Childhood and Adolescence

The first task will be to trace social development during childhood and adolescence, to observe the nature of interpersonal relationships at various ages and the factors that seem related to good adjustment with peers. In these early formative years, patterns of social interaction are established which often seem to persist throughout life.

SOCIAL INTERACTION IN EARLY CHILDHOOD

Interaction with own age peers is negligible for some months after birth (in part, of course, because there is little opportunity), but during the preschool years marked changes in social relations have been observed under experimental conditions. When placed in a playpen with another within three months of the same age, and with play material, children 6 to 8 months of age proved to be more interested in their environment than in their partners, treating the latter quite impersonally. Between 9 and 13 months, interest focused upon the play material to the extent that such social interaction as there was frequently involved nega-

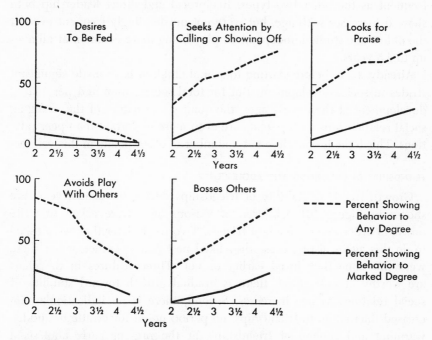

Figure 100. Growth Trends in Certain Aspects of Social Behavior. (Adapted from L. A. Hattwick and M. K. Sanders, Age differences in behavior at the nursery school level, *Child Development*, 1938, 9:27–47.)

tive "fighting" behavior. The other child seemed viewed as an obstacle; when play material was not present, interaction was positive and friendly. From about 13 months on to 25 months (the oldest age studied), friendliness and positive social relations were increasingly integrated with interest in play materials, the children having become "playmates" even though substantial negative reactions still existed (72).

Further social developmental trends, up to about four and a half years of age, are shown in Figure 100. Teachers' ratings on some 555 nursery school children were studied. Noted in the chart are increasing social independence in wanting to feed self (the curve for "desiring to be fed" drops); increased social interest, as shown in attention-getting behavior, praise-seeking, and the gradual disappearance of social avoidance behavior; and increased efforts at social dominance (bossing others). An earlier study (87, 88) had shown much the same trends for the same age period. "Parallel play" was the major social activity for 2-year-olds, but declined with age, being partially replaced by associative group play and coöperation. But even in the 4- to 4.5-year group, parallel play was as frequent as the other two types. Reciprocal and direct leadership both showed increases with age, but were not outstandingly frequent even at the oldest age studied, independent play being more common at all ages up to 4.5 years.

Already, then, before starting to school children have made significant strides in social development. But for total socialization and personality development at these early ages, the quality and nature of the changing social relationships with *parents* are even more important than peer relations. This topic is considered at a number of other points in this volume.

FRIENDSHIPS IN CHILDHOOD AND ADOLESCENCE

Growth trends in stability of friendships during the school years are shown in Figure 101. Children of various ages were asked to write down, in order, their three best friends. Two weeks later they were asked to do this again, listing those they liked best *now*, whether or not these were the same they listed earlier or not. Three features in the chart are worthy of note. First, there is gradual growth toward stability of social relations as age increases. Second, there is no indication of increased fluctuation in friendships, no period noted for erratic or sudden warming and cooling of friendships, at the pre- or early adolescent period as is often implied by writers who hold the view of adolescence as a period of storm and stress evidenced in part by extreme rapid vacillations in friendships. And, third, there is the suggestion that girls are more stable in their friendships than are boys.

Trends similar to but less marked than those in Figure 101 were also noted for rural children (48), and a later study, which extended the age range investigated downward, revealed that the trend for the entire 5- to 18-year age range was one of steady growth toward greater stability (47). Paralleling this trend of increased stability is an increasing tendency to turn to and depend on friends. At least when youngsters were queried as to what they would do if worried about something, increasing numbers checked "ask a friend about it" as they grew older, and decreasing numbers checked "talk to my mother and father about it" (111). Thus, the peer culture grows in importance in adolescence as a source of help and support—and also as a competitor to parental influence. Here is a source of conflict between home and friends but also an aid to emotional emancipation from parents.

What insights has research provided as to why children select particular friends? It is an elementary but basic fact that propinquity is a major factor in friendships. Children make friends with children who sit near them in school, live near them. College students choose their

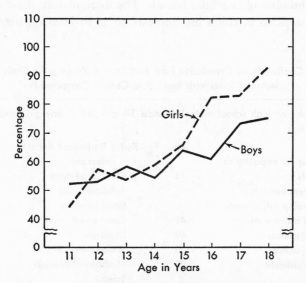

Figure 101. Increasing Stability of Social Relationships with Age as Shown by the Percentages of Boys and Girls Who Chose the Same Person as Their Best Friend (i.e., first of three choices) on Two Occasions Separated by a Two-Week Interval. (From G. G. Thompson and J. E. Horrocks, A study of the friendship fluctuations of urban boys and girls, *J. Genet. Psychol.*, 1947, 70:53–63.)

friends from the same residences (*120*), from the same floor when housed in large dormitories (*10*). Frequent and continuous opportunities to associate with others are essential to the development of friendships. In one study, lack of recent contact was the most frequent reason given by sixth-graders for not listing as a friend a person listed two weeks earlier (*3*). Parents who seriously restrict the social contacts of their children are in effect reducing opportunities for the development of close peer relations, in contrast to those who provide facilities for play and social experience in the home or who arrange for their children to have nursery school, camping, or other extra-home social experiences.

In addition to physical propinquity, based on geographic or sociological factors, similarity of interests and liking of the same activities (which are in part reflections of similarity in personality, intelligence, and other personal characteristics) result in particular people being thrown together in social groups and forming friendships. As shown in Table 75, friends tend to be like each other in various ways. Presumably, parents may help their children make friendships by helping them develop broad interests which will permit continuing social contact with a greater number of potential friends. The more mature person can himself take steps to broaden his interests so as to broaden his friendship potential.

TABLE 75. Coefficients of Correlation from Two Studies Showing the Similarity Between Mutual Friends with Respect to Certain Characteristics

I. Thirty pairs of high school mutual friends: 14 girl-girl, 7 boy-girl, and 9 boy-boy combinations

IQ	.46	Kuder Preference Record (Interests):	
Traits making for capacity to win friends	.74	Clerical interests	.54
Bell Adjustment Inventory (Personality Adjustment):		Artistic interests	.36
		Music interests	.28
Emotional adjustment	.49	Commercial interests	.24
Social adjustment	.49	Literature	.20
Home adjustment	.08	Social interests	.16
Health adjustment	.03	Mechanical interests	.13
		Science	.09
		Persuasive interests	.08

II. Thirty-eight pairs of mutual friends: early-teen-age boys

Socioeconomic status	.73	Behavior adjustment	.40
IQ	.55	Superiority	.15
Moral knowledge	.34	Self-criticism	.05
Number of play interests	.46	Criticism of others	.01

SOURCE: Data in I from M. E. Bonney, R. E. Hoblit, and A. H. Dreyer, a study of some factors related to sociometric status in a man's dormitory, Sociometry, 1953, 16:287–301. Data in II from H. S. Dimock, Rediscovering the Adolescent, New York, Association Press, 1937.

These factors (propinquity, similarity of interest) are the necessary but not the sufficient conditions for friendships. Friendships will develop between particular individuals to the extent that those individuals have psychological needs that are met in that friendship relation. A general social need may be hypothesized. But each individual personality is unique, as each friendship relation is unique in many respects. Dissimilar people may become friends, as, for example, a dominant and a submissive person. The friendship may satisfy the need of one to dominate and of the other to be dominated. But individual differences are such that another dominant person may need not a clinging vine but, instead, another dominant person. Whatever the nature of the need satisfaction relationship in individual friendships, each member must enjoy his own role in the friendship relationship, must see himself as a worth-while person (92).

This view that differences in needs will determine differences in friendships —even frequency of friendships—provides a tentative explanation of the differences between boys and girls in the frequency of friendships and attitudes they hold toward friendships. It was noted above that girls, at adolescence, have more stable friendships than boys. This same tendency is evident in other ways. Males spend less time with their best friends than do females (7). In a sociometric study of a college population, more mutual choices appeared among girls than among boys (30). In a study of attitudes of the two sexes toward friendships, girls showed many more feelings of emotional dependency (65). It is suggested that this frequently observed difference in dependency needs between the sexes is a reflection of the differential treatment from early babyhood on in the American culture.

CROSS-SEX CHOICES IN SOCIAL ATTRACTION

When youngsters are asked to name not their best friend (these are usually the same sex), but companions they would prefer for various activities, or people they would like to invite to a party, the opportunity exists to study heterosexual development. When responses to such questions are analyzed age for age, increasing cleavage between the sexes becomes evident up until roughly 12 years of age, following which the trend is reversed. The increasing cleavage during the elementary school years, based on the percentage of cross-sex choices made to the request to name choices for adjoining seats, is shown in the left-hand chart of Figure 102. The right-hand chart, from another study, shows the reversal of this trend during adolescence. In the latter instance, different questions were asked requesting choices of companions for various activities; thus the percentages for the two charts in the figure are not directly comparable. But the trend in the right-hand chart is unmistakably a reversal of the earlier age trend shown in the chart to the left.

Contrasts evident within the figures, other than the trends just noted, must be cautiously interpreted. Thus, boys appear to show greater and earlier heterosexual interest than females. It could well be that this finding is simply a reflection of greater reticence on the part of girls to write down names of boys on questionnaires. One study has noted that there is a great deal more cross-sex interaction apparent when the behavior itself is observed than when a sociometric test (choice of companions, etc.) is used (6). The trends shown in Figure 102 have been confirmed by other studies: one investigation used a paired-comparison procedure over the entire school age range (59), and in another interaction between the sexes was actually observed and rated (14).

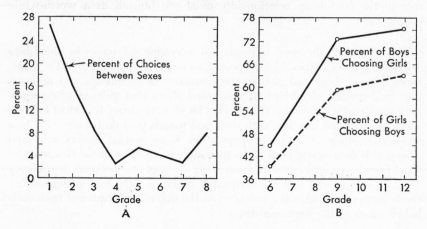

Figure 102. Percentage of Children in Various Grades Choosing the Opposite Sex Under Various Conditions (see text). Although the two charts are not comparable in all aspects, they combine to show the decreasing interest in the opposite sex during the early grades and the emerging new interest in the opposite sex in junior and senior high school. (Chart A from J. L. Moreno, Who Shall Survive? A New Approach to the Problem of Human Relations, Washington, D.C., Nervous and Mental Disease Publishing Company, 1934; Chart B based on data of R. G. Kuhlen and B. J. Lee, Personality characteristics and social acceptability in adolescence, J. Educ. Psychol., 1943, 34:321–340.)

Why are there such striking developments in relationships between the sexes? One explanation is that during the early years (roughly up to pubescence), youngsters are increasingly becoming identified with their own sex group and hence value increasingly the traits—as well as people—of that sex (59). Psychoanalytic writers (102) have given a more biological interpretation both to the identification with own sex and to the marked cleavage that exists at the prepubescent age. At this age, new sex pressures create anxieties in naïve youngsters who do not know how to handle the new urge. The active rejection of the opposite sex may be one means of dealing with this anxiety.

The decrease in social cleavage between the sexes from pubescence on is probably prompted in part by a biological urge toward heterosexuality and in part by the social expectation that youngsters will begin dating, abandon one-sex parties in favor of "boy-girl" parties, and in other ways evidence interest in the opposite sex. It is of some interest in this connection that individual differences in sex-social orientation are greatest around the age of pubescence (14). At young ages children are relatively homogeneous in this regard. At 13, some have reached pubescence and have become interested in the opposite sex, while the prepubescent children remain disinterested. Later when all are postpubescent, they are again fairly homogeneously interested in the other sex. This situation often creates problems for those attempting to deal with youngsters in junior high school, an age at which children differ greatly among themselves in this important aspect of behavior.

Since heterosexual adjustment represents one of the main developmental tasks of adolescence, the question arises as to whether developments in this direction can be promoted, thus perhaps reducing the marked sex cleavage and any accompanying anxiety, by broad social programs in the school or home planned to foster the earlier development of sex-social skills and to provide continuous opportunities for heterosexual contacts. Would youngsters in schools which have social dancing instruction and weekly school dances from the third grade on show less cleavage between the sexes at adolescence than those in other schools with little in the way of a social program? There is reason to expect that this might happen, but research validating this suggestion has not been reported to the writers' knowledge. In any event, here is a situation needing thoughtful study pointing toward the development of constructive programs in schools and more helpful efforts by parents. It is to be noted (in the right-hand chart of Figure 102) that large numbers (perhaps a quarter) of twelfth-graders do not choose the opposite sex, and about a third received no choices from the opposite sex. If heterosexuality is a desirable end result in development, then more positive efforts to promote it would seem called for.[1]

FACTORS RELATED TO SOCIAL ACCEPTABILITY

Whenever social choices are made, some people stand out as "stars," others are social isolates, and most lie between the extremes. Information which shows the characteristics of individuals who receive a disproportionately small number of choices in contrast to those who evidence

---

[1] The whole matter of heterosexual adjustment in adolescence and in marriage is such an important matter that the entire next chapter will be devoted to it.

a high degree of social acceptance should help identify areas of difficulty, the correction of which might foster better social development.

At the outset of this discussion it is worth noting that adults are not good judges of the extent to which children are accepted by their peers (8, 36). Apparently, they find it difficult to see children as other children see them; apparently, their values as to the desirability of certain traits differ from those of the children themselves. Indeed, even among children, social perception develops gradually. At early ages, they are relatively insensitive to the degree to which others are accepted by the group or the extent to which they themselves are accepted. The development of such "socioempathy" over the school

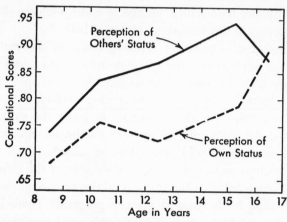

Figure 103. Perception of Own and Others' Sociometric Status for Various Age Levels. (After D. P. Ausubel, H. M. Schiff, and E. B. Gasser, A preliminary study of developmental trends in socioempathy: accuracy of perception of own and others sociometric status, *Child Development*, 1952, 23:113–128.)

years has been recently studied, and trends are graphed in Figure 103. The primary facts here are the obtained relationships (mean of the correlation coefficients) between the actual sociometric status and one's status as judged by his classmates. The increasing size of the correlations with age suggest that important improvements in accuracy of social perception are occurring and that the social acceptance of an individual may be becoming a more socially meaningful characteristic. It is noted in the next chapter, for example, that adolescents with high status are more frequently sought after as dates—and for that reason. Other data show similar growth in social perception of emotional expression presented in photographs (115) and suggest that only gradually do children become sensitive to the symbols of socioeconomic status or to social class distinctions (104).

A substantial number of studies have been made contrasting highly accepted individuals with those who are not well accepted at various age levels. Facts from one such study, presented in Table 76, emphasize personality differences. Although the groups involved in this investigation were delinquent girls committed to a "school," the kinds of information obtained seem especially suggestive of significant psychological differences. The girls were asked to indicate those with whom they would like to live, work, play, and/or study and to name any girls they would not want to include in these activities. From such choices it was possible to identify those who were acceptable and those who were unacceptable and to place other individuals on a scale between these extremes. Since these girls lived in cottages, it was possible also to get reports (complaints and commendations) from the housemothers regarding their behavior.

The table lists those traits mentioned as characterizing girls who were least acceptable, those who were of average acceptability, and those who were most acceptable. The table speaks for itself and warrants careful examination by the reader. The girls who were least acceptable by the other girls were more frequently the source of complaints registered by the housemothers, who complained about their nagging, whining, nervousness, resentfulness, and aggressiveness. "Cause and effect" circularity is probably evident here to the reader. Much of this behavior may be caused by social frustration, by lack of acceptability, but, in turn, the aggressive striking out and the belligerency are hindrances to the development of the state of affairs most needed—social acceptability.

The acceptable girls were sometimes the sources of complaints (e. g., for rebellious behavior or for overconfidence, which led them to start things without permission), but in the main they possessed commendable traits; were coöperative, even-dispositioned, and energetic; and showed initiative and the like. Perhaps most important was their sensitivity to human relations and group situations, as shown by their willingness to assume subordinate roles upon occasion, their insight into human nature, and their interest in others, as shown by their ability to assist girls who were especially difficult (problem girls) and their solicitous attitude toward newcomers to the group. While these data are from a special delinquent group and were obtained under special living conditions, their more general implications are apparent.

Physical traits also differentiate the well-accepted from those not so successful, as shown by a number of studies emanating from the University of California's Institute of Child Welfare. In certain investigations, early-maturing

TABLE 76. Behavior Traits Reported by Housemothers as Characterizing Frequently, Average, and Seldom-Chosen Residents in a "Training School for Girls"

Behavior Reported by Housemothers	Level of Social Acceptance		
	Bottom 15%[a] (N = 41)	Average (N = 41)	Top 15%[a] (N = 43)
Characterizes low-acceptability group			
Quarrelsome, irritable, chip on shoulder	15	3	1
Nagging, complaining, whining	8	4	
Nervous, jumpy behavior	8	4	
Aggressive, dominant behavior	12	6	2
Actively interrupting group activities	11		1
Passively interfering with group activities	13	1	1
Resentful of being criticized	16	9	8
Attention-demanding but not praise-seeking	11	5	1
Praise-seeking behavior	10	4	2
Characterizes high-acceptability group			
Rebellious behavior (refuses to do what is requested by person in authority)	4	7	11
Initiating behavior in making innovations without asking permission	2	4	13
Retaliatory behavior	2	5	14
Does not bring personal troubles to housemother (e. g., problems concerning home and family)	3	5	13
Coöperative behavior	7	28	40
Evenness of disposition	6	20	27
Requires no special attention of housemother		21	30
Makes most of vocational-avocational opportunities		17	31
Voluntarily does more than own share of work	7	18	25
Behavior shows planning and organization		13	26
Shows initiative	2	8	28
Willingness to accept temporary minor or background roles	3	13	26
Is ingenious in changing behavior of problem girls (e. g., forestalls tantrums, helps her gain recognition, deters others from excluding her, etc.)		8	37
Solicitous and encouraging toward new girls	2	9	39

[a] Actually those below (bottom 15%) and above (top 15%) one standard deviation from the mean.

SOURCE: Adapted from Helen H. Jennings, *Leadership and Isolation*, New York, Longmans, Green, 1943, pp. 145–148.

boys were shown to have better social acceptance than did those who were slow to develop (54, 55). And in another study, those who had more muscular body builds (the "mesomorphs") were judged by their classmates to possess more frequently those social traits which have been found to be associated with social acceptability (37).

Socioeconomic factors are also related to social acceptability, although it is difficult to assess their relationship in detail.[2] Several of the large-scale studies of social class have presented impressive evidence that social-class factors have pervasive influence and are of tremendous importance in determining social interaction at all ages (43, 45, 116). In one quantitative analysis of friendship

TABLE 77. Social Class of Self and Class of Listed Best Friend by Number and Percent[a]

Social Class of Namer	Social Class of "Best Friend"							
	I and II		III		IV		V	
	No.	%	No.	%	No.	%	No.	%
Boys								
I and II	15	71	6	29	0	0	0	0
III	8	11	51	70	14	19	0	0
IV	1	1	15	21	54	75	2	3
V	0	0	0	0	3	37	5	63
Girls								
II	10	71	4	29	0	0	0	0
III	3	4	58	80	12	16	0	0
IV	1	1	18	16	88	79	4	4
V	0	0	0	0	4	22	14	78

[a] This table is to be read across the rows. It includes all named best friends whether the named best friend is in or out of school. There were no class I girls.

SOURCE: Adapted from A. B. Hollingshead, *Elmtown's Youth*, New York, Wiley, 1949.

choices and reputation, it was noted that even at the ages of 10 or 11, children have friends and make judgments of others which appear to reflect the operation of social-class bias (117). Upper-class children were more frequently named as friends and were much more frequently nominated by their peers as having positive personal traits; lower-class children had negative traits at-

[2] Most sociometric studies have used procedures which request choice of companions for various activities, rather than intimate associates, and *from classroom groups*. And, often, the social-class variable is not even considered. One study (77) reports that the correlation between social acceptance and family socioeconomic status decreases over ages 14, 16, and 18, seemingly becoming a less important factor with increasing age. But this may be due to the increasing homogeneity of school groups as lower-class children drop out with advance in grades, a factor that could be important when choices are limited to school class groups. Other evidence (118), in fact, suggests that socioeconomic factors become more important in adolescence.

tributed to them and were less frequently mentioned as friends. By high school years similar choice of friends was evident, but there was much less tendency to attribute negative traits to the lower-class individuals; indeed, at this level, the upper-status group received its full share of mention for negative traits. This situation was interpreted as due to the fact that many of the lower-class children had dropped out of school, those who remained being the ones who were most like the upper-class groups in aspirations and values. Another study of social-class factors in friendship choices in a high school group has provided the facts presented in Table 77. In this study information was available on the social-class membership of all the youngsters, and thus it was possible to tabulate the "class choice" of individuals who were themselves in different class groups. It will be noted that in every comparison the youngsters from a particular class made most of their friendship choices from their own status-class group. This matter was touched upon earlier in Chapter 5.

CHANGING TRAIT VALUES WITH CHANGING AGE

The study cited a paragraph back shows something of the overall contrast between socially acceptable and socially unacceptable individuals at a particular age. But on the rapidly changing scene of childhood and adolescence, trait values shift from age to age, and it often happens that the traits parents attempt to promote in their children are not those valued or desired by the children themselves, or they may be those valued by children at one age but not at a later age. It is clearly important for social acceptance for children to have those characteristics valued *by their peer group.*

The several studies cited in this connection utilized essentially the same procedures. Children at different grade or age levels were asked to indicate those they liked, or would choose as companions, or thought popular. They were also asked to describe their classmates by writing down the names of those they thought fitted certain descriptions (e. g., "Here is someone who always seems rather sad, worried, or unhappy, who hardly ever laughs or smiles"). The investigators first sought to study the relationships between "personality traits" (as measured by these nominations) and social acceptability, and then to determine whether the same relationships held at various age levels.

Although children at the first-grade level seemed to be sensitive to a general factor of likableness and liked some children better than others, they did not seem sensitive to the specific traits producing this result. But by grades three and five, specific traits began to be differentially related to social acceptance. Thus, although one may assess the first-grade child's general status in his group, it is likely that little significance attaches to his scores on individual dimensions. But as early as the third and fifth grades, scores on separate item-pairs may prove useful in revealing more specifically how each child is perceived by his peers and may possibly suggest how he can be helped to better adjustment (*113*).

In an investigation of the adolescent years, the most socially accepted members of several sixth-, ninth-, and twelfth-grade classes were contrasted with the least accepted members. Notable changes were apparent. At the sixth grade, for example, the unaccepted boy or girl was considered "restless," but by the twelfth grade restlessness characterized the *popular* boy and girl. "Talkativeness" and "bossing" others were not related to acceptability at the sixth grade, but by the twelfth grade a clear relationship was apparent—the popular adolescent being the talkative and "bossy" one! In the sixth and ninth grades, the popular girls were more often judged to act older than their age. By the twelfth grade, such "sophistication" may be frowned on; at least, then, those judged to act older than their age were more often in the unaccepted group (*61*). Similar trends have been reported by another investigator, who summarized her findings in this way:

For the twelve-year-old girl, quiet, sedate, non-aggressive qualities are associated with friendliness, likability, good-humor and attractive appearance. Behavior which conforms to the demands and regulations of the adult world is admired. Tomboyishness is tolerated. At the fifteen-year-old level admiration for the demure, docile, rather prim, lady-like prototype has ceased. Instead, many of the criteria for the idealized boy, such as extroversion, activity and good sportsmanship are highly acceptable for the girl. The ability to organize games for parties involving both sexes and the capacity to keep such activities lively and entertaining are admired. In addition the quality of being fascinating or glamorous to the other sex has become important but is looked upon as relatively specific or unrelated to other desirable qualities. At the twelve-year-old level the idealized boy is skillful and a leader in games; his daring and fearlessness extend beyond his social group to defiance of adult demands and regulations. Any characteristic which might be construed as feminine by one's peers, such as extreme tidiness or marked conformity in the classroom is regarded as a weakness. However, some personableness and certain kindly, likable qualities tend to be associated with the more highly prized masculine qualities. At fifteen years, prestige for the boy is still in large measure determined by physical skill, aggressiveness and fearlessness. Defiance of adult standards has lost emphasis; though still acceptable and rather amusing to them, it tends to be associated with immaturity. In addition much greater emphasis is placed on personal acceptability, suggesting the effectiveness of rising heterosexual interest. (*110*, pp. 77–78.)

Such changes in trait value have important meanings for individual children. Dramatic illustrations can be found in research materials of individuals who were popular at one age but who did not develop the traits that were valued later, with a consequent loss of status. And the opposite may well occur. The wise parent will be sensitive to this changing social climate in making decisions involving social skills, dress, and degree of independence to be promoted in the varied social activities of their maturing offspring.

CONTINUITY VERSUS POTENTIAL CHANGE IN STATUS

The present emphasis upon *changing* values during the developmental years should not obscure the fact of general continuity of development. In general, those who are highly accepted at one age are well accepted at a later age. One study, for example, has shown that those who were leaders in junior high school tended to be leaders in high school (*64*). In another study, individuals who were leaders in adult life were identified and their high school backgrounds were compared with a group of nonleaders (*22*). Here again an element of continuity was apparent.

However, in any analysis of social acceptability or leadership and factors related thereto it becomes apparent that no specific formula for social success is possible. People low in traits associated with social acceptance are sometimes well-liked and sought-after folk, and some who seemingly have "everything" just don't "click." None of the facts presented in the foregoing pages should be interpreted to mean that efforts to promote the social acceptability of youngsters, or efforts to achieve social adjustment oneself, are doomed to failure. On the contrary, efforts to manipulate judiciously the social structure of a classroom (utilizing choices for committee membership, for example) have resulted in the improvement of social acceptance.[3] Play therapy has also been shown to affect sociometric status (*21*).

The circularity of cause and effect in personal characteristics and social acceptance has already been commented upon in an earlier reference in a negative way. But, this circularity can also have a positive "snowball" effect in that as increments in social acceptance occur the need for psychological defenses (aggression, belligerency, etc.) against lack of acceptance becomes less, and the individual thus has greater potential for social acceptance. A

[3] For a discussion of this matter together with practical suggestions as to how these ends might be achieved, see the booklet by Jennings (*51*).

great deal of tolerance, understanding, and objectivity on the part of adults, and peer groups, is often necessary to break the negative circular sequence so that a positive sequence can be established. Often the circle is broken when, for other reasons, a child changes schools or the family moves to a new neighborhood or city. In serious cases, say of delinquency, a change in environment may be utilized for rehabilitative purposes; a child may be placed in a foster home. In serious cases of social maladjustment, extensive psychotherapy may enable the individual to make a new start.

The importance of propinquity and of means of psychological contact with others through broad interests has already been commented upon. The possession of social skills makes a similar contribution to social acceptance and to friendship potential similar to the contributions made by broad interests and opportunities for contacts. And here is a fairly tangible means that schools and parents may utilize for the promotion of social development and adjustment. It has been shown that those youngsters who are most frequently chosen as companions by their classmates (in this instance at the ninth-grade level) report more frequently than those low in social acceptance that they can dance, swim, play tennis, sing, and carry on a conversation (11). They also have a broader range of activities. The less acceptable individuals in this same ninth-grade group indicated more "personal problems" of a persistent sort dealing with deficiencies in social skills (60). In general, as boys and girls (especially) develop through adolescence they develop more social know-how with respect to eating, meeting people, and other situations involving social interaction (63). They also seem to improve in tactfulness (34). When adolescents were asked, in another investigation, what had helped them develop social poise and adjustment, their replies emphasized opportunity for experience and imitation, or determination to learn:

"My home life helped me. I'm afraid if we students depended on the school for our social graces we wouldn't have any."

"I decided one night to 'do or die.' Went up to a girl and asked her. Just grit your teeth and do it. It isn't so bad after the first few tries."

"The more dances you go to, the more at ease you feel."

"I dated a fellow with a grand personality, and he taught me how to get along." (49.)

An examination of the total results of this study yields two main impressions: first, that learning of specific habits or skills, and through practice gaining poise in complex social situations, is fundamental; second, that the home and the school have typically made little special

effort to provide appropriate experiences. It would seem that both
agencies might make more constructive efforts to foster social development, perhaps along the lines suggested at several points in this discussion.

Interpersonal Relations and Status in the Adult Years

It is a notable characteristic of the adult years that subsequent to the
great upsurge of sex-social activities of the teens and early twenties,
there seems to be a steady decline in social interest. Figure 104 shows

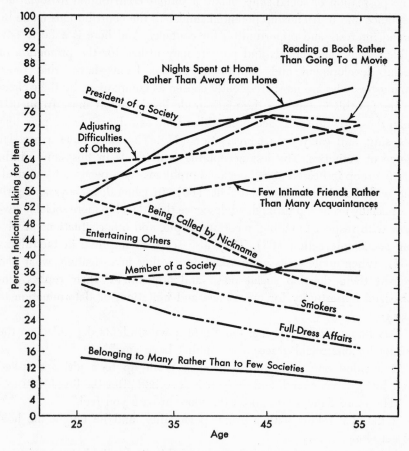

Figure 104. Change of Interest in Certain Social Activities and Interests with Increased
Age. The chart shows percentage of professional men at different ages liking the more
quiet and established, as compared with more active and varied, social contacts.
(Adapted from E. K. Strong, Jr., *Change of Interests with Age*, Stanford, Stanford
University Press, 1931, pp. 178–199.)

this shift for a group of professional men. Dress affairs, smokers, the familiarity of being called by a nickname, and entertaining others are all liked less with increasing age. Evenings spent at home reading a book rather than going to a movie, a few intimate friends rather than many acquaintances are liked better. These results, though reflecting a genuine change, should not obscure the psychological reality that the need for social interaction and for social status remains important throughout life.

SOCIAL INTERACTION AND COMPANIONSHIP IN THE ADULT YEARS

Sociometric studies at the adult community level show much the same results as at school age: some families stand out as "stars" with many social contacts with friends and neighbors; others are "isolates" in the sense that they have no such social interaction (16). In the adult years, as in childhood and adolescence, propinquity is a major factor in friendship formation. Common professional interest or occupational connection of husband often has very much to do with who associates with whom. And the informal, "passive" contacts within the neighborhood represent the starting point for many adult friendships.

One outstanding investigation, in a housing area at Massachusetts Institute of Technology populated by returned veterans aged 20 to 35, analyzed friendship formation with reference to the role of physical and "functional" distance. Neighboring apartments were only 22 feet apart, and apartments at opposite ends of the same floor were only 88 feet apart. Yet such small differences were significant influences in friendship formation. Where mailboxes or stairs were located, orientation of one's apartment toward street or toward court, and whether one occupied an "end" or "outer" apartment were all factors in influencing the frequency of passive contacts out of which friendship grew and helped determine the number of friends as well as who they were (29). Other research, although emphasizing the importance of propinquity, has suggested that the importance of neighborhood varies with socioeconomic status. A study of social intimacy, in a city of 100,000 population, noted that higher economic groups had more friends close by "in the neighborhood." Nevertheless, lower economic groups more frequently indicated neighbors as the source of friends. Further analysis revealed that the lower economic group moved residences more frequently, a fact which seemed to account for their more widespread social contacts. Length and stability of residence seemed the important factors in determining the number of friends nearby (101).

Age, too, will likely play a role in determining the extent to which the individual draws upon the immediate environment for his social contacts. A child knows everyone nearby—and the quality of cookies each housewife produces; the busy, young adult probably sees little of his neighbors; the middle-aged adult swaps gardening advice over the back fence and gets reacquainted with those who live near him. This pattern has been interestingly revealed in a study of the "acquaintances" and "associations" of the residents within a designated urban block. The "personal neighborhoods" of 20 individuals under 20 years of age, 15 between 21 and 40, and 20 over 40 years of age were studied. The findings indicated:

First, that children are the "best neighbors" in single family residential areas like the one studied . . . in the sense that their neighborly relations tie them to more neighbors, are less narrowly confined spatially, and are less restricted to their own age and sex groups than those of older people. Second, that young adults in this type of area—if not more generally—are the "worst" neighbors, in the sense that they are acquainted and associate with relatively few neighbors, that the acquaintances they do make are narrowly concentrated around their own homes, and that their associates among neighbors tend to be relatively selected in favor of their own sex groups. Third, older adults' acquaintance and association in personal neighborhoods are especially likely, in this type of area, to contain a disproportionate number of other oldsters. (108, pp. 75–76.)

For the three age groups—under 20, 21 to 40, 41 and over—the median number of acquaintances within the block was, respectively, 95, 41, and 78, and the median number of associations was 29.5, 10, and 23.5 respectively.

Beyond 65, companionship tends to decline, as shown in Table 78. This index of "overall companionship" is based on five types of association: live with husband or wife; see children or relatives at least once a week; live with someone; see adult friends at least once a week; see young friends at least once a week. Those with four or five types of companionship were considered to have a "high degree" of companionship; those with two or three types, a "moderate degree"; and those with none or only one type, a "low degree." From 60 on, the proportion evidencing "high degree" declines and the number having a "low degree" of companionship increases, this trend being most marked with women, in large part because of earlier marriage and longer life resulting in loss of marital companionship.

There is a paucity of data on the extent of social relations in old age, on factors related to acceptability, or on means by which social relationships might be promoted. Two studies, however, bear on such matters. Analysis of

TABLE 78.   Degree of Companionship in Old Age, by Age Periods[a]

Degree of Companionship	Percentage Distribution by Age Periods							
	60–64	65–69	70–74	75–79	80–84	85–89	90–94	95 Up
Males								
High	47	37	35	36	50	37	33	25
Moderate	43	52	51	49	39	53	68	50
Low	10	11	14	15	11	10	—	25
Total cases	68	87	110	107	56	19	6	4
Females								
High	47	33	28	30	18	10	8	25
Moderate	45	45	50	49	46	45	53	25
Low	8	21	22	21	36	45	39	50
Total cases	143	149	176	119	69	31	13	4

[a] Five types of companionship were included: live with husband or wife; see children or relatives at least once or twice a week; live with someone; see adult friends at least once a week; see young friends at least once a week. Those with a high degree of companionship had four or five types; those with moderate companionship had two or three; those with a low degree of companionship had one type or none. The small numbers of cases 90 and over should be noted.

SOURCE: Adapted from R. S. Cavan, E. W. Burgess, R. J. Havighurst, and H. Goldhamer, *Personal Adjustment in Old Age*, Chicago, Science Research Associates, 1949, p. 204.

the interpersonal choices, made within two residence halls at "Moosehaven"—a community for the aged in Florida operated by the Moose Lodge—indicated that a rather large proportion of the residents were "isolates" in the sense that they neither mentioned any other resident nor were mentioned by others in reply to the question, "With whom do you visit?" Some individuals chose others, but were not chosen; some had one intimate (reciprocal choice); some had two or more intimates; and some were mentioned by enough others to be classed as leaders. The members falling in each category are shown in the first three columns of Table 79. Of 64 persons, 27 (42 percent) were chosen by no one; 17 (27 percent) neither chose others nor were chosen by others. Here, indeed, is extensive social isolation within a community limited to old people and where rather extensive recreational and social opportunities exist. The next columns of the table show (but only for the "B" hall group) mean indexes of recreation, sense of usefulness, and feeling of happiness of each group, as well as average age. In general, social isolation is associated with low recreational participation and low feelings of usefulness and happiness. Also, those high in all of these respects had many mentions in the community news sheet.

Can anything be done to influence such older people into better social relationships with others? In a second study, special efforts were made by means of a seven-month activity program to improve social relationships among the residents of one home for the aged as compared with a "control" home not having the program. Sociometric procedures were utilized to check the degree of social interaction before and after the program. Although the results did not achieve statistical reliability, the trend was such as to suggest that the program did result in increased socialization and greater integration of the residents into the group structure (24).

TABLE 79. Social Acceptability and Average Scores on Recreational Activities, Usefulness, and Happiness of the Residents of a Community for Old People

Type of Social Relation	Social Acceptance			Average Score and Age, Hall "B"			
	Hall "A"		Hall "B"				
	17 Men	13 Women	34 Men	Recrea-tion	Use-fulness	Happi-ness	Age
Isolates							
Neither choose nor chosen by others	7	3	7	3.3	5.7	5.9	80.3
Choose, but not chosen by others	1	2	7	4.8	7.9	8.3	76.7
Intimates							
One reciprocated choice	3	0	10	5.0	7.4	7.1	78.5
Two or more reciprocated choices	2	7	3	5.7	6.9	4.0	74.3
Leaders	4	1	7	7.4	10.3	9.0	74.3

SOURCE: Adapted from E. W. Burgess, Social relations, activities, and personal adjustment, Amer. J. Sociol., 1954, 59:352–360.

Such facts emphasize again a life-cycle characteristic noted in an earlier chapter: an expanding social and psychological world in the first half of the life span and a decrease during the last half. This pattern is undoubtedly conditioned by many factors—maturity, time pressures, changes in energy level, need for status in the larger community. Without discounting the importance of warm, neighborly associations it is suggested that perhaps the "withdrawal" to the immediate level is more rapid or earlier than it need be. Other studies of the type cited in the preceding paragraph, not only in homes for the aged but (especially) in the typical community and neighborhood as well, are much needed to point the way to techniques by which older individuals may be helped to achieve and/or to maintain a better integration in social life.

ADULT GAINS AND LOSSES IN SOCIAL STATUS

In the adult years gains or losses in social status are apt to be judged in the more general status structure of society, that of social class. To become upwardly mobile,[4] an individual must, first, be fired by a drive for status or achievement, a drive that may have had its origins in emotional deprivation or which may simply reflect constant pressure to succeed from parents, teachers, and the general subculture. The latter pressure has sometimes been referred to as "middle-class anxiety" for success. Second, the individual must possess sufficient talent to translate this drive into actual achievement in an educational and/or economic sense. "Talents" may range anywhere from physical attractiveness to athletic, scientific, or artistic abilities. Third, he must possess appropriate social techniques and respond appropriately to various situations (go to the right place, *not* do certain things) so as to be evaluated favorably by others, especially by those in the next highest group.[5] Geographic mobility is also often an aid to upward mobility since by moving to a new locale points of origin may be obscured, and class-confining attitudes that might have retarded mobility in the home town may be escaped.

People vary a great deal, of course, in the degree to which they are oriented toward mobility and in the ways they respond to social frustration or success. Some try especially hard to conform; others strike out aggressively at social rebuffs; some simply withdraw quietly; some are unconcerned about and oblivious to the existence of a "class" structure. Some have the drive but not the capacity and skill to achieve mobility; others have the ability but not the need. With respect to mobility, one writer has classified people as "climbers" "strainers," "statics," "clingers," and "decliners," depending upon the direction of their status movement and their success in achieving new or hanging on to previous status (76).

The impression conveyed by much writing on social class is that upward mobility is "good" and "desirable," that it is the well-adjusted and success-oriented person who "makes the grade." It is, however, a good guess that actually many people are unconcerned about such matters and are nevertheless happy and well adjusted. Indeed, much informed opinion asserts that

[4] One writer has advanced the view that upward mobility must occur if the present status structure is to be maintained, since the upper classes have not in the past produced enough children to maintain their kind (76).

[5] This discussion is patterned somewhat after Carson McGuire's analysis of the prerequisites for upward social mobility as presented in Chapter 4 of Warner, *et al.* (117).

the drive for upward mobility is neurotic, the product of unhappy early experiences, and that the individual has many traumatic experiences along the way.

An interesting investigation of social-psychological correlates of upward mobility in unmarried career women touched upon such matters. The sample included the outstanding unmarried career women in a southern city. They were divided into two groups: 27 women whose occupational status differed substantially from that of their fathers and 33 whose occupational status was the same. Information about happiness as regards home and associates, as well as general happiness and areas of conflicts, was obtained through interviews. Table 80 shows that the mobile group had, in general, poorer relationships with their parents, fewer friends, more conflicts, especially with reference to career and personal conduct. Although differences with respect to geographic mobility (not shown in the table) were individually not statistically significant, every comparison made (number of cities worked in, number of states worked in, number born in the state, number of years residence in the city, etc.) reflected greater geographic mobility on the part of the occupationally upwardly mobile group.

TABLE 80. Contrasts Between Upwardly Mobile and Nonmobile Unmarried Career Women with Respect to Early Background and Social-Psychological Adjustment

	Mobile Group	Nonmobile Group
Percentage reporting		
Less than average attachment to parents	36	6
Parents showed favoritism toward a sibling	56	27
Mean number of		
Friends	8.9	17.8
Intimate friends in the city	5.6	9.4
Friendships of 5 or more years duration	3.2	8.2
Percentage reporting conflict in		
Religion	16	3
Politics	20	12
Career	40	18
Personal conduct	40	12
Percentage having experienced complete rejection by the general community	20	0
Number of cases	27	33

SOURCE: Adapted from Evelyn Ellis, Social psychological correlates of upward social mobility among unmarried career women, *Amer. Sociol. Rev.*, 1952, *17:*558–563.

Actual survey of an adult population as well as a life history analysis of a sample of oldsters indicates that upward social mobility with in-

creased adult age is, indeed, the characteristic trend. One investigation (19, pp. 167–169) involved an opinion poll of a national sample
of adults in which, among other things, the subjects were asked to name
the social class to which they thought they belonged. For successive
decades, from "under 30" through the thirties, forties, fifties to "over 60,"
the percentages identifying with the upper and middle social classes
were 66, 71, 79, 82 and 81 percent respectively, thus suggesting a steady
increase in social status (at least self-concept of status) with increased
age.

In still another research, a somewhat modified version of Warner's
social status index (42)[6] was computed for each of 45 men and 55 women
over 65 years of age (a representative sample of this age group in the
city studied) on the basis of life history information to show status at
birth (parents' status), at age 50, and at present. Table 81 presents the
proportion who gained or lost in status from birth to 50 and from 50
onward.

TABLE 81. Percentage of 45 Men and 55 Women, All Over 65, Who
Were Upwardly or Downwardly Mobile by Age 50 Compared to Parents'
Status, and Who Were Upwardly or Downwardly Mobile from Age 50
On. A Change of 5 Points or More in the Score Described in the Text Was
Required for a Person to Be Considered "Mobile"

	From Birth (Family) to Age 50	From Age 50 On
Percentage upwardly mobile		
Males	42	7
Females	31	11
Percentage not changing		
Males	38	71
Females	44	73
Percentage downwardly mobile		
Males	20	22
Females	25	16

SOURCE: Adapted from R. J. Havighurst and R. Albrecht, Older People, New
York, Longmans, Green, 1953.

It will be noted that the characteristic trend to age 50 was up, 36
percent being mobile upward and 23 percent downward. Moreover, this

[6] Occupation, source of income, ethnicity, and religion were given status-scale
values according to previous research results and assigned weights of 5, 4, 1, and 2
respectively to arrive at an "Index of Status Characteristics."

was thought to be an underestimate of the true amount of upward mobility, since those most upwardly mobile had probably moved away from the small city in which the study was conducted. Beyond age 50, losses outweighed gains in social status, even though in computing the status score retired people were given the same occupational status as they had before they retired. Thus, some people had lost their businesses or their jobs during the depression and never regained equivalent status—were really downwardly mobile. One is reminded here of the extreme examples of downward mobility in old age that are occasionally reported in the press. A former movie star or attorney, at one time with high income and status, may, through alcoholism, improvidence, or other circumstance, end up on skid row or in a cluttered room in a cheap hotel. Where losses in social status or forced drops in standard of living accompany old age, the adjustment problems may be acute, and a life which otherwise would have been happy may end in bitterness and despair.

There are, of course, important changes with age in status even when social class remains the same. Studies of attitudes toward different age groups in the American culture indicate that the forties are *thought* to be the years of greatest security, effectiveness, and social status, at least in middle-class society (*112*). The implied loss in status as people move into later maturity, a reflection of a culture which is not especially friendly to aging, is undoubtedly an important factor in determining differences in the level of personal adjustment of individuals of different ages. A new orientation in the American culture might, of course, markedly alter this picture. The American society has seemed overly geared to young people, has extolled the qualities of youth, has made aging something to be dreaded, has developed numerous incorrect stereotypes about the aging process that retard objective consideration of the values of each age of life. If the research results now becoming available were more widely disseminated, if cultural values were to change accordingly, if the status of people of all ages were determined on the basis of their actual qualities (age, after all, is only one factor making for individual differences), problems of the older years would be substantially reduced.

Social Interaction in Groups

A great many social activities of children and adults involve interactions in the context of informal or organized groups. Some groups are purely social in nature; others have goals of service to a community; some have educational or special interest functions. But they all provide opportunities for social interaction and participation and offer opportunities for friendships. In such relationships and activities a person often achieves a sense of usefulness and of making worth-while contributions, a feeling of *belonging*. At all ages these are important psychological dividends.

INFORMAL SOCIAL STRUCTURES IN CHILDHOOD AND ADOLESCENCE

At early ages the social groupings are very informal and often transitory, but gradually they assume greater stability and greater importance in the life of the youngster. As would be anticipated from data earlier presented relative to sex cleavage, the groupings in early childhood involve both sexes but gradually become unisexual in make-up and then return to heterosexuality. This pattern is readily observable by the parent who helps his children plan birthday parties or other social affairs. At the early elementary school stage, the child wants to invite both sexes; then the preference is likely to be for those of the same sex; later, boy-girl parties again become desirable.

By the fifth or sixth grade, as youngsters become more independent of the home and immediate neighborhood contacts and more socially perceptive, more stable and cohesive social groupings become possible. In adolescence, cliques tend almost to dominate the social scene. Figures 105 and 106 contain an illustration of the group structure existing among 15-year-olds in a California high school. These youngsters were asked to write down the names of their two best friends. Lines were then drawn to show the pattern of interrelationships. The "sociogram" thus created clearly exhibits the existence of a number of groups or cliques, especially among the girls. In the top left of Figure 105 is a group of 7 girls, each of whom makes her friendship choices from within the group. To the right are several groups composed of 3 or 4 members each. A large group of 19 girls is held together by interlocking, reciprocal choices; however, in a group this size, subgroups (as the one trio of individuals 5, 9, and 44) are likely to occur. Each of the three largest cliques also has a number of peripheral members. There are also a number of fairly isolated pairs and some complete isolates (at least in terms of the procedures followed here). The corresponding diagram for boys (Figure 106) shows structure but by no means the degree of cliquishness shown by the girls. This likely reflects a general difference between the sexes; as noted earlier in the chapter, girls rather consistently seem to have greater dependence on and need for warm friendship relationships than do boys.

The procedures utilized in constructing Figures 105 and 106 (i. e., choices for "best friend") are those which would tend to emphasize unisexual groups. Other types of observation bring out the strong heterosexual element that is nonetheless present in the adolescent clique arrangement. Parallel cliques among boys and girls may exist which are unisexual in their clique make-up and in perhaps most of their activities

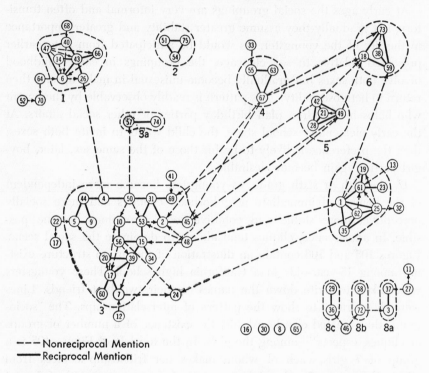

- - - Nonreciprocal Mention
——— Reciprocal Mention

Figure 105. Social Groupings Among 15-Year-Old Girls as Revealed by Their Choices of "Best Friend." (From H. E. Jones, *Development in Adolescence*, New York, Appleton-Century-Crofts, 1943, p. 44.)

but which regularly merge to form a larger clique (or adolescent "crowd") when heterosexual social activities are involved. Thus when one member of a "clique" has a party, she invites other members of her own clique and the boys from the "parallel" clique. Dates for school parties or dances, while on an individual basis, may well be almost exclusively between members of the two cliques. Such has been the state of affairs described in systematic efforts to study adolescent social behavior (45).

The facts already presented regarding social acceptability and friendship choices suggest the types of personal traits that will also make for congenial clique relationships. But more general lines of social class and school grade are also important determiners of membership in a particular clique. In one study, 86 percent of all clique ties were with class equals. It was also apparent "that the polar classes in the social

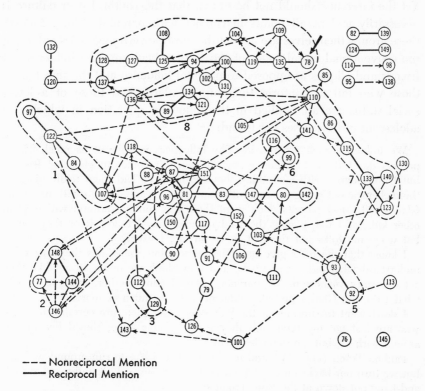

——— Nonreciprocal Mention
——— Reciprocal Mention

Figure 106. Social Groupings Among 15-Year-Old Boys as Revealed by Their Choices of "Best Friends." (From H. E. Jones, *Development in Adolescence*, New York, Appleton-Century-Crofts, 1943, p. 44.)

structure are isolated one from another insofar as intimate, personal time-consuming, ego-involving, face-to-face relations are concerned, for there are no clique ties between the class II's and the class V's" (45). Again and again in the study of social relationships, class lines are seen to be a pervasive influence.

The clique provides some of the most significant learning experiences in social development. In such groups, away from domination of parents and other adults, much of the learning to get along with others occurs;

opportunities for desirable growth of independence from family abound. The group or clique represents the powerful element of the adolescent peer culture that so often conflicts with parental pressures. But it is partially through the resolution of ideological and other conflicts between parental training and peer values that maturity of outlook grows. Yet the inference should not be drawn that the youthful peer culture is necessarily and at all points in conflict with parental values. Indeed, these groups themselves are among the most powerful agencies enforcing the conventional moral codes of the adult subculture. The influences of friends and cliques as opposed to parental influence and the rejection of those who fail to conform to group standards and those of a lower social status are all implied in the following quotation in which one adolescent girl discusses her friend:

We influence each other a lot. She influences me almost as much as my parents do. I listen to them, especially when it comes to choosing friends, but I don't agree with everything they tell me. I've had them really give me the dickens about going around with some girls I wanted to go with or maybe Gladys did. Most parents don't want their kids running around with certain other kids, and they'll give them advice and they'll follow it or they won't, but when my folks put the foot down on me, I listen.

I know that the folks give me good advice, but sometimes they just don't understand what kids want to do, and they think we ought to act like they acted twenty years ago. My parents, especially my mother, influence me in what I do, but Gladys probably influences me as much or more.

I don't want to run any of the kids down, but there are certain girls here who are just not my type, and they're not Gladys' type; they'd like to run around with us, but we don't let them.

Pauline Tryon (class IV) and her bunch would like to run around with us, but we turn our backs on them because they run around all night, cut school, and hang out down at the Blue Triangle.

There are some kids we'd like to go around with, but they don't want us to go with them. Gladys and I would like to go around with "Cookie" Barnett (class II) and her bunch, or the G.W.G.'s, but they snub us if we try to get in on their parties, or dances, or date the boys they go with. (45, p. 209.)

INFORMAL ADULT CLIQUES

Somewhat similar patterns of social relationships are apparent at the adult level. Informal adult cliques not infrequently are unisexual, existing within larger formal organizations or in the occupational context or in the more casual social life of tavern, golf course, bridge group, or poker club. But often adult cliques involve families, the husbands and wives if not the children.

The ways in which communities are structured into subgroups, cliques, and constellations of influence have been shown in a number of studies. In one Vermont village of about 1000 population studied some years ago, someone in almost every family (usually the housewife) was interviewed, and the request was made confidentially to indicate best friends. Ninety-four percent gave the requested information. Seven constellations, in addition to a fringe of isolates or semiisolates, could be identified. The most influential group (the "hub" of the village) consisted of businessmen, professional people, and skilled workers; another group consisted of executives, businessmen, and skilled workers. Three groups were composed of skilled and semiskilled individuals; one group was made up of semiskilled families; and one was a proletarian group of unskilled factory workers (68).

A recheck eight years later (67) showed that the same prestige group was still the hub of the village. However, its leader, a woman now past 70, had begun to retire from active community life and received only 9 choices as best friend compared to 17 earlier. She still had highest prestige though and was most frequently chosen to head a committee to welcome visiting dignitaries. Her successor as leader was a woman who eight years earlier received no choices—was an inconspicuous satellite—but who had made a name for herself through "great executive ability and interest in the community," and on the recheck was the most popular person in the village.

Several studies of university veterans' housing centers (16, 29) have also provided descriptions of adult communities, indicating the presence of cliques, usually smaller and more intimate than the larger constellation noted in the Vermont village.

The following quotation illustrates the changes that time (and age) brings in the more intimate clique relationships. The first account describes an upper-class group; the second, a lower-middle and working-class group.[7]

One such clique was just finishing its course in Prairie City at the time of our Study. It was formed at the turn of the century, as a 500 Club, by fourteen couples, mostly of upper-class status. They were young then, in their twenties and thirties. All were well-to-do; there were two lawyers who became judges, a banker, two large-scale farmers, several merchants. Many of the men were Masons and their wives members of the Eastern Star. All had large houses with servants.

The group was started accidentally by one couple entertaining the others.

[7] Quoted with permission of the publisher from R. J. Havighurst and Ruth Albrecht, *Older People*, New York, Longmans, Green, 1953, pp. 187–189.

When the guests returned the hospitality, they invited nearly the same people, because they were congenial, and so the social obligations became interlaced. They did many things besides playing 500. Picnics were favorite events, in which the children were included. Six of these children have intermarried within the group.

By 1948 all of the men and seven of the women in the original clique had died. The seven widows still living, all well along in the seventies or beyond, still got together to play cards or to have luncheon at the Country Club. Entertaining away from home was made necessary by the fact that several had given up their large houses to move into apartments too small for parties. As failing health made it more difficult to leave home, these ladies relied more and more on the telephone for communication. The tie gradually became more one of sentiment than of actual participation.

A clique of middle-aged and elderly women of lower-middle- and working-class status was formed some fifteen years ago in Prairie City, largely through the influence of one woman, Mrs. Bosten, who had recently moved into town with her husband from a farm. One day, shortly after their arrival, Mrs. Bosten had been working all morning in her garden when four unexpected visitors came to lunch. Her next-door neighbor brought over a pumpkin pie to help in the emergency, and after that they were good friends. The neighbor on the other side of the Bostens was drawn in next, and then a fourth woman in the vicinity, somewhat younger.

The four of them would take turns entertaining, usually with a card party, and they would invite other friends, together with the central nucleus of four. This clique had been going for some years when, with the coming of the war, the serving of refreshments began to be a problem, and it was decided to do without. . . .

Two of the women were then in their sixties, and a third in the seventies. When two of them became widows, they sold their homes and moved to other parts of town . . . and the clique died out. But Mrs. Bosten could not be without such a group, and she soon organized a birthday club of eight women, mostly younger than herself. Each woman on her birthday invited the others, and they all came with fifty cents, which they gave to the hostess for a present. This group fell apart when some personal difficulties arose between certain of the members. Now, Mrs. Bosten and her husband belong to a clique of eight couples, mostly younger than themselves, which meets about every three weeks at the home of one or another of the members for informal dinner and a game of 500 or pinochle. . . .

Thus, Mrs. Bosten has participated in three cliques during the fifteen years of her residence in Prairie City. She is now 65, and may have to rely mainly on younger people to organize a new clique if the present one disintegrates.

Notable in the above description are the inroads that change in residence, energy losses, and death, as well as interpersonal difficulties, make upon close friendships and social relationships as the adult years pass.

In the above-mentioned town, only 7 percent of those over 65 had close-knit clique relations, and 18 percent had loose group relations, such as giving and receiving invitations to dinners and parties. Most (71 percent) had only scattered social contacts in loosely assembled groups, as greetings at church services or conversations in cigar store or tavern (42). A study which dealt with lower-class adults of all ages in another city emphasized the importance of *kinship* associations as the typical informal group in the lives of laboring people. About two-fifths of husbands and wives had no intimate friends outside the family, but this did not necessarily mean social isolation. Rather, kin-groups were the important social contact. This finding has emphasized the continued importance in adult years of "primary" group relationships, a type of relationship often thought to be replaced in urban areas by less personalized "secondary groups" (26).

FORMAL GROUPS IN THE SCHOOL YEARS

Although many groups become closely knit and the members may even call themselves members of a "club" and concoct secret passwords and ritual, a formal structure is not usual. However, Cub Scout groups, "Brownies," and "Bluebirds"—the younger age organizations of Boy Scouts, Girl Scouts, and Camp Fire Girls respectively—open their membership to children as young as seven or eight and are very popular at these ages. As the later elementary school years merge into the junior high school, school clubs come onto the scene, and in adolescence the first peak of participation in formally organized groups occurs (75). Since such organizations typically exist in the context of the school (even when technically viewed as "extra-school"), the focus of this discussion will be upon the school's so-called extracurricular activities and their purposes and potential contributions or handicaps to desirable social development.

Participation in formal groups and organizations may make a number of contributions to the development and adjustment of youngsters. First, such groups provide experience in coöperative efforts to achieve certain ends, the joint planning of goals, methods, programs. Second, they provide experience in formal group procedures, as in conduct of a meeting and a presentation of ideas there. Third, they provide opportunities for the development of special interests and skills, as in a science or photography club. Fourth, they provide opportunity for social learning and a sense of "belonging." This may be an important outcome even in subject matter clubs where boys and girls may achieve a sense of integration with a group and learn social poise in the presence of the opposite sex under circumstances which direct attention away from these specific relationships. Fifth, participation in such groups provides opportunity for individual initiative and leadership to emerge. Such potential outcomes—and others may well come to the mind of the reader—provide ample reason for the development of a strong and varied extracurricular program in the school. Indeed, so intrinsic are some of these values to the objectives of the school that one wonders at the appropriateness of the label, "extra," a term which, unfortunately, seems to characterize the attitudes of some school groups to such programs.

Who participates in school activities? One analysis (Table 82) shows that those of higher economic status, those who are better adjusted, and those of better ability who make better grades are the most frequent participants. Nonparticipants were lower than participants in socioeconomic status, social adjustment as measured by the Bell Inventory, score on a vocabularly test (which provides as estimate of "intelligence"), and school achievement. And as degree of participation increased (one, two, and three or more activities), there were regular mean advances in all of these measures. In one large midwestern city

TABLE 82. Socioeconomic Status, Social Adjustment, Ability (Vocabulary Test), and School Achievement (Measured by Achievement Test) of Twelfth-Grade Boys Who Participated in Varying Numbers of Extracurricular Activities, as Revealed by Mean Scores on Various Tests[a]

Extent of Participation	Socioeco-nomic Status Scale	Social Adjustment Scale[b]	Vocabu-lary Test	School Achieve-ment Test
No activity	16.5	14.8	15.9	17.0
One activity	18.5	11.8	19.2	20.4
Two activities	21.5	10.4	20.3	20.9
Three or more	22.5	6.0	20.8	21.3

[a] Data for socioeconomic status and social adjustment are based on 121, 74, 46, and 30 cases in descending order; the number of cases in the same order for vocabulary and school achievement are 92, 53, 34, 22.

[b] Low scores show better social adjustment.

SOURCE: From H. P. Smith, The relationship between scores on the Bell Adjustment Inventory and participation in extracurricular activities, J. Educ. Psychol., 1947, 38:11–16, and H. P. Smith, A study in the selective character of secondary education: participation in school activities as conditioned by socio-economic status and other factors, J. Educ. Psychol., 1945, 36:229–246.

high school, 92 percent of the membership of sororities and fraternities were drawn from the top 30 percent of the group socioeconomically. The Hi-Y Club drew 74 percent of its membership from this group (100).

Further data on participation in school activities as related to social class in another small midwestern city are presented in Table 83. Not only are those of higher status more active in extracurricular activities, but they are more often elected to office. Attendance at athletic events, at high school dances, and at evening plays and parties is in every instance more frequent on the part of the upper-class children.

TABLE 83. Extent of Participation in Various High School Activities of Children from Different Social Status Levels

| | Social Class | | | |
	I and II	III	IV	V
Mean Number of Extracurricular				
Activities Participated in				
Boys	1.8	1.1	.8	.6
Girls	3.9	2.0	1.0	.1
Percentage Distribution of Elected Representa-				
tives	21.6	46.2	32.2	.0
Percentage distribution of student body	9.0	37.3	47.0	6.7
Attended evening plays and Parties				
Attended none (%)	.0	27	60	—
Attended most or seldom missed one (%)	89	56	12	—
Attended high school dances				
Did not attend (%)	14	41	63	—
Attended most or seldom missed one (%)	77	47	13	—
Attendance at athletic events				
Attended no games (%)	.0	12	24	46
Attended most or seldom missed one (%)	94	75	44	.0
Number of cases	35	146	163	26

SOURCE: Adapted from A. B. Hollingshead, *Elmtown's Youth*, New York, Wiley, 1949.

These findings lead one to suspect that the better social adjustment of the participants might not be a *product* of the extracurricular experience, even though a prime reason for the existence of the groups is to promote personal and social adjustment. Rather, it seems that it is, on the average, the better-adjusted individuals who "join." Those who most need the social experiences provided by such activities are often the very ones excluded from membership. Occasionally, this may be due to reticence in seeking out membership, in making application. But there is likely also a degree of snobbishness about the group members which results in social rejection of those with certain social lacks. The snobbishness of adolescent groups (and of many adult groups as well!) has been the subject of frequent comment. An attitude of complacency is suggested by the finding in one college that sorority members felt there should be no new organizations established, while nonmembers thought there should be; members thought sororities promoted desirable social traits, while fewer of the nonmembers thought so (50). A study of fraternities at Syracuse University some years ago also revealed a great deal of snobbishness and "institutional" thinking among the members (56). The feelings of rejection experienced by boys and girls of lower status with respect to extracurricular activities is dramatically shown in the following quotation:

> Frankly, for a lot of us there is nothing here, but just going to classes, listening to the teacher, reciting, studying, and going home again. We are pushed out of things. There is a group of girls here who think they are higher than us. They look down on us . . . they are a group of girls from the higher families. They have a club that is supposed to be outside of school, but it's really in the school. They . . . hog all of the offices. They're in all the activities. . . . Some of them will speak to us sometimes, but most of the time they just ignore us. . . . Last year, I was in the Home Makers' and the Cheer Club, but they ignored me. Now I'm not in anything. . . ." (45, pp. 202–203.)

How can school extracurricular groups be utilized more effectively to achieve their potential values? Some of the problems indicated above may be very difficult to deal with. But teachers themselves should avoid evidencing bias[8] and should make special efforts to reduce opportunities for bias in the operation of clubs. Recognizing the existence of a problem is the first step. A wider range of special interest and subject matter clubs pursued in the school context and utilizing school equipment may focus attention upon qualities of talent and achievement rather than upon social status. It has also been suggested that social clubs be encouraged to alter their pledging practices so as to produce a more heterogeneous membership, both as a means of bringing about more interstimulation and as a means of combating a group ideology adhered to by all (56, p. 203).

Status is, of course, only one factor influencing club participation.

[8] See a paper by Emil Heintz, His father is only the janitor *Phi Delta Kappan,* April, 1954, for an interesting account of class bias on the part of teachers in assigning grades.

Within any social class there exist wide differences in social acceptability and adjustment. More deliberate use might be made of clubs as a means of actively promoting social adjustment. In one university, counselors made special efforts to introduce shy, socially less well-adjusted students to organized social activities. A comparison made later of their social adjustment with that of a control group indicated gains as a result of this maneuver (2).

PARTICIPATION IN ORGANIZATIONS IN THE ADULT YEARS

Adults, rather than children or adolescents, are the "joiners" in American society, with the peak incidence of memberships being at about 50 years of age. There is an abrupt drop in participation in organizations as youngsters move out of school in which context many activities flourish. As adults in a new social context, young people must begin anew their contacts with formal groups.

Figure 107 shows age trends in club memberships for 4237 men and 2185 women, who constituted a national sample of college graduates (age was estimated from year of college graduation, assuming graduation at 22 years), and something of the degree of responsible participation as reflected in the holding of two or more offices and/or committee memberships. It will be noted that, in the case of males, there was in-

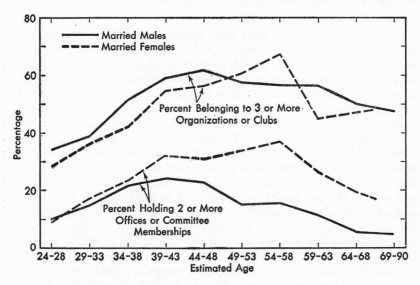

Figure 107. Organizational Activity as Related to Age. (Unpublished analysis by R. G. Kuhlen of *Time Magazine* survey data.)

creasing participation in organizational activities, with most frequent participation occurring during the estimated age range of 44 to 48 years. Offices and committee memberships were most frequently held during the age interval of 34 to 38 years. Increase in active participation in organizations during the earlier adult years may be due to the gradual establishment of the family and parent participation paralleling the participation of offspring. Membership in parent-teacher associations and participation of adults in boy or girl scout work probably parallels the activity of their youngsters in these or related activities. Also, special interest groups often actively solicit the participation of young adults.

Rather clear sex differences are apparent in the figure; the greatest frequency of feminine participation occurred in the 54- to 58-year age interval, about a decade later than the peak for men. Increasing participation on the part of women into the late fifties is likely, the writers venture, a product of their new-found freedom from family cares at a time when both social interests and energy level are still fairly high. Not only does such activity provide a means of using time, but may well fill a need to be useful when, with children gone, a mother may feel her major role in life is completed. By the time males are relieved of demands on their time, it may be relatively late to renew organizational contacts which were given up perhaps as energy level began to wane but as heavy work demands continued.

The general picture of group participation is seen, then, to parallel the trends of expansion and restriction noted so frequently in other chapters in this column. This life-cycle pattern appears in other studies, though there is not exact agreement as to peak ages or sex differences. Differences from study to study are likely due to differences in the groups investigated (college graduates, rural populations) as well as in the methods employed. Thus, a number of studies have employed the Chapin scale of participation in which membership is given a value of "1"; attendance, "2"; contribution, "3"; committee membership, "4"; and office position, "5." In a rural population in North Carolina, the mean social participation score was high in the teens, then dropped abruptly in the early twenties, but climbed steadily thereafter to a peak in the late forties for females and in the late fifties for males (in contrast to the data presented in Figure 107 for college graduates), and dropped in old age (73, 74, 75). Another investigator, working in a rural area, obtained a participation score of 4.9 for the age group 20 to 39; 6.9 for 55 to 64; and 3.5 for those over 75. In a small midwestern city it has been observed that associational membership in groups of mixed ages usually begins in the thirties, but that many do not join until 40 or 50. The peak participation in this locale was in the fifties, with a slow withdrawal beginning in the sixties (42). An age analysis for the various components of the participation scale would be desirable; it is likely that nominal membership, perhaps involving the paying of dues, continues beyond the age when active participation ceases.

Individual differences in participation in organizations are, of course, great. Socioeconomic status is an important factor, with the greater participation being among the upper socioeconomic groups (13, 42, 71); more urban than rural women spend time in club attendance (62). In Boulder, Colorado, in 1945, there were 268 organizations, or one for every 48 adult inhabitants. Yet 29 percent of the adults belonged to none, not even to a church. Of 8542 individual members, the average was about two memberships each. But 26 people belonged to 10 or more organizations; one person belonged to 16 (13)! In a working class group in New Haven, Connecticut, about 60 percent of men and 80 percent of women had no formal memberships (26). In Philadelphia, 78 percent of a sample belonged to no religious organization beyond general church membership; 85 percent belonged to no civic or charitable groups; 74 percent reported no affiliation with such occupational groups as union, business, or professional organizations, and of a representative sample of Philadelphia women, 55 percent belonged to no organization whatsoever (93).

What types of organizations appeal to people of different ages? Age distributions of memberships within a given type may vary greatly as a result of differences in policy or history. Thus, in the midwestern community mentioned earlier (42), one fraternal order (the "Eagles") had 15 percent of their membership under 30 and 7 percent 65 or above; however, the "Odd Fellows" had none below 40 but 43 percent aged 65 or over. In the broad sample of college graduates (4027 married men and 2185 married women) studied by one of the present writers, certain age differences in membership were apparent. Among the men, fraternities of the college type and patriotic societies were most popular at 24 to 28 years of age when 16 and 20 percent respectively belonged. At 39 to 43 years of age, 24 percent belonged to "historical, educational, and learned" types of organizations and 35 percent to "business, Rotary, and chamber-of-commerce" types. Male membership in "professional organizations" was highest at 44 to 48 years, with 53 percent belonging; lodge membership was highest at 54 to 58, with 42 percent belonging; and organizations dealing with "athletics, sports, recreation and hobbies" were most popular at ages 59 to 63 when 33 percent belonged.

The women showed somewhat similar shifts. Sorority interest continued at about 15 percent membership until the 39- to 43-year group; after this, membership declined. Lodge membership was highest at 59 to 63, but even then only 18 percent belonged. "Professional" organizations and "historical, educational, and learned" societies claimed greatest female membership among those 44 to 48 years of age (23 and 49 percent membership). Women's clubs were most popular at ages 49 to 53 (38 percent belonging). At 54 to 58, 30 percent belonged to "athletics, sports, hobby, and recreational" organizations, 30 percent to "religious and welfare," 20 percent to patriotic groups, and 18 percent to alumni groups.

The membership situation among those in the pre- and post-retirement age groups is worthy of special comment. As already noted in Figure 107, and confirmed by other studies (42, 18), membership declines and so does responsible participation as evidenced by the holding of offices and committee memberships. Other evidence shows withdrawal. Attendance decreases, and attitudes toward these organizations change. In one study, favorable attitudes toward clubs and organizations declined regularly from 50 percent of the women holding favorable views in the early sixties to 9 percent in the early nineties (18). In view of the potential adjustive value of club and organizational activities in old age, the reasons for this declining interest need examination. Cost of dues and related expenses may become prohibitive as budgets are reduced; physical infirmities as well as normal energy losses may make venturing out in unpleasant weather or for evening meetings uncomfortable or even dangerous; deafness or poor vision may limit social interaction. But the success of recently developed centers for older people suggests that such possible difficulties can be dealt with. Psychological factors may be important. Older people may feel ignored or rejected by other members or by the club leaders, may lack interest in group activities determined by younger members, or may disapprove of the actions and ideas of the younger people.

Special organizations for older people may avoid most of the above difficulties, provide opportunities for social contact with others of similar age and interests, and foster worth-while community activities, giving a sense of continued usefulness and worth. Such group activities were strongly recommended by Lillian Martin, a pioneer in the field of old age counseling, as a means of getting oldsters back into the stream of life and providing them with social support for rehabilitative efforts (70). Centers and programs exclusively for old people are not the only answer to the social needs of older people, however. Interaction with younger people has been shown to be notably characteristic of the better-adjusted oldsters when compared with those who are less well adjusted. Organizations which involve wide age ranges (such as churches or business organizations) might well plan subgroups which would somewhat adjust to the needs of older people but still keep them in the larger membership. It is unfortunate that even adult education programs often cater mainly to the interests of young or middle-aged adults, not satisfactorily serving the old.

Racial, National, and Religious Biases in Interpersonal Relations

Racial, national, and religious biases are a significant factor in all types of social relationships considered thus far in the chapter, but comment has been reserved for this separate section because the problem is of such magnitude that it might appropriately be designated the outstanding problem of modern times. How can groups—small ones within local communities, large ones among nations—of different racial, religious, and national origins learn to live together with mutual tolerance, appreciation, and respect?

EARLY DEVELOPMENT OF CONCEPTS AND BIAS

How early do youngsters begin to perceive themselves and others as being "Jewish," or "Catholic," or "Protestant," or "Negro"? And how early do biases emerge? One study showed Hawaiian children as young as three years of age perceiving the differences between Orientals and non-Orientals (103), but another indicated less recognition of differentiation between whites and Negroes in the preschool years (46), and other research has confirmed that at these ages, concepts of group membership and definitions of groups are vague and confused. By kindergarten and the first and second grades, all subjects in one study (91) were able to differentiate between Negro and white. However, 19 percent of these same white children and 53 percent of the Negro children did not know "Catholic"; 61 percent of the whites and 87 percent of the Negroes did not know the meaning of "Protestant"; and 21 percent of white children and 59 percent of the Negro children could not define "Jewish." Emerging concepts of "Jewish" and "American," according to the results of another study (40), show definition in terms of concrete activities at preschool ages but are not generalized into abstract concepts until about age 10.

It would be expected that the less explicit and evident differences among religious groups would require more time for perceptual and attitudinal discrimination to develop than would Negro-white differentiations. Differences between families and subcultures (the North and

South, for example) in the extent to which biases are made evident will influence the age at which children reared in those varying social contexts will develop concepts of religion or race. In neighborhoods or communities where conflicts are marked or where other circumstances (as having or not having religious education in the schools) focus attention, the awareness of group membership will likely be more pronounced and earlier in appearance.

Biases, in contrast to concepts and definitions, especially toward the Negro, may be evident in the early school years. Apparently, children may by then have already taken over the adult prejudices, believe in segregation ("white and colored can't play together"), show hostility ("I don't like nigger kids"), and think in stereotyped terms ("tough," "dirty," "Kill whites") (91). They seem also to be aware of the forbidden nature of the topics of race and religion, almost invariably being reserved or uneasy or tending to avoid the topic when mention of religion or race comes up. This was especially evident in Negro children at mention of Negro and white. From kindergarten to second grade there was an increase in *awareness* of group conflicts, patterns of exclusion, and forms of stereotyping and derogation and an increase in *acceptance* of prejudiced attitudes. However, there was no increase in the accuracy of information about groups over this age span (91). It is noteworthy that numerous studies have emphasized that these biases, which even at early ages are rather faithful reproductions of the prejudices of adults, are learned from adults and peers, *in the absence of direct experience with the groups themselves.* Thus, efforts to change children's attitudes will be handicapped to some degree by the inertia of the attitudes of the adult population.

Even at this early age, identification with a particular group carried with it recognized implications regarding social acceptance, anticipated conflicts with peers, security, or insecurity. Many children were threatened psychologically as a result of group prejudice. Negro and Jewish children often revealed the feelings of insecurity arising from anticipated rejection by others, sometimes even developing feelings of ambivalence toward their own group—expressions of self-hatred (91).[9]

[9] A paper by the late distinguished psychologist, Kurt Lewin, on "Bringing up the Jewish Child," *Menorah Journal*, 1940, 28:29–45, written for a Jewish audience and published in a magazine for Jewish women, stressed the importance of the Jewish child's developing a strong sense of membership in the Jewish minority group with positive feelings toward the group. This paper has been reprinted in Wayne Dennis (ed.), *Readings in Child Psychology*, Prentice-Hall, 1951, pp. 539–551.

By the time children have reached the fifth or sixth grade, they have taken over typical adult stereotypes regarding various national groups and begun to select their associates in such a way that cleavages among such groups become evident in social situations. A study of 1000 St. Louis school children (78, 79) showed substantial agreement in the preference ranking of 21 nations and races for grades 5, 6, 7, and 8, thus indicating the stability of the attitudes that have emerged by about 10 or 11 years of age. Other evidence (122, 123) suggests that, as in the case of attitudes toward the Negro, these biases develop with little if any contact with members of these groups. Concepts are often meager and incorrect.

By the same age (fifth grade), cleavages appeared in choices of whom to have sit next to one in the classroom. By this grade, "a greater number of Italian children begin to choose Italian neighbors; a great number of Japanese children begin to choose Japanese neighbors; a greater number of German children begin to choose German neighbors, etc." (82, p. 61). If choices of companions were made under conditions of freer choice than permitted by the classroom, even greater cleavage would likely appear. In one study in which children in grades 4 to 6 were asked to indicate their friends, 24 percent of those chosen by Jewish children were Jewish when the choice was limited to the classroom. But when choice could be from the whole school, 42 percent of their choices were Jewish; and when choice could be from outside the school (i. e., from the whole community), 72 percent of their choices were Jewish (38).

THE SHARPENING OF PREJUDICE IN ADOLESCENCE

It is apparent from the foregoing that by the time children reach adolescence they have already absorbed the prevailing social biases of adults and begin to select their associates accordingly. Further, their social relationships are then more likely to be perceived by their parents as possibly leading to marriage and conceivably involving intimacies of less acceptable males with their sexually mature daughters. It is likely that ethnic lines of cleavage will therefore tend then to be more sharply enforced, especially with girls.

This sharpening at adolescence of racial prejudice involving Negroes is well shown in the study from which Figure 108 was drawn. The chart also has the merit of exhibiting in quantitative terms something of the development of racial biases over the greater part of the school years.

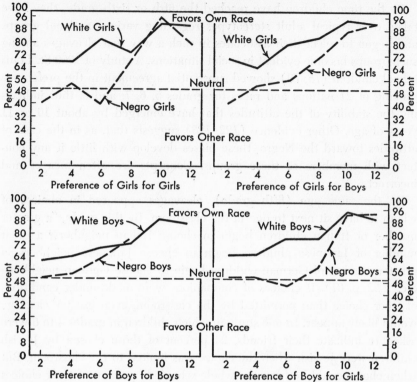

Figure 108. Extent to Which Negroes and White Children in Grades 2 Through 12 Prefer Their Own Race to the Other. (Based on data of H. L. Koch, The social distance between certain social, nationality, and skin pigmentation groups in selected populations of American school children, J. Genet. Psychol., 1946, 68:63–95.)

In this investigation children in various grades were asked to express preferences between youngsters whose names were paired together. Each child's name was paired with every other child's, and since this school contained substantial numbers of both Negroes and whites, it was possible to study preference of one race for its own members versus those of the other race. From the second grade through high school, the white children preferred their own race—and this preference became more marked with increased age. The Negroes chose one race about as readily as the other in the early grades, sometimes actually showing slightly greater preferences for whites. This slower development of own race preference is possibly a reflection of their attraction to the higher status group. Their preference for boys of their own race gradually but steadily emerges. However, a different trend is seen in their preference *for girls*. Both Negro boys and Negro girls show little racial preference for girls (they choose one race about as often as the other) until after the sixth grade. Then there is a sharp emergence of Negro preference for girls of their own age. Such sudden increase possibly results from the heightening at adolescence of social pressures brought by the whites. It would seem that Negroes of either sex are expected to "stay in their place" and white girls to associate only with "desirable" peers. It has been earlier noted that class lines are more sharply drawn as young people move into adolescence. In "class" relationships, too, greater concern is evident regarding the associates of girls—particularly upper-class girls.

Probably many northern communities show similar situations, but the reader should not infer that all communities or groups are alike in such matters. Attitudes may well be unfavorable toward Negroes in a community where they live in such numbers as to constitute a threat to the whites but more favorable in communities where there are only a few Negroes. One study (*80*), for example, found that in large urban areas, presumably having much direct contact with Negroes, children became strikingly more intolerant with increased age, whereas in small towns little or no trend toward intolerance was observed.

Probably there are similar trends as to attitudes with reference to other minority groups at adolescence, though these have not been so systematically studied. In a *Fortune* high school survey (published in 1942), 20 percent of Protestant youth said they would not consider marrying Catholics, and 52 percent would not marry Jews; 25 percent of the Catholics would not marry Protestants, and 59 percent would not marry Jews; of the Jews, about 25 percent would not marry Protestants, and about the same proportion would not marry Catholics (*31*). A recent study of selective association among various ethnic groups (non-Jewish white, Jewish, Chinese, Japanese, Negro) in a high school population revealed the ethnocentrism of the non-Jewish whites to increase with age and grade in high school (*66*). As might be expected on the basis of the facts so far presented, girls were more selective than boys. The investigators concluded that "*All* girls are bound by the social proprieties, but only boys of high status seem to be similarly restricted." This study also confirmed the implications of the marriage choices noted above that ethnic prejudice characterizes minority groups as well as majority groups. In many instances, they were even more selective than were the whites (*66*).

One further point should be made. It was noted earlier that even first- and second-graders are reticent in discussing religious and racial groups. This suggests that they are aware that the holding of biases is not considered desirable. Actually, children are exposed to a great many contradictory influences with respect to attitude development: the positive, favorable attitudes expressed as verbal "ideals" by parents, school, and church; the negative, emotional reactions that characterize the actual behavior of many of these very people who idealize on a verbal level. It might well be expected that children would learn two contradictory sets of values, one intellectual and one emotional, which would become increasingly divergent with increased age. A study of adolescent attitudes toward races conducted some years ago (80) suggests that such contradictory growth trends do indeed characterize the teens. Between the seventh and twelfth grades there was increasing *intolerance* in the instance of emotionalized, personal attitudes but increasing tolerance with respect to intellectualized attitudes. Not only do biases appear to be sharpened in adolescence; contradictions and ambivalences in attitudes also seem to be increased.

THE ADULT YEARS: AGE AND GROUP DIFFERENCES IN PREJUDICE

What happens during the adult years? As noted above, by the time youngsters reach adulthood there is almost complete cleavage between the Negro and white races as far as personal preference is concerned. Do biases become more or less pronounced from this point onward? Unfortunately, only a scattering of research results are available to provide an answer. In Table 84 are presented certain previously unpublished facts concerning the attitudes of a national sample of college graduates whose activities and attitudes have been described previously in this book. They were asked to indicate agreement or disagreement with a number of statements which (among other things) dealt with prejudice: "Children of minority groups or other races should play among themselves." "All Americans—Negroes, Jews, the foreign born, and others—should have equal opportunity in social, economic and political affairs." "Foreigners usually have peculiar and annoying habits." "Agitators and trouble-makers are more likely to be foreign citizens than native Americans." The general trend evident in the table is for responses to these items to show slightly increasing prejudice with age up to the forties or fifties, with a tendency for the curves to level off or reverse slightly from that point onward. Similar results were obtained with items dealing with internationalism (not shown in the chart). Up to the fifties, successive age groups were less internationally minded. Thereafter, the curves leveled off or reversed. Another study obtained similar results (1). For a group of average age of 34, 80 percent of whom were between 18 and 40 years of age, the correlation between age and ethnocentrism was .19, a value which while low was statistically reliable.

TABLE 84. Adult Age Trends in Bias Toward Various Groups as Reflected in the Percentage of a National Sample of College Graduates of Different Ages Who Agreed or Disagreed with Certain Statements[a]

Statement of Opinion	Sex	Age Group 24–28	39–43	54–58	64 and Over
"Agitators and trouble-makers are more likely to be foreign-born." (Agree)	M	24	38	60	66
	F	20	30	58	44
"Foreigners usually have peculiar and annoying habits." (Agree)	M	19	22	38	31
	F	13	12	24	20
"All Americans—Negroes, Jews, the foreign-born, and others—should have equal opportunity in vocational, economic, and political affairs." (Disagree)	M	12	15	13	20
	F	10	11	16	16
"Children of minority groups or other races should play among themselves." (Agree)	M	5	6	11	11
	F	6	4	6	9

[a] Only selected age groups are presented to show essential trends. Age is estimated from year of college graduation.

SOURCE: From unpublished analysis by R. G. Kuhlen of *Time Magazine* survey data.

Selected items from public opinion polls, some of which are presented in Table 85, show, in general, a trend toward increasing bias with increased adult age, but this is by no means an "across the board" matter.[10] There seems to be (within the age limits studied) no great increase in bias against admitting more Jewish exiles and Chinese to the country and no increase in concern about the influence of the Jews in this country. But there does seem to be increasing bias toward the close association of races in the armed services or on the job.

Perhaps the contrasts in these types of items involve the "intellectual decision" versus "emotional personal association" contrast noted above. It would be anticipated that different age trends would prevail in areas

[10] In this instance the facts relate to a more random sample of the general population than did Table 84 which was based on college graduates only.

of different ethnic group make-up and with respect to items differing in the amount of ego-threat involved. They would be more biased if a minority group constituted a personal threat, say, to economic security in hard times when jobs were hard to get or when a Negro family moved into a stable white neighborhood. With respect to age trends, it might be

TABLE 85. Adult Age Differences in Attitude Toward Minority Groups as Revealed by Percentages Responding in a Particular Way to Public Opinion Poll Questions[a]

	Age Group		
Attitude	18–30	31–47	48+
Would oppose a law requiring hiring of qualified persons regardless of race or color [b]	34	45	48
Think Negroes and whites should serve together in all branches of armed service	49	41	37
Think colored people in their state get a fair deal	54	72	59
Think Jews have too much power in this country	41	47	45
Think Jews have too much influence in business world	49	51	49
Would vote for a qualified Jew for President	49	47	40
Would allow more Jewish exiles into U.S.	19	22	22
Would allow Japanese who were moved inland to return to coast after the war	46	34	29
Would permit a limited number of Chinese to come into this country to become citizens	39	40	42

[a] Unless otherwise specified data are from R. P. Hinshaw, The relationship of information and opinion to age, unpublished Ph.D. dissertation, Princeton University, 1944. Questions were asked, in most instances, in about 1942 and have been rephrased into statements carrying the sense of the question and direction of the reply.

[b] From M. Strunk, The Quarter's Polls, Public Opinion Quart., 1945, Vol. 9. Age groups for this item are 21–29, 30–49, 50+.

anticipated that adults would be more concerned about race relations when they have reached the age where their children are adolescent, and less concerned later when their children are "safely" married.

What now of adult group differences in bias and prejudice, quite aside from the age of the members? Some differences have already been implied with respect to geographic location. Thus, on the question of attitude toward a law requiring employees to hire a qualified person regardless of race or color, 58 percent of those in New England and the mid-Atlantic states favored the proposition in contrast to 30 percent in the South. Forty-three percent of business and professional groups, 20 percent of farmers, and 52 percent of manual workers favor the law (15, p. 478).

People who belong to groups, at least at the high school level, are likely to be more prejudiced than nonmembers (66). This would seem a reasonable expectation as membership in an in-group, by its nature emphasizing exclusiveness, will limit choices of out-groups. But due consideration must be given to the nature of the specific group or organization. Some organizations might attract only the liberal and relatively unprejudiced, while others appeal only to the most snobbish and biased. Actually, as would be expected, organized groups show the same types of cleavages that individuals show. In New Haven, Connecticut, 90 percent of 177 women's organizations were racially exclusive; 76 percent were religiously exclusive; and more than half were structured along ethnic lines. Social class was another dimension running through these three divisional structures (80).

Table 86 contains the mean scores made by members of various groups on a scale of ethnocentrism, the scores on which reflect negative attitudes toward Jews and Negroes and positive attitudes toward the in-group (patriotism). Low scores indicate less bias. It will be noted that middle-class adults attending a labor school were least biased; a Unitarian women's group, the league of women voters, and working-class members of the labor school were also relatively low. An upper middle-class women's club and a suburban church group (both men and women) were the most ethnocentric groups of all. Presumably, such group differences are due to selective factors (the kind of people who join) as well as to the effect of the group on the members. In some instances, in-group membership itself may be a factor in producing biases toward out-groups.

Personality and Other Factors in Attitude Development and Modification

Social attitudes show a relatively high degree of patterning. Negative attitudes toward Jews, toward the Negro, and toward minority groups in general tend to go together, to be found in the same people, and to be related to other attitudes such as patriotism and political-economic conservatism (1). The same types of patterning have been found in various countries. Studies in Sweden, England, and Germany have shown relatedness among attitudes toward such diverse issues as war, Negroes, Jews, child-rearing methods, political issues, sex education, and capital

TABLE 86.   Mean Ethnocentrism Score of Members of Various Organizations. Low Scores Reflect Least Bias

Group	N	Mean Score
Suburban church group (men)	31	5.38
Suburban church group (women)	29	5.23
Upper middle-class women's club	36	5.05
International Longshoremen's Union (CIO) (new members)	26	4.60
United Electrical Workers (CIO) (Old members)	12	3.45
Parent-Teacher Association (men and women)	75	3.13
Labor school (working-class men)	15	2.41
Unitarian church group (women)	15	2.32
League of Women Voters	17	2.06
Labor school (Middle-class men)	9	1.27

SOURCE: Adapted from T. W. Adorno, Else Frenkel-Brunswik, D. J. Levinson, and R. N. Sanford, The Authoritarian Personality, New York, Harper, 1950, p. 194.

punishment (28). Those who expressed uncritical acceptance of religion and the church were more anti-Semitic than those who were critical of the church (1). And in one religious group, those who were most firm and orthodox in their views showed more bias toward the Negro and were more in favor of segregation (86).

PERSONALITY ORGANIZATION AND ATTITUDE FORMATION

A very stimulating and challenging study of attitudes led to the conclusion that "anti-Semitism or anti-Negroism, for example, are not isolated attitudes but are parts of a relatively unified ethnocentric ideology . . . [and that] . . . ethnocentrism itself is but one aspect of a broader pattern of social thinking and group functioning" (1, p. 207). Not only do ethnocentric individuals tend to reject all out-groups, but they seem able to find "in-group–out-group" distinctions in almost any context. It seems reasonable to surmise that the source of their bias lies within their own personalities rather than in the actual characteristics of the group. Further investigation, including extensive interviews and projective testing, confirmed this expectation. Deep-seated personality trends seemed to be involved which caused the prejudiced person to have a strong psychological need for an out-group on which to project prejudice.

Why would a person have such needs? Extensive research on college students and other adult groups (1) seemed to yield a picture of the ethnocentric person as one whose early childhood involved strict and rather arbitrary enforcement of narrow conventionalistic rules of conduct by parents who themselves had strong status needs, conformity being insisted upon as a necessary condition of social acceptance. The child apparently became unable to admit to himself his own weaknesses and incapacities and repressed many of his own hostilities and other impulses (such as sexual impulses, many expressions of which are not permitted by strict morality), with the result that he projected these traits upon others, especially out-groups. The prejudiced person was typically a rigid personality who thought in stereotyped terms and who, unable to tolerate ambiguity, was forced to see things in sharp black and white contrasts. In contrast, the unprejudiced person often had anxieties and problems—including the same kinds of inadequacies and impulses—but seemed able to admit and accept these traits and was a much freer, less defensive, more flexible person. This contrasting type of person was likely to have had a family background involving greater permissiveness, more direct and easy expression of affection, and greater individuation of treatment.[11]

These contrasting patterns of behavior between prejudiced and unprejudiced individuals, as well as contrasting family backgrounds, were evident as early as 11 years of age in a study done by one of the same investigators (33). And other research has confirmed the interrelationship of ethnic attitudes as early as the fifth grade (35, 39) and has also indicated at this young age a relationship between traditional family child-rearing practices and prejudice. Other studies suggest that these contrasts in behavior tendencies are evident in a wide variety of situations, including problem-solving, and show up in various ways in attitudes toward self and others (32). It has been shown, for example, that the prejudice-disposed type of person is lacking in self-insight compared to the unprejudiced (25) and that he is less sensitive to (i. e., less able to judge correctly) the characteristics of others in social situations (96).

Other less general but nonetheless dynamic interpretations of prejudice include the "scapegoat theory" which views prejudice as resulting from displacement of aggression growing out of general frustration (perhaps of an economic sort) upon a minority group, a group toward which hostility may be "safely" expressed in the culture. Bias may also be the result of fairly direct threat, as, for example, the threat of reduced property values if Negroes move into a neighborhood. It is likely that such bias would be directed toward *any* individual or family who threatened the standards and the property values of others in the neighborhood, perhaps by failing

---

[11] This formulation appears to have validity if it is not viewed as the *only* explanation of ethnic bias. It has, however, been criticized extensively (20). Other investigators have been unable to demonstrate unequivocally that "rigidity" is a general trait or that "rigidity" is highly correlated with bias. But there has also been some confirmation by other investigators.

to keep property in good repair. But the insecure or prejudice-prone individual is likely to react more vigorously to such threat, whether real or imagined.

If prejudice is deep-rooted in personality and is produced by such underlying dynamics as have been suggested, then the fundamental procedures for combating prejudice will be those which, instead of dealing with the surface symptoms (the specific prejudices themselves), will involve attempts to improve the adjustment of the individual and foster from early childhood the development of the type of personality which does not "need" to be prejudiced. The first type of method is that of psychotherapy; the second requires changes in child-rearing practices in the direction of greater permissiveness, greater and more consistent show of affection, and less authoritarian procedures.[12] It would be expected, in the light of this formulation, that efforts aimed at reducing prejudice toward a specific minority may reduce that prejudice only to have it crop out again with reference to some other group.

Research confirms the view that alterations in personality are likely to be paralleled by changes in attitudes toward others. Change during the process of psychotherapy includes a gradual increase in self-acceptance, a trend which is correlated with an increase in favorable attitudes toward others (97, p. 105). A number of other studies have confirmed, though not in a therapy situation, the relationship between acceptance of self and acceptance of others (85, 89). But therapy is expensive in both time and money, trained personnel is limited in supply, and there would be problems of getting prejudiced people to accept treatment. What about similar procedures adapted to groups—group discussions (or group therapy)—in school classes or the "acting out" of interpersonal problems in classroom "psychodramas"? Some evidence indicates that bias may be reduced through employing these procedures (119). Such group procedures, too, presumably make their impact upon prejudice by affecting personality, though less profoundly than does long-term personal therapy. Where such personality factors are involved in prejudice, it would seem that almost any method which promotes personal adjustment, and gives an individual a sense of security and self-acceptance, would

[12] The California group comments upon the difficulties of changing child-rearing practices since to a considerable degree such practices are (like prejudice itself) merely symptoms or manifestations of the parental personality structure. In summing up, however, these investigators say: "All that is really essential is that children be genuinely loved and treated as individual humans" (1, p. 975).

reduce one's need to project hostility onto others and have as a by-product the reduction of prejudice.

SOCIAL AND OTHER INFLUENCES UPON ATTITUDES

The foregoing emphasis upon personality factors should not obscure the role that factors external to the individual play in attitude development and change. Although social attitudes do tend to be intercorrelated, the correlations are not so high as to preclude the possibility that different factors may influence attitudes toward different groups. Thus, one investigator who studied attitudes in the "deep South" observed that of 258 persons who had attitudes favorable toward the Jews, 61 percent were anti-Negro. He concluded that "the problem of the 'American dilemma' cannot be solved by approaching it from the level of personality dynamics alone. Situational, historical, and cultural factors appear to be of considerable, perhaps major import" (90).

First is the matter of degree of contact with minority groups. It was noted earlier that attitudes toward Negroes and other minority groups may develop at a very early age, without the child's having direct experiences with members of that group. If the information and attitudes conveyed to him by his parents and others are notably inconsistent with the actual characteristics of the object of prejudice, further experience and information should result in some correction of concepts and some reduction in bias.

Usually, this does seem to happen. Of 46 graduate student subjects who participated, as part of an experiment, with Negroes in Harlem in a variety of social activities, all but 6 became less prejudiced as a result (98). Similar modification in attitude seems often to occur under normal living conditions. A study of neighborhoods in Minneapolis where only one or two Negro families lived found that those who lived nearest them had greater personal interaction *and were less biased* than those who lived farther away. This was especially true in areas where the Negroes had lived for 10 years or more but was still the case where they had resided for only 2 years (94). Presumably, this long-time experience resulted in neighbors learning to react to individual Negroes as individuals and thus in terms of personal qualities and also learning through experience that Negroes did not constitute a personal threat. In Duluth, Minnesota, where practically all Negroes live in predominantly white neighborhoods, 82 percent of the heads of the Negro families indicated that they had not been the object of neighborhood discrimination because of race (*114*). Such studies suggest that, over a long period of time, substantial gains in interrace relations may be hoped for.

However, increasing contact and experience may *not* reduce bias if there is a very strong institutionalized pattern of racial prejudice and subordination, as in the South, if the Negro group is large enough to constitute a threat or if "infiltration" has been substantial and recent. Thus, another Minneapolis study found bias toward the Negro greater in a neighborhood where infiltration had been recent and substantial than in a similar neighborhood with few Negro residents (*5*). And a study mentioned earlier (*80*) reported increases with ages in intolerance in cities where presumably the youngsters had much contact—but likely not the intimate contact involved in living near Negroes.

What about other methods of influencing social attitudes which are more manageable than transplanting people to new neighborhoods! A host of studies have investigated the influence on attitudes of courses of study, motion pictures, information presented in oral and written form, persuasive arguments, emotional appeal, and various devious propaganda subterfuges (*83*, p. 121). One critical review of such investigations concluded that ". . . the weight of evidence from published studies is that the stimuli tested (school and college courses, specific propaganda, personal contacts, information, and general education) do result in or are accompanied by attitude changes in a 'positive' direction. On the other hand, nearly half of the studies have found inconclusive results or no change in attitude" (*121*, p. 27). Such results demonstrate both the potential value of environmental manipulation in influencing attitudes and the importance of careful consideration of the method used, the group with whom it is used, the individual using it, the general social context (deep South, wartime, etc.), and other possible conflicting or facilitating factors. Clearly, it will be unreasonable for a teacher, parent, or other interested person to assume that specific efforts to change social attitudes will necessarily have the desired outcome.

Social group influence might be supposed especially helpful in efforts to change attitudes, since much social learning and reënforcement of that learning occur in groups to which people relate. It is in the group context, mainly, that the powerful influence of social rewards and punishments—approval and acceptance or disapproval and rejection—is brought to bear. In many instances, groups promote desirable attitudes and reenforce teachings of home, school, and church; in other instances, they represent counterpressures of such strength as essentially to negate efforts of other agencies. The group with which a person identifies represents an important factor in the nature of prejudices held (1). Simply knowing the opinions held by others, whether "experts" or one's colleagues in a classroom, will cause shifts in measured attitudes. Group-anchored attitudes have been found especially difficult to change (57). Recognition of these facts has led certain investigators to study the possibilities of enlisting the group itself as an instrument in attitude change. A recent summary of such work has emphasized that the degree of change produced will depend upon the extent to which the individual finds the group attractive and has a sense of belonging to it, the extent to which the attitudes involved are relevant to the basis of his attraction to the group, the extent to which decisions to change and information relevant to the change and the need to change are shared widely within the group, and the degree to which efforts to change the individual are in the direction of making him like the group or a deviate from its norms (17).

Seen in this connection, the group relations of adolescents and other age groups take on a new importance as formative and supporting influences in ideology generally. The cleavages among groups along racial, religious, ethnic, and social-class lines noted earlier in the chapter suggest the role of values in group formation. It is likely that these group associations will serve mainly to reënforce existing biases, unless imaginative and constructive efforts are made by participant leaders to utilize the group itself as a means of combating prejudice.

The total evidence thus indicates that a variety of interacting causes bring about social attitudes. They are rooted in culture patterns, are influenced by information and experiences which serve to confirm or deny the correctness of early conceptions, are susceptible to emotional appeals, and are modified by associates and groups who approve and reward certain values and disapprove others (95). Just how such experiences, social influences, and information are assimilated or reacted to will depend in part upon basic personality trends—upon the predispositions the individual brings to the situation. Sometimes these basic trends may be the primary cause of the attitudes held and be so all-pervasive as to render the individual almost impervious to efforts involving environmental manipulation. But even in these cases, procedures such as role-playing may change concepts of in-group–out-group relations, and authoritarian proscription (laws against segregation and discrimination) may take advantage of the prejudiced individuals' tendency to submit to strong authority. An illustration of the *interaction* of experience and personality in producing attitude change—or in rendering the experience ineffectual—follows:

In one notable study (84), attitude changes were studied in white children who for four weeks attended a summer camp which also enrolled about an equal number of Negro children. No segregation of any kind existed in the camp; the boys—all nonpaying clients from lower-class groups—lived, ate, and played together. The effects of this experience on attitudes varied from one youngster to another. Those who decreased in prejudice toward the Negro tended to be those boys who had relatively few aggressive needs, who had less feeling that punishment or retaliation would follow expression of aggression, and who tended to be rather well satisfied with the camp experience and were accepted by other boys in the camp. Those whose prejudice increased were boys who were dissatisfied with the camp experience, initially characterized by greater aggressive feelings and needs to defy authority, but expecting that expression of aggression would lead to punishment. For this reason they did not "act out" their aggression but instead displaced and projected it in the form of prejudice directed toward the Negro boys. The general conclusion seemed warranted that whether or not direct experiences with a minority group (or, presumably, vicarious experience and information) will reduce prejudice will depend in part upon the personality of the individual and in part upon the degree to which he feels the group experiences and associations to be rewarding.

Summary

The development of an individual's social life from early childhood to old age—of central importance to his welfare, effectiveness, happiness, and total psychological adjustment—may be summarized as follows:

1. Significant changes in social reactions are evident in the first years of life, and by the time the child starts school he has already developed certain patterns (e. g., competitiveness) typical of the culture. Childhood and adolescence represent periods of expanding social life and increasing stability of social relationships. Friendships and acceptance by peer groups become important. Specific friendships are best understood in terms of the ways in which, and the extent to which, one person satisfies needs of the other. Parents interested in good social development of their offspring should provide opportunities for them to be with others and help them to develop broad interests and social skills, thus increasing

their friendship potential. Parents should also be sensitive to the *changing* evaluations the peer groups place upon various traits as the child matures. It is how other children see the youngster (not how the parent sees him) that counts with the peer group.

2. The social scene becomes increasingly structured as children mature, cleavages appearing along racial, sociocultural, religious, and ethnic lines. Such distinctions become sharper at adolescence, especially for girls, as adults and other groups with higher status exert pressures. A characteristic cleavage along sex lines is most pronounced at the age of pubescence or somewhat earlier, and it is thought to be a product of development of sex role identification and possibly a defensive rejection of the opposite sex in an effort to reduce anxiety arising from new sex urges. The question is nonetheless raised as to whether more constructive efforts by home and school to promote easy social relations between the sexes might not reduce this split somewhat and make the heterosexual adjustments of adolescence easier.

3. Formal group interactions present important opportunities for social learning. Yet extracurricular activities are highly selective, most participants being the already better-adjusted and socially effective individuals from the upper socioeconomic levels. The question is raised as to whether schools might not make more constructive use of extracurricular programs to aid those who most need social experience.

4. The expansion of the social world continues during adolescence and into the adult years, until around the age of 50. From that point on, there is gradual withdrawal. This cycle of early expansion and later restriction of the social life is noticeable in various ways. There is psychosocial growth well beyond the years when many writers have assumed life to become relatively static and (presumably) opportunities for continued personality development minimal. The question is raised as to whether the social withdrawal occurring beyond age 50 is necessary or psychologically desirable. A more constructive gearing of social programs to *all* ages may result in opportunities for continued enrichment of living and a sense of belongingness at ages when it is much needed.

5. The strong influence of social-class lines is apparent in the pattern of social interaction at all ages. Snobbish enforcement of these lines in childhood and adolescence not only causes the rejected much unhappiness, but it probably has pervasive effects upon personality development as well as upon educational and vocational aspirations. The American middle-class success ideal is still much in evidence, and increased age

seems to bring some average increase in social-class level, though most are static, many are "clinging" or "straining," and some are definitely downwardly mobile. Some evidence suggests that drive for upward mobility and the upward mobility itself do not necessarily involve the good psychological adjustment often coupled in popular opinion with the "American success story." Hostilities and anxieties stemming from unhappy early family relations may provide the requisite drive but may also make for less warm social relationships along the way.

6. Prejudices against racial, religious, and ethnic groups other than one's own are evident early in life, apparently being "taken over" ready-made from adults. Imitation and learning as a result of approvals and disapprovals of peer groups are undoubtedly important factors in the development of prejudice, yet substantial evidence shows that prejudice is sometimes deep-rooted in the personality. Thus, different individuals may react quite differently to efforts to reduce bias by providing contacts with minority groups. Where basic personality factors are involved, methods directed at improving personal adjustment or altering the personality structure of the person, rather than aimed at the symptoms (the prejudice itself), are likely to be the more successful.

BIBLIOGRAPHY

1. Adorno, T. W., Frenkel-Brunswik, Else, Levinson, D. J., and Sanford, R. N., *The Authoritarian Personality,* New York, Harper, 1950.
2. Aldrich, Margaret G., An exploratory study of social guidance at the college level, *J. Educ. and Psychol. Meas.,* 1942, 2:207–216.
3. Austin, Mary C., and Thompson, G. G., Children's friendships: a study of the bases on which children select and reject their best friends, *J. Educ. Psychol.,* 1948, 39:101–116.
4. Ausubel, D. P., Schiff, H. M., and Gasser, E. B., A preliminary study of developmental trends in socioempathy: accuracy of perception of own and others sociometric status, *Child Development,* 1952, 23:113–128.
5. Bird, C., Monachesi, E. D., and Burdick, H., Infiltration and the attitudes of white and Negro parents and children, *J. Abnorm. and Soc. Psychol.,* 1952, 47:688–699.
6. Bock, R. D., A synthesis of time sampling and sociometric sampling, *Sociometry,* 1952, 15:263–271.
7. Bogardus, Ruth, and Otto, Phyllis, Social psychology of chums, *Sociol. and Soc. Res.,* 1936, 20:260–270.
8. Bonney, M. E., Sociometric study of agreement between teachers' judgments and student choices, *Sociometry,* 1947, 10:133–146.
9. Bonney, M. E., A sociometric study of the relationship of some factors

to mutual friendships on the elementary, secondary, and college levels, *Sociometry*, 1946, 9:21–47.

10. Bonney, M. E., Hoblit, R. E., and Dreyer, A. H., A study of some factors related to sociometric status in a men's dormitory, *Sociometry*, 1953, *16*:287–301.

11. Bretsch, H. S., Social skills and activities of socially accepted and unaccepted adolescents, *J. Educ. Psychol.*, 1952, *43*:449–458.

12. Burgess, E. W., Social relations, activities, and personal adjustment, *Amer. J. Sociol.*, 1954, *59*:352–360.

13. Bushee, F. A., Social organizations in a small city, *Amer. J. Sociol.*, 1945, *51*:217–226.

14. Campbell, E. H., The social-sex development of children, *Genet. Psychol. Monogr.*, 1939, *21*:461–552.

15. Cantril, H., *Public Opinion, 1935–1946*. Princeton, Princeton University Press, 1951.

16. Caplow, T., and Forman, R., Neighborhood interaction in a homogeneous community, *Amer. Sociol. Rev.*, 1950, *15*:357–366.

17. Cartwright, D., Achieving change in people: some applications of group dynamics theory, *Human Relations*, 1951, *4*:381–392.

18. Cavan, R. S., Burgess, E. W., Havighurst, R. J., and Goldhamer, H., *Personal Adjustment in Old Age*, Chicago, Science Research Associates, 1949.

19. Centers, R., *The Psychology of Social Classes*, Princeton, Princeton University Press, 1949.

20. Christie, R., and Jahoda, M. (eds.), *Studies in the Scope and Method of "The Authoritarian Personality,"* Glencoe (Illinois), The Free Press, 1954.

21. Cox, F. N., Sociometric status and individual adjustment before and after play therapy, *J. Abnorm. and Soc. Psychol.*, 1953, *48*:354–356.

22. Crowley, J. J., High school backgrounds of successful men and women, *School Rev.*, 1940, *48*:205–209.

23. Dimock, H. S., *Rediscovering the Adolescent*, New York, Association Press, 1937.

24. Donahue, Wilma, A study of the socialization of old people, *Geriat.*, 1953, *8*:656–666.

25. Dorris, R. J., Levinson, D. J., and Haufmann, E., Authoritarian personality studied by a new variation of the sentence completion technique, *J. Abnorm. and Soc. Psychol.*, 1954, *49*:99–108.

26. Dotson, F., Patterns of voluntary association among urban working-class families, *Amer. Sociol. Rev.*, 1951, *16*:687–893.

27. Ellis, Evelyn, Social psychological correlates of upward social mobility among unmarried career women, *Amer. Sociol. Rev.*, 1952, *17*:558–563.

28. Eysenck, H. J., Primary social attitudes: a comparison of attitude patterns in England, Germany, and Sweden, *J. Abnorm. and Soc. Psychol.*, 1953, *48*:563–568.

29. Festinger, L., Schachter, S., and Back, K., *Social Pressures in Informal Groups*, New York, Harper, 1950.

30. Flemming, E. G., Best friends, *J. Soc. Psychol.*, 1932, *3*:385–390.
31. *Fortune Survey:* Youth has its say about itself and the world, *Fortune*, 1942, *26*:8–20.
32. Frenkel-Brunswik, Else, Intolerance of ambiguity as an emotional and perceptual personality variable, *J. Personal.*, 1949, *18*:108–143.
33. Frenkel-Brunswik, Else, A study of prejudice in children, *Human Relations*, 1948, *1*:295–306.
34. Gibbons, C. C., and Porter, J. P., Some aspects of social adaptability among adolescents, *J. Appl. Psychol.*, 1939, *23*:508–520.
35. Gough, H. G., Harris, D. B., Martin, W. E., and Edwards, M., Children's ethnic attitudes: I. Relationship to certain personality factors, *Child Development*, 1950, *21*:83–91.
36. Gronlund, N. E., The accuracy of teachers' judgments concerning the sociometric status of sixth-grade pupils, *Sociometry*, 1950, *13*:197–225, 329–357.
37. Hanley, C., Physique and reputation of junior high school boys, *Child Development*, 1951, *22*:247–260.
38. Harris, Adeline, and Watson, G., Are Jewish or Gentile children more clannish? *J. Soc. Psychol.*, 1946, *24*:71–76.
39. Harris, D. B., Gough, H. G., and Martin, W. E., Children's ethnic attitudes: II. Relationship to parental beliefs concerning child training, *Child Development*, 1950, *21*:169–181.
40. Hartley, E. L., Rosenbaum, M., and Schwartz, S., Children's perceptions of ethnic group membership, *J. Psychol.*, 1948, *26*:387–398.
41. Hattwick, L. A., and Sanders, M. K., Age differences in behavior at the nursery school level, *Child Development*, 1938, *9*:27–47.
42. Havighurst, R. J., and Albrecht, R., *Older People*, New York, Longmans, Green, 1953.
43. Havighurst, R. J., and Taba, H., *Adolescent Character and Personality*, New York, Wiley, 1949.
44. Hinshaw, R. P., The relationship of information and opinion to age. Unpublished Ph.D. dissertation, Princeton University, 1944.
45. Hollingshead, A. B., *Elmtown's Youth*, New York, Wiley, 1949.
46. Horowitz, R. E., Racial aspects of self-identification in nursery school children, *J. Psychol.*, 1939, *7*:91–99.
47. Horrocks, J. E., and Buker, M. E., A study of the friendship fluctuations of preadolescents, *J. Genet. Psychol.*, 1951, *78*:131–144.
48. Horrocks, J. E., and Thompson, G. G., A study of the friendship fluctuations of rural boys and girls, *J. Genet. Psychol.*, 1946, *69*:189–198.
49. Hutson, P. W., and Kover, D. R., Some problems of senior-high-school pupils in their social recreation, *Educational Administration and Supervision*, 1942, *28*:503–519.
50. Jennings, Helen H., *Leadership and Isolation*, New York, Longmans, Green, 1943.
51. Jennings, Helen H., *Sociometry in Group Relations: A Work Guide for Teachers*, Washington, D.C., American Council on Education, 1948.

52. Johnson, B. E., An evaluation of normal school sororities, *J. Exper. Educ.*, 1938, 7:49–54.

53. Jones, H. E., *Development in Adolescence*, New York, Appleton-Century-Crofts, 1943.

54. Jones, H. E., Physical ability as a factor in social adjustment in adolescence, *J. Educ. Res.*, 1946, 40:287–301.

55. Jones, Mary C., and Bayley, Nancy, Physical maturing among boys as related to behavior, *J. Educ. Psychol.*, 1950, 41:129–148.

56. Katz, D., and Allport, F. H., *Students' Attitudes, A. Report of the Syracuse University Reaction Study*, Syracuse, (New York), The Craftsman Press, 1931.

57. Kelley, H. H., and Volkart, E. H., The resistance to change of group-anchored attitudes, *Amer. Sociol. Rev.*, 1952, 17:453–465.

58. Koch, H. L., The social distance between certain racial, nationality, and skin pigmentation groups in selected populations of American school children, *J. Genet. Psychol.*, 1946, 68:63–95.

59. Koch, H. L., A study of some factors conditioning social distance between the sexes, *J. Soc. Psychol.*, 1944, 20:79–107.

60. Kuhlen, R. G., and Bretsch, H. S., Sociometric status and personal problems of adolescents, *Sociometry*, 1947, 10:122–132.

61. Kuhlen, R. G., and Lee, B. J., Personality characteristics and social acceptability in adolescence, *J. Educ. Psychol.*, 1943, 34:321–340.

62. Leevy, R. J., Leisure time of the American housewife, *Sociol. and Soc. Res.*, 1950, 35:97–105.

63. Leevy, R. J., Social competence of high-school youth, *School Rev.*, 1943, 51:342–347.

64. Levi, I. J., Student leadership in elementary and junior high school and its transfer into senior high school, *J. Educ. Res.*, 1930, 22:135–139.

65. Lucina, Sister M., Sex differences in adolescent attitudes toward best friends, *School Rev.*, 1940, 48:512–516.

66. Lundberg, G. A., and Dickson, L., Selective association among ethnic groups in a high school population, *Amer. Sociol. Rev.*, 1952, 17:23–35.

67. Lundberg, G. A., and Kluge, N., A restudy of a Vermont village after eight years, *Sociometry*, 1946, 9:124–125.

68. Lundberg, G. A., and Steel, Mary, Social attraction patterns in a village, *Sociometry*, 1938, 1:375–419.

69. Mangus, A. R., and Cottam, H. R., Level of living, social participation, and adjustment of Ohio farm people, Wooster (Ohio), *Ohio Agr. Exp. Sta. Bull. 624*, 1941.

70. Martin, L. J., *A Handbook for Old Age Counselors*, San Francisco, Geertz Printing Co., 1944.

71. Mather, W. C., Income and social participation, *Amer. Sociol. Rev.*, 1941, 6:380–384.

72. Maudry, Maria, and Nekula, Maria, Social relations between children of the same age during the first two years of life, *J. Genet. Psychol.*, 1939, 54:193–215.

73. Mayo, S. C., Age profiles of social participation in rural areas of Wake County, North Carolina, *Rural Sociol.*, 1950, *15*:242–251.

74. Mayo, S. C., Social participation among the older population in rural areas of Wake County, North Carolina, *Social Forces*, 1951, *30*:53–59.

75. Mayo, S. C., and Marsh, C. P., Social participation in the rural community, *Amer. J. Sociol.*, 1951, *57*:243–248.

76. McGuire, C., Social stratification and mobility patterns, *Amer. Sociol. Rev.*, 1950, *15*:195–204.

77. McGuire, C., and Clark, R. A., Age-mate acceptance and indices of peer status, *Child Development*, 1952, *23*:141–154.

78. Meltzer, H., Children's thinking about nations and races, *J. Genet. Psychol.*, 1941, *58*:181–199.

79. Meltzer, H., The development of children's nationality preferences, concepts, and attitudes, *J. Psychol.*, 1941, *11*:343–358.

80. Minard, R. D., Race attitudes of Iowa children, *University of Iowa, Studies in Character*, 1931, Vol. 4, No. 2.

81. Minnia, Mhyra, Cleavage in women's organizations: a reflection of the social structure of a city, *Amer. Sociol. Rev.*, 1953, *18*:47–53.

82. Moreno, J. L., *Who Shall Survive? A New Approach to the Problem of Human Relations*, Washington, D.C., Nervous and Mental Disease Publishing Company, 1934.

83. Murphy, G., Murphy, L. B., and Newcomb, T. M., *Experimental Social Psychology*, New York, Harper, 1937.

84. Mussen, P. H., Some personality and social factors related to changes in children's attitudes toward Negroes, *J. Abnorm. and Soc. Psychol.*, 1950, *45*:423–441.

85. Omwake, K. T., The relation between acceptance of self and acceptance of others shown by three personality inventories, *J. Consult. Psychol.*, 1954, *18*:443–446.

86. O'Reilly, C. T., and O'Reilly, E. J., Religious beliefs of Catholic college students and their attitudes toward minorities, *J. Abnorm. and Soc. Psychol.*, 1954, *49*:378–380.

87. Parten, M. B., Leadership among preschool children, *J. Abnorm. and Soc. Psychol.*, 1932–1933, *27*:430–440.

88. Parten, M. B., Social participation among preschool children, *J. Abnorm. and Soc. Psychol.*, 1932–1933, *27*:243–269.

89. Philips, E. L., Attitudes toward self and others: a brief questionnaire report, *J. Consult. Psychol.*, 1951, *15*:79–81.

90. Prothro, E. T., Ethnocentrism and anti-Negro attitudes in the deep South, *J. Abnorm. and Soc. Psychol.*, 1952, *47*:105–108.

91. Radke, M., Trager, H. G., and Davis, H., Social perceptions and attitudes of children, *Genet. Psychol. Monogr.*, 1949, *40*:327–447.

92. Reader, N., and English, H. B., Personality factors in adolescent female friendships, *J. Consult. Psychol.*, 1947, *11*:212–220.

93. Reid, I. D., and Ehle, E. L., Leadership selection in urban locality areas, *Public Opinion Quart.*, 1950, *14*:262–284.

94. Rose, A. M., Atelsek, F. J., and McDonald, L. R., Neighborhood reactions to isolated Negro residents: an alternative to invasion and succession, *Amer. Sociol. Rev.*, 1953, *18*:497–507.

95. Sarnoff, I., and Katz, D., The motivational bases of attitude change, *J. Abnorm. and Soc. Psychol.*, 1954, *49*:115–124.

96. Scodel, A., and Mussen, P., Social perceptions of authoritarians and non-authoritarians, *J. Abnorm. and Soc. Psychol.*, 1953, *48*:181–189.

97. Sheerer, Elizabeth T., An analysis of the relationship between acceptance of and respect for self and acceptance of and respect for others in ten counseling cases, *J. Consult. Psychol.*, 1949, *13*:169–175.

98. Smith, F. T., *An Experiment in Modifying Attitudes toward the Negro*, New York, Teachers College, Columbia University, 1933.

99. Smith, H. P., The relationship between scores on the Bell Adjustment Inventory and participation in extracurricular activities, *J. Educ. Psychol.*, 1947, *38*:11–16.

100. Smith, H. P., A study in the selective character of secondary education: participation in school activities as conditioned by socio-economic status and other factors, *J. Educ. Psychol.*, 1945, *36*:229–246.

101. Smith, J., Form, W. H., and Stone, G. P., Local intimacy in a middle-sized city, *Amer. J. Sociol.*, 1954, *60*:276–284.

102. Spiegel, L. A., A review of contributions to a psychoanalytic theory of adolescence: individual aspects, in *The Psychoanalytic Study of the Child*, New York, International University Press, 1951, Vol. IV, pp. 353–393.

103. Springer, D. V., Awareness of racial differences by pre-school children in Hawaii, *Genet. Psychol. Monogr.*, 1950, *41*:215–270.

104. Stendler, C. B., *Children of Brasstown*, Urbana (Illinois), University of Illinois Press, 1949.

105. Stock, Dorothy, An investigation into the interrelations between the self-concept and feelings directed toward other persons and groups, *J. Consult. Psychol.*, 1949, *13*:176–180.

106. Strong, E. K., Jr., *Change of Interests with Age*, Stanford, Stanford University Press, 1931.

107. Sullivan, P. L., and Adelson, J., Ethnocentrism and misanthropy, *J. Abnorm. and Soc. Psychol.*, 1954, *49*:246–250.

108. Sweetser, F. L., *Neighborhood Acquaintance: A Study of Personal Neighborhoods*, New York, 1941, Privately printed Ph.D. dissertation in Political Science, Columbia University.

109. Thompson, G. G., and Horrocks, J. E., A study of the friendship fluctuations of urban boys and girls, *J. Genet. Psychol.*, 1947, *70*:53–63.

110. Tryon, C. M., Evaluation of adolescent personality by adolescents, *Monogr. of the Society for Research in Child Development*, 1939, Vol. IV, No. 4.

111. Tryon, C. M., *U C Inventory I. Social and Emotional Adjustment*, Berkeley, University of California, 1939 (two 40-page multigraphed booklets bound together).

112. Tuckman, J., and Lorge, I., The best years in life: a study in ranking, *J. Psychol.*, 1952, *34*:137–149.
113. Tuddenham, R. D., Studies in reputation III: Correlates of popularity among elementary school children, *J. Educ. Psychol.*, 1951, *42*:257–276.
114. Turbeville, G., The Negro population in Duluth, Minnesota, 1950, *Sociol. and Soc. Res.*, 1952, *36*:231–238.
115. Walton, W. E., Empathic responses in children, *Psychol. Monogr.*, 1936, *48*:40–67.
116. Warner, W. L., and Lunt, P. S., *The Social Life of a Modern Community*, New Haven, Yale University Press, 1941.
117. Warner, W. L., *et al.*, *Democracy in Jonesville*, New York, Harper, 1949.
118. West, J. (pseud.), *Plainville, U.S.A.*, New York, Columbia University Press, 1945.
119. Wieder, G. S., Group procedures modifying attitudes of prejudice in the college classroom, *J. Educ. Psychol.*, 1954, *45*:332–344.
120. Willerman, B., and Swanson, L., An ecological determinant of differential amounts of sociometric choices within college sororities, *Sociometry*, 1952, *15*:326–329.
121. Williams, R. M., Jr., *The Reduction of Intergroup Tensions: A Study of Research on Problems of Ethnic, Racial, and Religious Group Relations*, Social Science Research Council, Bulletin No. 57, 1947.
122. Zeligs, R., Racial attitudes of children as expressed in their concepts of races, *Sociol. and Soc. Res.*, 1937, *21*:361–371.
123. Zeligs, R., and Hendrickson, G., Factors regarded by children as the basis of their social attitude, *Sociol. and Soc. Res.*, 1935, *19*:225–233.

CHAPTER 12 •

• Heterosexual Development, Marriage, and Family Relationships

ONE highly significant aspect of interpersonal relations—that of heterosexual development and adjustment—was subordinated in the discussion of the previous chapter because the topic warrants more extensive consideration than could be accorded there. Few experiences in the life of the adolescent are as exciting as his relationships with the opposite sex; the event of marriage stands out in retrospect for most people as the major happy point of a lifetime; seldom are social relationships as meaningful for total life happiness or as enduring as the intimate relationships between spouses and within the family constellation. Little wonder that the achievement of heterosexual adjustment is considered one of the fundamental "tasks" of adolescence or that parents should, more than anything else, desire a happy marriage for their children and should evaluate their own life success partly in terms of the success of their marriage. What can be said of the social relationships leading to choice of mate? What factors condition the particular selection? How frequently and to what extent is good marital adjustment achieved and maintained as time passes? And what problems characterize human interaction in the family setting?

Dating and Courtship: From First Date to Marriage

DATING

On the average, children begin "dating" around 14 years of age. As Table 87 shows, slightly under half of a broad sample of high school freshman boys and girls were having dates whereas among high school seniors only 22 percent of the boys and 14 percent of the girls were *not* having dates. But some—about 10 percent of the ninth-graders and between 20 percent (for boys) and 35 percent (for girls) of the twelfth-graders—had dates as often as two or three times a week. The facts are, of course, for present-day America, and represent averages which may not characterize particular sections of the country or even particular neighborhoods.

TABLE 87.   The Percentage Frequency with Which High School
Freshmen and Seniors Had Dates

	Number of Cases	Number of Dates per Month			
		None	1–4	5–10	Over 10
Freshmen					
Boys	1276	54	21	16	10
Girls	1490	53	21	17	9
Seniors					
Boys	1408	22	29	29	20
Girls	1454	14	19	33	34

SOURCE: From H. H. Punke, Dating practices of high school youth, *Bull.* of *National Association of Secondary School Principals,* 1944, 28:47–54.

Some readers may be surprised to note that both boys and girls begin dating at about the same age, contrary to expectations in view of earlier pubescence of girls and their greater and earlier sex-social interests. It would appear that initial dating is occasioned not so much by the first inkling of biological interest in the opposite sex as by opportunity or expectation growing out of, for example, school social events. Although the timing of such activities may be a cultural adaptation to the facts of biological development, the timing seems not overly sensitive to general sex differences or, for that matter, to differences among individuals of the same sex. The grouping of children on a chronological age basis in classes in the public schools is likely a determining factor in this blurring of the impact of biological development on such overt behavior as dating, since it is in the school context that much of the social life of young people is initiated and carried on.

Dating practices depend upon many personal, family, and cultural factors. Physical attractiveness (*109, 111*), general personality and adjustment, social skills, and other personal attributes obviously enhance or detract from one's desirability as a "date." Thus in one study (*74*) college students who seldom or never dated, who started dating late in high school, and who have never had more than one "steady" were predominantly socially retiring and showed a slight tendency to be emotionally maladjusted. Those dating more frequently (one to three dates in two weeks), who started dating in junior high school, who started going steady in college, and who have had two to three "steadies" approximated the social and emotional norm. Those persons who started "going steady" in grade school or junior high school, who started "going steady" against their parents' wishes, and who had four or more "steadies" tended to be socially aggressive and emotionally maladjusted.[1] Such findings emphasize that "personality" is a factor in heterosexual relationships not only in terms of the attractiveness of one's personality to others but also as a determiner of one's own orientation toward the opposite sex.

Parents differ greatly in the extent to which they encourage or discourage dating. In Table 88 it will be noted that daughters more frequently than sons reported that fathers had discouraged them in their

TABLE 88. Attitudes of Mothers and Fathers Toward First Dating as Reported by College Students in Terms of Percentage Holding Different Attitudes[a]

	Prohibiting or Disapproving	Attitude Indifferent	Encouraging
Father's attitude toward			
Sons	8.5	70.7	20.8
Daughters	18.0	62.3	19.7
Mother's attitude toward			
Sons	7.3	57.6	35.1
Daughters	9.5	39.6	50.9

[a] Based on replies of 141 male and 258 female college students.

SOURCE: Adapted from C. Kirkpatrick and T. Caplow, courtship in a group of Minnesota students, Amer. J. Sociol., 1945, 51:114–125.

first dating whereas mothers had been more encouraging to their daughters than to their sons. Especially to be noted is the fact that the typical attitude of parents was mainly that of indifference to this important developmenal step—and that often parents were a handicap rather than an aid.

The original investigators call attention to the relevance of these data to Freudian theory: fathers show a slight tendency to be more inclined to resist the threatened emotional loss of their daughters than of their sons, whereas mothers tend to show a greater willingness to eliminate potential rivals

[1] Paraphrased from the original paper.

(daughters) from the family group by encouraging them to date. But they also point out ". . . since mothers were more inclined than fathers to encourage the dating of sons as well, the Freudian hypothesis must be qualified by the recognition that mothers may simply be more interested than fathers in the mating process; they perhaps acquire vicarious experience through identification." (53.)

Whatever the reasons that lead parents to encourage or discourage the social activities of their offspring, there can be little doubt that much of their motivation is unconscious. Whether the child is encouraged or discouraged may well reflect the parent's own status needs or ego defenses, and it is of some interest and significance that adults often exert close supervision over the dating of their offspring. In a study cited above (78) 20 to 25 percent of the freshmen and 7 to 10 percent of the seniors reported that they were usually or always chaperoned on dates. Such constant supervision is hardly conducive to the development of maturity and would seem to offer a decided handicap to the achievement of some of the potential values to be derived from dating.

One effect of parental pressures upon adolescent dating is to enforce the status lines of society. Clique membership was found in one study to be an important factor in dating, *but* both the adolescent clique and its dating patterns appeared to be a reflection of the adult social structure (46). Thus, a mother may carefully select youngsters invited to the child's first party, thereby influencing the circle of friends with which the child grows up. Or the youngsters themselves may enforce class lines. The child who dates an individual unacceptable to her clique mates (e. g., a youngster from a lower class) may be ostracized temporarily, and if the dating continues she may be permanently eliminated from clique membership. It is noteworthy in one study (46) that 61 percent of the daters belonged to the same social class and an additional 35 percent belonged in adjacent classes. Only 4 percent were separated by one intervening class. There were no dates between the class II's and the class V's.

There can be little doubt that the activity of "dating" plays an important role in the lives of young people, not only in terms of their current adjustment and personality development but also as preparatory for more stable heterosexual choices to be made later. In dating, adolescents find expression and satisfaction of many needs—for affection, for affiliation, for status, for dependence, and even for achievement, as well as for heterosexual needs. Such needs operate in all human relationships and are of especial importance in those relationships which are most intimate. While *who* is dated may sometimes be determined largely by situational factors (most extreme in the "blind" date) the kinds of people the individual continues to date will depend upon the extent to which those individuals meet personal psychological needs. Although some writers whose works have received a great deal of attention[2] take a rather dim view of dating practices, emphasizing status- and thrill-seeking aspects, the social and emotional experiences derived from dating are fundamental to desirable psychosocial development. Potentially valuable outcomes include greater social poise and competence, increased ability to adjust to others under diverse circumstances, greater experience in judging individuals objectively and sensibly, as well as broad experience with the opposite sex and opportunity to test compatibility of interests before emotional involvement becomes marked. In addition to their intrinsic value, all such outcomes should result in a better-based choice of mate (*12, 13*).[3]

LOVE AND COURTSHIP

Typically, heterosexual development involves a gradual transition from casual dating to courtship to formal commitment to marriage. Young people who have an initial date for a casual reason may find that a romantic interest has developed and a love affair emerged; that they are "going steady." Median age for first "going steady" appears to be around 15—i. e., slightly more than a year after dating first begins (*69*). And as in the case of first dating, sex differences were not statistically reliable. Although farther along the "courtship continuum" than "dating," "going steady" may or may not constitute a love relationship.

Falling in love, an overwhelming emotional experience, is exceedingly difficult to analyze and study psychologically. One writer has described the process as follows:

"Such affairs, in contrast to 'dating,' have marked directional trend; they may be arrested on any level, or they may be broken off at any point, but they may not ordinarily be turned back to a lesser degree of involvement; in this

[2] Waller (*103*), especially, interprets dating primarily as thrill- and status-seeking behavior on the part of young people who are definitely understood to be postponing marriage. Dating, according to this interpretation, serves no especially useful function and may have effects detrimental to later adjustment: dating and courtship is asserted to educate more for dating and courtship than for marriage, and it is argued the deception and exploitation so common in dating may injure and permanently interfere with the development of favorable love attitudes and their expression.

[3] It is of some interest that, when asked, youngsters tend to emphasize the educational and mate-selection functions as the major reasons for and values in dating (*68*). These are, however, probably "reasoned" assessments of dating or culturally acceptable answers rather than actual motivating factors.

sense they are irreversible. As this interaction process goes on, the process of idealization is reinforced by the interaction of personalities. A idealizes B, and presents to her that side of his personality which is consistent with his idealized conception of her; B idealizes A, and governs her behavior toward him in accordance with her false notions of his nature; the process of idealization is usually reinforced in such a way that it must necessarily lead to an increasing divorce from reality. As serious sentimental involvement develops, the individual comes to be increasingly occupied, on the conscious level at least, with the positive aspects of the relationship; increasingly he loses his ability to think objectively about the other person, to safeguard himself or to deal with the relationship in a rational way; we may say, indeed, that one falls in love when he reaches a point where sentiment-formation overcomes objectivity." (103)

But there is strong disagreement as to whether this description, which is essentially the popular stereotype of romantic love, actually holds. Burgess and Wallin (14, p. 170) report on the replies of 226 engaged couples to the question: "To what extent are you in love with your fiancé(e)?" Answers to be checked included "Head over heels," "Very much so," and "Somewhat or mildly." Slightly less than a quarter of both sexes checked "Head over heels" and close to 70 percent checked "Very much so." As one respondent said, "I am very much in love with my fiancée but not head over heels. As I interpret that term it would mean being blinded to all adverse or undesirable aspects of the relationship, and I don't think we are to that extent." Another said, "I think if I were head over heels in love with Bill I wouldn't let obstacles stand in the way of our marriage. As it is I don't let my heart rule my head. I know we can't live on love."

At what ages and how often *do* people fall in love—however they may define it for themselves? Most frequently in the teens and the early twenties, as Figure 109 shows. For girls the ages 16 to 20 included approximately two and a half love affairs each; boys averaged about one and a half during the same periods. Other studies confirm that the typical experience involves a succession of two or three love affairs during the teens (53, 61) in addition to an even greater number of infatuations (33).

Love affairs and infatuations are often short-lived and vary markedly in their courses. In the last study mentioned 29 percent of the infatuations and 5 percent of the love affairs lasted only from 1 to 4 weeks. The median girl reported that infatuations lasted about 6 weeks, and that after she fell in love she usually remained in love for about 36 weeks (33). The course of a love affair may show regular or cyclic trends, with perhaps 70 percent showing regular trends, i. e., built up steadily to a peak, remained steady, or declined steadily (54). Slightly more than 25 percent showed either fairly regular cycles of waxing and waning affection or involved irregular ups and downs. When college students were questioned as to their reactions to the breaking off of love affairs, about half reported no emotional trauma. In these cases adjustment seemed

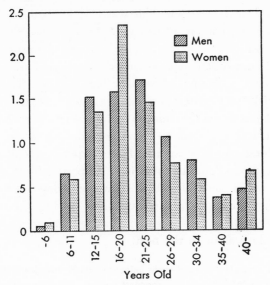

Figure 109. Average Number of Love Affairs per Person During Each of Various Age Periods. (Adapted from G. V. Hamilton and K. MacGowan, *What Is Wrong with Marriage?* New York, Boni, 1928, p. 257.)

almost immediate. On the other hand, about 10 percent took a year or more to readjust (*54*). The median college girl subject of one study (*33*) took about 4 weeks to become infatuated again after one of her love affairs had ended. The initial reaction to the lost love object according to one of the studies cited above varied from an upsurge of affection (15 percent) through ambivalent feelings (15 percent) to feelings of hostility in about 10 percent of the cases (*54*).

The mixed feelings that characterize going affairs, and the reaction to the termination of affairs, show something of the complexity and ambivalence of the emotions and the relationships subsumed under the caption of "love." A substantial number (between an eighth and a quarter) of college students reported that conflicts arose during the course of love affairs because of feelings of jealousy, possessiveness, criticism, or irritability arising from such factors and events as emotional tensions, dislike of friends, accusations of loss of interest, disagreement about the future. Substantial portions worried about becoming too involved or trapped in their relationships (*54*).

As one love affair follows another, there appears to be increasing movement toward marriage. In Table 89 are presented certain facts characterizing first, second, and third affairs described by a group of college students. As shown in the top two rows, with succeeding affairs a larger proportion experienced "love" as an emotional component, suggesting progress toward mate selection. This was true for both sexes. However, the investigator who conducted this study hypothesized that there likely exists a progressive sex differentiation in growth patterns in courtship. Women tend to marry somewhat earlier than men and are less burdened with the problem of financial adequacy for marriage. The outstanding problem for girls is to find a mate, whereas men have the responsibility of finding *both* a mate *and* the means to finance marriage. Thus, it might be expected that there would be increasing conflict, sex frustration, and unhappiness for males as economic forces separate them from girls in their own age group. This hypothesis is supported by the facts in the bottom four rows of the table which show increasing importance of unpleasant emotional components in love affairs for boys but a decreasing emphasis for girls. Boys also show an increasing number of sources of conflict from one love affair to the next.

TABLE 89.   Progress Toward Mate Selection with Progressive "Affairs" as Suggested by the Emotional Components Reported by College Students to Characterize First, Second, and Third Affairs with the Opposite Sex

| | | Affair | |
	First	Second	Third
Percentage mentioning love as an emotional component			
Girls	47	63	71
Boys	56	69	79
Ratio of pleasant to unpleasant emotional components			
Girls	1.29	1.56	1.78
Boys	1.83	1.57	1.40
Average number of sources of conflict mentioned			
Girls	2.0	2.5	2.0
Boys	1.8	2.5	2.7

SOURCE: Adapted from C. Kirkpatrick and T. Caplow, Courtship in a group of Minnesota students, *Amer. J. Sociol.*, 1945, 51:114–125.

There has been relatively little penetrating research into the psychological factors related to courtship development or, for that matter, to the selection of a mate.[4] An interesting series of papers (*109–113*) has been presented by Professor R. F. Winch who attempted to test certain Freudian hypotheses regarding courtship. Orthodox Freudian theory asserts that at adolescence

---

[4] See below for a further discussion of mate selection.

there is a resurgence of the Oedipus situation, i. e., a pubescent youngster becomes erotically attracted to the opposite sex parent. This attraction and subsequent attachment is presumed to be resolved, in part, through identification with the same-sex parent, and the adolescent is then left free to develop warm associations with same-age persons of the opposite sex. If this line of reasoning is correct, those individuals who had greater than average attachment to the opposite-sex parent, or those who had no same-sex parent in the home with whom to identify, would be somewhat slower in resolving the Oedipus situation and would be somewhat retarded in their courtship. These predictions were supported in the case of a group of male college students but not in the case of females, leading the investigator (after analyzing the family ties of the two sexes) to conclude that the Freudian biological emphasis was inadequate to explain courtship trends, but that cultural expectations and learning must be included as explanatory principles.[5]

In the course of these studies, the relationships of a number of specific variables were correlated with present courtship status. Although all relationships were low, among college women courtship status (i. e., how far advanced on a continuum including such levels as casual dating, exclusive dating, engagement, and marriage) was reliably and positively associated with the early dating situation, wish to be married, and appearance and negatively associated with "career drive" (109). Among college males, reliable and positive relationships with present courtship status obtained in the case of age, favorability of early dating situation, and wish to be married; strength of career drive was negatively correlated with courtship status (111).

MATE SELECTION: ENGAGEMENT AND MARRIAGE

As courtship advances, there develops a personal and social expectation that marriage will ensue, a state of affairs that is crystallized more formally and publicly upon announcement of the engagement. The engagement period usually permits greater intimacies and greater opportunity to interact with the prospective marriage partner in more situations (especially nonrecreational situations) than before, with the result that there can be more effective testing of the mutual adaptability of one to the other.

Length of engagement apparently averages somewhere between six months and a year (57, 66) and appears to be somewhat shorter now than in previous generations (57). Yet the time now appears to be utilized more realistically as a period of preparation for marriage, substantially more young married women reporting having discussed items pertinent to marriage than did their mothers and/or grandmothers (57, 62). If engagement is thus used constructively to consider problems of

---

[5] Another investigator (2) has failed to confirm Winch's finding of retarded courtship in the case of males who grew up in homes with the father absent.

marriage and as a means of testing personal and social compatibility, it would be anticipated that those couples who marry *without* a formal engagement would, as a group, be less well adjusted in their marriage and those who have short engagements should be less happy than those who have longer periods of engagements. And this is the case (*11, 66, 76*).[6]

The fact that many engagements do not terminate in marriage suggests either that the engagement period failed to demonstrate mutual compatibility or love or that external factors have made marriage impossible. Of 1000 engaged couples studied, 24 percent of the men and 36 percent of the women reported previous broken engagements, and 15 percent later broke the present engagement (*14*). Reasons for these broken engagements could be classified into five categories: slight emotional attachment, separation, parental opposition, cultural divergences, and personality problems.

According to recent figures (1949), American women married at a median age of 20.3 years and men at a median age of 22.7 (*37*).[7] Who married whom? And why? It is obvious, first, that people do not choose from *all* possible potential mates but only from among those they know at the time. Propinquity has been shown to be an important factor not only in marriage but also in engagement and first dating (*22, 98*). For example, in one recent study done in Columbus, Ohio, some 54 percent of a sample of 281 couples applying for a marriage license involved individuals who lived within 16 blocks of each other at time of first date (*22*). Fifty-three percent lived within this distance at time of applying for the marriage license. Even within a relatively circumscribed geographic area (which in itself tends to throw similar people together) certain influences assure that those most alike get together. Belonging to the same church results in sorting with respect not only to religion but also, to a degree, with respect to national origins and even socioeconomic status.

---

[6] The findings are, however, subject to other interpretations. Short engagements and unhappy marriages may, for example, be associated because they are both, in turn, associated with a third variable, perhaps unstable, unhappy home backgrounds which not only fail to generate the types of personality and adjustment that make for congenial marriages but also fail to influence the young person in the direction of long acquaintance and reasonable engagement periods prior to marriage.

[7] Age of marriage in the United States has been declining regularly during the past half century or so. This fact, evident in U.S. census figures, is at variance with the frequently encountered view that the American culture is steadily prolonging adolescence. In an economic sense, the latter may be true, but certainly marriage represents an important threshold marking entrance upon full-fledged adult responsibilities, and in this sense the adolescent period appears to be shorter now. Age at marriage varies widely with section of the country, race, and social-class level, as well as varying from country to country (*37, 98, 107*).

Meeting in college or in social clubs guarantees certain similarity with respect to such characteristics as cultural level, intelligence, economic status, level of ambition, interests. Parents, friends, or social institutions such as the church may influence against marriages involving another nationality, race, or faith. The total cultural pressures are so great that in New Haven, Connecticut, in 1948, to cite an example, no cross-race marriages occurred; religion was such an important consideration that 91 percent of the marriages involved partners from the same religious group; and in 58 percent[8] of the marriages, both partners came from the same class of residential area (45). Other studies show similar results (19, 100).

In the study of developmental psychology, special interest attaches to the role that developmental status as reflected in age plays in behavior of all types. The extent to which age is a factor in marriage will depend not only upon the degree to which people of like ages are thrown together[9] but also on the extent to which the individual finds those of particular ages attractive, proves attractive to those of different ages, or is pressured by social approval or disapproval into marriage with a mate of a particular age. The American culture tends to approve marriages between those of similar ages and to disapprove marriages between people of widely disparate ages. In first marriages, according to one study (44), the husband is only slightly older than the wife when he married before 23, but from that age upward the differential becomes greater and is about 6 years at 33 and after 40 about 10 years. When single men under 30 marry previously married women they marry women older than themselves on the average; after 30 they tend to marry women younger than themselves, but not so much younger as is true when marriages are first marriages for both parties. In other types of marriages (both second marriages; first for wife, second for husband) husbands tend to be older, the more so the older he is at the time of marriage. One writer (8), in analyzing marriages which occurred after 30, takes occasion to point out that men in their forties show no greater tendency to marry younger women than do those of other age groups, a fact he interpreted as contradicting the cultural stereotype of the "dangerous forties"—at least as regards any tendency "to run riot, so to speak, in their marrying habits."

In short, spatial factors and social pressures and expectations tend to define the "field of eligibles" from which a mate is chosen. The range of possibilities is further narrowed by the fact that people of similar interests and values tend to find each other's company congenial. It has been

---

[8] This was raised to 82.8 percent when consideration included those of the same class area plus those of an adjacent class.

[9] In a Wisconsin study, 26 percent of the men stationed at a military training center, who married, married women older than themselves, a circumstance thought to be due to the favorable supply of single women in these older age groups (98).

shown, for example, that those who marry tend to be alike in measured intelligence, general personality characteristics, in recreational interests, in moral and other attitudes and values, and in their friendships and social behavior such as drinking and smoking (15, 85). People tend to find irritating and annoying, or merely boresome, those whose interests and values are contrary to their own. Such differences may even be quite threatening: a very moral person is likely to be disturbed by immoral behavior on the part of an associate. In any event, people will tend to avoid, reject, or simply fail to seek out those with whom they have little in common, not only in day-by-day associations, but especially with respect to prospective marriage.

The group of potential marriage partners is limited even more by the conscious and/or unconscious "ideal conception" of a mate which the young person carries into his heterosexual social life. Over 25 percent of a sample of men and women reported that they were "very conscious" of an ideal conception of a mate, and another 30 percent were "vaguely conscious" of such an ideal. Interviews indicated that this ideal was especially effective in a negative sense, i. e., in eliminating individuals from consideration (14). The sources of such ideals are partly to be found in the culture in which the individual develops. But to a large degree they are likely found in the intimate associations within the family. Favorable attitudes to marriage are, for example, related to the marital happiness of parents (104). Some psychoanalytic theory holds that mates are selected to fit the image one has of his parents, particularly the opposite-sex parent. Research, however, fails consistently to support this notion (97). Indeed, detailed interviews with 50 young women emphasized that a great variety of types of relationships with parents might influence mate choice either positively or negatively. One may seek a husband "like father" or perhaps the exact opposite. Or perhaps, the positive traits of both parents may be combined into one's ideal of a mate—or if relationships with both parents have been unsatisfactory, both may be rejected (consciously or unconsciously) as a mate ideal.

As noted above, research has rather consistently demonstrated that "like marries like." Perhaps this is because the types of variables studied are those that define the *field* of potential mates. Since within this field choices are made in terms of the degree to which a particular person will satisfy the needs of a potential partner, may there not be a certain dissimilarity or complementariness? One group of writers (114, 115), who have so argued, propose that:

(1) The need or needs of A which are being gratified are *different in kind* from the need or needs being gratified in B; or (2) the need or needs of A which are being gratified are *very different in intensity* from the same needs in B which are also being gratified. . . . An example of (1) is found in the case of a person desirous of attention and recognition (recognition need) who finds gratification in relationship with a person who tends to bestow admiration on the former (deference need). Alternative (2) is illustrated in the interaction between a person who wants others to do his bidding (high dominance need) and one lacking the ability to handle his environment who is looking for someone to tell him what to do (low dominance need). (*114*)

To test this reasoning, an attempt was made to assess by means of interviews and projective test procedures the psychological needs of 25 young husbands and wives who were relatively homogeneous with respect to race, age, socioeconomic status, and religion. Comparisons, while not conclusive, tended to support the view that with respect to motivational patterns choices tend to be made so that personalities mesh or complement one another (*115*). In short, and probably quite unconsciously for the most part, people seek people as mates who in some respects are unlike themselves. This finding would seem to suggest that to an important degree progress toward mate selection is made through a process of rejection and selection rather than through "learning to be for each other" as a result of continued association. This inference is compatible with findings from another recent study (*56*).

ILLUSTRATIVE CASES

Quotations from reports of people regarding their own love affairs serve not only to show the differing patterns of falling in love and reaching an understanding about marriage but also to show vividly something of the complex dynamics of interpersonal relations that may precede marriage.

First date, falling in love, and becoming engaged may be greatly telescoped into a few short weeks or extended over quite a period of years. Rapid engagement was reported by one boy: "I think I became interested in her the first night we met. So much so that I took her home and made another date with her. I haven't the slightest idea what struck me. I really don't know. I don't think it was love at first sight. . . . I first felt I was in love with her about ten days after we met. I guess just about that time I told her I was in love. She expressed the same feeling. From that time on we went steady. Just about the same time we had an understanding to be married." Burgess and Wallin (*14*), from whose volume this quotation is taken, believe that in "a not inconsiderable minority couples progress from first meeting to formal engagement in a few months, if not weeks." But more typical of length of courtship is the following instance: "I was twenty when I first met my fiancé. We worked in the same office. We had our first date a couple of months after I started working there. We started keeping company after our first date. In about six months I felt I was falling in love with him. I think our falling in love was about mutual in time. He mentioned it first about the end of six months and I told him I felt practically the same way. About three or four months later I started wearing his fraternity pin." Although six months to a year after first date seemed about typical for deciding they wish to marry (14), some courtships of which the following is illustrative are fairly extended: "I first met her at a small dance arranged by some friends of hers. I was interested at first, although not madly in love. She was a lot of fun, a nice person to know. Within a week or two I called her for a date. In about six months we both seemed to enjoy each other's company so we just went places together. I first felt I was in love with her after a couple of years. It wasn't one of those great romantic loves. It just grew on me. It was sometime after that before we had an actual understanding about getting married."[10]

The outcomes of the marriages in the foregoing cases—or even whether these particular engagements resulted in marriage—are not reported. But the brevity of these quotations obscures the dynamics of the engagement, the role of the individual, his or her parents, and other potential mate choices. Something of the complex interplay of factors that occurs is illustrated in the following case, a case which is admittedly not typical. Indeed, it ended in divorce.

In my third year of high school, I started to have dates with a boy I had known for years, and fell very much in love with him. We became engaged after going together about three months. We were to be married when graduated, but the position Bob was to have did not materialize, so we postponed it. My family decided that I should go to a woman's college in the East, even though I preferred to go to the state university, which Bob was attending.

Late in the summer I had a date with a fellow seven years my senior, whom I had known for ten years. A week before I was to leave for school, my fiancé came home from the university, and we went to my father, asking him if we could get married. He told us he would give us his answer on the week end. The next night I went out with Dick. I suppose the reason he fascinated me was that he was older and had a steady income. By the week end I was out of the notion of getting married. My family encouraged my going out with Dick, because they would have done anything to keep me from marrying Bob.

I left for the eastern school still fascinated by Dick. During Christmas vacation I severed all relations with Bob. In February, Dick came to see me, and I found that some of the glamour had worn off. I saw him in relation to the people of my walk of life, and there were some things which were lacking.

When I came home in the summer, I had a date with Dick every night. He

[10] These quotations are from Burgess and Wallin (14), a volume containing an excellent treatment of this topic together with a substantial body of original data.

was very jealous and would check up on me several times a day. I did not see Bob during this time, so I could rationalize very well with myself that Dick was much better for me.

Several things happened at this time that made me decide that marriage was the best solution to my problems that looked so big to a girl of nineteen. First, my mother and I were having a great deal of conflict; second, I did not want to continue school; and, third, I wanted to spite Bob, for he hadn't even come to see me.

One day in August we were invited to a friend's home in the southern part of the state, so we planned to be married on our way there. We secured our license and went to a Justice of the Peace (this seemed to go with an elopement) and went on to my friend's. (66, pp. 115–116.)

Adjustment During Marriage

Apparently, the processes of mate selection described above are sufficiently effective and potentialities for adjustment sufficiently high that most marriages turn out to be reasonably successful. Terman (99) reported that the bulk of happiness scores of the 792 couples he studied were in the direction of high happiness, and his findings have been confirmed by other investigators (11, 66). To be sure, though, much unhappiness does exist, and many marriages terminate in divorce.

BACKGROUND AND PERSONALITY FACTORS IN MARITAL ADJUSTMENT

Three large-scale studies (and numerous minor studies) have been made of the factors related to marital adjustment (11, 66, 99). In two of these studies, the measure of happiness of marriage was based on a composite scoring procedure involving such items as own rating of happiness, interviewer's rating, number of satisfactions and complaints registered with reference to spouse. In the third investigation a comparison was made of a group of happily married couples with a group of divorced couples. Although differing in certain respects, the studies were in agreement on basic issues.

In the first place, well-adjusted and happily married people tend to come from the types of backgrounds that would likely have generated good personality and security in interpersonal relationships. As a group, they differ from those who are unhappily married with respect to the degree to which they rate their childhood as having been happy. In general, they grew up in happy families (they rated their own parents' marriage as happy), had few conflicts with parents, and experienced relatively little in the way of harsh or unduly restrictive discipline. They came to marriage with favorable attitudes toward sex, having encountered in their parents frank and encouraging attitudes or brief answers instead of evasion or rebuff in their response to their earlier sex curiosity. Thus, in the context of marriage as in other spheres of life there is an essential continuity of psychological growth and development with age, i. e., good adjustment at one age breeds good adjustment later.

Second, happily married couples tended to be more conventional and have stronger ties to social institutions. They were more frequently above the norm in education and were regular and frequent church attenders. They entered marriage with institutional sanctions which would tend to reënforce the marriage. They were, for example, more likely to have had parental approval of their marriage and to have had a church or home wedding with a minister, rabbi, or priest officiating. They were more likely to have had a reasonably long acquaintance, courtship, and engagement period and thus presumably had adequate opportunity for testing compatibility.

Third, happily married individuals were more likely to be relatively sociable, secure, well-adjusted, stable, and adaptable personalities. Home backgrounds are, of course, related to such outcomes. Serious conflicts between parents and with reference to children, unresponsiveness to needs of the children, strictness, harshness, and restrictiveness (all tending to be more frequent in backgrounds of the unhappily married) not only make for unhappiness in childhood but leave their mark upon the more persistent reaction patterns of the individual—his personality. As Terman (99, p. 110) has suggested, what comes out of marriage depends upon what goes into it in the way of attitudes, preferences, aversions, habit patterns, and emotional response patterns which constitute aptitude or ineptitude for marriage. People who are likely to be unhappy in marriage are those whose insecurities, hostilities, egocentricism, and general reaction patterns are such that they have difficulty finding happiness *anywhere*, not only because others have difficulty meeting their needs but also because they find difficulty in meeting the psychological needs of others. They may, for example, be incapable of either giving or receiving love. Terman's contrast, summarized below, between the personalities of well-adjusted and poorly adjusted husbands and wives is illustrative.[11]

[11] Although such personality characteristics may be the *product* of marriage, i. e., the product (on the positive side) of securities and satisfactions found in marriage that were previously lacking or (on the negative side) reaction to frustrations and insecurities arising from or in the marriage itself, it is likely that many of these personality contrasts existed prior to marriage. The following material is adapted from Cavan's (17) summary of Terman's (99) findings.

Unhappily Married Women. Unhappy wives are subject to emotional ups and downs, feeling now exultant, now sad without apparent reason. They worry needlessly, and useless thoughts run through their heads. Lacking in self-confidence, they are overly sensitive to criticism or any seeming domination by others. They are timid and easily discouraged. Unable to do exacting and painstaking work, they are unsteady and even flighty in work, unmethodical, and wasteful. They tend to be egotistic. To escape from their unhappiness they join numerous societies, seek romance, daydream, and visit fortunetellers; they often adopt radical ideas on religion, politics, and moral conventions.

Happily Married Women. Happy wives are serene, optimistic, and untroubled by extreme emotional reactions. They are steady workers. They are kindly, coöperative, and interested in others, especially in those who need help, such as children and old people. They seek conventional outlets through family excursions, educational movies, or personal correspondence.

Unhappily Married Men. Unhappy husbands are inclined to be gloomy, ill at ease, and sensitive to group opinions. In compensation, they tend to withdraw from situations that would test their ability and try to dominate those to whom they feel superior. Given to daydreams and fantasies, in imagination they play a superior role. They tend to be sporadic in work habits and lacking in thriftiness. More than the happy husbands, they express various radical attitudes.

Happily Married Men. They are even-tempered and stable, coöperative, and kindly in attitude toward their inferiors. Socially, they tend to be unselfconscious and are able to function in group relationships with initiative and responsibility. They tend to be conservative, cautious, and thrifty and to uphold prevailing conventions.

NEEDS AND EXPECTATIONS IN MARITAL ADJUSTMENT

Findings such as the foregoing may incorrectly lead to the conclusion that some people can never hope to find a happy marriage. Although it is probably true that some have the cards stacked somewhat against them, two points should be stressed. First, the contrasts in these studies have never been clear cut. Some people who fit closely the picture of the happy group are unhappy in their marriages, while some who in these terms would be unhappy have instead found substantial happiness. Second, it cannot be too strongly stressed that happiness in marriage involves a *meshing* of two personalities. Whereas two particular personalities may clash, these same parties may find others very congenial. Marriage has a dynamic quality and involves interaction and reciprocal relations between two people. Thus, each marriage is essentially unique, and no single formula for marital success can be identified. The success of a marriage will depend upon the continuing mutual satisfaction of the fundamental needs—biological, psychological, and social—of the two individuals concerned. As already noted, there is some premarital sorting out of people who marry, in terms of complementary needs. It is of some further interest in this connection that Terman found a correlation of .60 between husbands' and wives' happiness scores. Although this is a substantial relationship, Terman emphasized the exceptions in his interpretation: "It is significant in the suggestion it carries that the degree of satisfaction one finds in a marriage depends partly upon one's characteristic attitudes and so need not closely parallel the happiness of one's marital partner" (99).

A recent study (75) of marital adjustment has attempted to test the hypothesis that happiness or unhappiness in marriage is a function of the extent to which the expectations one has regarding his role or the role of his mate in marriage are unrealized. Thus the husband may be frustrated because he expects his wife to play the role of mother whereas she prefers being a clubwoman. Or the role of "husband" may not be filled to his wife's satisfaction by a man whose role as "professional man" takes precedence. Both marriages might be unhappy. The situation could well be different if, in the first illustration, the man *wanted* a clubwoman for a wife, and, in the second, if very active professional participation was what the wife *desired* in her husband. These specific behavior patterns represent ways in which certain more general needs —e. g., status needs—might be achieved. Expectation also relates to many rather specific behaviors—making decisions regarding food purchases, keeping clean and neat, kissing wife good-bye when leaving for work, initiating sex relations. Conflicts in marriage may exist when either the individual or his spouse fails to fulfill an expectation—whether the expectation is his own or his spouse's. It may be just as frustrating to an individual to be unable to (or know he does not) fulfill the expectations and needs of his spouse as it is to find his own expectations and needs unfulfilled.

The actual investigation of the relationship between happiness in marriage and role conflicts yielded a correlation of $-.83$, i. e., high happiness, low number of conflicts. Although this investigation seemed clearly to indicate that the number of role expectation conflicts was related to marital happiness, it also revealed that there was no special formula, in the sense of *particular* role expectations, for success in marriage. The investigator commented thus: "An example of 'no possibility of a special formula' is that the author interviewed certain couples who entered marriage expecting to be sexually promiscuous and with those expectations fulfilled their self-evaluation of happiness was number one [the highest]. Likewise the author interviewed couples who had expected fidelity for the self and the mate and were fulfilling these expectations and they also gave themselves a happiness rating of number one" (75). The evidence from another study (47) revealed that divorced couples exhibit a greater disparity in their attitudes toward the roles of husbands and wives in marriage than did married couples.

It has been noted in a recent study (116) that marital roles are partially an outgrowth of the individual's relationships with his own parents. *Husbands who were dominant* tended to have had conflicts with their own fathers and mothers while their wives had no such conflict and were attached to their mothers. In those instances where husband and wife played an *equalitarian role,* it was observed that the husband had little or no conflict with parents and was attached to his mother and that the wife's relationship to her own mother was one of attachment and absence of conflict. The *dominance of the wife* was positively related to conflict relationship with her own mother. Concerning his results this investigator commented as follows: "The association between parent-child conflict and dominant role in marriage can be explained in terms of psychological needs. It is expected that those young men or women who had more conflicts with their parents were more preoccupied with hostile and insecure feelings and reactions. A psychological need to release such hostility, to safeguard against anxiety, and against the danger of feeling unwanted seems obvious. The striving for power or domination is one of the ways to serve such purpose. In the marriage relationship it is but natural that they have the need to dominate their mates."

A clear and stable role structure within the family and in its relationships to the external social world—regardless of the nature of this structure, if it is accepted by the members—is more likely to be conducive to good family adjustment than a vacillating, uncertain one or one unacceptable to its members (*60*, pp. 56–60). One investigator (*43*) has, however, suggested that some types of family role structures may be more conducive to low tension in the family than others. Four patterns of husband-wife power interaction were identified: (1) husband dominant; (2) wife dominant; (3) "autonomous," with separate spheres of influence; (4) "syncratic," with joint coöperative determination. It was anticipated, in the study, that each of these patterns would be associated with a different level of adjustment or tension in the family. And it was found that autocratic structures had highest tension levels whereas syncratic structures had lowest. While under the syncratic arrangement tension in specific areas of relationships might be high, the effect of joint determination was to lower the tension, thus producing a generally harmonious family structure. In the autocratic (whether dominated by husband or wife) and in the autonomous structure, a reduction of tension in specific areas of relationships might be accomplished at the expense of an increase in general family tension.

A host of other factors have been studied in relation to marital success, but it is believed that almost any set of factors may best be considered from the point of view of their implications with respect to the creation or the satisfaction of needs of the particular individuals involved. Thus, the presence of children may "save" a marriage because the mother may find affectional outlets that are denied her in her relationships with her husband or because external social pressures to continue a marriage tend to be greater than if no children existed. But more fundamentally, children seem to fulfill an important psychological need characterizing most people, the birth of a child representing one of the happiest events in people's lives. People find in children a certain expansion of self—thus partially satisfying a need postulated by Buhler (9) to be fundamental in most lives—and find satisfactions (successes) denied them through identifying with their children. In general, though, adjustment in marriage increases not with number of children (indeed, the number is negatively correlated with adjustment) but with the ability of the couple to control fertility *in line with their desires* (21). Those of higher economic and cultural levels tend to be better adjusted in marriage (83) and to have a lower divorce rate (26). Economic factors may be related to marriage to the degree that finances provide basic satisfactions to the people involved (e. g., general economic security, or, perhaps, ability to purchase symbols of status) or are so inadequate as to represent serious limitations. Or finances may be related to marriage to the extent to which those from different cultural-economic backgrounds tend to vary in personality, needs, and adjustment or are subject to different cultural expectations regarding the conduct or continuation of marriage. Problems may be especially great when the partners of a marriage are from different levels (83). Age at marriage and age differences between spouses become important in terms of their implications with respect to psychological maturity, psychological adaptability to change in habit patterns necessitated by marriage, psychological needs related to age or which can be satisfied by a mate of a different age. Sex needs may be strong in youth; the need for continuation of name through children strong for the bachelor in his late thirties, the need for companionship strong in old age. A young woman closely attached to her father may find psychological and economic security in marriage to an older man.[12]

CHANGES IN MARITAL ADJUSTMENT WITH PASSAGE OF TIME

The findings presented in Figure 110 suggest that the happiest period of marriage is in its earliest days. The happiness measures in this study showed steadily falling marriage satisfaction from the early days of marriage to a low point 6 to 8 years after marriage, a rise, a second low point 15 to 17 years after marriage, with a fairly regular increase in happiness thereafter. The initial decline in this curve is confirmed by results from the Burgess-Cottrell study (11). Of all couples studied in the first year of

---

[12] Issues such as the foregoing have been investigated in the comprehensive studies of Terman (99), Burgess and Cottrell (11), and Locke (66) and have been the subject of numerous studies dealing with a single or a limited number of variables. Often, however, such research tends mainly to show the relationship of such factors to overall marital adjustment or divorce and does not show the relationship in terms of need satisfaction or frustration in *individual* marriages.

marriage, 56 percent had "good" adjustment and only 23 percent had "poor" adjustment. Of those married for 5 or 6 years only 29 percent rated as having "good" adjustment whereas 37 percent rated as poor in adjustment. Another study by Lang, cited by Burgess and Cottrell (*11,*

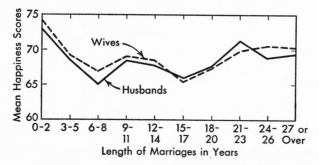

Figure 110. Mean Happiness Scores According to Length of Marriage. (By permission from *Psychological Factors in Marital Happiness,* by L. M. Terman, New York, McGraw-Hill, 1938.)

p. 248), suggested that, as rated by close acquaintances, happiness in marriage tends to decrease slightly beyond this point. The decline in happiness from 5 to 6 years of marriage to 16 (the limit of this study) was not so great as during the first few years.

Figure 111 represents other data relevant to the question of marital adjustment and marriage duration. There are shown divorce rates (including annulments) for marriages of varying duration. Separate figures are given for couples with and without children. It will be noted that divorce rates climb sharply immediately after marriage, reaching a peak for parent-couples 3 or 4 years after marriage and a year later for those without children. (In 1948, 55 percent of the total divorce decrees were granted to couples married less than seven years.) Thereafter, divorce rates steadily decline, especially rapidly in the case of those not involving children. It is of some interest in this connection that, although the chart covers the first 40 years of marriage, no notable secondary peaks of divorce occur. If there is a "dangerous" age in the forties, it does not show up in overall divorce statistics. If the breakdown were by various educational or other index of cultural level, however, somewhat different results might have been obtained.[13] Many divorces likely arise from mismatings which are rather promptly discovered after marriage. One would expect higher rates during times when more short-acquaintance marriages occur or when other circumstances (such as separation) are unfavorable. It is not sur-

[13] Kinsey (*51*), for example, has suggested that extramarital sex activity on the part of males decreases with age for lowest educational groups (8 years and less of education) but increases for those in the highest educational group (13 or more years of education).

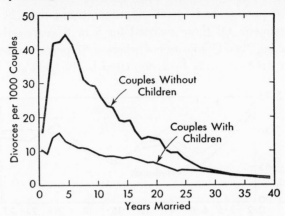

Figure 111. Divorce Rates for First 40 Years of Marriage, United States, 1948. (From P. H. Jacobson, Differentials in divorce by duration of marriage and size of family, Amer. Sociol. Rev., 1950, 15:235–244.) Rates are provisional. Final data on this subject will appear in Dr. Jacobson's forth-coming book on marriage and divorce, to be published by Rinehart and Company.

prising, then, that divorce rates were highest in 1946, immediately after World War II. And also that under ordinary circumstances separations resulting in divorce are most frequent in the first year of marriage and decrease thereafter.

It would seem, then, generalizing from the available data, that after 6 or 7 years, marriages, *on the average,* settle down to a moderate level of happiness and continue on that level.

What explanations may be offered for the decline in marital adjustment during the early years of marriage? A first possible explanation is that some of the decline may be due to growing discord in those marriages that will later be dissolved by divorce. A second explanation involves the notion presented in an earlier chapter that needs are arranged in a hierarchy of importance, and that basic needs must be satisfied before less basic needs are operative. Two important commonly frustrated needs of adolescence are (1) sexual needs and (2) need for independence and full acceptance as an adult. The first months of marriage represent high points in life with respect to satisfactions of both. Sexual needs can now be regularly satisfied, and marriage marks a milestone of independence—the setting up of a new and independent family. With these needs satisfied, others, not operative previously, may become important and may represent sources of friction. A third explanation of decreasing adjustment in early years of marriage may be that partners encounter different and perhaps not so congenial facets of each other's behavior. Many marriages are contracted in an aura of romantic idealism in which, prior to marriage, each partner (as suggested earlier) may tend to present his "best side" to his eventual mate. In the practical, round-the-clock relations of marriage, the *realities* of interacting personalities are encountered, perhaps with at least partial disillusionment, frustration, and friction.

Average curves such as those depicted in Figure 110 are notable, of course, for their smoothing out of contrasting trends characterizing individual cases. Many individual marriages are probably characterized by certain cycles or other less regular trends, and it is likely that these changes in one direction or the other are dependent largely upon changes in psychological needs and ability to satisfy those needs, changes in role, changes in personality or in circumstances that reveal previously unrecognized aspects of personality, improved adjustment due to learning or experience, and stresses or gains growing out of significant events characterizing the family cycle. Obviously such changes in circumstances are not confined to the early years of marriage.

In the first place, changes in marital adjustment may occur with age as needs and capacity to satisfy one's own needs and one's spouse's change. All of the conditions affecting need changes with age discussed in a previous chapter are relevant here. Physical decline, satisfaction or frustration of basic needs and their relation to higher level needs, and changing time perspectives are all important. Changes in one partner may be quite opposed to those occurring in the other, perhaps thus bringing personalities into more desirable matching or upsetting what hitherto had been a good match. For example, a husband may, after achieving vocational success and economic security at 40, wish to settle down to a more satisfying home life. But his wife, tied to the home by children thus far, may want to capitalize on her new freedom and better economic status in travel and more extensive social life. Sex needs of young adulthood may become less important with passing years, and companionship needs may become greater. A partner satisfying in one respect may not be so satisfying in the other. As described later in the chapter, the male's sex drive and capacity may be declining over the years, while his wife, having gradually broken free from inhibitions, may be experiencing increased desire. Personal incapacities to satisfy may be as threatening and frustrating as external threats. One investigator, noting a relationship between physical attractiveness of women and marital adjustment, comments that "this relationship might be reversed if these women, averaging about 30 years of age, staked too long their life adjustment upon fading charms (55). Such losses may prove to be significant threats to a woman who feels her ability to satisfy her husband and to maintain her own marital security depends upon physical attractiveness.

In the second place, age or time and the events that occur in time may result in important changes in role. A marriage may be happy during the period when a wife fills the role of mother, but become threatening to the husband when the children leave home and she fills the role of club- or career-woman, perhaps becoming a competitor. Or a woman, happy in the role of mother, may be at loose ends and dissatisfied when her children are no longer in the home. Occupational success, education, or other circumstances may change the social-class role of one partner without affecting the other, thus creating incompatibilities. Sometimes marriage and family adjustment is affected when the husband's and father's role is changed by prolonged unemployment (59, 60). The effects of hardship are often hard to predict and depend upon the conditions of the particular case. Hardship, indeed, may promote better adjustment.

In the Dickens' family, where the husband's dominance over his wife was slight because of her aggressiveness (and in a measure because of his passivity), a serious trouble involving debt as a result of death was unexpectedly solved through the husband's efforts. As a result of his act, the wife suddenly found herself freed of worry over the situation, and his dominance was elevated markedly. His statement follows:

"I never really knew until now what it means to be a father in a family. Why, since my wife's attitude's changed, my kids are real different to me. The boy and I are real friends. Last week we went to the Bronx Zoo on Sunday, he and I, and we both felt good about it. It seems too bad we had to get into a jam to have us feel like a family, doesn't it? I wish it could have happened five or six years ago—I'd of been a much better father to my kids, I know."

The permanence of this elevation of dominance is indicated in the wife's statement *eleven* months later:

"The Mister [she had always referred to him prior to the trouble as John, or more frequently as "he"] did something to all of us when he fixed that mess. He's never been the same since; it seems to me he's a bigger man. I don't know what to make of the change. Why, Jack and I think he's a much more important man than we did before. He's somebody to lean on now!"

"He's somebody to lean on now!" The strength and security for the family found in such a situation serves best to highlight the opposite effect, where trouble weakens and hamstrings the working of a satisfactory interaction which provides the *modus operandi* of adequate family life. (60, pp. 96–97.)

In the third place, overall marital adjustment may improve as specific problems are worked out, as one partner learns the idiosyncrasies of the other's personality and adapts thereto, or as the achievement of a sense of security (perhaps through actual "testing" of the marriage, or through vocational success) makes unnecessary defensive reactions which had become a source of friction. It is of some considerable importance for a young couple facing conflicts as the first flush of marital bliss is dissipated to recognize in a realistic way that conflicts are inevitable but not necessarily permanent. Problems have a way of getting themselves solved in time. Progress is made as one area of adjustment after another ceases to be a source of conflict and as techniques for dealing with family matters are worked out.

Table 90 contains some facts relevant to the foregoing, indicating the extent of adjustment in various areas of marital life and the length of time required to make adjustment. It is notable that in this sample of 409 marriages, which had lasted an average of 20 years, about 10 percent had never made an adjustment in each of the six areas of marriage adjustment listed. Adjustment with respect to religion and mutual friends was most frequently (as compared

TABLE 90. Percentage of 409 Couples Reporting Various Degrees of Present Adjustment in Six Areas of Marriage and Length of Time Required to Reach Adjustment

	Sex Rela- tions	Social Activ- ities	Religion	Spend- ing Income	In-Law Rela- tions	Mutual Friends
Present adjustment						
Satisfactory for both of us						
Spouses agreed	63	72	76	77	77	82
Spouses disagreed	16	10	8	8	8	7
Satisfactory for me but not						
for spouse	5	3	3	3	3	2
Satisfactory for spouse but						
not for me	4	3	3	3	3	2
Unsatisfactory for both but						
working toward better						
adjustment	2	3	3	6	2	3
At a standstill in adjustment	2	2	3	1	1	1
Time required to adjust						
From the beginning						
Spouses agreed	53	67	74	56	69	76
Spouses disagreed	12	10	7	11	11	8
1 to 12 months	13	4	2	9	4	5
1 to 20 years	10	5	7	13	7	3
Never adjusted	13	14	10	10	10	8

SOURCE: Adapted from J. T. Landis, Length of time required to achieve adjustment in marriage, Amer. Sociol. Rev., 1946, 11:666–677.

with other areas) good from the outset. Adjustments with respect to sex were most difficult to work out, with some 10 percent requiring over a year (from 1 to 20 years) to make a satisfactory adjustment and some 13 percent reporting never having achieved satisfactory sex adjustment. But failure to achieve a satisfactory sex adjustment need not mean the marriage itself is unsatisfactory. Although those who had never made an adjustment in an area were more likely to consider their marriage as "average" (as compared to "happy" or "very happy"), 5 percent of those rated as "very happy" reported never having made an adjustment with respect to spending of family income and 3 percent never made a satisfactory adjustment with respect to sex. Such exceptions add perspective to the generalization that the happier marriages tended to be those in which adjustments in various areas existed from the outset or were made early.

And, finally, there are certain critical events which are frequently part of the inevitable cycle of family life and which create periods of joy and deep satisfaction or, in some cases, become stressful episodes. People typically marry, establish homes, bear children; children marry, the family contracts, the breadwinner retires, one partner and then the other dies. Table 91 shows something of this cycle in family structure

TABLE 91.   Median Age of Husband and Wife at Each Stage of the Family Cycle, for the United States, 1940 and 1890

Staging of the Family Cycle	Median Age of Husband		Median Age of Wife	
	1940	1890	1940	1890
A. First marriage	24.3	26.1	21.6	22.0
B. Birth of first child	25.3	27.1	22.6	23.0
C. Birth of last child	29.9	36.0	27.2	31.9
D. Marriage of first child	48.3	51.1	45.6	47.0
E. Marriage of last child	52.8	59.4	50.1	55.3
F. Death of husband or wife	63.6	57.4	60.9	53.3
(Death of husband, if last)	69.7	66.4	—	—
G. (Death of wife, if last)	—	—	73.5	67.7

SOURCE: From P. C. Glick, The family cycle, Amer. Sociol. Rev., 1947, 12:164–169.

for two periods of time, 1890 and 1940, giving approximate ages for the occurrence of selected events. How people react to such events, and the significance of these happenings for marital adjustment, depends very largely on what the individuals concerned want, upon the preëxisting psychological relationships within the particular family, and the adjustment patterns of its individual members. The woman who reacts with much stress to the advent of pregnancy is likely to be somewhat maladjusted to begin with (*80*). Women (and men, too) differ markedly in their reactions to the husband's retirement; some look forward to it and enjoy it greatly while others are less happy than they were before as a result of reduced income and his continuous presence in the home (*102*). Reactions to pregnancy and birth of children, to menopause, to retirement, to death of spouse—all characteristic life-cycle events—will likely be a product of not only the degree of environmental stress involved but also the personality characteristics of the person (*84*).

In instances where marriage does not occur, children do not arrive, premature death of one partner or the other or divorce occurs, drastic alterations in the timing and course of the family cycle may occur. In many instances, a second cycle is begun with remarriage. Much more psychological research needs to be done on such matters; very little, for example, is known about the life cycle of adjustment of single individuals. In the case of remarriages of those previously divorced or widowed, such evidence as is available is essentially favorable. Bereaved individuals appear to be as happy and well adjusted in second marriages as are those who have been married only once. The same is true of previously divorced women in their second marriages, but it is not so true of previously divorced men (*66*). Thus, factors that have disrupted the first marriage (personal maladjustment, perhaps) need not be disruptive in marriage with a different partner. In fact, in the study just mentioned, 77 percent of 146 previously divorced individuals rated their present marriage as "happy" (32 percent) or "very happy" (45 percent); only 1 out of 10 rated their second marriage as unhappy or very unhappy.

What about relatively late first marriages? By 35, nearly all of those who ever become married have married; marriages after 35 may thus be defined as "late." Interestingly enough, in Terman's study both men and women marrying after 35 constituted on the average the happiest of the several groups studied, though the difference from other age groups was not statistically significant. And age differences between husbands and wives (a factor to be considered in late marriage) are apparently not too highly related to marriage happiness, according to Terman (*99*). In his analysis of age disparities, wives who were 4 to 10 years older than their husbands and husbands who were 12 or more years older than their wives were among the happiest. And their spouses were close to the average in happiness score!

Unfortunately, most of the research on marital adjustment has been conducted in the middle-class setting. Although probably very relevant to what the typical reader of this volume, likely a middle-class college student, will experience, such research often falls short of revealing what marriage and family living is like in other settings. The following thumbnail sketches[14] will illustrate that what is "true" in one family may be unheard of, and quite unbelievable, in another—and thus will provide some perspective to the present discussion.

Class II.   Marriage, which occurs in the middle twenties, is for life and not until divorce breaks it. In our sample, all adolescents were living with at least one parent, and 85 percent with both. Children are expected, and in most cases "parentage is planned"; thus, families are small in size. The mean number of children is 2.3 per family. Parents jointly accept the duty of rearing children correctly so the family will not be "disgraced" by their "misbehavior." Parents sacrifice time, energy, and their own desires "to rear the children properly" and "to give them advantages" they may not have had themselves. Education is believed to be the prime requisite to success. Thus, an education is indispensable in the family's plan for the children's future. In passing it may be well to point out that class II adults are the most highly educated group in Elmtown. Four out of five parents have completed high school and one-half have attended a college or university from one to four years. All have graduated from the eighth grade. The college-educated fathers are concentrated in the large professions; a few are in business. The noncollege fathers are in business enterprises of one kind or another. Those who have achieved success without a college education admit the lack of it, often in an indirect way, and indicate, none too subtly, their belief that they could have gone much further in business if they had had better educations. Both college and noncollege fathers and mothers emphasize the need for a college education to their children. The children expect their parents to assist them materially in reaching and consolidating a desirable future. The boys are headed for business or a profession. The girls are steered toward a desirable marriage after an education has been secured; for they must be trained for the kind of life that is expected of them. Girls are respected, well treated, and are not married off for the purpose of getting rid of them.

Class III.   Class III mothers marry, on the average, a year earlier in life than the class II mothers and give birth to their first child 18 months earlier in life than the class II's. The class III women also have more children than the class II women. The mean number of children is 3.6. Another difference

[14] These descriptions are adapted, by permission, from pp. 93–117 of A. B. Hollingshead, *Elmtown's Youth,* 1949, John Wiley and Sons, Inc. Because of space limitations as well as the small proportion of individuals involved, description of class I marriage and family patterns has been omitted.

is the birth practices in the two classes; among the class III's, practically all babies are delivered in the local hospital, whereas the class II mother goes to a city hospital. The families are equally stable in classes II and III. For instance, 82 percent of the class III children live with their own parents, whereas the figure was 85 percent for families in classes I and II. Strict sexual fidelity is required of the wives, but the husbands are known, on occasion, "to play around with other women." The wives do not "run around with other men" to any appreciable extent, and they bitterly condemn a woman who does. The children are the mutual concern of both parents and are reared without the aid of servants or domestic help. They are taught early in life that the family will help them as much as it can, but their future success will depend upon their own efforts rather than on their family or inherited wealth. Family decisions are made generally between husband and wife, but the wife exerts far more influence than her husband on things that pertain to the home, the garden, and the children. She makes decisions, usually independently, that affect the family "socially." The father generally plays the dominant role in an "economic" question, but with the advice, often the agreement, of his wife.

Class IV. The family pattern is sharply different from class III. Family stability so characteristic of the higher classes begins to give way to instability; exactly one-third of the families have been broken by separation, divorce, or death. This is a strong contrast to class III, where only 18 percent have been broken by these same factors. Males marry when they are in their early twenties, females in their late teens. Children normally are born from 10 to 18 months later. In our families, 55 percent of the class IV mothers gave birth to their first child before they were 20 years of age, whereas only 19 percent of the class III mothers gave birth to their first child before their twentieth birthday. Class IV women also have more children. The mean number per family is 4.3.

The roles of the wife and mother are encompassed by her domestic duties —cleaning, washing, ironing, mending, preparation of the family's meals, cutting out and making the children's clothes, particularly little girls'. There is no part-time help except in an emergency such as childbirth or illness; even then, it is dispensed with as soon as possible. Class IV housewives are discriminated against if they have ambitions to join the Women's Club or other "social" organizations. "Their place" is "in the home" or "on the job." They are judged by the way they keep their houses, dress their children, and manage the family budget. Emphasis is placed on wifely virtues—good housekeeper, good cook, good mother, good sewer, careful of her children's welfare. The husbands are judged as providers and by their moral actions. Neither the men nor the women are expected to do more than work hard, pay their bills, raise their family in the manner expected of this class, vote "right" in elections, and, above all, eschew any radical or "bolshevik" ideas.

Formal educational experience is limited almost exclusively to the public elementary and high schools. One-third of the fathers and a fifth of the mothers have not graduated from the eighth grade; one-sixth of the fathers and one-fourth of the mothers have attended high school, but only slightly more than one father out of twenty and one mother out of eleven have graduated from high school. Most class IV children aspire to a high school diploma, but the parents often are not convinced of its value, and they have few, if any, scruples about letting a child quit school or actually taking him out to work without a good reason.

There appears to be a definite attempt on the part of the factory workers to "get away from the wife" for a few hours at least once or twice a week. While the men are away, the women may call on a neighbor, putter about the house, or just relax from the labor, noise, and excitement of the daily grind of preparing meals, putting up lunches, cleaning the house, washing and ironing clothes, going to market, and caring for the children. The man's escape from home may be an adjustment to a tired, irritable, and frustrated wife who has a task that is too difficult for her to do "with what she has to do it with." The higher classes know little about the leisure activities of the class IV's, and they care less. This class is taken for granted, and the existence of its members is largely ignored except insofar as they perform economic and political functions.

Class V. Privacy in the home is almost nonexistent; parents, children, "in-laws" and their children, and parts of a broken family may live in two or three rooms. There is little differentiation in the use of rooms—kitchen, dining room, living room, and bedroom functions may be combined from necessity into a single use area. Bath and toilet facilities are found in approximately one home in seven. City water is piped near or into 77 percent of the homes within the city limits. . . .

The family pattern is unique. The husband-wife relationship is more or less an unstable one, even though the marriage is sanctioned either by law or understandings between the partners. Disagreements leading to quarrels and vicious fights, followed by desertion by either the man or the woman, possibly divorce, are not unusual. The evidence indicates that few compulsive factors, such as neighborhood solidarity, religious teachings, or ethical considerations, operate to maintain a stable marital relationship. On the contrary, the class culture has established a family pattern where serial monogamy is the rule. Legal marriages are restricted within narrow limits to class equals. However, exploitive sex liaisons between males from the higher classes frequently occur with teen-age girls, but they rarely result in marriage. Marriage occurs in the middle teens for the girls and the late teens or early twenties for the boys. Doctors, nurses, and public officials who know these families best estimate that from one-fifth to one-fourth of all births are illegitimate. Irrespective of the degree of error in this estimate, 78 percent of the mothers gave birth to their first child before they were 20 years of age. Another trait that marks the family complex is the large number of children. The mean is 5.6 per mother, the range, 1 to 13. There is little prenatal or postnatal care of either mother or child. The child is generally delivered at home, usually by a local doctor, the county nurse, or a midwife, but in the late 1930's some expectant mothers entered the local hospital. Hospital deliveries, however, are a recent innovation and not widely diffused. Death, desertion, separation, or divorce has broken more than half the families (56 percent). The burden of child care, as well as support, falls on the mother more often than on the father when the family is broken. The mother-child relation is the strongest and most enduring family tie.

Changes in Sex Interest and Sex Life

Because of the taboos that surround sex and discussion of sex, a factual account of this aspect of development has much to contribute to an understanding of social and marital relations. Although sex is obviously important in marriage, the emphasis of a separate section should not be interpreted as implying that it is the all-important factor in marital adjustment. Terman's conclusion, following extensive study of marital happiness, provides proper perspective: "Our data . . . indicate . . . that the influence of sexual factors is at most no greater than that of the combined personality and background factors, and that it is probably less" (99, p. 376).

DEVELOPMENT OF SEX INTEREST AND SEX BEHAVIOR IN CHILDHOOD AND ADOLESCENCE

The existence of erotic needs and erotic behavior dating from early infancy has long been assumed by Freud (7) and other writers and researchers and has been recently emphasized by Kinsey. Rather complete sex responses occur in some cases even in infancy (51, 52).[15] And almost as soon as they are able to talk children reveal their curiosity through question-asking (41). Contrary to the view urged by Freud and many others (7) that children enter a period of sexual quiescence—a latency period—between 4 or 5 years of age and pubescence, data on actual behavior indicate increasing interest in sex. The proportion of youngsters who are engaging in preadolescent sex play with others increases until 9 in girls and until 12 in boys, after which ages the incidence decreases. But (and this is an important point) the proportion who have at one time or another engaged in masturbation is steadily increasing (51, 52). As Kinsey has commented:

The cessation of pre-adolescent sex play in the later pre-adolescent years was taken by Freud and by many of his followers to represent a period of sexual latency. On the contrary, it seems to be a period of inactivity which is imposed by the culture upon the socio-sexual activities of a maturing child, especially if the child is female. Pre-adolescent masturbation is, on the other hand, usually carried over from the pre-adolescent to the adolescent and adult

[15] For reviews and discussion of the research literature on preadolescent sexuality, see Sears (87), Willoughby (108), Kinsey (51, 52), and Ford and Beach (34).

years, probably because it does not fall under the restraints which are imposed on socio-sexual activity. This provides further evidence that no biologic latency is involved in the discontinuity of the socio-sexual activities. (51, p. 116.)

Nonetheless, the advent of pubescence likely gives some impetus to the sex drive, and personal and social pressures for heterosexual activity increase. "When is petting right and when wrong?" was the most frequent problem raised for discussion in a survey of topics for young peoples' discussion groups (16). That most adolescents indulge in petting has long been well established (91). In one study some 18 percent of college students considered necking and petting necessary to popularity and 22 percent thought it a routine part of boy-girl relations (23). But most thought it not essential to popularity with the opposite sex (81). According to Kinsey, by 15 years of age about 40 percent of girls and slightly less than 60 percent of boys have indulged at one time or another in petting. By 20, these figures had increased to close to 90 percent for both sexes. And by 20 years of age, about 20 percent of each sex had experienced sexual climax through petting (51, p. 233; 52, p. 535).

Since one objection to adolescent petting is that it leads to greater sex liberties, with attendant dangers of pregnancy, venereal disease, or wantonness, figures on the incidence of premarital sex relations are pertinent. Various studies (39, 61, 99, 106) have indicated that between 25 and 35 percent of wives have had premarital intercourse and about 50 to 75 percent of husbands (39, 99, 106), but often such relations were with the future spouse. According to Kinsey's more recent and more extensive data, about 20 percent of females and 44 percent of males of educational level equivalent to college have had premarital coitus by age 20 (51, p. 333; 52, p. 550). But marked cultural differences exist. Males of low educational level were much less likely to pet to climax but were more likely to engage in premarital intercourse. Of course, in evaluating all such facts, special reservations must be made because of the difficulties in obtaining accurate information. Kinsey's research, for example, though extensive, likely contains errors because of sampling problems and interview procedures.

Petting or sexual intercourse may or may not involve a climax or orgasm, and the sexes differ markedly in the age at which this reaction is experienced. Despite the fact that girls show earlier physical signs of sexual maturity (about one and a quarter years earlier than boys, according to a recent paper [73]) and an earlier beginning of masturbation and orgasm experience, the general trends show a much slower *increase* in age incidence of orgasm among females. The facts, in the form of cumulative percentage curves, are shown in Figure 112. Apparently orgasm is experienced by the human male almost simultaneously with pubescence, and by the end of the teens almost all, if not all, have had this experience. This is not so for females. In contrast, development of sexual responsiveness in women to the point of orgasm is retarded to such a degree that it is not until approximately 20 years of age that half

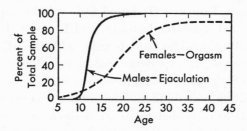

Figure 112. Accumulative Incidence of Orgasm with Age for the Two Sexes, Showing the Percentage at Each Age Who Have Experienced Orgasm, and the Slower Development of Women in This Respect. (Adapted from A. C. Kinsey, et. al., Sexual Behavior in the Human Female, Philadelphia, W. B. Saunders, 1953, p. 184.)

of the female population has experienced orgasm and by 35 only 90 percent have had the experience—69 percent of those who had never married and 95 percent of those who had ever been married. And for some women the orgasmic reaction is only seldom achieved during the entire span of marriage. The experience of erotic arousal is more general: about half of Kinsey's sample of women have had this experience by 15 and 89 percent by 20 (51).

Although Kinsey makes much of this "slower" development in the female and considers it a fundamental sex difference, the present writers venture the opinion that this difference is largely a product of the differential treatment that the sexes receive in sex instruction and the different social controls imposed upon them.[16] Margaret Mead, in her vivid contrast of the sexes in the American culture, points out that the learning and response pattern demanded of girls prior to marriage inevitably handicap them in their later sex adjustment. "Petting . . . requires a very special sort of adjustment in both male and female. The first rule of petting is the need for complete control of just how far the physical behavior is to go; one sweeping impulse, one acted-out desire for complete possession or complete surrender, and the game is lost, and lost ignobly. The controls on this dangerous game that is so like a ski-

[16] This is not to deny that biological differences, e. g., differences in the complexity of sex structures, may not also play a role.

slide, yet which must never be treated as a ski-slide, are placed in the hands of the girls. The boy is expected to ask for as much as possible, the girl to yield as little as possible. . . . The complete total relaxation of feminine surrender . . . is hardly available to women who have had to live through years of bridling their every impulse to yield and surrender" (*70*, pp. 290, 294).

One might conclude from the foregoing that indulgence in petting bodes ill for later marital adjustment. Or it might be argued that petting may result in fixation at an immature level of sexual response. Apparently neither is the case. Terman (*99*) found little relationship between adolescent petting and marital adjustment, and Kinsey (*51*, pp. 264–265) believes that petting provides most females with their first real understanding of a heterosexual experience and plays a highly significant and favorable role in their psychosexual development.

Whatever positive contributions premarital sex experiences make, it would be foolish to deny that there are dangers of unfortunate social consequences. How to handle this matter is a vexing problem for many parents, and there is no easy solution. Two suggestions, however, may be offered. The first relates to the provision for teen-agers of wholesome surroundings for their recreational activities wherein they can enjoy each other's company under the supervision of their own age mates and under the general (but not dominating or unduly restrictive) supervision of adults. This can be accomplished in the home, school, or community, but most desirably in all three. The second suggestion relates to the provision of adequate sex instruction so that such erotic experiences as youngsters may have will not be in the context of naïveté regarding sexual and reproductive functions and the possible consequences. But such instruction must be carefully handled, since unwholesome sex attitudes do appear to interfere with good marital adjustment in adult years (*99*).

The importance of adults facing directly the problem of sex education of their children is illustrated in Table 92 which shows sources of sex information reported by 190 college men and 174 college women. Most frequently mentioned were "books and pamphlets" and "friends of the same sex." Mother, friend of the opposite sex, school, father, and doctor ranked next in that order. It is apparent that these college students were essentially "on their own" when it came to getting sex information; only about half had received a major portion of their sex information directly from their parents. While it is undoubtedly true that the home is the best place for sex instruction, it is apparent that even in homes of better-educated parents this responsibility is not being discharged. Perhaps ignorance, embarrassment, or personal sex maladjustment of the parents stand in the way. Thus, there is a strong argument for objective presentation and discussion of the facts of human reproduction in schools. But in any event, instruction must be timed to interest and need, adjusted in detail and extent to the maturity level (intellectual maturity as well as maturity of experience and knowledge) of the individual, and handled in an objective, frank way. Children, like adults, are quick to sense embarrassment and implied taboos from actions and general behavior, and such factors may condition attitudes and/or influence the source of information they seek in the future even more than what is said.

Since the achievement of mature heterosexual orientation is one of the most significant developmental tasks of adolescence, parents may become greatly disturbed over failure of their offspring to become interested in the opposite sex or over undue attachment to a same-sex friend. Above all, it is desired that

TABLE 92. The Percentages of a Group of College Students Who
Stated That They Had Obtained Sex Information
from Various Sources

Source	Men	Women
Mother	18	55
Father	20	8
Brothers	5	5
Sisters	4	12
Friend of the same sex	64	64
Friend of the opposite sex	27	24
Doctor	24	5
School	20	30
Books and pamphlets	68	62
Other sources, such as church	11	8
Number of cases	190	174

SOURCE: Reprinted by permission from L. D. Rockwood and M. E. N. Ford, *Youth, Marriage, and Parenthood: The Attitudes of 364 University Juniors and Seniors Towards Courtship, Marriage, and Parenthood*, New York, John Wiley, 1945.

sex interests be *normal*. Recent studies, especially Kinsey's, have served to emphasize the great varieties of sexual behavior characterizing the human organism of both sexes. Actually many behaviors popularly thought to represent extreme deviation are fairly commonplace. The wide incidence of homosexual experience is a case in point. It is of some interest that according to one study (61) close crushes between girls in adolescence are practically universal (and some are recognized as having definite sexual components), yet practically all achieved mature heterosexual adjustment. Evidence currently available emphasizes the view that the development of aberrations in sexual behavior, including homosexuality, is more a function of circumstances of learning than of endocrine or other biological predisposition (5, 52). The preventative appears to be general rather than specific and to involve the development of broad interests, social skills, realistic attitudes toward sex and the "ideal" of the opposite sex, and adequate opportunity to meet and associate with the opposite sex.

SEX ADJUSTMENT IN MARRIAGE

It has been pointed out earlier that sex adjustments in marriage are somewhat more difficult to make than many other types of adjustment and take a longer time. Terman (99) has contributed more specific data on this question by comparing the extent to which married people desire sexual intercourse more or less frequently than they have it. He interpreted the ratio between the two as an indication of the degree of sex hunger or satiety characterizing the individual. In slightly more than half of the cases (53 percent of men, 54 percent of women) the ratio was close to unity, suggesting optimum satisfaction for the majority. More men (44 percent) than women (22 percent) reported preference exceeding performance to a degree suggesting sex hunger, whereas more women (24 percent) than men (3 percent) appear satiated. Those couples who were well matched with respect to sex drive averaged happier in their marriages than did either husbands or wives who were unequal in this respect. When the disparity was so great that one spouse was in a more or less chronic state of sex hunger while the other was in a state of satiety, their happiness dropped off significantly.

Orgasm capacity of the wife was another factor that seemed to Terman genuinely important to her own marital happiness as well as to her husband's. Those women who experienced orgasm regularly, and their husbands as well, had reliably higher happiness scores than those women of lesser capacity (and their husbands), whereas those who never experienced orgasm, and the husbands of this group, averaged lowest.

These two factors—relative strength of sex drive of the two spouses and orgasm capacity of wife—were the two sexual factors that seemed correlated with general happiness in marriage. Yet the problem is complex; sexual compatibility is influenced by psychological compatibility. "Couples who are psychologically well-mated are likely to show a surprising tolerance for the things that are not satisfactory in their relationships. The psychologically ill-mated show no such tolerance but instead are prone to exaggeration in their reports on sexual maladjustment" (99). Five percent of the husbands rated high in happiness by Terman had wives who never experienced orgasm, whereas 9 percent of a "low happiness" group of husbands had wives who always experienced orgasm.

Among "high happiness" wives, 7 percent never experienced orgasm, and 10 percent of the "low happiness" wives reported always having orgasms. Clearly there is no single formula for marital happiness.

The matter of *changing* sex adjustment, already mentioned, deserves further attention. Although the early teens appears to be the period of greatest sexual capacity (52) for those males who are sexually active, it will be recalled from the chapter on physical change that no significant decline in frequency of sexual activity occurs until the thirties. From that point onward there is a steady and regular decline until extreme old age. Figure 113, taken from another study, is in agreement with those findings. No acceleration in rate of decline in frequency of sexual *activity*

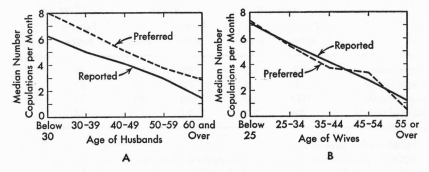

Figure 113. Showing Age Trends in Reported and Preferred Frequency of Sexual Intercourse for Husbands (A) and for Wives (B). (By permission from *Psychological Factors in Marital Happiness*, by L. M. Terman, New York, McGraw-Hill, 1938, pp. 272–273.)

is evident at the climacteric, but there appears to be some shift on the part of women in *desire* for sexual activity. But clearly, the menopause or "change of life" does not mark the end of the sex life. The coincidence of the curve for *desired* frequency of sexual relations with the curve for *reported* frequency in the instance of women and the greater desire as compared with reported frequency in the case of men suggests that in marriage, as prior to marriage, the pattern of sexual activity is determined largely by the female. Though frequency of intercourse declines with age, women increasingly react with orgasm. The median female of Kinsey's population experienced orgasm in 63 percent of coitus during the first year of marriage but 85 percent of the time during the twentieth year (51).

Contrary to the view expressed above, Kinsey argues that the pattern of sexual activity in marriage is largely determined by the male. The figures in Table 93, abstracted from his more extensive data, show trends with age for total sexual outlet (orgasm) from any sources for married and single males and females. Kinsey makes much of the fact that for single women there is no decline with age whereas for married women there is. He notes in this connection that the sexual life of single women is not dominated by male patterns (and does not decline) whereas sexual activities of married women largely reflect the capabilities of their husbands and thus must decline. Kinsey interprets these contrasting

TABLE 93.   Median Number of Times per Week Orgasm Is Experienced, from All Causes, Among Single and Married Males and Females Who Are Sexually Active at Those Ages

| | | Age | | | |
| | Adol.–15 | | 31–35 | | 46–50 | |
	Percent Active	Freq.	Percent Active	Freq.	Percent Active	Freq.
Single male	95	2.3	99	1.6	92	1.1
Single female	22	.5	70	.4	61	.5
Married male	100[a]	3.2[a]	100	2.1	99	1.2
Married female	78[a]	2.2[a]	94	1.5	94	.8

[a] In this instance, ages 16–20.

SOURCE: Based on A. C. Kinsey, et al., Sexual Behavior in the Human Female, Philadelphia, W. B. Saunders, 1953, p. 549 and A. C. Kinsey, et al., Sexual Behavior in the Human Male, Philadelphia, W. B. Saunders, 1948, p. 226.

trends as suggestive of fundamental differences (likely due, it is hypothesized, to hormonal differences) between the sexes with respect to sexual aging. The importance of this circumstance for changing marital adjustment is pointed out in the following quotation:

One of the tragedies which appears in a number of the marriages originates in the fact that the male may be most desirous of sexual contact in his early years, while the responses of the female are still undeveloped and while she is still struggling to free herself from the acquired inhibitions which prevent her from participating freely in the marital activity. But over the years most females become less inhibited and develop an interest in sexual relations which they may then maintain until they are in their fifties or even sixties. But by then the responses of the average male may have dropped so considerably that his interest in coitus, and especially in coitus with a wife who has previously objected to the frequencies of his requests, may have sharply declined. Many of the husbands in the sample reported that early in their marriages they had wanted coitus more often than their wives had wanted it. Many of the younger married females reported that they would be satisfied with lower coital rates than their husbands wanted. On the other hand, in the later years of marriage, many of the females had expressed the wish that they could have coitus more frequently than their husbands were then desiring it. Most of the decline in the male's interest may have represented physiologic aging; part of it may have been the product of a failure to work out effective relations in the earlier years of marriage; and part of it may have been a product of the fact that a number of the males—especially the better-educated males—were engaging in extramarital activities in their forties and fifties at the expense of coitus with their wives. (*51*, pp. 353–354.)

The present writers are inclined to agree with much of the foregoing quotation. Probably many such instances of contrary aging trends exist among married couples and cause problems of the type suggested. And the present writers agree with the largely psychological explanation given these trends *in this particular quotation*. But they do *not* believe Kinsey's data to constitute convincing evidence that a fundamental *biological* difference exists between the sexes with respect to sexual aging.[17] In fact, it is well known that aging effects in physiological functions are most apparent when the organism is behaving near the ceiling of its capacity and may hardly be noticeable when the organism is behaving at a lower level. Actually, cultural controls may so suppress experience and responsiveness among single women that aging effects might well be negligible. It is probably true that in the *present* culture, married women do experience increased psychological freedom and desire with respect to sex as inhibitions are, in the course of time, eliminated. But the writers venture the opinion that women who enter marriage with few inhibitions (and the proportion seems to be increasing) exhibit greater sexual capacity and need in their youth or young adult years.

Parent-Child Relationships During the Course of Life

The discussion thus far has concerned mainly relationships between husbands and wives. Relationships with other members of their families —notably their children or their own parents—are obviously important in understanding marriage and family life, not only because of the satisfactions children provide and the problems they create, but because of the pervasive effect of parent-child relationships upon personality growth and emotional development of youngsters. Some such issues have already been commented upon.

[17] Kinsey has emphasized biological determinants of these different age trends in many places in his more recent volume, and this interpretation has received wide publicity in the many popular reviews of his volume prior to its release. Hence, considerable space has been given here to a contrary interpretation of his data.

Freud and his followers (7) have long emphasized the tremendous importance for the child's development of his relationships with his parents, particularly his mother, during the first years of life. How feeding situations, toilet training, and sex behavior are handled during the first two or three years are deemed especially important. Biological developments are presumed to play an important role in the child's relationship with his parents. For example, around the fourth or fifth year and again at pubescence, it is presumed that the child experiences a strong attraction to the opposite-sex parent and experiences feelings of hostility toward the same-sex parent. Feelings of attraction and/or hostility between children and parents might thus be expected to show rather consistent age trends.

While granting the psychological importance of parent-child relationships from a very early age, one might well question the universality of these patterns as well as their essential biological basis. Homes differ in important ways; parents play different roles and behave differently toward their children. Thus, parents from rural, small-town, and urban areas have been shown to differ in the strictness of their discipline (96); families at different social levels have been shown to utilize different methods of child-rearing (27); and home environments in the same small-town setting and at about the same social level have been shown to differ in significant ways (3). Several studies (3, 20, 82) have produced evidence suggesting that homes differ in concern shown for the child, in degree of democratic guidance provided for children, in permissiveness, in parent-child harmony, in degree to which the parents are themselves sociable and well adjusted, in general level of activity, and in the degree to which parents suggest and direct the activities of the child.[18]

Clearly, homes differing in such respects pose quite different problems for the children growing up in them and represent quite different types of learning situations. In a very real sense each home is unique since the

[18] These seven dimensions, based on factorial analysis by Roff (82) of more specific data (3, 20), have been further reduced. It has recently been suggested that the basic information regarding home environment as suggested by the above studies relates to three questions: (1) How far does the home sustain and encourage dependence, and how far does it deny satisfaction to independence? (2) How far do its methods of child training reflect democratic practices and values, or to what extent are they authoritarian and undemocratic? (3) To what extent is there a strict orderliness in the home, or to what extent is the home lax and unorganized? (67).

home environment created by the parents represents extensions of their own unique personalities. The needs and conflicts of the parents are determiners of the pressures (or their lack) brought to bear on the children. For example, in one study it was shown that a parental need to have one's children appear to advantage in the eyes of others usually results in parents putting substantial pressure on their children to perform adequately (71). And the character of parent-child relationships may be expected to vary markedly from home to home and from parent to parent. Evidence exists, too, to suggest that the same home may provide different psychological environments—sometimes strikingly different—for different children (87, 95). Factors such as these are likely far more important in determining parent-child relations than the biological attraction and competition hypothesized by the Freudians and mentioned earlier. What now are the changes in parent-child relationships which occur, on the average, as the children mature?

Which parent does the child prefer? And does his preference change as he matures? According to the Freudian view mentioned earlier, one might expect increases at particular ages in preference for opposite-sex parent with corresponding decreases in preference for same-sex parent. Actually, no such trends and contrasts occur. In young ages there is greater preference on the part of children of both sexes for the mother, an increase over ages 5 to 9 in number expressing this preference according to one study (90), but also an increase in expression of no preference. By late adolescence and adulthood little preference is expressed on the average (39, 92). In those cases where strong preferences or conflicts do exist, there may be evidence of far-reaching and long-lasting effects, as in selection of mate and role in marriage. And these conflicts may be visited upon the next generation as well! In general, preferences for parents will depend upon who meets the child's needs. Little wonder that the typical child of either sex prefers his mother, or when asked to express preferences under various conditions (cut finger, needs toy fixed, wants money), will express preference for father or mother according to the situation (35), parents playing, as they do, different roles in children's lives.

As the child grows up, changes also occur in the extent of conflict with parents. Evidence from various studies (6, 65) seems to suggest that at least for girls friction with the family increases in the teens. In an investigation conducted in Austria, for example, in which children were asked to write about their relationships with their families, girls revealed increasingly bad relations up to 13 and better relations thereafter.[19] A recent study in this country utilized a "projective test" in which young-sters tell stories about pictures presented to them, with the expectation that they will unwittingly reveal their own attitudes in their stories. (Such pictures often elicit stories involving parents and their offspring.) The resulting stories suggested increases in tension between girls and their parents from 9 to 15 years of age. But after 15, the relative proportion of tension-revealing stories dropped off (65).

The situation in the case of boys seems to be somewhat different. Al-though the last study mentioned did not include boys, the European in-vestigation (also cited above) found that the age of 15 (corresponding roughly in terms of pubescent status with 13 in girls) did not stand out so clearly in their records (10). And scattered American evidence seems to confirm this view and to suggest that in general, boys have fewer con-flicts with parents (6, 79, 93, 101).

How can one account for these age trends and for the difference be-tween boys and girls? Although there may be some sex attraction (likely on an unconscious level) in some cases in the family situation and result-ing hostility toward the same-sex parent-competitor, the increasing con-flict with parents on the part of girls appears more likely due to the greater pressures put on daughters by their parents. The normal ven-turing of girls into more intimate relations with boys is likely to represent rather threatening problems to some parents and result in criticism or in-creasing restrictiveness—a circumstance that tends to generate aggression and hostility in the child. To what extent the parent in turn may become hostile toward the child is not clear, but challenging of parental authority or moral codes is likely to generate tension and hostility. And the parent may in some cases experience hostility growing out of unconscious envy of the adolescent's physical vigor and status at a time when he (or she) himself is slipping.

The above line of reasoning would seem also to explain the lesser con-flict on the part of boys with their parents. They have typically been given greater opportunities for independent experience, are not so closely supervised, and do not so regularly conduct their dating under super-vision of their own parents. Rather, they have at least some dates in the girl's home and conform to the rules (how late dates may last, for ex-ample) set by *her* parents. This opens girls more than boys to criticism

[19] Study by A. Buseman cited by Buhler (10).

by their parents, with resulting parent-daughter irritation. The parents of boys, on the other hand, may have little knowledge of their son's social life and fewer opportunities to criticize and supervise. Such an interpretation of the sources of parent-child conflict, in terms of the frustration-aggression hypothesis (31) mentioned in an earlier chapter, also recognizes that homes will vary greatly in the extent to which there is parent-child conflict, which parent is involved, and whether there is increase in such conflict at adolescence. Some homes have much; some little or none.

Evidence regarding particular points of parent-adolescent conflict supports the view outlined above that the increase in tension is due to frustrations of the youngsters posed by parents and to threats to the authority and moral codes of parents posed by the youngsters. It is noted in Table 94, for example, that a chief source of criticism of parents by

TABLE 94. Percentage Distribution of the Criticisms of Mothers and Fathers Offered by Their Adolescent Offspring

Types of Criticism	Criticisms of Mother		Criticisms of Father	
	Boys	Girls	Boys	Girls
Matters related to discipline and control	26	33	24	25
Temperamental traits and behavior	11	19	12	20
Personal habits and conduct	12	7	29	24
Educational adjustment and control	13	13	10	10
Ideas, attitudes, and beliefs	3	2	1	1
Work, self-sacrifice	12	8	9	3
Social adjustments and behavior	5	2	1	2
Miscellaneous, trivial	18	17	14	13
Number of criticisms	299	376	304	375

SOURCE: Adapted from L. H. Stott, Adolescents' dislikes regarding parental behavior and their significance, *J. Genet. Psychol.*, 1935, 26:169–176.

adolescents involves "matters related to discipline and control" and the chief causes of quarrels (Table 95) are related to social life, friends, and matters of money. Still another study depicting points of conflict between adolescents and their mothers emphasized the restrictive role played by parents (6).

The extent to which factors other than authority relationships may create parent-adolescent conflict is often difficult to study because they may operate without awareness of either party and they may be expressed so subtly that their symptoms may be referable to other influences. Thus, parents and adolescents, living in the intimate relationships of home life, are at significantly

Table 95.   Percentage Distribution of Causes of Quarrels with Fathers Reported by 989 Boys and 1142 Girls, and with Mothers Reported by 852 Boys and Girls

Types of Quarrels	Quarrels with Mother		Quarrels with Father	
	Boys	Girls	Boys	Girls
Relating to social life and friends	36	42	40	51
Relating to economic factors, work, and spending money	30	23	35	25
Related to clothes	6	17	1	5
Relating to education and vocation	8	3	7	5
Relating to other members of the family	5	5	2	4
Relating to other matters	15	9	15	11
Total percentage	100	99	100	101

SOURCE: Adapted from H. H. Punke, High-School youth and family quarrels, *School and Society,* 1943, *58:*507–511.

different phases of life: the adolescent is reaching his or her prime, the parent experiencing middle-age decline. The adolescent is hitching his wagon to a star; the parent at about the same time may have finally reached the conclusion that he will never achieve his early ambitions. When her daughter is reaching the full bloom of youthful beauty, the mother may be conscious of her own waning looks and the nearness of menopause. Cultural change has separated the generations with respect to values, particularly borderline moral issues, at a time when the adolescent is caught in the whirl of the most social years of life, and when the parents have settled down to a sedentary, home-restricted pattern of living. In all these differences are to be found sources of differences in viewpoint, sources of misunderstanding, and possibly origins of unconscious hostility (envy, jealousy) felt by a parent toward the young person. These matters, though discussed (25), have not been subjected to the type of research which might reveal their importance.

THE CHILD'S ACHIEVEMENT OF INDEPENDENCE FROM PARENTS

Optimal psychological growth involves the gradual achievement of emotional independence from parents and the development of self-reliance and capacity for self-direction. Yet to a considerable degree parents seem to resist the child's striving for freedom and for maturity. This resistance to independence and the failure of parents to permit as much decision-making on the part of children as might be desired, results, it is suggested, in a growth curve of self-reliance similar to the lower curve in Figure 114. Retarded during much of childhood, the child must grow up in a hurry at adolescence. This may well be a key factor in the causation of an adolescent period. The upper curve in Figure 114 shows steady growth through gradually widened opportunities and responsibilities and probably comes closer to the desirable situation. It may well be, however, that the lower curve may never reach an optimal adult level, since later experiences of independent behavior may not have the same psychological value as earlier experiences, and thus may result in a rather permanent lower level of adult maturity.

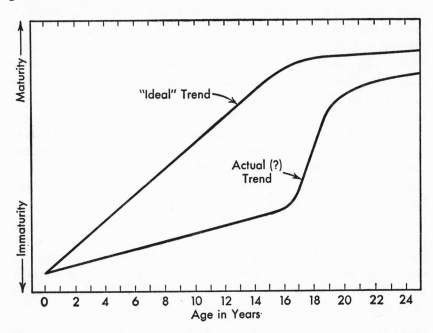

Figure 114. Schematic Diagram Suggesting How Emancipation from Parents and Self-Reliance Might Best Develop, and How It Probably Develops in the American Culture Under Conditions of Parental Resistance to Independence. The line suggesting "actual" development does not reach as high a level as the ideal trend on the assumption that late independence experiences are not as significant as early experiences.

Differences in the degree of independence are apparent at very young ages, even at the nursery school level (86). In part, such differences may be conditioned by inherited factors such as differences in energy level which result in greater or less interaction of the child with his environment or differences in size which result in differential treatment of children by their parents. Indeed, one study of "emancipation" from parents revealed height and weight to be among the factors most reliably associated with emancipation status (29), and another study (50) showed early-maturing boys to be more mature in behavior. One reason for such a relationship is suggested by other research showing that larger and more mature-looking children (those who mature earlier) tend to be granted more adult privileges and to have more expected of them (4).

But other influences are at work. Thus, the differences between parental treatment of first and second babies (likely due to changed attitudes and responsibilities of parents) may result in differences in the independence shown by the offspring. One study (86) noted that such treatment differences involved greater self-demand (rather than rigid schedule) feeding of second and later-born children and generally fewer nursing and feeding frustrations, less attention and babying at bedtime, and less cautioning about sickness and danger. Although such differences might be expected to be responsible for the slight positive relationship between dependency behavior and ordinal position apparent (in this study) at the preschool level, the analysis suggested nursing and weaning frustration in infancy to be the responsible factor.

Various studies have tended to emphasize the methods of control utilized by parents and the general quality of parent-child interaction as factors in child emancipation (1, 88, 89). Personality factors and maladjustments of the parents are probably important determiners of such differences. One notable study of instances of maternal overprotection has emphasized the variable of parent adjustment. Evidences of excessive maternal care obtained from case records involved such behaviors as the following:

(1) excessive contact, e. g., a mother sleeping with her fourteen-year-old son; (2) prolongation of infant care, e. g., breast feeding to age four years; (3) prevention of development of independent behavior, including such descriptive terms about the mother-child relationship as "she won't take any risks," "she always fights his battles"; (4) lack or excess of maternal control, shown in overindulgence of the child in regard to privileges or possessions, disregard on the child's part of eating time, sleeping time—in general, doing what he pleases, undeterred by the mother's commands or pleadings. (64)

The manifestations of these types of overprotection are apparent in the following case description:

Case 5
Excessive contact: Mother has slept with him the past three years. Up to age 7, she never let him go out with any adult (even father) except herself.

Prolongation of infantile care: When the patient is disobedient she puts him to bed in the afternoon, even now. She still prepares special food for him when he refuses to eat. She still sits by and coaxes.

Prevention of independent behavior: Mother delayed his schooling until he was 7 because she did not like him to leave her. She blocks the plan of sending him to boarding school. She kept him from having friends or learning bad things from other children. When he was sent to camp at 14, the mother visited him on the second day, found that his feet were wet and took him home.

Maternal control: General obedient, submissive response to maternal domination. Uses aggressive methods to maintain his dependency on the mother, insisting she walk to school with him, et cetera.

Study of the parents of 20 such instances of overprotection suggested the importance of frustrations and the resulting accentuation of certain psychological needs on the part of the mother as a determining factor in her treatment of the child. Thus, 13 of the 20 mothers had had experiences that might well increase maternal longing, e. g., long periods of sterility, spontaneous miscarriages. Sixteen instances of sexual maladjustment suggested the overprotection might well involve simple compensatory increase in mother love through blocking of other channels of expression. And 16 of the 20 overprotective mothers were found to have experienced severe privation of parental love in their own childhood, suggesting the possibility of an "affection hunger" which may have prompted the overprotective relationship (*64*).

There will, of course, be substantial differences among parents in different subcultures in their own psychological needs which find expression in their children and in the typical patterns of child-rearing and discipline practices. As already noted, such practices differ with social-class level and with size of town. One contrast calling for special comment is the differential treatment and expectations accorded boys and girls. In commenting upon such sex differences, one writer (*58*) suggests that the training of boys differs from girls in three important respects: (1) parents tend to speed up, often unwittingly but often deliberately, the emancipation of the boy by providing earlier and more frequent opportunities for independent action; (2) a higher degree of privacy in personal affairs is accorded boys compared with girls; and (3) the daughters of the family are held to a more exacting code of filial and kinship obligation. Such differences in treatment of the sexes should result not only in more rapid emancipation of boys from parents but also in a more *complete* emancipation and independence which may well characterize the average male throughout life. This expectation, especially the more rapid emancipation of boys, appears to be borne out in evidence from several studies (*24, 88, 89*).[20]

PARENT-CHILD RELATIONS AFTER CHILDREN REACH ADULTHOOD

The nature of the relationship between parents and their children, once the children have reached adulthood, has not yet been investigated to any considerable degree. Although modern mobility and urban life have probably resulted in less close ties between parents and their adult offspring compared to a generation or two ago, interaction probably typically continues throughout life, often with important reciprocal advantages between the generations, but often also with irritation, hostilities, and serious limiting demands of one generation upon the other.

It might be expected that the kind of relationship with parents established in the course of growing up would persist in an individual's life after he reached maturity. If he were largely "emancipated" by his late teens or early twenties, he would likely remain thus. If, on the other hand, he were still dependent, it is likely that his parents would continue to satisfy his dependency needs well into adulthood. One writer (*58*) has argued that the differential training received by boys and girls with respect to emancipation has as a major unintended consequence the creation of such strong ties to the girl's family of orientation that she has difficulty in accomplishing the necessary shift, psychoculturally, to the new family of procreation when she marries. Primary loyalty ties to her own family were thought to stand in the way of her developing equally strong loyalty ties in her own marriage. This writer suggests that consequently in-law problems in marriage, (i. e., parent-child relationship at an adult age) more frequently involve the wife's parents than the husband's parents.[21]

Actual investigation of the matter gives a much more favorable picture of in-law relationships than the prevalent "in-law" stereotype would sug-

[20] Winch (*110*) is of the view that mother-son ties are strongest and that emancipation problems are actually greater for the son because he not only has to break the identification with mother but also has to shift from a dependency role to one of independence. Girls, on the other hand, continue their identification with the female sex and their dependency role as they leave parents and marry. Although this may be true, it seems that greater emancipation training more than compensates for difficulties boys have.

[21] See the original article (*58*) for a discussion of contrary views. Komarovsky believes that arguments that conflict with husband's parents are more serious have grown out of the fact that in-law trouble involving the husband's dependence upon his parents, although rarer, may be more acute and, therefore, more obvious.

gest. As the data in Table 96 reveal, most people like their in-laws "considerably" or "very much," and about half of the men and two-fifths of the women queried in this study believed the spouse's family had strengthened their marriage, at least a little. Wives seem more dependent upon their parents than do husbands. They see them more frequently, and they more frequently report homesickness. But, contrary to the expectation expressed in the preceding paragraph, it is the husband's family (particularly his mother) who more frequently causes the difficulty when there is an in-law problem. This is suggested in Table 96 in the

TABLE 96. Percentage of Husbands and Wives (604 Couples, Married Three to Five Years) Reporting Various Attitudes, Judgments, or Behaviors with Respect to "In-Laws"[a]

	Husbands	Wives
Often homesick for father or mother	3	11
Sometimes homesick for father or mother	25	37
See parents 2 or 3 times a week or more	21	40
Like father-in-law "considerably" or "very much"	72	73
Like mother-in-law "considerably" or "very much"	66	61
Dislike father-in-law	7	7
Dislike mother-in-law	8	17
Spouse's family strengthened marriage "considerably" or "very much"	29	22
Spouse's family strengthened marriage "somewhat" or "little"	23	18
Spouse's family neither strengthened nor weakened marriage	40	54
Spouse's family weakened marriage	8	7

[a] N's on which various percentages are based ranged from 464 to 598.

SOURCE: Adapted from P. Wallin. Sex differences in attitudes toward "in-laws": a test of theory, *Amer. J. Sociol.*, 1954, 59:466–469.

fact that 17 percent of wives as compared to 8 percent of husbands disliked their mothers-in-law and that more husbands than wives thought their spouse's family had strengthened their marriage. Another study yielded more striking evidence: 9 out of 10 complaints regarding mothers-in-law were made by women (32).

Although this latter investigation[22] suggested that the prevalent cul-

[22] This exploratory study, though lacking many technical refinements, is reported in an interesting style and with much descriptive material, suggestions for further study, and an extensive bibliography (32). The book is recommended reading on the in-law question. In this study some 1337 individuals were asked, as members of small groups being interviewed, to write on a card the in-law relationship which in his or her experience had proved most troublesome and to give three reasons that made this relationship difficult.

tural stereotype of the "mother-in-law" problem (frequently expressed in hostility-laden humor) is on its way out, the mother-in-law is still most frequently mentioned as the most difficult in-law problem (Table 97). As will be noted "sister-in-law" ran a strong second. Brothers-in-law and fathers-in-law were the most troublesome in-law relationship for only about 5 percent of the respondents. A quarter of the respondents had no difficult in-law problems. When the replies regarding the nature of the mother-in-law complaints were analyzed, the three outstanding complaints—accounting for slightly over half of those mentioned—were meddlesomeness, possessiveness, and nagging.

TABLE 97.   The "In-Law" Named by 1337 Respondents as Representing the Most Difficult In-Law Relationship Experienced

In-Law	Percent Mentioning as "Most Difficult"
Mother-in-law	36.8
Sister-in-law	20.3
Brother-in-law	5.4
Father-in-law	5.0
Daughter-in-law	2.8
Other female in-laws (Aunt-in-law, etc.)	1.6
"All in-laws"	1.5
Son-in-law	.7
Other male in-laws	.1
No difficult in-laws	25.8
Total	100.0

SOURCE: Adapted from Evalyn Duvall, *In-laws: Pro and Con*, New York, Association Press, 1954.

To what extent the mother-in-law stereotype has created a certain predisposition to expect trouble with the mother-in-law, and trouble of a particular type, is, of course, difficult to ascertain. But it is of interest that sisters-in-law, with respect to whom no such cultural stereotype is clearly apparent, were also frequently mentioned as a problem. Much of the in-law friction appears to involve the women of the various families related by marriage. Perhaps this is because society assigns to women more than to men the role of responsibility for interfamily relations. Or perhaps women have more time for visiting with each other and hence greater opportunity for friction. Or perhaps the more submissive role of women makes them a safer target of criticism by their feminine in-laws than would be true of more dominant males. Such matters require much more research attention before answers will be forth-coming. It is clear, though, that the nature of these answers will depend very largely upon the group studied. Apparently the nature of traditional family relationship patterns varies greatly from culture to culture. For example, in groups roughly comparable in social characteristics, 76 percent of Jewish re-spondents mentioned mother-in-law as most difficult, compared to 25 percent of Baptists, and 12 percent of Roman Catholics (32).

When children are young it is the parents who occupy the favored role. But by the time the offspring reach adulthood, or by the time they reach 30, theirs is the favored role; the parents, now middle-aged or past, are likely experiencing status losses with respect to physical and mental traits as well as culturally. And thus the *direction* of the relationship be-tween parents and their children may change. It has been suggested, for example, by one author that there may be in middle age a third re-surgence of the Oedipus situation, but now with the parent evidencing attraction toward the young adult offspring of the opposite sex and view-ing the offspring's spouse as a competitor (28). And certainly the de-pendency relationship may change. Instead of the parent supporting the child and denying him the independence he wishes, the situation may be quite reversed in old age, though in the latter instance there may be considerable insecurity on the part of the oldster because of uncertainty as to whether economic support—let alone psychological support—will be forthcoming (30).

The overlapping of generations is such that the adult in his thirties or forties may well have as dependents not only his own children but a parent as well. Thus, in one study (49), 21 percent of a group of single teachers age 40 to 49 had their mothers as dependents; 5 percent had their fathers, and 3 per-cent had both. The percentages for married women teachers of the same age were 9, 4, 0, respectively, and for married men teachers of this age, 6, 0, 0, re-spectively. These figures are only suggestive since the respondents were by no means representative of the population at large, the women, for example, being all employed. In a recent analysis (42) of the "parent activities" of a group of people over 65, five levels of activity or participating roles were identified, with the category of mutual *independence* (rather than the dependence men-tioned above) being the major category. Eighty percent of 35 fathers and 70 percent of 43 mothers were independent of their children. Among the 35 fathers, 1 was dependent on his children and 1 was in a position of mutual dependence[23] with his children. Two of the fathers had no contact with their children. Of 43 mothers, all had contact with their children; 2 were dependent on their children; and 3 were in the category of mutual dependence.

[23] Defined as a situation in which the parent was furnishing the home and the children took care of him or the children had the home and the parent managed it.

Old people evidence a strong desire for continued independence, possibly accentuated by its threatened loss. Thus, in one study the majority expressed a strong desire to live alone rather than with their children. The investigator summed up her subjects' reactions as follows:

In the homes of their children they feel unwanted, neglected, and in the way. They resent the direction and "bossing" of their children, and even more so that of the "in-laws." They do not want to be treated as if they were old and feeble and helpless, incapable of doing any task properly. In their own homes they are independent, free to run their households in their own fashion. This last is very important. . . . Both men and women emphasized the personal freedom that homes of their own gave them. (72)

A second quotation from one old woman, queried by one of the present writers regarding her personal problems, is an interesting example of the psychological distance that develops between parents and their children during the adult years and of the restrictive "kindness" adults are apt to shower on their aged parents:

My chief anxiety or worry as I approached old age was the loss of my capacity due to illness, and thereby loss of independence in thought and action. Having been left a widow at 40 with two young children to support and educate, and, after being released from that responsibility, having to be the main support of aged parents, all of which prevented me from accumulating enough to make me independent in my old age. God never gave a woman a better son-in-law nor a sweeter daughter, but having lived in distant states since their marriage 20 years ago, our children are almost strangers. You have no tastes in common and above all your children rush you into the grave with mistaken kindness with their "don't"—trying to spare you instead of letting elderly people do what and as much as they are able of the things they like and enjoy. My mother died at 90, four years ago, and I can look back and see how I was unkind to her in the same way. I talked with a friend recently who said she tried to give her mother a "lady's" life, but if she had her back, she would let her take in washings if it would make her happy. The terrible let-down from an active, busy, full-day life is something that has to be experienced to be appreciated, but then individual temperaments vary and can't be judged as a whole. . . . So—when I feel that my body is imprisoned by don'ts and more don'ts, my mind and spirit is my own and free to wander over the pleasant experiences of the past. My work, though hard and exacting, was always a joy to me, and my great regret is that I could not have continued on until I dropped in the harness.

Yet with all such problems, it is well to note that the oldsters who were wary of living with their children nonetheless showed great pride in their offspring and liked to visit them and live near them. In fact, family relationships were named the most frequent source of comfort for the old and were often the most satisfying features of old age. Table 98 shows something of the role of grandparents and great-grandparents and the degree of interaction with their grandchildren. It is noteworthy that a quarter of this group of grandparents had occasional part-time responsibility for their descendants, and even as great-grandparents over half saw their descendants fairly often, played with them, and enjoyed them, although they took no responsibility for them.

TABLE 98. Percentage Distribution of the Roles of Grandparents and Great-Grandparents

Role	Grandparents		Great-Grandparents	
	Men	Women	Men	Women
Full responsibility for grandchildren or great-grandchildren	0	0	0	0
Occasional or part-time responsibility for descendants	20	28	0	6
Social participation only	73	70	57	57
Communication about descendants, no personal contact	0	0	29	31
No interest and no communication with or about descendants	7	2	14	6
Total	100	100	100	100
	N = 30	N = 40	N = 7	N = 16

SOURCE: From R. J. Havighurst and R. Albrecht, *Older People*, New York, Longmans, Green, 1953.

In view of this emphasis upon family relationships as a factor in the adjustment of old people, Table 99 is presented to give a general picture of the living arrangements of some 547 people 65 years of age and over in a midwestern town. Among the changes to be noted here are the *increases* from age 75 on in the number of individuals living alone in their own private homes or in institutions and the increase in middle-aged widows or widowers living with adult children and of older people living with adult children and grandchildren. Notable among the *decreases* beyond 75 are the number of married *couples* living alone in their own homes (this is especially great for women since they are usually married to slightly older men, and also have a greater average length of life than men) and the number of married couples living with adult children. Thus, the later years bring increasing solitude for many, while for others it may bring increasing (perhaps enforced) relationships with own adult children and grandchildren. Older individuals beyond 65 who have the good fortune to be married and have their spouses living prove to be better adjusted than widows, widowers, or those who remained single (*42*). Other studies (*18*, *38*) have indicated the better adjustment of older people who have been able to—or fortunate enough to—maintain their own homes. But, to quote one such investigator, much is to be said for various types of living arrangements:

TABLE 99. Percentage Distribution of a Sample of People Over 65 According to Living Arrangements

Household Pattern	Male		Female	
	65–74	75 Plus	65–74	75 Plus
One generation				
Lone person in				
Institution	3	8	1	7
Rooming house, hotel	3	7	2	0
Own private home	9	18	22	36
Married couple only	48	35	37	9
Subject and nonspouse	8	5	5	6
Two generations				
Married couple and adult children	21	9	8	2
Subject (widow) and adult children	5	9	21	31
Three generations				
Subject (with or without spouse), adult				
children and grandchildren	2	8	4	8
Number of cases	164	74	185	124

SOURCE: From R. J. Havighurst and R. Albrecht, *Older People*, Longmans, Green, 1953.

Each type of living arrangement has its advantages and disadvantages. Granting that it is often impossible for the old person to maintain his home until his death, what type of living arrangement seems best? Clearly, more institutions of the present type are not the answer; nor do rooming houses meet all the problems; homes with adult children have both advantages and disadvantages. A new type of living arrangement is needed that will combine the economic and physical security provided by the institution, the personal contacts found in the own home or the home of adult children, and the activities and sense of usefulness of the person who is still living independently. (*18*)

Summary

This chapter has surveyed the course of heterosexual relations, marriage, and family life from first date to final living arrangements in old age and widowhood. The major features of life-span developments in this important area of human satisfaction and adjustment are now summarized.

1. Dating begins on the average for both sexes at about 14 and "going steady" at about 15. These first intersex social engagements and ties are largely within the same social-class setting. They are influenced by social pressures from parents and peers but also by such individual factors as personality and attractiveness. Succeeding attachments increasingly involve a love component, but, apparently because of differential roles and responsibilities, tend to bring more conflicts for males than for females. Love affairs are most frequent in the teens and create disturbances in about half the cases when broken up. In total, these experiences make important contributions to psychological development and lay the base for intelligent mate selections. Yet parents all too often seem indifferent or actually handicap their youngsters in their early dating experiences.

2. Mates are chosen from the field of eligibles determined by such social factors as similarity in social class, religion, and age; mutuality of interests and values; and preconceptions growing out of family and other relationships of what the "ideal" partner should be. But since important psychological needs are satisfied in close human relationships, choices may involve a meshing of complementary needs (e. g., dominant and dependent) and thus a certain dissimilarity. Engagement periods are used more frequently now than in previous generations for realistic discussion of marriage issues, and they apparentely make contributions to marital happiness, very short or no engagement being associated with unhappiness in marriage.

3. Happiness in marriage is associated with background family factors characterized by happiness, stability, and good parent-child relations; with a marriage reënforced by social sanctions of home and church; with adequate premarriage testing of compatibility through engagement; and with good personality and personal adjustment. But since happiness involves the interaction of two personalities, marital happiness is also related to the extent to which the particular needs and expectations of one partner are satisfied by the particular individual he marries. Thus, people who may not be good marital risks in general or in one partnership might well be in another. This is borne out by the finding that over three-quarters of divorced individuals rated remarriages as happy or very happy.

4. Happiest years of marriage are the early years, marriages settling

down to a moderate level on the average after six or seven years. Changes in happiness during the course of marriage—gains and/or losses—may be explained by changing needs, roles, and expectations, which may result in couples who were well matched at one age being less so later, or those who at first were poorly matched becoming more alike with respect to their needs and expectations and their reciprocal capacity to satisfy each other's needs. Since some areas of adjustment take time to work out, gains may be expected in many instances as the result of learning to adjust. Tensions or basic satisfactions arise at the time of such important events in the family life cycle as pregnancy, unemployment, deaths, retirement, the nature of adjustment being a product largely of individual hopes and expectations as well as the psychological trends thus far characterizing the individuals and families involved.

5. Interest in sex is apparent very early, and though the existence of a sexual "latency" period is doubtful, the sex drive likely receives some impetus at pubescence. Although girls mature sexually earlier than boys, they are slower in achieving a complete sex response, likely because of training which develops strong inhibitions that must be unlearned in marriage. The gradual breakdown of such inhibitions may result in increasing sexual needs on the part of women during the years of marriage when their husbands are experiencing a decline in capacity to satisfy their needs. Here may lie the source of some marital problems. However, it appears that women are increasingly entering marriage with more relaxed sex attitudes and fewer inhibitions, with the result that more experience complete sex response early, a circumstance that may well alter the contrast just noted. Sexual satisfaction in marriage is to a considerable degree the product of good psychological adjustment between the partners rather than a product of any specific sex factor such as technique, contraceptive method, or even orgasm capacity of the wife, though the latter and optimal matching of husband-wife sex drives are, in general, related to marital happiness.

6. An important phase of psychological development involves the gradual emotional emancipation of children from parents and the development of mature independence and self-reliance. Evidence suggests that parents typically retard development much more than is desirable. In the course of development, increased friction develops between children (particularly girls) and their parents. Such conflict may be viewed, in part, as a product of the restrictions imposed by parents as children began to demand more freedom. In short, the resulting frustration leads

to hostility and aggression, and this is more evident in the case of girls because of the greater supervision and control exercised over them by parents. Gaps between the generations are created by differences in developmental status—biologically, socially, and with respect to time perspectives—and these gaps may represent sources of hostilities and misunderstandings. Rate of emancipation and degree of self-reliance seem largely related to manner of control utilized by parent, strict discipline being associated with dependence. Study of extreme instances of overprotection suggest that degree and type of control are functions of parents' personalities and adjustment.

7. Patterns and direction of intergeneration relations change as years pass and children move into the prime of life and parents beyond it. Evidence suggests that many of the negative features of intergeneration relations noted in popular conceptions (the mother-in-law issue, for example) are greatly overdrawn, though of course many instances of conflict do arise. Where in-law problems do arise, they more frequently involve the husband's mother. Actually, most relations are positive and mutually helpful. A common problem in old age, however, appears to be overprotection of the oldsters by their own adult children, with accompanying loss or threat of loss of independence on the part of the oldster. Even so, family relationships are the greatest source of comfort in old age. A special problem, and one not yet solved, is that of housing of old people, especially those whose spouses are no longer living, in such a way as to promote continued relationships with their children and the security of general social contacts and yet preserve their independence and sense of usefulness.

BIBLIOGRAPHY

1. Anderson, J. E., Parents' attitudes on child behavior: a report of three studies, *Child Development*, 1946, 17:91–97.
2. Andrews, R. O., and Christensen, H. T., Relationship of absence of a parent to courtship status: a repeat study, *Amer. Sociol. Rev.*, 1951, 16:541–543.
3. Baldwin, A. L., Kalhorn, J., and Breese, F. H., Patterns of parent behavior, *Psychol. Monogr.*, 1945, Vol. 58.
4. Barker, R. G., Wright, B. A., and Gonick, M. R., *Adjustment to Physical Handicap and Illness*, Social Science Research Council, Bulletin 55, 1946.
5. Beach, F. A., *Hormones and Behavior*, New York, Hoeber, 1948.
6. Block, V. L., Conflicts of adolescents with their mothers, *J. Abnorm. and Soc. Psychol.*, 1937, 32:193–206.

7. Blum, G. S., *Psychoanalytic Theories of Personality*, New York, McGraw-Hill, 1953.

8. Bossard, J. H. S., Marrying late in life, *Social Forces*, 1951, 29:405–408.

9. Buhler, Charlotte, Maturation and motivation, *Personal.*, 1951, 1:184–211.

10. Buhler, Charlotte, The social behavior of the child, in Murchison, Carl (ed.), *Handbook of Child Psychology*, Worcester, Clark University Press, 1931, Chap. 12, pp. 392–431.

11. Burgess, E. W., and Cottrell, L. S., *Predicting Success or Failure in Marriage*, New York, Prentice-Hall, 1939.

12. Burgess, E. W., and Locke, H. J., Comment on Lowrie's "Dating theories and student responses," *Amer. Sociol. Rev.*, 1951, 16:843–844.

13. Burgess, E. W., and Locke, H. J., *The Family*, New York, American Book Company, 1945.

14. Burgess, E. W., and Wallin, P., *Engagement and Marriage*, Philadelphia, Lippincott, 1953.

15. Burgess, E. W., and Wallin, P., Homogamy in social characteristics, *Amer. J. Sociol.*, 1943, 49:117–124.

16. Butterfield, O. M., *Love Problems of Adolescence*, New York, Emerson, 1939.

17. Cavan, R. S., *The American Family*, New York, Crowell, 1953.

18. Cavan, R. S., Family life and family substitutes in old age, *Amer. Sociol. Rev.*, 1949, 14:71–83.

19. Centers, R., Marital selection and occupational strata, *Amer. J. Sociol.*, 1949, 54:530–535.

20. Champney, H., The variables of parent behavior, *J. Abnorm. and Soc. Psychol.*, 1941, 36:525–542.

21. Christensen, H. T., and Philbrick, R. E., Family size as a factor in the marital adjustments of college couples, *Amer. Sociol. Rev.*, 1952, 17:306–312.

22. Clarke, A. C., An examination of the operation of residential propinquity as a factor in mate selection, *Amer. Sociol. Rev.*, 1952, 17:17–22.

23. Cuber, J. F., and Pell, Betty, A method for studying moral judgments relating to the family, *Amer. J. Sociol.*, 1941, 47:12–23.

24. Dale, E., *Children's attendance at motion pictures*, New York, Macmillan, 1935.

25. Davis, A., and Havighurst, R. J., Social class and color differences in child rearing, *Amer. Sociol. Rev.*, 1946, 11:698–710.

26. Davis, K., The sociology of parent-youth conflict, *Amer. Sociol. Rev.*, 1940, 5:523–535.

27. Davis, K., Statistical perspective on marriage and divorce, *Annals of the American Acad. of Polit. and Soc. Sci.*, 1950, 272:9–21.

28. Deutsch, Helene, *The Psychology of Women, A Psychoanalytic Interpretation*, Vol. II, New York, Grune and Stratton, 1945.

29. Dimock, H. S., *Rediscovering the Adolescent,* New York, Association Press, 1937.
30. Dinkel, R. M., Parent-child conflict in Minnesota families, *Amer. Sociol. Rev.,* 1943, 8:412–419.
31. Dollard, J., *et al., Frustration and Aggression,* New Haven, Yale University Press, 1939.
32. Duvall, Evalyn M., *In-laws: Pro and Con,* New York, Association Press, 1954.
33. Ellis, A., A study of human love relationships, *J. Genet. Psychol.,* 1949, 75:61–71.
34. Ford, C. S., and Beach, F. A., *Patterns of Sexual Behavior,* New York, Harper, 1951.
35. Gardner, L. P., An analysis of children's attitudes toward fathers, *J. Genet. Psychol.,* 1947, 70:3–28.
36. Glick, P. C., The family cycle, *Amer. Sociol. Rev.,* 1947, 12:164–169.
37. Glick, P. C., and Landau, E., Age as a factor in marriage, *Amer. Sociol. Rev.,* 1950, 15:517–529.
38. Gravatt, A. E., Family relations in middle and old age: a review, *J. Gerontol.,* 1953, 8:197–201.
39. Hamilton, G. V., *A Research in Marriage,* New York, Boni, 1928.
40. Hamilton, G. V., and MacGowan, K., *What Is Wrong with Marriage?* New York, Boni, 1928.
41. Hattendorf, K. W., A study of the questions of young children concerning sex, *J. Soc. Psychol.,* 1932, 3:37–65.
42. Havighurst, R. J., and Albrecht, Ruth, *Older People,* New York, Longmans, Green, 1953.
43. Herbst, P. G., The measurement of family relationships, *Human Relations,* 1952, 5:3–36.
44. Hollingshead, A. B., Age relationships and marriage, *Amer. Sociol. Rev.* 1951, 16:492–499.
45. Hollingshead, A. B., Cultural factors in mate selection, *Amer. Sociol. Rev.,* 1950, 15:619–627.
46. Hollingshead, A. B., *Elmtown's Youth,* New York, Wiley, 1949.
47. Jacobson, A. H., Conflict of attitudes toward the roles of the husband and wife in marriage, *Amer. Sociol. Rev.,* 1952, 17:146–150.
48. Jacobson, P. H., Differentials in divorce by duration of marriage and size of family, *Amer. Sociol. Rev.,* 1950, 15:235–244.
49. Johnson, G. H., Differences in the job satisfaction of urban teachers as related to age and other factors, unpublished Ph.D. dissertation, Syracuse University, 1951.
50. Jones, Mary C., and Bayley, Nancy, Physical maturing among boys as related to behavior, *J. Educ. Psychol.,* 1950, 41:129–148.
51. Kinsey, A. C., *et al., Sexual Behavior in the Human Female,* Philadelphia, W. B. Saunders, 1953.
52. Kinsey, A. C., *et al., Sexual Behavior in the Human Male,* Philadelphia, W. B. Saunders, 1948.

53. Kirkpatrick, C., and Caplow, T., Courtship in a group of Minnesota students, *Amer. J. Sociol.*, 1945, *51*:114–125.

54. Kirkpatrick, C., and Caplow, T., Emotional trends in the courtship experience of college students as expressed by graphs with some observations on methodological implications, *Amer. Sociol. Rev.*, 1945, *10*: 619–626.

55. Kirkpatrick, C., and Cotton, J., Physical attractiveness, age, and marital adjustment, *Amer. Sociol. Rev.*, 1951, *16*:81–86.

56. Kirkpatrick, C., and Hobart, C., Disagreement, disagreement estimate, and non-empathetic imputations for intimacy groups varying from favorite date to married, *Amer. Sociol. Rev.*, 1954, *19*:10–19.

57. Koller, M. R., Some changes in courtship behavior in three generations of Ohio women, *Amer. Sociol. Rev.*, 1951, *16*:366–370.

58. Komarovsky, M., Functional analysis of sex roles, *Amer. Sociol. Rev.*, 1950, *15*:508–516.

59. Komarovsky, M., *The Unemployed Man and His Family; the Effect of Unemployment upon the Status of the Man in 59 Families*, New York, Dryden Press, 1940.

60. Koos, E. L., *Families in Trouble*, New York, King's Crown Press, 1946.

61. Landis, C., *et al.*, *Sex in Development*, New York, Hoeber, 1940.

62. Landis, J. T., Length of time required to achieve adjustment in marriage, *Amer. Sociol. Rev.*, 1946, *11*:666–677.

63. Landis, P. H., Marriage preparation in two generations, *Marriage and Family Living*, 1951, *13*:155–156.

64. Levy, D. M., *Maternal Overprotection*, New York, Columbia University Press, 1943.

65. Liccione, J. V., The changing family relationships of adolescent girls, unpublished Ph.D. dissertation, Syracuse University, 1954.

66. Locke, H. J., *Predicting Adjustment in Marriage: A Comparison of a Divorced and a Happily Married Group*, New York, Henry Holt, 1951.

67. Lorr, M., and Jenkins, R. L., Three factors in parent behavior, *J. Consult. Psychol.*, 1953, *17*:306–308.

68. Lowrie, S. H., Dating theories and student responses, *Amer. Sociol. Rev.* 1951, *16*:334–340.

69. Lowrie, S. H., Sex differences and age of initial dating, *Social Forces*, 1952, *30*:456–461.

70. Mead, Margaret, *Male and Female*, New York, Morrow, 1952.

71. Merrill, Barbara, A measurement of mother-child interaction, *J. Abnorm. and Soc. Psychol.*, 1946, *41*:37–49.

72. Morgan, Christine M., The attitudes and adjustments of recipients of old age assistance in upstate and metropolitan New York, *Archives of Psychol.*, 1937, No. 214.

73. Nicolson, A. B., and Hanley, C., Indices of physiological maturity: Derivation and interrelationships, *Child Development*, 1953, *24*:3–38.

74. Nimkoff, M. F., and Wood, A. L., Courtship and personality, *Amer. J. Sociol.*, 1948, *53*:263–269.

75. Ort, R. S., A study of role-conflicts as related to happiness in marriage, *J. Abnorm. and Soc. Psychol.*, 1950, 45:691–699.

76. Popenoe, P., and Neptune, D. W., Acquaintance and betrothal, *Social Forces*, 1937–1938, 16:552–555.

77. Punke, H. H., Attitudes and ideas of high school youth in regards to marriage, *School and Society*, 1942, 56:221–224.

78. Punke, H. H., Dating practices of high school youth, *Bulletin of the National Association of Secondary School Principals*, 1944, 28:47–54.

79. Punke, H. H., High-school youth and family quarrels, *School and Society*, 1943, 58:507–511.

80. Robertson, G. G., Nausea and vomiting of pregnancy: A study in psychosomatic and social medicine, *Lancet*, 1946, 251:336–341.

81. Rockwood, L. D., and Ford, M. E. N., *Youth, Marriage, and Parenthood; The Attitudes of 364 University Juniors and Seniors Towards Courtship, Marriage, and Parenthood*, New York, Wiley, 1945.

82. Roff, M., A factorial study of the Fels parent behavior scales, *Child Development*, 1949, 20:29–45.

83. Roth, J., and Peck, R. F., Social class and social mobility factors related to marital adjustment, *Amer. Sociol. Rev.*, 1951, 16:478–487.

84. Sands, S. L., and Rothschild, D., Sociopsychiatric foundations for a theory of reactions to aging, *J. Nervous and Mental Diseases*, 1952, 116:223–241.

85. Schooley, M., Personality resemblance among married couples, *J. Abnorm. and Soc. Psychol.*, 1936, 31:340–347.

86. Sears, R. R., Ordinal position in the family as a psychological variable, *Amer. Sociol. Rev.*, 1950, 15:397–401.

87. Sears, R. R., *Survey of Objective Studies of Psychoanalytic Concepts*, New York, Social Science Research Council, Bulletin 51, 1943.

88. Sherman, A. W., Jr., Emancipation status of college students, *J. Genet. Psychol.*, 1946, 68:171–180.

89. Sherman, A. W., Jr., Personality factors in the psychological weaning of college women, *Educ. and Psychol. Meas.*, 1948, 8:249–256.

90. Simpson, M., Parent preferences of young children, Teachers College Contributions to Education, No. 652, New York, Teachers College, Columbia University, 1935.

91. Smith, G. F., Certain aspects of the sex life of the adolescent girl, *J. Appl. Psychol.*, 1924, 8:347–349.

92. Stagner, R., and Drought, N., Measuring children's attitudes toward their parents, *J. Educ. Psychol.*, 1935, 26:169–176.

93. Stott, L. H., Adolescents' dislikes regarding parental behavior and their significance, *J. Genet. Psychol.*, 1940, 57:393–414.

94. Stott, L. H., Home punishment of adolescents, *J. Genet. Psychol.*, 1940, 57:415–428.

95. Stott, L. H., Parent-adolescent adjustment, its measurement and significance, *Character and Personal.*, 1941–1942, 10:140–150.

96. Stott, L. H., *Personality Development in Farm, Small-town and City*

Children, Agriculture Experiment Station Research Bulletin, No. 114, University of Nebraska, 1939.

97. Strauss, A., The influence of parent-images upon marital choice, *Amer. Sociol. Rev.,* 1946, *11:*554, 559.

98. Sundal, A. P., and McCormick, T. C., Age at marriage and mate selection: Madison, Wisconsin, 1937–1943, *Amer. Sociol. Rev.,* 1951, *16:* 37–48.

99. Terman, L. M., *Psychological Factors in Marital Happiness,* New York, McGraw-Hill, 1938.

100. Thomas, J. L., The factor of religion in the selection of marriage mates, *Amer. Sociol. Rev.,* 1951, *16:*487–91.

101. Tryon, C. M., *U C Inventory I. Social and Emotional Adjustment,* Institute of Child Welfare, University of California Press, 1939.

102. Tuckman, J., and Lorge, I., *Retirement and the Industrial Worker,* Bureau of Publications, Teachers College, Columbia University, 1953.

103. Waller, W., The rating and dating complex, *Amer. Sociol. Rev.,* 1937, *2:*727–734.

104. Wallin, P., Marital happiness of parents and their children's attitude to marriage, *Amer. Sociol. Rev.,* 1954, *19:*20–23.

105. Wallin, P., Sex differences in attitudes toward "in-laws": a test of a theory, *Amer. J. Sociol.,* 1954, *59:*466–469.

106. Warner, Marie P., The premarital medical consultation, *Medical Woman's J.,* 1943, *1:*293–400.

107. Warner, W. L., and Lunt, P. S., *The Social Life of a Modern Community,* New Haven, Yale University Press, 1941.

108. Willoughby, R. R., Sexuality in the second decade, *Monogr. of the Society for Research in Child Development,* 1937, Vol. 2, No. 10.

109. Winch, R. F., Courtship in college women, *Amer. J. Sociol.,* 1949, *55:* 269–278.

110. Winch, R. F., Further data and observations on the Oedipus hypothesis: the consequences of an inadequate hypothesis, *Amer. Sociol. Rev.,* 1951, *16:*784–795.

111. Winch, R. F., Interrelations between certain social background and parent-son factors in a study of courtship among college men, *Amer. Sociol. Rev.,* 1946, *11:*333–343.

112. Winch, R. F., The relation between the loss of a parent and progress in courtship, *J. Soc. Psychol.,* 1949, *29:*51–56.

113. Winch, R. F., Some data bearing on the Oedipus hypothesis, *J. Abnorm. and Soc. Psychol.,* 1950, *45:*481–489.

114. Winch, R. F., The theory of complementary needs in mate selection: A test of one kind of complementariness, *Amer. Sociol. Rev.,* 1955, *20:*52–56.

115. Winch, R. F., Ktsanes, T., and Virginia, The theory of complementary needs in mate selection: an analytic and descriptive study, *Amer. Sociol. Rev.,* 1954, *19:*241–249.

116. Yi-Chuang Lu, Parent-child relationship and marital roles, *Amer. Sociol. Rev.,* 1952, *17:*357–361.

PART THREE .

. Preface to a "Life-Span" Psychology
of the Future

• Retrospect and Prospect: Major Concepts and Problems as Seen Integratively in the Life-Span View

A FINAL synthesizing task remains, not so much in summary as in the hope that bringing together the diverse materials of the preceding chapters may yield somewhat new, larger understandings and both more broadened and more personalized applications.

The Changing Person in the Rapidly Changing Scene

The first chapter emphasized the fact of extraordinary, rapid change in the last half century and more especially in the last 20 years. Technology, economic and social conditions, and culture all changed, not only rapidly, but with increasing tempo. And along with these depicted changes went changes in the family and the intimacies of life, in personality, and in life philosophy which were more subtle but as important and perhaps quite as rapid in nature. In this final chapter with emphasis on the future, this general fact of rapid and accelerating change presumably should be even more stressed.

It was also remarked early in this volume that the young reader might expect to live past the year 2000—a date seeming somewhat dramatic and a time by which a great deal more change can take place. Indeed, current expectation for length of life would give the average 20-year-old in 1960 an expectation of living until around 2015. But the past half century has seen an increase in average length of life of almost 20 years; barring atomic catastrophe, there should be some gains in life expectancy during the half century now under way. Ten more years (as through conquest of cancer and of arterial and cardiac diseases) would bring an average life span of 80 years with perhaps a substantial number reaching the century mark. Surely such prospects for long and perhaps very long living are to be pondered, regarding both their potentials and their problems. Indeed, suppose there is a "break-through" of the supposed constitutional hundred-year limit of maximal life span, and some do live to be 120! In any event, the prospect for the present young person (certainly for his children) is for a long life and conceivably even so long that the very concept of a life's span must be somewhat altered.

Surely that longer life of the immediate future will be healthier. It will (as stressed in a preceding paragraph) see accelerating changes in science, technology, and society. Already there are great (and rapidly growing) numbers of the old. With the dominance of the two-generation family and other changes in mode of life, the different age groups seem increasingly to be becoming somewhat separate subsocieties; people of 20, 40, 60, and 80 lead increasingly independent and increasingly different lives—one person, in his lifetime, leads several lives. But all this change means that, in practical fact, human nature is changing. Major features of that change, and adjustments seemingly desirable thereto, are now briefly to be considered in terms of the volume as a whole.

Psychological Reinterpretations

The suggestion was made in the first chapter that a life-span view might somewhat reconstitute understandings of certain basic psychological concepts; bringing together relevant implications regarding the concepts from several of the preceding chapters might both enlarge and reinterpret them further.

A FURTHER REINTERPRETATION OF "ABILITIES"

In Chapter 3, consideration of abilities as measured by tests led to the conclusion that the "classical" concept of a primarily constitutional general capacity, growing until the twenties and then declining, was both oversimplified and without recognition of certain possibilities for the more adequate nurture of "intelligence"—which the chapters on achievement and education further touched upon. The following concepts are now ventured, somewhat in review with also some reconstruing.

Basic in considering the organism's capacities throughout the life span would seem to be what may well be called its general organic potential and its basic curve of increase in the growth years, climax early in the "prime," and a slow decline in the following years. The various data on morbidity and mortality, growth and change in physique, and increase then lessening in strength and skill as measured and as shown in sports championships all show this elementary basic trend. So do measurements of abilities, the "champion accomplishments" of outstanding creative work, certain evidence regarding the work life, and sundry material on motivations and interests; all suggest a growth in the growth years, a climax in the "prime," and a slow decline in the following years. This basic organic potential might be thought of psychologically in terms of a general neural energy and plasticity (somewhat analogous to Spearman's general factor in intelligence) but with recognition also of the importance in various ways of the total organism—as in the sensitivities of artistic creation, the complex physiological involvements of powerful drives or urges, and the vitality sustaining the great efforts of notable accomplishment. Obviously, individuals differ greatly in their amount of such general organic potential and also in rate of decline after the prime. The assumption would seem reasonable (especially if the total organism is involved, as indicated above) that improvements in health, as well as less burdensome work, and more and richer leisure with wise recreation, might somewhat increase the organic potential and also retard the decline.

More specific stages or phases of the individual's potential were seen as also basically constitutional and emerging each in its own time and fashion. Thus, as the small child matures, he first develops mastery of his own body and then of speech. A little later he attains the capacity to use symbols, as in reading, and concepts, as in mathematics. Next, especially in the prime, the potential for creativity appears, and later in life, the capacity for leadership develops. Special musical or mechanical aptitudes emerge in some. It seems reasonable to assume that throughout life the constitutional substrata of abilities change not only in amount but somewhat in nature. One of the writers who has had opportunity to study an occasional centenarian has felt that these very old people had certain special qualities of personality and perhaps of abilities (a mellowness and detachment). Surely as the old and even the very old become major segments of the total population, their abilities should be broadly studied—not only as to possible deficits but also as to possible special characteristics that perhaps have some elements of merit. More generally, it might be expected that, with improved health at all ages and richer and more varied opportunities, distinctive abilities at different ages might more fully develop.

The nature and life history of basic capacities seem inadequately indicated by present tests of either "general intelligence" or "primary abilities," but they are suggested by broad developmental studies of interests and activities, and of careers both notable and ordinary in achievement. Though very inadequately, it might be said that the conventional tests of "general ability" measure a person's "literacy," using this term very broadly to mean his acquaintance with the intellectual tools and the fund of knowledge common among the more competent people of his time and his society. So understood, the findings of the nineteen thirties that older adults tested distinctly lower was a true picture of their lower literacy at that time; and the higher adult level and less decline with age shown by more recent testing are evidence of the more adequately schooled and widely informed present American population. As mentioned earlier, it is believed that tests that are wider in range and expressly planned to be descriptive of and somewhat "indigenous" to the adult years would describe more adequately the range and the age change of abilities throughout the life span. Thus, tests would be more accurate and fairer indications of competencies in adult life.

The two factors mentioned so far as being involved in actual realized abilities are essentially constitutional: a basic organic energy and plasticity and various developmental phases or features of total biological growth and change through the life span which may affect or express themselves in certain more or less special aptitudes. A third factor has been too narrowly labeled in the preceding paragraph as "literacy" and is more adequately expressed as effective acquaintance with the intellectual tools and the fund of knowledge needed for general competence in a person's community and in his time—acquaintance with the current culture. School, home, mass media of communication, and daily talk all contribute to this total, which is shaped by the culture of one's socioeconomic and age group. But the cultural expectations and the contributions from these various sources may be inadequate or even perverse. May school and college programs be sometimes bumbling and burdened with curricular deadwood? Are not the petty topics of the television quiz programs, and the chatter of the comedians, perverse in emphasis on the trivial? Is there not danger that Russian schools, which are less burdened with cultural relics and which place great emphasis on science, and Russian mass media, which are less "cheap," may produce a "literacy" in certain respects dangerously more effective than ours? Further, is not the "literacy" needed at 20 somewhat different from that needed at 40 or 60 or 80?

Obviously, the degree of literacy attained by the average American will be in proportion to his constitutional capacities to acquire a broad "literacy" and the advantages that make it available to him. But social classes and individuals differ as to their contacts with and acceptance of the contents, values, and points of view of the common culture. To call "general ability" simply literacy unduly narrows the concept to call attention to its limitations. But the proposed term also more clearly implies that such abilities can be increased in the general population by educational and related means and that the reader may in a very practical sense make himself more "intelligent."

Special fostering of functioning abilities is a fourth factor which may be more briefly reviewed. Special training in a profession, a trade, or a hobby may markedly develop an ability. Lively, intensive exercise of an ability usually not only maintains but improves it. Suitable opportunities and successes in one's field are especially helpful in nourishing abilities. This volume has attempted to make two special points in this connection. As instanced in an extreme by Mozart, a combination of encouragement, training, social facilitation, opportunity, and success experiences may operate powerfully to develop great ability, if congruent constitutional endowment is good. As notably instanced by Churchill, long and varied experience may bring certain types of abilities to fullest flower even in later life. Thus, in less outstanding people, education and career may also develop abilities, even though to a lesser degree.

In short, a life-span view of abilities would, first, stress a broad appraisal of a wide range of evidence regarding total intellectual effectiveness rather than special measures of "general" abilities, and that effectiveness would be seen as based on the total organism's adequacy. Secondly, the development and changes in the organism through the life span would be expected to involve varying phases if not forms of ability. Substantial individual differences would be expected, not only in total organic and neural energy, but also in special aptitudes and their times of emerging. These first two factors would be thought of as largely constitutional, though both health (physical and "mental") and exercise would somewhat affect them. But, clearly, the extent to which people acquire a literacy and effective familiarity with the current culture (and an easy alertness in operating in that culture) and special ability is much affected by the society in which they live. As exhibited in a graph in Chapter 4, the Western world in recent times seems to have produced more notable achievers than were produced in any period or locale before; also special localities at special times have, for reasons in part fairly evident, been especially productive of persons of superior achievement. This volume has taken the position that constitutional factors are less important and societal ones much more important than usually supposed. Longer life and the omnipresence of the culture through mass media should increase possibilities of progressive building up of abilities. Psychological and educational science *should* substantially improve methods of so doing. There seems no inherent reason why notable advances might not occur in these technologies, just as they have occurred in chemistry and engineering! But even without such special facilitation, further increases in average "intelligence" and improvements in finding and in fostering the capacities of the superior may be expected.

Perhaps once more it should be stated that the above position does not question the basic fact and basic importance of individual differences in constitutional intellectual capacities (or the value of current tests in displaying these differences). The writers do seek to increase recognition of the pervasive importance of the total socioeconomic and cultural environment in developing *and* maintaining such general and special abilities as are potential in each individual, and the probability that such developing and maintaining could be made much more effective than now.

Cumulative effects of these two kinds of gain—increase in average "literacy" or acquaintance with the common culture (or "general intelligence" as measured) and increase in the number of superior minds discovered *and* fostered—may add up to very important increases in the total abilities of a country. However, gains will probably not be simply cumulative. In a challenging paper on "human potentialities,"[1] Gardner Murphy has declared that "human nature and society are evolving together, not only along a line involving quantitative increase in this or that but into ever new qualities." And he gives examples from art and science of how there has been repeatedly "the development of a transmissible quality of new experience which then is further enriched as it is further transmitted. . . . I suggest that we be prepared to think of the humanity of a few generations hence as considerably altered from that which we know." For instance, might advances become as common and sweeping *and* accepted in the social sciences as is now the case in the physical sciences? Might the average American even come to act in accord with fact and reason instead of ballyhoo and prejudice? Might he become a truly rational being?

A LARGER CONTEXT FOR MOTIVATIONS AND VALUES

Earlier consideration of this topic began with "physiological tensions, urges, and discomforts" and pointed out how longer life involved change

[1] *J. of Social Issues,* Supplement Series No. 7, 1953.

in the pattern of these. They are indeed different at the ages of 10, 20, 40, 60, and 80. Muscular tone, glandular functioning, and tissue needs all change. Stressed were the pervasiveness, and the preëminent importance of social motivations and the need for social acceptance and security, for achievement, perhaps for defense against losses, and for gaining and then conserving status. Time perspectives change with age. It is well to reëmphasize the fact that lengthened lives plus a rapidly changing society and economy (and world scene) put all these considerations into flux. And there is in this country an "economy of abundance."

Unique as regards motivations and values would seem to be the situation of the many and increasing millions past 50 in this country whose children are grown, whose careers vocationally and socially have gone about as far as they are likely to go, who have a reasonable security and comfort—and 20 or more years ahead of them! These may be backward-looking years filled with regrets and the reviewing of earlier frustrations. But may there be a second career? The suggestion was made earlier that a mother coming into teaching in middle age might be especially competent. Or work adjusted to older years may be especially satisfying, as in the case of the elderly mechanic (mentioned in Chapter 6) who was happier than in his previous job in his sociable responsibility for the tool cage. But most important seems the possibility of greatly increasing the extent, status, and established social patterns of service types of undertaking. Now, some business and professional leaders give much time to such activities, and an occasional one upon retirement turns to such interests instead of to Miami. And devoted women serve as "gray ladies" in hospitals, are "friendly visitors," or give neighborly help when needed—as good neighbors have always done. But now that so many more people have so much more time and means, and for so much longer, might not the American culture be educated to evaluate such altruisms more highly and to provide even more social motivations for them?

The culture is flexible; it responds to advertising, to the shoutings of demagogues, and to fads. Not so many years ago the teachers of bridge were the most numerous and best paid of all "adult educators," and the hard-eyed competitions of that game set the tone of most middle- and upper-class social life. But it has already been pointed out that relaxed friendliness rather than competitiveness seems the more natural mood of the later middle and older ages. Now, their informal buffet entertaining and their do-it-yourself hobbies seem less class-differentiating and more coöperative than their former activities. The older people of the present time know the coöperative endeavors of the two world wars and the general distress of the Great Depression. The hypothesis is ventured that the rapidly growing and increasingly independent (economically and socially) subpopulation of those over 50 may well develop values and motivational patterns of great social worth.

Most communities have fine people who are similar to those in the following descriptions: the retired president of a big manufacturing company who made his second career out of leadership in community enterprises; the physician's wife whose children were grown and who was also busy in welfare; another wife from a lovely home who chose the county infirmary for volunteer work (though she often could not eat her dinner as a result of what she had seen that afternoon) and who helped to rehabilitate many people in that distressing institution; the elderly widower who rented most of his home at nominal rates to students with children because he knew of their difficulties in finding accommodations and who befriended them in many other ways. Kindliness and public spiritedness are, of course, not new; but it would seem that now sundry conditions were exceptionally favorable for the fostering of these traits in certain segments of the population of this country. It is to be hoped that there may be leadership in these directions rather than toward the inane placidities of the Florida trailer camp or the narrow evangelism of certain religious groups which seem especially to appeal to many older people.

The above paragraphs have propounded the view that the increasing prosperity and security, especially of older people, the increasing length of life in this country, and the increasing separateness of the generations might result in a subculture of the older groups which would have values and motivational patterns of especial merit. However, all these changes affect younger people, too, in some way. As mentioned in Chapter 10, one of the writers has, at decade intervals since 1923, inventoried the attitudes and interests of young people in a midwest area. In 30 years, the number of morally borderline types of conduct, such as smoking, flirting, immodesty, and extravagance, that were marked "wrong" decreased by almost 30 percent, and there was a substantial increase in number of declared interests of girls and young women. These findings seem to constitute evidence of the relaxing of Puritanic inhibitions and the expanding of feminine freedoms which are part of the changing culture emphasized in the first chapter. Certain interest increases seem worthy of special note. Thus, 20 percent more college men *and* women in 1953 than in 1923 indicated an interest in babies—a finding which agrees with today's trend among young college people toward earlier marriages and larger families. And about 20 percent more college men and women in 1953 than 30 years before indicated an interest in prayer and church.

These are mere bits of data and are of uncertain worth. But they may be indicative of two major trends in attitude toward life: (1) the feeling that America's abundance and a relaxation of old taboos make possible and respectable the satisfaction of the basic human needs and (2) the realization that upon the satisfaction of these basic needs, the need for a larger life philosophy becomes clearer. The preceding chapters on motivations, emotions, and values have for the most part been coldly factual. But these topics are, in essence, warm with feeling. Any useful understanding of them should help coördinate motivations and adjust them to realities, help reduce frustrations, and help find values of broad worth. To try to deal with these topics in terms of scientific knowledge, rather than dogma or prejudice or custom, tends toward a freer climate in which all this may more readily come about. The social scene, in which motives and emotions and values live, is rapidly changing, and lengthened life is changing perspectives. It does not seem unreasonable to anticipate that human personality may in the near future change substantially and develop a new maturity.

Certain Reintegrated Applications

It need hardly be said that the future should provide various enlarged opportunities for a psychology of the life span to be useful. The following samples are ventured, some of which the reader may think fanciful!

EDUCATION, WORK, AND LIFE VIEW

The preceding pages have suggested that the future will see rapid and often unpredictable changes. It would seem arguable on this assumption that, as already mentioned, much of the education to meet current needs and also to prepare for the future must be adult education, most of it made available as the need arises. As life is longer, preparation for later needs would seem to be less appropriate in childhood or adolescence— how impossible then wisely to prepare for an adulthood reaching far into the distance and in a future whose nature can hardly be anticipated. It would appear reasonable to expect that with lengthened life, increased leisure time (including time for adult education) and more rapid and unpredictable change, the present long preparatory type of full-time education will become increasingly questionable. The argument has also been stressed that the extensive training needed by superior minds for doing their superior work should not, as it often does at present, extend into the precious years of the young prime. It might also be assumed that there really will be increases in educational efficiency! Perhaps adult education will become a common and accepted phenomenon of adult life and the present practice of devoting all of one's time in youth and young adulthood to full-time education will be reduced.

The rate at which work is changing—some jobs becoming easy and semiskilled, while other work has become increasingly technical—has also been emphasized. Many people may need to modify or even change their careers in midlife. Work may be better adjusted not only to individuals of differing abilities and aptitudes but also to individuals of widely differing ages. But doesn't this mean that educators, industrial personnel men, and indeed all people who try to be intelligent about themselves will need to have an increasingly greater understanding about human development and change through the life span—about the basic topics of this volume? In fact, can there not be a gain from such understanding at all ages? The writers believe that a certain practical type of psychology is feasible and desirable in secondary schools. Even at that level, certain home economics teachers usefully discuss problems of child development and of family living. As has been suggested in discussing developmental tasks, young people beginning their careers and their families need educational help more, perhaps, than at any other time. If more people either have different jobs at different ages or find the changing of their job as they remain in it a major feature, periodical reconsideration of an individual's capacities and his possible opportunities would seem desirable. In any event, people may in effect have several careers and opportunities. It is already recognized that older people should study and plan with reference to retirement. Surely, it is no wild venture to assume that at all ages people will increasingly seek relevant information regarding problems of their own lives and of others as seen in the long perspective of a life span lived through.

Education almost life-span long, reshaped to fit development and need! Work similarly readjusted! Developmental psychology become a basic orientation in education and vocation, indeed in the thinking of every intelligent person! Surely expectations not unreasonable!

THE LIFE-SPAN VIEW AND THE COMMUNITY

The most prominent features of modern welfare provisions are for the greatly increased numbers of the aged. But the traditional concern of welfare is children, and their number is growing greatly, too. There may be ways in which these extremes of age can serve each other. A neighborhood news sheet recently carried this item: "Grandmother of seven will baby sit." Another grandmother has made a very profitable profession of "grandmothering"; when a couple with a family wishes to take a restful trip, she moves in and takes care of house and children with such relaxed efficiency that the mother often finds things in better shape on her return than when she left. On a recent visit to a Canadian city, one of the writers saw neighborhood parks which typically included a pleasant shaded area with settees for bowling on the green (none under 60 here) and near by were slides for little tots, tennis courts, box lacrosse for yeasty adolescents who like it a little rough, and a simple clubhouse with a big porch where any and all ages could sit and chat. Perhaps such easy proximity and casual association is better than the separateness of golden-age clubs, teen-age canteens, and other age groupings that are more usual in the United States. There should be simple experiments in the applied social psychology of age relations to appraise various physical setups and modes of recreation and association. And, as was said of teaching, perhaps certain types of professional social work could more often be prepared for and entered in middle age or even a little later. Various types of practical nursing care may perhaps be more readily prepared for and better rendered by older people than is at present recognized.

And again what about that growing group of those past the time of family-raising but not yet into the much-talked-about group of the old? Their most typical habitat is the apartment house. One of the writers has had especial opportunity to study one that housed mostly couples over 50, single women, and persons widowed or divorced. Most of the people had some church connection, but the church did not really seem to serve any of them. Family ties tended to be casual or lacking. Three women had affairs—one with shrewd profit, one with angry resentment at her situation, one under such criticism from relatives that she finally destroyed herself. Proximity brought casual neighboring; only illness and death were occasions for really helping each other. For the most part, the apartment house was an aggregate of people—mostly well intentioned and with diverse interests—but lacking social occasions or facilities which could bring about companionship and sharing of interests or give some social direction and purpose. However, the problem of the lonely person is yet more extensive. A census survey in 1956 reported (*Time*, May 14, 1956) that "over a five-year period, the number of Americans living alone has increased by one-third." Many are widowed or old, but some are young. Whatever their ages, what is the societal situation of these people? To what "community" do they belong? How should it serve them—and they it? Surely "psychological study of social issues" like these might make major contributions to community welfare.

Some Possible Personal Applications to the Reader

Now some last brief, personalized applications. The long life and the changing world make planning needful—and rich in potentialities.

For one thing, even the young reader around 20 should have a somewhat longer perspective than youth has had on problems of health and physical well-being. Many already do. For example, many young adults watch and control their weight not alone with reference to appearance but as a guard against possible health hazards of obesity. Possible relationships of smoking to lung cancer seem to have restrained some from smoking cigarettes. The young person may become aware of health problems of the middle and older ages as seen in older relatives, and these problems take on greater relevance to him since he knows he will probably reach these ages and that over long periods the insidious effects of neglect in self-care may be dangerously cumulative.

The analysis given earlier of factors involved in realized abilities is believed of certain practical applications to the reader. The broad concept of total organic growth to a peak in early adulthood, with a slow decline (in energy, quickness, readiness in learning) beginning shortly thereafter, suggests that the person of 20 may well be a "young man in a hurry," so that the fullness of his life may get under way in these precious years of the early prime.[2] The concept of a complex of constitutional capacities constantly changing all through a long life means that one should plan for 20 and 30 and 50 and even 80 with these changes in mind and keep them in mind when trying to understand and appreciate people of these ages. The notion that being "intelligent" means being "literate" in the essential intellectual tools and common knowledge of his

[2] A statement by Winston Churchill seems appropriate here. In *A Roving Commission*, he said of his younger years:

When I look back upon them I cannot but return my sincere thanks to the high gods for the gift of existence. All the days were good and each day better than the other. Ups and downs, risks and journeys, but always the sense of motion and the illusion of hope. Come on now, all you young men, all over the world, you are needed more than ever now. . . . You have not an hour to lose. You must take your place in life's fighting line. Twenty to twenty-five! These are the years! Don't be content with things as they are. . . . Enter upon your inheritance, accept your responsibilities. Raise the glorious flags again, advance them upon the new enemies, who constantly gather upon the front of the human army, and have only to be assaulted to be overthrown.

culture means not simply having the education of a high school graduate plus familiarity with the front-page news and the *Reader's Digest*. To keep intelligent through a long life, in a world rapidly changing, requires continuing planned effort. One should read certain of the critical magazines of opinion. One should no longer think of "getting an education" as a task that at 20 is completed. Continuing education for health, vocation, family living, and after-family living seem necessary to keep up with new knowledge about health, job, community, and the world scene which is now frighteningly and fascinatingly close.

One cannot feel secure in a job—automation may replace him or technological change remake or replace a whole vocational field—but one may have more than one career. In a long lifetime one may, in effect, have several careers. And a wise person, in a society sophisticated with reference to all these possibilities, will make these different careers different in pace and different in requirements and in opportunities, with each having satisfactions and status and involving associates developmentally appropriate.

The above comments have to do especially with the career of a man. For the young woman the career and the problem seem even more difficult. She must usually plan for some work in which she will engage before marriage and which may be a career if marriage does not come. Homemaking is increasingly being recognized as a career for which there should be education. Yet a wife may continue work at the beginning of marriage and perhaps thereafter, and she may wish to work again after a family is raised. A broken marriage may cause return to work. However, breaks in a career are especially likely to present problems. The young secretary may find that a few years from now when she had hoped that her skills might again be useful, mailable tape recordings have replaced her! Nevertheless, other and perhaps more interesting careers may then be available for those who have an understanding of abilities and opportunities at different ages.

However, work is becoming less preëmptive of life; what else may bulk large in the planning of a young person for his future? Hours and even days are added to leisure. With all this time of his own, what does he plan to do? Life reaches ahead with increasing leisure for years and years—does he have any plan for those years? If freedom from want is achieved—what does he want then? More sports, more inconsequential excitement, a faster and sportier car? Or may there be a new flowering of literature and the arts, with general interest therein or a more informed maturity of mind and increased understanding in dealing with human problems? May increased leisure result in increasing numbers of able young people finding absorbing interest in various constructive endeavors? Understanding, leadership, and social conscience are qualities that are sorely needed now, and there is an especial need for them in the handling of psychological problems, many of which have been the concern of this book. This thesis is eloquently stated in another Churchillian passage (in acceptance of the Nobel Prize in 1953):

The power of man has grown in every sphere except over himself. Never in the field of action have events seemed so harshly to dwarf personalities. . . . Rarely in history have brutal facts so dominated thought or has such widespread, individual virtue found so dim a collective focus. The fearful question confronts us: Have our problems got beyond our control? Undoubtedly, we are passing through a phase where this may be so. Well may we humble ourselves, and seek for guidance and mercy.

INDEXES .

Alexander, Grover Cleveland, 54
Alexander the Great, 129
Anderson, John E., 424, 427

Bauer, Marlene, 54
Bayley, Nancy, 81, 107
Blake, William, 130
Bose, R. G., 480
Bowerman, W. G., 137
Bridges, Robert, 132
Bryant, William Cullen, 130, 134
Buhler, Charlotte, 292
Burgess, E. W., 574, 589
Burns, Robert, 130
Byron, George Gordon, 199

Chatterton, Thomas, 130, 134
Chopin, Frederic, 140
Churchill, Winston, 129
Clague, Ewan, 168
Colt, Samuel, 130
Conrad, H. S., 83
Cottrell, L. S., 589
Cowley, Abraham, 130
Crane, Walter, 130
Curie, Marie, 141–142

Darwin, Charles, 134, 192
Davy, Sir Humphrey, 125, 131
Dvořák, Antonin, 140

Ellis, Havelock, 137

Faraday, Michael, 131
Frenkel-Brunswik, Else, 313

Galileo, 131
Galton, Francis, 134, 136–137
Garibaldi, Giuseppe, 131
Gibbon, Edward, 135
Gladstone, William E., 129
Goethe, Johann Wolfgang von, 132
Grant, Ulysses S., 142–143, 160
Green, William, 253

Hall, G. Stanley, 350
Handel, George Frederick, 140
Harlow, H. F., 273
Hartshorne, H., 444
Haydn, Franz Josef, 139
Herrick, C. J., 138
Hilgard, E. R., 91
Hoffman, Friedrich, 132
Hollingsworth, Leta S., 199
Holmes, Oliver Wendell, 130
Hoover, J. Edgar, 475

Jersild, A. T., 340
Johnson, Samuel, 135
Jones, Bobby, 54
Jones, H. E., 83

Kant, Immanuel, 135
Keats, John, 130, 134, 135, 199
Kelvin, Lord, 130

Lehman, H. C., 53, 123–124, 130, 131, 416
Lewin, K., 338, 351
Liberman, A. M., 313
Liebig, Justus von, 131
Liszt, Franz, 140
Lowell, A. Lawrence, 177

McCay, C. M., 64
McClelland, D. C., 287, 313
Martineau, James, 132
May, M. A., 444
Meany, George, 253
Mendelssohn, Felix, 140
Menuhin, Yehudi, 140
Mill, John Stuart, 141
Milton, John, 130
Morgagni, Giovanni Batista, 132
Mozart, Wolfgang Amadeus, 129, 134, 138–140, 146–147, 160, 199
Murphy, Gardner, 274, 638

Napoleon, 129
Naunyn, Bernard, 132

Oistrakh, David, 140
Oughtred, William, 132

Pacinotti, Antonio, 131
Perkin, William Henry, 130
Perkins, Frances, 113
Piaget, J., 443, 479
Pitt, William, the younger, 129
Pollak, O., 477, 479
Pope, Alexander, 130

Reuter, Walter, 253
Roosevelt, Franklin D., 113

Schubert, Franz, 134, 140
Scott, Barbara Ann, 54
Shelley, Percy Bysshe, 129, 134, 135, 199

Strong, E. K., Jr., 393
Symonds, P. M., 416

Tennyson, Alfred, 132, 134, 135
Terman, L. M., 107, 110, 192, 199, 444, 464, 584, 595, 599
Thorndike, E. L., 126, 299, 307, 314
Travis, Walter J., 54

Verdi, Giuseppe, 134, 140
Vischer, S. S., 132, 138

Wallen, P., 574
Wechsler, D., 83, 107, 114
White, William Allen, 143–145
Wills, Helen, 54
Winch, R. F., 576
Witty, P. A., 416
Wordsworth, William, 134, 135
Wundt, Wilhelm Max, 132

• Index of Subjects

Ability to learn, changes with age, 86–92, 635–636
  conventional tests, inadequacy of, 111–113, 635–636
  education, relation to, 103–108
  family resemblances, 93–95
  need for study, 113–114
  physique, relation to, 92–93
  racial differences, 95–97
  sex differences, 95
  socioeconomic status, relation to, 97–103
Accidents, 57–59, 237–238, 243–244
  industrial, 237–238, 243–244
  relation to age, 237–238
Activity need, 273–274
Adjustment, during marriage, 583–599
  interests for richer living, 426–429
  recreation and basic needs, 425–426
  relation of interests, 423–425
Age, and accidents and illness, 237–238
  adjustments for, 259
  ability to learn, changes in, 86–92, 635–636
  conservatism, trend, 494–498
  differences in moral values with, 448–452
  effect on functioning of vital organs, 59–61
  effect on vocational usefulness, 232–239
  psychological motivations, changes in, 289–292, 294–305, 311–313
  recreation related to, 412–414
  retirement, 239–243
  sensory adequacy, changes in, 54–56
  status, relation to, 250
Ages for notable achievement, age range, 130–132
  creative work, 123–127
  leadership, 127–130
Aggressive behavior, 331–334

Anger, 329–338
  age trends, 330–334
  causes, 334–336
  management, 336–338
Anxiety, *see* Emotional stress
Army Alpha test, 78–81, 105–106
Athletics, 52–54

Binet tests, 72, 82–83
Body proportions, 36–37
Body tissue and organs, 37–39, 59–61

Careers, 225–232, 639–641
Character, development; childhood and adolescence, 440–448; factors, 452–455; maturity and old age, 448–452
  gradations, 436–438
  inconsistency, 438–440
Civic attitude, 455–478
  crime during maturity and old age, 474–478
  juvenile delinquency, 468–474
  moral values, 455–459
  political behavior, 459–468
Conservatism, age trends, 494–498
Crime, 468–478
  during maturity and old age, 474–478
  juvenile delinquency, 468–474

Dating, 569–573
Death, leading causes of, 58
Divorce rate, 14–15

Economic changes, 11–14
Education, acceleration, 192–200
  adult, 167–169
  and ability to learn, 103–108
  coördination with development, 171–179
  flexibility, 202–205
  individual differences in development, 179–182
  lengthening and expansion, 166–167

Education—(*Continued*)
  motivations, 206–210
  of gifted persons, 191–192
  possibility of increased efficiency in,
    641–642
  problems of handicapped and mentally
    inadequate, 187–190
  rehabilitation and reëducation in adult
    life, 190–191
  social problems, 182–187
  vocational, 168, 637
Emotional development, anger, 329–338
  critical periods, 328–329
  infancy, 323–324
  old age, 325
  role of learning in, 326–327
Emotional stress, conditions that frustrate,
    359–361
  effects, 356–359
Engagement, 577–583
Expansion of activities and interests, 292–
    297

Family, changes in, 14–16
Family relationships, *see* Marital adjust-
    ment; Parent-child relationships
Fear, 327, 338–356
  adolescence, 342–346, 350–353
  adulthood, 346–349, 353–356
  childhood, 338–342, 349–350
Friendships, adult years, 522–530; factors,
    523–526; status changes, 527–530
  childhood and adolescence, 508–522;
    changing values with age, 518–520;
    heterosexual choices, 511–513; social
    acceptability, 513–518
  groupings, 530–545; adult, 534–537,
    541–545; childhood and adolescence,
    531–534, 537–541
Frustration, 329, 334, 359–363
  constructive handling, 361–363
  frustrating conditions, 359–361

General abilities, 71–117, 634–638
  changes after age of twenty, 82
  changes during growth years, 81–82
  growth during adult and older years,
    76–81
  growth during first twenty years, 72–
    75
  tests, 71–117
Goals, 280–284
Growth, maturity of, 41–42

Height and weight, changes in, 28–34
  influences affecting, 34–36

Henmon-Nelson verbal-type test, 99, 100
Hobbies, 390–391, 428
Homeostasis, 61
Hours of work, 246–247

Illness, 56–59, 237–238
  related to age, 237–238
  See also Mental disease
Initial jobs, 223–224

Juvenile delinquency, 468–474

Labor, earnings, 221–222
  hours of work, 246–247
  initial jobs, 223–224
  lunch hours, 245
Labor force, 216–220
  proportion of women, 217–218
Labor unions, 251–253
Life expectancy, 3–7, 633–634
Love and courtship, 573–577
Lunch hours, 245

Marital adjustment, 583–599
  background, 583–584
  change of sex interest, 599–604
  needs and expectations, 585–595
  personality factors, 584–585
  sex adjustment, 604–607
  social class, relation to, 596–599
Menopause, 42–43
Mental disease, 148–157
  case histories, 151–157
Merrill-Palmer scale, 104
Moral values, 436–478
  age differences during adulthood, 448–
    452
  civic attitudes, 455–459
  development during childhood and ad-
    olescence, 440–448
  gradation in character, 436–438
  inconsistency in character, 438–440
Morbidity, *see* Illness
Mortality, life expectancy, 3–7, 633–634
  reduction of, 3–6, 633–634
  variation with age, 56
Motion pictures, 407–409
Motivations, 271–317
  physiological, 271–279
  psychological, 279–317

Notable achievement, age range, 130–132
  case histories of notable achievers,
    139–145
  creative work, 123–127
  development of notable achievers, 147–
    148

Notable achievement—(*Continued*)
environment, effects of, 135–137
intellectual traits, 134–135
leadership, 127–130
major factors, 133–138
Nurture, importance of, 159–160

Occupational contrasts, 417–422
Otis nonverbal test, 99
Otis self-administering test, 77

Parent-child relationships, 607–622
after children reach adulthood, 616–622
child's emancipation, 612–616
"in-law" problems, 616–619
while children are maturing, 608–612
Physical development, adult life, 49–52
childhood and youth, 46–49
early years, 44–46
Physiological tension, 271–279
activity need, 273–274
age differences, 275–278
individual differences, 274–275
infant, 271–272
Physique, changes with age, 27–66
relation to ability to learn, 92–93
Planning for life, 1–3, 641–642
Play, *see* Recreation
Population increase, 6–8
Proportion of women in labor force, 217–218
Psychological motivations, 279–317
age changes, 289–292, 294–305, 311–313
money income, 305–309
need to achieve, 287–292
occupational, 280–284
social, 284–286
time perspectives, 303–305
Psychological services in industry, 258–261
Puberty, 39–41

Radio and television, 404–407
Reading interests, books, 402–404
magazines, 400–402
newspapers, 399–400
Recreation, 16–17, 379–416, 425–426
adult life, 386–395
age differences, 412–414
changing interests, 393–395
early childhood, 380–381
effects of mass media, 409–412
motion pictures, 407–409
radio and television, 404–407

Recreation—(*Continued*)
reading interests, 399–404
school years, 381–386
sex contrasts, 414–416
Religious values, 478–494
early development, 479–481
factors, 490–492
in adolescence, 481–486
in adult years, 486–490
philosophy of life, 492–494
Retirement, 239–243

Self-understanding, 1–2
Sensory adequacy, changes with age, 54–56
hearing, 55
other senses, 55–56
vision, 54–55
Social interaction, adult years, 522–530;
factors, 523–526; status changes, 527–530
early childhood, 506–508
groupings, 530–545; adult, 534–537, 541–545; childhood and adolescence, 531–534, 537–541
later childhood and adolescence, 508–522; change in status, 520–522; changing values with age, 518–520; heterosexual choices, 511–513; social acceptability, 513–518
other factors, 553–560
racial and other prejudices, 545–560; adolescence, 547–550; adult years, 550–553; early years, 545–547
Society, changes in, 14–20, 641–644
Special training, 637
Standards of conduct, 440
Stanford-Binet test, 75, 98, 100
Status, 97–103, 248–251, 285–286
relation of ability to learn to socioeconomic, 97–103
Study, need for, 113–114

Technology, 8–11
Terman-McNemar test, 73
Tests, Army Alpha, 78–81, 105–106
Binet, 72, 82–83
conventional, inadequacy of, 111–113, 635–636
general abilities, 71–117
Henmon-Nelson verbal-style, 99, 100
Otis nonverbal, 99
Otis self-administering, 77
Stanford-Binet, 75, 98, 100
Terman-McNemar, 73
Types of work, 220–221

Unemployment and layoffs, 217, 219–220, 224–225, 244

Unions, *see* Labor unions

Vocational planning, 253–256
Vocational usefulness, 232–239

Wechsler-Bellevue scale, 72
Wechsler scale, 77
Weight, *see* Height and weight

Women in industry, 217–218
Women, proportion of, in labor force, 217–218
Working conditions, 245–251, 256–258
    lunch hours, 245
    status, 248–251, 256–258
Worries, adolescence, 342–346, 350–353
    adulthood, 346–349, 353–356
    childhood, 338–342, 349–350